Lexical Roots of Old Cree

Lexical Roots of Old Cree

An Etymological Dictionary

Kevin Brousseau

Mercury Series
Indigenous Histories and Contemporary Cultures Paper 147
Canadian Museum of History
and the University of Ottawa Press

Legal Deposit: Fourth Quarter 2025
Library and Archives Canada

Co-published by the **Canadian Museum of History** *and the* **University of Ottawa Press**

Cover image:
CMH V-A-18, Garter, Nehiyaw, Manitoba, © CMH.

Production Team

Copyediting	Lauren McClellan
Typesetting	Interscript
Cover design	Benoit Deneault

The University of Ottawa Press gratefully acknowledges the support extended to its publishing list by the Government of Canada, the Canada Council for the Arts, the Ontario Council for the Arts, the Federation for the Humanities and Social Sciences through the Awards to Scholarly Publications Program, and the University of Ottawa.

Photo of the author (back cover):
Joe Alvoeiro

Library and Archives Canada Cataloguing in Publication

Title: Lexical roots of Old Cree: an etymological dictionary / Kevin Brousseau.
Names: Brousseau, Kevin, 1981- author.
Description: Includes bibliographical references and index. | Introductory text in English. Dictionary in Cree.
Identifiers: Canadiana (print) 2025021749X | Canadiana (ebook) 20250217589 | ISBN 9780776645490 (softcover) | ISBN 9780776645506 (PDF)
Subjects: LCSH: Cree language—Etymology—Dictionaries. | LCSH: Cree language—Lexicology, Historical. | LCSH: Cree language—History. | LCGFT: Etymological dictionaries.
Classification: LCC PM988 .B76 2025 | DDC 497/.323203—dc23

The Mercury Series

The best resource for peer-reviewed research on the history, archaeology, and culture of Canada is proudly published by the Canadian Museum of History and the University of Ottawa Press.

La collection Mercure

Le Musée canadien de l'histoire et Les Presses de l'Université d'Ottawa publient avec fierté la meilleure ressource en ce qui a trait aux recherches évaluées par les pairs dans les domaines de l'histoire, de l'archéologie et de la culture canadiennes.

For this book/Pour ce livre

Series Editor/Direction de la collection:
Pierre M. Desrosiers
Editorial Committee/Comité éditorial:
Laura Sanchini, Janet Young, Katie Pollock, and Salina Kemp
Managing Editor/Responsable de l'édition:
Jenny Ellison
Coordination: Pascal Scallon-Chouinard

How To Order

All trade orders must be directed to the University of Ottawa Press:

Web: www.press.uottawa.ca
Email: puo-uop@uottawa.ca
Phone: 613-562-5246

All other orders may be directed to either the University of Ottawa Press (as above) or to the Canadian Museum of History:

Web: www.historymuseum.ca/boutique
Email: publications@historymuseum.ca
Phone: 1-800-5550-5621 (toll-free) or 819-776-8387 (National Capital Region)
Mail: Mail Order Services
Canadian Museum of History
100 Laurier Street
Gatineau, QC, K1A 0M8

Pour commander

Les libraires et les autres détaillants doivent adresser leurs commandes aux Presses de l'Université d'Ottawa :

Web : www.presses.uottawa.ca
Courriel : puo-uop@uottawa.ca
Téléphone : 613-562-5246

Les particuliers doivent adresser leurs commandes soit aux Presses de l'Université d'Ottawa (voir plus haut), soit au Musée canadien de l'histoire :

Web : www.museedelhistoire.ca/boutique
Courriel : publications@museedelhistoire.ca
Téléphone : 1-800-5550-5621 (numéro sans frais) ou 819-776-8387 (région de la capitale nationale)
Poste : Service des commandes postales
Musée canadien de l'histoire
100, rue Laurier
Gatineau (Québec) K1A 0M8

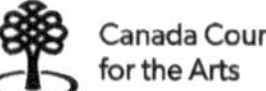

Land Acknowledgement
Reconnaissance territoriale

The Canadian Museum of History and the University of Ottawa Press are located on the traditional, unceded territory of the Algonquin Anishinabeg. This land has held, and continues to hold, great historical, spiritual, and sacred significance. We recognize and honour the enduring presence of the Algonquin people. We also know that you, our readers, are joining us from many places near and far, and we acknowledge the traditional owners and caretakers of those lands.

Le Musée canadien de l'histoire et Les Presses de l'Université d'Ottawa sont situés sur le territoire traditionnel non cédé des Anishinabeg (Algonquins). Ce territoire a eu, et continue d'avoir, une grande importance historique, spirituelle et sacrée. Nous reconnaissons et honorons la présence pérenne du peuple algonquin. Nous avons aussi conscience que notre lectorat provient de nombreux endroits, proches et lointains, et nous reconnaissons les gens qui sont les propriétaires et les gardiens traditionnels de ces terres.

Indigenous Histories and Contemporary Cultures
Histoire autochtone et cultures contemporaines

Created in 1972, this sub-collection brings together works that engage with Indigenous histories and cultures. Its previous title, *Ethnology*, reflected out-dated terminology rooted in colonial approaches. The new title, *Indigenous Histories and Contemporary Cultures*, centres Indigenous voices and perspectives and honours the enduring presence of First Nations, Inuit and Métis Peoples. This renaming is part of the Canadian Museum of History's commitment to ensuring that Indigenous histories and cultural knowledge are represented with respect and that our work is guided by Indigenous perspectives and authority.

Créée en 1972, cette sous-collection rassemble des œuvres qui traitent de l'histoire et des cultures autochtones. Son ancien nom, « Ethnologie », reflétait une terminologie désuète ancrée dans une approche coloniale. Son nouveau nom, « Histoire autochtone et cultures contemporaines », met l'accent sur les voix et les perspectives autochtones, et rend hommage à la présence pérenne des Premières Nations, des Inuit et du peuple métis. Ce changement de nom s'inscrit dans le cadre de l'engagement du Musée canadien de l'histoire à veiller à ce que l'histoire et les connaissances culturelles autochtones soient représentées avec respect, et à ce que son travail soit guidé par les perspectives et l'autorité autochtones.

Abstract

Lexical Roots of Old Cree: An Etymological Dictionary is a dictionary of derivational morphemes of Old Cree, the postulated ancestor of Cree, Innu, Naskapi, and Atikamekw dialects. It is the result of over two decades of research on historical and contemporary Cree dialects. Built from extensive linguistic fieldwork with nearly a hundred fluent speakers and supported by lexical databases and textual corpora, it offers a detailed reconstruction of Old Cree lexical roots with ample evidence from various dialects included.

Lexical roots—the smallest meaningful units of words—are central to Cree's polysynthetic structure. By meticulously reconstructing these roots, this dictionary provides critical insights into how words were formed in Old Cree and how they continue to be structured in modern dialects.

Beyond linguistic reconstruction, this work addresses practical challenges in Cree lexicography, particularly those arising from orthographic variations and dialectal differences. It serves as a valuable resource for lexicographers, linguists, and community members engaged in language preservation and revitalization. At a time of rapid linguistic erosion, this dictionary not only documents Cree's rich lexical heritage but also supports ongoing efforts to sustain and strengthen the language for future generations. It stands as a testament to the knowledge generously shared by fluent speakers and to the enduring vitality of Cree linguistic traditions.

Résumé

Lexical Roots of Old Cree: An Etymological Dictionary est un dictionnaire des morphèmes dérivationnels du vieux cri, l'ancêtre présumé des dialectes cri, innu, naskapi et atikamekw. Il résulte de plus de deux décennies de recherche sur les dialectes cris historiques et contemporains. Élaboré à partir d'un vaste travail linguistique sur le terrain auprès d'une centaine de locuteurs parlant couramment cri et s'appuyant sur des bases de données lexicales et sur des corpus textuels, il offre une reconstruction détaillée des racines lexicales de l'ancien cri accompagnée de nombreuses preuves provenant de divers dialectes.

Les racines lexicales – les plus petites unités significatives des mots – sont au cœur de la structure polysynthétique du cri. En reconstruisant méticuleusement ces racines, ce dictionnaire fournit des informations essentielles sur la façon dont les mots étaient formés en ancien cri et sur leur structure dans les dialectes modernes.

Au-delà de la reconstruction linguistique, cet ouvrage aborde les défis pratiques de la lexicographie crie, en particulier ceux qui découlent des variations orthographiques et des différences dialectales. Il constitue une ressource précieuse pour les lexicographes, les linguistes et les membres de la communauté engagés dans la préservation et la revitalisation de la langue. À une époque de détérioration linguistique rapide, *Lexical Roots of Old Cree* documente non seulement le riche patrimoine lexical du cri, mais soutient aussi les efforts en cours pour maintenir et renforcer la langue pour les générations futures. Il témoigne des connaissances généreusement partagées par les locuteurs parlant couramment le cri et de la vitalité persistante des traditions linguistiques cries.

Table of Contents

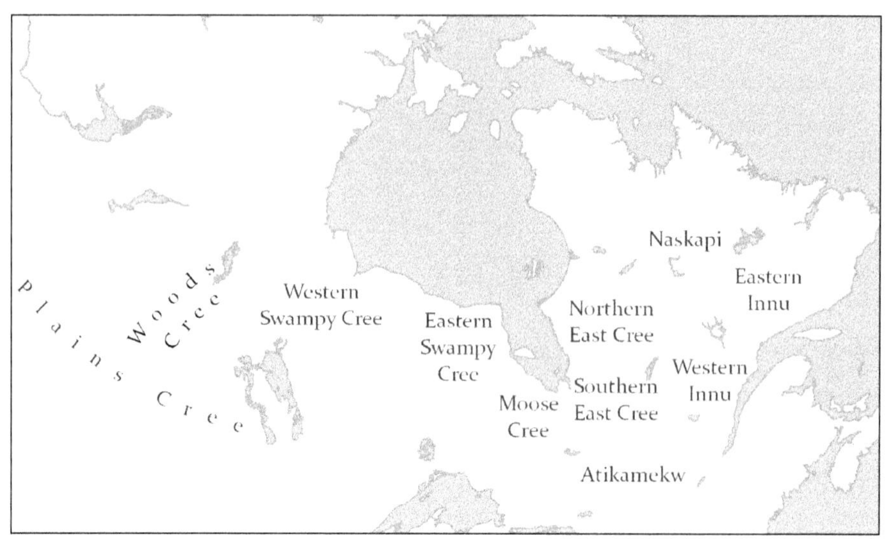

Approximate distribution of contemporary Cree dialects. Map created by John E. Bishop.

List of Tables

Preface

This etymological dictionary of lexical morphology is the product of over two decades of research on multiple contemporary and historical dialects of Cree.[1] My fondness for dictionaries and interest in historical linguistics started in childhood when I first browsed a list of Proto-Indo-European roots appended to an English dictionary, inevitably resulting in this publication.

Personal interest aside, I would contend that this work is necessary for a few reasons. From a scholarly perspective, consider that Proto-Algonquian reconstructions have been largely supported, inasmuch as Cree is implicated, by a Plains Cree dataset. Given that this dialect has merged a few historically distinctive phonemes, this is far from ideal. A dataset from a phonologically conservative dialect of Cree would have been preferable, but a large enough dataset from such a dialect has been unavailable until the recent publications of Atikamekw, Moose Cree, and Woods Cree dictionaries. The availability of such datasets finally allows for a proper reconstruction of Proto-Cree, which we term Old Cree, thereby improving the usefulness of Cree as a whole in the task of reconstructing Proto-Algonquian and consequently Proto-Algic.

From a practical perspective, an etymological dictionary is immensely useful for lexicographers, not only for the investigation of lexical lacunae but also as an orthographic signpost. This is not to suggest a circular logic—the carefully reconstructed roots presented in this dictionary can in practice support work that would otherwise be stalled by local controversies surrounding orthography, an unfortunate reality for too many communities at a time of precipitous linguistic erosion. Furthermore, the reconstruction of Old Cree is useful in dispelling folk etymologies proliferating partly because of this erosion and partly because of dialectal isolation, both of which have resulted from a recent history of assimilatory policies, such as coerced, and at times enforced, sedentarization and residential schools.

As a synthesis of cross-dialectal and diachronic research, the reconstructions presented in this work depend on an enormous quantity of data, much of which only became available in recent decades. Though I am responsible for collecting a significant quantity of data from my fieldwork in multiple dialects over the last couple of decades, the amount of data required to support such work necessarily involves many people over many lifetimes. I would like to highlight some of the people to whom I am intellectually indebted.

1. Though I had plans to produce a dictionary of lexical morphology for years, the project truly started to take shape in 2020 when I committed to it using an online, open-source lexicography platform (https://www.lexonomy.eu). By November 2022, the data were fully revised and migrated to a professional lexicography platform (https://oldcree.com). Since then, the data have been evolving steadily, to the point that a print publication became inevitable.

The manuscript dictionaries of Jesuits Antoine Silvy, Bonaventure Fabvre, Pierre-Michel Laure, and Jean-Baptiste de La Brosse must be acknowledged. These dictionaries of the dialects spoken in the Saguenay and its surrounding regions between the 1680s and 1760s constitute the earliest extensive and systematic documentation of the Cree language. As these dictionaries were compiled for personal use, they only became available as scholarly publications in recent decades: Fabvre's dictionary in 1970, Silvy's in 1974, and Laure's in 1988. While La Brosse's dictionary has yet to be published, John E. Bishop, toponymist at the Cree Nation Government, generously shared the copy he had typed out—for this I wish to thank him. Other historical works of benefit to my endeavour include the Reverend Edwin Watkins' multidialectal dictionary, published in 1865, the Oblate Albert Lacombe's dictionary of Plains Cree, published in 1874, and the Oblate George Lemoine's dictionary of Western Innu, published in 1901.

By the latter half of the twentieth century, a new wave of publications had begun, each glossary or dictionary informing the production of the next. Although we must recognize each of these, along with their editors, a few publications stand out for having filled a gap in the lexicographic record. Jean-Pierre Béland's *Atikamekw Morphology and Lexicon*, a dissertation published in 1978, provided a substantial dataset on what was then a largely undescribed dialect. Marguerite MacKenzie's collaborations, first with Annie Whiskeychan of Waskaganish and subsequently with others from various communities, led to the publication of the Cree School Board's dictionaries of Southern and Northern East Cree, initially published as a single volume in 1987. Lynn Drapeau's publication of her *Dictionnaire montagnais-français* in 1991 was a monumental achievement that laid the foundation for the modern multidialectal dictionary of Innu, published in 2013. I must acknowledge her work and offer my thanks for providing me with a digital copy of her lexical database to assist me in my work. In the late 1970s, Colin Charles of Lac La Ronge in northern Saskatchewan began working on a dictionary of Woods Cree, a dialect of great importance to the reconstruction of Proto-Cree consonant clusters. I must acknowledge this important work, and I thank Minnie McKenzie for sending me a copy of the latest edition of this dictionary.

I must also acknowledge every fluent speaker of the language who has graciously given me their time during my various research endeavours over the last two decades. I am indebted to them for generously sharing their knowledge. Having worked with nearly a hundred knowledgeable speakers of various dialects over the years, I must refrain from naming them all, lest I turn this section into a tedious list reminiscent of biblical genealogy, or worse, give offence by inadvertently omitting an appreciated contributor. Suffice it to say this group includes speakers of Western Innu, Northern and Southern East Cree, Atikamekw, Moose Cree, and Eastern Swampy Cree, in addition to the Abitibi dialect of Anishinabe—all dialects for which I have previously undertaken fieldwork. Speakers who were questioned deliberately for this study are acknowledged by name in the relevant entries. Regarding dialects for which I am not actively involved in fieldwork, speakers who provided forms are also acknowledged by name in the relevant entries. These include: Woods Cree speakers Solomon Ratt and Tom Roberts of Stanley Mission; Western Swampy Cree speakers Ellen Cook of Misipawistik and Ida Bear; Atikamekw speakers Joey Awashish of Opitciwan, Nicole Petiquay of Wemotaci, and Paul Niquay of Manawan; and Western Innu speaker Kim Picard of Pessamit.

I have invested a considerably larger portion of my time investigating the dialects of Moose Cree and Southern East Cree, the latter being the dialect spoken by my family and me. I have accumulated substantial datasets in these dialects that have resulted in the publication of a number of dictionaries. I must therefore offer a special acknowledgement to the speakers of these dialects, collaborators with whom I have built long-term relationships based on mutual respect. I must also acknowledge Geraldine Govender at Moose Cree First Nation for her unwavering support, which has led to the publication of what is presently the largest dictionary of any Cree dialect, the *Dictionary of Moose Cree*, now in its fourth edition.

Through the years I have benefited from the continued fellowship of scholars and our many conversations regarding the Cree language and its history. These scholars include: Manon Tremblay at Concordia University, whose support and massive lexical database of Plains Cree has proved helpful on numerous occasions; Vincent Collette at Université du Québec à Chicoutimi, a longtime associate who has years of fieldwork experience in various Cree dialects and shares my interest in historical linguistics; Conor Quinn, a scholar of Eastern Algonquian languages who has on a few occasions helped me think through challenging reconstructions; and John E. Bishop, toponymist at the Cree Nation Government. The toponymic database at the centre of his work is built on close collaboration with hundreds of monolingual speakers of the various dialects of East Cree, many of whom produce highly conservative pronunciations. The existence of this dataset, and the work required to build it, is greatly appreciated for its excellent representation of conservative East Cree phonology and morphology. Its multitude of archaic and even obsolete forms has helped elucidate the morphophonological and semantic features of certain lexical roots under consideration in this work. Lastly, I must offer my thanks to the peer reviewers, and to Richard Rhodes at the University of California for his valuable comments during my presentation of this work at his conference on Proto-Algonquian, which was held to honour the memory of the late David Pentland.

Note on Transcriptions

< >	grapheme/orthographic transcription
/ /	phoneme/phonemic transcription
[ ]	phone/phonetic transcription
*	proto-form

Old Cree reconstructions listed in this work are largely transcribed using the values of the Standard Roman Orthography, with the addition of the grapheme <ı>, which represents a vowel that may have been phonetically identical to <i> but behaved differently at morphological boundaries. This reconstructed vowel is the Old Cree reflex of Proto-Algonquian *e and is alphabetized as such in this volume. Aside from this addition, readers accustomed to the way the Standard Roman Orthography is used to represent their own dialects will have little difficulty with the entries in this dictionary. However, this standard has not been adopted by speakers of certain dialects and an explanatory note is therefore warranted. Note that the International Phonetic Alphabet has been used wherever a phonetic transcription was necessary.

East Cree dialects are generally represented in a syllabic orthography, though an alphabetic system is used by the editors of the Cree School Board's dictionaries. Their practice is based on the Standard Roman Orthography with some adjustments, such as use of the graphemes <ch> rather than <c>, <sh> rather than <š>, and <e> rather than <ē>, the latter of which mirrors the lack of a diacritic in syllabics to represent this particular phoneme. Other than this long vowel, for which there is no corresponding short vowel, long vowels are represented optionally as double vowels or by use of a circumflex. These orthographic idiosyncrasies have also been adopted for the dialect of Naskapi spoken in Kawawachikamach, except for the use of the circumflex. This orthography is reproduced in this work for Northern East Cree and Naskapi forms. On the other hand, Southern East Cree forms in this work derive mostly from my fieldwork and represent conservative forms transcribed using the Standard Roman Orthography, excluding the use of the diacritic over the letter <e>. The few Southern East Cree cognates sourced from the Cree School Board dictionary are identified as such and spelled using their orthography.

The orthography used by the three Atikamekw communities is based partly on French spelling rules. It omits vowel length and aspirates and represents the Standard Roman Orthography letters <š> as <c> and <c> as <tc>. To aid the reader, Standard Roman Orthography equivalents are provided in square brackets.

Innu communities speak multiple phonologically distinct dialects. Despite this, they have managed to adopt a standard orthography that also omits vowel length and aspirates, but have ensured that their dictionary includes phonetic keys for the various dialectal forms. These keys are included in this work whenever an Innu form is cited, with long vowels indicated by use of a macron rather than a colon.

Table 1.1. Grapheme Correspondences – Contemporary Dialects (excluding phonological or morphophonological processes represented orthographically)

Old Cree	Plains		Woods	Swampy		Moose	Atikamekw	East Cree		Innu	
	South	North		West	East			South	North	West	East
a	a	a	a	a	a	a	a	a	a	a	a
ā	ā	ā	ā	ā	ā	ā		ā	ā		
ı	i	i	i	i	i	i	i	i	i	i	i
ē	ē	ī	ī	ē	e	e	e	e	ā	e	e
i	i	i	i	i	i	i	i	i	i	i	i
ī	ī	ī	ī	ī	ī	ī		ī	ī		
o	o	o	o	o	o	o	o	o/u	u	u	u
ō	ō	ō	ō	ō	ō	ō		ō/ū	ū		
p	p	p	p	p	p	p	p	p	p	p	p
t	t	t	t	t	t	t	t	t	t	t	t
k	k	k	k	k	k	k	k	k	k	k	k
c	c	c	c	c	c	c	tc	c/ch	ch	tsh	tsh
m	m	m	m	m	m	m	m	m	m	m	m
n	n	n	n	n	n	n	n	n	n	n	n
s	s	s	s	s	s	s	s	s, sh	s	sh	sh
š					š	š	c	š/sh	sh		
r	y	y	ð/θ/ th	n	n	l	r	y	y	l/ń	n/ń
h	h	h	h	h	h	h	h, Ø	h	h	h, Ø	Ø
w	w	w	w	w	w	w	w	w	w	u	u
y	y	y	y	y	y	y	y	y	y	i	i

Aside from the orthographic representation of contemporary dialects, historical records vary substantially in their transcriptions of Cree, largely due to variations in the orthographic systems used by lexicographers. For example, French-speaking lexicographers represented vowel quality using continental vowels while English speakers adhered to the values of the post-Great Vowel Shift. Vowel length contrasts, however, were only occasionally represented by French speakers, while English speakers regularly—though at times inaccurately—attempted to represent some of them.

While consonants were represented in a fairly straightforward manner, there are certain details worth mentioning. Early French-speaking lexicographers occasionally used the letter <t> to represent what was likely pronounced [ts] or [tʃ], reflecting a convention common to this day in contemporary Canadian French. These lexicographers had not fully grasped the phonemic inventory of Cree and consequently vacillated in their use of voiced and unvoiced consonants, and while they largely marked intervocalic aspirates, they neglected preconsonantal aspirates almost entirely. Later lexicographers, such as Watkins and Lacombe, made substantial improvements on these points. It should also be noted that each of the historical dictionaries, excluding those by Laure and Lacombe, is a record of multiple dialects, each with its own phonological and morphophonological innovations. To use these dictionaries effectively, it is essential to understand this as well as the idiosyncrasies of the orthographies used by each lexicographer. Note that certain historically compiled word lists and dictionaries were omitted from this work due to their limited utility in the reconstruction of Proto-Cree. These include short word lists compiled by English-speaking Hudson Bay Company workers over the past few centuries, with the exception of James Isham's from 1743 and Alexander MacKenzie's from 1801. Manuscript dictionaries compiled by French-speaking Oblate missionaries in the century following the compilation of La Brosse's dictionary were not consulted.

Table 1.2. Grapheme Correspondences – Historical Dictionaries (excluding occasional errors, minor idiosyncrasies, and phonological or morphophonological processes represented orthographically)

Old Cree	Silvy	Fabvre	Laure	La Brosse	Watkins[2]	Lacombe	Lemoine
	ca. 1680	ca. 1690	ca. 1726	1766	1865	1874	1901
a	a	a/ă	a	a	ă, u	a	u/ ă
ā	a	a/ā	a	a	a, o[3]	ā	a/ā
ı	i	i/ĭ	i	i	i	i	i/ĭ
ē	e	e/ē	e	e	ā	e	e
i	i	i/ĭ	i	i	i, e	i	i/ĭ
ī	i	i/ī	i	i	e	i	i/ī
o	8[4]	8	u	u	oo	o/u	u
ō	8	8	u	u	oo	o	u/ū
p	p/b	p/b	p/b	p/b	p	p/b	p
t	t/tt/d	t/tt/d	t/tt/d	t/tt	t	t	t/tt
k	k/g	k/g	k/g	k/g	k/g	k	k
c	tch/t	tch/t	tch/t	tsh/t	ch	tch/tj	tsh/ts
m	m	m	m	m	m	m	m
n	n	n	n	n	n	n	n
s	s/ss	s/ss	s/ss	s/ss	s	s	sh
š	ch	ch	ch	sh	s/sh		
r	r, l, n, y	r, l, n, y	r	r	y, n	y	l
h	h/Ø	h/Ø	h/Ø	h/Ø	h/ò[5]	h[6]	Ø
w	8/u[7]	8/u	u	u	w, o	w	u
y	i/ï	i/ï	i	i	y		i

2. Refer to this column for Faries and Mackay (1938), a revised edition of Watkins (1865) that follows, for the most part, the orthography set by its predecessor.
3. When preceding w.
4. Ligature of Latin o and u.
5. Inverted apostrophe over the preceding vowel to represent preconsonantal aspiration.
6. Intervocalic h only. Preconsonantal aspiration was marked by gemination of the affected consonant.
7. The latter was preferred in word final position when preceded by a vowel, likely representing a contraction of Old Cree word-final *wa or *wi. For example, "m8teu" replaced Old Cree *mōhtēwa, "woodworm."

Abbreviations

PA	Proto-Algonquian
CINA	Cree-Innu-Naskapi-Atikamekw (as a dialect continuum)

Cree Dialects[8]

PC	Plains Cree
WC	Woods Cree
WSC	Western Swampy Cree
ESC	Eastern Swampy Cree
MC	Moose Cree
AT	Atikamekw
SEC	Southern East Cree
NEC	Northern East Cree
WI	Western Innu
EI	Eastern Innu
NSK	Naskapi

Algonquian Languages

ABEN	Abenaki[9]
ANISH	Anishinabe[10]
MENO	Menominee
MESK	Meskwaki
MIAMI	Miami
MIGM	Mìgmaq
PASS	Passamaquoddy

8. The following labels are glottonyms used by Algonquianists and should not be interpreted as ethnonyms representing discrete ethnic groups.
9. The spelling of this glottonym is inherited from a Gallicized form of the endonym "Wôbanaki," alternatively spelled "W8banaki." All three spellings are used commonly among Abenaki communities and organizations.
10. Variant spellings of this term include Anishinaabe, Nishnaabe, and Anicinape. The term is used here to refer to any of the dialects of the Anishinabe language group, including dialects commonly referred to as Ojibwe, Odawa, Algonquin, and Severn. Note that speakers of the Severn dialect use the related term "Anishinini" rather than "Anishinaabe."

Grammar

NA	noun, animate
NI	noun, inanimate
P	particle
VAI	verb, animate intransitive
VII	verb, inanimate intransitive
VTA	verb, transitive animate
VTI	verb, transitive inanimate

Alphabetization

The alphabetization of Proto-Cree lexical roots is as follows: a, ā, c, ɩ, ē, h, i, ī, k, m, n, o, ō, p, r, s, š, t, w, y.

Introduction

Dialects of Cree, Innu, Naskapi, and Atikamekw (henceforth CINA) have long been understood as being closely related. Though mutual intelligibility among these dialects varies, ranging from nonexistent to fully intelligible, the group has come to be described as a dialect continuum.[11] In general, mutual intelligibility ranges from nonexistent between geographically distant regions to fully intelligible between neighbouring communities. There are exceptions, however, where intelligibility is nonexistent despite geographic proximity or the intelligibility between two dialects is asymmetric. Variations in intelligibility depend on the accumulation of isoglosses, the number of which tends to accumulate with time and distance. The occasional lack of mutual intelligibility suggests certain linguistic varieties are more akin to distinct languages than dialects, though "dialect" remains the conventional term. There is no doubt, however, that all these linguistic varieties, whether dialects or languages, descend from a single ancestor we refer to as Old Cree.

Although no record exists of this ancestral language, it is possible to reconstruct it to a great extent by systematically comparing its descendants. This comparative method has been used to reconstruct other ancestral languages, which are termed protolanguages. While "Proto-Cree" is technically the correct name for the reconstruction of the ancestral Cree language, "Old Cree" is used here instead as a more accessible term for lay readers and linguists alike.

Other names, however, have been used in the linguistic literature, including "Common Cree" and "Pre-Cree." We have rejected these terms for a number of reasons. While the former is technically an acceptable synonym for Proto-Cree or Old Cree, it lacks a reference to the past and is ambiguous in that it evokes the notion of a *lingua franca*. Examples of "common" used as a synonym of "proto-" include "Common Germanic" as a synonym of "Proto-Germanic," "Common Slavic" for "Proto-Slavic," and "Common Romanian" for "Proto-Romanian." Note that the use of this adjective for protolanguages is usually restricted to lower-level protolanguages. Along these lines, Goddard (1979) distinguishes major genetic groupings from minor ones within the Algonquian language family, classifying the Eastern Algonquian branch as a major group and the Cree dialect continuum as a minor group, hence his use of the term "Common Cree." The earliest known reference to Common Cree is in the summary of a paper presented by Cooper in 1925 at the New National Museum. Cooper contrasts the term with Atikamekw in the context of a discussion of the reflexes of Proto-Algonquian *r (1925). It is unclear whether Common Cree was used to refer to Proto-Cree or Plains Cree. While Goddard tends to refer to Proto-Cree as Common Cree (cf. Goddard: 1979, 1981, 1994), he also occasionally uses the term Common Cree-Montagnais (1991). Other references include Costa (1996) and Grossman *et al.*

11. Cf. Wolfart (1973) and MacKenzie (1980).

(2018). Note that Rhodes (2021) refers unambiguously to Proto-Cree and other lower-level protolanguages such as Proto-Ojibwean, Proto-Meskwakian, and Proto-Miami-Illinois, proposing that the last three, along with an ancestral form of Shawnee, derive from a higher-level protolanguage termed Proto-Core Central Algonquian.

On the other hand, Pre-Cree would technically refer to an earlier state of the language postulated on the basis of internal reconstruction rather than the comparative method.[12] In fact, the term Pre-Cree could appropriately be applied to a state situated between Proto-Algonquian and Proto-Cree, one that can only be postulated by an internal reconstruction of Proto-Cree. The use of this term is ambiguous in the literature. The earliest known reference is in Pentland (1978), where Proto-Cree and Pre-Cree appear to be used interchangeably. Pentland (1979, p. 34) offers a specific definition of Pre-Cree-Montagnais, describing it as "the unattested descendent [*sic*] of Proto-Algonquian which split into Cree and Montagnais just before the first contact with Europeans."

Mackenzie (1979) postulates a reconstruction of the phonological system of "Pre-Cree" without defining the term and without presenting any corroborative evidence. Mackenzie (1980) later defines the term as "a form of the Cree language intermediate between Proto-Algonkian and the present-day dialects" and also states that "it is unlikely that any protolanguage ever existed in a single undifferentiated form at any time," echoing Pentland's (1979, p. 33) assertion that a unified Proto-Algonquian, "though theoretically convenient, cannot have existed in fact." Of course, the nature of language is such that idiosyncrasies arise continuously, resulting in idiolectal, dialectal, and sociolinguistic variability, none of which is at odds with the theoretical exercise of reconstructing a protolanguage. Paradoxically, however, Mackenzie (1980) adds that "it will further be assumed that all the dialects under study can be derived from the Pre-Cree level by the application of a set of ordered rules," strongly suggesting the existence of a protolanguage.

The term continues to be used in this way by Mackenzie (1994), Oxford (2014), and Kang (2017). Finally, Collette (2020) refers to "Pre-CINA, the common ancestor of Cree-Innu-Naskapi-Atikamekw," without any additional comments.[13]

As the protolanguage from which all dialects of CINA are descended, it is important to distinguish Old Cree from its own ancestor, Proto-Algonquian, which itself descends from Proto-Algic. The transition from Proto-Algic to Proto-Algonquian to Old Cree involved a series of linguistic innovations that would have likely rendered these languages mutually unintelligible. It is only by using the comparative method that the existence of each of these languages can be postulated: by comparing dialects

12 While the comparative method and internal reconstruction both aim to postulate an earlier state in the history of a language, the former is done by comparing data from languages thought to descend from a single ancestor and the latter is done using only language-internal evidence of the language in question.

13. Collette (personal communication) clarified that he in fact intended to refer to a protolanguage.

of CINA to arrive at Old Cree, by comparing the latter with other Algonquian languages to arrive at Proto-Algonquian, and, finally, by comparing Proto-Algonquian with Wiyot and Yurok to arrive at Proto-Algic.

In order to reconstruct Old Cree, the comparative method requires the identification of cognate sets among its descendent dialects and languages, from which regular sound correspondences can be determined. It is from these correspondence sets that the phonemes proper to the protolanguage are deduced, allowing us to reconstruct the ancestral forms supported by the cognate sets. While the cognates used are fully inflected words, the majority of reconstructions presented in this etymological dictionary are morphemes, the basic building blocks of this polysynthetic language. This decision keeps the dictionary concise and useful and allows us to circumvent the time-consuming task of reconstructing every possible derivation. Such an endeavour would require substantial internal reconstruction and would significantly delay the publication of this work. This decision also ensures we do not erroneously reconstruct whole words that may never have been spoken prehistorically, such as the word for "gun," which could theoretically be reconstructed despite the fact that guns are a recent addition to the material culture. Additionally, we presently limit our reconstructions to lexical morphemes, 2,275 of which were included in this work.[14] Since most reconstructions in this dictionary are morphemes, we have omitted dashes to indicate incomplete words, as their use would have been superfluous.

Entries in this dictionary may be presented with three different types of corroborative data. The first type includes a set of cognates from the various dialects descended from Old Cree. This evidence is necessary for any reconstruction to be considered valid. The second type of data includes cognates from sister languages, those descended from Proto-Algonquian but not Old Cree. Though this type is unnecessary, it is nonetheless corroborative, often providing external proof that can help bolster a reconstruction when evidence of the first type is scarce. The third type is the Proto-Algonquian reconstruction as presented in the dictionaries of either Aubin (1975) or Hewson (1993). Unfortunately, the late David Pentland's Proto-Algonquian dictionary had yet to be published and was unavailable during the preparation of this publication. While the reconstructions of Old Cree forms must in no way be influenced by this last type of information, their concordance with Proto-Algonquian reconstructions nonetheless testifies to their accuracy and that of the comparative method. As might be expected, Old Cree provides new evidence for the reconstruction of Proto-Algonquian forms. Any discordance, therefore, must compel us to re-evaluate the latter. Note that any Proto-Algonquian reconstruction not cited from Aubin (1975) or Hewson (1993) is original to this work, notwithstanding the possibility of it being included in Pentland's dictionary of Proto-Algonquian.

14. Multimorphemic forms are occasionally listed for convenience or when the underlying morphology is unclear. In these cases, the assumed underlying morphemes are cross-referenced.

At the risk of belabouring the point, it must be emphasized that all reconstructions presented in this etymological dictionary of Old Cree are the result of a rigorous use of the comparative method. Each dialect of CINA was systematically consulted and referenced when necessary. As such, the evidence for every reconstruction is carefully documented and presented transparently to the reader.

Morphology

In order to identify cognate sets for comparison, it is imperative that the morphology of this protolanguage and its descendants be understood to some degree. What follows is a brief overview of Old Cree word classes, inflectional morphology, and derivational morphology—enough to prepare the reader for the corroborative evidence presented in this dictionary.

Old Cree is a polysynthetic, head-marking language with complex agglutinative morphology. Its lexical words can be divided into three classes: NOUN, VERB, and PARTICLE. GENDER is either ANIMATE or INANIMATE. NUMBER is either SINGULAR or PLURAL. PERSON is FIRST, SECOND, and THIRD. There are two plural first persons. The first includes the person to whom one is speaking and is termed INCLUSIVE. The other excludes the person to whom one is speaking and is termed EXCLUSIVE.

Nouns and verbs are formed by inflecting a stem that minimally contains a lexical root that serves as the initial component. Beyond this, the stem may also contain a series of derivational morphemes concatenated according to their associated templatic positions.[15] These morphemes, or lexical roots, have been consequently labelled according to these templatic positions as INITIAL, MEDIAL, or FINAL. When a stem consists only of an initial, or is derived by the combination of an initial and final with an optional medial, it is termed a primary stem. This stem can further be assigned to the initial position to derive new nouns and verbs. When this results in a change of lexical category or a change in valency, it is termed a secondary stem.[16] Lastly, particles are formed by the suffixation of one of a number of particle-forming finals to a stem that consists minimally of an initial but may also contain a medial.

INITIALS may either be functional verb or noun stems that only require inflections to become fully formed words or they may minimally require the addition of a final. MEDIALS may be identified as CLASSIFIERS or instances of NOUN INCORPORATION. FINALS are identified as either ABSTRACT, CONCRETE, DERIVED, or NOUN INCORPORATION, and are provided with grammatical classifications such as VERB, NOUN, TRANSITIVITY, and ANIMACY.

Nouns are inflected for GENDER, animate or inanimate; NUMBER, singular or plural; OBVIATION, proximate or obviative; and PERSON, as a marker of possession. Obviation marks an animate noun as less salient in a discourse that contains another, more salient third-person participant of the animate gender. Inanimate nouns are automatically assigned obviation in a discourse containing an animate noun. With regard to person, nouns are divided into INDEPENDENT and DEPENDENT classes. The former occurs independently of person markers while the latter requires them. Animate nouns possessed by a proximate third person require the obviative marker,

15. Cf. Bloomfield (1946) and Goddard (1990).

16. Cf. Goddard (1990).

while inanimate nouns do not. Nouns may also take various types of DIMINUTIVE suffixes and likely other types of inflections, such as PRETERITE and possibly DUBITATIVE suffixes.

Table 1.3. Examples of Independent Noun Inflections (*niska, *Canada goose*; *koskoski, *snowshoe crossbar*)

	singular	**plural**	**obviative**
animate[17]	*niska	*niskaki	*niskahi
inanimate[18]	*koskoski	*koskoskahi	*koskoskıriwi

---

17. Evidence of the animate singular marker includes historical and contemporary sources of bisyllabic words such as *kōna, "snow," and *niska, "Canada goose." The marker continues to be explicitly retained in dialects such as PC and WC due to a phonological constraint on monosyllabic words, a constraint that does not apply to function words. The marker also continues to be retained in AT on animate noun stems ending in sibilants, such as *namekosa* /namēkossa/, "lake trout," *macamekosa* /māʒamēkossa/, "speckled trout," and *okaca* /okāšša/, "walleye." Additional evidence of this marker can be deduced from eastern dialects such as SEC, in which word-final short vowels have been dropped but only after the process of palatalizing a preceding /k/ took place. If we compare the same two words used in table 1.3, we understand that, in SEC, *niska and *koskoski became *nisk* and *koskosc* respectively, a development that displays clearly the palatalization of word-final /k/ in the latter and its preservation in the former. Similar evidence for the animate plural marker includes the palatalized plural marker /ac/ in SEC and WI (as spoken in Mashteuiatsh) and /ic/ in NEC and Naskapi. Also note that, in Old Cree, the third-person indicative verbs of the independent order featuring animate subjects share the same singular and plural markers as animate nouns. Knowing this, consider the SEC subjective verb paradigm in which the third-person singular marker is /ā/ and its plural marker is /acī/, both matching the Old Cree singular and plural markers, with the exception of vowel-lengthening. Contemporary evidence of the animate marker can also be seen for independent indicative VAI verb stems ending in /n/ in SEC, WI, and EI. For singular third persons in these dialects, the inflection *wa is contracted to [u], for instance: *takohšinwa, "s/he arrives," is contracted in SEC (Waswanipi) to [təkʊ̯ʃinu] and in WI (Pessamit) to [təkuʃənu]. In other dialects the final animacy marker is dropped along with the third-person marker, resulting in a reflex of /takohšin/.
18. The singular and plural inanimate markers benefit from historical sources such as Silvy (ca. 1680). Consider the following entries from his dictionary: "mini pl. minai. bleuets" and "8tchach pl. 8tchatai. Mufle d'orignal." The lenition of stem final *t_2 (see phonology section below) is also evident in the latter example, a fact that explains disparate contemporary forms *ocāš* in MC and *ocāt* in SEC, *ocāt* being derived by back-formation from the plural form. In a similar fashion, consider the palatalization of stem final /k/ in eastern dialects as discussed in the previous note. Regarding the plural, contemporary dialects that maintain a shortened form continue to pronounce it [ah] despite spelling it <a>. In SEC, this form is maintained in stems ending in sibilants and occasionally /kw/, but is contracted to [h] in noun stems ending in semivowels or other stops. For example, consider SEC *mīniša,* "berries," [mi:nʃah] and *oyākana,* "dishes," [uja:kənh].

As above, a properly formed noun requires the inflection of a noun stem that consists minimally of an initial. Many concrete nouns are of this type, consisting of a lexical root that serves as an initial and its inflection. However, stems of abstract nouns and certain types of concrete nouns are morphologically derived by suffixing a FINAL to preexisting verb or noun stems. For example, the initial and fully functional verb stem *ēškē, "to chisel through ice to capture beaver," could theoretically accommodate three different noun finals to produce two concrete nouns and one abstract noun: *ēškani, "an ice chisel;" *ēškahpi, "a place where one chisels through ice to capture beaver;" and *ēškēwini, "the art of chiselling through ice to capture beavers."

The complexity of a polysynthetic language can be fully appreciated by parsing verbs of any Algonquian language, Old Cree being no exception. This complexity is due to agglutination of both derivational and inflectional morphology, the latter of which will only be superficially discussed here, and to various types of REDUPLICATION. Verbs are of four distinct morphosyntactic classes: ANIMATE INTRANSITIVE (VAI), INANIMATE INTRANSITIVE (VII), TRANSITIVE ANIMATE (VTA), and TRANSITIVE INANIMATE (VTI). Class is determined by the verb final. Each class has its own set of inflectional paradigms for marking PERSON, TENSE, and MOOD. As with nouns, verbs may also accommodate diminutive suffixes.

Animate intransitive verbs involve an animate subject and are typically monovalent.[19] However, a subset of this class is bivalent, the second participant being an inanimate object.[20] Another subset of this class is ambitransitive, in which case the optional second participant is also an inanimate object.[21] Inanimate intransitive verbs either refer to an inanimate subject or are impersonal.[22] As such, they are either monovalent or avalent. Transitive animate verbs typically refer to two animate participants and are bivalent, but a subset of these verbs are trivalent, the primary object being assigned to the animate recipient or benefactive while the secondary object remains unmarked for animacy.[23] Transitive inanimate verbs are typically bivalent with an animate subject and inanimate object.[24] However, verbs referring to emotional or mental states can be ambitransitive. In these cases, the absence of a direct object simply attributes the emotional or mental state to the subject.[25]

Particles refer to words that are not inflected. They can be either grammatical or lexical, though only lexical particles are of interest for the purposes of this dictionary. Unlike grammatical particles, lexical particles are derived by the suffixation of a particle-forming final to an initial optionally followed by a medial. Although they

19. VAI (monovalent), *mīcihsowa, "s/he eats"
20. VAI (bivalent), *mīciwa, "s/he eats it"
21. VAI (ambivalent), *minwa, "s/he drinks" or "s/he drinks it"
22. VII (monovalent), *wāpāwi, "it is white;" (avalent), *kimiwanwi, "it rains"
23. VTA (bivalent), *wicipitēwa, "s/he pulls h/;" (trivalent), *wicipitamawēwa, "s/he pulls something for h/"
24. VTI (bivalent), *wicipitamwa, "s/he pulls it"
25. VTI (ambivalent), *mirwērihtamwa, "s/he likes it" or "s/he is happy"

are not inflected in the classical sense, they can be attenuated by the suffixation of a diminutive suffix and may also undergo reduplication.

It is important to note that entries in this dictionary do not consist of fully inflected nouns, verbs, or particles. Rather, they consist of lexical roots identified by their templatic positions as either initial, medial, or final. A few semantically null morphemes termed ACCRETIONS are also provided with their own entries, as are PREFINALS, lexical roots that contribute to the sense of subsequent finals. An effort was made to identify the base forms of lexical roots, separated from any surrounding derivational or inflectional morphology. On occasion, internal reconstruction is required to divorce an initial from its associated finals or a prefinal from its associated finals. This is done only when absolutely necessary to obtain the base form of a root under investigation, typically to reconstruct a final vowel that is obscured due to morphological processes. For example, consider *nakwē, "snare," for which the evidence of its final vowel is provided by its derived medial *akwē, and by analogy of other roots that make use of the finals to which this particular root is limited.

Phonology

Now that some basic notions of Old Cree morphology have been covered, cognates can be readily identified and compared in order to reconstruct the phonological system. The caveat to identifying the elements of such a system is that they must be understood essentially as phonemic distinctions that only approximate actual phonetic values. So, while a level of confidence does exist regarding the phonetic value of most of these phonemes, a fact that informs our choice of characters, the ambiguity that remains must be acknowledged.

The present evidence requires that eight vowels be postulated, four short and four long, namely *a, *ɩ, *i, *o and *ā, *ē, *ī, *ō. Thirteen consonants must be postulated as follows: *c, *h, *k, *m, *n, *p, *r, *s, *š, *t_1, *t_2, *w, *y. These vowels and consonants are supported by regular correspondence patterns. For the most part these patterns are straightforward. However, highly divergent dialects can complicate and even obscure the patterns until the phonological innovations are clarified. Typically, divergence increases the farther east a dialect is spoken, with those spoken in eastern Québec and Labrador being the most divergent. On the other hand, dialects spoken at Opitciwan and Moose Factory qualify as rather conservative phonologically.

The vowel system is largely preserved in southern Plains Cree, Swampy Cree, Moose Cree, Atikamekw, the inland dialect of Southern East Cree, and the Western Innu dialect spoken at Mashteuiatsh. The phonetic distinction between *ɩ and *i, if any, is unclear and appears obscured in contemporary dialects and the historical record.[26] However, they continue to be phonemically distinct such that only *i will trigger lenition of a preceding *t. As a result, we recognize *ɩ as a distinct phoneme at morpheme boundaries where lenition will occur as a regular morphophonological process. Intramorphemically, the same phoneme may be recognized where a preceding *t is not lenited, but its recognition serves no purpose, as there is seemingly no phonetic distinction between this phoneme and *i and no active phonological process to prove its presence, and as the non-lenited forms are inherited during the transition between

26. Possible evidence of its retention phonetically may be supported by the Southern East Cree variant spoken by elderly people in Oujé-Bougoumou, Québec. All supportive examples feature stressed syllables where the reflex of Old Cree *ɩ is pronounced [ɛ]. For instance, the reflex of Old Cree *ɩwi, a final that forms verbs from noun stems, as in SEC e *apināniwic*, "people are sitting," was recorded as [ɛ: apɪna:ˈnɛwtʃ] from the speech of a local elder. The VTI passive, as in SEC *tōtikaniwiw*, "it is done," is commonly pronounced [tu:ˈtɛkənu:] and even [tu:ˈtɛ:kənu:] by younger speakers. Compare the NEC pronunciation of the same word, [tu:ˈtɪkɪnu:]. Finally, consider that distal demonstratives appear to be derived from neutral forms, such as SEC *nete*, "over there," from *anite*, "there," [ˈnɛ:tɛ:] and [anˈtɛ:h] respectively, where the change of stress appears to have lengthened the ellipsed vowel to [ɛ:]. Aside from these demonstratives, corroborative evidence outside this dialect is lacking at present.

Proto-Algonquian to Old Cree. Its recognition intramorphemically would be necessary at the Pre-Cree level only. Note, however, that a merger of *ɪ towards the modern reflexes of *i is underway in Plains Cree, Woods Cree, Swampy Cree, Moose Cree, and Atikamekw, evidenced by the unexpected lenition of *t to the dialectal reflexes of *c.[27]

In the coastal dialects of East Cree, the phonetic distinction between *a and *i is progressively merging with the latter, though the phonemic distinction remains such that only reflexes of *i will trigger lenition of *t and *k.[28] The phonetic distinction of short vowels *a, *ɪ, and *i are lost in the Western Innu dialect spoken at Pessamit in favour of a shwa, but remain distinct morphophonologically as above. The distinctive status of *ē is lost in favour of the contemporary reflexes of *ī in Northern Plains Cree and Woods Cree and to the reflexes of *ā in Northern East Cree and Naskapi as spoken in Québec. In Northern East Cree and Naskapi, the merger occurred after *ē triggered the palatalization of *k. Note that, in many contemporary dialects, the modern reflexes of *a, *ā, and *ē will include rounded backed allophones when preceded by, and sometimes necessarily surrounded by, *w.

In many dialects the presence of an *h either before or after a short vowel will trigger tensing, and arguably lengthening, of that vowel. For example, tensing of short vowels preceded by *h occurs in Moose Cree for vowels *a and *i and for *i in Atikamekw and East Cree. Lengthening of a short vowel followed by *h occurs in some varieties of Plains Cree, Woods Cree, and Eastern Innu. In East Cree, a following sibilant or aspirate leads to devoicing of the preceding short vowel, unless the syllable in which it is found carries stress.

Word-initial *a is tensed, and arguably lengthened, in Atikamekw. This process occurs in East Cree for word-initial *ɪ and *o, pronounced [i] and [u] respectively, unless it is unstressed and followed by a sibilant or aspirate.

Old Cree *c remains a distinct phoneme in all contemporary dialects where modern reflexes vary phonetically between [ts] and [tʃ]. This phoneme is distinct from the phonetically identical allophone of *t. The evidence available to support the reconstruction of Old Cree requires that these phonemes be kept distinct, unlike in Proto-Algonquian where, according to Pentland (1983), every *c (traditionally spelled *č) should be recognized as an allophone of *t.

On the other hand, the status of Old Cree *t as a distinct phoneme is complicated by the fact that it derives from two Proto-Algonquian phonemes, *t and *θ, the reflexes

---

27. Compare Old Cree *poštɪškamwa, "s/he puts it on," to SEC *poštɪškam* and MC *pohciškam*. This change also occurs intramorphemically. Compare Old Cree *witihciyi, "h/ hand," with *ocihciy* in dialects spoken west of SEC. This phonological change is incomplete and many exceptions can be found in dialects where such examples have been noted.

28. Compare Old Cree *ē wāpamaka, "when I see him or her," with Inland SEC (Waswanipi) [ɛ: wɑ:pmək] and Coastal SEC (Waskaganish) [ɛ: wɑ:pmɪk]. This merging of /a/ and /i/ into [i] in the coastal dialects leads to a loss of distinction between the conjunct indicative inflections for the 2nd → 3rd person and 3rd → 1st person, both realized as [ɪ̱t], or [i̱t] when tensed by a preceding aspirate.

of which can only be distinguished by their allophony at morpheme boundaries. As such, their distinction is lost intramorphemically.[29] The allophones of $^*t_1$ include [t], [c], and [s], while the allophones of $^*t_2$ include [t] and [š].[30] As this dictionary lists allomorphs that display the allophones of each phoneme, no distinction is made between $^*t_1$ and $^*t_2$ in headwords.

The aspirate *h is retained intervocalically in all contemporary dialects west of Pessamit. All dialects to the east, including the variant spoken at Pessamit, lose the aspirate intervocalically. In this same region, it is lost as a preaspirate in consonant clusters, except in Eastern Innu communities represented by the tribal council Mamit.[31] Note, however, that only in the Western Innu dialect spoken in Pessamit and Uashat was the aspirate lost without affecting any surrounding vowels. In Eastern Innu dialects, the preaspirate triggered a lengthening of preceding short vowels prior to being lost. In dialects spoken to the west of Pessamit, consonantal preaspiration, with exception of sibilants, is either retained outright or as a reflex realized as gemination of the following consonant. Reflexes of preaspirated sibilants are retained only in Atikamekw as gemination of the affected sibilants.

Old Cree *k is retained in all contemporary dialects of Cree. However, in all dialects spoken east of Moose Cree and Atikamekw, a process of palatalization occurs when the phoneme precedes *ɩ, *i, *ē, or *ī. In NEC and Naskapi, this process occurred prior to the change from *ē to [ā]. The adoption of this phonological change is incomplete in Western Innu and East Cree, with the SEC variant spoken at Waswanipi retaining many archaisms, particularly in the speech of monolingual elders.[32]

---

29. In other words, $^*t_2$ cannot be postulated intramorphemically. For example, Old Cree *atimwa, "dog," is diminutivized as *acimošiš* in Moose Cree, *acimošš* in SEC, and *acimos* or *acimosis* in Plains Cree when diminutive consonant symbolism is applied. The [t] never alternates with [š], despite deriving from Proto-Algonquian *aθemwa.
30. Note the complementary distribution of [t] and [c] in the Moose Cree VTI verb *nāṯam*, "s/he fetches it," and its passive form *nāc̱ikātew*, versus the complementary distribution of [t] and [š] in its VTA counterpart *nāṯew* and its imperative *nāš̱*.
31. These four communities are Ekuanitshit (also known as Mingan), Natashquan (also known as Nutashkuan), Pakuashipi, and La Romaine (also known as Unaman-shipit).
32. Consider SEC *mākoškam*, "s/he presses it (with foot or body weight)," and its WI cognate *makushkamᵘ*, where the /k/ in the final is retained in the non-third person constructions such as *ni mākošḵen* and *nimakushḵen* respectively. Compare this to the palatalized form cited by Silvy (ca. 1680) as "ni mag8chten," rendered as *ni mākoscēn* using a modern Roman orthography. Similarly, consider the same verb in NEC, *mākušḵim*, where the loss of phonetic distinction between /a/ and /i/ does not trigger palatalization, nor does the passive inflection -ɩkiniwi-, as in *mākuškikiniwiu*. In Waswanipi, it is not uncommon to hear middle-aged people reminisce about the way their late grandparents and great-grandparents spoke, which they often describe as closer to the dialects spoken at Moose Factory and Opitciwan. With the closure in 1892 of the HBC post at Migiskan, a southern outpost of Waswanipi, the community likely came under increasing influence of SEC as trappers reoriented their summer trade towards more northern posts. Words commonly pronounced with a retained *k include *ayamihcikew*, "to pray," *mīkis*, "bead," *otakišiy*,

Old Cree *m and *n are retained in all contemporary dialects. However, numerous speakers of Eastern Swampy Cree at Fort Albany and Kashechewan (more so speakers of the latter) hypercorrect /n/ to [l], suggesting a change is underway due to the influence of neighbouring Moose Cree. A similar phenomenon can be observed in Pessamit where Western Innu is spoken.[33] Additionally, contemporary Moose Cree, Coastal Southern East Cree, Northern East Cree, Naskapi, and Western Innu as spoken by some families in Pessamit undergo a process whereby /n/ is assimilated into that particular dialect's reflex of Old Cree *r when both occur within the same lexical morpheme and are separated only by a vowel.[34]

Old Cree *p is retained as a distinct phoneme in all contemporary dialects.

Evidence suggests that Old Cree *r was retained as a phoneme until recently in dialects spoken in the Saguenay region of Québec, the southern and eastern James Bay coasts, the western Hudson Bay region, and as far west as Lake Athabasca.[35] It is today retained as /r/ only in Atikamekw. However, its distinctiveness as a phoneme has been retained in Woods Cree as /ð/ and as /l/ in Moose Cree and Western Innu as spoken in Mashteuiatsh and Pessamit. In all other dialects, the phoneme has lost its distinctive status in favour of either /y/, as in Plains Cree, East Cree, and Naskapi, or /n/, as in Swampy Cree, Eastern Innu, and Western Innu as spoken in Matimekosh, Uashat, and Maliotenam.[36] Dialectal reflexes that maintain the distinctive status of Old Cree *r, namely /r/, /ð/, and /l/, can be considered the same phonemically, despite their minor phonetic differences. In fact, they are phonetically distinguished more so by their manner of articulation than their place of articulation. This can explain why some elderly monolingual speakers of the Atikamekw dialect in Opitciwan vary their

---

"intestine," *oškihtesiw*, "water lily," and *wākinākan*, "tamarack," among many others. Words where Old Cree *r is retained as /l/ include *alakahkway*, "leech," *pāhpalakisiw*, "northern hawk owl," and *pipiko-alīkiš*, "toad," among others. Note that examples of archaisms similar to these are to a lesser extent also heard in neighbouring SEC communities, suggesting the palatalization of /k/ and the change to /y/ as the reflex of Old Cree *r likely took place in the not-so-distant past.

33. The extent of this change has not been documented. Compare Old Cree *nōrkwātamwa, "s/he licks it," with [nu:kwa:təm] and [lu:kwa:təm], both occurring in Pessamit (personal communication with Kim Picard of Pessamit).

34. Compare Old Cree *ıriniwa, "man," with MC *ililiw*, Coastal SEC *iyiyiw*, NEC *iyiyiu*, Naskapi *iyiyiu*, and WI (Pessamit) *illu* and *ilnu*. In Pessamit this process appears incomplete, with the latest dictionary displaying the change for certain roots but not others. For instance, Old Cree roots *nāraw, "ruin," *narim, "upwind," and *nēhiraw, "of or allied to the local people," are realized as [la:lu:], [lələm], and [lɛ:lu:], whereas *nīram, "weak," is presented as [ni:ləm].

35. Cf. Pentland (1978).

36. As explained in the above footnote concerning the contemporary reflex of Old Cree *k, the SEC variant spoken at Waswanipi retains many archaisms in this regard. Additionally, as per Mackenzie (1980), the Naskapi dialect spoken at Kawawachikamach may have changed their reflex of Old Cree *r from /n/ to /y/ in recent history.

pronunciation freely between a tap [ɾ] and an approximant [l]. In fact, it is possible that the Old Cree speakers varied the pronunciation of this phoneme as well.

The two Old Cree sibilants, *s and *š, are highly unstable and have remained distinct only in Eastern Swampy Cree, Moose Cree, Atikamekw, Coastal Southern East Cree, and Northern East Cree, excluding the variant spoken at Whapmagoostui. However, they can be subject to diminutive consonant symbolism and their place of articulation can be influenced by a nearby sibilant or /t/. These phonological processes can obscure the exact phonemic identity of these sibilants in contemporary dialects, and it is only with the careful comparison of cognate sets that their identity becomes clear in Old Cree. Outside of these dialects, *š merges with *s in Plains Cree, Woods Cree, and Western Swampy Cree, while the inverse occurs in Inland Southern East Cree, the Northern East Cree variant spoken at Whapmagoostui, and the Western Innu variant spoken at Mashteuiatsh. In the other Western Innu variants and in Eastern Innu, both sibilants have either merged into /š/ or /h/.[37]

Old Cree semivowels *w and *y are retained in every contemporary dialect. In most dialects these affect the place of articulation of a following vowel. For instance, reflexes of *ā are backed in nearly every dialect when preceded by a /w/. Similarly, in Plains Cree and Moose Cree, /a/ is raised to [ɛ] when it follows *y. These effects are typically not displayed in standard orthographies.

Having reviewed the Old Cree vowels and consonants, a brief overview of consonant clusters is in order. Note that the semivowel *w can occur after any consonant and is thus excluded from clusters listed in table 1.4.

Table 1.4. Old Cree Consonant Clusters

	h	s	š	r
c	*hc			
k	*hk	*sk	*šk	*rk
p	*hp	*sp		*rp
r	*hr			
s	*hs			
š	*hš			
t	*ht		*št	

37. For instance, in Pessamit, *s and *š have merged into one phoneme with three allophones; /h/ in word-initial position and intervocalically, /š/ in word-final position, and /ss/ when rendering the diminutive *ɩšihš, which has undergone a contraction. For example, Old Cree *sākihēwa, "s/he loves h/," *apihšāhšiwi, "it is small," *namēhsa, "fish," and *nāpēšihša, "boy," are rendered as [ha:tʃje:w], [əpha:hu:], [nəmɛ:ʃ], and [na:pɛ:ss] by Kim Picard of Pessamit.

While many of the above consonant clusters occur intramorphemically, many result from morphophonological processes that arose during the Pre-Cree period. For example, the combination of *t_2 with *p and *t result in *sp and *ht respectively.[38] The combination of *m with *k or *t result in *hk and *ht respectively.[39] The combination of *n and *t results in *ht.[40] The lenition of *št when following *i or *ī results in *hc.[41]

Consonant clusters beginning with *r must be postulated due to evidence from Woods Cree, which is supported externally by cognates from Algonquian languages such as Anishinabe and Meskwaki. However, while the existence of *rk is well supported by numerous roots, 23 of which were identified in this volume, the existence of *rp hinges on the Woods Cree root for "lung."

Evidence for the pair of preaspirated sibilants comes from Atikamekw, a dialect that has retained the distinction between these Old Cree clusters and their unaspirated counterparts. In this dialect, Old Cree *hs is retained as a voiceless and geminated sibilant /s/, while the reflex of Old Cree *s intervocalically becomes a nongeminated and voiced sibilant /z/. Similarly, Old Cree *hš is retained as a voiceless and geminated /ʃ/, while Old Cree *š intervocalically becomes a nongeminated and voiced sibilant /ʒ/. Unfortunately, the published Atikamekw data sets are limited in scope and much fieldwork was required to review all intervocalic sibilants reconstructed in Old Cree. In the end, preaspirated sibilants were identified in 228 entries (*hs in 144 entries and *hš in 84 entries), 22 of which required support from other Algonquian languages due to the lack of an Atikamekw cognate. Thankfully, the regular correspondence of these consonant clusters across other Algonquian languages testifies to the reliability of the Atikamekw data in this regard and to our confidence in these reconstructions. In the end, 26 entries did not benefit from the necessary evidence to confirm the presence or lack of a preaspirated sibilant.

38. Cf. *ɩspitamwa, "s/he pulls it thus or thither" & * ɩhtōtamwa, "s/he does it thus."
39. Cf. *ahšahkēwa, "s/he feeds people" & *wāpahtamwa, "s/he sees it."
40. Cf. *tihkākohtēwi, "the expanse of snow melts."
41. Cf. *pištahamwa, "s/he hits it accidentally," versus *pihcipowa, "s/he poisons h/self," or, etymologically, "s/he eats accidentally."

Morphophonology

A number of regular morphophonological processes that occur at morpheme boundaries are listed below in order of application. Dictionary entries for morphemes that trigger these processes are also provided, in most cases, with a description of the triggered sound changes. Given the nature of this publication, these changes are described as replacement rules. Additionally, entries for morphemes that undergo the sound changes when triggered by neighbouring morphemes include the resulting allomorphs. This brief overview of Old Cree morphophonology is by no means exhaustive; it serves mainly to provide context to the sound change rules included in the dictionary.

1. [m] → [h] / _ [k, t][42]
[n] → [h] / _ [k, p, t]
[t_2] → [s] / _ [p]
[t_2] → [h] / _ [t]

2. [t_1] → [c] / _ [y][43]
[t_2] → [š] / _ [y]
[št_1] → [hc] / _ [y]
[št_2] → [hš] / _ [y]

3. [y] → Ø / C_[44]

4. C+C → CiC[45]

5. [t_1] → [c] / _ [i, ī]
[t_2] → [š] / _ [i, ī][46]
[št_1] → [hc] / _ [i, ī]
[št_2] → [hš] / _ [i, ī]

---

42. *ahšam + *kē → *ahšah̲kēwa, "s/he feeds people"
43. *sīht + *yā → *sīhc̲āwi, "it is tight"
44. *sīht + *yā → *sīhc̲āwi, "it is tight"
45. *man + *pit → *mani̲pitamwa, "s/he pulls it off"
46. *ıt_2 + *tācimo → *ıš̲itācimowa, "s/he crawls thither"

6. [aw, ay] → [ā] / _ [ι][47]
   [ē] → [a] / _ [ι][48]
   [iw, iy] → [ī] / _ [ι]

7. [a, ι, i, o] → Ø / V_[49]

In addition to the above regular morphophonological processes, certain morphemes trigger sound changes that have no obvious phonological explanation, as in the first example below, or that do not follow the above patterns, as in the spirantization of *t_1 in the last two examples below. These idiosyncratic adjustments are likely inherited from Proto-Algonquian and are listed in the dictionary when identified. For example:

1. [ē] → [ā] when preceding *kē^{1}, *m^{2}, *n^{1}, *so^{1}, *tē^{2}, *t^{3}, *t^{4}, *tiht^{1}, or *tiht^{2}.[50]

2. [t_1] → [s] when preceding *āpaht, *āpam, *āpi, and *ī^{1}.[51]

3. [t_1] → [si] and [št_1] → [hsi] when preceding *i + *n, *naw, *sk, or *skaw.[52]

---

47. *rēkaw + *ιwi → *rēkāwiwa, "s/he is sandy"
48. *pīhtokē + *ιmihki → *pīhtokamihki, "indoors"
49. *kīwē + *aho → *kīwēhowa, "s/he travels home by canoe"
50. *witāpē + *tiht → *witāpātihtēwa, "s/he hauls sth for h/"
51. *kīmōt + *āpi → *kīmōsāpiwa, "s/he spies;" *mīt + *ī → *mīsīwa, "s/he defecates"
52. *mwēšt + *skaw → *mwēhsiskawēwa, "s/he arrives too late for h/"

Relationship to Proto-Algonquian

As a protolanguage descending from Proto-Algonquian, Old Cree is characterized by a number of phonological, morphological, and lexical innovations. In other words, applying the comparative method to the various CINA dialects allows us to reconstruct a language that is quite different from Proto-Algonquian. Notwithstanding this dictionary's focus on derivational morphology, a few innovations that distinguish Old Cree from its ancestor are presented here.

The basic phonological inventory of Old Cree is conservative. Except for PA *e and *θ, which result in reflexes distinguished only by morphophonological processes, all phonemic distinctions are fully retained. Some contractions occur, however, and most consonant clusters undergo changes that result in a loss of distinction. Additionally, PA postconsonantal *y is lost in Old Cree, except in stem-final position where it is extended to *iy.[53]

Table 1.5. Vowel Correspondences

Proto-Algonquian	*a	*ā	*e	*ē	*i	*ī	*o	*ō
Old Cree	*a	*ā	*ɩ	*ē	*i	*ī	*o	*ō

Table 1.6. Consonant Correspondences

Proto-Algonquian	*c	*h	*k	*m	*n	*p	*r	*s	*š	*t	*θ	*w	*y
Old Cree	*c	*h	*k	*m	*n	*p	*r	*s	*š	*t_1	*t_2	*w	*y

Table 1.7. Consonant Cluster Correspondences

Proto-Algonquian	*ʔc *hc *nc	*hk *nk	*hp *mp *ʔm[54]	*ʔr *hr *nr	*ht *nt	*hθ *nθ	*çk[55]	*çp	*ck *θk *xk	*cp *θp *xp	*šk	*ʔt	*ʔθ	*ʔs *hs *ns	*ʔš *hš *nš
Old Cree	*hc	*hk	*hp	*hr	*ht_1	*ht_2	*rk	*rp	*sk[56]	*sp	*šk	*št_1	*št_2	*hs	*hš

53. Cf. PA *myāθkesiwa, "s/he is deformed" → Old Cree *māskɩsiwa; but PA *aʔsenya, "stone" → Old Cree *ahsiniya.
54. Alternatively *hm (cf. Goddard, 1974).
55. Likely PA *rk (cf. Goddard, 1979).
56. Cowan (1977) argued that PA *xk and *θk were retained as distinct clusters in a dialect of Montagnais from the late seventeenth-century, basing his claims on the two multidialectal Jesuit dictionaries compiled during that era. A counterargument is offered in Goddard (1994) that addresses Cowan's limited statistics and explains away the variant cluster reflexes, asserting that they are suggestive of a coming merger between Old Cree *s and *š in that region. Note that a similar variance between <s> and <sh> is present in East Cree dictionaries compiled by the Cree School Board due to the involvement of informants of various dialectal backgrounds that treat this pair of Old Cree phonemes in different ways.

A reconstruction of Old Cree inflectional morphology has yet to be undertaken, so few remarks will be made regarding the subject. However, innovations include the loss of distinction between OBJECTIVE and ABSOLUTE verb forms, resulting in merged paradigms.[57] Passive inflections for conjunct transitive animate verbs for non-third persons have been lost in favour of the theme sign *ιkawi, onto which regular conjunct inflections are suffixed. Non-third person inflections for conjunct transitive animate verbs that feature an inanimate subject, otherwise known as inverse forms in Cree grammar, are suppleted by the inverse marker *ιko, onto which regular conjunct inflections are suffixed. The inflectional morphology for transitive inanimate verb class II merges with animate intransitive verbs ending in *ā, while class III verbs acquire the class I theme sign *am.[58] Innovative verb paradigms include the *h preterite and possibly the *htay preterite.[59] Regarding nominal inflections, the PA inanimate plural

57. Cf. Pentland (1999). Despite the merging of paradigms, the remnants of a system that marks the presence of a definite object or event may have persisted in Old Cree. See the following footnote for more details.
58. Compare PA transitive inanimate verb *nepyētōʔmi, "I bring it," with Old Cree *nipētāna, which displays a suppletion of the expected variants of the class II theme sign *aw by VAI class morphology. Similarly, a loss of the class III zero theme in favour of the class I theme *am can be seen when comparing PA transitive inanimate verb *nātwa, "s/he fetches it," with Old Cree *nātamwa. For a discussion on verb classes in PA, see Pentland (1999).
59. The *htay preterite is also reported by the Jesuit Louis Nicolas for a 17th century dialect of Anishinabe (Daviault, 1994), but it may represent an areal feature as it not reported for other Anishinabe dialects or Algonquian languages. It has been proposed as an innovation in Cree by Goddard (1979). However, in Goddard (2007) and Oxford (2014), a PA origin, or possibly a Pre-Cree origin, is suggested due to the retention of the third-person prefix in this paradigm, which the authors consider an archaism. In other words, it is assumed that the third-person prefix would have been lost in Cree proper. However, it would be remiss of me not to present some evidence of the retention of the third-person prefix. In an early Cree grammar by La Brosse (1768), third-person verbs of the independent order include the third-person marker regardless of tense and morphosyntactic class. Questions remain, however, regarding the possible triggering of the prefix in the context of a definite object or event, harking back to the Proto-Algonquian distinction between absolute and objective paradigms, in which case the prefix would have been optional. For instance, La Brosse includes the third-person prefix in all VTA and VTI paradigms, but only in some VAI paradigms such as "api-" and "mitshisu-," "to sit" and "to eat" respectively, excluding it from the verb "katauashishi-," "to be good-looking." His grammar includes a note that hints at the optional nature of the prefix, stating in a translation from the original Latin: "*Ni, ki, et u sont les marques des première, deuxième et troisième personnes, bien que parfois les sauvages les omettent; cependant on se fait mieux comprendre si on les ajoute*" (La Brosse, 2018:285). In Lacombe's grammar of Plains Cree, appended to his voluminous dictionary, the third-person marker is included for the *h preterite. Consider the example of "o kiwa," the third-person *h preterite of Plains Cree *kīwē-*, "to return" (Lacombe, 1874:56). A trace of the third-person prefix, reconstructable as *wi(t) in Old Cree, survives in some contemporary Cree dialects as a nominalizing agentive prefix. Note that modern dialects that employ

marker *ari is replaced in Old Cree by *ahi. Finally, the diminutive suffixes in Old Cree become *ιhš and *ιšihš.

A few lexical innovations will conclude our cursory comparison. The PA word for "sun" is lost in favour of Old Cree *pīhsimwa. PA *nekwetwi, "one," is replaced in Old Cree by *pēyakwi.[60] The PA word for "fox" is lost in favour of *mahkēhšiwa. The PA word for "birch" is replaced by Old Cree *waškwaya. The same initial is used for birch bark, but as an inanimate noun: *waškwayi. Innovations to kinship terminology include extended stems for mother and father. Compare PA *nōhθa and *nekya, "my father" and "my mother" respectively, with Old Cree *nōhtāwiya and *nikāwiya.[61] Finally, the "shaking tent," a form of divination common to many Algonquian people, receives the name *kosāpahcikani in Old Cree, derived from the verb stem referring to this type of divination. Many other lexical innovations remain to be identified as research in Algonquian languages advances.

---

the *htay preterite do so only in a mixed set where their reflex of the *pan preterite is used for third persons and *htay for non-third persons.

60. Despite this replacement, the PA initial *nekweto is maintained as the initial *nikoto in Old Cree for derivational purposes.

61. Old Cree vocative forms *nōhtā and *nēkā are vestiges of the aforementioned PA forms.

References

Primary Sources

Plains Cree

Lacombe, A. (1874). *Dictionnaire de la langue des Cris.* Montréal: C.O. Beauchemin & Valois.

LeClaire, N., Cardinal, H., Hunter, E., & Waugh, E. H. (1998). *Alberta elders' Cree dictionary.* University of Alberta Press.

Mandelbaum, D. G. (1979). The Plains Cree: An ethnographic, historical, and comparative study. *Canadian Plains Studies, 9.* University of Regina Press.

Wolfart, C. H. (2023). *Memoir 26: Essays on the language of two Plains Cree autobiographies.* Algonquian and Iroquois Linguistics.

Wolfart, C. H. (2022). *Memoir 24: Studies in Plains Cree Grammar and Style.* Algonquian and Iroquois Linguistics.

Wolfart, C. H. (1973). Plains Cree: A grammatical study. *Transactions of the American Philosophical Society, 63*(5), 1–90.

Wolvengrey, A., & Ahenakew, F. (2001). *nēhiýawēwin: itwēwina, Cree: Words.* https://itwewina.altlab.app[62]

Woods Cree

Charles, C. (2021). *Colin Charles Cree dictionary.* Lac La Ronge Indian Band.[63]

Western Swampy Cree

Ochékiwi Sípī Cree Dictionary Committee. (2014). *Cree Dictionary: Swampy Cree.* Fisher River Cree Nation.[64]

Eastern Swampy Cree

Ellis, C. D. (Ed.). (1995). *âtalôhkâna nêsta tipâcimôwina / Cree legends and narratives: From the west coast of James Bay.* University of Manitoba Press.

MacKenzie, M. (2007). *Wasaho Ininíwimowin dictionary (Fort Severn Cree).* Kwayaciiwin Education Resource Centre.[65]

62. Source of the Plains Cree cognates listed in the dictionary entries unless stated otherwise. Speakers listed by name are from the dictionary's audio recordings, available online at https://itwewina.altlab.app.
63. Source of the Woods Cree cognates listed in the dictionary entries unless stated otherwise.
64. Source of the Western Swampy Cree cognates listed in the dictionary unless the name of a particular speaker is listed, in which case the cognate was provided directly by that speaker.
65. Cognates taken from this dictionary are listed "ESC (Severn)." Cognates without this designation and without any other source information listed are taken directly from

Michelson, T. (1936). *Field notes on Cree at James Bay and Hudson Bay* [Manuscript, NAA MS 3411, Folder 2]. Suitland: National Anthropological Archives.

Moose Cree

Brousseau, K. (2023). The dictionary of Moose Cree *(web edition)*. https://moosecree.ca/dictionary/[66]

Atikamekw Cree

Béland, J.-P. (1978). *Atikamekw morphology and lexicon.* [Doctoral dissertation, University of California]. https://escholarship.org/uc/item/7fk44815

Chachai, V., Junker, M.-O., & Petiquay, N. (2022). *Dictionnaire Atikamekw en ligne.* https://dictionnaire.atikamekw.atlas-ling.ca[67]

Southern East Cree

Blacksmith, A., Diamond, P., Weistche, P., Junker, M.-O., & MacKenzie, M. (2018). *The eastern James Bay Cree dictionary on the web: English-Cree and Cree-English, French-Cree and Cree-French (southern dialect).* www.dictionary.eastcree.org/words

Brousseau, K. (2023). *An illustrated dictionary of flora and fauna: Southern James Bay Cree.* Aanischaaukamikw Cree Cultural Institute.[68]

Cree Nation Government. (2022). *Place names database.* (J. Bishop, Ed.). Cree Nation Government.

Northern East Cree

Bobbish-Salt, L., Duff, A., Visitor, L., Salt, R., Junker, M.-O., & MacKenzie, M. (2018). *The eastern James Bay Cree dictionary on the web: English-Cree and Cree-English, French-Cree and Cree-French (northern dialect).* www.dictionary.eastcree.org/words[69]

Cree Nation Government. (2022). *Place names database.* (J. Bishop, Ed.). Cree Nation Government.

fieldwork data gathered by the author. The speakers who provided these forms are from Peawanuck, Attawapiskat, Kashechewan, or Fort Albany.

66. Source of the Moose Cree cognates listed in the dictionary entries unless stated otherwise.
67. Source of the Atikamekw cognates listed in the dictionary entries unless stated otherwise, and excluding examples provided by Joey, Patrick, and Monique Awashish, all of Opitciwan, and Nicole Petiquay of Wemotaci. Other speakers listed by name are from the online dictionary's audio recordings.
68. Southern East Cree cognates listed in the dictionary entries are taken from my own lexical database, partially published under this title, unless stated otherwise.
69. Source of the Northern East Cree cognates listed in the dictionary entries unless stated otherwise.

Western Innu

Cooter, D. (1975) *Étude du montagnais de la Pte-Bleue : La langue actuelle et son lien avec le passé (cahier 1)*. Études Amérindiennes.

Lemoine, G. (1901). *Dictionnaire français-montagnais : avec un vocabulaire montagnais-anglais, une courte liste de noms géographiques et une grammaire montagnaise*. W.B. Cabot and P. Cabot.

Drapeau, L. (1991). *Dictionnaire montagnais-français*. Presses de l'Université du Québec. Mailhot, J., MacKenzie, M., & Junker, M.-O. (2013). *Online Innu dictionary*. www.dictionary.innu-aimun.ca/Words[70]

Eastern Innu

Armitage, P. (2008). *As we walk across our land*. https://www.innuplaces.ca/

Mailhot, J., MacKenzie, M., & Junker, M.-O. (2013). *Online Innu dictionary*. www.dictionary.innu-aimun.ca/Words

Naskapi

MacKenzie, M., & Jancewicz, B. (2015). *Naskapi lexicon* (web edition). https://dictionary.naskapi.atlas-ling.ca[71]

Historical Dialects

Fabvre, B. (1970). *Racines montagnaises*. (L. Angers & G. McNulty, Eds.). Université Laval.[72]

Faries, R., & Mackay, J. A. (1938). *A dictionary of the Cree language: as spoken by the Indians of the provinces of Québec, Ontario, Manitoba, Saskatchewan and Alberta*. Toronto: Church of England in Canada.

Isham, J. (1949). *James Isham's observations on Hudson's Bay, 1743, and notes and observations on a book entitled A voyage to Hudson's Bay in the Dobbs galley, 1749*. (E. E. Rich & A. M. Johnson, Eds.). Champlain Society.[73]

Laure, P. (1988). *Apparat français-montagnais*. (D. E. Cooter, Ed.). Presses de l'Université du Québec.[74]

La Brosse, J.-B. de. (1766). *Radicum montanarum silva* [Manuscript, HR 1026.M75R 7-8]. Ottawa: Deschâtelets Archives.[75]

La Brosse, J.-B. de. (2018). *À la recherche d'un signe perdu : Jean-Baptiste de La Brosse, S.J., éléments de langue montagnaise (1768)*. (J.-F. Cottier & R. Lambert-Bretière, Eds.). Chemins de traverse.

Le Jeune, P. (1633). *Brève relation du voyage de la Nouvelle France, fait au mois d'Avril dernier par P. Paul le Jeune de la Compagnie de Jésus*. Paris: Sebastien Cramoisy.

---

70. Source of the Western and Eastern Innu cognates listed in the dictionary entries unless stated otherwise.
71. Source of the Naskapi cognates listed in the dictionary entries unless stated otherwise.
72. Referenced as Fabvre (ca. 1690) in the dictionary entries.
73. Referenced as Isham (1743) in the dictionary entries.
74. Referenced as Laure (ca. 1726) in the dictionary entries.
75. Referenced as La Brosse (ca. 1766) in the dictionary entries.

Le Jeune, P. (1635). *Relation de ce qui s'est passé en la Nouvelle France en l'année 1634.* Paris: Sebastien Cramoisy.[76]

Mackenzie, A. (1801). *Voyages from Montreal on the river St. Laurence, through the continent of North America, to the frozen and Pacific Oceans, in the years 1789 and 1793: With a preliminary account of the rise, progress, and present state of the fur trade in that country.* T. Cadell, Jun. & W. Davies.

Silvy, A. (1974). *Dictionnaire montagnais-français.* Presses de l'Université du Québec.[77]

Thwaites, R. G. (Ed.). (1897). *The Jesuit relations and allied documents: Travels and explorations of the Jesuit missionaries in New France, 1610–1791; The original French, Latin, and Italian texts, with English translations and notes* (Vol. 9). The Burrows Brothers Company.

Watkins, E. A. (1865). *A dictionary of the Cree language: as spoken by the Indians of the Hudson's Bay Company's territories.* London: Society for Promoting Christian Knowledge.

Algonquian Languages

Abenaki

Day, G. M. (1994). *Western Abenaki dictionary, volume 1: Abenaki-English. Mercury Series* (No. 128).

Day, G. M. (1995). *Western Abenaki dictionary, volume 2: English-Abenaki. Mercury Series* (No. 129).

Anishinabe

André, L. (1690). *Dictionnaire Algonquin* [Manuscript, MS 14, Folder 8]. Montréal: The Archives of the Jesuits in Canada.

Baraga, F. (1878). *A dictionary of the Otchipwe language, explained in English.* Montréal: Beauchemin & Valois.

Baraga, F. (1853). *A dictionary of the Otchipwe language, explained in English.* Cincinnati: Jos. A. Hermann.

Cuoq, J. A. (1886). *Lexique Algonquin.* Montréal: J. Chapleau & Fils.

Daviault, D. (1994). *L'algonquin au XVIIe siècle: Une édition critique, analysée et commentée de la grammaire algonquine du Père Louis Nicolas.* Presses de l'Université du Québec.

Dumont, M., & Papatie-Dumont, M. (1985). *Lexique algonquin/français.* Conseil de bande du Lac Simon.

Dumont, V. (1999). *Lexique anicinabe.* Conseil de bande du Lac Simon.

McGregor, E. (2004). *Algonquin lexicon: Third edition.* Kitigan Zibi Education Sector.

Rhodes, R. A. (1993). *Eastern Ojibwa-Chippewa-Ottawa dictionary.* Mouton de Gruyter.

Lippert, C., & Gambill, G. T. (2023). *Freelang Ojibwe Dictionary.* https://www.freelang.net/online/ojibwe.php

Livesay, N., & Nichols, J. D. (2012–2021). *The Ojibwe people's dictionary.* https://ojibwe.lib.umn.edu

Kwayaciiwin Education Resource Centre. (2014). *Anihshininiimowin Oji-Cree dictionary: Severn River and Winisk River (draft edition).* Kwayaciiwin Education Resource Centre.

76. Referenced as Le Jeune (1634) in the dictionary entries.
77. Referenced as Silvy (ca. 1680) in the dictionary entries.

Meskwaki

Goddard, I., & Thomason, L. (2014). *A Meskwaki-English & English-Meskwaki dictionary.* Mundart Press.[78]

Bloomfield, L. (1975). Menomini lexicon. *Publications in Anthropology & History, 3.*[79]

Miami

Baldwin, D., & Costa, D. J. (2005). *A Miami-Peoria dictionary.* Miami Nation.

Miami Tribe of Oklahoma. (2017). *Miami-Illinois: Indigenous languages digital archive.* https://mc.miamioh.edu/ilda-myaamia/dictionary[80]

Mìgmaq

Metallic, E. N., Cyr D. E., & Sévigny, A. (2005). *The Metallic Mìgmaq-English Reference Dictionary.* Presses Université Laval.

Passamaquoddy-Maliseet

Francis, D. A. & Leavitt, R. M. (2008) *A Passamaquoddy-Maliseet Dictionary.* The University of Maine Press.

Proto-Algonquian

Aubin, G. F. (1975). *A Proto-Algonquian dictionary.* National Museums of Canada.

Hewson, J. (1993). *A computer-generated dictionary of Proto-Algonquian.* National Museums of Canada.

Secondary Sources

Bloomfield, L. (1946). Algonquian. In H. Hoijer et al. (Eds.), *Linguistic structures of Native America* (pp. 85–129). Viking Fund Publications in Anthropology.

Brightman, R. A. (1993) *Grateful prey: Rock Cree human-animal relationships.* University of California Press.

Collette, V. (2020). An old Iroquoian loanword in Algonquian languages: **Šôriyâwa* 'silver.' *Anthropological Linguistics, 62*(3), 195–258. https://www.jstor.org/stable/27136159

Collette, V. (2021). Animate intransitive consonant stems in North East Cree. Paper presented at the 53rd Algonquian Conference.

Commission de Toponymie du Quebec. (1980). *Dossier des enquêtes en milieu amerindien: Inventaire toponymique: Archipel de Mingan.*

Commission de toponymie. (n.d.). *Wemotaci.* Retrieved December 17, 2023, from https://toponymie.gouv.qc.ca/CT/toposweb/fiche.aspx?no_seq=261561

78. Source of the Meskwaki cognates listed in the dictionary entries unless stated otherwise.
79. Source of the Menominee cognates listed in the dictionary entries unless stated otherwise.
80. Referenced as ILDA in the dictionary entries along with the year the website was accessed.

Cooper, J. M. (1926). Proceedings of the Academy and affiliated societies: Anthropological society. *Journal of the Washington Academy of Sciences, 16*(5), 138–40.

Cooper, J. M. (1933). The northern Algonquian supreme being. *Primitive Man, 6.3*(4), 41–111. https://doi.org/10.2307/3316465

Cooper, J. M. (1945). Tête-de-boule Cree. *International Journal of American Linguistics, 11*(1), 36–44. https://doi.org/10.1086/463849

Costa, D. J. (1996). Reconstructing initial change in Algonquian. *Anthropological Linguistics, 38*(1), 39–72. https://www.jstor.org/stable/30028443

Cowan, W. (1977). xk/θk Proto-Algonquien dans le montagnais du 17e siècle. In W. Cowan (Ed.), *Papers of the 8th Algonquian Conference* (pp. 143–150). Carleton University.

Denny, J. P. (1991). The Algonquian migration from Plateau to Midwest: Linguistics and archaeology. In W. Cowan (Ed.), *Papers of the 22nd Algonquian Conference* (pp. 103–124). Carleton University.

Flannery, R. (1995). *Ellen Smallboy: Glimpses of a Cree woman's life*. McGill-Queen's University Press.

Goddard, I. (1974). Remarks on the Algonquian independent indicative. *International Journal of American Linguistics, 40*(4), 317–327. https://doi.org/10.1086/465328

Goddard, I. (1979). Comparative Algonquian. In L. Campbell & M. Mithun (Eds.), *The languages of Native America: Historical and comparative assessment* (pp. 70–132). University of Texas Press.

Goddard, I. (1981). Against the evidence claimed for some Algonquian dialectal relationships. *Anthropological Linguistics, 22*(7), 271–297. https://www.jstor.org/stable/30027878

Goddard, I. (1990). Primary and secondary stem derivation in Algonquian. *International Journal of American Linguistics, 56*(4), 449–483. https://doi.org/10.1086/466171

Goddard, I. (1991). Algonquian linguistic change and reconstruction. In P. Baldi (Ed.), *Patterns of change, change of patterns: Linguistic change and reconstruction methodology* (pp. 55–70). Walter de Gruyter.

Goddard, I. (1994). The west-to-east cline in Algonquian dialectology. In W. Cowan (Ed.), *Papers of the 38th Algonquian Conference* (pp. 187–211). University of Manitoba.

Goddard, I. (2007). Reconstruction and history of the independent indicative. In H. C. Wolfart (Ed.), *Papers of the 38th Algonquian Conference* (pp. 207–271). University of Manitoba.

Grossman, E., Antonov, A., & Jacques, G. (2018). A cross-linguistic rarity in synchrony and diachrony: Adverbial subordinator prefixes exist. *STUF - Language Typology and Universals, 71*(4), 513–538.

Kang, E. B. (2017). Morphological variation in the conjunct order among the Cree dialects. *Toronto Working Papers in Linguistics, 39*, 1–17. https://twpl.library.utoronto.ca/index.php/twpl/article/view/28491

Long, J. S., Preston, R. J., & Oberholtzer, C. (2006). Manitu concepts of the eastern James Bay Cree. In H. C. Wolfart (Ed.), *Papers of the 37th Algonquian Conference* (pp. 451–492). University of Manitoba.

MacKenzie, M. (1979). Fort Chimo Cree: a case of dialect syncretism? In W. Cowan (Ed.), *Papers of the 10th Algonquian Conference* (pp. 127–136). Carleton University.

MacKenzie, M. E. (1980). *Towards a dialectology of Cree-Montagnais-Naskapi*. [Doctoral dissertation, University of Toronto].

MacKenzie, M. (1992). Negative markers in East Cree and Montagnais. In W. Cowan (Ed.), *Papers of the 23rd Algonquian Conference* (pp. 174–184). Carleton University.

Masty, E. (2014). *Mind's eye: Stories from Whapmagoostui* (S. Marshall, Ed.). Aanischaaukamikw Cree Cultural Institute.

Michelson, T. (1939). Linguistic classification of Cree and Montagnais-Naskapi dialects. *Bureau of American Ethnology, Bulletin 123*, 69–95.

Oxford, W. R. (2014). *Microparameters of agreement: A diachronic perspective on Algonquian verb inflection* (Publication No. 3634426) [Doctoral dissertation, University of Toronto]. ProQuest Dissertations & Theses.

Pentland, D. H. (1978). "A historical overview of Cree dialects." In W. Cowan (Ed.), *Papers of the 9th Algonquian Conference* (pp. 104–126). Carleton University.

Pentland, D. H. (1979). *Algonquian Historical Phonology* [Doctoral dissertation, University of Toronto].

Pentland, D. H. (1979). An early Iroquoian loanword in Algonquian. *Algonquian Linguistics* 4(3), 27-29.

Pentland, D. H. (1981). The Proto-Algonquian word for 'corn.' *Algonquian and Iroquoian Linguistics* *6*(3), 35–37.

Pentland, D. H. (1982). French loanwords in Cree. *Kansas Working Papers in Linguistics, 7,* 105–117. https://doi.org/10.17161/KWPL.1808.3620

Pentland, D. H. (1983). Proto-Algonquian [č] and [š]. In W. Cowan (Ed.), *Papers of the 14th Algonquian Conference* (pp. 379–396). Carleton University.

Pentland, D. H. The morphology of the Algonquian independent order. In D. H. Pentland (Ed.), *Papers of the 30th Algonquian Conference* (pp. 222–266). University of Manitoba.

Rhodes, R. (2021). The case for Core Central Algonquian. In L. Thomason, D. J. Costa, & A. Dahlstrom (Eds.), *Webs of relationships and words from long ago: A festschrift presented to Ives Goddard on the occasion of his 80th birthday*. Mundart Press.

Skinner, A. (1911). Notes on the Eastern Cree and Northern Saulteaux. *Anthropological Papers of the American Museum of Natural History, 9*(1).

Etymological Dictionary

A

a

FINAL (ABSTRACT)

— forms particles when suffixed to certain consonant-final initials

evidence | PC ēskwa, *wait;* WC kiðipa, *hurry;* MC sōhka, *strongly, effortfully;* Laure (ca. 1726) "suka, *avec effort*" compare | *ci, *ēr[2], *i[3], *nē[4]

acaškw (~ *acaško)

MEDIAL, FINAL (NOUN INCORPORATION)

— muskrat

evidence | PC nōtacaskwēw, *to hunt muskrats;* WC nōcacaskwīw, *to kill many muskrats;* MC kitohicaškwew, *to call muskrat;* SEC nōcicaškwew, *to harvest muskrats;* WI (Pessamit) shipaitshashkueu [ʃīpītʃəʃkwēw], *to pull a muskrat pelt onto a stretcher;* EI (Unaman-shipit) uishinautshashkᵘ [wīhɨnāwtʃahkw], *muskrat testicle;* Watkins (1865) "Nutowuchuskwāo, *v.i.3. He is hunting rats*" see | *wacaškw

acēn

INITIAL (NOUN, ANIMATE)

— man-eating humanoid, cannibal

evidence | SEC (Waswanipi) acenacīšš, *place name, literally 'small acen mountain'* (Bishop, 2022); NEC achān, *a cannibal giant, a monster;* WI (Pessamit) atshen [tʃēn], *a cannibal giant;* atsheniss [tʃēnīss], *son of a cannibal giant (in a particular folktale);* EI (Mamit) atshen [atʃēn], *a cannibal giant;* Watkins (1865) "uchān, *n.an. a cannibal;*" Laure (ca. 1726) "atchen, *loup-garou. Espèce d'animal que voient ou s'imaginent voir nos sauvages, lequel (à ce qu'ils disent) mange les hommes. Cet animal est comme un homme, à la réserve qu'il n'a point de tête et qu'il mange par les épaules. Certains prétendent en avoir tué.;*" *also* "atsenu, *bête imaginaire que croient sottement voir les sauvages dans leur chemin, loup-garou;*" Silvy (ca. 1680) "atchen, *loup-garou;*" "nit'atcheniȣin, *j'en suis un;*" Le Jeune (1636, Chapter VII; Thwaites, 1897) *"But that Atchen (a sort of werewolf), would come in his place to devour them"* | MIGM jenu, *a cannibalistic giant and kidnapper of children in the Mi'gmaq myth and legend of the Ice Heart;* PASS Cinu, rock giant (name of being in oral traditions who eats people) compare | *wīhtikow discussion | An isogloss runs with Moose Cree and Atikamekw grouping with more westerly dialects, and Northern East Cree and Western Innu grouping with more easterly dialects. While the dialects spoken to the east of this line display the above root, those spoken to the west instead use the root ***wīhtikow**. This lexical feature can be appreciated in the name for the northern shrike *(Lanius borealis)*, appropriately named "wīhtikōwi-wīškacān" in Moose Cree and "atshenishkatshan" in Western Innu, both translating to "cannibal grey jay." The Southern East Cree dialect has retained both roots, though in lexicalized derivatives only. In this dialect the word "atōš" has come to replace both roots in common speech.

*aci

FINAL (VERB, ANIMATE, INTRANSITIVE, CONCRETE)

— affected by the cold

evidence | PC āhkwaciw, *to be frozen;* MC maškawaciw, *frozen hard;* SEC šīhkaciw, *to feel cold;* Laure (ca. 1726) "ni-chipatsin, *je suis dur au froid*" | ANISH mashkawaji, *to be frozen stiff* (Livesay & Nichols, 2021) origin | PA ***aci** (Aubin, 1975; Hewson, 1993) see | *at[5], *i[2] paired with | *atin[2]

*aciraw

INITIAL

— a short while

evidence | PC aciyaw, *a short while;* MC acilaw, *a short period of time; just in case;* WI (Pessamit) atshilu [tʃəlu], *the last time (in the past);* Silvy (ca. 1680) "atchirau, *pour la dernière fois*" | ANISH ajina, *a little while* (Livesay & Nichols, 2021); Cuoq (1886) "atcina, *pour peu de temps, pour un moment*"

*acit (~ *acic)

INITIAL

— upside down

evidence | PC acicipayiw, *to fall head first;* WC acitakocin, *to hang upside down;* MC acitaštew, *placed upside down;* SEC acitinam, *to hold sth upside down;* Laure (ca. 1726) "nit-atchitakutau, *je le pends par les pieds*" | ANISH ajidagoode, *to hang upside down* (Livesay & Nichols, 2021); MESK achichīkwēsēwa, *to fall and hit one's face on the ground* origin | PA ***acit** (Hewson, 1993) compare | *acitaw

*acitaw

INITIAL

— downwards

evidence | WC acitawi-, *downwards;* MC acitawāpiw, *to look downwards;* SEC acitawipayihow, *to swoop, speaking of a bird;* EI (Unaman-shipit) atshitauapu [atʃitawapu], *to sit with one's upper body bent forward* | MESK achitawenamwa, *to tip sth up, as to drink from it* compare | *acit

aciw[1]

INITIAL

— decrease

evidence | WC aciwāpīkinam, *to shorten sth string-like manually;* MC aciwakihtam, *reduce price;* SEC aciwipayihow, *to lose weight;* EI (Sheshatshiu) atshunam[u] [tʃūnəm], *to make sth smaller by removing part of it by hand;* Laure (ca. 1726) "nit-atchiuittan, *je rapetisse*"

*aciw[2]

MEDIAL, FINAL (NOUN INCORPORATION)

— hill, mountain

evidence | PC āmaciwew, *to climb up;* sōskwaciwēw, *to slide downhill;* posākanaciy, *place name, Touchwood hills;* WC paskitāmaciwīw, *to go over a hill;* MC nīhtaciwew, *descend a slope;* šōškociwepalihow, *to make oneself slide down;* SEC kospāmaciwehtahew, *to take sb up the slope;* WI (Pessamit) shakatshueu [ʃākətʃwēw], *to arrive at the summit;* EI (Sheshatshiu) Manitu-utshu [məntūtʃu], *place name, Manitu-utshu Mountain;* Laure (ca. 1726) "nit-amatchiuan 3. -ueu, *je monte la côte*" | ANISH zaagajiwe, *to come out over a hill* (Livesay & Nichols, (2021) origin | Old Cree ***waciwi** see | *waciw

*ah

FINAL (VERB, TRANSITIVE, INANIMATE, CONCRETE)

— **1** by use of a tool

— **2** by striking (with fist or tool)

— **3** sing

— **4** travel on foot

— **5** travel by canoe

— **6** swim

— **7** be in the sky, fly

evidence | [1]PC itaham, *to handle sth so by use of a tool;* MC pīmaham, *twist using tool;* SEC masinaham, *to write sth;* Laure (ca. 1726) "nit-achitaskuahen 3. -himu, *je coupe sur un billot avec une hache*" [2]PC tāwaham, *to hit a target;* MC otāmahikew, *to strike;* SEC pištaham, *to hit sth accidentally;* Laure (ca. 1726) "n-utuskuanahen, *je lui donne des coups de coude*" [3]PC naskwaham, *to respond in song;* MC ililiwahamāsow, *to sing in Cree;* AT itahamaso, *to sing thus;* SEC mōsoham, *to sing one's moose hunting song;* NEC pikuniwiham, *to sing w/o looking at the lyrics;* Laure (ca. 1726) "ni-naskuehimauau, *je l'aide à chanter;*" Silvy (ca. 1680) "nit'itahen, *je chante ainsi*" [4]MC lālaškekaham, *walk alongside the muskeg;* SEC otahāmew, *to take a step;* WI (Pessamit) taussekaimᵘ [tāwssēkīm], *to walk right in the middle of a muskeg* [5]PC nataham, *to paddle upstream;* WC wāsakāmīham, *to paddle along close to the shoreline;* SEC cīweham, *to travel home by canoe;* Laure (ca. 1726) "ni-nakatahunan, *nous nous entre-quittons (par eau);*" Silvy (ca. 1680) "ni pitchita8ahen, *j'entre à la voile dans les terres*" [6]WC nātakāmīham, *to swim towards the shore;* MC sākaham, *to swim out of one's tunnel or lodge;* SEC pīhcitawaham, *to swim into the mouth of a river* [7]MC pimaham, *to migrate, as a bird;* WI (Pessamit) ishpaimᵘ [ʃpīm], *to fly high;* Silvy (ca. 1680) "abita8ham, *midi*" | [1]ANISH bajiishka'an, *to prick sth (using sth)* (Livesay & Nichols, 2021) [2]ANISH bita', *to accidentally hit sb* (Livesay & Nichols, 2021) [3]ANISH ina'am, *to sing a certain way* (Livesay & Nichols, 2021) [4]ANISH biida'adoo, *to follow a trail here* (Livesay & Nichols, 2021) [5]ANISH biinjidawa'o, *to enter a river or bay from a lake in a boat* (Livesay & Nichols, 2021) origin | PA ***ah** (Aubin, 1975; Hewson, 1993) paired with | *ahw

*ahak

MEDIAL (NOUN INCORPORATION)

— scales

evidence | SEC cikahacew, *to still have one's scales, speaking of a fish;* NEC iyihichaau, *to have scales, speaking of a fish;* kaahkihaachaasiu, *to have dry scales;* Fabvre (ca. 1690) "8abahakesi8, v. 8abarakesi8, *sorte (de) carpe*" see | *ahakay

*ahakay

INITIAL (NOUN, DEPENDENT ANIMATE)

— scale

evidence | PC Lacombe (1874) "*écaille,* wāhākay, ak;" WC wahakay, *a fish scale;* MC wahakayak, *fish scales;* AT (Wemotaci, Jeannette Coocoo) ohokai [ohokī], *a fish scale;* SEC (Waswanipi) wahakay, *a scale;* NEC uhākīh, *one's scales, speaking of a ish;* Watkins (1865) "waùkai, wuàkai, *scale*" compare | *arahakay see | *ahak, *ay²

*ahan

FINAL (VERB, INANIMATE, INTRANSITIVE)

— pulse, throb, swell

evidence | MC mihkohan, *to be inflamed;* pahkahan, *to pulsate or throb;* SEC pehkātahan, *to pulsate slowly;* NEC pihkihan, *to throb;* WI (Pessamit) pakain [pəkīn], *to give a shooting pain; to throb or palpate;* Laure (ca. 1726) "ashtehanu, *la fièvre diminue;*" Fabvre (ca. 1690) "pakahin, *cela bat, v.g. battemt de cœur*" see | *ah, *an²

*ahc

MEDIAL

— ground

evidence | PC piskwahcāw, *to be a mound;* WC pāhkwāhcāw, *to be dry ground;* MC pasahcāw, *be a ditch, trench, or furrow in the ground;* papeskohcāw, *to be lumpy ground;* SEC išpahcāw, *to be high ground*

*ahcāhkw¹ (~ *ahcāhko)

INITIAL (NOUN, ANIMATE)

— force that permeates living objects and inanimate things; spirit, mana

evidence | WC āhcāhk, *a soul; a ghost;* ahcāhkowan, *to be a soul or be imbued with a soul;* MC ahcāhkʷ, *a soul or spirit;* ahcāhkoš, *a soul or spirit;* SEC ahcāhkʷ, *a soul; sentient force that permeates people and objects; a pompom;* NEC ahcāhkʷ, *a soul; a pompom;* WI (Pessamit) atshakᵘ [tʃākʷ], *a soul, a spirit;* EI (Ekuanitshit) atshakushinu [ātʃākuhinu], *to cast a shadow;* EI (Sheshatshiu) atshakush [ātʃākuʃ], *a soul; a shadow;* Watkins (1865) "Achàk, *n.an. A spirit, a soul, a ghost;*" Laure (ca. 1726) "atchakuch *pl.* -ets, *fantôme, spectre;*" Silvy (ca. 1680) "atchak8, *âme*" see | *ahcāhkw² compare | *cīpay discussion | The translation of Christian texts over the centuries resulted in a shift in meaning of many words related to traditional beliefs, including the above. Evidence of the original meanings remain, however, thanks to the safekeeping of traditional stories and beliefs in certain parts of Cree country. For instance, the above word is traditionally used to refer to a sort of sentient force that permeates living objects and inanimate objects. This force was propitiated by anointing the object in question. People would anoint themselves by greasing the top of their heads, while butchered animals received it on their skulls. The identification with the top of the head is what lead to the sense of "pompom" in East Cree dialects and explains the traditional practice of decorating and hanging animal skulls from ritual poles or trees. The practice of anointing objects was also widespread until recently and painting one's hunting equipment was thought to achieve the same effect. A Cree folktale that explicitly mentions this belief is that of the comb who betrays a fugitive who forgot to anoint it to buy its silence.

*ahcāhkw[2]

MEDIAL, FINAL (NOUN INCORPORATION)

— force that permeates living beings and inanimate things; spirit, mana

evidence | MC atihkohcāhkʷ, *hornet;* AT pisiskiwahcāhkoš, *Aegolius spp.;* SEC maskohcāhkoš, *Aegolius spp.;* tōmahcāhkwenew, *to anoint the skull of an animal;* wāpamahcāhkwew, *to scry;* Laure (ca. 1726) "ni-uabamatchakuasun, *je me mire dans l'eau;*" Silvy (ca. 1680) "8abatchak8man; 8abatchak8mau, *miroir*" see | *ahcāhkw[1]

*ahcāp

INITIAL

— bow

evidence | PC ahcāpāhtik, *bow stick;* WC āhcāpāsk, *elm;* Watkins (1865) "Uchapache, *n.in. A bowstring;*" Laure (ca. 1726) "atchabasku, *arc (le bois);*" Silvy (ca. 1680) "achabatchi, *la corde de l'arc*" see | *ahcāpiy

*ahcāpiy

INITIAL (NOUN, ANIMATE)

— bow

evidence | PC ahcāpiy, *a bow;* MC ahcāpiyāpiy, *a bowstring;* SEC ahcāpiy, *a bow;* EI (Sheshatshiu) atshapitsheu [ātʃāpītʃēw], *to make a bow;* Silvy (ca. 1680) "achabi, *arc*" | ANISH Cuoq (1886) "atchap(in), *la corde d'un arc*" see | *ahcāp

*ahcē

INITIAL

— (of animals) pregnant

evidence | WC āhcīsow, *to be pregnant;* SEC ahceyāpišīwiw, *to be a pregnant lynx;* EI atsheshtimu [ātʃēhtamu], *to be a pregnant dog;* Watkins (1865) "úchāsew, *v.i.1. She is with young (as a cow or mare);*" Silvy (ca. 1680) "atchemisk8, *femelle de castor pleine*" | Possibly akin to ANISH anjiko & MESK achihkwiwa, *to be pregnant*

*ahciw

MEDIAL, FINAL

— pubes

evidence | PC miyahciwāna, *pubic hair;* MC mīlahciwāna, *pubic hair;* AT (Wemotaci, Nicole Petiquay) orakatci [orakahciy], *one's vagina;* Silvy (ca. 1680) "miratchi8an, *pilus pudendorum utriusque sexus*"

*ahkē

INITIAL (VERB, ANIMATE, INTRANSITIVE)

— grind bones

evidence | PC ahkāmasiniy, *round hand-held stone for crushing chokecherries;* NEC ahchāu, *to break bones to make broth;* EI atsheuatsheu [ātʃēwātʃēw], *to use sth to grind caribou bones;* Watkins (1865) "Ukamusinne, *n.an. The upper stone for pounding berries, meat, &c.*" Laure (ca. 1726) "nit-akan 3. atseu, *je hache des os;*" Fabvre (ca. 1690) "akaten 8skana, *piller des* *os, hacher menu;*" Silvy (ca. 1680) "akanasini, *pierre à piler*" | ANISH "akkee, *he extracts marrow*" (Bloomfield, 1946); MENO ahkɛ·w, *to break bones for marrow* origin | PA ***ahkē** (Aubin, 1975) discussion | In the absence of a Woods Cree cognate, the reconstruction of the consonant cluster is indirectly supported by Anishinabe and Menominee cognates.

*ahkēhšiw

MEDIAL, FINAL (NOUN INCORPORATION)

— fox

evidence | PC osāwahkēsiw, *a red fox;* MC šīpahahkešiwew, *to stretch a fox pelt;* SEC pahkonahcešiwew, *to skin a fox;* EI (Sheshatshiu) uapatsheshish [wāpātʃēʃīʃ], *an arctic fox* see | *mahkēhšiw

*ahkorē

FINAL (VERB, INANIMATE, INTRANSITIVE, CONCRETE)

— fire burns

evidence | ESC kišahkonew, *to be hot flame;* MC išpahkolew, *high flames;* AT (Opitciwan, Joey Awashish) kicikorew [kiʒīhkorew], *fire burns fast;* SEC matwehkoyew, *fire burns audibly;* Watkins (1865) "oosawŭkwunāo, *it has a yellow or green flame;*" Fabvre (ca. 1690) "Kichakȣneȣ, *Le feu e(st) gr(an)d*" | ANISH gizhakone, *to be a hot flame* (Livesay & Nichols, 2021); MENO wi·nwahkonɛ·w, *to blaze up* origin | PA ***ahkorē**

*ahkw[1]

MEDIAL

— POINTED PROJECTILE

evidence | PC cikahkwēw, *to throw a dart;* WC pimotāhkwīw, *to shoot an arrow;* MC pimotahkwew, *shoot arrow;* SEC pimotahkwātew, *to shoot an arrow at sb;* Fabvre (ca. 1690) "kigakȣatan, n. tau, *darder, lancer dard sur a(nim)al;*" Silvy (ca. 1680) "ni pimȣtakȣan 3. -eȣ, *je tire mon arc*"

*ahkw[2]

MEDIAL

— strand

evidence | WC pīmināhkwān, *rope;* WI (Pessamit) piminakuaniapi [pīmənəkwānjāpī], *a cord, line, or string;* Laure (ca. 1726) "ni-piminakuan, *je file*" | ANISH biiminakwe, *to twist fiber to make cord, string, rope, or twine* (Livesay & Nichols, 2021) limited to | pīm

*ahkwan[1]

INITIAL (NOUN, DEPENDENT INANIMATE)

— ankle

evidence | PC mahkwanēyāpiy, *an Achilles tendon;* WC māhkwan, *a heel;* MC ohkwan, *one's ankle;* SEC nahkwan, *my ankle;* NEC uhkun, *one's ankle or wrist;* WI (Washau) ukunikan [ukunəkən], *a malleolus;* Laure (ca. 1726) "nakuanigan, *l'os de la cheville du pied;*" Silvy (ca. 1680) "makȣan, *le talon*" see | *ahkwan[2]

*ahkwan[2]

MEDIAL, FINAL (NOUN INCORPORATION)

— ankle

evidence | MC kotikohkwanešin, *to sprain or dislocate one's ankle;* SEC pācihkwanepayiw, *one's ankle(s) swells;* EI (Sheshatshiu) kutikuakunepanu [kutukwākunēpənu], *to dislocate one's ankle or wrist;* Silvy (ca. 1680) "piskȣgȣan, *cheville du pied*" see | *ahkwan[1]

*aho

FINAL (VERB, ANIMATE, INTRANSITIVE, CONCRETE)

— travel by canoe

evidence | PC kīwēhow, *to travel home by water;* MC itahow, *canoe thither;* kīwehow, *to return by canoe;* SEC pimahonān, *a canoe route* | ANISH biinjidawa'o, *to enter a river or bay from a lake in a boat* (Livesay & Nichols, 2021); MENO asiahow, *to push or paddle back* see | *ah, *o

*ahor
FINAL (VERB, TRANSITIVE, ANIMATE, CONCRETE)

— transport by water

evidence | PC kīwēhoyēw, *to take sb home by water;* MC itaholew, *transport thither by canoe;* SEC itahoyew, *to transport thither by boat* see | *aho, *r paired with | *ahotā

*ahotā
FINAL (VERB, ANIMATE, INTRANSITIVE, CONCRETE)

— transport by water

evidence | PC kīwēhotāw, *to take sth home by water;* MC itahotāw, *transport thither by canoe;* SEC pimahotāw, *to transport sth by boat* see | *aho, *tā paired with | *ahor

*ahp
PREFINAL

— tie

see | *ahpiso, *ahpit[1], *ahpit[2], *ahpitē

*ahpin
INITIAL (NOUN, INANIMATE)

— rawhide

evidence | PC ahpin, *hide, rawhide, parchment;* ahpinēkin, *parchment;* WC āhpin, *a dressed hide;* WSC (Misipawistik, Ellen Cook) ahpinihkew, *to prepare a rawhide* | MIAMI ampenaïa, *peaux avec le poil pelleterie* (Largillier - ILDA, 2017)

*ahpinat (~ *ahpinaš)
FINAL (VERB, TRANSITIVE, ANIMATE, CONCRETE)

— harm, kill

evidence | PC kīmahpinatēw, *to fight sb dirty or illegally;* NEC wāyutihpinitāu, *to kill a large number of them;* WI (Pessamit) tshishkamapinateu [tʃīʃkəmpəntēw], *to kill sb outright;* Laure (ca. 1726) "tchimapinatitunaniu, *duel (deux se tuent en cachette)*" see | *ahpinē, *t[5] compare | *nat[2], *pinat

*ahpinē
FINAL (VERB, ANIMATE, INTRANSITIVE, CONCRETE)

— feel pain or be in a particular state due to pain

evidence | PC māhpinēw, *to moan or cry in pain;* WC mātāhpinīw, *to start have labour pains;* MC itahpinēw, *to suffer from a certain kind of pain;* SEC wīsakahpinew, *to suffer from intense pain;* NEC pātihpināu, *to return home due to feeling sick;* WI (Pessamit) uishakapineu [wīʃəkəpənēw], *to have a cramp or sharp pain;* tshishkamapineu [tʃīʃkəmpənēw], *to die suddenly or instantly;* Silvy (ca. 1680) "ni nanekatapinechinin, *je souffre, étant malade*" compare | *āspinē, *nē[3], *pinē[2]

*ahpiso
FINAL (VERB, ANIMATE, INTRANSITIVE, CONCRETE)

— tied

evidence | PC kotahpisow, *to try tying oneself;* MC itahpisow, *be tied thus;* AT sakappiso-, *to be tied up* (Béland, 1978); SEC sīhtahpisow, *to be tied tightly* | ANISH inapizo, *to be tied thus* (Livesay & Nichols, 2021) origin | PA ***ahpiso** (Hewson, 1993) see | *ahp, *so[1]

*ahpit[1] (~ *ahpiš)
FINAL (VERB, TRANSITIVE, ANIMATE, CONCRETE)

— tie

evidence | PC asahpitēw, *to tie things together in a bunch;* MC itahpitew, *tie sb thus;* SEC sīhtahpitew, *to tie sb tightly;* Laure (ca. 1726) "ni-kachkapiten, *je ferme en liant quelque chose*" | ANISH inapizh, *to tie sb thus* (Livesay & Nichols, 2021) origin | PA ***ahpiθ** (Hewson, 1993) see | *ahp, *t[3]

*ahpit[2] (~ *ahpic)
FINAL (VERB, TRANSITIVE, INANIMATE, CONCRETE)

— tie

evidence | PC asahpitam, *to tie things together in a bunch;* MC itahpitam, *tie sth* *thus;* SEC sīhtahpitam, *to tie sth tightly* | ANISH inapidoon, *to tie sb thus* (Livesay & Nichols, 2021); MESK takwapitōwa, *to tie sth together with sth else* origin | PA ***ahpit** (Hewson, 1993) see | *ahp, *t[4]

*ahpitē

FINAL (VERB, INANIMATE, INTRANSITIVE, CONCRETE)

— tied

evidence | PC akwahpitēw, *to be tied on;* MC itahpitew, *be tied thus;* SEC sīhtahpitew, *to be tied tightly* | ANISH inapide, *to be tied thus* (Livesay & Nichols, 2021); MENO ahsa·hpetɛw, *to be tied in a bundle or sheaf* origin | PA ***ahpitē** (Hewson, 1993) see | *ahp, *tē[2]

*ahr[1]

INITIAL (VERB, TRANSITIVE, ANIMATE)

— set

evidence | MC alew, *to set sth or sb; to sit sb;* SEC (coastal) ahyew, *to set sth or sb; to sit sb;* EI (Sheshatshiu) aneu [ānēw], *to place sth or sb; to sit sb* origin | PA ***aʔr** (***aʔl**, Aubin, 1975), from ***ap** + ***r** see | *ahr[2], *ap[1], *r paired with | *aštā[1]

*ahr[2]

FINAL (VERB, TRANSITIVE, ANIMATE, DERIVED)

— set

evidence | PC māmawahēw, *to place things together;* MC acitalew, *set sth upside down;* SEC itahyew, *to set sth thus* see | *ahr[1]

*ahrakēmak

MEDIAL

— bark

evidence | Fabvre (ca. 1690) "Papak8rakemak8, *pins à flocons;*" Silvy (ca. 1680) "papag8eratchemak, *onguent d'écorce de pin à flocons, contre la brûlure*" | ANISH bapakwanagemag(oog), *Norway Pine* (Lippert & Gambill, 2023); Cuoq (1886) "pakwanakemak," cf. "*les arbres du genre sapin, c.-à-d., à rameaux toujours verts*" see | *ēmak

*ahrakēsk

MEDIAL

— bark

evidence | PC Lacombe (1874) "makkayakeskisiw, *une grande écorce;*" MC pinalakeskiškamawew, *to knock the bark down for sb using one's feet or body;* SEC (Waskaganish) pāpakohīceskahwew, *to peel the bark from a tree;* WI (Pessamit) pelatshessipitshikan [pēltʃēssəpəttʃəkən], *a tool for removing bark from a tree;* Fabvre (ca. 1690) "Papag8rakeskahikan e8, *Leuer ecorce du bois de fraine*" | ANISH gīzhikanagek, *cedar bark* (Livesay & Nichols, 2021) see | *wahrakēskw

*ahrakēskw

FINAL (NOUN INCORPORATION)

— bark

evidence | Laure (ca. 1726) "michtanaratchesku, *sa deuxième pellicule*" see | *wahrakēskw

*ahrap[1]

INITIAL

— **1** fishing net

— **2** netlike, have many holes or spaces

evidence | [1]MC alapihkānāhtikʷ, *a netting needle;* SEC ahyapihcew, *to make a fishing net* [2]PC ayapikamāw, *to be plenty of inlets on the lake;* MC alapekan, *for a sheet-like object to have many holes;* WI (Pessamit) alapau [ləpāw], *to be full of holes* | [1]ANISH asabike, *to make a net(s)* [2]ANISH asabaa, *to have small holes or be a mesh* (Livesay & Nichols, 2021) see | *ahrapiy[1]

*ahrap[2]

MEDIAL (NOUN INCORPORATION)

— fishing net

evidence | WC mīsahaðapīw, *to mend a net;* MC nātalapew, *to check one's fishing net;* SEC (Waskaganish) manahīpew, (Waswanipi) manahapew, *to remove one's fishing net* | ANISH agoodasabii, *to hang up a net* (Livesay & Nichols, 2021) see | *ahrapiy[1]

*ahrapiy[1]

INITIAL (NOUN, ANIMATE)

— fishing net

evidence | MC alapīšiš, *a small net; a netted amulet;* SEC ahyapiy, *a net,* pronounced [ahīpī] in Waskaganish and [ahapī] in Waswanipi; EI (Sheshatshiu) anapi [ānəpī], *a net;* Laure (ca. 1726) "arabi -a, *filet, rets à poisson;*" Silvy (ca. 1680) "arabi, *rets*" | ABEN ahlab, *a net* (Day, 1995); ANISH asab(iig), *a net(s)* (Livesay & Nichols, 2021); MENO aqnap(yak), *net(s), spiderweb(s)* origin | PA ***aʔrapya** (***aʔlapya**, Aubin, 1975; Hewson, 1993) see | *ahrap¹, *ahrap², *ahrapiy²

*ahrapiy[2]

FINAL (NOUN INCORPORATION)

— fishing net

evidence | MC asakolapiy, *a fishing net with a small mesh;* SEC (Waswanipi) namewahyapiy [namewhapī], *sturgeon net;* Silvy (ca. 1680) "pachkahahabi, *rets à grande maille*" see | *ahrapiy¹

*ahrā

FINAL (VERB, ANIMATE, INTRANSITIVE, CONCRETE)

— set fishing net

evidence | WSC (Ida Bear) namēwanān, *place where a net is set for sturgeon;* AT (Opitciwan, Joey Awashish) nameworanan [namēwarānān], *place where a net is set for sturgeon;* SEC (Waswanipi) namewahāw [namēwhāw], *to set a net for sturgeon;* otōlipīwahāw [utūlipīwhāw], *to set a net for land-locked cisco* | ANISH aazhawasaa, *to string a net across* (Livesay & Nichols, 2021) see | *ahr², *ā²

*ahs

INITIAL

— bunch, group

evidence | PC asahpitam, *to tie things together in a bunch;* Lacombe (1874) "asāpokow, ok, *(a.a.) il se rassemble en tas, par le courant;*" WC asapiw, *to be piled up, such as a fishing net;* MC asilāwak, *to fly together as a group;* EI (Unaman-shipit) ashakutau [ahakutāw], *to hang things in a bundle;* Laure (ca. 1726) "assirheuets, *bande d'oiseaux;*" Silvy (ca. 1680) "assipariȣetch, *ils sont en bande, les poissons*" | MENO ahsa·hpetɛw, *to be tied in a bundle or sheaf;* MIAMI "Nitansingȣenan, *je plisse des souliers;*" "Nitansinacȣne, *je prend a la fois plusieures buches pour faire du feu*" (Largillier - ILDA, 2017) discussion | In the absence of an Atikamekw cognate, the preaspirate in this reconstruction is indirectly supported by Menominee and Miami-Illinois.

*ahsan

INITIAL

— compacted, compressed solidly

evidence | PC Lacombe (1874) "asaninew, *il le durcit avec la main;*" WC asanapiw, *to be packed, such as snow;* asanāw, *to be hard or dense;* NEC asināu, *to be indurated, speaking of an area of inflammation;* EI (Sheshatshiu) ashinatauakᵘ [ʃɨntāwākʷ], *sand compressed into the consistency of rock* | ANISH asanii, *to have bark that is hard to get off, speaking of a tree* (Livesay & Nichols, 2021); asanaa, *be compacted* (Lippert & Gambill, 2023) discussion | In the absence of an Atikamekw cognate, the preaspirate in this reconstruction is indirectly supported by Anishinabe.

*ahsām[1]

INITIAL (NOUN, ANIMATE)

— snowshoe

evidence | PC asāmak, *snowshoes;* AT asamatikw [assāmāhtikw], *a snowshoe frame;* SEC asāmihcew, *to make snowshoes;* EI (Sheshatshiu) ashamashkᵘ [ʃāmāʃkʷ], *a snowshoe frame or birch used for making snowshoes;* Silvy (ca. 1680) "assamichich, *petite raquette*" see | *ahsām², *ɪm² compare | *ākim¹, *mahkwatoy

*ahsām[2]

MEDIAL, FINAL (NOUN INCORPORATION)

— snowshoe

evidence | PC nātasāmawēw, *to fetch snowshoes for sb;* MC kikasāmohtew, *walk with snowshoes;* AT akossa:me-, *to have wet snow on one's snowshoe* (Béland, 1978); SEC nīmasamew, *to bring snowshoes along;* WI (Pessamit) tatusham [tətəʃām], *so many pairs of snowshoes;* Silvy (ca. 1680) "nit'abahassaman 3. -e8, *je détisse des raquettes*" see | *ahsām[1]

*ahsāwēw

INITIAL (NOUN, ANIMATE)

— yellow perch (Perca flavescens)

evidence | WC asāwīsis, *a perch;* WSC osāwēsis, *a perch;* MC asāwew, *a yellow perch;* AT (Opitciwan, Patrick Awashish) asawew [assāwēw], *yellow perch;* SEC asāwew & osāwew, *a yellow perch;* Fabvre (ca. 1690) "Assa8e8, *poisson q(u'o)n peut appeler perche*" | ANISH asaawe, *a perch* (Livesay & Nichols, 2021) origin | PA ***aʔsāwēwa** (Hewson, 1993)

*ahsin[1]

INITIAL

— rock

evidence | WC asināpiy, *a net sinker;* SEC asināpiy, *a net sinker* see | *ahsiniy

*ahsin[2]

MEDIAL (NOUN INCORPORATION)

— rock

evidence | PC sīkahasinēw, *to pour cement;* pimwasinātēw, *to throw a rock at sb;* MC āwatasinew, *to carry a stone(s) from one place to another;* SEC pimosinātaham, *to throw a stone at sth;* WI (Pessamit) pimushineu, *to throw a projectile by hand;* Silvy (ca. 1680) "ni pim8sinatau, *je lui rue une pierre*" | ANISH moona'asinii, *to dig up rocks or mine ore* (Livesay & Nichols, 2021) origin | Old Cree **ahsiniya**, from PA ***aʔsenya** (Aubin, 1975) see | *ahsiniy

*ahsiniy

INITIAL (NOUN)

— rock

evidence | PC asiniy, *NA a rock; NI a bullet;* MC asiniy, *NA a rock; a bullet;* AT asini [assiniy], *NA rock; bullet;* asinikan [asinīhkān], *a brick; cement;* SEC asiniy, *NA rock;* asinīskāw, *to be rocky;* WI (Pessamit) ashini [ʃənī], *NA a useful rock; worked stone;* EI (Sheshatshiu) ashini [əʃinī], *NI rock; bullet;* Laure (ca. 1726) "assini *pl.* -a, *pierre, roche, caillou;*" "assinichets, *gravier;*" Silvy (ca. 1680) "assini *pl.* -nia, *pierre;*" "assini8igamik, *mur, maison de pierre*" | ANISH asin, *NA rock* (Livesay & Nichols, 2021) see | *ahsin[1], *ahsin[2]

*ahsisiy

INITIAL (NOUN, INANIMATE)

— waterweed

evidence | PC asisiy, *seaweed, waterweed;* MC asisiy, *seaweed;* AT (Wemotaci, Jeannette Coocoo) asisi [assiziy], *aquatic plant* | ANISH Cuoq (1886) "Anzisi, *n, plante aquatique qui porte de petits paquets d'herbe réunis sur une longue tige. D'autres la nomment Anzins; le chevreuil se montre friand de cette herbe, ce qui donne souvent aux chasseurs la facilité de le tuer*" see | *ahs compare | *nīpisiy

*ahsiw

FINAL (NOUN, ANIMATE)

— large bird

evidence | PC Lacombe (1874) "asponasiw, *aigle;*" MC mištasiw, *giant mythical man-eating bird;* AT -ssiw, *bird* (Béland, 1978); (Opitciwan, Joey Awashish) piresiw [pirēssiw], *large bird;* (Opitciwan, Joey Awashish) piponasiw [piponssiw], *gyrfalcon;* SEC piponasiw, *gyrfalcon* | ANISH binesi, *bird of a large species* (Livesay & Nichols, 2021)

*ahš

INITIAL

— feed or provide with food

evidence | PC asahtowak, *to feed each other;* WC asāhkīw, *to give food;* MC ašahtam, *to provide sth with food;* ašamew, *to provide sb with food; to feed sb;* AT aššam-, *to feed sb* (Béland, 1978); SEC ašamāwasow, *to feed children;* Silvy (ca. 1680) "nit'achakan, *je donne à manger;*" "nit'achatȣnan, *nous nous entre-donnons des vivres*" | ANISH ashange, *to feed people* (Livesay & Nichols, 2021); MENO ahsa·mɛ·w, *to give sb food, to feed sb* limited to | *am[1]

*ahšākēw

INITIAL (NOUN, ANIMATE)

— lobster

evidence | WC asākīw, *a crayfish;* MC ašahākew, *a lobster;* ašahākešīš, *a crayfish;* EI (Sheshatshiu) ashatsheu [ʃātʃēw], *a lobster;* Fabvre (ca. 1690) "Achakěȣ, *Hȣmar, grosse ecrevisse;*" Silvy (ca. 1680) "achatcheȣ, *grosse écrouele*" | ANISH ashaageshiinh, *a crayfish, a crab* (Livesay & Nichols, 2021); ahshaake, *a crayfish* (Oji-Cree, 2014); MIAMI saahkia, *a crayfish* (ILDA, 2017) origin | PA ***ahšākēwa** (Aubin, 1975; Hewson, 1993) discussion | In the absence of an Atikamekw cognate, the preaspirate in this reconstruction is indirectly supported by Anishinabe and Miami-Illinois.

*ahšit (~ *ahšic)

INITIAL

— in addition, also

evidence | PC asici, *in addition;* MC ašitakihtam, *to count sth in;* AT aššic, *with, adding to* (Béland, 1978); EI (Sheshatshiu) ashitinam[u] [əstnəm], *to add sth to the mixture;* Fabvre (ca. 1690) "Achitĭnen n nau, *mesler en aiȣtant*" | ANISH (Abitibi dialect) ahšic, *in addition, with*

*ahšo (~ *ahšaw)

INITIAL (VERB, ANIMATE, INTRANSITIVE)

— on guard

evidence | PC aswēyihcikēw, *to be on guard against things;* MC ašōw, *to be on guard;* ašohikan, *a blind;* ašomew, *to threaten sb;* AT (Opitciwan, Joey Awashish) acohikan [aššohikan], *a blind;* SEC ašawāpamew, *to watch for sb;* Silvy (ca. 1680) "nit'achaȣabin, *je fais le guet*" | ANISH ashwii, *to be prepared, ready to act, or on guard* (Livesay & Nichols, 2021)

*ahšot (~ *ahšoc)

INITIAL

— against

evidence | MC ašocišimew, *to lay sb against sth;* ašotahpitam, *to tie sth against sth;* AT (Wemotaci, Nicole Petiquay) acotcikwatam [aššocikwātam], *appliquer quelque chose en cousant;* a:ššotapi-, *to sit on sth* (Béland, 1978); NEC ashtishkiwāu, *to hold sb against sth with one's foot or body* | ANISH Baraga (1878) "Ashotakamigishima, (nind). *I put him down on the ground*" discussion | This root has fallen in with ***ahšit** in many contemporary dialects.

*aht[1]

MEDIAL (NOUN INCORPORATION)

— beaver pelt

evidence | PC manahtēw, *to get pelts;* MC šīpahāhtew, *stretch pelt;* AT (Opitciwan, Joey Awashish) tacopitateu [taʒopitahtēw], *to stretch a pelt over a frame;* NEC sichipitihtāu, *to stretch and lace a pelt on a frame;* EI shipaitakan [ʃīpējtākən], *pelt stretcher* origin | Old Cree ***ahtaya**, from PA ***aʔθaya** (Hewson, 1993) see | *ahtay[1] compare | *ahtay[2]

*aht[2]

FINAL (VERB, TRANSITIVE, INANIMATE, ABSTRACT)

— conveys the semantic role of patient to a participant

evidence | PC tahkahtam, *to stab sth;* wāpahtam, *to see sth;* MC tahkahtam, *to stab* *sth;* ašahtam, *to provide sth with food;* SEC tahkahtam, *to stab sth* paired with | *am[1]

*aht[3] (~ *ahc)

FINAL (VERB, TRANSITIVE, INANIMATE, CONCRETE)

— by use of mouth or teeth

evidence | MC kāhcitahtam, *catch sth with one's mouth;* SEC mākohtam, *to bite sth;* Laure (ca. 1726) "ni-nichuatten uaua, *couple d'œufs, je les mange;*" Silvy (ca. 1680) "n'ȣtaten, *j'attire avec la bouche*" | ANISH ginibanjige, *to eat quickly* (Livesay & Nichols, 2021); MENO se·wahcekɛ·w, *to eat sweet things* origin | PA ***ant** (Aubin, 1975; Hewson, 1993), from ***am** + ***t** paired with | *am[2]

*ahtan

INITIAL (NOUN, ANIMATE)

— ornamental band such as a bangle or ring

evidence | PC (Mackwacīs, Louise Wildcat & Rosie Roan) ahcanis, *finger ring;* Lacombe (1874) "attan, ak, *(n.r.) bracelet, gros anneau;*" "Atchanis, ak, *jonc, anneau;*" WC āhcanis, *NA a finger ring;* WSC (Misipawistik, Ellen Cook) ahcanis, *a ring;* Watkins (1865) "ootùchunisew, *he has a ring;*" Isham (1743) "ar tun nuck, *hand cuffs*" | ANISH Cuoq (1886) "anan, *bracelet qu'on met au-dessus du poignet;*" "Ananin mesakindagwakin, *des bracelets de prix*"

*ahtay[1]

INITIAL (NOUN, ANIMATE)

— beaver pelt

evidence | PC ahtay, *a pelt;* MC ahtewat, *a bag for beaver pelts;* NEC ahtī, *beaver pelt;* WI (Pessamit) ataitapan [tītāpān], *beaver pelt used for wrapping supplies when hauling them on snow;* EI (Sheshatshiu) atai [ātēj], *a beaver pelt;* Laure (ca. 1726) "attatibis, *babiche faite de peau de castor;*" Fabvre (ca. 1690) "Atai, *pl* aïak, *peau de castor passée*" | MESK asaya, *skin of a small or medium size animal* origin | PA ***aʔθaya** (Hewson, 1993) see | *aht[1], *ay[2], *ahtay[2]

*ahtay[2]

FINAL (NOUN INCORPORATION)

— beaver pelt

evidence | PC Lacombe (1874) "Wettatayesiw, ok, *(a.a.) elle n'est pas chère (fourrure);* MC peyakohtayesiw, *to be worth one dollar;* SEC nīšohtay, *two dollars; two made beavers;* Fabvre (ca. 1690) "Achkătai, *peau de castor frais o(u) passée;*" Silvy (ca. 1680) "matatas, *robe de castor*" see | *ahtay[1] compare | *aht[1]

*ahw

FINAL (VERB, TRANSITIVE, ANIMATE, CONCRETE)

— **1** by use of a tool

— **2** by striking (with fist or tool)

evidence | [1]PC cīkahwew, *to chop sth;* MC pīmahwew, *twist sth using tool;* SEC masinahwew, *to write sb's name;* Silvy (ca. 1680) "nit'abahȣau assam, *j'en défais la tissure*" [2]PC tāwahwew, *to hit a target;* MC otāmahwew, *to strike sb;* SEC pištahwew, *to hit sb accidentally* | [1]ANISH obajiishka'waan, *to prick sb (using sth); to give sb an injection* (Livesay & Nichols, 2021) [2]ANISH obita'waan, *to accidentally hit sb* (Livesay & Nichols, 2021) paired with | *ah

*ak[1]

INITIAL

— reckon

evidence | PC akimew, *to count sb;* MC akihtam, *to count sth;* SEC acihtāsow, *to count;* Silvy (ca. 1680) "nit'atchimisȣn, *je me compte, je me mets du nombre*" | ANISH agindaaso, *to count* (Livesay & Nichols, 2021) origin | PA ***ak** (Aubin, 1975) limited to | *m[1], *ht[4]

*ak[2]

ACCRETION (POST-INITIAL, POST-MEDIAL)

evidence | PC wāwiyakihkotam, *to whittle sth round;* ispākonakāw, *to be deep snow;* tāpwēwakēyimēw, *to believe in sb;* MC kinwātakan, *long burrow, tunnel, hole or bore;* tepakelihtākwan, *be fit or suitable;* SEC miywākonakāw, *nice expanse of snow;* tepaceyihtākosiw, *to be consider fit or suitable* | ANISH anaamoonag, *under the boat* (Livesay & Nichols, 2021) compare | *ak³, *ēmak

*ak³

PREFINAL

— smell or taste like

limited to | *akan, *akisi compare | *ak²

*akahc

MEDIAL (NOUN INCORPORATION)

— rectum

evidence | PC kisipikahcēw, *to be constipated;* WSC (Misipawistik, Ellen Cook) kipwakahcīw [kipwakascīw], *to be constipated;* MC wīnakahcew, *to have a smelly bowel movement;* SEC (Waswanipi) cipakahcew, *to be constipated;* NEC chipikihchāu, *to be constipated;* WI (Pessamit) lipatikatsheu [ləpātəkətʃēw], *to have one's buttocks uncomfortably wet or soiled;* EI (Unaman-shipit) uinikatsheu [wīnakātʃēw], *to stink when farting or shitting;* Laure (ca. 1726) "chipikatcheuin, *constipation, resserrement de ventre*" | ANISH gibishaganzhii, *to be constipated* (Livesay & Nichols, 2021) see | *akahciy

*akahciy

INITIAL (NOUN, INANIMATE)

— **1** pot-hook

— **2** rectum

evidence | [1]SEC akahciy, *a hook for hanging a pot over a fire;* NEC akihchī, *a hook for hanging pots over the fire;* WI (Pessamit) akatshi [kətʃī], *a hook for hanging a kettle;* Watkins (1865) "Ukàche, *n.in. A hook, a pot-hook;*" Fabvre (ca. 1690) "agăsi, *crochet de bois à pendre ch(au)diere*" [2]WSC (Misipawistik, Ellen Cook) okahciy [okasciy], *one's rectum;* SEC okahciy, *one's rectum;* WI (Pessamit) ukatshi [ukətʃī], *one's anus or buttocks* see | *akahc

*akahšiy

FINAL (NOUN, INANIMATE)

— fruit-bearing shrub

evidence | PC okāminakasiy, *a briar;* WC okāwiminakasiy, *a thorn;* SEC (Waswanipi) kāwakašiy, *a rose bush;* EI (Sheshatshiu) minakashi [mīnəkəʃī], *a berry bush;* Silvy (ca. 1680) "kaȣachiminanagachi, *cerisier*" | ANISH bawa'iminaanaganzh, *a pin cherry bush* (Livesay & Nichols, 2021); MENO ka·ka·kemenakɛ·hsyan, *staghorn sumacs* compare | *ɩmihšiy discussion | In the absence of an Atikamekw cognate, the preaspirate in this reconstruction is based by analogy on the root ***ɩmihšiy** and is also indirectly supported by Anishinabe and Menominee.

*akan

FINAL (VERB, INANIMATE, INTRANSITIVE, CONCRETE)

— smell or taste like

evidence | PC iskotēwakan, *to smell like fire;* MC paštewakan, *to smell like smoke;* wīpimīwakan, *to smell like grease or oil;* NEC wīshtimukin, *to smell like dog;* WI (Pessamit) uimishkukan [wiməškukən], *to smell like beaver; to taste like real, good beaver* (Drapeau, 1991); Silvy (ca. 1680) "ȣichtemaugan, *cela sent le pétun*" paired with | *akisi see | *wī

*akarkway

INITIAL (NOUN, ANIMATE)

— leech

evidence | PC akahkway, *a bloodsucker, a leech;* WC akaðkway, *a leech;* SEC akahkway, *a leech;* EI (Shashatshiu) akakuai [kākwēj], *a leech;* Silvy (ca. 1680) "akakȣai *pl.* aïak, *sangsue*" | MESK akashkwāha, *a bloodsucker* discussion | Note that the variant ***arakarkway** can be reconstructed on the basis of SEC (Waswanipi) alakahkway, ESC (Severn) alikahkway, and a variant WC form cited by Pentland (1979:77) as being from Lac La Ronge, aθakaskway.

*akaskw (~ *akasko)

INITIAL (NOUN, ANIMATE)

— blunt arrow

evidence | PC akask, *knob-shaped arrow;* akaskocēpihk, *arrowroot;* WC wakaskow, *to have arrows;* MC okaskwa, *one's arrow(s);* WI (Pessamit) nakashk^u [nəkəʃkʷ], *my arrow;* EI (Mamit) akashkutsheu [akahkūtʃēw], *to make an arrow(s);* Silvy (ca. 1680) "akask8, *trait, matelas ou bâton à tête*" | MESK akahkwi, *a wooden blunt arrow* compare | *amahkw, *ašisoy, *atohs discussion | ***Akaskwa** is one of a few independent nouns in Old Cree that does not, despite its form, require an epenthetic **t** when possessed.

*akat (~ *akac, *akas)

INITIAL

— shame

evidence | AT akatciw [akaciw], *to be shy; to be embarrassed; to be ashamed;* Laure (ca. 1726) "atatchiuin, *honte, vergogne, pudeur;*" "nit-atatchimau, *je lui fais honte;*" Fabvre (ca. 1690) "Atatchĭm8n 8, *Hont(eu)x à parler, L estre, Le faire;*" Silvy (ca. 1680) "nit'atatchin, *je suis honteux*" | ABEN agaji, *to be ashamed* (Day, 1994); ANISH agadendan, *to be ashamed of sth;* agajiwin, *shame* (Livesay & Nichols, 2021)

*akā

FINAL (VERB, ANIMATE, INTRANSITIVE, CONCRETE)

— move along or across an open expanse of water

evidence | PC misakāw, *arrive by boat;* nātakāsiw, *to wade towards the shore;* MC mišakāw, *arrive by boat;* SEC nātakāskow, *to walk on ice towards the shore* origin | PA ***akā** (Hewson, 1993) compare | *akām²

*akām[1]

INITIAL

— across

evidence | PC akāmaham, *to cross by canoe;* MC akāmihk, *across the water;* SEC akāmašcec, *across the muskeg;* Silvy (ca. 1680) "agamits, *l'autre bord*" origin | PA ***akām** (Aubin, 1975; Hewson, 1993)

*akām[2]

MEDIAL, FINAL

— along or across an open expanse of water

evidence | PC āsowakāmēw, *to cross a body of water;* WC ðāðakāmīham, *to paddle along the shore;* MC lālakām, *along the shore;* ātakāmešin, *blocked by a body of water;* SEC kweskakām, *across the water* | MENO a·sawaka·m, *at the opposite side* origin | PA ***akām** (Hewson, 1993) see | *akā, *ɪm⁴

*akāw

INITIAL

— to be unable or barely able despite wanting, to be frustrated

evidence | PC akāwātam, *to desire sth;* Lacombe (1874) "akāwātew, *(v.a.),* tam, siwew, tchikew, *il le désire inutilement, sans pouvoir se le procurer...;*" "akāwihew, *(v.a.),* ttam, hiwew, tchikew, *même verbe que akāwimew, mais celui-ci désigne une action sur, etc., tandis que l'autre indique la parole; v.g., on joue un tour à quelqu'un, on lui fait espérer inutilement, on dira: akāwihaw, il est frustré;*" "akāwan, wa, (a.in.), *ce qui ne réussit pas;*" "akāweyimew, *(v.a.),* ttam, miwew, tchikew, *il pense qu'il agit sans but, il le pense ne pas avoir son esprit: v.g., n't'akāweyimaw ata e māmitjimot, quoiqu'il se vante, je ne le pense pas cable;*" WC akāwāc, *hardly, just a little bit of a thing;* akāwātīw, *to desire sb, to want to have sb;* ESC akāwāc, *hardly;* MC akāwātamawew, *to desire sth from sb;* Laure (ca. 1726) "nit-akahumau, *détracter, calomnier, je détracte, je calomnie*" | ANISH agaawaadan, *to hope for sth or desire sth* (Livesay & Nichols, 2021); MENO aka·wa·nɛ·w & aka·wa·tam, *he longs for him, it;* MESK akāwi, *barely, for just a short time;* akāwātamātisowa, *to desire sth for oneself*

*akiht

FINAL (VERB, TRANSITIVE, INANIMATE, DERIVED)

— reckon

evidence | WC wīhtakīhtam, *to sell sth cheap;* MC kištakihtam, *to think highly of sth;* SEC itacihtam, *to price thus* | MIAMI ilakintam-, *to price sth at a certain amount* (ILDA, 2017) paired with | *akim

*akikw[1] (~ *akiko)

INITIAL (NOUN, ANIMATE)

— nasal mucus

evidence | PC akik, *snot, nasal discharge;* MC akikʷ, *phlegm, snot; a common cold;* SEC otacikomiw, *to have a cold;* EI (Sheshatshiu) atshikᵘ [ətʃukʷ], *snot* | ANISH agigokaa, *to have a cold* (Livesay & Nichols, 2021) origin | PA ***akikwa*** see | *akikw²

*akikw[2]

MEDIAL (NOUN INCORPORATION)

— to have a runny nose or excessive nasal mucus

evidence | WI (Pessamit) uinatshikueu [wīntʃəkwēw], *to have a snotty nose;* EI (Unaman-shipit) uinatshikueu [wīnatʃukwēw], *to have a snotty nose;* Laure (ca. 1726) "ni-punatchikuan, *je suis désenrhumé;*" Silvy (ca. 1680) "ni nechtȣtchikȣan, *les flegmes m'étouffent*" cf. MC otakikomiw, *to have a cold;* Silvy (ca. 1680) "atchigȣ, *flegme, rhume*" see | *akikw¹

*akim

FINAL (VERB, TRANSITIVE, ANIMATE, DERIVED)

— reckon

evidence | PC itakimēw, *to count sb thus, to price sb thus, to hold sb in such esteem;* MC kištakimew, *to think highly of sb;* SEC itacimew, *to price thus* paired with | *akiht

*akinē

INITIAL

— one after the other

evidence | PC akinēnam, *to pick one up after the other;* Lacombe (1874) "akinepayiw, ok, a, ... *ça arrive l'un après l'autre;*" WC akinīskawīw, *to pass in front of rows of people;* MC akineškam, *to walk to one after the other successively;* NEC īchināham, *to go from place to place by vehicle;* Watkins (1865) "Ukenāskum, *v.t.in.6. He passes through the whole of them*"

*akinēpikw (~ *akinēpiko)

INITIAL (NOUN, ANIMATE)

— snake

evidence | PC kinēpikwasakay, *a snakeskin;* MC kinepikoskāw, *to be many snakes;* SEC acinepikʷ, *a snake;* NEC achināpikw, *a snake;* WI (Pessamit) atshinepikᵘ [tʃənēpukʷ], *a snake;* EI (Sheshatshiu) atshinepikᵘ [ətʃɨnēpukʷ], *a snake;* Laure (ca. 1726) "tchinebiku, *couleuvre ordinaire;*" "mikuaskateu attchinebikuchich, *couleuvre d'une autre espèce;*" Silvy (ca. 1680) "kinebigȣ, *couleuvre*"

*akisi

FINAL (VERB, ANIMATE, INTRANSITIVE, CONCRETE)

— smell or taste like

evidence | PC mēyakisiw, *to smell like feces;* MC askīwakisiw, *to smell or taste earthy or mossy;* NEC wīyimiskuchisiu, *to smell or taste like beaver;* WI (Pessamit) uitsheshiutshishu [witsešiwtšu], *to smell like fox* (Drapeau, 1991) paired with | *akan see | *wī

*ako[1] (~ *akw)

INITIAL

— **1** wear as a cloak

— **2** adhere, cling, stick

evidence | ¹PC akohp, *blanket;* MC akohon, *cloak;* SEC akohp, *dress, coat;* EI

(Sheshatshiu) akup [əkūp], *coat, dress, or skirt;* Watkins (1865) "Ukoohoon, *A cloak, a robe*" ²PC akwahpitēw, *to be tied on;* WC akohcin, *to float;* MC akwākonew, *have snow stuck on oneself;* akoštaham, *to stitch or pin sth on;* SEC akosīw, *to climb up or be perched;* AT akorew, *to hang sb;* Silvy (ca. 1680) "ak8am8, *cela tient, v.g. la terre aux souliers*" | ¹ANISH agwinaan, *a shawl* (Livesay & Nichols, 2021); MESK akwihēwa, *to put a robe or blanket on sb to wear* ²ANISH agogin, *to grow attached to sth* (Livesay & Nichols, 2021); MESK akotēwi, *to adhere because of heat* origin | PA ***ako** (Aubin, 1975; Hewson, 1993), possibly akin to ***akwan**

*ako²

FINAL (VERB, ANIMATE, INTRANSITIVE, DERIVED)

— wear as a cloak

evidence | MC aspakow, *to wrap oneself with sth for protection from the cold;* NEC aspikuwin, *sth used as a shawl;* WI ashpaku [ʃpuku], *to wrap oneself with sth for protection from the cold;* Laure (ca. 1726) "aspagun, *manteau, mon manteau*" see | *ako¹

*akocin

FINAL (VERB, ANIMATE, INTRANSITIVE, DERIVED)

— **1** to hang

— **2** to be in the sky

evidence | PC pētakocin, *to come through the air;* WC acitakocin, *to hang upside down;* MC iškwākocin, *to be the end of a month;* SEC itakocin, *to hang thus* origin | PA ***akocin** (Hewson, 1993) see | *ako¹, *cin paired with | *akotē

*akohp

MEDIAL, FINAL (NOUN INCORPORATION)

— cloak, robe

evidence | PC nātakohpēw, *to fetch a blanket(s);* MC oškakohpew, *to wear new dress;* SEC miyokohpew, *to wear a nice coat or dress;* Silvy (ca. 1680) "ni keachag8pan, *j'ai une vielle robe*" see | *ako¹, *ihp

*akor

FINAL (VERB, TRANSITIVE, ANIMATE, DERIVED)

— to hang sb

evidence | MC acitakolew, *to hang sb upside down;* SEC (Waskaganish) āhtakoyew, *to hang sb elsewhere;* NEC pīmikuyāu, *to hang sb up crooked;* NSK kuiiskukuyaaw, *to hang sb straight;* cf. ESC akonew, *to hang sb;* AT akorew, *"accrocher quelqu'un ou quelque chose d'animé (mot rare)"* | MIAMI "Nipang8ac8ra, *je le pend pour le faire seicher*" (Largillier - ILDA, 2017) origin | PA ***akor** (***akol**, Hewson, 1993), cf. ***akoθ** (Hewson, 1993) see | *ako¹, *r, *t⁵ paired with | *akotā discussion | This form has been supplanted by reflexes of ***akot** in many dialects including Plains Cree, Woods Cree, the inland dialects of Southern East Cree, Western Innu, and Eastern Innu. Both forms are used in Atikamekw, with ***akor** being considered a rare form. Laure recorded a reflex of ***akot** circa 1726 in "nit-atchitakutau, *je le pends par les pieds.*" This either suggests the change is quite old or that both forms may be correctly reconstructed for Old Cree. Alternatively, the historically correct form may in fact be ***akot**. In such a case the change to ***akor** may be via areal diffusion of the Old Anishinabe form ***akōr**, which itself could be a reflex of either PA ***akor** or ***akoθ**, the latter being supported by contemporary southern Anishinabe dialects.

*akorē

INITIAL

— overhang

evidence | MC akolekotew, *to overhang;* akolātam, *to deposit a scent mark by urinating on sth, speaking of an animal raising its leg in order to urinate on sth;* AT akoreaw [akorēyāw], *"être en suspension (se dit de l'air entre l'eau et la glace), c'est l'espace entre l'eau et la glace où le castor prend de l'air frais en hiver"* | MENO aki·niatam, *to urinate against sth, speaking of a dog* origin | PA ***akwiryē**

*akotā

FINAL (VERB, ANIMATE, INTRANSITIVE, DERIVED)

— to hang sth

evidence | PC tapahtakotāw, *to hang sth low;* MC išpakotāw, *to hang sth high;* SEC itakotāw, *to hang sth thus* origin | PA ***akotā** (Hewson, 1993) see | *ako[1], *tā paired with | *akor

*akotē

FINAL (VERB, INANIMATE, INTRANSITIVE, DERIVED)

— **1** to hang

— **2** to be in the sky

evidence | MC itakotew, *to hang thus;* SEC miyokotew, *to hang nicely;* WI (Pessamit) kuishkukuteu [kwīʃkukutēw], *to hang straight;* Laure (ca. 1726) "puskutekuteu, *à demi ouvert*" | ANISH ajidagoode, *to hang upside down* (Livesay & Nichols, 2021); MESK akwanakōtēwi, *to overhang* origin | PA ***akotē** (Hewson, 1993) see | *ako[1], *tē[3] paired with | *akocin

*akwan

INITIAL

— cover

evidence | PC akwanāhkwēw, *to have one's face covered;* MC akwanaham, *cover sth;* SEC akwanisekāw, *overhanging cliff;* Silvy (ca. 1680) "nit'akȣanahȣsȣn, *je me couvre, me cache*" | ANISH agwanoge, *to cover a lodge* (Livesay & Nichols, 2021); MESK akwanakōtēwi, *to overhang* origin | PA ***akwan** (Hewson, 1993), possibly akin to ***ako**

*akwā

INITIAL

— **1** come or take out of water

— **2** remove from over the fire

evidence | PC akwāpitam, *to pull sth out of water;* MC akwānam, *take out of water or off the fire;* SEC akwāpayiw, *to drive ashore;* Silvy (ca. 1680) "nit'akȣanau, *je le débarque, mets à terre avec la main*" | ANISH agwaanizhikaw, *to chase sb ashore* (Livesay & Nichols, 2021); MESK akwāhwēwa, *to fish sb out of the water or take off the fire using a stick* origin | PA ***akwā** (Aubin, 1975)

*akwāko (~ *akwākw)

INITIAL

— **1** mould

— **2** rust

evidence | PC akwākomākwan, *to smell mouldy;* MC akwākohtin, *be mouldy or rusty;* SEC akwākopayiw, *to become mouldy;* Silvy (ca. 1680) "akȣakȣchin, *il est moite*" | ANISH agwaagoshi, *to be mouldy* (Livesay & Nichols, 2021) origin | Possibly akin to ***ako**.

*akwāwē

INITIAL (VERB, ANIMATE, INTRANSITIVE)

— place or hang flesh on a rack to dry, smoke, or roast

evidence | PC akwāwānihkēw, *to make a drying rack;* MC akwāwew, *to hang meat or fish on a rack to dry, smoke, or roast;* AT akwawanatikw, *cache pour fumer la viande;* NEC akwāwān, *thinly cut deboned beaver meat hung to dry;* Fabvre (ca. 1690) "(nit) agȣaȣan ȣïas, *estendre chair sur perches*" origin | Query obscure noun incorporation.

*akwē

FINAL (VERB, ANIMATE, INTRANSITIVE, DERIVED)

— snare

evidence | MC tāpakwew, *to set a snare(s);* SEC nātakwew, *to check a snare(s);* WI manakueu [mənəkwēw], *to remove a snare* |

ANISH giitagwen, *to remove sb from a snare* (Livesay & Nichols, 2021) see | *nakwē

*akwēp

INITIAL

— bulky, cumbersome

evidence | PC Lacombe (1874) "akwebisiw, *il est embarrassant, et, embarrassé;*" MC akwepan, *be bulky or cumbersome;* SEC akwepisīw, *to be encumbered;* Fabvre (ca. 1690) "Ak8episin i8, *auoir beauc(ou)p de bagage*"

*am[1] (~ *ah)

FINAL (VERB, TRANSITIVE, ANIMATE, ABSTRACT)

— conveys the semantic role of patient to a participant

evidence | PC tahkamew, *to stab sb;* asahkēw, *to feed people;* WC wāpamīw, *to see sb;* MC tahkamew, *to stab sb;* SEC maskamew, *to rob sb;* WI (Pessamit) ashameu [ʃəmēw], *to feed sb* see | *aht[2]

*am[2] (~ *ah)

FINAL (VERB, TRANSITIVE, ANIMATE, CONCRETE)

— by use of mouth or teeth

evidence | MC kāhcitamew, *catch sb with one's mouth;* SEC mākomew, *to bite sb;* Fabvre (ca. 1690) "Tak8atemau piki8, *mascher braye, La tenir en La b8che;*" Silvy (ca. 1680) "ni mag8amau, *je prends avec les dents;*" "ni kaskamau, *je casse avec les dents;*" "tak8akan 3. -e8, *je mords*" origin | PA ***am** (Aubin, 1975) paired with | *aht[3]

*amahciho

FINAL (VERB, ANIMATE, INTRANSITIVE, CONCRETE)

— experience a sensation

evidence | PC mātamahcihow, *to start experiencing pain;* MC itamahcihow, *feel thus;* SEC cihkāwātamahcihow, *to feel right* | ANISH dakamanji'o, *feel a chill* (Livesay & Nichols, 2021) see | *amaht

*amahcihtā

FINAL (VERB, ANIMATE, INTRANSITIVE, CONCRETE)

— experience a sensation

evidence | WC kosikwamahcihtāw, *to feel sth is heavy;* MC itamahcihtāw, *feel sth thus;* SEC nisitomahcihtāw, *to recognize the feeling of sth* see | *amaht, *htā

*amahkw

INITIAL (NOUN, ANIMATE)

— needle used for lacing or weaving

evidence | WC amāhkos, *a small snowshoe weaving needle made of wood;* MC amahk^{w}, *a needle used for lacing a snowshoe frame; a needle used for weaving strips of rabbit fur;* SEC kamahk^{w}, *your needle for lacing or weaving;* NEC amihkw, *a snowshoe lacing needle;* WI (Pessamit) namak^{u} [nəmuk^{w}], *my netting needle for babiche;* EI (Mamit) amak^{u} [amāhk^{w}], *a netting needle for babiche;* Silvy (ca. 1680) "namak8a, *aiguille à tirer raquettes*" compare | *akaskw, *ašisoy discussion | ***Amahkwa** is one of a few independent nouns in Old Cree that does not, despite its form, require an epenthetic **t** when possessed.

*amaht

PREFINAL

— experience a sensation

evidence | PC mātamahcihow, *to start experiencing pain;* MC itamahcihow, *feel thus;* SEC nisitomahcihtāw, *to recognize the feeling of sth* | ANISH maadamandam, *to start to have pain* (Livesay & Nichols, 2021); MESK menwamatamwa, *to feel good* origin | PA ***amant** see | *amahciho, *amahcihtā

*amatihso

INITIAL (VERB, ANIMATE, INTRANSITIVE)

— to feel uneasy or vulnerable due to some unseen presence

evidence | MC amatisototawew, *to feel uneasy or vulnerable due to sb's unseen presence;* AT (Wemotaci, Nicole Petiquay) amatiso [amatissow], *être en présence de quelque chose de surnaturel;* SEC amatisow, *to feel uneasy or vulnerable due to some unseen presence;* Fabvre (ca. 1690) "Amatis8n 8, *au(oi)r l'allarme de L'ennemy*" | ANISH amaniso, *to sense an unseen presence* (Livesay & Nichols, 2021) origin | PA ***amaθehso** (Hewson, 1993)

*amā

INITIAL

— spook, scare off

evidence | PC amāhēw, *to scare an animal away;* MC amāhew, *spook animal;* SEC (Waskaganish) amāhīpew, *to scare fish away from an area by leaving a net in too long;* Fabvre (ca. 1690) "Amamau, *faire fuir a(nim)al en parlant*"

*amēhs

MEDIAL, FINAL (NOUN INCORPORATION)

— fish

evidence | PC nōtamesew, *to fish;* MC mōmesew, *eat fish;* AT (Opitciwan, Joey Awashish) momesew [mōmēssēw], *eat fish;* SEC nōtamesew, *to fish;* Laure (ca. 1726) "ni-tepamesan, *je suis soûl, las de poisson;*" Silvy (ca. 1680) "atames, *poisson puant*" origin | Old Cree ***namēhsa** see | *namēhs

*amēkohs

FINAL (NOUN, ANIMATE)

— trout

evidence | PC māsamēkos, *a speckled trout;* AT (Wemotaci, Jeannette Coocoo) macamekos [māʒamēkos], *a speckled trout;* Laure (ca. 1726) "machameguch, *petite truite*" see | *namēkohs compare | *amēkw

*amēkw

MEDIAL, FINAL (NOUN INCORPORATION)

— fish

evidence | MC sāsamekwew, *fry fish;* SEC pīwahamekwew, *to scale fish;* NEC wāpimākw, *a beluga whale;* Fabvre (ca. 1690) "Niganameg8an, *p(ar)tie de poiss(on) entre La teste et La queue;*" Silvy (ca. 1680) "marameg8, *barbue (poisson)*" | MIAMI myaalameekwa, *catfish* (ILDA, 2017) origin | PA ***amēkw** (Aubin, 1975), ultimately from PA ***namēkwa**, *lake trout* (Aubin, 1975) see | *namēkohs compare | *amēkohs

*amiskw[1] (~ *amisko)

INITIAL (NOUN, ANIMATE)

— beaver

evidence | PC amisk, *beaver;* amiskwāyow, *a beaver tail;* MC amiskoskāw, *to be many beavers;* SEC amiskopiy, *a beaver pond;* WI (Pessamit) amishkushtau [məʃkustāw], *to set a trap for beaver;* Laure (ca. 1726) "amisku, *castor;*" Silvy (ca. 1680) "amisk8ar8, *queue de castor;*" Le Jeune (1634) "Amiscouakhi, *castors*" | ANISH amikokaa, *to be many beavers* (Livesay & Nichols, 2021); MESK amehkwa, *a beaver* see | *amiskw[2]

*amiskw[2] (~ *amisko)

MEDIAL, FINAL (NOUN INCORPORATION)

— beaver

evidence | PC nitawamiskwēw, *to search for beaver;* WC patamisk, *three year old beaver;* MC pahkonamiskwew, *skin beaver;* SEC nōtamiskwew, *to harvest beavers;* WI (Pessamit) patamishk[u] [pətaməʃkʷ], *a three-year old beaver;* Laure (ca. 1726) "nit-askauamiskuan 3. -eu, *je l'attrape à l'affût (castor);*" Fabvre (ca. 1690) "n8tchiamisk8an e8, *u8loir tuer ou pr(en)dre castors;*" Silvy (ca. 1680) "ni nata8amisk8an, *je vais au castor*" | ANISH andawamikwe, *to hunt or trap beaver* (Livesay & Nichols, 2021) origin | Old Cree ***amiskwa** see | *amiskw[1]

*amo

FINAL (VERB, INTRANSITIVE)

— attached, fixed, or stuck to

evidence | WC wīmāmow, *to be a detour;* MC itamow, *fixed or stuck thus;* SEC cikamohtāw, *to stick sth on;* Laure (ca. 1726) "panakuabegamu, *lâche, qui n'est pas bien tendu;*" Silvy (ca. 1680) "ak8am8, *cela tient, v.g. la terre aux souliers*"

*amotay[1]

INITIAL (NOUN, DEPENDENT INANIMATE)

— crop

evidence | PC omotay, *crop of a bird; beard of a buffalo or moose;* NEC umutī, *crop of a bird;* WI (Pessamit) umutai [umutī], *one's belly;* Laure (ca. 1726) "pirechich uamutai, *jabot d'un oiseau*" see | *amotay[2]

*amotay[2]

FINAL (NOUN INCORPORATION)

— crop

evidence | PC wēskwamotayēw, *five-year-old bull moose;* Laure (ca. 1726) "pireu amutai, *vessie de perdrix*" see | *amotay[1]

*an[1]

INITIAL

— lose

evidence | PC Lacombe (1874) "ānihuw, ok, *(v.n.) il dépérit, il maigrit, par exemple un animal après avoir trop travaillé;*" NEC anihū, *to be gone for a long time;* Watkins (1865) "unnehoo, *v.refl.4. He brings bad luck upon himself (by the improper performance of heathen rites);*" Fabvre (ca. 1690) "annĭh8n 8, *tarder à venir;*" "anĭtan, *perdre, égarer q(uel)q(ue) ch(os)e;*" Silvy (ca. 1680) "nit'anichinin, *je m'égare, je me perds;*" cf. AT (Wemotaci, Nicole Petiquay) itaniho [itanhow], *to be gone for a certain length of time;* SEC itanihow, *to be gone for a certain length of time;* NEC itinihū, *to be gone for a certain length of time* | MENO ane·hɛ·w, *to win from sb;* MESK anihēwa, *to defeat sb*

*an[2] (~ *ah)

FINAL (VERB, INANIMATE, INTRANSITIVE, ABSTRACT)

— forms stative verbs

evidence | WC ispīhtāyawan, *to be such a time of the year;* MC alakaškekan, *wide sheet;* wīhkašin, *to be delicious;* SEC yikoskwan, *cloudy;* Fabvre (ca. 1690) "Pigan, *cela e tr8blé, v.g. eau*" | ABEN tekwigwan II, *to be heavy;* MENO we·hkan II, *to taste good* compare | *ɪn[4]

*anakw

MEDIAL (NOUN INCORPORATION)

— sleeve(s)

evidence | MC mīšahanakwew, *patch a sleeve;* SEC tahkonakweyāw, *to have short sleeves;* Silvy (ca. 1680) "ni kechtanag8an 3. -e8, *je dévêts mes manches*" see | *anakway

*anakway

INITIAL (NOUN, ANIMATE)

— sleeve

evidence | PC anakway, *a sleeve;* NEC anikui, *a sleeve;* Laure (ca. 1726) "nanaguaiets, *manche de femme;*" Silvy (ca. 1680) "anag8eia, *pl.* -eiak, *manches*" see | *anakw, *ay[2]

discussion | ***Anakwaya** is one of a few independent nouns in Old Cree that does not, despite its form, require an epenthetic **t** when possessed.

*anarkitiy

INITIAL (NOUN, DEPENDENT ANIMATE)

— rump of a bird, uropygium

evidence | ESC (Severn) onakitiy, *a tail feather of bird;* MC wanahkitiya, *its rump, speaking of a bird;* AT (Opitciwan, Joey Awashish) onikiti [onihkitiy], *rump of a bird* | ANISH onashkid, *its tail, speaking of a bird;* cf. Cuoq (1886) "wewebanackitiieni, *il frétille de la queue (en parlant des oiseaux)*" discussion | In the absence of a Woods Cree cognate, the reconstruction of the consonant cluster is indirectly supported by Anishinabe cognates.

*anask

MEDIAL

— top of a tree

evidence | WC cimanaskatōhtak, *tree with its top broken off;* MC kīškanaskisiw, *to be broken off at the top, speaking of a tree;* NEC chiminischipiyiu, *to break off, speaking of a dead tree;* WI (Pessamit) pishkutanassiu [pəʃkutnəssīw], *to have a rounded top, speaking of a tree;* Watkins (1865) "Chimunuskut, *n.indec. [sic] A tree broken by the wind*" |

ABEN gezibanakw, *a tree squeak* (Day, 1994) compare | *wanasko

*anāskē

INITIAL (VERB, ANIMATE, INTRANSITIVE)

— lay material down as flooring

evidence | PC anāskān, *matting, flooring;* MC anāskew, *to lay conifer boughs down for flooring;* AT (Opitciwan, Joey Awashish) anaskan [anāskān], *conifer branch flooring;* NEC anāschāu, *to lay conifers down for flooring;* WI (Pessamit) anashkatam[u] [nāʃkətəm], *to put a floor in sth;* EI (Sheshatshiu) anashkan [ənāʃkən], *plank of a canoe;* Silvy (ca. 1680) "anaskan, *litière des cabanes*" | ANISH anaakanashkoon, *reeds, rushes* (Livesay & Nichols, 2021); MENO ana·hkow, *to lay a mat(s);* MESK anāhkēwa, *to lay sth down as a mat to sit or lie on*

*anihtoy

INITIAL (NOUN, INANIMATE)

— fishing spear, leister

evidence | PC Lacombe (1874) "Anittuy, a, *(n.r.) dard fait avec un bois;*" NEC nihtuyi, *a harpoon for hunting sturgeon or whale;* nihtukin, *barb of a harpoon;* EI (Sheshatshiu) nitukan [ntūkan], *a harpoon with detachable head;* Watkins (1865) "*Harpoon, n.* Unetookun;" Laure (ca. 1726) "anitui, *bâton à tuer le castor;*" Fabvre (ca. 1690) "Anit8gan, *le fer du harpon ou d'au(tre)fois os;*" Silvy (ca. 1680) "anit8i, *bâton à tirer le castor*" | ANISH anit, *a fish spear* (Livesay & Nichols, 2021); MENO ani·htiy, *spear, fish spear;* neta·nihtiy, *my fish spear*

*anikwacāhs

INITIAL (NOUN, ANIMATE)

— squirrel

evidence | PC anikwacās, *a squirrel;* WC anikwacās, *a squirrel;* ESC (Severn) anikwacāsh, *a squirrel;* AT (Wemotaci, Jeannette Coocoo) anikotcac [anikocāš], *a squirrel;* anikoca:šš, *a squirrel* (Béland, 1978); SEC anikocāš, *a squirrel; a squirrel-like rodent such as the chipmunk or flying squirrel;* NEC anikuchāsh, *a squirrel;* WI (Pessamit) anikutshash [nukutʃāʃ], *a squirrel; a red squirrel;* EI (Sheshatshiu) anikutshash [nukutʃāʃ], *squirrel; red squirrel;* Watkins (1865) "Unikwuchas, *n.an. A squirrel;*" La Brosse (1766) "Anikutshash, *Sciuris;*" Laure (ca. 1726) "anikutchach *pl.* -ets, *écureuil [roux];*" Fabvre (ca. 1690) "Anik8chas, *petit Escurieux*"

*aniskamē

INITIAL

— line for fastening a cloak or robe

evidence | PC āniskamātēw, *to button sb up;* Lacombe (1874) "āniskamān, ak, *(n.f.) épinglette, agraffe;*" Isham (1743) "a nis ko mon, *strings to a beaver coate or loose garment;*" Laure (ca. 1726) "aniskaman *pl.* -a, *corde attachant la robe par devant sur les épaules;*" Fabvre (ca. 1690) "Aniskăman = magan, *Corde, Lien de l(eu)r robbe qui l'agraffe;*" Silvy (ca. 1680) "aniskamagan, *corde à attacher une robe*" | ANISH anikamaanan, *suspenders; shoulder straps of a traditional Anishinaabe dress* (Livesay & Nichols, 2021); anakamaan, *button;* anakamaaneyaab, *laced upright holding main lacing to crossbar* (Lippert & Gambill, 2023); MENO neta·nehkama·nan, *my suspenders* origin | Query obscure noun incorporation.

*anoht (~ *anohc)

INITIAL

— during the course of the present day

evidence | PC anohc, *now; today;* MC anohc, *at the present time, now; today; during the course of a specified period of time;* anohcīhkān, *recently;* SEC anohcīš, *now; today;* EI (Sheshatshiu) anutshish [nūtʃīʃ], *now, currently, today; in the near future; recently, a short while ago;* Laure (ca. 1726) "anutch, *incessamment, tout à l'heure;*" Silvy (ca. 1680) "an8ch, *maintenant*"

*anot (~ *anoš)

INITIAL (NOUN, INANIMATE)

— line used for securing legging to belt

evidence | Isham (1743) "Man no ta pee, *A String the women wears, about their waste, wch. they tie their Stockings;*" Laure (ca. 1726) "anuchi pl. -a, *corde attachant, serrant les culottes;*" "nit-anuchikahun, nit-anichikan 3- -kau, *je les attache;*" Fabvre (ca. 1690) "An8chi [breve noted over 8], *corde qui tient L(eu)rs mitas à la ceinture;*" "An8tēbi, *Ceinture à La q(ue)lle ils attachent l(eu)rs bas;*" Silvy (ca. 1680) "nit'an8chikan, *je lie mes bas*" | ANISH anoonihsh, *cloth, rag, old clothes* (Oji-Cree, 2014) origin | Likely PA ***anweθ**.

*anow

MEDIAL (NOUN INCORPORATION)

— cheek(s)

evidence | MC mihkonawew, *have red cheeks;* SEC pācinawepayiw, *to have swelling cheeks;* Laure (ca. 1726) "n-utamanuaiuau, *je lui baille un soufflet sur la joue;*" Silvy (ca. 1680) "ni mamik8an8an, *j'ai les joues rouges*" | ANISH oziiganowe, *to have wrinkled cheeks* (Livesay & Nichols, 2021); MESK mamākanowēwa, *to have big cheeks* origin | Old Cree ***-anoway** see | *anoway

*anoway

INITIAL (NOUN, DEPENDENT INANIMATE)

— cheek

evidence | PC maniway, *a cheek;* WI (Pessamit) unuai [ūnwī], *one's cheekbone;* Watkins (1865) *"Cheek, n.* unoowai or anoowai;" Silvy (ca. 1680) "man8ai *pl.* man8eïa, *joue*" | ANISH onow, *one's cheek* (Livesay & Nichols, 2021); MESK nenowayi, *my cheek;* MIAMI ninowaya, *my cheeks* (ILDA, 2017) see | *anow, *ay²

*ap¹

INITIAL

— sit

evidence | PC apiw, *to sit;* MC apisow, *sit by source of heat to warm up;* SEC apiw, *to sit;* Silvy (ca. 1680) "nit'aïapisites8n, *je me chauffe les pieds*" origin | PA ***ap** (Aubin, 1975; Hewson, 1993) paired with | *aštē¹

*ap²

MEDIAL (NOUN INCORPORATION)

— inner thigh(s)

evidence | PA Lacombe (1874) "wikkwepān, ak, *(n.f.) pantalons, culottes;*" MC tōhkapeštāw, *to part one's thighs;* SEC kāhkapeyiw, *to part one's thighs;* Laure (ca. 1726) "nit-aragabegabauin 3. -uiu, *j'écarte les jambes [debout]*" see | *apay

*apahkw

MEDIAL, FINAL (NOUN INCORPORATION)

— thatch, cover of a dwelling

evidence | MC āhtapahkwew, *change roof of dwelling;* AT (Wemotaci, Jeannette Coocoo) okitapokw [okitapokkw], *on the roof;* WI (Pessamit) takutapak^{u} [təkutəpuk^{w}], *on top of the tent, on the roof;* EI (Sheshatshiu) pashapakueu [pāʃəpākwēw], *faire sécher sa toile, sa tente;* Silvy (ca. 1680) "ni rachabak8enen, *je retire, je rabaisse l'écorce*" | ANISH ogidabak, *on top of the roof* (Livesay & Nichols, 2021) | ANISH Cuoq (1886) "Ackatai, *peau crue*" origin | Old Cree ***apahkwaya**, *thatch,* ultimately from PA ***apahkwaya** (Hewson, 1993) see | *apahkway

*apahkway

INITIAL (NOUN, ANIMATE)

— thatch, cover of a dwelling

evidence | NEC apihkui, *covering for a shelter;* WI (Pessamit) apakuai [pukwī], *tent covering, heavy canvas;* EI (Sheshatshiu) apakuai [əpākwī], *tent covering, heavy canvas;* Laure (ca. 1726) "matutichin-apakuai, *les écorces pour la suerie*" | MENO apa·hkiy, *reed, bullrush* origin | PA

***apahkwaya** (Hewson, 1993) see | *apahkw, *apahkwē, *ay[2]

*apahkwācīhš

INITIAL (NOUN, ANIMATE)

— bat (flying mammal of the order Chiroptera)

evidence | PC apahkwācīs, *a bat;* SEC apahkwācīš, *a bat;* Laure (ca. 1726) "apakuatchich *pl.* -ets, *chauve-souris*" compare | *apahkway

*apahkwē

INITIAL (VERB, ANIMATE, INTRANSITIVE)

— thatch, cover a dwelling

evidence | PC apahkwēw, *to thatch a dwelling, to cover a dwelling with a roof;* MC apahkwāsow, *to cover or roof one's dwelling;* SEC apahkwān, *canvas;* Silvy (ca. 1680) "nit'abak8aten, 3. -tam, *j'abrie, couvre, bouche, v.g. maison, etc.*" | ANISH apakwe, *to put on a roof, to cover the lodge with bark* (Livesay & Nichols, 2021) see | *apahkway

*apahšoy

INITIAL (NOUN, INANIMATE)

— pole for supporting a tipi

evidence | PC apasoyāhtik, *a tipi pole;* WC apasoy, *a tent pole;* AT (Wemotaci, Nicole Petiquay) apacowatikw [apaššowāhtikw], *a lodge pole;* SEC apašoy, *a tipi pole;* EI (Sheshatshiu) apashui [pəʃwi], *a long pole used in different types of dwellings to create a frame;* Silvy (ca. 1680) "apach8i, *perche*" | ANISH abanzh, *a lodge pole; a rafter* (Livesay & Nichols, 2021)

*apay

INITIAL (NOUN, DEPENDENT INANIMATE)

— inner thigh

evidence | ESC (Fort Severn) wapay, *one's groin;* MC opay, *one's inner thigh;* cf. AT orakapai [orakapay], *one's groin* see | *ap[2]

*api

FINAL (VERB, ANIMATE, INTRANSITIVE, DERIVED)

— sit

evidence | PC nahapiw, *to sit down;* MC āhtapiw, *to sit elsewhere;* SEC miyopiw, *to sit comfortably;* Laure (ca. 1726) "ni-nichtamapin, *je tiens le premier rang*" | MENO saka·hkapew AI *"to be put away, to be safe in a proper place, to sit in one's proper place"* origin | Old Cree ***apiwa**, from PA ***apiwa** (Aubin, 1975; Hewson, 1993) see | *ap[1], *i[2] paired with | *aštē[2]

*apihkan

INITIAL (NOUN, ANIMATE)

— thwart, crosspiece

evidence | WC apīhkan, *a crossbar or a canoe;* MC apihkan, *a thwart;* AT (Wemotaci, Jeannette Coocoo) apikan [apihkan], *a thwart of a canoe;* NEC apihkin, *a crosspiece of a canoe;* EI (Sheshatshiu) apikan [əpīkən], *a thwart of a canoe*

*apihkē

INITIAL (VERB, ANIMATE, INTRANSITIVE)

— plait, braid

evidence | WC apīhkīw, *to braid or plait;* MC apihkān, *a plait;* SEC apihkēw, *to plait;* Silvy (ca. 1680) "nit'abikaten, *je tresse*" | ANISH apike, *to braid* (Livesay & Nichols, 2021) origin | PA ***apihkē**, cf. ***apihkāni** (Hewson, 1993) see | *apihs, *ihkē

*apihs

INITIAL (NOUN, INANIMATE)

— a string or rope

evidence | AT (Wemotaci, Nicole Petiquay) apisa [apissa], *strings;* SEC apis, *string, rope;* NEC apis, *string;* EI (Mamit) napish [napih], *my cord, string, rope, or strap* origin | Likely PA ***apihsi**, diminutive of ***apyi**. see | *apihkē, *āp[2], *āpihkē, *āpiy discussion | ***Apihsi** is one of a few independent nouns in Old Cree that does not, despite its form, require an epenthetic **t** when possessed.

*apiht[1]

INITIAL (NOUN, ANIMATE)

— **1** flint

— **2** dark blue or purplish hue

evidence | [1]PC Lacombe (1874) "ahpit, ak, *sac, pour le tabac;*" ESC apiht, *flint; a sparkplug;* SEC (coastal) Apihtipiy, *flint lake, place name known as Lac Abitibi in French;* NEC apiht, *flint;* Watkins (1865) "Upèt, *n.an. See* Apèt;" "Apèt, *n.an. A fire-steel; a fire-bag;*" Laure (ca. 1726) "apit, *batte-feu;*" Fabvre (ca. 1690) "Apit, *baste feu fuzil à faire feu*" [2]PC ahpīhtisiw, *to be bruised;* MC apihcihkwešin, *to sustain a bruise on one's face after impact;* apihtahwew, *to inflict a bruise on sb;* AT (Wemotaci, Jeannette Coocoo) apitisiw [apihtiziw], *to be bruised;* SEC apihtisiw, *to be a dark blue color;* WI (Pessamit) apitau [pətāw], *to be purplish;* EI (Sheshatshiu) apitshimineu [pītʃiminēw], *to be purple;* Watkins (1865) "Ăpetów [*sic*], *v.imp. It is blue (as a bruise), it is livid, it is bruised, it is a bruise;*" Laure (ca. 1726) "abitau; ka iabitatch, *contusion, meurtrissure;*" "abitabıu, *les yeux battus*" | ANISH Cuoq (1886) "Apis, *v. Piwanak;* cf. Piwanak, ...ok, *silex, pierre à fusil;*" "Apisaje, *avoir la peau livide;*" MENO apɛ·hnen, *to be dark-colored or blue;* apɛ·s, *prenoun, dark-colored, blue* origin | PA ***apehθa*** see | *apiht[2] discussion | The expected allormorph ***apihš*** appears to be unattested and is replaced instead in some contemporary dialects with reflexes of ***apihc**.

*apiht[2]

MEDIAL, FINAL (NOUN INCORPORATION)

— flint

evidence | MC pāhpākapihtesiw, *a yellow rail;* Watkins (1865) "Pewapiskapèt, *n.an. A fire-steel;*" Silvy (ca. 1680) "papakapitechich, *espèce d'oiseau*" see | *apiht[1] discussion | Corroborative evidence for this noun incorporation largely consists of the name of the yellow rail (Coturnicops noveboracensis), a bird known for its distinctive call that sounds like two stones repeatedly clicking together. The Moose Cree name, as well as its cognate in Silvy (ca. 1680) translates to "one that repeatedly clicks the flint."

*apiskw (~ *apisko)

INITIAL (NOUN, ANIMATE)

— large bird of prey

evidence | PC apiskwak, *large eagles;* WSC (Misipawistik, Ellen Cook) apiskway, *osprey;* Watkins (1865) "Upisk, *n.an. A large eagle;*" EI (Ekuanitshit, Anasthasie Napess) "apiskuatshistun, *le nid des apisk (sorte d'aigles)*" (Commission de Toponymie du Quebec, 1980) | MIAMI apeehkoohsia, *turkey vulture* (ILDA, 2017)

*apišt (~ *apihš)

INITIAL

— small

evidence | PC apistacihkos, *antelope;* apisīs, *a little;* WC apiscākamisin, *to be a little quantity of liquid;* MC apihciškiš, *cackling goose;* apišipakāw, *to have small leaves;* AT apištiriniššak, *gnomes, elves;* apišša:ššin, *to be small;* (Béland, 1978); SEC apišitonešiw, *to have a small mouth;* WI (Pessamit) apishtapeushu [pəstāpēwʃu], *to be a small man;* EI apishtiss [apistiss], *brant;* Laure (ca. 1726) "nit-apichirauanach, *je suis petit de stature;*" Silvy (ca. 1680) "nit'apistatanach, *j'ai petit ventre, je mange peu*" | MENO apɛ·hsos(-ok), *deer;* MIAMI "apechikitchiȣa, *il a une petite queüe*" (Largillier - ILDA, 2017)

*apoy[1] (~ *apō)

INITIAL (NOUN, ANIMATE)

— paddle

evidence | MC apoyāhtikʷ, *wood for making a paddle;* apōhkew, *to make a paddle;* SEC apoyāhtik[w], *wood for making a paddle;* NEC apūhchāu, *to make a paddle;* EI (Sheshatshiu) aputsheu [apūtʃēw], *to make a paddle;* Laure (ca. 1726) "apuai, *aviron;*" "nit-apukauau 3. -ueu, *je lui fais un aviron;*" Silvy (ca. 1680) "ap8i *pl.* ap8iak, *aviron;*" "ap8iask, *érable*"

*apoy[2]

MEDIAL, FINAL (NOUN INCORPORATION)

— paddle

evidence | WC māhkapoyīw, *to have a big paddle;* MC kinwāskopoyew, *to use a long paddle;* oškapoy, *a new paddle;* WI (Pessamit) natuapuieu [nātwāpujēw], *to have a paddle broken in two;* Fabvre (ca. 1690) "N8tapïan e8, *le rame fortem(en)t*" | ANISH bookwaboye, *to break a paddle* (Livesay & Nichols, 2021)

*apwē[1]

INITIAL (VERB, ANIMATE, INTRANSITIVE)

— **1** sweat

— **2** roast

evidence | [1]ESC apwesiw, *to sweat;* MC apwecihcew, *have sweaty hands;* SEC (Waswanipi) apwehkwāmiw, *to sweat during sleep;* Silvy (ca. 1680) "nit'ap8echtig8anan, *je sue à la tête*" [2]ESC apwew, *to roast over an open fire on a frame;* MC apwātam, *to roast sth over fire,* AT apwan [apwān], *viande rôtie;* Silvy (ca. 1680) "nit'ap8an, *je fais rôtir*" | [1]ANISH abwezo, *to sweat* (Livesay & Nichols, 2021) [2]ANISH abwaan, *a roast* (Livesay & Nichols, 2021)

*apwē[2]

FINAL (VERB, ANIMATE, INTRANSITIVE, DERIVED)

— roast

evidence | PC sakapwew, *to roast on string;* MC maskatepwew, *to cook fish or meat directly on embers;* SEC cīštahāpwān, *meat roasted on a skewer;* Silvy (ca. 1680) "ni papatchiga8ab8an 3 -e8, *je fais tomber la graisse, rôtissant*" | ANISH ningwa'abwe, *to cook sth under the ashes* (Livesay & Nichols, 2021)

*ar

INITIAL

— cover or bury

evidence | PC ayākonēham, *to cover sth with snow;* WC aðiskam, *to cover sth with one's foot;* NEC iyiham, *to cover sth with earth or snow;* WI (Pessamit) alakuneu [lākunēw], *to be covered with snow;* Watkins (1865) "ayuchistin, *v.imp. the track is covered (e.g. by drifting snow);*" Laure (ca. 1726) "arauatchipitaganiuets, *le champ est hersé, le grain est enterré;*" Silvy (ca. 1680) "rak8neu, *la neige s'arrête dessus*"

*arahak

MEDIAL (NOUN INCORPORATION)

— scales

evidence | MC kispakalahakew, *to have thick scales* | MESK mamākinahakēwa, *to have large scales* see | *arahakay

*arahakay

INITIAL (NOUN, DEPENDENT ANIMATE)

— scale

evidence | ESC (Severn) manahakay, *scale of a fish;* MC walahakay, *scale of a fish or reptile;* Silvy (ca. 1680) "8arahagai, *écaille de poisson*" | ANISH wanahakayak, *fish scales* (Oji-Cree, 2014); MESK onahakayani, *scales (of a fish);* MIAMI "arahagaïaki, *écailles de poisson, cosses de pois ou fèves*" (Largillier - ILDA, 2017) compare | *ar, *ahakay see | *arahak, *ay[2] discussion | Comparative evidence limited to Atikamekw, Western Innu, and a historical source from the Saguanay region (Laure, ca. 1726) allow for the reconstruction of the variant ***arakay**. This form, however, is likely a contraction of ***arahakay**, a form that is supported by sources drawn from a much larger geographic area.

*arahsit[1]

INITIAL (NOUN, DEPENDENT ANIMATE)

— foot of an ungulate

evidence | MC walasit, *the foot of an ungulate or rabbit;* AT (Opitciwan, Joey Awashish) orisit [orissit], *foot of a moose;* (Wemotaci, Nicole Petiquay) warisitai [warizitay], *foot of a moose;* SEC (Waswanipi) wayasit, *foot of an ungulate;* WI (Pessamit) ulashit [uləʃət], *foot of a caribou or moose;* EI (Sheshashiu) unasht [unəst], *foot of a caribou or moose;* Silvy (ca. 1680) "ȣarasit *pl.* -sitak, *l'ongle ou corne du pied*" | ANISH ninasidan, *my hooves* (Lippert & Gambill, 2023) see | *arahsit²

*arahsit²

MEDIAL, FINAL (NOUN INCORPORATION)

— foot of an ungulate

evidence | PC pitikwayasit, *club foot;* WC kaskitīwaðasit, *a Blackfoot;* MC wāpalasitew, *to have white feet;* NEC uchishtiwiyisitān, *the space in the split in the hoof;* EI (Sheshatshiu) muanashteu [mwānəstēw], *to eat caribou feet;* Laure (ca. 1726) "taskarasitan, *pied fourchu d'un animal;*" Silvy (ca. 1680) "tachkarasitan, *fourchure du pied de l'orignal*" see | *arahsit¹

*arak

INITIAL

— wide apart

evidence | AT orakapai [orakapay], *one's groin;* NEC iyikipāhtāu, *to walk with legs apart;* WI (Pessamit) alakapepu [ləkəpēpu], *to sit with legs apart;* Laure (ca. 1726) "nit-aragabegabauin 3. -uiu, *j'écarte les jambes [debout];*" Silvy (ca. 1680) "aragabechagan, *haut-de-chausses;*" cf. PC tastawayakap, *between legs;* MC oteštakalapew ([*sic*], likely a contraction of earlier oteštakalakapew, in reference to the taller front of the caribou), *a vicious mythical caribou* compare | *arakašk limited to | *ap²

*arakaskw¹ (~ *arakasko)

INITIAL (NOUN, DEPENDENT ANIMATE)

— palate

evidence | PC mayakask, *a palate;* MC olakaskwa, *one's palate;* WI (Pessamit) ulakashkua [uləkəʃkwē], *one's palate;* Laure (ca. 1726) "uragasku *pl.* -ets, *le palais de la bouche;*" Silvy (ca. 1680) "aragaskȣ, *palais de la gorge*" | ABEN walakw, *uvula, palate* (Day, 1995); ANISH onagaskway, *one's palate* (Livesay & Nichols, 2021)

*arakaskw² (~ *arakasko)

MEDIAL, FINAL (NOUN INCORPORATION)

— palate

evidence | MC māskalakaskwew, *to have a deformed palate*

*arakašk

INITIAL

— wide

evidence | PC ayakaskāw, *to be wide;* MC alakaškekan, *wide sheet;* alakaškisitew, *have broad feet;* SEC ayakaščikotew, *to have a wide beak* compare | *arak

*arakāsk

INITIAL

— volar aspect (of hand or foot)

evidence | ESC manakāskicihcān, *the palm of a hand;* MC olakāskisitān, *the sole of one's foot;* olakāskicihcān, *the palm of one's hand;* AT orakaskisitan [orakāskizitān], *the sole of one's foot;* SEC (Waswanipi) wayakāscisitān, *the sole of one's foot;* EI (Sheshatshiu) unakashtan [unəkāstān], *the sole of one's foot;* Laure (ca. 1726) "uragatchisitan, *la plante du pied;*" Fabvre (ca. 1690) "Aragastitĭchan, *paume de la main;*" Silvy (ca. 1680) "maragastisitan *pl.* -tanak, *la plante des pieds large*" | ANISH onagaakininj, *one's palm;* onagaakizid, *one's sole* (Livesay & Nichols, 2021)

*arāwat (~ *arāwac, *arāwas)

INITIAL

— useless(ly)

evidence | SEC ayāwatan, *to be useless;* ayāwacimow, *to talk uselessly;* NEC iyāutāyihtim, *to think sth is done unnecessarily;* Laure (ca. 1726) "nit-arauatchimun, *je parle, pas correctement*"

*arihs

INITIAL

— plain, unseasoned

evidence | ESC anisipiy, *plain water;* MC alisāw, *to be plain tasting;* AT (Opitciwan, Joey Awashish) arisipi [arissipiy], *spring water;* (Wemotaci, Nicole Petiquay) arisaw [arissāw], *to be plain tasting* | MIAMI "Aressip8gan8i, *fade*" (Largillier - ILDA, 2017) compare | *pīrihs

*arihsā

INITIAL

— refrain, resist

evidence | PC ayisac [*sic*], *unwillingly;* Lacombe (1874) "Isāhew, *il le modère, il le corrige;*" ESC anisāc, *unwillingly;* MC alisāhow, *to restrain oneself;* AT (Opitciwan, Joey Awashish) arisaho [arissāhow], *to restrain oneself, to avoid overexerting oneself;* SEC ayisāc, *unwillingly, resistingly*

*arihš

INITIAL

— root of unknown meaning that is always affixed to *riniw, possibly an ancient ethnonym

evidence | PC ayisiyiniw, *human being;* WC aðisiðiniw, *human being;* AT (Wemotaci, Nicole Petiquay) aricíriniw [arišširiniw], *a human being;* SEC ayišiyiniw, *human being;* NEC nishīyiyiu, *a modern day man;* Watkins (1865) "Ayiseyinewew, *v.i.1. He is a man, he is human;*" Laure (ca. 1726) "kassinau arichiriniuets, *le monde, parlant de tous les hommes qui le composent;*" Fabvre (ca. 1690) "Arichirini8, *homme, peuple, na(ti)on*" | ANISH anishinaabe, *human being, Ojibwe* (Livesay & Nichols, 2021); anihshinini, *person, Native, Oji-Cree* (Oji-Cree, 2014); MESK aneshinenīhaki, *common people*

*ariw

INITIAL

— more, exceed

evidence | PC ayiwihēw, *to outdo sb;* MC aliwikāpawīštawew, *to be taller than sb;* WI (Pessamit) alumu [lūmu], *to be installed or fixed with a portion in excess;* EI (Mamit) anu [anu] *more than; preferably;* Laure (ca. 1726) "ariui ka tchichachtetch, *canicule, temps où il fait plus chaud;*" Silvy (ca. 1680) "nit'ari8eriten, *j'estime, j'aime plus cela*" | MENO ani·w, *more, farther, beyond, too far*

*arīk

INITIAL (NOUN, ANIMATE)

— toad

evidence | WC aðīkis, *a frog;* MC alīkiš, *a toad;* AT arikic [arīkiš], *crapaud, frog;* WI (Pessamit) alik [līk], *a toad;* EI (Mamit) anik [anīk], *a toad;* Silvy (ca. 1680) "arik *pl.* arikak, *grenouille*"

*arkatē

FINAL (VERB, ANIMATE, INTRANSITIVE, CONCRETE)

— due to hunger

evidence | PC nōhtēhkatēw, *to be hungry;* MC kawahkatew, *die of hunger;* SEC nōhtehkatew, *be famished;* WI (Pessamit) shipakateu [ʃīpəkətēw], *to withstand hunger well* | ANISH noondeskade, *to be hungry* (Livesay & Nichols, 2021) origin | Query obscure noun incorporation. discussion | In the absence of a supportive Woods Cree form, this reconstruction is indirectly supported by an Anishinabe cognate.

*arkwat

MEDIAL

— tooth

evidence | PC Lacombe (1874) "tāwākwatew, *il a un espace entre les dents;*" WC (Stanley Mission, Tom Roberts) tawaðkotiw, *to be gap-toothed;* SEC tūhkatū, *one's front teeth are missing* (CSB, 2018); Watkins (1865) "Towukootoo, *v.i.4. He has a space between his teeth, he has lost some teeth;*" Silvy (ca. 1680) "ni ta8ak8at8n, *j'ai perdu une dent;*" "ni ta8ak8tipitau, *je lui casse une dent, je l'arrache*" | ANISH dawaskono, *to be gap-toothed* (Lippert & Gambill, 2023) origin | PA ***arkwaθ** limited to | *taw compare | *at[4]

*arōmin

INITIAL (NOUN, ANIMATE)

— wild rice (Zizania spp.)

evidence | PC ayōminask, *linseed meal;* ayōmināpoy, *oatmeal porridge;* WSC (Ida Bear) anōminak, *oats;* ESC anōmināpoy, *oatmeal porridge;* MC alōminak, *oats;* SEC ayōmināpow, *oatmeal porridge;* ayōminac, *oats;* NEC ayūminich, *rolled oats;* NSK iyuuminich, *rolled oats;* Watkins (1865) "Unoomin, *n.an. Oatmeal;*" Isham (1743) "a'tho me nuck, *oatmeal;*" cf. WSC (Ida Bear) wāpanōminak, *white rice;* MC (Moose Factory) wāpalōmin, *a grain of barley;* SEC (Waswanipi) wāpayōmin, *a grain of white rice* | ABEN malomenal, *grains of wheat, also used for oats, barley, and wild rice* (Day, 1994); ANISH manoomin, *wild rice* (Livesay & Nichols, 2021); MENO mano·mɛnan, *wild rice; rice; oats;* MESK manōmini, *rice; wild rice;* MIAMI naloomini, *a grain of wild rice* (ILDA, 2017) origin | PA ***marōmini** see | *min⁴ discussion | The above reflex is unique among Algonquian languages for lacking an initial consonant as in Abenaki, Anishinabe, Menominee, Meskwaki, and Miami. As an innovation that departs from Proto-Algonquian ***marōmini**, this reflex is likely attributable to Old Cree. Its conspicuous absence in eastern dialects is likely due to the more westerly geographic distribution of wild rice. As in other languages, however, its sense would change with the adoption of new trading partners. It is here reconstructed as a single root as its separation from what is likely the final ***min** would result in a cranberry morpheme. Note also that the basic noun derived from this root is animate in Old Cree while inanimate in other Algonquian languages. The Atikamekw form **mirōmin**, "a grain of rice," is a old loanword from a neighbouring Anishinabe dialect, modified by analogy with the root ***miro**.

*arōskan

INITIAL (NOUN, ANIMATE)

— raspberry

evidence | PC ayōskanak, *raspberries;* SEC ayōskanāhtikʷ, *a raspberry bush;* EI (Sheshatshiu) anushkan [nūʃkən], *a raspberry;* Laure (ca. 1726) "aruskan *pl.* -ets, *framboise;*" "aruskaniminagachi -a, *framboisier*" | MENO ano·hkan, *raspberry* origin | PA ***arōθkana** (***alo·θkana**, Hewson, 1993)

*arwā

INITIAL

— subsided (speaking of weather)

evidence | MC alwāštin, *calm, windless weather;* SEC aywāštin, *calm, windless weather;* Laure (ca. 1726) "aruaspun, *beau temps après la neige;*" Silvy (ca. 1680) "ar8atan, *beau temps après la pluie*" | ANISH anwaatin, *calm weather* (Livesay & Nichols, 2021)

*arwē

INITIAL

— rest

evidence | WC aðwīpiw, *to have a rest;* MC alwesiw, *to rest;* SEC aywepiw, *to sit and rest;* Silvy (ca. 1680) "nit'ar8epin, *je me repose en chemin, étant las de porter*" origin | PA ***arwē** (***alwe**, Hewson, 1993)

*asakātihp[1]

INITIAL (NOUN, INANIMATE)

— crown of the head

evidence | ESC (Severn) osakātihp, *the crown of one's head;* MC osakātihp, *the crown of one's head;* AT (Wemotaci, Nicole Petiquay & Opitciwan, Joey Awashish) oskatip [oskatihp], *the crown of one's head;* EI (Sheshatshiu) ushakatip [uʃəkātīp], *the crown of one's head;* Laure (ca. 1726) "asakatip, *crâne;*" "nasakatip, *mon crâne;*" "nisakatipi, *le sommet de la tête*" see | *tihp², *asakātihp² discussion | The Atikamekw form appears to have been influenced by ***skahtikw**, "forehead." As a result, the absence of a preaspirated sibilant cannot be confirmed.

***asakātihp²**

MEDIAL, FINAL (NOUN INCORPORATION)

— crown of the head

evidence | MC paškosakātihpew, *to be bald at the top of the head;* Silvy (ca. 1680) "8astitasagatip, *sommet de la tête*" see | *asakātihp¹

***asāk**

MEDIAL

— clothes

evidence | PC postasākēw, *to put one's coat on;* WC kispakasākīw, *to be wearing a thick coat;* MC āhtasākew, *to change clothes;* Watkins (1865) "Mùkusakāo, *v.i.3. He wears a large coat*" see | *asākay discussion | This reconstruction suffers from the lack of an Atikamekw cognate to confirm the absence of a preaspirated sibilant.

***asākay**

FINAL (NOUN, INANIMATE)

— clothes

evidence | PC kispakasākay, *a thick coat;* WC wāpiskasākay, *a white coat;* Watkins (1865) "kinwusakai, *a long coat*" see | *asāk, *ay² discussion | This reconstruction suffers from the lack of an Atikamekw cognate to confirm the absence of a preaspirated sibilant.

***asiskitān**

INITIAL (NOUN, INANIMATE)

— calf of the leg

evidence | PC asiskitān, *calf of the leg;* WC asiskitān, *calf of the leg;* WI (Pessamit) utashtan [utəstān], *one's calf;* EI (Sheshatshiu) utashtana [utəstāna], *one's calf;* Lemoine (1901) "*Mollet, son* —, utĕshtān;" Watkins (1865) "Usiskitan, Usiskiskitan, *n.in. The calf of the leg;*" Laure (ca. 1726) "utassistitan *pl.* -a, *le gras de la jambe;*" "utachissitan, *le gras de la jambe*" compare | *rān discussion | The absence of a preaspiration on the first sibilant cannot be confirmed due to the lack of an Atikamekw cognate and the quality of the sibilants cannot be confirmed based on the cognates cited above.

***asiwē**

INITIAL

— to put in a container

evidence | PC asiwacikēw, *to place sth or things into;* WC asiwasow, *to be inside a container;* MC asiwalew, *to put sth in a container;* SEC asiwatāw, *to put sth in a container;* NEC asuwitāu, *to put sth in a container* | ANISH asiwaso, *to be in a container* (Oji-Cree, 2014); MENO ase·wanɛw, ase·wataw, *to sow or plant sth;* neta·sewana·w, neta·sewato·n, *I sow or plant sth;* MIAMI "assi8atagane, *semence*" (Largillier - ILDA, 2017)

***ask¹**

INITIAL

— lie in wait

evidence | MC askamawew, *to lie in wait for sb;* AT (Opitciwan, Joey Awashish) askataw [askatāw], *to lie in wait;* SEC askamawew, *to lie in wait for sb;* EI (Unamanshipit) ashkusseu [ahkawssēw], *to lie in wait for geese;* Laure (ca. 1726) "nit-askauamiskuan 3. -eu, *je l'attrape à l'affût (castor)*" | ANISH akamaw, *to lie in wait for;* (Livesay & Nichols, 2021); MESK ahkamawēwa, *to lie in wait for sb;* ahkawāpamēwa, *to watch over sb* | limited to | *am³, *aw³

***ask²**

MEDIAL (NOUN INCORPORATION)

— **1** land

— **2** moss

evidence | WC nātaskīw, *to go gather moss;* MC misaskeham, *run aground;* likohaskān, *grave;* AT tipahaskew, *survey land;* SEC pimitaskāw, *to be an expanse of land lying crosswise, place name;* NEC pāsischāu, *to dry moss;* Laure (ca. 1726) "ni-tchimutaskan, *empiéter, j'empiète sur sa terre;*" Silvy (ca. 1680) "michastetin sipi8, *la rivière, l'eau* *a fond;*" "michastcheparin eg8, *elle trouve le fond v.g. la sonde;*" "ni tataskan 3. -e8, *je suis de ce pays*" origin | PA ***askyi** (***axkyi,** Hewson, 1993) see | *askiy

*ask[3]

PREFINAL

— erect, build

evidence | PC kistaskisow, *to stand solidly, as a tree;* WC māmawaskitīwa, *to stand in a bunch or cluster;* MC itaskilew, *to erect sth thus;* išpaskitew, *to be tall, speaking of sth erected;* āyitaskitāw, *to erect sth firmly* | ANISH dabasakide, to stand low (Livesay & Nichols, 2021) limited to | *r, *ɩso[2], *tā, *tē[3]

*askamik

MEDIAL

— **1** ground

— **2** moss

evidence | [1]PC mostaskamik, *on the surface of the ground;* MC kilaskamikāw, *to be slippery ground;* SEC maškawaskamikāw, *to be hard ground;* WI (Pessamit) enashkamit [ēnəʃkəmət], *flat on the ground or moss* [2]MC wāpaskamikʷ, reindeer lichen; SEC mihkoskamikāw, *to be an expanse of red sphagnum;* WI (Pessamit) enashkamit [ēnəʃkəmət], *flat on the ground or moss;* Silvy (ca. 1680) "nichkaskamigau, *lieu ou terre humide*" | ABEN kitakamigw, *the land as opposed to water, the mainland* (Day, 1994); ANISH maanakamigaa, *to be poor ground* (Livesay & Nichols, 2021)

*askawiy

INITIAL (NOUN, INANIMATE)

— open water on an otherwise frozen body of water

evidence | PC Lacombe (1874) "Askawiw, *(v.im.) il y a mare, mais cela s'entend seulement quand dans la glace, il y a des places où l'eau n'est pas gelée;*" SEC (Oujé-Bougoumou, Charlie Bosum) aškawiy, *an unfrozen area on an otherwise frozen body of water;* SEC (Oujé-Bougoumou, Jean-Pierre Bosum) aškawiw [aškawiw], *to be an area of open water out on an otherwise frozen body of water;* EI (Ekuanitshit) ashkui [ahkawī], *ice-free area on a lake;* EI (Sheshatshiu) ashkui [əʃkwī], *ice-free area on a lake;* cf. SEC (Oujé-Bougoumou, David Mianscum) piponaškawiy [pipunškwī], *an area of open water on an otherwise frozen body of water;* WI (Pessamit) pipunishkun [pupunəʃkūn], *to be a place where the lake never freezes* discussion | While the existence of this root is secure in Old Cree, the quality of the sibilant cannot be confirmed based on the dialectal reflexes cited above.

*askihkw[1] (~ *askihko)

INITIAL (NOUN, ANIMATE)

— pot

evidence | PC askihkos, *a little pail or pot;* MC askihkohkew, *to make a pot;* SEC ascihkʷ, *a pot;* WI (Pessamit) assikᵘ [ssukʷ], *pail, pot, kettle;* EI (Unaman-shipit) assikuiapi [assīkwjāpī], *handle of a kettle or pail;* Silvy (ca. 1680) "astik8, *chaudière*" see | *askihkw[2]

*askihkw[2] (~ *askihko, *ēskihkw, *ēskihko)

MEDIAL, FINAL (NOUN INCORPORATION)

— pot

evidence | PC akotaskihkwēw, *to hang a kettle over the fire;* sāsēskihkwān, *a frying pan;* MC nīmaskihkwew, *to take a pot along;* SEC newescihkʷ, *four potfuls;* WI (Pessamit) akuessikueteu [kwēssukwētēw], *to stick to the bottom of the pot while cooking;* uapassikᵘ [wāpəssukʷ], *white enamelled kettle;* Silvy (ca. 1680) "ni tchipestik8an 3. -e8, *je fais chaudière*" | ANISH niimakikwe, *to take a pot along* (Livesay & Nichols, 2021); MIAMI ahsenahkihkwi, *pottery* (ILDA, 2017) see | *askihkw[1] discussion | Evidence of the allomorph ***ēskihkw** dates back to the seventeenth century, though the factors triggering its use are unclear. It may simply represent a doublet.

*askisin

MEDIAL, FINAL (NOUN INCORPORATION)

— moccasin

evidence | PC kikaskisinēw, *to have shoes on;* MC oškaskisinew, *to have new shoes;* AT (Opitciwan, Joey Awashish) kikaskisinew [kikaskizinēw], *to have shoes on;* SEC poštascisinew, *to put on one's shoes;* WI (Pessamit) ushkassin [uʃkəssən], *a new pair of shoes;* Silvy (ca. 1680) "ni michtig8astisinikan, *je fais des souliers de bois*" | ANISH nabanekizine, *to only have one shoe on* (Livesay & Nichols, 2021) origin | Old Cree ***maskisini**, from PA ***maskeseni** (***maxkeseni**, Hewson, 1993) see | *maskisin discussion | Some contemporary dialects such as SEC, NEC, WI, and EI feature a reflex of ***ēskisin** as an allomorph, particularly as a final rather than a medial.

*askiy

INITIAL (NOUN, INANIMATE)

— **1** earth

— **2** moss

— **3** country, territory

evidence | MC otaskīmiw, *to have moss;* AT askiwiw [askīwiw], *to be covered in earth or moss; to be made of clay;* SEC otascīw, *to have land, to have a hunting territory;* ascīwikamik^{w}, *moss covered lodge;* WI (Pessamit) assiu [ssjū], *to be made of earth; to be rotted and decomposed;* EI (Unamanshipit) assi [assī], *earth; moss; land; country;* Laure (ca. 1726) "astchi, *pays, terre*" | ANISH aki, *earth, land, ground; a country, a territory; moss* (Livesay & Nichols, 2021) origin | PA ***askyi** (***axkyi,** Hewson, 1993) see | *ask²

*askō

INITIAL

— be next, succeeding

evidence | PC askōtowak *to follow one another;* askowiskawēw, *to come next after sb;* WC askwawīw [*sic*], *to be next in line to sb;* WI aiashku [ājāʃku], *"gradually, bit by bit, one after the other;"* Watkins (1865) "Uskooiskowāo, *v.t.an. He is next to him (either by position or birth);*" Fabvre (ca. 1690) "Eïask8, *de iour à autre, alternatiuem(en)t*" | ANISH Cuoq (1886) "Akawinek ni nidjanisak, *mes enfants meurent l'un après l'autre;*" MENO ahko·wekapowew, *to stand next in order;* MESK ahkōwēwa, *to come next after sb;* MIAMI ahkoow-, *to follow sb, to come after sb* (ILDA, 2017) compare | *aškoht

*askw¹

MEDIAL, FINAL (NOUN INCORPORATION)

— cloud, sky

evidence | PC mamēnaskwāw, *to be partly clouded;* WC wāsīskwan, *clear sky;* MC nihcikānaskwan, *to be dark clouds;* SEC yikoskwan, *cloudy;* kaškawanaskw, *a cloud;* WI (Pessamit) petashkuan [pētəʃkwən] *clouds approach;* itashkuau [ītəʃkwāw], *the sky has a certain appearance;* Laure (ca. 1726) "tchiuetin-askuanu, *les nuages en viennent (du nord-ouest);*" Silvy (ca. 1680) "8is8a8ask8an, *le ciel est jaune*" | ANISH ningwakwad, *to be cloudy* (Livesay & Nichols, 2021) see | *waskw, *wāskw compare | *āwaskw

*askw²

MEDIAL, FINAL (NOUN INCORPORATION)

— bear

evidence | PC nōtaskwēw, *to trap bear;* MC wāpask^{w}, *polar bear;* WI (Pessamit) makusheshkueu [mukuʃēʃkwēw], *to hold a bear feast;* Fabvre (ca. 1690) "n8task8an e8, *à la chasse de l(')8rs;*" Silvy (ca. 1680) "ab8task8an, *cette montre (de l'ours)*" | ANISH noozhek, *a female bear* (Livesay & Nichols, 2021) origin | Old Cree ***maskwa** see | *maskw

*asp

INITIAL

— protective layer

evidence | PC aspēyimow, *to trust;* MC aspapiw, *to sit on a cushion;* SEC aspinam, *to take or hold sth using a protective material* |

ANISH apenimonodan, *to depend or rely on sth* (Livesay & Nichols, 2021); MESK ahpahikani, *patch*

*aspin

INITIAL

— since

evidence | WC aspin, *since, ago; gone;* MC aspin, *since; to be gone or absent;* SEC aspin, *since;* NEC aspin, *from time to time;* Laure (ca. 1726) "migu aspin ni-uabamau, *je le vois peu souvent;*" Silvy (ca. 1680) "aspin mitchis8ian, *la dernière fois que je mange*" | ANISH Nicholas (ca. 1670) "apin, *pour la dernière fois*" (Daviault, 1994)

*aš

MEDIAL (NOUN INCORPORATION)

— skin

evidence | PC kispakasēw, *to have thick skin;* MC kalakašew, *have itchy skin;* SEC māskašew, *to have a scar;* Laure (ca. 1726) "pinacheu tchinebiku, *muer, le serpent mue (peau);*" Silvy (ca. 1680) "ni pita8achan, *j'ai la peau enflée*" | ANISH nibiiwazhe, *to have wet skin* (Livesay & Nichols, 2021) compare | *ašak, *ašakay²

*ašak

MEDIAL (NOUN INCORPORATION)

— skin

evidence | PC mihkwasakēw, *to have red skin;* WC kispakasakīw, *to have thick skin;* MC lōskašakew, *have soft skin;* AT (Wemotaci, Jeannette Petiquay) mirocakew [miroʒakēw], *to have nice skin* origin | Old Cree ***-ašakay** compare | *aš¹, *ašakay²

*ašakay¹

INITIAL (NOUN, DEPENDENT ANIMATE)

— skin

evidence | PC masakay, *skin;* MC ošakaya, *one's skin;* AT (Wemotaci, Jeannette Coocoo) ocakai [oʒakay], *one's skin;* EI (Sheshatshiu) ushakaikup [uʃəkējkūp], *a fur coat;* Watkins (1865) "Musukai, *n.in. The skin, the cuticle (when not removed from the body, or, if removed, whilst still in an unprepared state). This word is applied to human beings, birds, and fish, but to scarcely any quadrupeds except pigs.* Nusukai, *my skin;*" Laure (ca. 1726) "kasagai, *ta peau*" see | *aš¹, *ašak, *ay², *ašakay²

*ašakay²

MEDIAL, FINAL (NOUN INCORPORATION)

— skin

evidence | PC oskasakay, *a new skin;* WC kinosīwasakay, *fish skin;* MC wīlipašakayew, *have dirty skin;* Laure (ca. 1726) "ni-manasakahienau, *j'habille un poisson, ôtant sa peau*" compare | *aš¹, *ašak see | *ašakay¹

*ašākw (~ *ašāko, *ašāh, *ašāš)

INITIAL (NOUN, INANIMATE)

— **1** mark, streak

— **2** tattoo

evidence | PC asāswēw, *to tattoo sb;* Watkins (1865) "assasoo, *v.pass.4. He is tattoed;*" Isham (1743) "ar sar so win, *to marke or disfigure;*" Laure (ca. 1726) "nit-achasun, *je suis marqué sur le corps;*" Fabvre (ca. 1690) "nit achās8n, achak8m, *ma petite marq(ue);*" Silvy (ca. 1680) "achak8a, 8atachak8chich, *raies ou marques qui sont aux écorces;*" "nitachak8n, *ma marque noire faite au corps*" | ANISH azhaaso, *to apply a medicinal tattoo* (Livesay & Nichols, 2021); André (ca. 1690s) "nit'achassoua, *il le marque avec le feu;*" MENO asa·qtɛw, *to be marked; to be pictured, depicted, or written*

*ašē

INITIAL

— move backwards

evidence | PC asēpayiw, *to drive backwards;* MC ašepiw, *to sit farther back;* AT ašeh-, *to move sth back by tool* (Béland, 1978); SEC ašāpayiw, *to move backwards;* EI (Sheshatshiu) ashetateu [ʃētātēw], *to follow sb's tracks backwards;* Fabvre (ca. 1690) "nit

Achebăk8n 8, *retirer de son sein;*" Silvy (ca. 1680) "nit'achegaba8in, *je m'éloigne, me retire, étant debout*" | ANISH azhegaabawi, *to stand back* (Livesay & Nichols, 2021) origin | PA ***ašyē*** (Aubin, 1975)

*ašēsin

INITIAL (NOUN, INANIMATE)

— vamp

evidence | PC asēsin, *vamp;* MC asesinihkew, *to make a vamp;* AT (Opitciwan, Joey Awashish) aseson [azezon], *vamp;* SEC (Waskaganish) asesin, *vamp;* (Waswanipi) ašešon, *vamp;* NEC sāsiniū, *to be used for the vamp;* EI (Sheshatshiu) asheshinikuatam[u] [ʃēʃinukwātəm], *to sew a vamp onto sth;* Laure (ca. 1726) "utiteu achechin, *le soulier est brûlé dessous;*" Silvy (ca. 1680) "achasin, *pièce faisant le dessus du soulier*" | ABEN azazenal, *moccasin side flaps* (Day, 1995); ANISH aseson, *vamp* (Oji-Cree, 2014); Cuoq (1886) "asezon, *c'est le dessus d'un soulier sauvage, d'un mocassin*" origin | PA ***asēseni*** (Hewson, 1993) compare | *maskisin

*ašikē

INITIAL (VERB, ANIMATE, INTRANSITIVE)

— have insulating material in the moccasins one is wearing

evidence | PC asikan, *a sock;* WC asikan, *a sock;* MC ašikew, *to wear moccasin linings or socks;* AT acikanikew [aʒikanihkew], *to make socks;* SEC ašikan, *a sock* | ANISH azhige, *to use sth as footwear lining* (Livesay & Nichols, 2021); MENO ase·kan, *blade of grass, wisp of hay*

*ašisoy

INITIAL (NOUN, INANIMATE)

— ice chisel

evidence | PC āsoyāhtik, *handle of an ice chisel;* WC asisoy, *chisel;* NEC asisui, *ice chisel;* EI (Unaman-shipit) nassui [nasswī], *my ice chisel;* Watkins (1865) "ăssisoi, *n.in. an ice-chisel;*" Isham (1743) "arsisue, *a broad ice chissel;*" Fabvre (ca. 1690) "Achis8ïask8, *L(on)g baston à prendre poisson*" compare | *akaskw, *amahkw discussion | This reconstruction suffers from the lack of an Atikamekw cognate to confirm the absence of any preaspirates. Note that ***ašisoyi*** is one of a few independent nouns in Old Cree that does not, despite its form, require an epenthetic **t** when possessed.

*ašišk

INITIAL

— raw

evidence | PC asiskisiw, *to have an open wound;* WC asiskīkin, *rawhide;* asiskisiw, *to be raw;* Laure (ca. 1726) "asistchéugu, *viande fraîche;*" Silvy (ca. 1680) "achichkames, *poisson frais;*" "achichtisi8 amisk8, *castor frais, non boucané*" cf. NEC chikishishkāu, *to be raw or uncooked* compare | *ašk[1] discussion | The absence of a preaspiration on the first sibilant cannot be confirmed due to the lack of an Atikamekw cognate.

*ašiškiw

INITIAL (NOUN, INANIMATE)

— mud

evidence | PC asiskiy, *mud, clay, soil;* WC asiskīwākamiw, *to be muddy water;* MC ašiškīwihtakiškam, *to muddy the floor with one's feet;* AT ašiški:win-, *to cover or plaster sb or sth with mud by hand* (Béland, 1978); WI (Pessamit) ashissu [ʃəssu], *mud, clay;* EI (Unaman-shipit) ashissu [ahassu], *mud, clay;* Watkins (1865) "Usiske, *n.in. Clay, mud;*" "Usiskew, *n.in. Clay;*" "Usiskewun, *v.imp. It is clayey, it is earthern;*" Silvy (ca. 1680) "achichti8, *ordure, boue*" | ABEN azesko, *mud* (Day, 1995); ANISH azhashki, *mud* (Livesay & Nichols, 2021); MESK ashishkiwi, *mud* see | *ıškiw[1]

*ašiw

INITIAL

— dull

evidence | AT (Wemotaci, Nicole Petiquay) aciwotin [aʒiwhtin], *to be blunted;* ašiwa:-, *to be blunt* (Béland, 1978); Laure (ca. 1726) "achiuau, *il est émoussé;*" Silvy (ca. 1680) "achi8au, *il est émoussé, ne coupe plus*" | ANISH azhiwaa, *to be dull* (Livesay & Nichols, 2021) compare | *šī

*ašk[1]

INITIAL

— raw

evidence | PC askekin, *raw hide;* MC aškāw, *to be raw;* SEC aščipow, *to eat raw meat;* Silvy (ca. 1680) "nit'achtib8n, *je mange cru*" | ANISH ashkin, *to be raw (as meat)* (Livesay & Nichols, 2021); MENO askɛ·n, *to be raw;* MESK ashkenwi, *to be raw* compare | *ašišk

*ašk[2]

MEDIAL

— herbaceous vegetation, grass

evidence | PC timaskāw, *to be tall grass;* MC išpaškāw, *to be tall grass;* SEC osāwaškāw, *to be green grass* | ANISH Cuoq (1886) "Packwackaige, *sarcler*" see | *aškw[1]

*aškat

MEDIAL (NOUN INCORPORATION)

— abdomen

evidence | PC māyaskatēw, *to have an upset stomach;* MC kitoweškatew, *stomach rumbles;* SEC mošeškatew, *to be naked;* Silvy (ca. 1680) "ni 8a8iechkatan 3. -e8, *j'ai le ventre rond*" see | *aškatay

*aškatay

INITIAL (NOUN, DEPENDENT INANIMATE)

— abdomen

evidence | PC maskatay, *stomach covering, abdominal wall;* MC oškatay, *one's abdomen, one's belly;* EI (Sheshatshiu) ushkatai [uʃkətāj], *one's abdomen* see | *aškat, *ay[2]

*aškēk

MEDIAL

— muskeg

evidence | WC tāwaskīkamon, *path or road runs right through the muskeg;* MC akāmaškek, *across the muskeg;* WI (Pessamit) pitassekau [pītəssēkāw], *to be a long muskeg to travel through* origin | Old Cree ***maškēkwi** see | *maškēkw

*aškimē

INITIAL (VERB, ANIMATE, INTRANSITIVE)

— lace snowshoe frame

evidence | PC askimēw, *to lace snowshoes;* MC aškimātew, *to lace sth, speaking of a snowshoe;* SEC aščimaneyāpiy, *babiche for lacing the cental part of a snowshoe;* WI (Pessamit) assimeu [ssəmēw], *to lace a snowshoe* | ANISH ashkime, *to weave snowshoe webbing* (Livesay & Nichols, 2021) see | *ɪm[2]

*aškinē

FINAL (VERB, INTRANSITIVE, DERIVED)

— full

evidence | MC osāmaškinew, *to be overfilled;* SEC sākaščinew, *to be full;* Silvy (ca. 1680) abit8chtinebe8, "*il est mi-plein, v.g. vase*" see | *mōškinē

*aškohsiw (~ *aškohsiwak)

MEDIAL, FINAL (NOUN INCORPORATION)

— herbaceous vegetation, grass

evidence | WC kīskaskosiwahikan, *a scythe;* MC tapahtaškošiwakāw, *to be short grass;* nōtaškošiwew, *to make hay;* NEC pīkwāshkushiwikāu, *to be thick grass;* WI (Pessamit) tshimashkushuesseu [tʃəməʃkuʃwēssēw], *to mow the lawn;* Laure (ca. 1726) "ni-muchiuaskusiuatsinen, *j'ôte les mauvaises herbes de mon champ ou jardin;*" "menistiguaskasiu, *touffe d'herbes, ramassée comme un petit fort*" see | *maškohsiw, *ak[2]

*aškoht (~ *aškohc)

INITIAL

— be next, succeeding

evidence | PC "ayaskoc, *one after the other,*" pronounced on the Itwēwina dictionary website by Mary Jean Littlechild of Maskwacīs as [āyāskohc]; WC askohciskawīw, *to be next in command to sb;* MC aškohcihew, *to take revenge on sb;*

AT ackotci posiw [āškoci-pōsiw], *“se déplacer d'un véhicule à un autre;”* (Wemotaci, Jeannette Coocoo) aiackotc [āyāškohc], *“chacun son tour, l'un après l'autre;”* Watkins (1865) “Uskòochipuyew, *v.imp. It follows;”* “Uskòoch, *prep. or adv. After, next;”* Laure (ca. 1726) “askut, *enfin;”* Fabvre (ca. 1690) “Askȣt, *enfin;”* “ïaskȣech, *L'un apres l autre;”* “ïaskȣk, aïaskȣts, *le 2e, celuy d'apres le 1er”* | ANISH “ayäckot, *à tour de rôle”* (Dumont, 1999); MENO “ahko·qc, *next in order”* compare | *askō discussion | While the existence of this root is secure, its form may be inaccurate as the corroborative evidence is marred by inconsistencies regarding vowel length and the final preaspirate. It is also nonproductive in most dialects and obsolete in some. For example, the Moose Cree form is supported only by historical literature from the nineteenth century, sources that do not mark preaspirations and are rife with vowel length inconsistencies. Note that speakers of the contemporary Atikamekw dialects routinely lengthen short vowels in word-initial position.

*aškotē[1]

MEDIAL (NOUN INCORPORATION)

— grassy clearing after a fire

evidence | Silvy (ca. 1680) “ȣraskȣteïau, *belle terre sans broussaille”* | ANISH zhiibeshkodeyaa, *to be open prairie* (Lippert & Gambill, 2023) see | *maškotēw

*aškotē[2]

FINAL (VERB, INANIMATE, INTRANSITIVE, DERIVED)

— grassy clearing after a fire

evidence | SEC (Oujé-Bougoumou) kā mošawaškotēšiy, *place name, literally ‘grassy clearing’* (Bishop, 2022); NEC (Chisasibi) ā pimiciškotāšic, *place name, literally ‘small grassy clearing that extends crosswise, crossway meadow;’* (Whapmagoostui) ā cāhkiškotāc, *place name, literally ‘steep meadow’* (Bishop, 2022); Laure (ca. 1726) “muchauaskuteu, *lande, pays brûlé et terre desséchée;”* Silvy (ca. 1680) “muchaȣaskȣteȣ, *où le feu a brûlé les arbres”* see | *maškotē

*aškotēw

FINAL (NOUN INCORPORATION)

— grassy clearing after a fire

evidence | WI (Uashat) Upishkuteu [upiʃkutēw], *place name, Opiscotéo Lake* | ANISH mishawashkode, *on the open plain, open prairie* (Livesay & Nichols, 2021); MESK ahkwashkotēwiwi, *the meadow goes so far* see | *maškotēw discussion | The comparative evidence also supports analyzing this root as the verb final ***aškotē**, though the Western Innu place name listed above does suggest its use as a noun final is accurate, at least in more recent times.

*aškōraw

INITIAL

— fail to obtain

evidence | ESC aškōnōsiw, *to fail to obtain what is sought;* MC aškōlōsiw, *to fail to obtain what is sought;* Laure (ca. 1726) “achkurau, *sans rien;”* Fabvre (ca. 1690) “Askȣrau pakitinȣ passisigan, *le fuzil a raté Il est tombé decliné sans rien faire”* | ANISH Cuoq (1886) “Ackona ni tagocin, *j'arrive corps nu, c'est-à-dire, sans avoir rien tué, rien pris;”* “Nind ackonawis, *je suis corps nu, je n'apporte rien, je n'ai rien pris”*

*aškw[1] (~ *aško)

MEDIAL, FINAL (NOUN INCORPORATION)

— herbaceous vegetation, grass

evidence | PC osāwaskwa, *yellow grass;* MC pīhtaškwātam, *to stuff sth with grass;* AT wapocockw [wāpoʒoškw], *rabbit root;* SEC wacaškwāyōšk^w, *cattail & blueflag* | ANISH anaakanashkoon, *reeds, rushes* (Livesay & Nichols, 2021) see | *ašk², *w¹ compare | *maškohsiw

*aškw[2]

MEDIAL (NOUN INCORPORATION)

— **1** birch

— **2** birch bark

evidence | AT pa:pakoniškwewe-, *to debark a birch tree* (Béland, 1978); SEC opaškweskaw, *to be a narrows marked by the presence of many birch trees;* WI (Pessamit) shipeshkuepakau [ʃīpēʃkwēpəkāw], *to be a way through an area of scattered birch trees* | ANISH nookashkweyaa, *to be soft birch bark* (Livesay & Nichols, 2021) see | *waškway compare | *aškway, *aškwēmak

*aškway

MEDIAL, FINAL (NOUN INCORPORATION)

— birch bark

evidence | WC manaskwayīw, *to gather birch bark;* SEC manaškwayew, *to remove bark from a birch;* WI (Pessamit) uashuakanashkuai [wāʃwānəʃkwī], *a birchbark torch used for fishing by torch-light;* EI (Sheshatshiu) pakunashkuaieu [pākunəʃkwjēw], *to peel the bark from a birch* see | *waškway compare | *aškwēmak

*aškwēmak

MEDIAL

— bark

evidence | AT masinackwemakitin [masinaškwēmakihtin], *to be imprinted on paper;* pikiwockwemokw [pikīwaškwēmak^w], *waxed paper;* Laure (ca. 1726) "pikuaskuemagu, *gargousse;*" Silvy (ca. 1680) "ragachk8emagachi8, *cela est léger*" | ANISH biimashkwemaginigan, *a bark torch;* nagamoshkwemagoon, *birch bark song scrolls* (Livesay & Nichols, 2021) see | *aškw², *ēmak

*ašt

MEDIAL (CLASSIFIER)

— string-like

evidence | PC pīmastēhikan, *spinning wheel;* MC pašaštehwew, *to whip sb;* SEC wehtašteyāw, *to be easy to pull, speaking of a trigger;* Silvy (ca. 1680) "ni pich8achtebarin, *je tombe en trébuchant*" | ANISH Cuoq (1886) "Nind abatewa sesap, *je détord le fil*"

*aštahciko

INITIAL (VERB, ANIMATE, INTRANSITIVE)

— store for later use, cache

evidence | PC astahcikon, *a cache;* MC aštahcikow, *to store things for later use, to cache things;* Silvy (ca. 1680) "nit'achtatgig8n, *je fais une cache de bois*" | ANISH asanjigo, *to store, cache, or stash sth* (Livesay & Nichols, 2021)

*aštaw (~ *aštawak)

MEDIAL (NOUN INCORPORATION)

— beaver or muskrat lodge

evidence | ESC (Severn) newastaw, *four beaver lodges;* MC newaštaweyāw, *to be four beaver lodges;* NEC pāyikushtiu, *one beaver family or lodge;* wāskwāhtāmishtuwikuhch, *the back of the beaver lodge opposite to the door side;* WI (Pessamit) peikushtueshuat [pējkustwēʃūt], *they are one family in a lodge, speaking of beavers;* EI (Mamit) nishushtu [nīhwahtaw], *two beaver families (one per lodge)* see | *wīšt

*aštawē

INITIAL (VERB, ANIMATE, INTRANSITIVE)

— fletch

evidence | WC astowīw, *to fletch an arrow;* MC aštahwān, *a fletch;* aštahwew, *to fletch an arrow(s);* Watkins (1865) "Ustawāo, *v.i.3. He is fletching (arrows), he is putting on quills (i.e. to the arrow);*" Silvy (ca. 1680) "nit'achta8aten, *je mets des plumes aux flèches*" | ANISH Cuoq (1886) "Asawate anwi, *la flèche a son fer, ses plumes;*" MIAMI ahsawaankatia, *a feather* origin | PA ***aʔθawē**

*aštā[1] (~ *aštw)

INITIAL (VERB, ANIMATE, INTRANSITIVE)

— set

evidence | PC aštāw, *to set sth, to place sth;* WC astwātowin, *a bet;* MC aštowew, *to set sth* *aside for sb;* SEC aštāw, *to set sth, to place sth;* WI (Pessamit) ashtuau [stwāw], *to set sth aside for later use;* Silvy (ca. 1680) "nit'achtan 3. -tau, *je mets une chose en quelque lieu;*" "nit'achtȣan 3. -au, *je garde le reste de table, des vivres;*" "achtȣatcheȣin, achtȣatȣin, *partie au jeu, jeu*" origin | PA ***aʔtāwa*** (Aubin, 1975), from ***ap*** + AI final ***tā*** see | *aštā², *ap¹, *tā paired with | *ahr¹ compare | *aštō discussion | The ***aštw*** allomorph surfaces only for further derivation when suffixing either the antipassive ***ā*** or the benefactive ***aw***. Its origin predates what is otherwise a loss of morphological distinction in Old Cree between Proto-Algonquian transitive inanimate verb class II and animate intransitive verbs ending in ***ā*** (cf. Pentland, 1999). Note that contemporary dialects have all contracted ***aštw*** + ***aw*** to a reflex of ***aštow***, but the underlying form is revealed when vowel-lengthening processes occur, resulting in reflexes of ***aštwā*** as expected.

*aštā² (~ *aštw)

FINAL (VERB, ANIMATE, INTRANSITIVE, DERIVED)

— set

evidence | PC āhtastāw, *to move sth;* MC cīpataštāw, *to place sth upright;* itaštowew, *to place sth in a certain position or place for sb;* SEC nīpiteštāw, *to place things in a row* origin | Old Cree ***aštāwa*** see | *aštā¹ discussion | The ***aštw*** allomorph surfaces only for further derivation when suffixing either the antipassive ***ā*** or the benefactive ***aw***.

*aštā³

INITIAL

— a nonproductive root of uncertain meaning found only in reflexes of *aštāskamikwi, "moss," and *aštākanaškwi, "reed"

evidence | PC astāskamikwa, *moss;* astākanask, *a reed;* WC astākanask, *a reed;* Watkins (1865) "Ustakunusk, *n.in. A reed*" | ANISH aasaaganashk(oon), *reed;* aasaakamig, *moss* (Livesay & Nichols, 2021); MENO aqna·hkameko·wew, *to be covered with moss* origin | PA ***aʔθā***

*aštākipiy

INITIAL (NOUN, INANIMATE)

— algae

evidence | MC aštākipiy, *algae* | ANISH ataagib, *algae* (Livesay & Nichols, 2021) origin | PA ***aʔtāk***, unknown meaning, + ***epyi*** see | *ɩpiy discussion | The above reconstruction is supported by variants used in Western and Eastern Innu, spelled *ashtatshipek*ᵘ and pronounced in Pessamit as [stāʧəpēkʷ] and in Sheshatshiu as [stāʧipēkʷ].

*aštē¹

INITIAL (VERB, INANIMATE, INTRANSITIVE)

— sit

evidence | MC aštew, *to sit, to be placed;* SEC aštew, *to sit, to be placed;* EI (Sheshatshiu) ashteu [əstēw], *to be placed; to be set, speaking of a trap* origin | PA ***aʔtēwi*** (Aubin, 1975), from ***ap*** + II final ***tē*** see | *aštē², *ap¹, *tē³ paired with | *ap¹

*aštē²

FINAL (VERB, INANIMATE, INTRANSITIVE, DERIVED)

— sit

evidence | PC nahastēw, *to be put away;* MC itaštew, *to sit thus;* SEC nehpemaštew, *to be placed at the ready* | MENO saka·hkaqtɛw II, *"to be put away, to be safe in a proper place, to sit in one's proper place"* origin | Old Cree ***aštēwi*** see | *aštē¹ paired with | *api

*aštihs¹

INITIAL (NOUN, ANIMATE)

— mitten

evidence | PC astis, *mitten;* MC aštisak, *mittens;* EI (Mamit) ashtish [ahtɨh], *a mitten;* Fabvre (ca. 1690) "Achtis *pl* sak, *mitaines, mȣffles*" see | *aštihs²

*aštihs[2]

MEDIAL, FINAL (NOUN INCORPORATION)

— mitten

evidence | PC postastisēw, *to put on one's mittens;* MC āhtaštisahew, *to change sb's mittens;* AT (Wemotaci, Nicole Petiquay) ririkastisak [rīrīkastissak], *gloves;* EI (Sheshatshiu) pishakanashtish [pīʃākənəstəʃ], *a leather mitten;* Silvy (ca. 1680) "ni kestastisan, *j'ôte mes mitaines*" see | *aštihs¹ discussion | Contemporary dialects such as SEC, NEC, WI, and EI feature a reflex of ***ēštihs** as an allomorph, particularly as a final rather than a medial.

*aštihs[3]

INITIAL

— backstrap sinew

evidence | PC astisēwakwa, *lengthwise muscles on back;* Watkins (1865) "Ustisāwuk, *Sinewy flesh (e.g. that from the back of the animal)*" see | *aštihsiy

*aštihsiy

INITIAL (NOUN, INANIMATE)

— backstrap sinew

evidence | PC astisiy, *thread made from sinew;* MC aštisiy, *backstrap sinew;* SEC aštisiy, *backstrap sinew;* EI (Sheshatshiu) ashtish [əstəʃ], *tendon close to the muscle on each side of the backbone of a caribou or moose;* Watkins (1865) "Ustise, *n.in. A sinew;*" Isham (1743) "Ar stis se, *a sinew;*" Fabvre (ca. 1690) "Astich, achtich, *tandon, nerf... dont ils c8sent*" | ANISH atis, *sinew* (Livesay & Nichols, 2021); MENO aqteh, *plural* aqtɛ·hsyan, *sinew* origin | PA ***aʔtehsyi** (***aʔtehsi**, Hewson, 1993) see | *aštihs³ discussion | In the absence of an Atikamekw cognate, the preaspirate in this reconstruction is indirectly supported by Anishinabe and Menominee.

*aštimw (~ *aštimo)

MEDIAL, FINAL (NOUN INCORPORATION)

— dog

evidence | PC macastim, *a bad dog;* MC nōtaštimwew, *to be busy taking care of dogs;* WI (Pessamit) aimishtimueu [īmīstəmwēw], *to talk to a dog(s);* Laure (ca. 1726) "aiatastimu, *chien emprunté à d'autres;*" Fabvre (ca. 1690) "N8tinastim8an e8, *battre q(ue)lq(ues) chiens*" | ANISH giiwosewasim, *a hunting dog* (Livesay & Nichols, 2021); MENO keta·kaqnɛm(-ok), *spotted dog* origin | PA ***aʔθemw** (Aubin, 1975), possibly related to PA ***aθemwa** (Aubin, 1975), *dog* see | *atimw

*aštor

INITIAL

— make canoe

evidence | WC astoðiw, *to make a canoe;* MC aštoliw, *to build a canoe;* AT actoriw [aštoriw], *to make a canoe;* NEC ashtuyiu, *to make a canoe;* WI (Pessamit) ashtulu [stlu], *to make a canoe;* EI (Mamit) ashtunu [ahtunu], *to make a canoe;* Silvy (ca. 1680) "nit'acht8ra8au, *nob. je lui fais un canot*" | ANISH atoono, *to make a canoe* (Livesay & Nichols, 2021) see | *aštō, *or

*aštotin[1]

INITIAL (NOUN, INANIMATE)

— headgear, hat, cap

evidence | PC astotinihkawēw, *to make a hat for sb;* MC aštotiniškīš, *an old or worn out hat;* AT actotinikaso [aštotinihkāzow], *to make a hat for oneself;* SEC aštotinihcew, *to make a hat, cap, or tuque;* NEC ashtutin, *a hat, a cap;* NSK astutin, *a hat;* Fabvre (ca. 1690) "Acht8tin, *calotte, petit bonnet*" | MIAMI kitehtoleni, *your hat* (ILDA, 2017); "atatt8reni, *Chapeau gris*" (LeBoullenger - ILDA, 2017) origin | PA ***aʔtoθeni** see | *aštotin² discussion | This root and its derivatives have been replaced in WI and EI by reflexes of the morphologically transparent ***akwanıskwēhoni**, a word that coexists with reflexes of ***aštotini** in SEC and NSK.

*aštotin[2]

MEDIAL, FINAL (NOUN INCORPORATION)

— headgear, hat, cap

evidence | WC māhkastotinēw, *to have a large cap;* MC mīšahaštotinew, *to patch a hat;* maškošīwaštotin, *a straw hat;* SEC oškaštotinew, *to wear a new hat;* NSK chikistuutinaaw, *to wear a hat or cap* | MIAMI atehtoleni-, *to wear a hat, put on a hat* (ILDA, 2017) see | *aštotin[1]

*aštō

INITIAL

— set or place in a particular position, sit or come to sit in a particular position

evidence | WC astōkamiw, *to be still water;* astōpākan, *a receptacle for storing water;* MC aštōpaliw, *to congeal;* aštōkamipaliw, *to become still, speaking of water;* Watkins (1865) "Astoogumin, *v.imp. It is still water;*" Laure (ca. 1726) "achtupan, *réservoir d'eau;*" Fabvre (ca. 1690) "Acht8s8an e8, *cacher en neige l'orig(na)l*" | ANISH atoobaan, *a large container for liquid* (Livesay & Nichols, 2021) compare | *aštā[1], *aštor discussion | This root is a vestigial variant of ***aštā** that survived what is otherwise a loss of morphological distinction in Old Cree between Proto-Algonquian transitive inanimate verb class II and animate intransitive verbs ending in ***ā** (cf. Pentland, 1999). Compare the Anishinabe word *odatoon,* "to put in a certain place" (Livesay & Nichols, 2021), a cognate of Old Cree ***aštāwa**.

*at[1] (~ *aš)

INITIAL

— rotten

evidence | WC atāwi, *a rotten egg;* EI (Mamit) atameshu [atamēhu], *to be a rotten fish;* EI (Sheshatshiu) atamesh [təmēʃ], *rotten fish;* Watkins (1865) "Utawe, *n.in. An addle egg, a rotten egg;*" Laure (ca. 1726) "atames, *poisson puant;*" "attames, *poisson infecte;*" "achipimissu, *anguille puante, vieille;*" Fabvre (ca. 1690) "Achinămes et attames, *poisson puant;*" Silvy (ca. 1680) "atimisk8, *castor puant;*" "atin, *il est pourri*" | ABEN alikō, *to be rotten;* MENO ana·mɛk (-ok), *dead fish washed ashore;* MESK anenwa, anetwi, *to rot;* cf. ANISH bigishkanimaagozi, *to smell rotten* (Livesay & Nichols, 2021); MIAMI šaakwalet-, *to rot* origin | PA ***aθ** (Hewson, 1993) see | *atin[3], *atit

*at[2]

MEDIAL (CLASSIFIER)

— soft substance

evidence | PC kīskatāwahkāw, *to be a steep bank;* MC pinatawepaliw, *fur falls out;* mākotinam, *to press sth soft;* nōtimatinam, *to shape soft substance into a ball;* SEC piskotāwahkāw, *to be a mound of sand;* NEC ishiwātāwihkāu, *to be a narrow point of elevated ground;* Watkins (1865) "Ayuchistin, *v.imp. The track is covered (e.g. by drifting snow)*" | ANISH onadinige, *to form, shape, knead, or mold a soft substance by hand* (Livesay & Nichols, 2021) origin | PA ***at**

*at[3]

MEDIAL (NOUN INCORPORATION)

— stomach

evidence | PC iyiwatēw, *to have an empty stomach;* MC šīwatew, *be hungry;* SEC wīnatew, *to bring up a foul smelling burp or vomit;* WI (Pessamit) liutew [ljūtēw], *to have an empty stomach;* Silvy (ca. 1680) "nit'apistatanach, *j'ai petit ventre, je mange peu*" | ANISH mangimisade, *to have a big belly* (Livesay & Nichols, 2021) origin | PA ***at** see | *atay

*at[4]

MEDIAL

— mouth

evidence | WC sākatīmīw, *to hold sth partly sticking out of one's mouth;* SEC tāwatiw, *to open one's mouth;* Fabvre (ca. 1690) "Takuatemau piki8, *mascher braye, La tenir en La b8che"* | ANISH daawani, *to open one's mouth;* zaaganendan, *to have sth sticking out of one's mouth* (Livesay & Nichols, 2021) origin | PA ***aθ***

*at[5]

PREFINAL

— affected by the cold

origin | PA ***at*** (Aubin, 1975) see | *aci, *atin[2], *atihtā, *atim[3]

*atahkw[1] (~ *atahko)

INITIAL (NOUN, ANIMATE)

— star

evidence | WC acāhkos, *a star;* MC atahk^w, acahkoš, *a star;* AT atcakoc [acahkoš], *a star;* SEC acahkoš, *a star;* NEC achihkush, *a star;* Silvy (ca. 1680) "attak8, *étoile*" | ANISH anang, *star* (Livesay & Nichols, 2021) origin | PA ***aθankwa*** (Aubin, 1975) see | *atahkw[2] discussion | Bloomfield's reconstruction presented in Aubin (1975) and the form reconstructed by Hewson (1993) are erroneously reconstructed with a long vowel in the second syllable due to the use of insufficient data. A Plains Cree form containing the lengthened vowel was used for both reconstructions, highlighting the limitations of using a dialectal dataset for PA reconstructions. Additionally, Bloomfield's form cites the use of an Ojibwe form that also exhibits this long vowel, though this form is dubious as modern forms across dialects continue to employ the original short vowel. Note, however, that Goddard's reconstruction presented in Aubin (1975) is correct, as is the reconstruction for "morning star," by Hewson (1993), ***wāpanaθankwa***.

*atahkw[2] (~ *atahkwak)

MEDIAL, FINAL (NOUN INCORPORATION)

— star

evidence | PC wāpanacāhkos, *morning star;* MC ocekatahk^w, *Big Dipper;* SEC wāsetahkokan, *starry night;* WI (Pessamit) utshekatak^u [utʃēkətuk^w], star; Laure (ca. 1726) "uachetakuaganu, *les étoiles luisent;*" Fabvre (ca. 1690) "8achetak8akesi8, *luir, luisent etoilles*" see | *atahkw[1], *ak[2]

*atakay

INITIAL (NOUN, INANIMATE)

— penis

evidence | MC atakay, a penis; mištatakay, *a giant penis, mythological figure;* AT (Opitciwan, Joey Awashish) takai [takay], *expression of surprise;* SEC takay, *exclamation used to express anger or annoyance;* NEC tikī, *exclamation used to express anger or annoyance;* Isham (1743) "U'tuk kie, *the pinis*" compare | *ītakay

*atam

INITIAL

— **1** please

— **2** salute

evidence | PC atamihēw, *to please sb;* MC atamiskātowak, *to greet one another;* WI (Pessamit) atamishkueu [təməʃkwēw], *to give sb a gift or to greet sb;* Fabvre (ca. 1690) "Kit Atamichkă8in, *tu me salue, fais du bien;* kit Atamiskātin 2 na8au, *Ie te salue 2 u8s autres*" | ANISH anamikaage, *to greet people* (Livesay & Nichols, 2021); MENO ana·mehkatwan, *greeting, handshaking, saying farewell* origin | PA ***aθam*** (Hewson, 1993)

*ataniy

INITIAL (NOUN, DEPENDENT ANIMATE)

— tail feather

evidence | PC wataniy, *a tail feather;* MC wataniy, *a tail feather;* EI (Mamit) utani [watanī], *feathered tail of a bird;* Watkins (1865) "Mitunne, *n.in. The tail of a bird;*" Laure (ca. 1726) "perechich-uatani -a, *queue d'oiseau;*" Fabvre (ca. 1690) "8abita kisk8e 8atani, *queue d aigle blanche*" | MENO wana·n(yan), *tail feather(s), bird tail(s)*

***atap (~ *atapēk)**

MEDIAL (NOUN INCORPORATION)

— fine root

evidence | NEC mūnitipāw, *to dig up roots;* WI (Pessamit) tashkatapeneu [tāʃkətəpēnēw], *to split a root lengthwise;* Laure (ca. 1726) "sakatapetichiu *enraciné, qui a des racines;*" Fabvre (ca. 1690) "gasiskatapetĭchen, *c8per racine qui le c8d;*" "Tachtigamatăban, *f(en)dre racines pr c8dre*" | ANISH daashkadabiibizh, *to split a tree runner with ones hands* (Livesay & Nichols, 2021) see | *watapiy

***atay**

INITIAL (NOUN, DEPENDENT INANIMATE)

— stomach

evidence | PC matay, *a belly, a stomach;* SEC (Waswanipi) watay, *one's stomach;* Laure (ca. 1726) "uatai, *panse, ventre*" see | *at[3], *ay[2]

***atā[1]**

INITIAL

— trade, barter

evidence | PC atāmēw, *to buy from sb;* WC atāwīw, *to barter; to buy;* MC atāwākew, *to sell sth;* AT atawan [atāwān], *merchandise;* SEC atāwew, *to sell sth;* NEC atāwāsiu, *a trader or merchant;* WI (Pessamit) atautitamueu [tāwtətəmwēw], *to make a sale for sb;* Watkins (1865) "Utawāo, *v.i.3. He barters, he exchanges, he trades, he buys, he deals;*" Laure (ca. 1726) "nit-atauatitau, *je traite pour lui;*" Fabvre (ca. 1690) "kit atamĭtin, *Ie te traite, vens, achete cela;*" Silvy (ca. 1680) "ata8e8in, *traite, marché*" | ANISH adaawe, *to buy* (Livesay & Nichols, 2021); MESK atāmēwa, *to sell sth to sb* limited to | *wē[1], *m[3]

***atā[2]**

PREFINAL

— breathe

limited to | *am[2], *aht[3] discussion | Alternatively, this prefinal may in fact be the medial ***at[4]**, *mouth*, followed by the post-medial accretion ***ē**, onto which the ablauting final ***m** is suffixed.

***atāht**

FINAL (VERB, TRANSITIVE, INANIMATE, CONCRETE)

— breathe on, breathe in

evidence | PC mahkatāhtam, *to take a deep sigh or breath;* MC āpawatāhtam, *to thaw sth with one's breath;* SEC pāhkotāhtam, *to be thirsty;* Laure (ca. 1726) "ni-nechtutaten, *j'en suis hors d'haleine*" origin | contraction of **atām + t** see | *atā[2], *aht[3] paired with | *atām[2]

***atām[1]**

INITIAL

— **1** under the surface

— **2** suspect or attribute guilt

evidence | [1]PC atāmihtak, *under the boards;* NEC itāmākunich, under the snow; Fabvre (ca. 1690) "Atamĭrau nihiak, *au dedans de mon corps, de ma chair*" [2]PC atāmimēw, *to accuse or blame sb;* MC atāmelimew, *to blame sb;* WI (Pessamit) atamelitam[u] [tāmēltəm], *to suspect sth;* Laure (ca. 1726) "ui-utchimauiu atamerimaganiu, *on le soupçonne de vouloir être roi*" | [1]ABEN alōmdona, *inside the mouth* (Day, 1994); ANISH anaamoonag, *under the boat* (Livesay & Nichols, 2021); MENO ana·ma·kon, *under the snow* [2]ANISH anaamim, *to blame sb* (Livesay & Nichols, 2021) origin | PA ***aθām** (Aubin, 1975)

***atām[2]**

FINAL (VERB, TRANSITIVE, ANIMATE, CONCRETE)

— breathe on, breathe in

evidence | MC ospatāmew, *to aspirate sth;* SEC āpawatāmew, *to thaw sth with one's breath;* WI (Pessamit) ishkutameu [ʃkutāmēw], *to inhale sth through one's nose* see | *atā[2], *am[2] paired with | *atāht

*atāmo

FINAL (VERB, ANIMATE, INTRANSITIVE, CONCRETE)

— **1** breathe

— **2** vocalize

evidence | [1]PC kakwātakatāmow, *to have a difficult time breathing;* MC nōhtetāmow, *to be short of breath;* SEC cipotāmow, *to suffocate* [2]PC itatāmow, *to sing thus;* MC sōhkatāmow, *to sing strongly;* EI (Sheshatshiu) nanamatamu [nənəmutāmu], *to have a quivering or trembling voice;* Laure (ca. 1726) "chai tchika-sukatamun, *ta voix se fortifie*" | [1]ANISH gibitanaamo, *to stop breathing* (Livesay & Nichols, 2021) [2]ANISH baapaganaamo, *to have a shaky voice* (Livesay & Nichols, 2021) see | *atā², *am², *o

*atān

INITIAL (NOUN, ANIMATE)

— stone on which food is pounded, a bed stone, a nether millstone

evidence | SEC atān, *NA a mortar or anvil;* NEC atān, *NA smooth rock used as an anvil for pounding dried fish into powder;* NSK ataan, *NI stone anvil or mortar for crushing bones before boiled;* WI (Uashat) atān [tān], *NI a mortar, a stone on which bones or meat are pounded;* EI (Sheshatshiu) atān [ətān], *NI a mortar, a stone on which bones or meat are pounded;* Watkins (1865) "Utan, *n.an. The under pounding-stone*"

*atē

MEDIAL (CLASSIFIER)

— a certain thickness, breadth, or width

evidence | MC alakaškatesiw, *to be a wide fishing net;* ispihtatešam, *to cut sth a certain thickness;* ispihtateyāw, *to be a certain thickness;* mahkatesiw, *to be a large fishing net from top to bottom;* Watkins (1865) "ayukuskutāmoon, *Broad (as a path);*" Fabvre (ca. 1690) "chaga8atesi8 arabi, *rez etroite*" | ANISH inigokwadeyaa, *to be a certain width* (Livesay & Nichols, 2021)

*atēwē

MEDIAL

— snow crust being strong enough to walk on

evidence | PC waskitatēwēnam, *to walk on the snow's crust;* MC itatewew, *to travel thither over the snow's crust;* NEC ushtitāwāyāu, *snow surface freezes after rain in winter* | ANISH biidadewe, *to walk hither on the snow crust* (Livesay & Nichols, 2021) see | *watē

*aticiy

INITIAL (NOUN, INANIMATE)

— unripe berry

evidence | NEC atichīsh, *an unripe berry;* SEC aticīwan, *to be an unripe berry;* WI (Pessamit) atitshi [tətʃī], *a green blueberry;* EI (Ekuanitshit) atitshimin [atɨtʃīmɨn], *a pea;* Silvy (ca. 1680) "atitchimin *pl. -mina, pois*" | ANISH anijiiminaaboo, *pea soup* (Livesay & Nichols, 2021); MESK anechīmini, *a pea* origin | PA ***aθecyi** discussion | The Atikamekw reflex of this root, **aritci**, pronounced [aricī], is an early borrowing from a neighbouring Anishinabe dialect. In this dialect, as well as coastal Southern East Cree, Moose Cree, Eastern Swampy Cree, and Plains Cree, the word for "pea" derives from a loanword from an early Anishinabe dialect, likely spread via trade routes.

*atih

INITIAL

— dye, color

evidence | PC atisikan, *dye;* MC atihtew, *to be dyed, to be ripe;* AT atisam [atissam], *to dye sth;* atisārikwew [atissārihkwēw], *to dye one's hair;* SEC atisam, *to dye sth;* Fabvre (ca. 1690) "Atisa8ian, *racines r8ges p(ou)r teindre pore epy*" | ANISH adiso, adite, *to be ripe, dyed, or colored* (Livesay & Nichols, 2021); MENO atɛ·hsow AI, atɛ·htɛw II, *to be dyed, colored, ripe* limited to | *s, *sw, *so², *tē⁴ discussion | Further derivatives are based on the transitive inanimate verb stem ***atihs**.

*atihkw¹ (~ *atihko)

INITIAL (NOUN, ANIMATE)

— caribou

evidence | PC atihk, *a caribou; a goat;* MC atihkoskāw, *to be many caribou;* NEC atihkukin, *a caribou bone;* EI (Unamanshipit) atikuminan [atīkumɨnān], *a bearberry;* Silvy (ca. 1680) "attik8, *cerf*" origin | PA ***atehkwa*** (Aubin, 1975; Hewson, 1993) see | *atihkw²

*atihkw² (~ *atihko)

MEDIAL, FINAL (NOUN INCORPORATION)

— caribou

evidence | PC apistacihkos, *antelope;* MC mowatihkwew, *to eat caribou;* WI (Pessamit) amutikᵘ [āmūtəkʷ], *un caribou vigilant et rusé;* EI (Mamit) nutikueu [nawatīkwēw], *to chase after caribou;* Fabvre (ca. 1690) "N8tattik8an e8, *à la chasse des cer(f)s, carib8s;*" Silvy (ca. 1680) "ni g8tattik8an, *je goûte du cerf;*" "irinatik8, *caribou*" see | *atihkw¹

*atihkwan (~ *atihkwanak)

MEDIAL, FINAL (NOUN INCORPORATION)

— branch, knot

evidence | MC nikotwāsotihkwanēsiw, *to have six branches;* NEC ītāmitihkuniū, *to be knots on the inside;* WI (Pessimit) passetikunatshiu [pəssētukuntʃīw], *to branch, speaking of a tree;* Watkins (1865) "Sukutìkwunewew, *v.i.1. He is branchy, he is thick with branches (i.e., the tree)*" see | *watihkwan

*atiht (~ *atihc)

INITIAL

— not centered

evidence | AT atitapiw [atihtāpiw], *loucher;* SEC atihtahwew, *to miss one's target by shooting to the side;* NEC atihch, *not centered;* atihtāpiu, *to be cross-eyed;* atihtiham, *miss target by shooting by its side;* WI (Pessamit) atitaim [tətīm], *to shoot wide of what one is trying to hit;* atitshapakutitau, *loucher;* EI (Mamit) atitapu [atītāpu], *loucher;* Laure (ca. 1726) "nit-atitahigan, *je le couche de travers;*" Silvy (ca. 1680) "nit'atit8tan, *je passe par où il passe, je vais en delà;*" "nit'atitchetinen, nit'atitetinen, *en pliant une robe, je fais passer un pli plus que l'autre;*" "nit'atitchabin, *je suis louche, tournant les yeux de côté et d'autre*"

*atihtā

FINAL (VERB, ANIMATE, INTRANSITIVE, CONCRETE)

— affect by exposure to the cold

evidence | PC āhkwatihtāw, *to freeze sth;* NEC mishkiwitihtāu, *to freeze sth;* Laure (ca. 1726) "maskauatitaganiu, *endurci par la gelée*" see | *at⁵, *ıhtā¹ paired with | *atim³

*atim¹

INITIAL

— progressively become farther from, withdraw

evidence | PC atimipahtāw, *to run away;* MC atimohtew, *to walk away;* SEC atimipayiw, *to drive away* | ANISH animose, *to walk away* (Livesay & Nichols, 2021); MENO anɛ·mapew, *to sit facing away;* MESK anemāmowa, *to flee away* origin | PA ***aθem*** (Hewson, 1993)

*atim²

INITIAL (VERB, TRANSITIVE, ANIMATE)

— overtake

evidence | PC atimēw, *to overtake sb;* MC atimaham, *to catch up by paddling;* SEC atiminehwew, *to overtake sb;* Silvy (ca. 1680) "nit'attimau, *je l'attrape*" | ANISH adim, *to catch up to sb, to overtake sb* (Livesay & Nichols, 2021) origin | PA ***atem*** (Hewson, 1993) see | *ım³

***atim**[3]

FINAL (VERB, TRANSITIVE, ANIMATE, CONCRETE)

— affect by exposure to the cold

evidence | PC āhkwatimēw, *to freeze sb;* ESC āhkwatimēw, *to freeze sb;* SEC maškawatimew, *to freeze sb;* WI (Pessamit) shikatimeu [ʃīkətəmēw], *to cause sb to catch a chill* see | *at⁵, *ɪm³ paired with | *atihtā

***atiman**

INITIAL (NOUN, INANIMATE)

— snowshoe harness

evidence | ESC atiman, *a snowshoe harness;* SEC atiman, *a snowshoe harness;* EI (Sheshatshiu) atiman [ətɨmɨn], *a snowshoe harness or strap;* Silvy (ca. 1680) "attiman, *corde tenant le pied à la raquette*" | ANISH adimanike, *to put the foot strap on snowshoes* (Livesay & Nichols, 2021) origin | PA ***atemani** see | *ɪm²

***atimā**

INITIAL

— in opposite positions, inverted

evidence | MC atimāskisinew, *to wear one's shoes on the wrong feet;* SEC atimāškam, *to wear sth on the opposite side;* atimāštisew, *to wear one's mittens on the wrong hands;* NEC atimāyāpitikuhch, *on the blunt side of a blade;* cf. Watkins (1865) "Utimapesim, *n.in. The north*"

***atimw (~ *atimo)**

INITIAL (NOUN, ANIMATE)

— dog

evidence | PC atimotihkom, *a woodtick;* WC acimosis, *a puppy; a pussywillow;* MC atimoskāw, *to be many dogs;* SEC atimʷ, *a dog;* atimotāpāneyāpiy, *a dog harness;* WI (Pessamit) atimussikananish [təmūssəkānānəʃ], *a pussywillow;* Laure (ca. 1726) "attimuchich, petit chien;" Silvy (ca. 1680) "attimȣ, *chien;*" "attimȣstiȣan, *museau de chien*" | ANISH animosh, *a dog;* animogan, *a bone of a dog* (Livesay & Nichols, 2021); MENO anɛ·m(ok), *a dog(s)* origin | PA ***aθwi**, *arrow* (Aubin, 1975), akin to Old Cree ***atohsi** see | *aštimw

***atin**[1]

MEDIAL

— hill, mountain

evidence | MC išpāmatināw, *high bank or hill;* SEC nīhtatin, *at the foot of a hill or mountaint;* WI (Pessamit) upatinau [upətnāw], *to be a mountainous rise* | ABEN menadena, *tio be mountains here and there* (Day, 1994); ANISH mangadinaa, *big hill* (Livesay & Nichols, 2021) origin | PA ***aten** (Hewson, 1993)

***atin**[2]

FINAL (VERB, INANIMATE, INTRANSITIVE, CONCRETE)

— affected by the cold

evidence | PC sōhkatin, *to be frozen solid;* MC maškawatin, *frozen hard;* SEC wāšetin, *to be frozen clear* | ABEN gebaden, *to be frozen shut, to be frozen over* (Day, 1994); ANISH mashkawadin, *to be frozen solid* origin | PA ***aten** (Aubin, 1975) see | *at⁵, *ɪn⁴ paired with | *aci

***atin**[3]

FINAL (VERB, INANIMATE, INTRANSITIVE, DERIVED)

— rotten

evidence | PC pikiskatin, *to be rotten;* WC wīcīkatitin, *to be putrid from rotting;* MC malōkatatin, *to be soft from decay;* Watkins (1865) "Māstututin, *v.imp. It rots;*" "Pikiskutin, *v.imp. It is putrid, it is rotten;*" Laure (ca. 1726) "pitchiskatinu uhias, *viande pourrie*" see | *at¹, *ɪn⁴ paired with | *atit discussion | This root has been reshaped in some dialects by analogy of its animate counterpart.

***atipihs**

INITIAL (NOUN, INANIMATE)

— thin babiche

evidence | PC atipis, *rawhide string used for lacing snowshoes;* MC atipisihkew, *to make thin babiche;* AT (Opitciwan, Joey Awashish) atipisak [atipissak], *lines of babiche;* EI (Sheshatshiu) atipish [ətɨpəʃ], *fine babiche for weaving front and back of snowshoe;* Laure (ca. 1726) "attibis-iets, *la petite babiche, lacée finement*"

*atit

FINAL (VERB, ANIMATE, INTRANSITIVE, DERIVED)

— rotten

evidence | PC pikiskatiw, *to be rotten;* WC pikiskatiw, *to be rotten;* MC malōkatatiw, *to be soft from decay;* Watkins (1865) "Pikiskutitew, *v.i.1. He is putrid, he is rotten;*" Laure (ca. 1726) "pitchiskatitu-names, *poisson pourri*" see | *at[1], *ɪt[3] paired with | *atin[3] discussion | This final has been reshaped in all modern dialects by analogy of its inanimate counterpart.

*ato[1] (~ *atw)

INITIAL

— **1** point at

— **2** choke on bone

evidence | [1]MC itohikew, *to point at;* SEC atohwew, *to point at sb* [2]MC atohow, *to choke on a bone;* SEC atohow, *to choke on a bone* | MIAMI alohw-, *to aim at sb* (ILDA, 2017) origin | PA ***aθo*** see | *ato[2], *ato[3], *atohs

*ato[2]

INITIAL

— work

evidence | MC atoskew, *work;* SEC atutew, *assign work;* WI (Pessamit) atusseu, *work*; EI atusseu, *work;* Silvy (ca. 1680) "nit'at8tau, *je l'emploie*" | ANISH anokii, *work* (Livesay & Nichols, 2021) origin | PA ***aθo*** (Aubin, 1975) limited to | *t[3] see | *ato[1], *kē[2] compare | *nip[2] discussion | Note that the extended form ***atoskē*** is an antipassive formed from the VTA stem ***atot*** + ***kē***. The root itself likely shares the same origin as its homonym, the sense of the transitive verb stem likely evolving from something akin to "pointing sb toward a task" to "assigning a task." Only by forming the antipassive does the root acquire the basic sense of "working."

*ato[3] (~ *atw)

MEDIAL

— arrow

evidence | MC pīhtatwān, *quiver;* Laure (ca. 1726) "pitatuan, *carquois, trousse à mettre des flèches, on le porte sur le dos*" | MESK pītanwāna, *quiver* origin | PA ***aθwi***, *arrow* (Aubin, 1975), akin to Old Cree ***atohsi*** see | *ato[1], *ato[2], *atohs

*ato[4] (~ *atw)

MEDIAL, FINAL (CLASSIFIER)

— stick-like

evidence | PC sīsipāskwat, *maple sugar, sugar;* WC cimanaskatōhtak, *tree with its top broken off;* ākat, *a curved pole used for finding beaver tunnels under the ice;* MC pīkotowiw, *to be rotten, speaking of a tree;* SEC pīkotōhtak[w], *rotten wood;* NEC ākitu, *curved stick for finding beaver tunnels under the ice;* WI (Pessamit) nakat [nākət], *my curved stick used to probe for beaver;* pishkuashkut [pəʃkwāʃkut], *knotty outgrowth on a tree;* Watkins (1865) "Chimunuskut, *n.indec. [sic] A tree broken by the wind;*" Laure (ca. 1726) "agatu -a; agaturiu *rel., bâton croche pour sonder le castor;*" "pakahatuetau, *jouons à la crosse;*" Fabvre (ca. 1690) "Pagahat8an, *b8les à I8er;*" "chinipask8at, *Eau qui déc8le d'arbre v.g. Eau d'érable;*" "Rigat8i mitai, *v.g. uieux p8ry bois*" | ANISH giishkanakad, *a stump;* baaga'adowe, *to play lacrosse* (Livesay & Nichols, 2021); MESK pākahatowēwa, *to play lacrosse or baseball* origin | PA ***ato***

*atohs

INITIAL (NOUN, ANIMATE)

— pointed arrow

evidence | PC atos, *an arrow; a bullsnake;* AT (Opitciwan, Joey Awashish) atosak [atossak], *arrows;* SEC atos, *an arrowhead;*

WI (Pessamit) atush [təʃ], *arrowhead;* natush *my arrowhead;* EI (Mamit) atush [atuh], *an arrowhead;* Fabvre (ca. 1690) "Pakichinȣ attȣs, *La fleche, Le trait the;*" Silvy (ca. 1680) "atȣs, *flèche;*" "atȣsaskȣ, *le bois de la flèche*" origin | PA ***aθōnsi** (Aubin, 1975) see | *ato¹, *ato², *ato³ compare | *akaskw discussion | ***Atohsa** is one of a few independent nouns in Old Cree that does not, despite its form, require an epenthetic **t** when possessed. Note that this word is treated as animate in contemporary dialects, with the exception of Eastern Innu, as well as in Fabvre's example from the 1690s, contrary to Aubin's assignment of the inanimate gender in Proto-Algonquian.

*atonisk

MEDIAL, FINAL (NOUN INCORPORATION)

— clay

evidence | PC wāpatonisk, *white clay; white face paint;* MC wāpatonisk, *clay;* WI (Pessamit) uapatunishk [wāpətūnəʃk], *clay;* Laure (ca. 1726) "uabatunisk, *terre grasse, argile*" | ANISH (Abitibi dialect) wāpanonihk, *clay; common family name* see | *matonisk

*atōsp

INITIAL

— alder

evidence | NEC utūspiskāu, *to be many alders;* WI (Pessamit) atushpishkau [tuʃpəʃkāw], *to be many alders* see | *atōspiy

*atōspiy

INITIAL (NOUN, INANIMATE)

— alder

evidence | PC atōspiy, *an alder;* MC atōspīskāw, *to be many alders;* AT atospi [atōspiy], *an alder;* SEC atōspīwāpow & otōspīwāpow, *a decoction of alder bark, a traditional medicine;* EI (Sheshatshiu) atushpi [tūʃpī], *an alder;* Silvy (ca. 1680) "atȣspi, *aulne, arbre*" see | *atōsp

*atōt (~ *atōs)

INITIAL

— on

evidence | PC atōspow, *to eat off of sth;* MC atōspow, *eat off of a dish;* NEC atutipiu, *sit on;* Laure (ca. 1726) "mokmaniriu atutapiu, *le couteau est dessous lui;*" Silvy (ca. 1680) "atȣtapiȣagan, *siège relevé*" | MENO ato·sɛhkam, *to stand on sth;* ato·tapew, *to sit on sth*

*atwēmo

FINAL (VERB, ANIMATE, INTRANSITIVE, DERIVED)

— cry

evidence | WC kakwātakatwīmow, *to lament;* MC kipihtatwemow, *to stop crying;* SEC cipihtatwemow, *to stop crying;* Laure (ca. 1726) "ka papamatuemut, *inconsolable, qui gémit toujours*" | ANISH maadademo, *to start to cry* (Livesay & Nichols, 2021); MENO tana·ti·mow, *to weep there, then, through that time* see | *matwē, *ımo

*aw¹

INITIAL

— have

evidence | PC awihiwēw, *to lend sth;* MC awihāsomew, *to borrow from sb;* SEC awihew, *to lend sth to sb;* Laure (ca. 1726) "nit-auin nitchichigu, *je me sers de mes yeux;*" Fabvre (ca. 1690) "Aȣĭtan 3 tau, *pouuoir posse;*" Silvy (ca. 1680) "nit'aȣiasȣn, *j'emprunte;*" "aȣȣina, *hardes, bagages*" compare | *awahkē

*aw²

MEDIAL

— fur

evidence | PC āhtawēw, *to change one's pelage;* MC pinatawepaliw, *fur falls out;* NEC yākāutiwāu, *to have sandy fur;* Silvy (ca. 1680) "nit'abȣtaȣechchimau, *je le mets à contre poil;*" "ni sagaȣan 3. -eȣ, *le poil me vient*"

*aw[3] (~ *ā)

FINAL (VERB, TRANSITIVE, ANIMATE, ABSTRACT)

— **1** produces transitive animate verb stems when suffixed to certain transitive inanimate verb stems

— **2** adds a benefactive argument when suffixed to transitive inanimate themes and to animate intransitive verb stems ending in *tw as allomorphic variants of *tā

evidence | [1]PC tōtawēw, *to do sth to sb;* WC miskawīw, *to find sb;* MC ohtiškawikāpawīštawew, *stand facing sb;* SEC pīkoškawew, *to break sth under one's weight* [2]PC tōtamawew, *to do sth for sb;* WC otinamawīw, *to take sth for sb; to buy sth for sb;* MC akwanahamawew, *to cover sth for sb;* kātowew, *to hide sth from sb;* ki kātwātin, *I hide sth from you;* otāmihtitowew, *to hit sb with sth;* tetāwihtowew, *to separate sth down the middle for sb;* AT katowew [kātowēw], *hide sth from sb;* SEC petamawew, *to bring sth for sb;* petowew, *to bring sth for sb;* ci petwātin, *I bring sth for you*; ayamihtowew, *to read sth for sb;* pimipayihtwāsow, *to run a business for oneself;* Silvy (ca. 1680) "ni miskamaȣau, *je trouve pour lui;*" "nit'achtȣau, *je lui garde qqch de mon manger*" origin | PA ***aw** (Aubin, 1975) compare | *w², *tw² discussion | Note that contemporary dialects have all contracted ***tw** + ***aw** to a reflex of ***tow**, but the underlying form is revealed when vowel-lengthening processes occur, resulting in reflexes of ***twā** as expected.

*awahkē

INITIAL (VERB, ANIMATE, INTRANSITIVE)

— to own a person or animal

evidence | PC awahkēwin, *slavery;* MC awahkew, *to have a pet, to have a slave (archaic);* SEC awahkān, *a pet;* Fabvre (ca. 1690) "Aȣakan, *Esclaue, prisonnier, captif*" compare | *aw¹

*awahs

INITIAL

— far side, beyond

evidence | PC awasāpisk, *beyond the rocks;* MC awasewehtew, *to walk out of sight behind a bend or corner;* AT awasatin [awassatin], *on the far side of the mountain;* (Opitciwan, Joey Awashish) awasite [awassitē], *farther;* SEC awas! *go away!;* Laure (ca. 1726) "auassité, *là, de l'autre côté, plus loin*" | ANISH awasaatig, *on the other side of a tree or pole* (Livesay & Nichols, 2021)

*awahtān

FINAL (VERB, INANIMATE, INTRANSITIVE, DERIVED)

— rain

evidence | PC pīsawācāsin [*sic*], *to be windy with rain;* MC pōnawahtān, *to cease raining;* SEC sōhkawahtān, *to rain strongly;* NEC mimihkiwihtān, *large raindrops;* Laure (ca. 1726) "minauatanu, *une pluie soudaine;*" cf. Laure (ca. 1726) "auatanu, *pluie menu*" see | *awan, *tān²

*awan

FINAL (VERB, INANIMATE, INTRANSITIVE, DERIVED)

— fog

evidence | PC yīkwawanipayiw, *to be a sudden fog;* MC kaškawan, *to be foggy;* SEC mātawanipayiw, *to be an ice fog;* Laure (ca. 1726) "tapatauanu, *petit nuage sur la rivière;*" Fabvre (ca. 1690) "Kachkaȣan, *Brȣillards*" | cf. ANISH awan, *to be foggy*

*awanān

INITIAL (NOUN, ANIMATE)

— landlocked salmon, ouananiche (Salmo salar)

evidence | AT (Wemotaci, Jeannette Coocoo) wananic [wanāniš], *ouinaniche;* SEC awanāniš, *landlocked Atlantic salmon;* NEC uwinān, *landlocked salmon;* NSK unaan, *ouananiche;* WI (Pessamit) unan [ūnān], *ouananiche;* EI (Sheshatshiu) unan [unān], *ouananiche;* EI (Mamit) unan [wanān], *ouananiche;* Laure (ca. 1726) "auananich *pl.* -chets, *ouananiche, espèce de petites truites qui se trouvent dans ces rivières;*" cf. SEC awanāw, *landlocked Atlantic salmon*

*awāhs

INITIAL (NOUN, ANIMATE)

— child

evidence | PC awāsis, *a child;* Lacombe (1874) "awāsissiwiw, ok, *(a.a.) il est enfant;*" WSC (Misipawistik, Ellen Cook) nic awāsimis, *my child;* MC awāšiš, *a child;* kit awāšimiš, *your child;* AT (Wemotaci, Nicole Petiquay) awacak [awāššak], *children;* awacicak [awāššiššak], *little children, contrasting with the accepted variant* awacicak [awāʒiššak], *children;* (Opitciwan, Joey Awashish) awaca [awāšša], *a child;* awacak [awāššak], *children;* nit awacim, [nit awāššim], *my child;* awacic [awāššiš], *a baby;* awacicak [awāššiššak], *babies;* nit awacimic [nit awāššimiš], *my baby;* SEC awāššīwiw, *to be a child;* NEC awāshish, *a child;* WI (Pessamit) auassikashu [wāssīkāʃu], *to act like a child;* Laure (ca. 1726) "esku auachissiban, *il n'était pas grand encore;*" Fabvre (ca. 1690) "a8achisets, *enfants;*" Silvy (ca. 1680) "a8achich, *un enfant;*" "m8ska8ate8 a8achis, *l'enfant pleure*" see | *āwahs compare | *nīcān discussion | Suffixation of the diminutive ***ɩhš** produces the stem from which most contemporary reflexes are derived.

*awē

INITIAL

— near a source of heat

evidence | PC awasam, *to warm sth up;* Lacombe (1874) "āwatew, a, *(a.in.) il y a un bon feu;*" MC awasow, *to warm oneself up by a source of heat;* AT (Opitciwan, Joey Awashish) nit awason [nit awazon], *I warm myself up;* SEC awasow, *to warm oneself up by a source of heat;* Laure (ca. 1726) "nit-auasun, *je me chauffe auprès du feu;*" Silvy (ca. 1680) "nit'a8as8n, *je me chauffe*" | ANISH awazo, *to warm oneself by the fire* limited to | *s, *sw, *so², *tē⁴

*awēhsīhs

INITIAL (NOUN, ANIMATE)

— beast, wild animal

evidence | MC awesīs, *a wild animal;* AT (Wemotaci, Nicole Petiquay) awesis [awēssis], *an animal;* awessiss, *animal* (Béland, 1978); SEC awesīs, *a wild animal;* EI (Sheshatshiu) aueshish [wēʃiʃ], *an animal, a quadruped;* Watkins (1865) "owāses, *n.an. A wild animal, a beast, a brute;*" Laure (ca. 1726) "auechich -ets, *bête, privée ou sauvage;*" Fabvre (ca. 1690) "A8esis, *a(nim)al, beste terrestre*" | ABEN awaas, *a wild animal;* ANISH awesiinh, *a wild animal* (Livesay & Nichols, 2021); MENO awɛ·hse·hsɛh, *a bear cub;* MIAMI aweehsa, *a wild animal* (ILDA, 2017) compare | *pišiskiw

*awēt

INITIAL (NOUN, ANIMATE)

— beaver under a year of life

evidence | WC awīcisis, *baby beaver under a year old;* MC awetiš, *a beaver during its first year of life;* SEC awetiš, *a beaver during its first year of life;* WI (Uashat) auetiss [wētīss], *a beaver less than a year old;* Laure (ca. 1726) "auetich, *castor d'un an;*" Fabvre (ca. 1690) "a8etich, *petit castor;*" "A8etǎtach, *peau de petit castor*" | ANISH Cuoq (1886) "Awenicenj, *jeune castor, jeune rat-musqué*" origin | PA ***awēθ**

*awihso

FINAL (VERB, ANIMATE, INTRANSITIVE, DERIVED)

— gather fruit, pick berries

evidence | MC natawawisow, *to go pick berries;* NEC chiyikiwāwisū, *to pick more than one kind of berry* | ANISH gaadawinzo, *to hide berries being picked* (Livesay & Nichols, 2021) see | mawihso

*awik

INITIAL

— dusk

evidence | MC awikāw, *be dusk;* SEC awikāšteyāw, *be overcast;* WI (Pessamit) ukau [ukāw], *crépuscule*

*awip

INITIAL

— calm water

evidence | WI (Pessamit) aupinashteu [ūpənāstēw], *to be calm water in warm weather;* EI (Ekuanitshit) aupishu [āwpɨhu], *to be calm water;* Silvy (ca. 1680) "nit'a8ibinichin, *j'ai du beau temps, calme*" | ABEN awiben, *to be calm* (Day, 1995); ANISH awibaa, to be calm, windless (Livesay & Nichols, 2021) limited to | *ɪn[4]

*ay[1]

INITIAL (NOUN)

— a person, animal, or thing

evidence | MC ayahāšiš, *a small thing; a young animal, bird, or person;* aya, *word used to attract attention;* SEC ayāpew, *a buck;* ayihe, *an animal, person, or thing for which one cannot recall the name;* WI (Pessamit) aie [ājē], *dear, sweetie dear, sweetie (term of address for spouse);* Silvy (ca. 1680) "nitaim, *mon chien*" | ANISH ayaabe, *a male deer;* odayan, *one's dog; one's horse* (Livesay & Nichols, 2021); Nicholas (ca. 1670) "aïa! *hau, holà*" (Daviault, 1994)

*ay[2]

MEDIAL, FINAL (NOUN, CLASSIFIER)

— sheet-like

evidence | PC masakay, *skin;* WC atihkway, *a caribou skin;* manaway, *a cheek;* SEC ohtawakay, *one's ear;* EI (Ekuanitshit) manuai [mānwēj], *the hide of a caribou or moose dried with fur on;* Watkins (1865) "Utikwai, *n.in. A deer skin;*" "Uchikwas, *n.in. A small deer-skin, a piece of deer-skin;*" Laure (ca. 1726) "matutichin-apakuai, *les écorces pour la suerie;*" Fabvre (ca. 1690) "Atai, *pl* aïak, *peau de castor passée;*" Silvy (ca. 1680) "nichkaïau nitag8p, *ma robe est mouillé d'eau, de neige fondue dessus;*" "michtattik8ai, *peau de cerf*" | ANISH Cuoq (1886) "Askikwei, n, *peau de loup-marin*"
discussion | Though nonproductive in contemporary dialects, reflexes of this final are found in a large number of sheet-like materials, body parts, and hollow organs.

*ayaht (~ *ayahc)

INITIAL

— different, foreign

evidence | PC ayahtokamik, *unfamiliar or strange lodge;* MC ayahtelihtam, *to consider sth different;* ayahciliw, *a foreigner;* WI (Pessamit) aitan [ītn], *be different;* EI (Ekuanitshit) aitan [ajātan], *be different;* Laure (ca. 1726) "aiatastimu, *chien emprunté à d'autres;*" Silvy (ca. 1680) "ïatisi8 mistig8, *ce bois est d'une autre espèce*"

*ayak

FINAL (ABSTRACT)

— forms particles that convey a specified number of ways or places when suffixed to numerals

evidence | PC pēyakwayak, *in one way, in one place;* WC nīswayakinam, *to see double;* MC mištetoyakinākwanwa, *to be many kinds;* SEC nīšwayac, *two kinds;* NEC nīshuyich, *two ways or kinds;* WI neuit [nēwīt], *in four ways, in four places;* Watkins (1865) "Nāwuyuketow, *v.t.in.2. He divides it into four parts*" | MESK taswayaki, *so many kinds, groups, pairs*

*ayam

INITIAL

— talk

evidence | PC ayamihēw, *to speak to sb;* WC ayamihāw, *to pray;* ESC ayamiw, *to talk;* MC ayamiw, *to speak;* AT aiamihaw [ayamihāw], *to pray;* SEC (Waswanipi) ayamihkwāmiw, *to talk in one's sleep;* NEC ayimihtāu, *to read sth;* WI (Pessamit) aimishtimueu [īmīstəmwēw], *to talk to a dog(s);* EI (Sheshatshiu) aimieu [ējmjēw], *to talk to sb; to telephone sb;* Watkins (1865) "Ayumètow, *v.t.in.2. He reads it;*" Laure (ca. 1726) "nit-aiamin 3. -iu, *je tiens conseil;*" Silvy (ca. 1680) "aïamihitȣin, *harangue*"

*ayawiš

INITIAL

— within the same day

evidence | PC iyawis, *entirely, wholly;* ESC (Severn) ayawish, *just for the day, answers to 'how long will you be gone?;'* MC ayawiš, *within the same day, for the day;* NEC iyuwisaau, *to be fresh food;* Watkins (1865) "Yowusi-kesikow, *n.in. The same day;*" Fabvre (ca. 1690) "Aïaȣich minaïaȣich, *derechef, encore;*" "Iaȣich, *sans interruption*" | ANISH Nicholas (ca. 1670) "iaouich, *le mesme jour*" (Daviault, 1994) discussion | The absence of a preaspiration on the sibilant cannot be confirmed due to the lack of an Atikamekw cognate.

*ayā

INITIAL (VERB, INTRANSITIVE)

— **1** be (in a certain location or condition)

— **2** have

evidence | [1]PC ayāw, *to be in a certain place or condition;* WSC (Misipawistik, Ellen Cook) ayāw, *to be in a certain place or condition;* SEC miyo-ayāw, *to be well* [2]PC ayāw, *to have or own sth;* ayānis, *article of clothing;* WC ayānis, *article of clothing;* ESC ayāwew, *to have sb;* MC ayāw, *to have sth;* SEC (Waswanipi) ayān, *article of clothing;* NEC iyāu, *to have sth;* EI (Sheshatshiu) aiau [jāw], *to buy sth;* Watkins (1865) "Ayow, *v.t.in.2. He has it, he possesses it;*" Laure (ca. 1726) "nit-aian 3. aiau, *cela m'appartient;*" Fabvre (ca. 1690) "kit Aïaȣin, *tu te sers de moy;*" Silvy (ca. 1680) "nit'aïan, *je possède cela*" | [1]ANISH ayaa, *to be in a certain place or condition* [2]ANISH odayaan, odayaawaan, *to have or own sth, sb* (Livesay & Nichols, 2021) compare | *tē[1]

ayākwām

INITIAL

— cautiously, carefully

evidence | PC ayākwāmīw, *to be cautious;* yākwā, *look out!;* Lacombe (1874) "Yākwāmeyimew, *il est attentif auprès de lui, prévenant;*" WC ayākwāmisiw, *to be careful;* WSC (Misipawistik, Ellen Cook) yākwāmisiw, *to be cautious;* ESC (Severn) āyākwāmīw, *to be cautious;* MC yākwāmihew, *to warn sb;* yākwā, *be careful!;* AT (Wemotaci, Jeannette Coocoo) ekwamictowew [ēkwāmīštawēw], *to be wary of sb, to be careful regarding sb;* SEC yākwā! *Be careful!;* NEC iyākwāmimāu, *to caution sb;* WI (Uashat) akua [ākwā, jākwā], *carefully; be careful!;* EI (Sheshatshiu) iakua [jākwā], *carefully; be careful!;* Watkins (1865) "Yakwamisewin, *n.in. Carefulness;*" Laure (ca. 1726) "ka iaguamuet, *circonspect, qui prend garde en parlant;*" "nit-iagua-mituneriten, *je prends garde à cela, j'y pense;*" "iagua ni-mituneriten, *je prends mes sûretés;*" "aiaguamiu, *mine effaré*" | ANISH Cuoq (1886) "Angwam, *et plus ordinairement* Aiangwam, *gare! attention!;*" MENO aya·kuamemɛw, *to warn sb, to tell sb to be on their guard*

*ayēskaw

INITIAL

— ready

evidence | MC ayeskawaštāw, *to place sth at the ready;* SEC ayeskaweyimow, *to feel ready;* NSK ayaaskuwiistim, *to get ready for sth;* WI (Pessamit) aieshkuiu [ējēʃkwīw], *to get ready;* EI (Unaman-shipit) aieshkushtau [ajēhkwahtāw], *to place sth at the ready;* Watkins (1865) "Ayāskowegapowew, *v.i.1. He stands ready*"

*ayēsko

INITIAL

— tire, tired

evidence | PC ayēskosiw, *to be tired;* MC ayeskocāpiw, *to have tired eyes;* SEC ayeskomow, _tired from vocalizing (e.g., wailing);_ Laure (ca. 1726) "nit-aieskupuaman, _je suis las dans les cuisses_" | ANISH ayekozi, _to be tired_ (Livesay & Nichols, 2021); MESK ayīhkwiwa, _to be tired_

*ayirimo

INITIAL (VERB, ANIMATE, INTRANSITIVE)

— sneeze

evidence | PC Lacombe (1874) "āyeyimow, ok, _éternuer;_" WC āyīðimow, _to sneeze;_ MC elimow, _to sneeze;_ AT (Opitciwan, Joey Awashish) nit aierimon [nit ayērimon], _I sneeze;_ SEC āyimwew, _to sneeze;_ NEC āyiyimū, _to sneeze;_ NSK iyaayimuw, _to sneeze;_ WI (Pessamit) alimu [āləmu], _to sneeze;_ Laure (ca. 1726) "nit-airimuskagu tchistemau, _j'éternue, prenant du tabac;_" Silvy (ca. 1680) "nit'airim8n, _j'éternue_"

*ā[1]

ACCRETION (PREMEDIAL, PREFINAL)

evidence | PC ispākonakāw, _to be deep snow;_ cahkāsikēw, _to shine;_ MC kinwānakāw, _long island;_ cākāhkahtew, _to be consumed by fire;_ SEC itākamāw, _lake is thus_

*ā[2]

FINAL (VERB, ANIMATE, INTRANSITIVE, ABSTRACT)

— forms the antipassive when suffixed to transitive animate verb stems and to animate intransitive verb stems ending in *tw as allomorphic variants of *tā

evidence | PC pakitahwāw, _to set a fishing net;_ WC ayamihāw, _to pray;_ ESC pāhtakomāw, _to drive or funnel caribou into a killing zone outlined by poles;_ MC masinahikepalihtwāw, _to type;_ SEC (Waswanipi) namewahāw, _to set a net for sturgeon;_ WI (Pessamit) pitaunau [pətūlāw], _to catch fish in a net;_ ashtuau [stwāw], _to set sth aside for later use;_ Silvy (ca. 1680) "nit'acht8an 3. -au, _je garde le reste de table, des vivres_" compare | *ıkē, *kē[2], *kēmo, *wē[2]

*ācim

FINAL (VERB, TRANSITIVE, ANIMATE, DERIVED)

— give an account of

evidence | MC tipācimew, _to relate an account about sb;_ SEC miywācimew, _to relate a good account about sb;_ Silvy (ca. 1680) "ni maratchimau, _je lui dis de sales paroles_" paired with | *ātot

*ācimo

FINAL (VERB, ANIMATE, INTRANSITIVE, DERIVED)

— give an account

evidence | WC takwācimow, _to arrive with news;_ MC tipācimow, _to relate an account;_ SEC petācimow, _to bring news_ | MESK menwāchimowa, _to speak well_ see | *ācim, *o

*ācištaw

INITIAL

— barely, only a little

evidence | PC Lacombe (1874) "ātchistāweyimew, _négliger;_" WC ācistawīðimīw, _to begrudge sb;_ MC ācištawi-kiskelihtam, _to barely know sth;_ Watkins (1865) "Achistowisew, _He is very ill, he is in the last stage of illness;_" Fabvre (ca. 1690) "Achista8isin i8, _fantas(tique), fascheux_"

*āciwahs

FINAL (VERB, TRANSITIVE, INANIMATE, CONCRETE)

— boil

evidence | PC kaskāciwasam, _to boil sth tender;_ MC aciwāciwasam _to boil sth down;_ AT (Opitciwan, Joey Awashish) pekwatciwosam [pēhkwāciwssam], _to boil sth dry;_ WI (Pessamit) pitshishkatshusham[u] [pətʃəʃkātʃūʃəm], _boils sth until it disintegrates_ see | *wih, *s paired with | *āciwahsw

*āciwahso

FINAL (VERB, ANIMATE, INTRANSITIVE, CONCRETE)

— boil

evidence | PC kwāskwēyāciwasow, *to be at a full boil, speaking of a kettle;* MC macimākwāciwasow, *to smell bad while boiling;* EI (Unaman-shipit) pakuatshushu [pākwātʃwahu], *to boil dry* paired with | *āciwahtē see | *wih, *so²

*āciwahsw

FINAL (VERB, TRANSITIVE, ANIMATE, CONCRETE)

— boil

evidence | PC pāskāciwaswēw, *to cause sth to burst by boiling;* MC aciwāciwaswew *to boil sth down;* WI (Pessamit) pitshishkatshushuue [pətʃəʃkātʃūʃwēw], *boils sth until it disintegrates* see | *wih, *sw paired with | *āciwahs

*āciwahtē

FINAL (VERB, INANIMATE, INTRANSITIVE, CONCRETE)

— boil

evidence | PC mēstāciwahtēw, *to boil dry;* MC kaškāciwahtew, *to be boiled tender;* Laure (ca. 1726) "ikatchiuateu, *l'eau de la chaudière est consumée;*" Silvy (ca. 1680) "tchimatchiȣatechiȣ, *elle bout doucement*" paired with | *āciwahso see | *wih, *tē⁴

*āciwan

MEDIAL

— rapids

evidence | PC wapāciwanāhk, *place name, Patuanak, literally 'at the narrowing rapids;'* MC nīhtāciwaneyāpokow, *to drift down the rapids;* EI (Unaman-shipit) apituatshuan [āpītawātʃwan], *halfway along a rapids* see | *ā¹, *ciwan

*āh¹

PREFINAL

— by action of wave(s) see | *āhan, *āhotē, *āhoko

*āh² (~ *āš)

PREFINAL

— shine light

origin | PA ***ā?** limited to | *s, *so², *sw, *tē⁴ see | *āhs, *āhso², *āhsw, *āštē²

*āhan

FINAL (VERB, INANIMATE, INTRANSITIVE, CONCRETE)

— waves run

evidence | MC māmahkāhan, *large waves;* SEC wāsāhan, *breaking waves* see | *āh¹, *an²

*āhāhsiw

INITIAL (NOUN, ANIMATE)

— American crow (Corvus brachyrhynchos)

evidence | PC āhāsiw, *a crow;* WC āhāsīsis, *a young crow;* ESC āhāsciw, *a crow;* AT (Wemotaci, Jeannette Coocoo) ahasiw [āhāssiw], *a crow;* SEC āhāsiw, *a crow;* WI (Masheuiatsh) ahashu [āhāʃu], *a crow;* EI (Mamit) ahashu [āhu], *a crow;* Watkins (1865) "Ahasew, *n.an. A rook;*" Laure (ca. 1726) "hahachiu, hahatchiu, hahach, *corneille;*" Silvy (ca. 1680) "ahassȣ, *corneille*" | ANISH aa'aasi, *a crow* (Lippert & Gambill, 2023)

*āhāwēw

INITIAL (NOUN, ANIMATE)

— long-tailed duck (Clangula hyemalis)

evidence | ESC āhāwew, *long-tailed duck;* MC āhāwew, *a long-tailed duck;* SEC āhāwew & āhāwešīš, *a long-tailed duck;* EI (Sheshatshiu) ahaueu [āhāwēw], *a long-tailed duck;* Silvy (ca. 1680) "aihaȣeȣ, *espèce d'oiseau, comme une sarcelle*" | MENO aqawɛ·w, *brant*

*āhk[1]

INITIAL

— pretend

evidence | PC āhki, *pretend, make-believe;* ESC (Severn) āhke, *let's pretend;* MC āhki, *pretend, make-believe;* SEC (Oujé-Bougoumou) ayāyāhc, *pretend*

*āhk[2]

MEDIAL

— move one's wings

evidence | ESC kitoweyāhkešip, *common goldeneye;* MC tašwāhkew, *to spread one's wings;* SEC pehpewāhcew, *to flap one's wings without moving around;* WI (Pessamit) pimueuiatsheu [pmwēwījātʃēw], *to make a sound from one's wings in passing;* Watkins (1865) "Sowákāo, *It closes its wings*"

*āhkato

PREFINAL

— affect by drying, affected by dryness

see | *āhkatos, *āhkatoso, *āhkatotē

*āhkatos

FINAL (VERB, TRANSITIVE, INANIMATE, CONCRETE)

— affect by drying

evidence | MC maškawāhkatosam, *to harden by drying;* AT (Opitciwan, Joey Awashish) akwakatosam [āhkwāhkatozam], *to dry sth severely;* SEC pāštāhkatosam, *to crack sth by drying it;* WI (Pessamit) itakatushamᵘ [ītākəttʃəm], *to dry sth in a certain way;* Laure (ca. 1726) "ni-maskauagatusen, *je durcis du cuir*" see | *āhkato, *s paired with | *āhkatosw

*āhkatoso

FINAL (VERB, ANIMATE, INTRANSITIVE, CONCRETE)

— affected by dryness

evidence | PC wākāhkatosow, *to be bent from dryness;* MC kāspāhkatosow, *be brittle and dry;* SEC pāštāhkatosow, *to crack from dryness* paired with | *āhkatotē see | *āhkato, *so[2]

*āhkatosw

FINAL (VERB, TRANSITIVE, ANIMATE, CONCRETE)

— affect by drying

evidence | MC maškawāhkatoswew, *to harden by drying;* SEC pāštāhkatoswew, *to crack sth by drying it;* WI (Pessamit) itakatushueu [ītākəttʃwēw], *to dry sth in a certain way* see | *āhkato, *sw paired with | *āhkatos

*āhkatotē

FINAL (VERB, INANIMATE, INTRANSITIVE, CONCRETE)

— affected by dryness

evidence | MC ispihtāhkatotew, *to be dried to a certain extent;* AT (Opitciwan, Joey Awashish) akwakatotew [āhkwāhkatotēw], *to be severely dry;* SEC pāštāhkatotew, *to crack from dryness;* Silvy (ca. 1680) "maska8agat8te8, *il est durci au feu, v.g. le soulier*" paired with | *āhkatoso see | *āhkato, *tē[4]

*āhkay

INITIAL (NOUN, ANIMATE)

— vulva or vagina

evidence | PC mitāhkay, *a vulva or vagina;* MC āhkay, *a vulva or vagina;* SEC (coastal) āhkay, *a vulva or vagina;* Isham (1743) "Aur kie, *the sanctum sanctorum;*" Laure (ca. 1726) "nitagaïa, ni takachs, *circa mulieres*"

discussion | In the absence of a Woods Cree cognate, the status of the preaspiration cannot be confirmed.

*āhko (~ *āhkw)

INITIAL

— **1** hurt, sick

— **2** grievous, severe

evidence | [1]MC āhkohew, *to hurt sb;* SEC āhkosiw, *to be hurt or sick;* Silvy (ca. 1680) "nit'ak8his8n, *je me blesse*" [2]PC āhkwaciw, *to be frozen;* MC āhkomākwan, *to smell harsh;* SEC āhkwātisiw, *to be fierce or dangerous*

origin | PA ***āhkw** (Aubin, 1975)

*āhkom

FINAL (VERB, TRANSITIVE, ANIMATE, DERIVED)

— have or take as kin

evidence | WSC (Ida Bear) tāpāhkomēw, *to adopt sb as replacement for a deceased loved one;* MC pešwāhkomew, *to be closely related to sb;* Laure (ca. 1726) "nit-itakumau 3. -meu, *je l'appelle en qualité de parent;*" Silvy (ca. 1680) "nit'itak8mau, *je lui suis parent en tel degré*" | MESK inākomēwa, *to be related to sb in such a way* origin | Old Cree ***wāhkomēwa** see | *wāhko

*āhkw (~ *āhko)

MEDIAL, FINAL (NOUN INCORPORATION)

— spawn, roe

evidence | PC mowāhkwēw, *to eat roe;* SEC pāšcināhkwākan, *club moss, traditionally used to help burst roe when preparing the roe for cooking;* NEC pāsāhkwān, *dried fish eggs;* Laure (ca. 1726) "aichaueskatesi-uakuets, *œufs au lait de haring*" | ANISH ogaansaakwag, *pickerel roe* (Lippert & Gambill, 2023) see | *wāhkw

*āhkwap

INITIAL

— retreat to one's den

evidence | SEC āhkopiw, *to retreat to one's den, speaking of a porcupine;* otāhkopiy, *porcupine den;* NEC āhkupihikū, *to have a hard time killing a porcupine that has retreated to its den;* WI (Pessamit) akupu [ākupu], *to hide, speaking of a porcupine;* EI (Mamit) akupu [ākwapu], *to hide, speaking of a porcupine;* Laure (ca. 1726) "utakuapiu -a, *caverne à porc-épic;*" Silvy (ca. 1680) "ag8appi8, ak8appi8, *il est caché*"

*āhoko

FINAL (VERB, ANIMATE, INTRANSITIVE, CONCRETE)

— by action of wave(s)

evidence | PC pimāhokow, *to drift along in the current;* MC pīkwāhokow, *to be damaged by the waves;* SEC wepāhokow, *to be swept away by the waves*

*āhotē

FINAL (VERB, INANIMATE, INTRANSITIVE, CONCRETE)

— by action of wave(s)

evidence | PC kwētipāhotēw, *to be tipped over by the waves;* MC pīkwāhotew, *to be damaged by the waves;* SEC wepāhotew, *to be swept away by the waves*

*āhpi

FINAL (VERB, ANIMATE, INTRANSITIVE, DERIVED)

— laugh

evidence | PC tatāhpiw, *to laugh there;* MC ništāhpiw, *to laugh hysterically;* SEC cīwāhpiw, *to frolic, speaking of an animal;* WI (Pessamit) tshiuapishtueu [tʃīwāpīstwēw], *to want to play with sb, speaking of a dog* | ANISH gawaapi, *to fall over from laughing so hard* (Livesay & Nichols, 2021) see | *pāhp

*āhpiskan[1]

INITIAL (NOUN, INANIMATE)

— jaw

evidence | PC mitāpiskan, *a jaw, a chin;* MC āpiškan, *exclamation used as an expression of anger or annoyance;* NEC utāhpishkin, *one's jaw;* WI (Pessamit) utapissikan [utāpəssəkən], *one's jawbone;* EI (Unamanshipit) utapissikan [utāpɨssakan], *one's jawbone;* Watkins (1865) "Apiskunekākun, *n.in. The jaw;*" Laure (ca. 1726) "nitabiskan, *os de la mâchoire d'en bas*" | ABEN -dōpikan, *chin, jaw* (Day, 1995); MENO neta·hpɛhkan, *my chin;* MIAMI -taampihkan-, *jaw* (ILDA, 2017) origin | PA ***āʔmiskan** (***wetāʔmixkani**, Pentland, 1979) see | *āhpiskan[2] discussion | Regarding this root the Jesuit Pierre Laure (ca. 1726) curiously wrote, "*comme c'est un mot de 'maratauanerie' servez-vous de nitamikan,*" "maratauanerie" being a Gallicized form of ***mārātwāni**, referring to the use of profanity. He elsewhere states in Latin that the word is a "*pejor injuria quae ad Gallorum boulgres [*sic*] spectat* [a worse injury which is directed against the Gauls].” Although this sense has not been corroborated by contemporary data, the word does continue to be used as an expression of anger or annoyance by a few elderly Moose Cree speakers in Moose Factory, a use that was also recognized by an elderly woman from Waswanipi. Reflexes of the synonym Laure refers to, reconstructible as the noun stem ***tāmihkan**, continues to be used in Moose Cree, Atikamekw, and Southern East Cree. However, reflexes of its medial forms, ***tāmihkan** and ***āmihkan**, enjoy a much broader distribution, essentially found in all dialects between eastern Ontario and Labrador. However, this root represents an early borrowing, likely from Anishinabe, that is derived from the same Proto-Algonquian root as the proper Old Cree reflex ***āhpiskan**.

*āhpiskan[2]

MEDIAL, FINAL (NOUN INCORPORATION)

— jaw

evidence | PC tāwāpiskanēpitēw, *to pull sb's jaw open;* nanamitāpiskanēwaciw, *one's jaw trembles from the cold;* SEC wewepāhpiškanepayiw, *one's jaw moves from side to side* (CSB, 2018); NEC chīnāhpishkināu, *to have a pointy jaw;* Laure (ca. 1726) “ni-tauabiskanebitau, *je lui ouvre, fends la tête, je lui ouvre jusqu'au menton;*” Silvy (ca. 1680) “ni tag8abiskanechkan 3. -kau, *je ferme la bouche*” | MESK nenekāpihkanēshkēwa, *one's jaw is quivering* see | *āhpiskan[1]

*āhs

FINAL (VERB, TRANSITIVE, INANIMATE, CONCRETE)

— shine light on, generally in reference to the sun

evidence | PC cahkāsikēw, *to shine;* MC cahkāsam, *to shine a beam on sth;* AT cakka:ssikew, *to shine, speaking of the sun* (Béland, 1978); NEC shāpwāsim, *to shine through sth;* SEC wāpāsicew, *sun shines white;* Silvy (ca. 1680) “he paripasak piissim8, *par où passe le soleil, le rayon*” see | *āh[2], *s paired with | *āhsw

*āhsik (~ *āhso)

FINAL

— suffix forming numbers above five

evidence | PC nikotwāsik, *six;* WC nikotwāsik, *six;* nikotwāsosāp, *sixteen;* WSC (Misipawistik, Ellen Cook) nikotwāsik, *six;* nikotwāswāw, *six times;* mitātaht-nikotwāsosāp, *sixteen;* MC nikotwāsohtak, *six pieces of firewood;* AT (Wemotaci, Nicole Petiquay) nicowaso [nīʒwāsso], *seven;* nicwaso [nišwāsso], *eight;* SEC nikotwāswāw, *six times;* NEC nīshwāshch, *seven;* Laure (ca. 1726) “nichuachu, *huit;*” Silvy (ca. 1680) “nik8t8achik, *six;*” “nich8achitch, *8*” | ANISH nishwaaswi, *eight* (Livesay & Nichols, 2021) discussion | The allomorph listed above appears to have been used only for further derivation with the numeral stem functioning as an initial.

*āhso[1] (~ *āhsw)

INITIAL

— lean against for support

evidence | PC āswāskokāpawiw, *to stand leaning against sth stick-like;* ESC (Severn) āswahikanāhtik, *a support stick for a beaming pole;* AT (Wemotaci, Nicole Petiquay) acotin [āššohtin], *to lean on sth;* SEC āsow, *to lean against sth for support;* NEC āsuhtin, *to lean on sth;* WI (Pessamit) ashutin [āʃətn], *to lean against sth at one of its extremities;* Laure (ca. 1726) “nit-asussimau 3. -meu, *je l'appuie*” | ANISH aason, *to support sb with one's hands* (Livesay & Nichols, 2021)

*āhso[2]

FINAL (VERB, ANIMATE, INTRANSITIVE, CONCRETE)

— affected by light, generally in reference to the sun

evidence | PC nēstwāsow, *to be fatigued by the sun's heat;* MC wīlipāsow, *to be* *tanned;* AT -a:sso-, *by heat* (Béland, 1978); EI (Sheshatshiu) shiuashu [ʃīwāʃu], *to be blinded by the sunlight;* Silvy (ca. 1680) "ni chi8as8n, *je suis ébloui de soleil, de neige*" | ANISH gashkaaso, *to be sunburned* (Livesay & Nichols, 2021) see | *āh², *so² paired with | *āštē²

*āhso³

FINAL (VERB, ANIMATE, INTRANSITIVE, ABSTRACT)

— forms the antipassive when suffixed to transitive inanimate verb stems or animate intransitive verb stems that syntactically require an object

evidence | PC pōsihtāsow, *to load a boat or vehicle;* AT (Opitciwan, Nadia Awashish) akitaso [akihtāssow], *to count;* SEC otināsow, *to shop;* EI (Sheshatshiu) akuanashu [kwānāʃu], *to unload a boat or vehicle* | ANISH agwaanaaso, *to unload a boat or vehicle* (Livesay & Nichols, 2021)

*āhsw

FINAL (VERB, TRANSITIVE, ANIMATE, CONCRETE)

— shine light on, generally in reference to the sun

evidence | PC kīhkāyāsowēw, *to shine brightly;* MC cahkāswew, *to shine a beam on sb;* AT -a:ssw-, *by heat* (Béland, 1978); Silvy (ca. 1680) "ni chi8as8g8n, *la neige m'éblouit*" see | *āh², *sw paired with | *āhs

*āhswē

INITIAL

— beyond

evidence | WC āswīpaðiw, *to go past a given point;* MC āšweham, *to shoot beyond sth;* SEC āsweham, *to shoot beyond sth* (CSB, 2018); NEC āswāshkim, *to go beyond sth;* Watkins (1865) "Aswāapùtum, *v.t.in.6. He sees or looks beyond it, he misses it (in reading);*" Fabvre (ca. 1690) "Ach8eg8ask8tin *passer en sautant;*" Silvy (ca. 1680) "nit'as8ek8ask8atin, *je saute*" | ANISH aanzwekaw, *to miss sb in the road* (Lippert & Gambill, 2023) discussion | In the absence of an Atikamekw cognate, the preaspirate in this reconstruction is indirectly supported by Anishinabe.

*āhš

INITIAL

— a nonproductive root of uncertain meaning found only in reflexes of *āhši-mwākwa, "red-throated loon," a waterbird known for having a stronger, fishier taste when compared to the common loon

evidence | ESC (Severn) āshimwākwa, *a red-throated loon;* AT (Wemotaci, Jeannette Coocoo & Opitciwan Joey Awashish) acimwakw [āššimwākʷ], *red-throated loon;* NEC āshimwākʷ, *red-throated loon;* EI (Sheshatshiu) ashi-muakᵘ [āʃīmwākʷ], *a red-throated loon;* Silvy (ca. 1680) "achim8ak, *plongeon à long bec*" | MENO a·ʔsehtaw, *to infect sth* discussion | It is unclear if early Jesuit sources refer to this root or to ***at**, "rotten," in entries such as Silvy (ca. 1680) "achim8s, *orignal puant;*" "achinames, *poisson puant,*" though the latter seems more likely. An Anishinabe cognate might be found in the following entry from Cuoq (1886), though not without some uncertainty due to the nonphonological orthography: "Aci! *interjection d'étonnement, de répulsion, d'horreur, de dégoût, d'impatience. Aci se place devant certains mots et quelquefois s'y incorpore:* Aciwiias, *ô la mauvaise viande!* Acikikons, *fi du poisson! il est pourri.*"

*āhši

FINAL (VERB, ANIMATE, INTRANSITIVE, CONCRETE)

— by action of wind

evidence | MC pīkwāšiw, *to be broken by the wind;* AT (Wemotaci, Jeannette Coocoo) itaciw [itāššiw], *to be blown thither in the wind;* SEC itāšiw, *to be blown thither;* Silvy (ca. 1680) "nit'achaïachin, *je recule par la force du vent contraire*" | ANISH bengwaashi, *to blow dry* (Livesay & Nichols, 2021) origin | PA ***āhši** (Aubin, 1975) paired with | *āštan see | *āšt, *i²

*āht (~ āhc)

INITIAL

— **1** move

— **2** change

— **3** more so

evidence | ¹PC āhcipayiw, *to move;* MC āhcīw, *to move;* āhtapiw to sit elsewhere; SEC (Waskaganish) āhtakoyew, *to hang sb elsewhere;* Silvy (ca. 1680) "nit'attinen, *je tourne, mets d'une autre façon*" ²PC āhtawēw, *to change one's pelage;* MC āhtapahkwew, *change roof of dwelling;* SEC āhcitāsew, *to change socks* ³PC āhci, *more; nevertheless;* MC āhcipiko, *more and more, increasingly;* SEC ayāyāhc, *in spite of, nonetheless;* EI (Sheshatshiu) aiat [ājāt], *more and more;* Silvy (ca. 1680) "hatchi, *encore mieux, davantage*" | ANISH aanjinaagwad, *to change appearance* (Livesay & Nichols, 2021); aanjigo, *more* (Lippert & Gambill, 2023) origin | PA *ānt (Aubin, 1975)

*āhtak

MEDIAL (NOUN INCORPORATION)

— **1** conifer

— **2** conifer branch with needles still attached

evidence | PC nēyāhtakāw, *to be a promontory covered in jack pines;* WC ohcikawāhtakāw, *to drip in warm weather, speaking of trees;* MC Pīwāhtakinamʷ, *December, in reference to the scattering of dry conifer needles;* NEC mināhtikāu, *to be a spot covered with boughs;* piniwāyāhtikihīchāu, *to chop boughs from a young tree for flooring;* Laure (ca. 1726) "chechegataku, *épinette blanche;*" "sagatagau, *sapinière abondante;*" Silvy (ca. 1680) "sesegatakȣ, *espèce d'arbre*" | ANISH bashkwaandagaa, *to be bare of boughs* (Livesay & Nichols, 2021) origin | PA ***āntak** (nominal form ***āntakw**, Aubin, 1975; Hewson, 1993) see | *ā¹, *šiht, *ak² compare | *āšiht, *ɩht⁴ discussion | This root also comes to refer to the conifer branch or its needles by metonymy in most dialects. Note that Pentland (1983) identifies the Proto-Algonquian nominal form of this root, ***āntakw**, as a derivative of the initial ***šent**, which he instead reconstructed as ***θint** (i.e., **ā + (θ)int + ak + w**). The possibility of a variant form of this root, one without the premedial accretion, is raised by Silvy (ca. 1680) "ȣaratatchisten, *j'éparpille la litière,*" equivalent to contemporary MC **walāhtakiškam** and reconstructible in Old Cree as ***wahrāhtakiškamwa**. Use of ***(ɩ)htak** to refer to the traditional conifer bough flooring suggests that its modern use in reference to modern-day floors could be a semantic extension of this root rather than a derivative of the homophonous root referring to wood, cf. Old Cree ***ɩht(ak)** from PA ***ehθ(ak)**.

*āhtawī

FINAL (VERB, ANIMATE, INTRANSITIVE, CONCRETE)

— move along a surface located above ground or floor

evidence | PC iskwāhtawīw, *to climb up or so far;* ESC (Severn) kospāhtawīw, *to go upstairs;* MC āšawāhtawīw, *to climb across;* SEC nīšāhtawīw, *to climb down;* NEC nihtāwāhtiwīu, *to climb skillfully;* WI (Pessamit) upatueuiu [upātwēwīw], *to climb a tree, speaking of a porcupine;* Laure (ca. 1726) "ni-rachatauan, *je descends d'un arbre;*" Silvy (ca. 1680) "chanaskataȣeȣ, *écureuil volant*" | ANISH aazhawaandawe, *to climb across* (Livesay & Nichols, 2021); MENO ehkuahtawɛw, *to climb up; to go up a ladder or stairway*

*āhtikw (~ *āhtiko)

MEDIAL, FINAL (NOUN)

— **1** tree

— **2** stick, pole

evidence | PC kawāhtikwēw, *to fell trees;* MC nōtāhtikwew, *to log;* SEC cimahāhtikwew, *to cut poles;* WI (Pessamit) atamatik[u] [tāmātuk[w]], *at the heart of a tree;* Silvy (ca. 1680) "tchipaïatik, *croix*" origin | PA ***āhtekw** (Aubin, 1975; Hewson 1993)

*āk

INITIAL

— prod

evidence | WC ākat, *a curved pole used for finding beaver tunnels under the ice;* MC ākatehtam, *to gag on sth;* SEC ākatenitisow, *to make oneself gag or retch using one's figher;* NEC ākitu, *curved stick for finding beaver tunnels under the ice;* Laure (ca. 1726) "agatu -a; agaturiu *rel., bâton croche pour sonder le castor*" | ANISH āgade, *to burp* limited to | *at³, ato⁴

*ākan¹

FINAL (NOUN, ANIMATE)

— suffixed to transitive animate verb stems, denoting the theme or patient of such a verb

evidence | PC kiskinwahamawākan, *a student;* MC cīmākan, *a canoe companion;* EI (Mushuau) atamakan [ətāmākēj], *a merchant, a trader;* Silvy (ca. 1680) "ni 8itchimagan, *celui qui demerue avec moi*" origin | PA ***ākan** (Aubin, 1975)

*ākan²

FINAL (NOUN, INANIMATE)

— suffixed directly to an initial to form concrete nouns

evidence | PC pakamākan, *a club, a bat, a sledgehammer;* WC tatākan, *a wedge for splitting logs;* MC kištākan, *a stake;* SEC šinotākan, *a binding line for nets;* NEC wiyākin, *a dish;* EI (Sheshatshiu) shimakan [ʃimākən], *caribou spear; sword;* Fabvre (ca. 1690) "Pakamāgan *pl.* găna, *massüe, casse teste;*" Silvy (ca. 1680) "chin8tagan, *maître à rets, corde, etc.*"

*ākaw (~ *ākō)

INITIAL

— out of sight or concealed behind

evidence | PC ākawāskwēyāhk, *in the shade of a dense forest;* MC ākōcāpahpisow, *to be blindfolded;* ākawaštāw, *place sth out of sight;* NEC ākiwāyihtam, *to faint;* WI (Pessamit) akauashk[u] [ākuwāʃk[w]], *out of sight behind a tree;* Fabvre (ca. 1690) "Aga8achtepăgau, *bel ombre d'arbre feuilles etc;*" Silvy (ca. 1680) "nit'ag8achtechim8n, *je m'ôte le jour, je me mets à l'ombre*" origin | PA ***ākaw** (Aubin, 1975)

*ākim¹

INITIAL (NOUN, ANIMATE)

— snowshoe

evidence | AT akimaskw [ākimāsk[w]], *ash tree (Fraxinus spp.);* WI (Pessamit) atshimashk[u] [ātʃəmāʃk[w]], *ash tree;* Watkins (1865) "akimask, *n.an. An ash (tree);*" Laure (ca. 1726) "akimasku, *frêne;*" Fabvre (ca. 1690) "Akimask8, atchimask8, *fresne, bois, arbre*" | ABEN ōgemakw, *a snowshoe frame* (Day, 1995); ANISH aagimike, *to make snowshoes* (Livesay & Nichols, 2021); MENO a·kem, *snowshoe;* MESK ākema, *snowshoe* origin | PA ***ākema** (Aubin, 1975; Hewson, 1993) see | *ākim², *ım² compare | *ahsām¹, *mahkwatoy discussion | This initial has been replaced in all dialects by ***ahsām** when referring to snowshoes. It survives only in reference to ash trees, the distribution of which extends over regions where AT and WI are spoken. As amedial, this root has been retained in SEC and NEC as a synonym of ***ahsām**. The distinction, if any, between ***ākima** and ***ahsāma** in Old Cree is irretrievable from the extant comparative evidence.

*ākim[2]

MEDIAL

— snowshoe

evidence | SEC (Oujé-Bougoumou) ohtācimew, *to come from a certain direction on snowshoes;* NEC akwāchimāu, *to have wet snow stick to one's snowshoes* | ABEN boskwōgem, *a broken snowshoe frame (Day, 1995);* ANISH babaamaagime, *to snowshoe about* (Livesay & Nichols, 2021) see | *ākim[1]

*ākiskow

INITIAL (NOUN, ANIMATE)

— sharp-tailed grouse (Tympanuchus phasianellus)

evidence | PC āhkiskow, *a prarie chicken;* MC ākiskow, *a sharp-tailed grouse;* AT akisko [ākiskow], *a sharp-tailed grouse;* SEC āciskow, *a sharp-tailed grouse;* Fabvre (ca. 1690) "Atisk8, *Espece d oiseau*" | ANISH aagask(oog), *a sharp-tailed grouse* (Livesay & Nichols, 2021)

*ākon (~ *ākoh, *ākonak)

MEDIAL, FINAL (NOUN INCORPORATION)

— snow

evidence | WC ðikwākonīpaðiw, *to get covered in snow from a fall;* MC tihkākohtew, *snow melts;* AT tcakakotew [cāhkākohtēw], *snow melted away;* SEC ošāšākonacišin, *to slip on snow;* NEC miyimiwākunikāu, *damp expanse of snow;* wāpushwākun, *freshly-fallen, light snow;* Laure (ca. 1726) "etagunatsinamu, *piste sur la neige;*" Silvy (ca. 1680) "ni pitag8nan 3. -e8, *la neige entre dans mes habits*" origin | PA ***ākon** see | *ā[1], *kōn, *ak[2]

*ākw (~ *āko)

MEDIAL, FINAL (NOUN INCORPORATION)

— porcupine

evidence | MC mowākwew, *to eat porcupine;* SEC nāpeyāk[w], *male porcupine;* tshisheiak[u] [tʃʃējāk[w]], *an adult porcupine;* Fabvre (ca. 1690) "n8tak8an e8, *à la chasse de porc epy*" origin | Old Cree ***kākwa** see | *kākw

*ākwāt (~ *ākwāc)

INITIAL

— more than half, towards the end

evidence | PC ākwātaskinēw, *to be more than half full;* ākwāc, *more than halfway; quite a lot;* MC ākwā-kīšikāw, *to be late in the day;* ākwā-nīpin, *to be late summer;* SEC ākwā-tipiskāw, *to be late in the night;* Silvy (ca. 1680) "ag8a tibiskau, *il est tout-à-fait nuit*"

*ākwīhtaw

INITIAL

— superimpose

evidence | PC Lacombe (1874) "ākwettāwikwātew, *(v.a.)* tam, siwew, tchikew, *il les coud l'un sur l'autre, il le double;*" MC ākīhtawaštāw, *to superimpose sth;* SEC ākwīhtawiškam, *to wear an extra layer;* WI (Pessamit) akuetushinu [ākwētūʃənu], *to lie on top of another;* Fabvre (ca. 1690) "nit ag8ita8ichimā8ak, *mettre plusieurs choses nobles l'une sur l'autre, y mettre ainsy*" | ANISH Nicholas (ca. 1670) "agouita, *l'un sur l'autre*" (Daviault, 1994)

*ām[1]

INITIAL

— **1** go over edge or apex

— **2** spawn, speaking of fish

evidence | [1]PC āmaciwew, *to climb up;* ESC āmāhtawīw, *to climb out of a vehicle;* MC āmipew, *to overflow;* SEC āmitišinew, *to push sb off sth;* NEC āmutāpiyiu, *to fall out of a canoe;* WI (Pessamit) amipalu [āmpəlu], *to fall from where one was perched;* Watkins (1865) "Amuchewāo, *v.i.3. He ascends a hill or bank;*" "Amuskināpāyow, *v.imp. It runs over (speaking of a liquid);*" Silvy (ca. 1680) "amitin, *cela tombe d'en-haut;*" "nit'am8tenau, *je le jette par-dessus bord, à l'eau*" [2]PC āmīw, *to go upstream to spawn;* MC āmīw, *to spawn;* WI (Pessamit) amu [āmu], *to spawn;* EI (Sheshatshiu) amiu [āmjū], *to spawn;* Silvy (ca. 1680) "ami8ets namesset, *les poissons sont en troupe, frayent ensemble*" | [2]aamiwag, *to spawn* (Livesay & Nichols, 2021)

*ām[2] (~ *āh)

MEDIAL (NOUN INCORPORATION)

— **1** path

— **2** take steps

evidence | PC nātahāhtēw, *to go for sb by following their tracks;* MC tāpahāmew, *to walk in the footsteps of another;* SEC otahāmew, *to take a step* origin | Old Cree ***ā** + ***mēwi**, from PA ***myēwi**, *road* (Aubin, 1975) see | *ɪm[1], *mēw

*āmiso

FINAL (VERB, ANIMATE, INTRANSITIVE)

— gather fruit, pick berries

evidence | PC nitāmisow, *to pick berries;* SEC nātahāmisow, *to go get berries by boat;* NEC pānihāmisū, *to clear snow to access berries underneath;* Laure (ca. 1726) "ni-natamisun, *j'en vais chercher à cueillir;*" "ni-natahamisun, *j'en vais chercher à cueillir en canot*" | This reconstruction suffers from the lack of an Atikamekw cognate to confirm the absence of a preaspirate.

*āmo

FINAL (VERB, ANIMATE, INTRANSITIVE, CONCRETE)

— flee

evidence | PC itāmow, *to flee thither;* WC pītāmōhkīw, *to scare or chase away;* MC takwāmow, *to arrive fleeing;* SEC petāmow, *to flee hither* | MESK anemāmowa, *to flee away;* MIAMI maacaamwi-, *to run away* (ILDA, 2017)

*āmow

INITIAL (NOUN, ANIMATE)

— bee

evidence | PC āmow, *a bee, a wasp;* MC āmowak, *bees;* āmōskāw, *to be many bees;* SEC āmow, *a bee;* EI (Sheshatshiu) amu [āmu], *a bee, a wasp;* Silvy (ca. 1680) "amȣ, *abeille, guêpe*" | ANISH aamookaa, *to be many bees or wasps* (Livesay & Nichols, 2021)

*ān

INITIAL

— disapprove, rebuke

evidence | PC ānimēw, *to call sb bad, to declare sb's conduct reprehensible;* Lacombe (1874) "ānittawew, *(v.a.) ttam, ttākew, tchikew, il lui désobéit, il n'approuve pas ses paroles;*" EI (Mamit) animeu [ānɨmēw], *to criticize sb, to say sth bad about sb;* Laure (ca. 1726) "nit-animau, *je le réprimande;*" Silvy (ca. 1680) "nit'animau, *je le reprends*" compare | *ānwē

*āniskē

INITIAL

— from one to another, successive

evidence | MC āniskeyāspinew, *to have a hereditary disease;* AT aniskehew, *transmettre quelque chose à quelqu'un;* NEC ānischāyāpihkātim, *to tie things one after the other;* Watkins (1865) "Aniskāskowāo, *v.t.an. He succeeds him*" | ANISH aanikegamaa, *to be a chain of lakes;* (Livesay & Nichols, 2021) compare | *ānisko

*ānisko (~ *āniskaw)

INITIAL

— link, extend

evidence | PC āniskohpitam, *to tie sth on as an extension;* MC āniskawāw, *to have an extension;* SEC āniskawaškošiw, *horsetail plant;* WI (Pessamit) anishkumu [ānəʃkūmu], *to be installed or fixed as an extension;* Watkins (1865) "Aniskootapāo, *v.i.3. He makes a knot*" compare | *āniskē

*ānwē

INITIAL

— doubt, disbelieve, disapprove

evidence | PC ānwēhtawēw, *to disbelieve sb;* WC ānwīhtamowin, *disbelief;* MC ānweyelihcikew, *to disapprove or criticize;* SEC ānwehtam, *to disbelieve sth;* NEC ānwāyihtim, *to be displeased with sth;* Laure (ca. 1726) "nit-anuerimau, *mécontent, je le suis de lui;*" Fabvre (ca. 1690) "An8ēten 3 tam n tau ta8in, *Improuuer q(ue)lq(ue) ch(os)e 2 q(uelqu'u)n, 2 tu m'impr(ouu)e*" | ANISH aanwetam, *to doubt or disbelieve* (Livesay & Nichols, 2021) compare | *ān

*āp[1]

INITIAL

— undo

evidence | PC āpahwēw, *to unharness or untie sb;* WC āpīhtakahikan, *a lock;* MC āpihtenam, *to open a tent flap;* SEC āpaham, *to open sth, to untie sth;* Silvy (ca. 1680) "nit'abahassaman 3. -e8, *je détisse des raquettes*" | ANISH ābābīgise, *to unravel* (Livesay & Nichols, 2021); MENO a·penam, *to untangle sth*

*āp[2]

MEDIAL (CLASSIFIER)

— to have or use string-like object

evidence | PC otāpēw, *to pull a load;* MC sīhtahāpew, *to weave tightly;* WI (Pessamit) takuapeu [təkwāpēw], *to have a short hauling line* origin | PA noun final ***āpy*** compare | *āpēk, *āpihkē, *āpiy see | *apihs

*āpah

PREFINAL

— expose to smoke

limited to | *s, *so[2], *sw, *tē[4] see | *āpahs, *āpahso, *āpahsw, *āpahtē

*āpahs

FINAL (VERB, TRANSITIVE, INANIMATE, CONCRETE)

— expose to smoke

evidence | MC pāhkwāpasam, *to dry sth superficially by smoking;* AT akwapisam [akwāpissam], *to smoke sth;* SEC akwāpasam, *to smoke sth* see | *āpah, *s paired with | *āpahsw

*āpahso

FINAL (VERB, ANIMATE, INTRANSITIVE, CONCRETE)

— be exposed to smoke

evidence | PC wīsakāpasow, *to smart from smoke;* MC akwāpasow, *to be smoke-dried;* SEC šāpwāpasow, *to be thoroughly smoked* | ANISH wiisagaabaso, *one's eyes hurt from the smoke* (Livesay & Nichols, 2021) see | *āpah, *so[2] paired with | *āpahtē

*āpahsw

FINAL (VERB, TRANSITIVE, ANIMATE, CONCRETE)

— expose to smoke

evidence | PC kipwatāmāpaswēw, *to suffocate sb with smoke;* MC pāhkwāpaswew, *to dry sth superficially by smoking;* AT akwapiswew [akwāpisswēw], *to smoke sth;* SEC akwāpaswew, *to smoke sth* see | *āpah, *sw paired with | *āpahs

*āpaht

FINAL (VERB, TRANSITIVE, INANIMATE, DERIVED)

sound change | ...t_1 → ...s

— to see

evidence | PC nahāpahtam, *to see sth clearly;* MC kītawāpahtam, *to look for sth in vain;* SEC kanawāpahtam, *to look at sth* origin | Old Cree ***wāpahtamwi*** paired with | *āpam[2]

*āpahtē

FINAL (VERB, INANIMATE, INTRANSITIVE, CONCRETE)

— **1** be exposed to smoke

— **2** produce smoke

evidence | [1]MC išpāpahtew, *smoke ascends;* SEC miywāpahtew, *to produce smoke well;* EI uinipapateu [wīnipāpātēw], *to produce black smoke* [2]MC kāhkāpahtew, *to be cured superficially by smoking;* AT rikwapitew [rikwāpihtēw], *to be covered in smoke;* WI (Pessamit) laluapateu [lālūwāpətēw], *to be spoiled or unusable because of the smoke;* Laure (ca. 1726) "tibiskabateu uasku, *le ciel est caché par une épaisse fumée*" | ANISH biidaabate, *to come hither, speaking of smoke* (Livesay & Nichols, 2021) see | *āpah, *tē[4] paired with | *āpahso

*āpam[1]

INITIAL

— behind

evidence | WC āpamīw, *to turn around;* MC āpamākonak, *behind a snowbank;* WI (Pessamit) apamishkuat [āpməʃkwāt], *behind the door* | ANISH aabamigaabawi, *to turn back while standing* (Livesay & Nichols, 2021); MENO a·pame·qtaw, *to turn sharply round, to wheel back*

*āpam[2]

FINAL (VERB, TRANSITIVE, ANIMATE, DERIVED)

sound change | ...t_1 → ...s

— to see

evidence | PC nahāpamēw, *to see sb clearly;* MC āpasāpamew, *to look back at sb;* SEC kosāpamew, *to divine sb by use of the shaking tent;* kanawāpamew, *to look at sb;* Silvy (ca. 1680) "ni maȣabamau, *je vais, je viens le voir*" origin | Old Cree ***wāpamēwa*** paired with | *āpaht

*āpas

INITIAL

— turn back

evidence | MC āpasāpiw, *to look back;* AT (Wemotaci, Nicole Petiquay) apasapiw [āpazāpiw], *to look back;* SEC āpasāpamew, *to look back at sb;* NEC āpisāpiu, *to look back;* WI (Pessamit) apashapatam [āpəʃāpətəm], *to look back at sth* | ANISH ābanābi, *to look back* (Livesay & Nichols, 2021) origin | PA ***āpaθ*** discussion | The evidence suggests this root was nonproductive, forming words only with finals relating to sight. We reconstruct it as above given the lack evidence for the expected allomorph ***āpat***.

*āpat (~ *āpac, *āpas)

INITIAL

— use

evidence | PC āpatisiw, *to be used, to be useful;* MC āpacihtāw, *to use sth;* AT apasinakon [āpazinākon], *to look useful;* SEC āpatan, *to be used;* EI (Sheshatshiu) apatenitamᵘ [āpətēntəm], *to consider sth important;* Silvy (ca. 1680) "abatgitagan, *nécessité, ce dont on a besoin*" | ANISH aabajichige, *to use sth* (Livesay & Nichols, 2021) origin | PA ***āpat*** (Hewson, 1993)

*āpatonisk (~ *āpatoniskak)

MEDIAL, FINAL (NOUN INCORPORATION)

— clay

evidence | MC maškawāpatoniskāw, *to be an expanse of hard clay;* SEC cīškāpatoniskāw, *to be a steep bank of clay;* Laure (ca. 1726) "marugabatuniskatchichiu, *terre tendre, molle*" see | *wāpatonisk

*āpaw

INITIAL

— thaw

evidence | MC āpawinam, *to thaw sth manually;* SEC āpawāyāw, *to be a thaw;* NEC āpuwīu, *to thaw in warm weather, speaking of ice;* EI (Sheshatshiu) apupanu [āpūpənu], *the weather warms up;* Silvy (ca. 1680) "abaȣiteȣ, *cela est dégelé*" | ANISH aabawaate, *to be warm from the sunshine* (Livesay & Nichols, 2021)

*āpākwē

FINAL (VERB, ANIMATE, INTRANSITIVE, CONCRETE)

— thirst

evidence | PC nipahāpākwew, *to die of thirst;* MC mōskwāpākwew, *to cry of thirst;* SEC nōhteyāpākwew, *to thirst* | ANISH noondeyaabaagwe, *to be thirsty* (Livesay & Nichols, 2021) see | *nipākwē

*āpān

MEDIAL

— a nonproductive root referring to "body of water" and found only in reflexes of ***wiškāpānēwatinwi***

evidence | WSC (Misipawistik, Ellen Cook) oskāpānēwatin, *to be a newly frozen body of water;* MC oškāpānētin, *to be a newly frozen body of water;* AT (Opitciwan, Joey Awashish) ockapanewotin [oškāpānēwatin], *to be a newly frozen body of water;* tackapanewotin [tāškāpānēwatin], *to be split, speaking of ice on a body of water;* (Wemotaci, Nicole Petiquay) ockapanetin [oškāpānētin], *to be a newly frozen body of water;* SEC oškāpānētin, *to be a newly frozen body of water;* NEC ushkāpānātin, *to be the first freezing of a body of water in the fall;* WI (Mashteuiatsh) "ushkâpanêtin shîpi, *la rivière est nouvellement gelée*" (Cooter, 1975) | ANISH oshkaabaanedin & oshkaabaanewadin, *to be newly frozen ice* (Lippert & Gambill, 2023)

*āpāwar

FINAL (VERB, TRANSITIVE, ANIMATE, CONCRETE)

— affect by use of water

evidence | PC kicistāpawayēw, *to wash sb;* SEC ništāpāwayew, *to drown sb;* WI (Pessamit) likapuleu [līkāpwēwlēw], *to cause sth to become undone or collapse by putting it in water;* Laure (ca. 1726) "ni-meiauabauarau namesh, *je dessale du poisson*" see | *āpāwē, *r

*āpāwatā (~ *āpāwac, *āpāwatw)

FINAL (VERB, ANIMATE, INTRANSITIVE, CONCRETE)

— affect by use of water

evidence | MC kicištāpāwatāw, *to wash sth;* Laure (ca. 1726) "ni-tchichistabauatchitunan, *je me lave la bouche*" see | *āpāwē, *tā

*āpāwē

FINAL (VERB, INTRANSITIVE, CONCRETE)

— affected by water

evidence | MC mōskwāpāwew, *to cry from being wet;* SEC yōskāpāwew, *to be softened by water;* WI (Pessamit) itapaueu [ītāpuwēw], *to be wet to a certain point;* Silvy (ca. 1680) "ni kiȣeabaȣan, *je reviens à cause de la pluie*" | ANISH biigwaabaawe, *to get ruined in the water* (Livesay & Nichols, 2021); MENO sa·puapa·wɛ·w AI, *to be wet through*

*āpēk

MEDIAL (CLASSIFIER)

— string-like

evidence | WC aciwāpīkinam, *to shorten sth string-like manually;* MC tahkwāpekan, *to be a short string-like object;* SEC āpišāpecikwayawešiw, *to have a skinny neck;* NEC piswāpākiham, *to trip over sth string-like;* Laure (ca. 1726) "panakuabegamu, *lâche, qui n'est pas bien tendu*" | ANISH naanwaabiig, *five strands or strings* (Livesay & Nichols, 2021); MIAMI kinwaapiikatwi, *to be a long string* (ILDA, 2017) origin | Likely from PA noun final ***āpy** + ***ak**. compare | *āp², *āpihkē, *āpiy see | *apihs

*āpēw

FINAL (NOUN, ANIMATE, NOUN INCORPORATION)

— male (typically human)

evidence | PC oskāpēw, *a young man;* MC kīšāpew, *adult man;* ayāpew, *a buck or bull;* WI (Pessamit) apishtapeushu [pəstāpēwʃu], *to be a small man;* EI aiapeshish [ajāpēhīh], *young buck or bull* | ANISH ayaabe, *a buck, a male deer;* moozhaabe, *a bachelor* (Livesay & Nichols, 2021) origin | Old Cree ***nāpēwa** compare | *nāpēw²

*āpi

FINAL (VERB, ANIMATE, INTRANSITIVE, DERIVED)

sound change | ...t_1 → ...s

— **1** to see

— **2** eye

evidence | PC pākāpiw, *to have swollen eyes;* MC pasakwāpiw, *to close one's eyes;* SEC itāpiw, *to look in a particular direction;* WI (Uashat) tshimushapu [tʃīmūʃāpu], *to spy;* Silvy (ca. 1680) "ni mamakabin, *j'ai de grands yeux*" | MESK ahkwāpiwa, *to see a certain distance* origin | Old Cree ***wāpiwa** see | *wāp

*āpihkē

MEDIAL (CLASSIFIER)

— by use of string-like object

evidence | PC iskwāpihkēpitēw, *to pull sb a certain distance using a rope;* MC kinwāpihkeyāw, *to be a long string-like object;* itāpihkātam, *to tie sth thus;* SEC sakāpihcenew, *to hold sb with a leash;* Silvy (ca. 1680) "ni 8anabitcheparihau, *je mêle, j'embrouille du fil*" origin | Possibly the premedial accretion ***ā** + ***apihkē**, *to plait.* compare | *āp², *āpēk, *āpiy see | *apihkē, *apihs

*āpihtaw

INITIAL

— half

evidence | MC āpihtawāhkahtew, *to be half-burnt;* SEC āpihtawakocin, *to be the middle of the month;* EI (Sheshatshiu) apitu [āpītu], *halfway;* Silvy (ca. 1680) "abita8ham, *midi*" origin | PA ***āpehtaw** (Hewson, 1993)

*āpikohšīhš

INITIAL (NOUN, ANIMATE)

— mouse

evidence | PC āpakosīs & wāpakosīs, *a mouse;* WC āpakosīs, *a mouse;* ESC āpikošīš & wāpikošīš, *a mouse;* MC āpikošīš & wāpikošīš, *a mouse;* AT (Wemotaci, Nicole Petiquay) apokocic [āpokoššiš], *a mouse;* (Opitciwan, Patrick Awashish) apokocic [āpokoššiš], *a mouse;* SEC āpikošīš, *a mouse;* NEC āpikushīsh, *a mouse;* WI (Pessamit) apikushish [āpukuʃīʃ], *a mouse;* EI (Mamit) apikushish [āpukuhīh], *a mouse;* Laure (ca. 1726) "apikuchich -ets, *souris, petit rat;*" Fabvre (ca. 1690) "Apik8chich, *petite s8ris;*" "8abik8chich, abik8chich, *petite s8ris, mus;*" Silvy (ca. 1680) "8apik8chich, *souris*" discussion | As the more widespread variant, the above reconstruction is favored over the alternative ***wāpikohšīhš**. The latter is most likely a hypercorrection of what is otherwise an opaque root.

*āpirko (~ *āpirkw)

INITIAL

— untie, unfastened, open

evidence | WC āpiðkopaðiw, *to become untied;* MC āpihkopaliw, *to become untied;* SEC āpihkonam, *to unfasten;* Silvy (ca. 1680) "abik8chkau, *il est détaché, délié, v.g. d'une bande, etc.*" | ANISH odaabiskonaan, *to undo sth by hand* (Livesay & Nichols, 2021) see | *āp¹

*āpis

INITIAL

— revive

evidence | PA āpisisin, *to revive; to come back to life;* MC āpisihkwašiw, *to be wakeful;* āpisīweyihtam, *to regain consciousness;* AT (Wemotaci, Nicole Petiquay) apisiweritam [āpizīwerihtam], *to be conscious;* NEC āpisihāu, *to revive sb;* WI (Pessamit) apishikushu [āpəʃəkuʃu], *to wake up;* Watkins (1865) "Apissewāyètum, *v.i.6. He revives;*" "Apissisin, *v.i.7. He revives (after fainting)*" | ANISH aabiziishin, *to come back to life; to revive* (Livesay & Nichols, 2021); MENO a·pese·hcekan, *reviving medicine;* MESK āpesīwa, *to come back to life* origin | PA ***āpes**

*āpištān

FINAL (NOUN INCORPORATION)

— marten

evidence | SEC nāpeyāpištān, *a male marten;* NEC uchākāpishtān, *a fisher;* WI (Pessamit) takuakapishtan [təkwākāpəstān], *a marten in fall coat* see | *wāpištān, *āpištāniw

*āpištāniw

MEDIAL (NOUN INCORPORATION)

— marten

evidence | MC nōtāpištāniwew, *to harvest marten;* SEC natawāpištāniwew, *to go hunt martens;* Laure (ca. 1726) "ni-pakuanabistaniuan, *j'écorche une martre*" see | *wāpištān, *āpištān

*āpit

MEDIAL, FINAL (NOUN INCORPORATION)

— tooth, teeth

evidence | PC kāsāpitēw, *to have sharp teeth;* MC cīpwāpitew, *to have pointy teeth;* SEC ciyakāpitew, *for one's gums to itch when teething;* Laue (ca. 1726) "ni-nikabiterin, *je desserre les dents;*" Silvy (ca. 1680) "8ik8abita, *dents de derrière*" | ANISH zaagaabide, *to teeth* (Livesay & Nichols, 2021) origin | PA ***āpit** (Hewson, 1993) see | *ā¹, *īpit

*āpitin

INITIAL

— once

evidence | SEC (Waswanipi) āpitinišino, *to die instantly in a collision;* SEC āpitinīu, *to manage to take all of one's load in one trip* (CSB, 2018); NEC āpitin, *all at once, only once;* āpitinihwāu, *to kill sb instantly with a shot;* Silvy (ca. 1680) "abitin, *une fois*" | ANISH Nicholas (ca. 1670) "apitin & apitim, *une fois*" (Daviault, 1994)

*āpiy (~ *ēyāpiy)

FINAL (NOUN, INANIMATE, CLASSIFIER)

— string-like object

evidence | PC asināpiy, *sinker;* maskisinēyāpiy, *a moccasin string; a shoelace;* MC nakwākanāpiy, *snare line;* SEC pīwāpiskweyāpiy, *a wire;* Silvy (ca. 1680) "p8nisitass8ineabi, *cable d'ancre*" origin | PA noun final ***āpy** compare | *āp², *āpēk, *āpihkē see | *apihs

*āpo¹

INITIAL

— bring token of hunt

evidence | WC (Stanley Mission, Solomon Ratt) āpohtān, *edible innards of moose;* SEC āpotowew, *to bring token of hunt back to sb;* EI aputan [āpūtān], *token brought back from hunt;* Watkins (1865) "Apooyāo, *v.t.an. He sends it to him;*" Laure (ca. 1726) "nit-abutan 3. -teu, *je porte la montre de ma chasse;*" Silvy (ca. 1680) "ab8task8an, *cette montre (v.g. de l'ours tué)*" | MIAMI aapwee-, *return, come back;* aapool-, *to bring sb back* (ILDA, 2017) limited to | *r, *tā

*āpo²

MEDIAL, FINAL (NOUN)

— **1** liquid

— **2** lid (for container containing liquid)

evidence | ¹PC sīwāpoy, *soda pop;* MC alōmināpow, *oatmeal porridge;* SEC cōcōšināpoy, *milk;* Laure (ca. 1726) "tutuchunabui, *lait;*" Fabvre (ca. 1690) "Agahap8an e8, *distribuer la s8ppe, le potage*" ²PC akwanāpowēhikan, *lid;* MC kipahāpwew, *to insert a wad into a cartridge;* SEC (Waswanipi) kā akwanāpwehikaniwitmanicōš, *water beetle;* NEC akunāpuwāham, *to cover sth with a lid;* WI (Pessamit) akunapuatam [kunāpwātəm], *to cover sth with a lid;* Laure (ca. 1726) "tchipahabuagan, agunabuagan, *couvercle de pot;*" Silvy (ca. 1680) "kipab8ate8 8a8itagan, *le baril est bouché, enfoncé*" | ¹ANISH zhoominaaboo, *wine* (Livesay & Nichols, 2021) ²ANISH baakaabowenan, *to lift the cover or lid off sth containing a liquid* (Livesay & Nichols, 2021)

*āposk

MEDIAL

— burnt land

evidence | MC paškwāposkitew, *to be barren from a forest fire;* SEC oškāposcitew, *to be a newly burnt area;* Watkins (1865) "Wesapooskichāsin, *v.imp. It is a small patch of burnt woods*" see | *wīposk

*āpošw (~ *āpošo)

MEDIAL, FINAL (NOUN INCORPORATION)

— hare

evidence | PC mistāpos, *jackrabbit;* MC kakemotāpošwew, *to steal hares;* AT sasapocwew [sāssāpoʒwēw], *to fry rabbit;* SEC mowāpošwew, *to eat hare;* NEC sichipiskunāyāpush, *rabbit snared around the back;* Laure (ca. 1726) "ni-natauabuchuan, *je chasse au lièvre;*" Fabvre (ca. 1690)

"Mistab8ch, v. michtabuch, *gr(an)d Lieure*" origin | Old Cree **wāpošwa** see | *wāpošw

*āpot (~ *āpoc)

INITIAL

— **1** fold over onto itself

— **2** turn inside out

evidence | PC āpotinam, *to turn sth inside out;* MC āpocipitam, *to pull sth inside out;* Silvy (ca. 1680) "nit'ab8ta8echchimau, *je le mets à contre poil*" origin | PA ***āpot** (Hewson, 1993)

*ārahkw

INITIAL (NOUN, ANIMATE)

— thrush (Catharus spp.)

evidence | PC Lacombe (1874) "ayak, wok, (n.r.) ayakus, ak, *petit oiseau qui crie la nuit;*" ESC (Severn) ānak, *a hermit thrush;* AT (Opitciwan, Joey Awashish) arako [ārahkow], *a thrush;* WI (Pessamit) aluk[u] [āluk[w]], *a thrush* | ANISH aanak, *a thrush;* aanakoog, *thrushes* (Livesay & Nichols, 2021)

*ārim

INITIAL

— **1** difficult

— **2** active, animated, agitated, restless

evidence | [1]WC āðimisiw, *to be troublesome;* MC āliman, *to be difficult;* AT ariminikatew [āriminihkātēw], *donner un nom difficile à quelqu'un;* SEC āyimacihtākwan, *to be expensive;* Silvy (ca. 1680) "nit'arimimau, *je lui fais de la peine par mes paroles*" [2]SEC āyimohtew, *to be busy walking around, to walk around non-stop;* NEC āyimisiu, *to be busy or active;* Isham (1743) "ar the ma ta go sin, *a great talker;*" Laure (ca. 1726) "nit-arimiparihun, *je me meux sans cesse dans mon lit par la fièvre;*" Silvy (ca. 1680) "nit'arimichkan 3. -au, *je vais çà et là;*" "nit'arimitag8sin, *je discours*" | ANISH odaanimimaan, *to reprimand sb* (Livesay & Nichols, 2021); MENO a·nemɛsew, *to be in a bad state, to be dangerously ill*

*ārimō

INITIAL

— talk about

evidence | PC āyimōhtowak, *to gossip about one another;* MC ālimōtam, *to speak about sth;* AT arimomitiso [ārimōmitizow], *to speak about oneself;* SEC āyimōmew, *to speak about sb;* NEC āyimutim, *to talk about sth;* Watkins (1865) "Anemoomāo, *v.t.an. He accuses him;*" Silvy (ca. 1680) "nit'arim8itama8a8, *je lui demande une chose difficile*" compare | *ārim

*ārkikw[1] (~ *ārkiko)

INITIAL (NOUN, ANIMATE)

— seal

evidence | WC āðkikos, *a baby seal;* MC āhkikoskāw, *to be many seals;* SEC āhcik[w], *a seal;* Silvy (ca. 1680) "atchik8, *loup-marin;*" "askhik8, *loup-marin*" | ANISH Cuoq (1886) Askik, *loup-marin* see | *ārkikw[2]

*ārkikw[2] (~ *ārkiko)

MEDIAL, FINAL (NOUN INCORPORATION)

— **1** seal

— **2** otter

evidence | WC pitahikīwāðkikos, *small otter that makes holes in dams;* MC pahkonāhkikwew, *to skin a seal;* SEC nōtāhcikwew, *to harvest seals or otters;* EI muatshikueu [mwātʃukwēw], *to eat seal or otter;* Laure (ca. 1726) "ni-pakuanastchikuan, *j'écorche du loup-marin;*" Silvy (ca. 1680) "ni nata8astik8an, *je vais au loup-marin*" origin | Presumably from Old Cree ***ārkikwa**, "seal;" compare Old Cree ***nikikwa**, "otter." Alternatively, the present situation may represent a merger of medials derived from these two separate nouns, either at the Old Cree level or at various points in time as the dialects branched off. see | *ārkikw[1]

*āro[1] (~ *ārw)

MEDIAL, FINAL (NOUN)

— tail

evidence | PC amiskwāyow, *beaver tail;* MC wewepālowestāw, *to wag one's tail;* SEC wacaškwāyow, *muskrat tail;* NEC kākwāyui, *porcupine tail;* Laure (ca. 1726) "tchinuarueu, *l'animal a la queue longue;*" "ni-kutatchitan attikuarui, *je respecte la queue de caribou*" | ANISH miishaanowe, *to have a furry tail;* animwaanow, *a dog's tail* (Livesay & Nichols, 2021); MESK sākānowekāpawa, *to stand with one's tail in sight*

*āro[2]

FINAL (VERB, ANIMATE, INTRANSITIVE)

— accumulation of snow

evidence | MC akotālow, *an accumulation of snow on a branch;* AT (Opitciwan, Joey Awashish) akotanokon [akotānokon], *to be snow accumulated on a branch;* SEC mihtāyow, *an accumulation of snow on a branch;* WI (Pessamit) pimitalushtin [pmətālūstən], *to be a snowdrift across the road;* WI (Uashat) mitanu [mɨtānū], *to be a conifer loaded with snow;* Laure (ca. 1726) "akutaru, *neige, elle tient aux arbres;*" Watkins (1865) "mìtaiyoo, *n.an. A tree covered with snow (so as to resemble a pillar or cone);*" Fabvre (ca. 1690) "ak8tar8g8n, ag8tar8, *la neige e(st) suspendue aux harts;*" "mitar8ets, *la neige tient aux arbres;*" Silvy (ca. 1680) "patchichim8ar8sti8, *la neige tombe des arbres;*" "ni rig8ar8n, *je suis plein de neige*" | ANISH Cuoq (1886) "ningwano, *être couvert de neige, être enneigé*" discussion | This root has been reanalysed as an animate noun final in contemporary dialects with lengthening of the final vowel or the addition of a word-finaly.

*āsiyān[1]

INITIAL (NOUN, ANIMATE)

— loincloth

evidence | PC āsiyān, *loincloth; diaper; menstrual pad;* MC otāsiyāniw, *to have a loincloth, diaper, or sanitary pad on;* AT asianekin [āziyānēkin], *sanitary napkin;* a:siya:n, *pamper, underwear* (Béland, 1978); SEC āsiyān, *a diaper;* WI (Pessamit) ashian [āʃjān], *fly of pants;* Silvy (ca. 1680) "assian, *brayet*" | ANISH aanziyaan, *a breech cloth; a diaper* (Livesay & Nichols, 2021) origin | PA ***āsiyāni** (Hewson, 1993) see | *āsiyān[2]

*āsiyān[2]

MEDIAL, FINAL (NOUN INCORPORATION)

— loincloth

evidence | PC mīskotāsiyānēhēw, *to change sb's diaper;* ESC (Severn) onātowewāsiyān, *algae;* MC kehcitāsiyānew, *to remove one's diaper;* SEC āhtāsiyānahew, *to change sb's diaper;* NEC āhchitāsiyānihāu, *to change sb's diaper;* WI (Pessamit) nutshitashianeneu [nūtʃətāʃjānēnēw], *to fondle a man;* Laure (ca. 1726) "ni-tchestassianan 3. -eu, *je quitte mon brayet;*" Silvy (ca. 1680) "ni p8chtasianan, *je prends mon brayet*" see | *āsiyān[1] discussion | Some contemporary dialects exhibit a reflex of ***tāsiyān**, an allomorph containing an epenthetic t derived from the possessive form of the noun.

*āsk

PREFINAL

— intensifier for finals relating to heat and cold

limited to | *aci, *atin[2], *atihtā, *atim[3], *s, *so[2], *sw, *tē[4] see | *āskaci, *āskatin, *āskatihtā, *āskatim, *āskis, *āskiso, *āskisw, *āskitē

*āskaci

FINAL (VERB, ANIMATE, INTRANSITIVE, CONCRETE)

— freeze

evidence | PC maskawāskaciw, *to be frozen stiff;* WI (Pessamit) itashkatshu [ītāʃkətʃu], *to be frozen to a certain point* see | *āsk, *aci paired with | *āskatin

*āskatihtā

FINAL (VERB, ANIMATE, INTRANSITIVE, CONCRETE)

— freeze

evidence | PC maskawāskatihtāw, *to freeze sth solid;* WI (Pessamit) itashkatitau [ītāʃkətətāw], *to let sth freeze to a certain point* see | *āsk, *atihtā paired with | *āskatim

*āskatim

FINAL (VERB, TRANSITIVE, ANIMATE, CONCRETE)

— freeze

evidence | PC maskawāskatimēw, *to freeze sb solid;* WI (Pessamit) itashkatimeu [ītāʃkətəmēw], *to let sb freeze to a certain point* see | *āsk, *atim[3] paired with | *āskatihtā

*āskatin

FINAL (VERB, INANIMATE, INTRANSITIVE, CONCRETE)

— freeze

evidence | PC kispakāskatin, *to be frozen thick;* MC kipwāskatin, *to be blocked by ice;* WI (Pessamit) itashkatin [ītāʃkətn], *to be frozen to a certain point* see | *āsk, *atin[2] paired with | *āskaci

*āskaw

INITIAL

— sometimes, occasionally

evidence | PC āskaw, *sometimes;* MC āskaw, *sometimes;* AT askawin [āskawīn], *occasionally, sometimes;* SEC āskaw, *sometimes;* NEC āskiu, *sometimes, once in a while;* WI (Pessamit) ashku [āʃkū], *as, when, while;* Fabvre (ca. 1690) "Askau, aïaspich, *de tems et tems, d espace en espace*"

*āskikan

MEDIAL, FINAL (NOUN INCORPORATION)

— chest

evidence | PC tāwāskikan, *in the middle of the chest;* MC māskāskikanew, *to have a chest wall deformity;* SEC šīwāscikanew, *to have heartburn;* Watkins (1865) "Ootamaskikunāwāo, *v.t.an. He hits him on the breast*" see | *skāskikan

*āskis

FINAL (VERB, TRANSITIVE, INANIMATE, CONCRETE)

— burn

evidence | PC mēstāskisam, *to burn all of sth;* MC šīkwāskisam, *to burn up the contents of sth;* AT (Wemotaci, Nicole Petiquay) tcakaskisam [cākāskizam], *to burn sth all up, to consume sth with fire* | ANISH ginibaakizige, *to get drunk fast* (Livesay & Nichols, 2021) see | *āsk, *s paired with | *āskisw discussion | Contemporary eastern dialects favor reflexes of ***āhkahs**, a root that may not trace back to Old Cree and that is likely a combination of ***ā** + ***ıhkahs**. Reflexes of both roots are productive in Moose Cree.

*āskiso

FINAL (VERB, ANIMATE, INTRANSITIVE, CONCRETE)

— be burnt

evidence | PC mēstāskisow, *to be all burnt up;* MC šīkwāskisow, *to have one's contents burnt up;* AT tcakaskisow [cākāskizow], *to be all burnt up, to be consumed by the fire;* Silvy (ca. 1680) "ni rarastisȣn, *je brûle qqch à moi*" | ANISH daashkaakizo, *to split in the fire* (Livesay & Nichols, 2021) see | *āsk, *so[2] paired with | *āskitē discussion | Contemporary eastern dialects favor reflexes of ***āhkahso**, a root that may not trace back to Old Cree and that is likely a combination of ***ā** + ***ıhkahso**. Reflexes of both roots are productive in Moose Cree.

*āskisw

FINAL (VERB, TRANSITIVE, ANIMATE, CONCRETE)

— burn

evidence | PC mēstāskiswēw, *to burn all of sth;* MC šīkwāskiswew, *to burn up the contents of sth;* AT tcakaskiswew [cākāskizwēw], *to burn sth all up, to consume sth with fire* see | *āsk, *sw paired with | *āskis discussion | Contemporary eastern dialects favor reflexes of ***āhkahsw**, a root that may not trace back to Old Cree and that is likely a combination of ***ā** + ***ıhkahsw**. Reflexes of both roots are productive in Moose Cree.

*āskitē

FINAL (VERB, INANIMATE, INTRANSITIVE, CONCRETE)

— be burnt

evidence | PC mēstāskitēw, *to be all burnt up;* MC šīkwāskitew, *to have one's contents burnt up;* AT tcakaskitew [cākāskitēw], *to be all burnt up, to be consumed by the fire;* Laure (ca. 1726) "kaskaskastchiteu, *tout en feu, pénètre, embrasé;*" Silvy (ca. 1680) "kichachtite8, *il fait chaud, le soleil brûle*" | ANISH zhaabwaakide, *to be burned through* (Livesay & Nichols, 2021) see | *āsk, *tē[4] paired with | *āskiso discussion | Contemporary eastern dialects favor reflexes of ***āhkahtē**, a root that may not trace back to Old Cree and that is likely a combination of ***ā** + ***ıhkahtē**. Reflexes of both roots are productive in Moose Cree.

*āsko (~ *āskw)

MEDIAL, FINAL (CLASSIFIER)

— stick-like

evidence | PC apwānāsk, *a roasting stick;* ispāskosiw, *to be a tall tree;* ESC maciteweyāskweyāw, *to be a wooded point;* MC wanaskwāskwan, *to be the tip of sth stick-like;* tāpitawāskweyāw, *to be an expanse of trees of equal height;* SEC tōhkāskoham, *to spread sth apart using sth stick-like* | ANISH dewe'iganaak, *a drumstick* (Livesay & Nichols, 2021)

*āspat (~ *āspac)

INITIAL

— to lean against

evidence | PC āspatapi-, *to lean against sth; to have a back, speaking of a stove* (Wolfart, 2022); MC āspataskitāw, *to lean sth in an upright position against sth else;* AT (Opitciwan, Joey Awashish) aspitciw [āspiciw], *to lean against sth while getting up;* WI ashpatashtau [āʃpətəstāw], *to place sth leaning against sth else;* Laure (ca. 1726) "nit-aspitauiganéchimun, *je suis appuyé sur le dos;*" "aspatchichimu, *appuyé*" | ANISH (Abitibi dialect) āhpacihšimo, *to lean against sth;* MENO a·hpatahow, *to walk using a cane* origin | PA ***āspat** (***a:mpat** by Aubin (1975) due to insufficient evidence).

*āspinat (~ *āspinaš)

FINAL (VERB, TRANSITIVE, ANIMATE, DERIVED)

— harm or affect negatively thus

evidence | PC māyāspinatēw, *to beat or maim sb* (Wolfart, 2023); MC pakwanawāspinatew, *to curse sb with illness behind their back;* NEC iyāspinitāu, *to harm sb in a certain way* see | *āspinē, *t[5]

*āspinē

FINAL (VERB, ANIMATE, INTRANSITIVE, DERIVED)

— **1** have illness

— **2** harm or affect negatively thus, of transitive clauses derived from the above stem

evidence | PC wāpāspinēw, *to have leprosy;* WC macāspinīw, *to have a venereal disease;* MC pakwanawāspinatew, *to curse sb with illness behind their back;* SEC itāspinew, *to have a certain illness;* Laure (ca. 1726) "tchi-manaspinan 3. -eu, *tu tombes en délire*" | ANISH inaapine, *to be afflicted or sick in a certain way* (Livesay & Nichols, 2021); MENO we·qsaka·hpenɛw, *to be painfully or seriously ill* origin | PA ***āθpenē** (Hewson 1993) see | *ā[1], *ıspinē compare | *ahpinē, *nē[3]

*āspon

INITIAL

— disagreeable, unpleasant

evidence | PC āsponisiw, *to be greedy or stingy;* Lacombe (1874) "Asponeyimow, *il est égoïste;*" MC āsponelimew, *to think sb is taking inappropriately or is being greedy;* NEC āspunisīu, *to be greedy;* Laure (ca. 1726) "aspunichiu, *morne, triste;*" "tchit-aspunihau, *tu le mets de mauvaise humeur, tu l'offenses;*" Fabvre (ca. 1690) "asp8nĭsin i8, *etre de mauuaise hum(eu)r chag(ri)n;*" "asp8ni kichigau, *laid ternis*"

*āš

INITIAL

— presage, herald a bad omen

evidence | MC āšimew, *to foretell a bad outcome for sb;* AT (Opitciwan, Joey Awashish & Véronique Chachai) acihew [āʒihēw], *to herald a bad omen regarding sb;* WI (Pessamit) ashieu [āʃjēw], *to presage sb's death* | MENO a·se·wesew, *to get a bad omen*

*āšihk

INITIAL

— fervently

evidence | MC āšihkāpamew, *to stare at sb;* SEC āšihkwew, *to scream;* WI (Pessamit) ashitshelitakuan [āʃətʃēltākwən], *to be encouraging;* Laure (ca. 1726) "nit-achitchimau, *je le rends fervent, je l'encourage;*" Fabvre (ca. 1690) "Achik8an e8, *chanter, parler haut*" | ANISH aazhikwe, *to scream* (Livesay & Nichols, 2021)

*āšihkw (~ *āšihko)

MEDIAL, FINAL (NOUN INCORPORATION)

— **1** pine or pine-like tree

— **2** branch of a pine or pine-like tree with needles still attached

evidence | AT (Opitciwan) kakatciwackw [kāhkākīwāšk[w]], *Canada yew;* SEC oyoweyāšihk[w], *a white pine;* NEC muwāshihkwātāu, *to eat its needles, speaking of a conifer;* WI (Pessamit) uluiashik[u] [ulwīāʃuk[w]], *a pine tree;* utatakuakanashik[u] [utətəkwānāʃuk[w]], *a conifer branch with no needles;* EI (Unaman-shipit) pinashikuashtan [pɨnāhīkwāhtan], *conifers lose their needles because of the wind;* kauashik[u] [kāwāhīhk[w]], *branch of a black spruce;* EI (Sheshatshiu) assiuashik[u] [ssīwāʃuk[w]], *a Canada Yew;* Laure (ca. 1726) "ureuasiku, pin blanc;" Fabvre (ca. 1690) "Kakaki8achik mistik, *pruch(e), arbre;*" Silvy (ca. 1680) "8reachig8, *pin dont l'écorce est mince*" origin | Either from Old Cree premedial accretion ***ā** + unattested noun ***šihkwa**, *pine,* or inherited as a whole from PA ***āšenkw**, from premedial accretion ***ā** + noun stem ***šenkw** (cf. ***šenkwa:xkwa**, Aubin, 1975; Hewson, 1993). see | *ā[1] discussion | Though the noun whence this root is derived is unattested in contemporary Cree dialects and the historical record, reflexes of the Proto-Algonquian root ***šenkw** are attested in Ojibwe and Meskwaki.

*āšiht (~ *āšihtak)

MEDIAL, FINAL (NOUN INCORPORATION)

— **1** conifer

— **2** conifer branch with needles still attached

evidence | PC napakāsiht, *balsam fir;* WC minahikwāsīht, *a spruce bough;* MC kāwāštakāw, *rough or prickly conifer bough flooring;* AT (Wemotaci, Jeannette Coocoo) irinacit [irināʒit], *balsam fir;* -a:šitt-, *fir* (Béland, 1978); askiwacit, *Canada yew;* NEC nātāshihtāu, *to fetch conifer branches;* WI (Pessamit) manashteu [mənāstēw], *to gather conifer branches;* mushtashtat [mūstāstət], *on the conifer bough flooring;*" Fabvre (ca. 1690) "Tepachitan e8, *aur assez de sapin pr La Cabane;*" Silvy (ca. 1680) "irinachit, *sapin à faire une litière*" origin | Old Cree ***šihta**, *a conifer* see | *ā[1], *šiht compare | *āhtak

*āšitaw

INITIAL

— cross

evidence | SEC āšitawikotešīš, *crossbill;* WI ashtukuteshish [āstūkutēʃīʃ], *crossbill;*

Laure (ca. 1726) "achitauaskueu, *nuit, environ 3 heures du soir;*" Fabvre (ca. 1690) "Achita8ask8e8, *La 2 p(ar)tie d'après midy*" | MESK āshitawāhēwa, *to retaliate against sb.* compare | *āšitē, *āšitonē

*āšitē

INITIAL

— **1** cross

— **2** in turn

evidence | MC āšitemew, *to talk back to sb;* AT aciteckowew, *to pass sb on foot;* a:šitem-, *to contradict sb, to dispute with sb* (Béland, 1978); PC āsitēmēw, *to talk back to sb;* SEC āšiteyāhtik^{w}, *a cross;* NEC āshtāshkiwāu, *to cross sb on foot without noticing them;* Watkins (1865) "Asitāaskootin, *it lies across;*" Laure (ca. 1726) "nit-achiteskauau, *je passe sans l'apercevoir;*" Fabvre (ca. 1690) "Achitehau = hin = hitin, *rendre reciproq(ue) à qlqn*" | ANISH aazhide-waagosh, *cross fox* (Livesay & Nichols, 2021); MIAMI aašitehkam-, *to meet up with sth, to come across sth* compare | *āšitaw, *āšitonē

*āšitonē

INITIAL

— cross

evidence | SEC āšitoneštāw, *to write an X (as on a ballot);* WI (Pessamit) ashitunetitau [āʃətnēttāw], *to lay sth down with one end crossing sth else;* Watkins (1865) "Asitoonāaskootin, *it lies across;*" Laure (ca. 1726) "nit-achitunepitunerin, *je croise mes bras*" compare | *āšitaw, *āšitē

*āškā

FINAL (VERB, INANIMATE, INTRANSITIVE, CONCRETE)

— waves run

evidence | PC mahkāskāw, *to be big waves;* MC āšteyāškāw, *waves subside;* NEC pātāshkāwich, *waves come in* | ANISH agwaayaashkaa, *waves come ashore* (Livesay & Nichols, 2021)

*āškēw (~ *āškēwak)

MEDIAL

— ember, firebrand

evidence | MC (Moose Factory, Hilda Jeffries) āhtāškewakaham, *to stir the embers;* AT (Opitciwan, Joey Awashish) otapackewakaham [otāhpāškēwakaham], *to pull the embers towards oneself using sth;* SEC (Oujé-Bougoumou, Gerry Bosum) otāšcewakahikan, *a fire poker;* NEC utāshchāukiham, *to gather the coals together;* WI (Pessamit) tauasseu [tāwāssēw], *in the middle of the fire or embers;* utasseukaim [utāssēwkīm], *to pull the embers towards oneself using sth* see | *ak[2] compare | *āškišēw, *ıšēw

*āškišēw (~ *āškišēwak)

MEDIAL, FINAL (NOUN)

— ember, firebrand

evidence | WC iskwāskisīw, *a firebrand;* kwīskāskisīnam, *to turn the wood over the fire;* WSC (Misipawistik, Ellen Cook) otāskisēwakaham, *to pull the embers towards oneself;* MC (Moose Factory, George Quachegan) kwetipāškišewakaham, *to turn a firebrand over using sth;* mihkwāškišew, *an ember;* iškwāškišew, *a firebrand;* SEC (Oujé-Bougoumou, David Bosum) iškwāšcišew, *charcoal;* Watkins (1865) "Iskwaskisāo, *v.imp. It is a burning billet, a firebrand;*" Laure (ca. 1726) "iskuastchicheu, *pl. -a, braise, charbons allumés;*" "ni-cheguasticheuahen, *je mets les tisons dessous*" see | *ak[2] compare | *āškēw, *ıšēw discussion | This reconstruction suffers from the lack of an Atikamekw cognate to confirm the absence of a preaspirate.

*āšo (~ *āšaw)

INITIAL

— go across

evidence | PC āsowakāmēw, *to cross a body of water;* MC āšawāhtawīw, *to climb across;* AT (Wemotaci, Nicole Petiquay) acokew [āʒokēw], *to cross over a bridge or object serving as a bridge;* SEC āšawipahtāw, *to run across;* Fabvre (ca. 1690) "Acha8ahen n h8rau, *passer dela l(')eau*" | ANISH aazhawagaako, *to go across on the ice* (Livesay & Nichols, 2021); MENO a·sawaka·m, *at the opposite side*

***āšt (~ *āhš)**

PREFINAL

— by action of wind

origin PA ***āʔθ** see | *āštan, *āhši

***āštam**

INITIAL

— near side

evidence | PC āstam, *come!* MC āštamakām, *on the near shore;* SEC otāštamihkʷ, *one's face;* EI (Sheshatshiu) ashtamashteu [āstəmāstēw], *to be in the sun* | ANISH aasamajiw, *on the side of a hill, on the hill* (Livesay & Nichols, 2021) origin | PA ***āʔθam** (Hewson, 1993)

***āštan**

FINAL (VERB, INANIMATE, INTRANSITIVE, CONCRETE)

— by action of wind

evidence | PC nīhtāstan, *to be blown down;* MC wepāštan, *to be blown away;* SEC itāštan, *to be blown thither;* Silvy (ca. 1680) "8e8epachtan, *le vent pousse, ouvre la porte*" paired with | *āhši see | *āšt, *an²

***āštawē¹**

INITIAL (VERB, ANIMATE, INTRANSITIVE)

— extinguish

evidence | PC āstawēham, *to extinguish sth;* MC āštawešātam, *to extinguish sth by urinating;* SEC (Waswanipi) āštawepayin, *fire goes out;* Laure (ca. 1726) "achtaueu, *éteindre, feu éteint*" compare | *āštē¹

***āštawē²**

FINAL (VERB, ANIMATE, INTRANSITIVE, DERIVED)

— shine, speaking of a heavenly body

evidence | ESC sāsākāstawepaniw, *light rises and fall;* MC palipāštawew, *sun or moon's light pierces through;* SEC cīhkāyāštawew, *moon or sun shines brightly;* Laure (ca. 1726) "tchichigastaueu, *clair de lune*" compare | *āštē²

***āštē¹**

INITIAL

— abate, subside

evidence | MC āšteyāškāw, *waves subside;* AT actepectan [āštepeštān], *la pluie cesse;* SEC āšteyawesiw, *to have one's anger subside* compare | *āštawē¹

***āštē²**

FINAL (VERB, INANIMATE, INTRANSITIVE, DERIVED)

— **1** affected by light, generally in reference to the sun

— **2** shine, speaking of a light

evidence | MC mihkwāštew, *red light;* SEC āpawāštew, *to thaw in the sun;* cīšikāštew, *moonlight;* Laure (ca. 1726) "tchichachteu, *âpre, en parlant de feu, du soleil;*" "maskauachteu, *durci au soleil;*" Fabvre (ca. 1690) "Aga8achtepăgau, *bel ombre d'arbre feuilles etc*" origin | PA ***āʔtē** (Aubin, 1975) paired with | *āhso² see | *āh², *tē⁴ compare | *aštawe²

***āštim**

FINAL (VERB, TRANSITIVE, ANIMATE, CONCRETE)

— expose to wind

evidence | PC nātāstimēw, *to fetch sb by wind;* MC pāhkwāštimew, *to dry sth in the wind;* SEC papāmāštimew, *to fly sth about in the wind;* EI (Unaman-shipit) tshitashtameu [tʃītāhtamēw], *to let sth go in the wind* | ANISH dakaashim, *to cool sb in the wind* (Livesay & Nichols, 2021) see | *āšt, *ɪm³ paired with | *āštitā

***āštitā**

FINAL (VERB, ANIMATE, INTRANSITIVE, CONCRETE)

— expose to wind

evidence | PC Lacombe (1874) "webāstitaw, *il le vanne;*" MC pāhkwāštitāw, *to dry sth* *in the wind;* WI (Pessamit) uepashtatau [wēpāstətāw], *to let sth go in the wind;* Silvy (ca. 1680) "ni pakȣachtatan 3. -tau, *je fais sécher au vent, à l'air*" | ANISH webaasidoon, *to let sth blow away* (Livesay & Nichols, 2021) see | *āšt, *ɪtā paired with | *āštim

*āt¹ (~ *āc)

INITIAL

— give an account of

evidence | PC ācimēw, *to tell about sb;* MC ātotam, *give account of sth;* EI (Sheshatshiu) atshimeu [ātʃɪmēw], *to tell a story or a fact about sb* | MENO a·totam, *to narrate about sth* compare | *āt², *ātarōhkē

*āt² (~ *āc, *ās)

INITIAL

— held back by, blocked by

evidence | PC āsiskawēw, *to arrive before sb, to get ahead of sb;* WC ācihtin, *to be caught between two objects;* MC ātakāmešin, *blocked by a body of water;* NEC ātāpischinam, *to lock sth manually;* WI (Pessamit) atipeu [ātəpēw], *to be blocked by the rising tide;* Silvy (ca. 1680) "nit'achiskaȣau, *je le devance à porter nouvelles*" compare | *āt¹

*āt³ (~ *ātak)

MEDIAL (NOUN INCORPORATION)

— burrow, tunnel, hole

evidence | PC yāwātakan, *deep hole;* MC kipohātew, *to block a tunnel;* kinwātakan, *long burrow, tunnel, hole or bore;* SEC yāwātakan, *deep hole;* Silvy (ca. 1680) "kinȣatagan, *cela est profond, v.g. un puits*" origin | PA ***āθ** + ***ak** see | *wāt¹, *āt⁴

*āt⁴ (~ *āš)

FINAL (NOUN, INANIMATE)

— burrow

evidence | Laure (ca. 1726) "maskuach *pl.* maskuata, *ours, caverne à ours, antre*" | ANISH amikwaazh, *underwater trench and tunnel entrance to a beaver lodge;* makwaazh, *a bear den* (Livesay & Nichols, 2021) origin | PA ***āθ** see | *wāt¹, *āt³

*āt⁵ (~ *ās)

PREFINAL

— be (thus), have (a certain) character or personality

evidence | PC macātisiw, *to be bad or wicked;* WC kistātan, *to be great;* MC itātisīw, *to have a certain character;* SEC māyātan, *to be bad;* āhkwāsinākwan, *to look dangerous;* NEC chīshātin, *to be ready-made;* WI (Pessamit) shukatishiu [ʃūkāttʃīw], *to be solid or sturdy;* EI kushtatshu [kustātʃu], *to be afraid*

*āt⁶ (~ *āc)

FINAL (VERB, TRANSITIVE, INANIMATE, CONCRETE)

— consider, deem, or feel a certain emotion about

evidence | PC akāwātam, *to desire sth;* MC mihtātam, *to regret sth;* WI (Pessamit) shikatamᵘ [ʃīkātəm], *to hate sth* paired with | *āt⁷ compare | *ēriht

*āt⁷ (~ *āš)

FINAL (VERB, TRANSITIVE, ANIMATE, CONCRETE)

— consider, deem, or feel a certain emotion about

evidence | PC akāwātēw, *to desire sb;* MC milawātew, *to like sb;* WI (Pessamit) shikateu [ʃīkātēw], *to hate sb* paired with | *āt⁶ compare | *ērim

*ātakā

FINAL (VERB, ANIMATE, INTRANSITIVE, DERIVED)

— swim

evidence | PC pētātakāw, *to swim hither;* MC pimātakāw, *swim along;* SEC itātakāw, *to swim thither* see | *nāt, *ātakā

*ātarōhkē

INITIAL (VERB, ANIMATE, INTRANSITIVE)

— tell folktale

evidence | PC ātayōhkawēw, *to tell sacred stories or legends to sb;* WC ācaðōhkan, *character from legends;* MC ātalōhkew, *to tell* *a folktale;* WI (Pessamit) atalutsheu [ātlūtʃēw], *to tell a legend or myth;* Laure (ca. 1726) "atarukaniu, *on dit des fables*" | ANISH aadizooke, *to tell a sacred story* (Livesay & Nichols, 2021); MENO a·tɛqno·hkɛ·w, *to tell a sacred story;* MESK ātesōhkēwa, *to tell a sacred story;* MIAMI aalhsoohkaani (ILDA, 2017) compare | *āt[1]

*ātaw[1]

INITIAL

— fail, disregard, reject

evidence | PC ātawinawēw, *to disdain sb's appearance;* MC ātawihtāw, *to fail at sth;* SEC ātaweyihtam, *to reject sth;* āta, *even though;* Laure (ca. 1726) "nit-atuspiten 3. -tamu, *je ne le trouve pas bon, cela n'est point à mon goût*" | ANISH aanawendaagozi, *to be rejected;* aana-, *in vain; without result; in spite of* (Livesay & Nichols, 2021); MIAMI aalawinam-, *to refuse sth* (ILDA, 2017) origin | PA ***āθaw** (Hewson, 1993)

*ātaw[2]

INITIAL

— gaunt

evidence | SEC ātūsīu, to be lean, speaking of a fish (CSB, 2018); Laure (ca. 1726) "atuastim, *chien maigre;*" nit-atuastchiganin, *j'ai maigreur à la poitrine;* nit-atuikatan 3. -teu, *j'ai maigreur aux jambes;*" Silvy (ca. 1680) "Ataȣachtimȣ, *chien maigre*"

*ātiht

INITIAL

— a few, some

evidence | PC ātiht, *some;* MC ātiht, *some;* AT atita [ātihta], *some;* SEC (Nemaska) ātiht, *a few;* EI (Mamit) aiatit [ājātīht], *certain people;* Watkins (1865) "Atèt, *n. indec. A part of them, some of them; a few. (Not often used in this latter sense);*" Laure (ca. 1726) "atit, *les uns et les autres, d'aucuns*" | ANISH aanind, *some* (Livesay & Nichols, 2021); MIAMI aalinta, *some, part* (ILDA, 2017) origin | PA ***āθent** (Hewson, 1993)

*ātikw

MEDIAL (NOUN INCORPORATION)

— waves

evidence | MC petātikwew, *waves come hither;* NEC wāyātikwāu, *trough in the waves;* WI tshipuatikueu, *waterway blocked by waves* | cf. MENO teko·w AN, *wave* origin | PA ***tekowa**, *wave* (Hewson, 1993)

*ātim

MEDIAL

— channel

evidence | WI (Pessamit) uakatimiu [wākātəmīw], *to be a curved channel;* MC kīškātimāw, *precipice at channel bed;* SEC kaškātimīw, *underwater precipice* see | *ā[1], *tim

*ātot

FINAL (VERB, TRANSITIVE, INANIMATE, DERIVED)

— give an account of

evidence | PC itātotam, *to tell thus about sth;* MC tipātotam, *to relate an account about sth;* SEC macātotam, *to tell bad news about sth* paired with | *ācim

*āw[1]

INITIAL

— to be (a specified thing or person)

evidence | PC Lacombe (1874) "āweyimew, ttam, miwew, tchikew, *il commence à le reconnaître dans sa pensée, il en découvre la signification, le sens;*" MC āwiw, *to be a specified person;* SEC āwan, *to be a specified thing;* Watkins (1865) "Awinowāo, *v.t.an. He recognizes him*" | ANISH aawan, *to be a certain thing* (Livesay & Nichols, 2021) origin | Possibly ***ay** + ***ɩw**

*āw[2] (~ *āwak)

MEDIAL, FINAL (NOUN INCORPORATION)

— egg

evidence | PC askāwi, *raw egg;* MC nānatawāwew, *to look for eggs;* AT manawan [manāwān], *egg-gathering place (place* *name);* WI (Pessamit) neuaukashtau [nēwāwkəstāw], *to have four eggs in one's nest;* Laure (ca. 1726) "nichuauets, *deux œufs;*" "uiskuenauan -a; uskanauan, *coque d'œuf;*" Silvy (ca. 1680) "chichipau, *œuf de canard*" see | *wāw[1]

*āwahk

MEDIAL (CLASSIFIER)

— granular substance

evidence | PC ohpwēyāwahkāstan, *to be a sandstorm;* MC wāpāwahkisiw, *to be a white granular substance;* SEC piskotāwahkāw, *to be a pile of sand;* waweyāwahkaham, *to prepare the sandy ground using sth;* ošetāwahk^w, *a sandy ridge, an esker;* Laure (ca. 1726) "arauatchipitaganiuets, *le champ est hersé, le grain est enterré;*" Silvy (ca. 1680) "mina8a8atchipari8, *on ne voit plus la piste*" | ANISH gizhaawangide, *to be hot sand* (Livesay & Nichols, 2021) origin | PA ***āwank** (Hewson, 1993)

*āwahs

MEDIAL (NOUN INCORPORATION)

— child(ren)

evidence | PC asamāwasow, *to feed children;* AT (Wemotaci, Jeannette Coocoo) kanawerimawasow [kanawērimāwassow], *to be pregnant;* aššama:wasso, *to feed one's own child* (Béland, 1978); MC wīhpemāwasow, *to sleep with children;* SEC pekatehāwasow, *to burp a child* | ANISH minogi'aawaso, *to raise one's children well* (Livesay & Nichols, 2021) see | *ā[1], *awāhs limited to | *o

*āwaskw

MEDIAL

— sky

evidence | MC mihkwāwaskwan, *to be a red sky;* SEC mihkwāwaskwan, *to be a red sky;* NEC mihkwāuskwāu, *to be a red sky;* WI (Pessamit) mekuaushkuan [mēkwāwʃkun], *to be red cloud at sundown;* Watkins (1865) "Mìkwowuskwun, *v.imp. The sky is red, the cloud is red;*" Silvy (ca. 1680) "mamik8a8ask8ach [*sic*], *le ciel est rouge*" limited to | *mirko see | *wāskw compare | *askw[1]

*āwatō

INITIAL

— convey, carry from one place to another

evidence | PC āwatōpew, *to haul water;* WC āwatōpīw, *to haul water;* SEC āwatōsiw, *fallfish;* WI (Pessamit) autuatameu [āwtūtāmēw], *to carry people on one's back in several trips;* EI (Ekuanitshit) autuateu [āwatwatēw], *to carry things on one's back in several trips* see | *āwē, *tā compare | *aštō discussion | This root is a vestigial variant of ***āwatā** that survived what is otherwise a loss of morphological distinction in Old Cree between Proto-Algonquian transitive inanimate verb class II and animate intransitive verbs ending in ***ā** (cf. Pentland, 1999). Compare the Anishinabe word *odaawadoon,* "to haul sth" (Livesay & Nichols, 2021), a cognate of Old Cree ***āwatāwa**.

*āwatōhsiw

INITIAL (NOUN, ANIMATE)

— fallfish (Semotilus corporalis)

evidence | AT (Opitciwan, Monique Awashish & Patrick Awashish) awatosiw [āwatōssiw], *fallfish;* SEC āwatōsiw, *fallfish;* WI (Pessamit) autushu [āwtūʃu], *type of unidentified fish* | ANISH aawadoosi, *mullet, dart* (Lippert & Gambill, 2023) see | *āwatō discussion | Literally "one who carries things," this fish is named for its habit of piling pebbles into small mounds. As the English name suggests, they are often found at the base of waterfalls or rapids. The French Canadian "ouitouche" is likely a Gallicized form of a cognate from a neighbouring Algonquian language, possibly Anishinabe.

*āwē

INITIAL

— convey, carry from one place to another

evidence | MC āwalew, *to carry sb from one place to another;* āwatāw, *to carry sth from one place to another;* NEC āuchikutisū, *to haul a kill back in several trips;* WI (Pessamit) autau [āwtāw], *to transport things in several trips;* EI (Mamit) autshitapeu [āwatʃitāpēw], *to transport things in several trips by toboggan* | ANISH aawadoon, *to haul sth;* aawadaatigwe, *to haul logs* (Livesay & Nichols, 2021) see | *āwatō limited to | *r, *tā

*āwikan

MEDIAL, FINAL (NOUN INCORPORATION)

— spine, back

evidence | PC māskāwikanēw, *to have a deformed back;* MC pēšāwikanew, *to have a striped back;* EI (Unaman-shipit) tshinuaukanu [tnwāwkanu], *to have a long back;* Watkins (1865) "Munowikun'ātin, *v.imp. The keel gets broken off;*" Laure (ca. 1726) "nit-aspitauiganéchimun, *je suis appuyé sur le dos;*" Silvy (ca. 1680) "pisk8a8igan, *bosse du dos*" | ANISH dewaawigane, *to have a sore back* (Livesay & Nichols, 2021) compare | *tahtakwākan

*āwimat (~ *āwimaš)

INITIAL

— be in heat

evidence | ESC āmatahkešīwiw, *to be a fox in heat;* MC āmataštimow, *to be a dog in heat;* āmacimōsow, *to be a moose in heat;* Laure (ca. 1726) "auimatachtimu, elle est en chaleur;" Fabvre (ca. 1690) "A8imatachk8ek, *Les 8rs sont en chal(eu)r*" | ANISH aamanasimo, *to be a dog in heat* (Livesay & Nichols, 2021); MENO awe·manasow, *to be a rutting deer;* MESK āmanwa, *to have sexual inclinations, to have sex, to rut (deer)* discussion | The expected allomorph ***āwimaš** has yet to be corroborated by written sources, but is indirectly supported by cognates from Anishinabe, Menominee, and Meskwaki.

*āwiy

MEDIAL, FINAL (NOUN INCORPORATION)

— porcupine quill

evidence | NEC chihkāwiyāu, *pricked by porcupine quill;* WI (Pessamit) tshipatshikauieu [tʃīpətʃəkāwījēw], *pricked by porcupine quill;* Laure (ca. 1726) "uichuauauiets, *porc-épic teint en jaune;*" Fabvre (ca. 1690) "Atisa8ian, *racines r8ges p(ou)r teindre pore epy;*" Silvy (ca. 1680) "8s88a8ietch, *brins de la queue du porc-épic*" origin | Old Cree ***kāwiya**, *porcupine quill* see | *kāwiy²

*āyaw

MEDIAL

— bottom of a body of water

evidence | PC kīskāyawāw, *to be a sharp drop underwater;* MC kīškāyawištikweyāw, *to be a deep river;* NEC chīškāyiwāu, *underwater precipice;* Silvy (ca. 1680) "kichkaïa8au, *écore, raide, falaise*" | ANISH apiitaayawaa, *to be so deep* (Lippert & Gambill, 2023) discussion | In combination with the final ***yā**, the resulting sequence ***āyawā** seen in the examples above is contracted to a reflex of ***āyā** by some speakers of contemporary dialects.

*āyā

FINAL (VERB, INANIMATE, INTRANSITIVE, CONCRETE)

— be certain weather, season, or time

evidence | PC tahkāyāw, *to be cold weather;* WC kīkisīpāyāw, *to be morning;* MC kweskwāyāu, *to be a change of season;* SEC āpawāyāw, *to be a thaw;* NEC chīshuwāyāu, *to be warm weather;* yūskāyāu, *to be mild weather in winter;* WI (Pessamit) pakuaiau [pākwājāw], *to dry up after the rain* | ANISH dakaayaa, *to be cool weather* (Livesay & Nichols, 2021)

*āyihkam

INITIAL

— deal with, compel

evidence | PC āhkamihtāw, *to keep at sth;* Lacombe (1874) "akamihew, *(v.a.)* ttaw, hiwew, tchikew, *il s'occupe beaucoup de lui;*" "akameyimow, ok *(v.n.) il prend courage, il s'empresse, v.g.,* akameyimow e wi ayamihāt, *il prend courage pour prier;* akameyimuk tchi kiskinohamākawiyek, *empressez-vous de vous faire instruire;*" WC āhkaminam, *to look after sth cooking or baking;* āhkamīðimow, *to persevere;* ESC (Attawapiskat, Bill Louttit) āhkamihtāw, *to deal with or take care of sth;* MC āyihkamimew, *to compel sb verbally;* AT (Wemotaci, Nicole Petiquay) aikamitaw [āyihkamihtāw], *to tend to sth cooking;* SEC āyihkamihtāw, *to persevere;* NEC āyihkimihāu, *to force sb;* WI (Pessamit) aikamieu [ājkəmjēw], *to force or compel sb;* EI (Sheshatshiu) aikam [ājkəm] *reluctantly; in spite of everything;* Watkins (1865) "Ayekumehāo, *v.t.an. He forces him, he constrains him;*" "Akumetow, *v.t.in.2. He takes care of it;*" Laure (ca. 1726) "nit-aikamimau, *je le mets dans la nécessité, je le contrains;*" Fabvre (ca. 1690) "Akamerĭten 3 tam8, *se haster de marcher*" discussion | Elision of the second syllable accounts for the alternate form, **āhkam**, found in dialects west of MC and in one historical source from the 1600s. In addition, note that a doublet, ***āyihkē**, can be reconstructed from the AT words **āyihkēw** (VAI), **āyihkam** (VTI), and **āyihkawēw** (VTA). These three forms have been confirmed for the communities of Wemotaci (Nicole Petiquay) and Opitciwan (Joey Awashish) and carry the sense of "dealing with or tending to (sth or sb)." Alternatively, given the lack of corroborative evidence outside this dialect, this form may have resulted from a reanalysis of ***āyihkam** as a VTI, leading to the VTA form and the VAI by back-formation.

*āyit (~ *āyic, *āyis)

INITIAL

— **1** solidly in place, firmly, securely

— **2** necessarily, without fail

evidence | [1]PC āyītahpisow, *to be tied firmly or securely;* ESC (Severn) āyitisiw, *to be firm or steady;* MC āyitāpihkātam, *to tie sth firmly or securely;* āyicimew, *to enjoin sbi;* NEC yāiyisinākuhtāu, *to secure sth;* yāiyitisīu, *to be trustworthy;* Laure (ca. 1726) "nit-aitamutuau, *j'enharnache un cheval*" [2]MC yālitel, *must, necessarily;* SEC yāyitēy, *make sure;* NEC yāyitāi, *make sure, for sure;* Watkins (1865) "Yayitā, Yayitān, adv. Rather; *without fail, by all means*" | ANISH aayiijigwaadan, *to sew sth securely* (Lippert & Gambill, 2023) see | *ēr[2] discussion | The Moose Cree word 'yālitel' is likely a hypercorrected form in a similar fashion to its cognate for the root ***pēhk**. Compare the Swampy Cree cognate of this word from Watkins (1865), "Yayitān," which maintains the Old Cree ***y** in ***āyit**.

C

*cahcahkarow

INITIAL (NOUN, ANIMATE)

— red-winged blackbird (Agelaius phoeniceus)

evidence | WC cāhcāhkaðōs, *a black bird;* MC cahcahkalow, *a red-winged blackbird;* SEC cahcahkayow & cahcahkalow, *a red-winged blackbird;* WI (Pessamit) tshatshakalu [tʃətʃəkəlu], *a rusty blackbird;* EI (Mamit) tshatshakanu [tʃātʃākanwī], *a rusty blackbird;* Laure (ca. 1726) "tchatchakaru -ets, *ortolan, hortolan, ceci est le nom de l'étourneau;*" Silvy (ca. 1680) "tchatchakarau, *espèce d'oiseau*" | ANISH (Abitibi dialect) cahcahkanō & cahkanō, *red-winged blackbird*

*cahk

INITIAL (NOUN, ANIMATE)

— small

evidence | PC cahkasinâsow, *to be dotted;* cahkâpês & cahkâpêw, *Man-in-the-Moon;* WC câhkipîhikan, *a dot or syllabic final;* MC cahkasinaham, *to mark sth with a spot or dot;* cahkâsam, *to cast a beam of light on sth;* SEC cahkâpêš, *a character in traditional tales who retires to the moon after his many adventures; sturgeon head bone said to resemble a man;* AT (Wemotaci, Jeannette Coocoo) Tcikapec [cihkâpêš], *Tcikapec, the legendary hero;* WI tshakashtau [tʃəkəstāw], *to make a small mark, a period;* EI (Ekuanitshit) Tshakapesh [tʃakāpēh], *Tshakapesh, character in stories;* Fabvre (ca. 1690) "Tchakabech, *petit garçon fabuleux*" | MESK chakeshîhiwa, *to be small;* chakinâkâhi, *a small bowl* compare | *tahk²

*camohk

INITIAL

— kerplunk

evidence | PC camohkaham, *to make a loud splash, such as a beaver with its tail;* MC camohkihtin, *to hit the water with a kerplunk;* NEC chimuhkâskuhîkin, *pole used for scaring fish into a net*

*câhk

INITIAL

— front end elevated

evidence | MC câhkakohtin, *to float with front end elevated;* SEC câhkâskwešin, *to lie with one's head elevated;* WI (Pessamit) tshakalueu [tʃākālwēw], *to have one's tail raised;* EI (Sheshatshiu) tshakatinau [tʃākətnāw], *to be a mountain with a steep slope at its peak* | ANISH jaangaakweni, *to poke one's head up* (Livesay & Nichols, 2021) origin | PA ***cānk** compare | *mōhkit

*câk

INITIAL

— deplete

evidence | MC câkinam, *use up*; AT tcakakotew [câkâkohtêw], *snow melted away;* WI (Pessamit) tshatshineu [tʃātnēw], *to use sth all up;* Laure (ca. 1726) "ni-tchakatauan, *j'ai tout traité;*" Silvy (ca. 1680) "tchatchipariȣ, *il est tout coule, v.g. le sablier*"

*cât (~ *câš)

INITIAL (NOUN, DEPENDENT INANIMATE)

— snout, muzzle

evidence | ESC (Severn) ochâsh, *one's snout; one's nose;* MC ocâš, *one's nose; one's snout;* NEC uchât, *one's muzzle;* EI (Sheshatshiu) utshat [utʃāt], *one's snout;* Silvy (ca. 1680) "ȣtchach *pl.* ȣtchatai, *mufle d'orignal*" | MENO necias, *my nose;* ocianowawan, *their noses* origin | PA ***tyāθ**

*cêpihk

MEDIAL, FINAL (NOUN INCORPORATION)

— primary root

evidence | PC wâpicêpihk, *unidentified plant;* MC môskicepihkopitew, *to pull out the roots of a tree;* NEC mûnichâpihchipiyiu, *to become uprooted;* Silvy (ca. 1680) "ni mȣnaitchebikan, *je tire, j'amène (je déracine);*" cf. MC ocepihkiwan (obsolete form) & ocepihkowan, *to have roots;* SEC ocepihc, *primary root;* Fabvre (ca. 1690) "ȣtchepik, ȣtchebik *pl.* kȣa, *racines d'arbres*" see | *wicêpihk

*cêšt[1] (~ *cêhc)

INITIAL (NOUN, DEPENDENT INANIMATE)

— sinew

evidence | PC ocêstatay, *gristle, muscle, tendon;* SEC ucheshtitai, *the top part of the abdomen of a moose that is cut out in a circle shape* (CSB, 2018); ocêšteyâpiy, *a ligament or tendon;* NEC uchâshtiû, *to be gristly, speaking of meat;* EI (Sheshatshiu) utshesht [utʃēst], *one's tendon;* Laure (ca. 1726) "ȣtchestaiabiu, *nerveux, plein de nerf;*" Fabvre (ca. 1690) "nikech, nitchech, *mon nerf, neru(us)*" | ANISH Cuoq (1886) "Ni tcictatan, *mes nerfs;*" MENO neci·qtan, *my cord, my sinew (in body)* see | *cêšt²

*cēšt² (~ *cēhc, *cēštak)

MEDIAL (NOUN INCORPORATION)

— sinew

evidence | WI (Pessamit) papeshkutsheshtipalu [pəpēʃkutʃēstəpəlu], *to have lumps on the body caused by arthritis;* Laure (ca. 1726) "ni-kuetibitchestatchiparihun, *je me suis foulé un nerf;*" Silvy (ca. 1680) "ni kitchichg8tchechtichigan, *je dépouille un os, un nerf de la chair*" see | *cēšt¹

*ci

FINAL (ABSTRACT)

— forms particles when suffixed to certain initials

evidence | PC wanaskoc, *at the tip;* WC kīhcināc, *certainly;* MC tāwic, *in the middle of a body of water;* kisiskāc, *quickly;* AT pecotcik [peššocihk], *close;* SEC ayisāc, *unwillingly, resistingly;* WI (Pessamit) tshitshit [tʃītʃət], *near* compare | *a, *ēr², *i³, *nē⁴

*cicāskay

INITIAL (NOUN, DEPENDENT INANIMATE)

— crotch, groin

evidence | PC ocicāskāhk, *in the crotch;* MC ocicāskay, *one's groin;* AT (Opitciwan, Joey Awashish) otcitcaskai [ocicāskay], *one's groin;* SEC nicicāskay *my crotch or groin;* NEC uchichāskī, *one's groin;* WI (Pessamit) utshitshashkai [utʃətʃāʃkī], *the skin around one's groin;* EI (Sheshatshiu) utshitshashkai [utʃāʃkī], *the skin around one's groin* see | *cicē

*cicē

INITIAL (VERB, ANIMATE, INTRANSITIVE)

— dirty with excrement

evidence | MC cicew, *to dirty oneself with excrement;* cicān, *a shit stain;* SEC cicāhtam, *to dirty sth with excrement;* EI (Sheshatshiu) tshitshameu [tʃitʃāmēw], *to get sth dirty with shit*

*cikā

INITIAL

— abrupt narrowing

evidence | WSC (Ida Bear) cikāyāskonawew, *to have a narrow waist;* SEC cikāyāw, *to narrow;* NEC chikāsikusiu, *to be narrow, speaking of ice;* WI (Pessamit) tshikashiu [tʃəkāʃīw], *to have a notch, a deep gash*

*cikēmā

INITIAL

— of course, certainly

evidence | PC cikēmā, *certainly, of course;* MC cikema & cikemānima, *of course;* SEC cemekā, *of course;* SEC (Waswanipi) cēmānim, *of course;* NEC chāmākā, *no wonder, nevertheless* | ANISH jigemaa, *of course* (Lippert & Gambill, 2023)

*cim

INITIAL

— **1** cut short, sever

— **2** suffer from

evidence | ¹PC cimikwayawēw, *to have a short neck;* WC cimisāwātam, *to cut sth down short;* cimipitonīw, *to have short arms;* SEC cimahāhtikwew, *to cut poles;* cimāw, *to be cut short;* WI (Pessamit) tshimishamᵘ [tʃəməʃəm], *to cut sth off;* EI (Sheshatshiu) tshimikateu [tʃiməkātēw], *to have an amputated leg;* Watkins (1865) "Chimiskiwunāo, *He has a short nose;*" Laure (ca. 1726) "ni-tchimitakakuanesuau, *je rogne les ailes à l'oiseau;*" Fabvre (ca. 1690) "Tchimip8tan e8, *sier, cier de trauers;*" Silvy (ca. 1680) "ni tchimipiten, *je déchire qqch;*" "tchimar8eu, *il est sans queue*" ²WI (Pessamit) tshimapakueu [tʃəmāpākwēw], *to be very thirsty;* tshimakateshkaku [tʃəməkətēʃkāku], *to become skinny because of sth;* EI (Sheshatshiu) tshimakateu [tʃimākətēw], *to be skinny;* Laure (ca. 1726) "tchimapakueu, *pépie (l'oiseau a grande soif);*" "ni-tchiminesin, *je suis languissant, les forces me manquent;*" Silvy (ca. 1680) "ni tchimapag8an 3. -e8, *j'ai grande soif;*" "ni tchimakatan, 3. -e8, *j'ai fort faim*" | [1]MENO teme·ka·tɛ·w, netɛ·mekatɛ·m, *to have a stub leg* discussion | The sense of this root in western dialects has shifted from "severed" to "short" when referring to body parts. This appears to be an innovation as it is without evidence in Eastern Swampy Cree, Moose Cree, Atikamekw, or eastern dialects. Evidence for the figurative second sense appears to be limited to contemporary dialects spoken along the north shore of the St. Lawrence River but is supported by evidence dating back to the seventeenth century.

*cimē[1]

FINAL (VERB, ANIMATE, INTRANSITIVE, CONCRETE)

— **1** travel by canoe

— **2** swim

evidence | PC isicimēw, *to paddle or swim thither;* WC kisīcimīw, *to paddle fast;* MC išicimew, *to swim thither or travel thither by canoe;* SEC cihcicimew, *to paddle off, to start swimming;* Silvy (ca. 1680) "ni nita8itchiman 3. -e8, *je nage bien*" | MENO anɛ·meceme·w, *to swim or paddle off yon way*

*cimē[2]

INITIAL

— erect

evidence | WC cimaðīw, *to erect sth;* MC cimatāw, *to erect sth;* AT tcimaso [cimazow], *to be erect;* SEC cimayew, *to erect sth;* EI tshimaneu [tʃimanēw], *to erect sth;* Silvy (ca. 1680) "tchimateu, *il est debout*" limited to | *r, *ɪso[2], *tā, *tē[3]

*cin

FINAL (VERB, ANIMATE, INTRANSITIVE, ABSTRACT)

— to be suspended or snagged

evidence | PC sakicin, *to get snagged on sth;* MC sakāskocin, *snagged on sth stick-like;* SEC akocin, *hangs* | ANISH badakijin, *to be pricked* (Livesay & Nichols, 2021)

*cišk[1]

INITIAL (NOUN, DEPENDENT INANIMATE)

— **1** anus

— **2** bum

evidence | PC ociskiw, *to have an anus;* MC kicišk, *your anus;* SEC micišc, *a bum; an anus; a word used to express anger or annoyance;* WI (Pessamit) utshiss [utʃəss], *one's penis;* EI (Mamit) utshiss [utʃɨss], *one's bum;* Laure (ca. 1726) "utchistchk *pl.* -a, *cul, podex*" see | *cišk[2]

*cišk[2]

MEDIAL (NOUN INCORPORATION)

— **1** anus

— **2** bum

evidence | MC opīwāwiciškew, *to have a hairy bum;* SEC nānāmiciščešīš, *spotted sandpiper (Actitis macularius);* Silvy (ca. 1680) "ni tapitistenau f. *je mets mon doigt dans son derrière*" | MENO moqcecehkɛw, *to have a bare buttocks* see | *cišk[1]

*cištēmāw

INITIAL (NOUN, ANIMATE)

— tobacco

evidence | PC cistēmāw, *tobacco;* WC cistīmāwakan, *to smell like tobacco;* ESC cištemāw, *tobacco;* MC cištēmāw, *tobacco;* cištemāwakan, *to smell like tobacco;* AT tcictemaw [cištēmāw], *tobacco;* SEC cištemāwimākosiw, *to smell like tobacco;* EI (Sheshatshiu) tshishtemau [tʃɨstēmāw], *tobacco, a cigarette;* Silvy (ca. 1680) "ni saskah8au tchistemau, *j'allume le pétun*" origin | PA ***θeʔθēmāwa** (Hewson, 1993) discussion | The expected Old Cree reflex, ***tištēmāwa**, is supported by a variant pronunciation [tištēmāw], provided on various occasions by Susan Cheechoo of Moose Factory. Given that she is known for her highly conservative pronunciation, this form cannot be ignored until further fieldwork clarifies its status as either an archaism or innovation.

*ciwan

FINAL (VERB, INANIMATE, INTRANSITIVE, CONCRETE)

— water flow, current

evidence | PC sōhkiciwan, *strong flowing current;* MC peciciwan, *the tide flows;* AT opitciwan [opiciwan], *narrows in a river, place name;* SEC peciciwan, *tide comes in* | ABEN molōjoan, *to be a deep current* (Day, 1994); ANISH baazhijijiwan, *to overflow* (Livesay & Nichols, 2021); MENO se·pa·cewan, *to flow under*

*cīhcīko (~ cīhcīkw)

INITIAL

— **1** remove meat from bone

— **2** devoid of one's natural covering

evidence | PC cīhcīkwahtam, *to nibble or gnaw the meat off sth*; MC cīhcīkoštikwānēw, *to eat what remains of the meat on a skull*; cīhcīkotawēw, *to have patchy fur*; cīhcīkwāw, *to be debarked, degrained, defleshed, or epilated*; SEC cīhcīkopitam, *to pull meat off of a bone*; NEC chīhchīhkwāyiwāu, *to have a bare tail* | ANISH jiichiigwaanowe, *to have a bare skinny tail* (Livesay & Nichols, 2021); MENO ci·qcekuahtamowɛ·w, *to gnaw sth bald for sb*

*cīhcīkw (~ *cīhcīko)

INITIAL (NOUN, ANIMATE)

— wart

evidence | MC ocīhcīkomiw, *to have warts;* SEC nicīhcīkom, *my wart;* EI (Sheshatshiu) tshitshik[u] [tʃītʃīk[w]], *a wart;* Silvy (ca. 1680) "n'8tchichig8mititchan 3. -e8, *j'ai des verrues aux mains*" | ANISH jiichiigom, *a wart* (Livesay & Nichols, 2021); MENO neci·qcekwam, *my wart*

*cīhk

INITIAL

— **1** enjoy

— **2** cheerful, happy

evidence | PC cīhkēyihtākwan, *to be important or well-liked;* WC cīhkīðimīw, *to like sb, to esteem sb;* WSC (Misipawistik, Ellen Cook) cīhkēnimēw, *to delight in the thought of sb, to be enthused about sb*; cīhkispitam, *to enjoy the taste of sth*; cīhkipēw, *to be cheerful under the influence of alcohol, to be a happy drunk*; ESC (Severn) cīhkenihtam, *to be interested in sth* | ANISH ojiikimaan, *to make sb excited or happy by what one says;* jiikamanji'o, *to feel good or happy;* ojiikaabamaan, *to enjoy seeing sb; to like what one sees in sb* (Livesay & Nichols, 2021); MENO ci·hkenakwat, *to look clear*

*cīhš[1]

INITIAL

— remove superficial layer

evidence | AT ci:ššа:skoh(w)-, *to cut sb or sth away from a tree; to take sb or sth off from skin* (Béland, 1978); SEC (Waswanipi) cīšāskohikan, *a two-handed flesher;* WI (Pessamit) tshishakunetin [tʃīʃākunētn], *to brush on the snow in passing*; EI (Sheshatshiu) tshisham[u] [tʃīʃəm], *to cut the meat off a bone* | ANISH jiishaakwa'ige, *to scrape hides;* MENO ci·hsi·kenɛw, *to skin sb*

*cīhš[2]

INITIAL

— cheat, mislead

evidence | PC cīšimēw, *to mislead sb by speech;* MC cīšihew, *to cheat or mislead sb;* AT (Wemotaci, Nicole Petiquay) tcicihew [cīššihēw], *to cheat or mislead sb;* SEC cīšihew, *to fool sb* | ANISH jiishi'iwe, *to trick, fool, or entice people* (Livesay & Nichols, 2021)

*cīk[1]

INITIAL

— near

evidence | PC cīkaskamik, *close to he ground;* MC cīkāsk[w], *near trees;* WI (Pessamit) tshitshit [tʃītʃət], *near;* Silvy (ca. 1680) "tchigagamich, *proche de l'eau;*" Laure (ca. 1726) "ni-tchikaskamitchiparin, *je rampe comme un serpent"* | ANISH jiigaabik, *by a rock* (Livesay & Nichols, 2021)

*cīk[2]

INITIAL

— **1** scratch itch

— **2** chop

evidence | [1]WC cīhcīkīw, *to scratch oneself to relieve an itch;* MC cīhcīkipitam, *to scratch sth to relieve an itch;* WI (Pessamit) tshitshiku [tʃītʃīku], *for an animal to scratch itself* [2]PC cīkaham, *to chop sth;* MC cīkahikan, *axe;* SEC cīkaham, *to chop sth* | [2]MENO ce·kekaham, *to hew sth*

*cīm

INITIAL (VERB, TRANSITIVE, ANIMATE)

— travel with by canoe

evidence | WC cīmīw, *to accompany sb by canoe;* MC cīmākan, *a canoe companion;* SEC cīmew, *to accompany sb by canoe;* Silvy (ca. 1680) "ni tchimau, *je l'embarque en canot"*

*cīp

INITIAL

— twitch

evidence | PC cīpipayiw, *to jerk or twitch;* MC cīhcīpāpiw, *to feel one's eye twitch;* WI (Pessamit) tshitshipitunu [tʃītʃīpətnu], *avoir la lèvre qui tressaille;* Watkins (1865) "Chechepipuyew, *v.imp. It quivers;"* Laure (ca. 1726) "ni-tchitchipikuamin, *je me remue en dormant"* | ANISH jiibaabi, *to wink* (Livesay & Nichols, 2021); MENO ce·peqtaw, *to give a sudden jump, to start with surprise*

*cīpat (~ *cīpac)

INITIAL

— place upright or vertically

evidence | PC cīpacikāpawiw, *to stand very straight;* MC cīpataštāw, *to place sth upright;* SEC cīpatapiw, *to sit up straight;* NEC chīpitāskuhīkin, *a dead bird propped up with a stick as a decoy* | ANISH jiibadabi, *to sit stiffly* (Livesay & Nichols, 2021)
compare | *cīpē

*cīpay

INITIAL (NOUN, ANIMATE)

— soul of a dead person

evidence | PC cīpay, *a ghost; a corpse;* MC cīpayēkin[w], *a burial shroud;* cīpayimeskanaw, *path taken by the souls on their way to the afterlife, traditionally identified with the Milky Way;* SEC cīpay, *a ghost;* WI (Pessamit) tshipaiatik[u] [tʃīpjātuk[w]], *a crucifix, a cross;* Laure (ca. 1726) "tchipai *pl.* -ats, *âme d'un trépassé;"* Silvy (ca. 1680) "tchipaï, *l'âme de trépassé;"* "tchipaïakana, tchipenakana, *obsèques, festin des morts"*
compare | *ahcāhkw[1]

*cīpē

INITIAL

— place upright or vertically

evidence | Laure (ca. 1726) "ni-tchipestchikuan, *je mets la chaudière au feu;"* Fabvre (ca. 1690) "ki tchipestik8atin pl na8au, *ie la (chaudiere) fais pr toy pl pr u8s;"* Silvy (ca. 1680) "ni tchipestik8an 3. -e8, *je fais chaudière"* | MENO ce·panɛw TA, ce·pataw TI, *to stand or fix sb or sth upright in or on sth* compare | *cīpat discussion | Evidence for this root is limited to a construction referring to placing a pot over a fire for cooking. It has since become obsolete in contemporary dialects, but its doublet, ***cīpat**, derived from an unattested applicative stem, continues to be used productively in most dialects.

*cīpo (~ *cīpw)

INITIAL

— pointed

evidence | PC cīpohkotam, *to whittle sth to a point;* MC cīpwāpitew, *to have pointy teeth;* NEC chīpuham, *to taper sth with a tool* | ANISH jiibwaa, *to be pointed* (Livesay & Nichols, 2021)

*cīrawē

INITIAL

— have as kin

evidence | AT (Wemotaci, Nicole Petiquay) tcirowemew [cīrowēmēw], *to be related to sb;* (Wemotaci, Jeannette Coocoo) tcirowetowin [cīrowēhtowin], *kinship;* WI (Pessamit) tshilueshkueu [tʃīlwēʃkwēw], *to be familiar with sb;* EI (Sheshatshiu) tshinuemeu [tʃīnwēmēw], *to be related to sb;* Laure (ca. 1726) "ni-tchirauemau, *je l'ai pour parent*" | ANISH Cuoq (1886) "tcinawendiwin, *parenté;*" MESK chīnawēmēwa, *to be related to sb;* MIAMI ciilaweem-, *to be a near relative with sb* (ILDA, 2017) compare | *wāhko discussion | An isogloss runs with East Cree dialects grouping with more westerly dialects and Western Innu grouping with more easterly dialects. While the dialects spoken to the east of this line display the above root, those spoken to the west instead use reflexes of the root ***wāhko**. The Atikamekw dialect has retained both roots as synonym.

*cīskē

INITIAL

— garter

evidence | PC sīskēpisow, *to put on a garter;* ESC (Severn) cīskepison, *a garter;* MC cīskepison, *a garter;* NEC chīschāhpisun, *a garter;* EI (Sheshatshiu) tshissepishun [tʃīssēpəʃun], *a garter;* Isham (1743) "ke ska pe sun, *a carter;*" Silvy (ca. 1680) "chistchepisȣn, *jarretière*"

*cīšt (~ *cīhš)

INITIAL

— **1** pierce

— **2** cause piercing pain

evidence | [1]PC cīstahwēw, *to pierce or prick sb;* MC cīštaham, *to pierce sth;* SEC cīštahāpwān, *meat roasted on a skewer;* EI (Sheshatshiu) tshishtaim^{u} [tʃīstējm], *to pierce sth using a stick; to cook sth over a fire with a stick;* Laure (ca. 1726) "ni-tchitchitahen tchistaskuan, *j'enfonce un clou dans la muraille*" [2]PC cīstinam, *to pinch sth;* MC cīhcīšinesiw, *to suffer from an intermittent stabbing pain;* SEC cīštinew, *to pinch sb* | ANISH jiisibizh, *to pinch sb* (Livesay & Nichols, 2021) origin | PA ***cīʔθ**

*cītaw

INITIAL

— stiff

evidence | PC sītawāw, *to be stiff;* ESC cītawāskopaniw, *to stiffen;* MC cītawekipaliw, *to stiffen, speaking of a sheet-like object;* AT tcitowarikwew [cītowārihkwēw], *to have stiff hair;* NEC chitiwihtāu, *to stiffen sth;* WI (Pessamit) tshituau [tʃītwāw], *to be stiff;* Silvy (ca. 1680) "tchitaȣaskȣan, *raide, difficile à plier, bois, etc.*" | ANISH ziidawaawigane, *to have a stiff back* (Livesay & Nichols, 2021)

*cīwē

INITIAL

— high-pitched noise

evidence | WC cīwīskihtīw, *to have ringing in one's ears;* ESC cīweyāstan, *to make a whistling noise in the wind;* MC cīwehtawakew, *to have tinnitus;* cīwetāmow, *to wheeze;* SEC cīwekašīš, *dragonfly;* NEC chīwāyāu, *to be quiet and favorable for echoes;* Laure (ca. 1726) "tchiueteu, *le fruit fait du bruit, la pomme en cuisant fait du bruit;*" Silvy (ca. 1680) "tchiȣeachtan, *il bruit, vent;*" "tchiȣesȣ kakȣa, *le porc-épic vesse, siffle en rôtissant*" | ANISH jiiwede, *to sizzle* (Livesay & Nichols, 2021)

ɩ

*ɩc

MEDIAL

— **1** abdomen, belly

— **2** (classifier) soft and hollow

evidence | [1]PC pakocēnēw, *to gut sb;* ESC (Severn) sakicepisow, *to be snared by the*

middle; MC kalakicenew, *to tickle sb at the waist;* pōtācepaliw, *to become bloated;* WI (Pessamit) pakatsheneu [pākātʃēnēw], *to cause sb's belly to burst while handling them;* Silvy (ca. 1680) "ni pik8tchenau, *je l'ouvre par le ventre*" [2]MC tamakocenam, *to squeeze out the contents of sth;* NEC pishkuchāham, *to break sth open (such as a bag) using sth* | [1]ANISH biskijiitaa, *to bend of flex one's body;* dewijiizi, *to have a stomachache* (Livesay & Nichols, 2021) [2]ANISH maagojiibidoon, *to squeeze sth soft and hollow* (Livesay & Nichols, 2021)
origin | PA ***ecy** (Aubin, 1975) see | *ɩciy
discussion | Dialects east of Swampy Cree have extended the sense of this root to "penis" and, in the case of Moose Cree, "vagina."

*ɩciy

FINAL (NOUN, INANIMATE)

— **1** abdomen, belly

— **2** (classifier) soft and hollow

evidence | ESC (Severn) omeciy, *partially digested contents of an animal or fish stomach, dirty laundry;* opihkwāciy, *swim bladder;* MC opihkwāciy, *swim bladder;* EI (Sheshatshiu) umetshi [umētʃī], *partially digested food in the paunch of a caribou or moose* see | *ɩc

*ɩh

FINAL (VERB, TRANSITIVE, ANIMATE, ABSTRACT)

sound change | ē → a

— suffixed to animate intransitive verb stems to form causative verbs

evidence | PC matotisahēw, *to have sb hold a sweat lodge;* sākaskinahēw, *to fill sth up;* MC āhtāsiyānahew, *to change sb's diaper;* SEC pīhtokahew, *to bring sb indoors;* Watkins (1865) "kupuhāo, *v.t.an. He disembarks him, he puts him on shore;*" Fabvre (ca. 1690) "Naska8etahau, *pr(en)dre qlqn. en chemin par terre;*" Silvy (ca. 1680) "ni pit8kahau, *je le porte dedans*" paired with | *ɩhtā², *tā

*ɩhkahs

FINAL (VERB, TRANSITIVE, INANIMATE, DERIVED)

— apply direct heat, cook

evidence | PC itihkasam, *to cook sth thus;* MC tepihkasam, *to cook sth enough;* SEC itihkasam, *to cook sth thus* see | *pihkah
paired with | *ɩhkahsw

*ɩhkahso

FINAL (VERB, ANIMATE, INTRANSITIVE, DERIVED)

— affected by the application of direct heat, cooked

evidence | PC kāspihkasow, *to be cooked until crisp;* WC mīstihkasow, *to be burnt up;* MC tepihkasow, *to be cooked enough;* EI (Unaman-shipit) itikashu [itīkahu], *to be burnt or cooked to a certain extent;* Laure (ca. 1726) "ka katchitchekasut, *victime de flammes de l'enfer;*" "ni-nikustiguanikasun, *je me frise;*" Silvy (ca. 1680) "ni p8tik8s8n, *le feu vole dans ma manche*" see | *pihkah
paired with | *ɩhkahtē

*ɩhkahsw

FINAL (VERB, TRANSITIVE, ANIMATE, DERIVED)

— apply direct heat, cook

evidence | PC itihkaswēw, *to cook sth thus;* MC tepihkaswew, *to cook sth enough;* SEC itihkaswew, *to cook sth thus;* Silvy (ca. 1680) "ni 8ihikass8au, *je rôtis*" see | *pihkah paired with | *ɩhkahs

*ɩhkahtē

FINAL (VERB, INANIMATE, INTRANSITIVE, DERIVED)

— affected by the application of direct heat, cooked

evidence | PC Lacombe (1874) "pikinikkattew, *il est réduit en cendres;*" MC tepihkahtew, *to be cooked enough;* SEC itihkahtew, *to be cooked thus;* WI (Pessamit) utikateu [utəkətēw], *the fire comes from a certain direction or place* see | *pihkah paired with | *ɩhkahso

*ıhkē

FINAL (VERB, ANIMATE, INTRANSITIVE, CONCRETE)

— make

evidence | PC mīwatihkēw, *to make a sacred bundle;* MC cīmānihkew, *to make a canoe;* SEC asāmihkawew, *to make snowshoes for sb;* Silvy (ca. 1680) "nit'achabikan, *je fais un arc*" origin | PA ***ehkē** (Aubin, 1975)

*ıhki

FINAL (NOUN, ABSTRACT)

— **1** forms the locative when suffixed to nouns

— **2** forms the simulative when suffixed to nouns

evidence | MC mīwatihk, *in the bag;* AT pecotcik [peššotcihk], *close;* (Opitciwan, Joey Awashish) tcimaniki [cīmānihki], *in the canoe;* SEC nipīhc ispokwan, *to taste like water;* WI (Pessamit) assit [ssīt], *on the ground, on land;* Laure (ca. 1726) "nitaspiskuechimunitch nit-atutapin, *je suis assis dessus (l'oreiller);*" Silvy (ca. 1680) "agamits, *l'autre bord*" origin | PA ***enki** compare | *ımihki discussion | Fieldwork with elderly Opitciwan speakers in 2010 confirmed the retention of the archaic form **ıhki** as a productive suffix. New investigations in 2023 with a younger speaker reconfirmed this finding but also provided evidence that the archaic form is in competition with the shorter form **ıhk** for nouns and that the latter is the only form used for particles. Michelson (1939) reports the use of this archaic form in a particle for the dialect spoken at Opitciwan. Other Atikamekw communities use only the shorter form.

*ıhkop

MEDIAL

— bush, thicket

evidence | PC piskohkopāw, *to be a clump of willows;* MC tapahtihkopāw, *to be a short bushed;* nehkopāw, *to be a bushy point;* WI (Pessamit) ishikupau [īʃəkupāw], *to be a stretch of alders extending in a certain direction or having certain characteristics*

*ıhkot[1] (~ *ıhkoc)

FINAL (VERB, TRANSITIVE, INANIMATE, DERIVED)

— carve

evidence | PC masinihkotam, *to carve sth;* MC aciwihkotam, *to whittle sth down;* itihkotam, *to carve sth thus;* SEC wayihkotam, *to shape sth by carving* paired with | *ıhkot[2]

*ıhkot[2] (~ *ıhkoš)

FINAL (VERB, TRANSITIVE, ANIMATE, DERIVED)

— carve

evidence | PC masinihkotēw, *to carve sth;* MC itihkotew, *to carve sth thus;* SEC wayihkotew, *to shape sth by carving* paired with | *ıhkot[1]

*ıhkw[1] (~ *ıhko)

INITIAL (NOUN, ANIMATE)

— louse

evidence | PC ihkwa, *a louse;* AT iko [ihko], *a louse;* SEC ihkʷ, *a louse;* Silvy (ca. 1680) "ik8a, *pou*" | ANISH ikwa, *a louse* (Livesay & Nichols, 2021); MENO ehkuah, *louse;* otɛ·hkoman, *one's lice* see | *ıhkw[2], *tihkom

*ıhkw[2]

MEDIAL (NOUN INCORPORATION)

— louse

evidence | Silvy (ca. 1680) "ni pachkamik8an 3. -e8, *je mange un pou entre les dents*" origin | Old Cree ***ıhkwa** see | *ıhkw[1] compare | *tihkom

*ıhkwahši

FINAL (VERB, ANIMATE, INTRANSITIVE, CONCRETE)

— affected by sleep or sleepiness

evidence | PC kawihkwasiw, *to fall asleep;* MC šākōtihkwašiw, *to be overcome by sleepiness;* AT a:piccikkošši-, *to be continually sleeping, be always in bed* (Béland, 1978);

SEC cišihkwašiw, *to be sleepy;* WI (Pessamit) nekatikushu [nēkātəkuʃu], *to suffer from insomnia;* Silvy (ca. 1680) "ni kaȣikȣachin, *je me rendors*" | ANISH gawingwashi, *to fall asleep* (Livesay & Nichols, 2021); MENO sɛ·kehkuaqsew, *to have a nightmare* origin | PA ***enkwaʔši** (Aubin, 1975) see | *ıhkwašt, *i²

*ıhkwašt (~ *ıhkwahš)

PREFINAL

— affected by sleep or sleepiness

evidence | PC nōhtēhkwastimēw, *to make sb sleepy;* SEC cišihkwašiw, *to be sleepy* | MENO sɛ·kehkuaqsew, *to have a nightmare* origin | PA ***enkwaʔθ** see | *ıhkwahši, *ıhkwaštim

*ıhkwaštim

FINAL (VERB, TRANSITIVE, ANIMATE, CONCRETE)

— affect with sleep or sleepiness

evidence | PC nōhtēhkwastimēw, *to make sb sleepy;* SEC koštācihkwaštimikow, *to have a nightmare because of sth;* WI (Pessamit) nekatikushtimeu [nēkātəkustəmēw], *to prevent sb from sleeping* origin | PA ***enkwaʔθem** see | *ıhkwašt, *ım³

*ıhkwāmi

FINAL (VERB, ANIMATE, INTRANSITIVE, CONCRETE)

— sleep

evidence | PC mītihkwāmiw, *to defecate in one's sleep;* MC ayamihkwāmiw, *to speak in one's sleep;* SEC (Waswanipi) itihkwāmiw, *to sleep thus;* Silvy (ca. 1680) "ni chitchikȣamin, *je pisse au lit en dormant*" origin | PA ***enkwāme** (Aubin, 1975)

*ıhp

FINAL (NOUN, ABSTRACT)

sound change | ē → a

— suffixed to animate intransitive verb stems, forming nouns that generally refer to objects or places where particular activities are performed

evidence | PC onikāhp, *portage;* MC mātokahp, *abandoned camp;* AT akop, *robe;* SEC āmiyihkahp, *fishing site for spawning fish;* NEC āshkihp, *place where one hunts beaver by chiseling into a beaver lodge;* WI (Pessamit) mitshuap, *dwelling;* Laure (ca. 1726) "matugapi, *massure, vieille cabane;*" Silvy (ca. 1680) "matȣgap, *cabane délaissée*" compare | *ın², *n¹, *win

*ıhs

MEDIAL, FINAL (NOUN)

— useful metal or rock

evidence | PC atos, *arrow;* matotisahēw, *to have sb hold a sweat lodge;* AT ato:ss, *arrow head* (Béland, 1978); SEC matotisān, *sweatlodge;* NEC mītunisān, *rock used for pounding dry fish into powder;* WI (Pessamit) matish [mātəʃ], *knife used for bloodletting; gunflint;* Laure (ca. 1726) "pakamichanasku, *coin, massue de bois;*" Fabvre (ca. 1690) "Matis *pl.* matisets/k, *pierres à fuzil;*" "Mitȣnīsan, *Pierre de desȣs à piler;*" Silvy (ca. 1680) "matȣtisan, *suerie;*" "pagamisanaskȣ, *maillet, marteau;*" "atȣs, *flèche*" | ANISH madoodison, *a sweat lodge* (Livesay & Nichols, 2021); MESK mātesi, *knife;* MIAMI maalhsi, a knife (ILDA, 2017) compare | *ıhsēk

*ıhsēk

MEDIAL (CLASSIFIER)

— **1** useful metal or rock

— **2** rock face, cliff

evidence | ¹AT atisekaham [ātisekaham], *verrouiller ou barrer quelque chose;* EI (Unaman-shipit) tatushetshipanu [tātuhētʃɨpanu], *to be split, speaking of sheet-metal;* EI (Sheshatshiu) atishekaueu [ātəʃēkāwēw], *to lock sb in;* Laure (ca. 1726) "ni-patabichekahen 3. -himu, *je rive le clou;*" "ni-teuessekaikan 3. -tseu, *sonner, je sonne la cloche;*" Fabvre (ca. 1690) "Kaȣisekipȣtāgan, *une lime à limer;*" Silvy (ca. 1680) "mokmanisekȣ, *verge de fer*" ²MC išpisekāw, *high cliff;* SEC wīhpisekāw, *to be a hollow in a cliff;* NEC ā itisākāshish, *place name in*

Wemindji territory; WI (Pessamit) ne<u>shek</u>au [nēʃēkāw], *rock face jutting out into the water;* pimit<u>ishek</u>au [pmətəʃēkāw], *to be a rock face across the route;* lal<u>ishet</u> [lāləʃēt], *along the foot of a cliff;* EI uema<u>shek</u>aimᵘ [wēmāʃēkējm], *to go beyond a cliff on foot;* Watkins (1865) "Min<u>isāk</u>, *n.in. A rock, a rocky island;*" Laure (ca. 1726) "pitchitau<u>icheg</u>au, *(fleuve) qui coule entre deux chaînes de montagnes;*" Silvy (ca. 1680) "papeskȣ<u>seg</u>ȣ, *lieu plein de rochers*" compare | *ɩhs discussion | A tantalizing clue to the origin of this root is the Naskapi word *isaakw,* 'iron, metal,' and the Eastern Innu (Mushuau) cognate *nishek*ᵘ, 'iron.' Without further evidence these words are precluded from being etymologically related. In the end, the above root may be a combination of Old Cree ***ɩhs** (query, PA ***ehsy**, or ***eʔsy**) and the post-medial accretion ***ak**.

*ɩhsihtā

FINAL (VERB, ANIMATE, INTRANSITIVE, CONCRETE)

— portage a canoe

evidence | MC lālakāme<u>štāw</u>, *to portage along the shore;* AT (Opitciwan, Joey Awashish) nasipe<u>ctaw</u> [nāzipēšštāw], *to portage a canoe down the bank;* (Manawan, Paul Niquay) matape<u>ctaw</u> [matāpēšštāw], *to reach a body of water while portaging a canoe;* SEC (Oujé-Bougoumou) kaskame<u>štā</u>kan, *place name, literally "shortcut portage"* (Bishop, 2023); NEC īt<u>isihtā</u>u, *to carry one's canoe in a certain direction;* NSK atim<u>isiihtaa</u>w, *to portage a canoe in the opposite direction;* naat<u>isiihtaa</u>w, *to go to portage a canoe;* WI (Pessamit) nashipe<u>shta</u>u [nāʃəpēstāw], *to go down to the water's edge while portaging;* EI (Unamanshipit) [pētɨstāw], *to come portaging one's canoe;* Fabvre (ca. 1690) "nat<u>isita</u>n, *aller au lac, y prendre castors*" | ANISH pim<u>isatò</u>, *to carry a canoe* (McGregor, 2004)

*ɩhsimo

FINAL (VERB, ANIMATE, INTRANSITIVE, CONCRETE)

— from or pertaining to one's throat, generally in reference to drinking

evidence | PC mik<u>isimo</u>w, *to bark;* MC mik<u>isimo</u>w, *to bark;* tep<u>isimo</u>w, *to quench one's thirst;* AT (Opitciwan, Joey Awashish) tep<u>isimo</u> [tēpissimow], *to quench one's thirst;* SEC nōhtā<u>simo</u>w, *to not drink enough;* tep<u>isimo</u>w, *to quench one's thirst;* NEC tāko<u>simū</u>, *to choke on a liquid;* WI (Pessamit) tep<u>ishimu</u> [tēpəʃəmu], *to quench one's thirst;* Laure (ca. 1726) "ni-téb<u>isimu</u>n, *je me rassasie de boire de l'eau*" | cf. MENO tɛ·p<u>eqse</u>w, *to drink enough, to quench one's thirt* compare | *ɩmo

*ɩhš

FINAL (NOUN, DIMINUTIVE)

sound change | v + ɩhš → v̄hš

— conveys a sense of smallness, generally use for things that tend to cluster or group together

evidence | PC ēs<u>is</u>, *mollusk;* mīn<u>is</u>, *a berry;* WC manicō<u>s</u>, *a bug;* ESC pineshī<u>sh</u>, *a bird;* MC nīpī<u>š</u>ak, *leaves;* pilešī<u>š</u>ak, *birds of a smaller species such as songbirds;* AT (Opitciwan, Monique Awashish) oka<u>c</u>a [okāšša], *a walleye;* (Wemotaci, Jeannette Coocoo) potco<u>c</u> [pōcoš], *tadpole;* (Wemotaci, Nicole Petiquay) nipi<u>c</u>a [nīpišša], *leaves;* SEC manicō<u>š</u>ac, *vermin, bugs;* mīn<u>iš</u>a, *berries; blueberries;* nīpī<u>š</u>ac, *leaves;* WI (Pessamit) piku<u>sh</u> [pukuʃ] *biting midge;* Silvy (ca. 1680) "pirechi<u>ch</u>, *petit oiseau*" compare | *ɩšihš

*ɩhšawē

INITIAL

— angled edge, wedge-shaped

evidence | PC <u>isawē</u>hkwak, *glover's needle;* MC <u>ayišawe</u>sitepalihow, *to invert or evert one's feet;* AT acawe-caponikan [aššawe-šāponikan], *glover's needle;* SEC šawehkokʷ, *leather needle;* NEC ishiwātāwihkāu, *to be a narrow point of elevated ground;* WI (Pessamit) ishueiau [ʃwējāw], *to has an edge, ridge, or crest;* Laure (ca. 1726) "nit-ichauekuten, *je coupe en carré;*" Silvy (ca. 1680) "aïcha8eïau, *cela est quarré*" | ANISH ashaweshk, *sword;* ashawese, *to tilt over or flip* (Livesay & Nichols, 2021)

*ɩht¹ (~ *t)

INITIAL (VERB, ANIMATE, INTRANSITIVE)

— happen, fare

evidence | PC ihtiw, *to fare so;* MC ihtiw, *to fare thus;* SEC ayihtiw, *to do thus* NEC ā ihtik, *to fare thus;* Fabvre (ca. 1690) "nititin 2 kititin 3 t8a *faire fais*" | ANISH ayindi, *to have sth the matter* (Livesay & Nichols, 2021) paired with | *in¹ discussion | Most modern dialects have reshaped the above verb stem from Old Cree ***ɩht** to reflexes of ***ɩhtɩ**, reassigning the epenthetic vowel *ɩ—obtained from the conjunct or the independent first- or second- person forms—as a final without transposition. However, in NEC, as demonstrated by Collette (2021) and the above example, the Old Cree conjunct indicative inflection for the third-person singular for stems ending in consonants continues to be used, providing evidence for the above form.

*ɩht²

MEDIAL

— ear

evidence | PC kakēpihtēw, *to be deaf;* Lacombe (1874) "tābitebisun, ak, *pendant d'oreille;*" MC osihtew, *to have hearing;* SEC cipihtew, *to be deaf;* Silvy (ca. 1680) "nit"apichichitanach, *j'ai de petites oreilles;*" "ni kistiteh8n, *je me perce l'oreille*" | ANISH gagiibishe, *to be deaf* (Livesay & Nichols, 2021); MENO ke·skɛhtɛsosow, *to cut off one's own ear* compare | *ɩht³

*ɩht³

FINAL (VERB, TRANSITIVE, INANIMATE, CONCRETE)

— hear

evidence | PC tēpihtam, *to be near enough to hear sth;* MC itihtam, *to hear sth thus;* SEC miyohtam, *to like the sound of sth* compare | *ɩht² paired with | *ɩhtaw

*ɩht⁴ (~ *ɩhtak)

MEDIAL (NOUN INCORPORATION)

— wood

evidence | PC kīhkēhtakāhk, *in the corner;* WC āwacinihtīw, *to haul loads of fire-wood;* MC tāhtāškahihtew, *to split firewood;* manihtew, *to gather or chop firewood;* kāsīhtakinam, *to wipe the floor clean;* SEC kāwihtakāw, *to be rough wood or floor;* mōhtew, *a woodworm;* NEC mustihtic, *on the floor;* misihtikw, *a whole log;* WI (Pessamit) nikuteu [nəkutēw], *to chop firewood;* ititakau [ītətəkāw], *to have a certain appearance, speaking of firewood or worked wood;* Silvy (ca. 1680) "ni 8ipitagahen, *je troue, je creuse*" | ANISH bagidinise, *to put wood on the fire* (Livesay & Nichols, 2021); nibiiwisagaa, *to be a wet floor* (Livesay & Nichols, 2021); MIAMI manehsee-, *to gather firewood* (ILDA, 2017) origin | PA ***mehθ-**, *firewood* (Aubin, 1975; Hewson, 1993) see | *miht², *ak² compare | *āhtak

*ɩhtaw (~ *ɩhtā)

FINAL (VERB, TRANSITIVE, ANIMATE, CONCRETE)

— hear

evidence | PC nahihtawēw, *to obey sb;* SEC itihtawew, *to hear sb thus;* Silvy (ca. 1680) "ni nisit8ta8au, *je l'entends*" | MIAMI palehtaw-, *to mishear sb* (ILDA, 2017) see | *ɩht³, *aw³ paired with | *ɩht³

***ɩhtā¹** (~ ***ɩhc, *ɩhtw**)

FINAL (VERB, ANIMATE, INTRANSITIVE, ABSTRACT)

— forms causative verbs

evidence | PC āhkwatihtāw, *to freeze sth;* maskawāskatihcikēw, *to freeze things;* MC mawatihtāw, *to visit sth;* SEC maškawatihtāw, *to freeze sth;* EI (Sheshatshiu) mashkutitau [məʃkūtītāw], *to freeze sth* paired with | *ɩm³ discussion | The ***ɩhtw** allomorph surfaces only for further derivation when suffixing either the antipassive ***ā** or the benefactive ***aw**. Its origin predates what is otherwise a loss of morphological distinction in Old Cree between Proto-Algonquian transitive inanimate verb class II and animate intransitive verbs ending in ***ā** (cf. Pentland, 1999). Note that contemporary dialects have all contracted ***ɩhtw** + ***aw** to a reflex of ***ɩhtow**, but the underlying form is revealed when vowel-lengthening processes occur, resulting in reflexes of ***ɩhtwā** as expected.

***ɩhtā²** (~ ***ɩhc, *ɩhtw**)

FINAL (VERB, ANIMATE, INTRANSITIVE, ABSTRACT)

sound change | ē → a

— suffixed to animate intransitive verb stems to form causative verbs

evidence | PC matotisahtāw, *to take sth into the sweat lodge;* sākaskinahtāw, *to fill sth;* MC āpihtawaškinahtāw, *to fill sth halfway;* masinahikepalihtwāw, *to type;* SEC ayamihtāw, *to read sth;* ayamihtowew, *to read sth for sb;* pimipayihtwāsow, *to run a business for oneself;* ayamihcikew, *to read; to pray* paired with | *ɩh discussion | The ***ɩhtw** allomorph surfaces only for further derivation when suffixing either the antipassive ***ā** or the benefactive ***aw**. Its origin predates what is otherwise a loss of morphological distinction in Old Cree between Proto-Algonquian transitive inanimate verb class II and animate intransitive verbs ending in ***ā** (cf. Pentland, 1999). Note that contemporary dialects have all contracted ***ɩhtw** + ***aw** to a reflex of ***ɩhtow**, but the underlying form is revealed when vowel-lengthening processes occur, resulting in reflexes of ***ɩhtwā** as expected.

***ɩhtāko** (~ ***ɩhtākw**)

PREFINAL

— make sound

evidence | PC miyohtākosiw, *to have a pleasant voice;* MC nōhtākohtāw, *to turn the sound on;* SEC itihtākwan, *to sound thus;* Silvy (ca. 1680) "ni maskassitag8sin, *je discours admirablement*" see | *ɩhtaw, *ɩko

***ɩkē**

FINAL (VERB, ANIMATE, INTRANSITIVE, ABSTRACT)

sound change | ...aw + ɩkē → ākē

— forms the antipassive when suffixed to transitive animate verb stems ending in *aw

evidence | PC natotamākēw, *to request sth from people;* MC paskilākew, *to win;* SEC nātamācew, *to assist* compare | *ā², *kē², *kēmo, *wē²

***ɩkit**

FINAL (VERB, ANIMATE, INTRANSITIVE, CONCRETE)

— have a certain size

evidence | PC ispīhcikitiw, *be a certain size;* MC mišikitiw, *to be big;* AT itikitiw, *be a certain size;* SEC ispišicitiw, *be a certain size* | ANISH inigini, *be a certain size* (Livesay & Nichols, 2021); MESK inekinwa, *be a certain size;* MIAMI ilekili-, *be a certain size* (ILDA, 2017) origin | PA ***ekeθ** (***-ekeθe**, Aubin, 1975) discussion | In most modern dialects, this root has been regularized as a prefinal followed by the epenthetic vowel ***ɩ**, the latter of which is treated as a verb final without transposition. However, in WI, as demonstrated by Collette (2021), the Old Cree conjunct indicative flexion for the third-person singular for stems ending in consonants continues to be used, providing evidence for the above form.

*ɩko (~ *ɩkw)

PREFINAL

sound change | aw + ɩko → āko

— forms the mediopassive when suffixed to transitive animate verb sterms

evidence | WC macinikwan, *to be bad footing;* MC tipahamākosiw, *to be paid for sth one does;* SEC miyonikwan, *to offer good footing;* WI (Pessamit) aimikushiu [īmīkuʃīw], *to arrange to be spoken to by sb;* Silvy (ca. 1680) "8atenig8an, *la neige porte*"

*ɩkosi

FINAL (VERB, ANIMATE, INTRANSITIVE, ABSTRACT)

sound change | aw + ɩkosi → ākosi

— forms the mediopassive when suffixed to transitive animate verb stems

evidence | PC itihtākosiw, *to sound thus;* MC milonākosiw, *to look good;* AT peššona:kosi-, *to be close* (Béland, 1978); SEC cišitewinikosiw, *to have a fever;* Laure (ca. 1726) "niui-mugusin, *je veux être mangé*" see | *ɩko, *ɩsi

*ɩkwan

FINAL (VERB, INANIMATE, INTRANSITIVE, ABSTRACT)

sound change | aw + ɩkosi → ākwan

— forms the mediopassive when suffixed to transitive animate verb stems

evidence | PC itihtākwan, *to sound thus;* MC kāwinikwan, *to feel rough to the touch;* SEC miyonākwan, *to look good* see | *ɩko, *an²

*ɩm¹ (~ *ɩh)

MEDIAL (NOUN INCORPORATION)

— path

evidence | PC mitihtam, *to track sth;* MC mitimew, *to follow a path;* AT mitimeapiskipariw [mitimeyāpiskipariw], *to follow train tracks driving;* NEC mitihtāu, *to track sb;* WI (Pessamit) mitimepatau [mətəmēpətāw], *to follow a path running or driving;* Watkins (1865) "Mitịtāo, *v.t.an. He tracks him;*" "Mitimāo, *v.i.3. He follows (as in a track or path);*" Laure (ca. 1726) "ni-mititau, *je suis la piste;*" Silvy (ca. 1680) "ni mitiman meskanau, *je suis le chemin*" | ANISH Nicholas (ca. 1670) "nimitira, *je le suis*" (Daviault, 1994); MENO metɛ·hnɛw, *to track sb;* metɛ·mow, *to follow a path or trail* origin | PA epenthetic ***e** + ***myēwi**, *road* (Aubin, 1975) limited to | *mit see | *ām², *mēw

*ɩm²

MEDIAL, FINAL (NOUN, ANIMATE)

— snowshoe

evidence | PC asām, *snowshoe;* ESC atiman, *a snowshoe harness;* MC aškimātew, *to lace sth, speaking of a snowshoe;* AT akimaskw [ākimāskʷ], *ash tree (fraxinus spp.);* SEC nōtimēw, *to walk without snowshoes;* WI (Pessamit) pishimeu [pəʃəmēw], *to put a line through holes pierced around a frame;* Silvy (ca. 1680) "mak8at8m, *pl.* -t8mak, *raquettes rondes*" see | *ahsām¹, *aškimē, *atiman, *ākim¹, *pišimē, *nōtimē discussion | The majority of forms onto which this root is affixed would appear to be cranberry morphemes if isolated. However, a couple of words suggest that this root continued to be productive in Old Cree. Its existence is therefore postulated, if only tentatively. Note that reflexes of ***nōtɩmēwa** are widely attested and the initial is likely parsable as ***nōt**, from PA ***nōθ**. Another productive example can be found in an early variant of Old Cree ***mahkwatoy**, which Jesuit sources from the sixteenth and seventeenth centuries record as "mak8at8m" and "makuatum," parsable as ***mahkwatoy** + ***ɩm**. The medial also figures in Old Cree ***mōhkomāni**, "knife."

***ɩm³ (~ *m)**

FINAL (VERB, TRANSITIVE, ANIMATE, ABSTRACT)

— forms causative verbs

evidence | PC nōhtēhkwastimēw, *to make sb sleepy;* MC pāhkwāštimew, *to dry sth in the wind;* akohcimew, *soak in water;* SEC teštacišimew, *to lie sb down with trunk elevated* paired with | *ɩtā, *ɩhtā¹ discussion | The presence of allomorphy without any obvious conditioning environment suggests these two forms have different origins. However, we propose them together here as allomorphs as they are semantically identical and both pair up with ***ɩtā** or ***ɩhtā**.

***ɩm⁴**

FINAL (NOUN, INANIMATE)

sound change | ē → a

— a place

evidence | WC waðawītimiskwāht, *just outside the doorway;* MC walawītim, *outside;* išpimīwan, *to have a second storey;* SEC oskotim, *a beaver dam;* NEC wiyiwītimishkwāhch, *just outside the doorway;* WI (Pessamit) ishpimitakᵘ [ʃpəmətukʷ], *upper floor* discussion | This root appears to alternate with ***tim**, though it is unclear whether the ***t** precedes the above root or belongs to an allomorph.

***ɩmihki**

FINAL (NOUN, ABSTRACT)

sound change | ē → a

— forms locative nouns when suffixed to certain initials

evidence | PC māmihk, *downriver;* WC pīhtokamīhk, *indoors;* AT ntimik, *en amont;* MC walawītimihk, *outside;* SEC išpimihc, *above;* WI pitukamit, *à l'intérieur (d'une habitation, d'un édifice)* see | *ɩm⁴, *ɩhki discussion | This root appears to alternate with ***timihki**, though it is unclear whether the ***t** precedes the above root or belongs to an allomorph.

***ɩmihšiy**

FINAL (NOUN, INANIMATE)

— shrub

evidence | AT (Opitciwan, Joey Awashish) piremici [pirēmiššiy], *any number of small evergreen shrubs of similar appearance such as the Labrador tea and sheep laurel;* mikkwa:pemiššya:ttikw, *dogwood* (Béland, 1978); SEC maskomišiy, *mountain ash;* NEC miskumishī, *mountain ash;* WI (Pessamit) pilemishi [pəlēməʃī], *generic term for Labrador tea and sheep laurel;* Laure (ca. 1726) "uikupimichi *pl.* -a, *bâton de bois blanc*" | ANISH bagaaniminzh, *a hazelnut bush* (Livesay & Nichols, 2021); Cuoq (1886) "Wikopiminj, *arbre à tille, tilleul, bois-blanc du Canada;*" MENO aski·qtemi·hsyak, *white oaks;* MESK mīshimishi, *bur oak* origin | PA ***eminšy** (Hewson, 1993) compare | *akahšiy

***ɩmo**

FINAL (VERB, ANIMATE, INTRANSITIVE, CONCRETE)

— vocalize

evidence | PC kisīmow, *to speak angrily;* pwātimow, *to speak Dakota;* WC nīmow, *to growl;* MC ililīmow, *to speak Cree;* SEC ayeskomow, *tired from vocalizing (e.g., wailing);* Laure (ca. 1726) "n-utabenatkimun 3. -tekimu [*sic*], *je parle abénaqui;*" Silvy (ca. 1680) "nit'haïachtchimem8n, *je parle gaspésien*" see | *m³, *o

***ɩn¹**

FINAL (NOUN, INANIMATE, CONCRETE)

— island

evidence | SEC Mōson, *moose island (Moose Factory Island);* ciyāškonāpiskʷ, *gull island;* EI (Unaman-shipit) Tshiashkunapishkᵘ [tʃjāhkunāpɨhkʷ], *Durocher Lake, literally, 'gull island'* origin | akin to PA ***menehsyi** see | *min[3] compare | *ɩnak

*ɩn[2]

FINAL (NOUN, ABSTRACT)

sound change | ē → a

— suffixed to animate intransitive verbs and forms nouns that generally refer to objects

evidence | AT minikwakan, *tasse, verre;* MC otāmahikan, *hammer;* SEC pišiman, *lace around snowshoe frame from which the netting is weaved;* NEC uchikwāchikin, *a fish hook;* Laure (ca. 1726) "takuahigan, *mortier, vase à piler;*" Fabvre (ca. 1690) "chik8man, *meslange de bluets et uiandes;*" Silvy (ca. 1680) "pi8ichigan, *retaille d'étoffe, de peau, etc.*" compare | *ɩhp, *n[1], *win

*ɩn[3]

FINAL (VERB, TRANSITIVE, CONCRETE)

— **1** by use of hand

— **2** travel on foot

evidence | [1]PC itinam, *to hold sth thus by hand;* WC aciwāpīkinam, *to shorten sth string-like manually;* MC nōtimatinam, *shape soft substance into a ball;* SEC wewacikwenitowac, *to hug one another;* Laure (ca. 1726) "ni-patchitinan 3. -nau, *je le sème;*" Silvy (ca. 1680) "ni mitchiminen, *je retiens, je soutiens*" [2]PC Lacombe (1874) "oskinam, *il vient de passer (sa piste fraîche);*" WC pisikwāhcinam, *to misstep on ground;* macinikwan, *to be bad footing;* MC kotāwākonenam, *to sink in the snow as one walks;* itinikwan, *to offer such a footing, speaking of terrain;* SEC pīcinam, *to make the water turbid from walking through it;* Laure (ca. 1726) "etagunatsinamu, *piste sur la neige;*" Fabvre (ca. 1690) "Nassitaminen, *au(oi)r peine à marcher par chemin facheux;*" Silvy (ca. 1680) "ni t8anen, ni t8at8anen, *j'enfonce dans la neige*" | [1]MENO āpenam, *to untangle sth;* MESK sakikwēnēwa, *to take or hold sb by the neck* origin | PA ***en** (Aubin, 1975)

*ɩn[4]

FINAL (VERB, INANIMATE, INTRANSITIVE, ABSTRACT)

— forms stative verbs

evidence | PC āhkwatin, *be frozen;* WC apiscākamisin, *to be a little quantity of liquid;* MC kīšowākamin, *to be warm liquid;* Silvy (ca. 1680) "atin, *il est pourri*" see | *atin[2], *htin[1], *htin[2] compare | *an[2]

*ɩnak (~ *ānak)

MEDIAL (NOUN INCORPORATION)

— island

evidence | WC iskwānakāw, *island measures a certain length;* MC apišānakāw, *small island;* SEC mahkānakāw, *to be a large island;* NEC piskunikāu, *to be an island with a hill;* wīpichīnakʷ, *walrus island;* EI (Unaman-shipit) Tshiashkunakua, *Tshiashkunakua Islands, literally 'gull islands;'* Laure (ca. 1726) "auachanatch, *derrière l'île*" see | *ɩn[1], *ak[2]

*ɩnawē

FINAL (VERB, ANIMATE, INTRANSITIVE, CONCRETE)

— cook

evidence | PC paminawasow, *to prepare a meal, to cook;* NEC piminiwitāu, *to cook for sb;* EI (Sheshatshiu) itinueu [itnwēw], *to cook thus;* Laure (ca. 1726) "paminauaniu, *cuisine, apprêt du manger;*" Silvy (ca. 1680) "ni pamina8an 3. -e8, *je fais la cuisine*"

*ɩnāhki

FINAL (NOUN, ABSTRACT)

— in the land of the, among the

evidence | PC pwātināhk, *in Dakota country;* MC ililīnāhk, *among the people;* SEC iyinīnāhc, *among the Cree* | ANISH Cuoq (1886) "Natowenang, *chez les Iroquois*" see | *ɩhki

***ɩp** (~ ***ɩpēk, *ɩpēh, *ɩpēš**)

MEDIAL (NOUN INCORPORATION)

— **1** water

— **2** drink

evidence | PC kāskipāsow, *to shave oneself;* kisīpēkīw, *to bathe;* MC otāmipekaham, *strike surface of the water;* kisīpekinam, *to wash sth;* šōpesam, *to warm up sth liquid;* šōpeštew, *to be warm liquid;* SEC sīnipātam, *wring water out of sth;* wīhcipew, *to like drinking alcoholic beverages;* NEC akutipāyāu, *dew;* WI (Pessamit) mushepeiau [mūʃēpējāw], *open water in winter;* atipeu [ātəpēw], *to be blocked by the rising tide;* Laure (ca. 1726) "ni-chibiban -beu, *je porte bien la boisson;*" "ni-tchitabetchissen, *j'enfonce avec le pied;*" Fabvre (ca. 1690) "Kataȣatibeachiȣ, *fleuue, r(ivière) belle sans sault, riuiere sans trop de rapide(s);*" Silvy (ca. 1680) "abitȣchtinebeȣ, *il est mi-plein, v.g. vase;*" "ȣassipechteȣ, *l'eau reluit*" | ANISH agawaatebiigisin, *to be reflected in the water* (Livesay & Nichols, 2021); MIAMI kiihpoopii-, *to have enough to drink* (ILDA, 2017) origin | PA ***nepyi** (Hewson, 1993), optionally followed by post-medial accretion ***ak** to form Old Cree ***ɩpēk**. Its allomorph ***ɩpēh** occurs when followed by heat finals ***s**, ***sw**, and ***so**, while ***ɩpēš** occurs when followed by heat final ***tē**. see | *nipiy, *ak², *ē

***ɩpēštān**

FINAL (VERB, INANIMATE, INTRANSITIVE, CONCRETE)

— rain

evidence | PC tahkipēstāw, *cold rain;* MC atimipeštān, *drizzle retreats;* AT actepectan [āštepeštān], *la pluie cesse;* SEC mamenipeštān, *scattered showers;* Laure (ca. 1726) "mamatchipestanu, *la pluie tombe dur;*" Silvy (ca. 1680) "papakibestan, *il pleut un peu d'une nuée grosse*" origin | Old Cree ***ɩpēk** + ***tān** see | *ɩp, *tān²

***ɩpiy**

FINAL (NOUN INCORPORATION)

— **1** water

— **2** body of water

evidence | MC amiskopiy, *beaver pond;* AT arisipī, *drinking water;* SEC Wāswānipiy, *torch-fishing lake;* SEC (coastal) Apihtipiy, *flint lake, place name known as Lac Abitibi in French;* Watkins (1865) "Tàkipe, *n.in. Cold water*" origin | PA ***nepyi** (Hewson, 1993) see | *nipiy

***ɩr**

INITIAL

— allow, tolerate

evidence | PC iyinamawēw, *to allow sb to do sth;* MC ilinam, *to allow sth;* Laure (ca. 1726) "eka irinauinan ka sagutchihiguiats, *ne nous y laisse pas succomber;*" Silvy (ca. 1680) "nit'iriten, *je souffre, j'endure*"

***ɩraman**

MEDIAL, FINAL (NOUN INCORPORATION)

— ochre

evidence | Laure (ca. 1726) "ka mitcheturamanemagatch, *qui est de plusieurs couleurs;*" Silvy (ca. 1680) "kastiteraman, *peinture noire*" | MIAMI oonsaalamoni siipiiwi, *Salamonie River* (ILDA, 2017) origin | PA ***eraman** see | *wiraman

***ɩrēm**

INITIAL

— many, much

evidence | NEC iyāmh, *a great deal, a large portion, too much;* WI (Pessamit) alem [lèːm], *many, a large quantity;* EI (Mamit) anem [anēma], *many, a large quantity;* Watkins (1865) "yāma, *adv. A great deal;*" "Yammaispuyew, *v.imp. It requires a great deal;*" Laure (ca. 1726) "irima, *beaucoup, grandement;*" Silvy (ca. 1680) "irima, *beaucoup*" | ANISH Nicholas (ca. 1670) "irima, *beaucoup*" (Daviault, 1994) limited to | *a

*ɩrihtē

INITIAL (VERB, INANIMATE, INTRANSITIVE)

— be bare ground as snow melts

evidence | PC iyihtēw, *to thaw;* MC ilihtew, *to be bare ground as the snow melts;* EI (Ekuanitshit) initeu [īnītēw], *to be exposed earth when the snow melts;* Silvy (ca. 1680) "irite8, *il n'y a plus de neige*" | ANISH Cuoq (1886) "inite, *elle est découverte (en parlant de la terre, quand la neige est fondue)*"

*ɩrikā

INITIAL

— inflame, provoke

evidence | AT airikamew [āyirikāmēw], *provoke sb verbally;* SEC āyiyikānesiw, *to suffer from an infection;* āyiyikāhēw, *provoke sb;* NEC īyikānāsiu & āyikānāsiu, *to be infected;* WI (Pessamit) ailikaneshu [jājləkānēʃu], *to have an infected or inflamed wound;* ailikameu [jājləkāmēw], *narguer verbalement qlqn;* Laure (ca. 1726) "tapue tchiui-airikahin, *tu pousses ma patience au bout;*" Fabvre (ca. 1690) "Aïats iriganēsin i8, *deuenir plus mal, desesperé;*" Silvy (ca. 1680) "nit'aïrigahau, *je le gausse*"

*ɩrikohko (~ *ɩrikohkw)

INITIAL

— such an amount, size, extent, or degree

evidence | PC iyikohk, *so much, to such a degree or extent; until; more;* WC iðikohk, *as much as; until;* ESC (Severn) inikohk, *as much as; until; up to;* MC ilikohk, *a certain quantity, extent, or degree;* AT irikokosiw [irikohkoziw], *to be a certain size* | ANISH inigokobagad, *to has leaves of such a size* (Livesay & Nichols, 2021); MENO enekoh, *so much, so many, so big*

*ɩrin (~ *ɩrih)

INITIAL

— common, ordinary

evidence | PC iyinisip, *mallard duck;* MC ililimin, *blueberry;* AT irināhtik^w, *maple tree;* SEC iyihkway, *eastern paper birch;* (inland) iyinascisin, *moccasin;* (coastal) iyiyames, *freshwater whitefish;* NEC iyihpī, *drinking water;* EI (Sheshatshiu) innasht [īnnāst], *balsam fir;* Laure (ca. 1726) "iripi, *boisson, eau pure;*" Silvy (ca. 1680) "irinikoman, *fer, métal;*" "irinatik8, *caribou*" origin | PA ***eren** (***elen**, Aubin, 1975) see | *ɩriniw

*ɩriniw

INITIAL (NOUN, ANIMATE)

— **1** man

— **2** human being

evidence | PC iyiniw, *a man; a person; a First Nations person;* iyinīwiw, *to heal;* iyinīhkahēw, *to heal sb;* MC ililīmow, *to speak Cree;* ililīskāw, *to be many people;* ililīhkahew, *to keep sb alive;* SEC iyiniw, *a Cree person; a Native American person;* iyinīwiw, *to be alive;* "iyinīhkān, *a statue;*" WI (Pessamit) ilnu [īlnu], *a human being; an Innu; a First Nations person;* Laure (ca. 1726) "nit-iriniuin, *je vis;*" "nit-irinikahau, *je le sauve;*" Fabvre (ca. 1690) "irinikăhau, *resusciter qlqn;*" Silvy (ca. 1680) "irini8, homme;" "nit'irinikas8n, *je me fais homme, je m'incarne;*" "irini8i8in, *vie*" | ANISH inini, *a man* (Livesay & Nichols, 2021) see | *ɩrin, *ɩrinī discussion | Verbal derivatives of this root take on a number of unexpected senses, such as ***ɩrinīwi**, "to be alive," ***ɩrinīhkah**, "to heal sb," and likely also ***ɩrinīsi**, "to be wise."

*ɩrinī

INITIAL

— wise

evidence | PC iyinīsiw, *to be wise;* WC iðinīsiw, *to be wise;* WI (Pessamit) ilnishu [īlnīʃu], *to be intelligent or wise; to be cunning, speaking of an animal;* Laure (ca. 1726) "nit-irinisihau, *je le rends sage;*" Silvy (ca. 1680) "nit'irinisin, *j'ai de l'esprit, de l'industrie*" origin | Likely ***ɩriniw** + ***ɩsi** limited to | *ɩsi

*ɩripē

INITIAL

— tilt

evidence | WC iðipīyāw, *to slant;* MC ilipeštew, *to sit on a slant;* AT aripetakaw, *être incliné, d'un plancher;* Fabvre (ca. 1690) "Iribechkau 8rágan, *le plat 8ragan panche*" | ANISH anibekamigaa, *to be a sloping ground* (Livesay & Nichols, 2021)

*ɩriwē

INITIAL

— oppose, resist

evidence | PC iyiwēskam, *to go to sth against orders;* MC iliwemototākew, *to voice opposition;* NEC iyiwāshkiwāu, *to overcome sb, to come out ahead;* Laure (ca. 1726) "nit-iriuechin, *indigner, je m'indigne, je hais*"

*ɩrk

INITIAL

— remove liquid

evidence | WC iðkaham, *to bail water;* MC ihkaštew, *low tide;* SEC ihkahipew, *to bail water;* Laure (ca. 1726) "ikatchiuateu, *l'eau de la chaudière est consumée*" | ANISH iskate, *for a liquid or body of water to go down or dry up* (Livesay & Nichols, 2021); MENO ehka·qtɛw, *to dry up, speaking of a body of water*

*ɩrkaw

MEDIAL

— **1** fish flesh

— **2** wood grain

evidence | PC Lacombe (1874) "yoskikkawew, *il a la chair molle (chair du poisson);*" SEC ayāpišihkawew, *fish has small-flaked flesh or tree is fine-grained;* itihkawew, *fish has such flesh or tree has such grain;* NEC itihkiwāu, *fish has such flesh;* pāsihkiwāyāskusiu, *to have rings (speaking of a tree);* EI (Mamit) mikukueu [mīkūkwēw], *fish has red flesh* | ANISH nookiskawe, *fish has soft flesh* (Livesay & Nichols, 2021) see | *wirkawēw discussion | In the absence of a Woods Cree cognate, the reconstruction of the consonant cluster is indirectly supported by Anishinabe.

*ɩro

MEDIAL

— deer, quadruped

evidence | SEC mātāhtiyow, *to find tracks of a moose or caribou;* SEC nātiyow, *to go after a moose or caribou;* WI (Pessamit) natulu [*sic*] [nātlu], *to go fetch caribou or moose that have been already located;* Laure (ca. 1726) "ni-natirun, *je cherche la piste de l'orignal;*" Fabvre (ca. 1690) "Natir8n 8, *Aller tuer L(')a(nim)al qn a desia (déjà) dec8uert autrefois, auant cela*"

*ɩsi

FINAL (VERB, ANIMATE, INTRANSITIVE, ABSTRACT)

— forms stative verbs

evidence | PC kanātisiw, *to be clean;* MC āhkosiw, *to be sick or hurt;* AT (Wemotaci, Jeannette Coocoo) kakitisiw [kākītiziw], *to be sore;* (Wemotaci, Nicole Petiquay) kockosiw [koškoziw], *to wake up;* SEC mihkosiw, *to be red* | ANISH aabadizi, *to be useful or used;* MESK asāwesiwa, *to be yellow* origin | PA ***esi** (Aubin, 1975) paired with | *an², *ɩn⁴ compare | *ɩt³

*ɩsiko (~ *ɩsikw)

MEDIAL, FINAL

— ice

evidence | MC kilisikošin, *to slip on ice;* AT pokonesikohike-, *to make a hole in the ice* (Béland, 1978); SEC cišipisikwāw, *to be the end of an expanse of ice;* NEC kāchichāsikw, *iceberg;* WI (Pessamit) ussitishikᵘ [ūssətəʃəkʷ], *on the surface of the ice* | ANISH babigozigwaa, *bumpy ice* (Livesay & Nichols, 2021) compare | *ɩsko²

***ɩsk¹ (~ *āsk)**

MEDIAL, FINAL (NOUN INCORPORATION)

— **1** Canada goose (Branta canadensis)

— **2** goose

evidence | MC kitohiskew, *to call Canada geese;* SEC nōtāscew, *to harvest Canada geese;* wāpisk, *snow goose;* NEC pishkusk, *moulting goose;* muwāschāu, *to eat Canada geese;* EI apishtiss [apɨstɨss], *brant;* EI (Sheshatshiu) makushesseu [mukuʃēssēw], *to take part in a goose feast;* Laure (ca. 1726) "uabis *pl.* uabiskets, *oie, anser*" origin | from PA ***neska** (***nexka**, Aubin, 1975; Hewson, 1993) see | *nisk¹

***ɩsk²**

PREFINAL, FINAL (NOUN)

— conveys a frequentative action such as a habit or abundance

evidence | PC kīskwēpēsk, *drunkard;* misposkin, *to snow often;* WC mātosk, *a cry baby;* mātoskiw, *to be a cry baby;* MC kilāškišk, *liar;* wākinākaniskikamāw, *to be a lake marked by the presence of tamaracks;* SEC cimotisk, *thief;* minahikoskatināw, *to be a hill or mountain with many white spruce;* Silvy (ca. 1680) "ni p8etchit8chtin, *je suis un péteur*" origin | PA ***eθk** (Aubin, 1975) see | *ɩski, *ɩskā discussion | The alternate ***ɩški** form is likely a result of diminutive consonant symbolism providing a pejorative coloring. Also note the duplication of the final in Moose Cree *kilāškišk*, displaying a formation based on the lexicalized stem *kilāski-*, "to lie."

***ɩskan**

INITIAL

— from beginning to end of a period of time

evidence | MC iskanapiw, *to stay all day;* iskani-kīšikāw, *all day;* SEC iskanapiw, *to stay all day;* iskanitipiskwepiw, *to sit all night;* NEC iskinitiwishtāu, *all week;* WI (Pessamit) ishkanitshishikuekuamu [ʃkəntʃīʃəkwēkwāmu], *to sleep all day;* EI (Unaman-shipit) ishkaninipina [hkanīpɨna], *all summer;* EI (Ekuanitshit) ishkanitipishkua [ihkantɨpɨskwa], *all night;* Watkins (1865) "Yiskin-tipiskow, Yiskune-tipiskow, *n.in. All night long;*" La Brosse (1766) "Hiskan, *Tandiù, omnem durationem;*" "hiskantibiskau, *tota nox;*" "Riskanapin, *Moror tolâ dies;*" Laure (ca. 1726) "niskan-tibiskuetanu, *il a plu toute la nuit;*" "riskani pipun, *tout l'hiver;*" Fabvre (ca. 1690) "Hiskan tibiskau, *t8te la nuict;*" "Richkanapin i8, *sei8rner, rester encore t8t Le I8r;*" "Riskanapi8 *pl.* 8ek, *il, ils demeurent La t8t Le I8r;*" Silvy (ca. 1680) "hiskan, *durant;*" "ni riskanapin, *je demeure encore ce soir*" | ANISH Nicholas (ca. 1670) "rikanap, *rester à un endroit pour la nuit;*" "hikan, *toute*" (Daviault, 1994); Cuoq (1886) "Nikanend,i, *Être absent pour toute la journèe et ne revenir au logis que le lendemain;*" MESK ahkani, nahkani, & nehkani, *for the duration of;* nehkanipepōnwe, *all winter* discussion | All Jesuit sources list forms that support the reconstruction of ***riskan** rather than the above form. However, these documents are complex and include a mix of dialectal forms in addition to a number of early Anishinabe loans. Any use of these sources as corroborative evidence must therefore be careful and informed. In this light, one must contend with the fact that no contemporary dialect has maintained evidence of the initial consonant and that Silvy (ca. 1680), Fabvre (ca. 1690), and La Brosse (1766) list forms that also support the above reconstruction in addition to the ***riskan** forms, suggesting the latter is either an obsolete dialectal variation or a loan from a neighbouring language. Contemporary evidence is limited, however, in that all western dialects except for Moose Cree have replaced this root with the Anishinabe loan "kapē." Note, however, that the corroborative evidence presented above for both

Anishinabe and Meskwaki also support the reconstruction of Proto-Algonquian forms that vary regarding the presence, or lack thereof, of the initial consonant.

*ɪskanaw

MEDIAL, FINAL (NOUN, INANIMATE)

— tracks, path

evidence | PC itiskanawēw, *to make tracks thither;* WC paskīskanaw, *off the road;* MC pimohteskanaw, *walkway;* SEC pimiskanawew, *to leave tracks as one walks along;* WI (Pessamit) itishkanueu [ītəʃkənwēw], *to leave tracks or footprints which lead in a certain direction;*" Laure (ca. 1726) "pimiskanaueuets iriniuets, *il y a des pistes d'hommes*" see | *mēskanaw

*ɪskā

FINAL (VERB, INANIMATE, INTRANSITIVE, CONCRETE)

— abundance of

evidence | PC mihtiskāw, *to be lots of potential firewood;* MC amiskoskāw, *to be many beavers;* SEC (coastal) iyiyāšihtiskāw, *to be many balsam firs* | ANISH amikokaa, *to be many beavers* (Livesay & Nichols, 2021) see | *ɪsk² compare | *ɪski

*ɪski

FINAL (VERB, ANIMATE, INTRANSITIVE, CONCRETE)

— conveys the habitual aspect

evidence | PC pēkatēskiw, *to burp frequently;* WC tāhkwāhkīskiw, *to be in the habit of biting;* ESC ayamiskiw, *to talk a great deal;* MC maskahtweskiw, *to be a robber;* kilāskiskiw, *to be a liar;* nipeškiw, *to sleep much;* AT kirāskiw, *to lie;* Silvy (ca. 1680) "nit'acht8atchestin, nit'acht8atchechtin, *je suis adonné au jeu*" | ANISH mawishki to be a crybaby (Livesay & Nichols, 2021); MENO sɛ·kesi·hkiw, *to be given to fear;* MIAMI kilaahkii-, *tell a lie* (ILDA, 2017) see | *ɪsk², *i² compare | *ɪskā discussion | The alternate ***ɪški** form is likely a result of diminutive consonant symbolism providing a pejorative coloring. Also note the duplication of the final in Moose Cree *kilāskiskiw*, displaying a formation based on the lexicalized stem *kilāski-*, *"to lie."*

*ɪsko¹ (~ *ɪskw)

INITIAL

— **1** particular length or height

— **2** up

evidence | ¹PC iskwāpihkēpitēw, *to pull sb a certain distance using a rope;* WC iskwānakāw, *island measures a certain length;* MC iskwāskwan, *to be sth stick-like of a certain length;* SEC iskwāw, *to be a certain length;* Silvy (ca. 1680) "isk8egan, *il est de cette longueur*" ²MC iskopaliw, *to go up;* SEC iskwāpihcepayiw, *to be pulled up by sth string-like;* NEC īskwāhtiwīu, *to climb up;* EI (Sheshatshiu) ishkupitamᵘ [iʃkupɨtəm], *to lift sth quickly;* Silvy (ca. 1680) "nit'isk8etginau, *je relève ses habits*" | ¹MESK ahkwāpiwa, *to see a certain distance* ²MENO ehkuahtawɛw, *to climb up; to go up a ladder or stairway*

*ɪsko²

FINAL (VERB, ANIMATE, INTRANSITIVE, CONCRETE)

— travel over ice

evidence | PC pimiskohtēw, *to walk over the ice;* SEC nātakāskow, *to walk on ice towards the shore;* NEC tiskimiskū, *walk directly across the ice;* WI (Pessamit) itishkupitshu [ītəʃkupətʃu], *to pull toboggan thither over the ice;* Silvy (ca. 1680) "ni petisk8tan 3. -e8, *je viens en deçà sur la glace*" compare | *ɪsiko

*ɪskw (~ *āskw)

MEDIAL

— head

evidence | PC nawakiskwēnēw, *to bend down sb's head by hand;* MC itiskweliw, *to move one's head thus;* SEC cāhkāskwešin, *to lie with one's head elevated*

***ɩskwam (~ *ɩskwamak)**
MEDIAL (NOUN INCORPORATION)
— ice
evidence | PC mowiskwamēw, *to eat ice;* MC nāciskwamew, *to fetch ice;* SEC maniskumeham, *to remove ice from sth;* nātiskomew, *to fetch ice;* (Waswanipi) kā opiskomakāw-sākahikan, *place name, literally "frozen narrows lake"* (Bishop, 2022); NEC tāskum, *out on the ice;* kā wāyāwihciskumikāc, *place name, literally "frozen lake in a sandy depression"* (Bishop, 2022); NSK mishtiskumikw, *place name, literally "large frozen lake"* (Bishop, 2022); EI (Natuashish) ka uauatshishkumakashit, *place name, literally "lesser winding frozen lake"* (Bishop, 2022) see | *miskwamiy

***ɩskwē**
INITIAL
— female
evidence | SEC iskwešip, *a female duck;* WI (Pessamit) ishkueleu [ʃkwēlēw], *a female grouse;* Laure (ca. 1726) "iskuechtim, *chienne;*" Silvy (ca. 1680) "isk8eak8, *femelle du porc-épic*" see | *ɩskwēw¹

***ɩskwēw¹**
INITIAL (NOUN, ANIMATE)
— woman
evidence | MC iskwewihow, *to be dressed like a woman;* SEC iskwewāspisow, *to be dressed like a woman;* WI (Pessamit) ishkueukupeu [ʃkwēwkupēw], *to wear a dress or skirt;* Silvy (ca. 1680) "isk8e8, *femme;*" "nit'isk8e8apin, *je suis assis comme les femmes*" origin | PA ***eθkwēwa** (Aubin, 1975; Hewson, 1993) see | *ɩskwē, *w¹, *ɩskwēw²

***ɩskwēw²**
MEDIAL, FINAL (NOUN INCORPORATION)
— woman
evidence | PC wīhpēmiskwēwēw, *sleep with a woman;* MC nōcihiskwewew, *to pursue a woman for romantic affairs;* SEC natomiskwewew, *to ask for the permission to marry a woman;* nātoweskwew, *an Iroquois woman;* Silvy (ca. 1680) "ni n8tisk8e8atau, *je la recherche en mariage*" | ANISH gimoodikwewe, *to steal someone's wife* (Livesay & Nichols, 2021) see | *ɩskwē

***ɩso¹**
FINAL (VERB, ANIMATE, INTRANSITIVE, ABSTRACT)
sound change | aw + ɩso → āso
— reflexive
evidence | PC sikitisow, *to urinate on oneself;* WC otinamāsow, *to take or buy sth for oneself;* AT kiwenamaso [kīwēnamāzow], *to regain what one has given;* SEC tōtāsow, *to do to oneself;* Silvy (ca. 1680) "nit'ak8anah8s8n, *je me couvre, me cache*" discussion | Dialects such as Atikamekw, Moose Cree, and the Southern East Cree dialect spoken at Waswanipi also make use of the extended variant ***ɩtɩso**, possibly borrowed from the neighbouring Anishinabe language.

***ɩso²**
FINAL (VERB, ANIMATE, INTRANSITIVE, ABSTRACT)
sound change | ē → a
— forms stative verbs
evidence | PC cimasow, *to stand upright, to be erected;* WC asiwasow, *to be in a container;* AT (Opitciwan, Nadia Awashish) tcimaso [cimazow], *to be upright, erected;* SEC cimasow, *to be erected* paired with | *tē³

***ɩspiht (~ *ɩspihš)**
INITIAL
— such an amount, size, extent, or degree
evidence | PC ispīhtēkan, *to be such a size, speaking of sth sheet-like;* ispīhcāw, *to be a certain size;* ispisiskāw, *to go so fast;* WC ispīhtāyawan, *to be such a time of the year;* ispisīw, *to have so much strength;* MC ispihcinākwan & ispišinākwan, *to be at a certain distance;* AT aspi:c, *so much, so far* (Béland, 1978); SEC ispišāw, *to be a certain size or quantity;* NEC ishpishīu, *to have*

enough time for; WI (Pessamit) ishpitapu [īʃpətāpu], *to have eyes of a certain size;* EI (Sheshatshiu) ishpishau [iʃpəʃāw], *to be a certain size;* Laure (ca. 1726) "egu ispitatet, *jusqu'au ventre;*" "egu ispichatch utenau, *le village est de cette grandeur;*" Silvy (ca. 1680) "ispitag8nik, *de la neige jusque-là;*" "ispichau, *de cette grandeur;*" "nit'ispichigaba8in, *je suis de cette grandeur, de cette hauteur*" | ANISH apiichibatoo, *to run at a certain speed* (Livesay & Nichols, 2021); MENO ahpi·hciwɛw, *to have so much muscular strength* discussion | An isogloss exists whereby contemporary dialects west of Southern East Cree, including Atikamekw, favor a reflex of ***ɩspihc** rather than ***ɩspihš** as a productive allomorph. The latter is nonetheless present in most of these dialects, likely in what might be considered lexicalized forms. Early sources support the allomorph ***ɩspihš** rather than ***ɩspihc**, suggesting the latter is a recent innovation, perhaps due to influence from neighbouring Anishinabe dialects. Evidence from Moose Cree also suggests that the transition from ***ɩspihš** to ***ɩspihc** is rather recent. While contemporary speakers productively use a reflex of ***ɩspihc**, the 1876 translation of the King James Bible overwhelming made use of a reflex of ***ɩspihš** when the allomorph was required—293 instances of ***ɩspihš** against 54 of ***ɩspihc** to be exact.

*ɩspinē

INITIAL (VERB, ANIMATE, INTRANSITIVE)

— **1** be ill thus

— **2** harm or affect negatively thus, of transitive clauses derived from the above stem

evidence | PC ispinēw, *to be sick in such a way; to be sick unto death; to be dead;* ispanēmēw, *to berate sb thus;* ispanatēw, *to attack or kill sb thus or there* (Wolfart, 2023); Fabvre (ca. 1690) "Ispinehigan 3 ke8, *priser, estimer tant;*" Silvy (ca. 1680) "nit'ispineh8au, *je lui vends tant*" | MENO ehpɛ·nɛ·w, *to fare ill, to suffer, to be sick, to die, in that way;* ehpɛ·nanɛw, *to deal with sb in that way, especially of adverse action; to injure sb or do away with sb that way;* MESK ahpenēweni, *disease* see | *ɩt[1], *pinē[2], *āspinē discussion | Though a derived stem, this entry is included to corroborate and elucidate the relationship between ***pinē** and ***āspinē**. While the initial in the above stem is ***ɩt**, the stem as a whole also participates as an initial in further derivation, as demonstrated in the evidence above. Note that this stem is obsolete in most contemporary dialects.

*ɩš

FINAL (VERB, TRANSITIVE, CONCRETE)

— cut

evidence | PC pistisam, *to cut sth accidentally;* MC itišam, *to cut sth thus;* AT ta:škiš-, *to split sth by knife* (Béland, 1978); SEC sehkwešam, *to cut sth into a flared shape;* Silvy (ca. 1680) "pi8ichigan, *retaille d'étoffe, de peau, etc.*" origin | PA ***eš** (Aubin, 1975) paired with | *ɩšw

*ɩšē

FINAL (VERB, ANIMATE, INTRANSITIVE)

— give birth to, bear child

evidence | PC nītisān, *my sibling;* WC nīcisān, *my sibling;* MC kīwašišān, *an orphan;* Silvy (ca. 1680) "pik8atichanicha, *bâtard;*" "ni pik8atichan 3. -eu, *j'ai un enfant d'autre que de mon mari*" compare | *ōšē

*ɩšēw (~ *ɩšēwak)

MEDIAL, FINAL (NOUN, INANIMATE)

— ember, firebrand

evidence | NEC āmisāuchipiyiu, *to be a burning log that rolls away from the fire;* nishtiwishāukiham, *to put the unburned ends of firewood together;* Watkins (1865) "Nistowisāwukinum, *v.t.in.6. He scrapes the embers together;*" Laure (ca. 1726) "nit-aiaticheuenen 3. -namu, *j'attise le feu;*" Fabvre (ca. 1690) "n 8pichenen, 3 nam8, *Leuer un tison du feu;"* Silvy (ca. 1680) "n'8tichenen, *j'approche, v.g. le feu;"* "ni 8aska8ichenen, *je remue le feu"* compare | *āškēw, *āškišēw discussion | This reconstruction suffers from the lack of an Atikamekw cognate to confirm the absence of a preaspirate.

*ɩšihš

FINAL (NOUN, DIMINUTIVE)

sound change | v + ɩšihš → v̄šihš

— **1** conveys a sense of smallness

— **2** conveys infancy or youth

— **3** conveys the state of being yet unmarried

evidence | PC pisīsis, *a baby lynx;* MC nāpešiš, *a boy; a man who is yet to be married; in jest, a man who is married but has yet to father any daughters;* sīpīšiš, *a small river;* AT (Wemotaci, Nicole Petiquay) wapococic [wāpoʒoʒiš], *a baby hare;* SEC nāpešš, *a boy; a man who is yet to be married; in jest, a man who is married but has yet to father any daughters;* WI (Pessamit) mashkuss [muʃkūss], *a bear under one year old;* EI (Unaman-shipit) emikuaniss [ēmīkwāniss], *a teaspoon;* EI (Sheshatshiu) ishkuess [iʃkwēss], *a girl; an unmarried woman;* Silvy (ca. 1680) "assamichich, *petite raquette;"* "attim8chich, *petit chien"* compare | *ɩhš

*ɩšk[1]

INITIAL

— tired

evidence | PC iskiskawēw, *to wear sb out by treading;* WC iskapiw, *to be tired from sitting;* MC iškilānew, *to have tired calves;* SEC iščikāpawiw, *to be tired standing;* WI (Pessamit) issiu [ssīw], *to be uncomfortable or stiff* | MESK ashkapiwa, *to be tired of sitting*

*ɩšk[2]

FINAL (VERB, TRANSITIVE, INANIMATE, CONCRETE)

— **1** by use of foot or body

— **2** have on or in one's body, wear article of clothing

evidence | [1]WC nisiwanātiskam, *to spoil sth by treading on it;* MC ašiškīwihtakiškam, *to muddy the floor with one's feet;* SEC pīkoškam, *to break sth under one's weight* [2]PC miyoskam, *to fit sth well;* WC postiskam, *to put sth on;* MC itiškam, *to wear sth thus;* SEC panahkoškam, *to wear an article of clothing loosely* | ANISH debishkan, *to fit sth* (Livesay & Nichols, 2021); MIAMI aašitehkam-, *to meet up with sth, to come across sth* origin | PA ***ešk*** (Aubin, 1975) paired with | *ɩškaw compare | *sk[2]

*ɩškaw (~ *ɩškā)

FINAL (VERB, TRANSITIVE, ANIMATE, CONCRETE)

— **1** by use of foot or body

— **2** have on or in one's body, wear article of clothing

evidence | [1]WC nisiwanātiskawīw, *to spoil sth by treading on it;* MC ašiškīwihtakiškawew, *to muddy the floor with one's feet;* SEC pīkoškawew, *to break sth under one's weight;* WI (Pessamit) takushiteshkueu [təkuʃətēʃkwēw], *to step on sb's foot* [2]PC miyoskawew, *to fit sth well;* WC postiskawīw, *to put sth on;* MC itiškawew, *to wear sth thus;* SEC panahkoškawew, *to wear an article of clothing loosely* | ANISH debishkan, *to fit sth* (Livesay & Nichols, 2021); origin | PA ***eškaw*** (Aubin, 1975) paired with | *ɩšk[2] compare | *skaw

*ɩškā

FINAL (VERB, INTRANSITIVE, ABSTRACT)

— **1** forms both stative and dynamic verbs

— **2** travel by water

evidence | [1]PC ohpiskāw, *to rise into the sky;* MC pīkoškāw, *to be broken;* kipihciškāw, *to stop walking;* SEC waniškāw, *to rise from a reclined position;* Laure (ca. 1726) "pekuatiskau, *mon habit est troué;"* Fabvre (ca. 1690) "Iribechkau 8rágan, *le plat 8ragan panche;"* Silvy (ca. 1680) "abik8chkau, *il est détaché, délié, v.g. d'une bande, etc.;"* "kachkatichkau, kachkatchipari8, *il est rompu, épointé, cassé"* [2]PC papāmiskāw, *to paddle or swim about;* MC atimiškāw, *to paddle or swim away;* pimiškāw, *to paddle or swim along;* NEC pātāshtimishkāu, *to paddle or swim hither;* WI (Pessamit) atimishkau [təməʃkāw], *to move away by canoe or swimming;* Silvy (ca. 1680) "ni pimishkan 3. -kau, *je navigue*" | ²ANISH animishkaa, *to go away in a canoe* (Livesay & Nichols, 2021); MENO pemɛ·skaw, *to go by canoe; to move along; to travel past* origin | PA ***eškā** (Aubin, 1975; Hewson, 1993)

*ɩškiw¹ (~ *ɩškiwak)

MEDIAL (NOUN INCORPORATION)

— mud

evidence | PC yipātiskiwakisimow, *to muddy or dirty oneself;* micimoskiwēw, *to be stuck in the mud;* SEC nešciwakāw, *to be a muddy point;* WI (Pessamit) kutaussutshipalu [kutāwssūtʃəpəlu], *to sink into the mud;* Laure (ca. 1726) "pinissiuagahigana, *plâtras, débris d'un bâtiment;*" Fabvre (ca. 1690) "mar8kisti8ăgau, *terre molle, uase, on y enf(on)ce*" origin | Old Cree ***ašiškiwi** see | *ašiškiw

*ɩškiw²

FINAL (NOUN, PEJORATIVE)

— conveys a sense of diminished quality or value, typically as a result of aging

evidence | MC āšokaniškīš, *a dilapidated bridge;* wīštiškīš, *an abandoned beaver or muskrat lodge;* AT (Opitciwan, Joey Awashish) maskisinickica [maskiziniškišša], *old, worn out shoes;* atimockic [atimoškiš], *darn dog!;* SEC aštotiniščiš, *an old, worn out hat;* wīshtischī, *old beaver lodge* (CSB, 2018); NEC umwāhtiwāschī, *a dead tree whose bark was eaten a long time ago;* NSK asaamischiis, *an old, worn-out snowshoe;* Silvy (ca. 1680) "nichtisti8, *mon mari qui m'a quittée*" discussion | Contemporary dialects that retain this final typically suffix the diminutive ***ɩhš** onto it, producing reflexes of ***ɩškīhš**.

*ɩško¹ (~ *ɩškw)

INITIAL

— remain (after consumption or destruction of the rest), be leftover

evidence | WC iskwascikana, *leftovers;* MC iškohcikan, *leftovers;* SEC iškopayiw, *to have some left;* NEC ishkupwāu, *to leave some of sth uneaten*

*ɩško²

PREFINAL

— eat, feed see | *ɩškor, *ɩškoro, *ɩškotā

*ɩškor

FINAL (VERB, TRANSITIVE, ANIMATE, CONCRETE)

— feed

evidence | SEC cipiškoyew, *to make sb choke on sth;* WI (Pessamit) uishashkuleu [wīʃāʃkulēw], *to attract sb with food;* EI (Unaman-shipit) tepishkuneu [tēpɨhkunēw], *to satiate sb;* Silvy (ca. 1680) "ni nip8chk8rau, *je le tue de trop manger*" see | *ɩško², *r paired with | *ɩškotā

*ɩškoro

FINAL (VERB, ANIMATE, INTRANSITIVE, CONCRETE)

— eat

evidence | PC osāmiskōyow, *to eat too much;* nōhtāskoyow, *to not have enough to eat;* MC tepiškolow, *to eat enough;* WI ishpitishkulu [īʃpətəʃkwəlu], *to swallow a certain quantity;* Silvy (ca. 1680) "ni nechtt8sk8r8n, *je suis mal de trop manger*" see | *ɩškor, *o

*ɩškotā

FINAL (VERB, ANIMATE, INTRANSITIVE, CONCRETE)

— feed

evidence | Fabvre (ca. 1690) "ni nip8chk8tan nihiau, *tuer son corps à force de m(an)ger*" see | *ɩško², *tā paired with | *ɩškor

***ɩškotēw**

INITIAL (NOUN, INANIMATE)

— fire

evidence | PC iskotēwakan, *to smell like fire;* MC iškotehkēw, *to build a fire;* AT ickotewatikw [iškotēwāhtikw], *a match;* SEC iškotewāpow, *alcohol;* WI (Pessamit) ishkutekan [ʃkutēkān], *kitchen;* Laure (ca. 1726) "iskuteuabui, *eau de vie;*" Silvy (ca. 1680) "ichk8te8, *feu*" see | *škotaw, *škotēw

***ɩškōr**

FINAL (VERB, TRANSITIVE, ANIMATE, CONCRETE)

— affect by the weight of a load or by the applied pressure of a moving body

evidence | MC māhtakoškōlew, *to weigh sb down with sth heavy;* NEC tipāpāshkuyāu, *to weigh sb* paired with | *ɩškōtā

***ɩškōso**

FINAL (VERB, ANIMATE, INTRANSITIVE, CONCRETE)

— be affected by the weight of a load or by the applied pressure of a moving body

evidence | PC nayawiskōsow, *to be weary under a burden;* MC kotāwākoneškōsow, *to sink in the snow under the weight of a load;* AT apitcickoso [āhpiciškōzow], *to be crushed to death;* SEC wepiškōsow, *to be swept away by the applied pressure of a moving body;* Laure (ca. 1726) "patiskusu, *la bête a manqué à s'y prendre (dans la trappe);*" Silvy (ca. 1680) "pa8ichk8s8, *il est renversé, répandu, qqch. tombant dessus*" | ANISH zaginikeshkoozo, *to be trapped by the forepaw* (Livesay & Nichols, 2021) paired with | *ɩškōtē

***ɩškōtā**

FINAL (VERB, ANIMATE, INTRANSITIVE, CONCRETE)

— affect by the weight of a load or by the applied pressure of a moving body

evidence | MC māhtakoškōtāw, *to weigh sb down with sth heavy;* NEC tipāpāshkutāu, *to weigh sth* paired with | *ɩškōr

***ɩškōtē**

FINAL (VERB, INANIMATE, INTRANSITIVE, CONCRETE)

— be affected by the weight of a load or by the applied pressure of a moving body

evidence | PC kawiskōtēw, *to collapse under the weight;* MC māhiškōtew, *to be swept downstream by the applied pressure of a moving body;* SEC wepiškōtew, *to be swept away by the applied pressure of a moving body* | ANISH nabagishkoode, *to be flattened by weight or pressure* (Livesay & Nichols, 2021) paired with | *ɩškōso

***ɩškwā**

INITIAL

— end

evidence | WC iskwāpaðiw, *to end;* MC iškwākocin, *to be the end of a month;* AT ickwaparitaw [iškwāparihtāw], *to finish sth;* ickwaso [iškwāsow], *to be burnt, to burn;* SEC (Waswanipi) iškwāpayin, *to end;* Watkins (1865) "Iskwayoosan, n.an. *The last child, (i.e. the youngest of the family)*" | ANISH ishkwaase, *to come to an end* (Livesay & Nichols, 2021) compare | *ɩškwē

***ɩškwāhtēm**

INITIAL (NOUN, INANIMATE)

— doorway

evidence | PC iskwāhtēm, *a door;* MC iškwāhtemāhtik^{w}, *a doorframe;* SEC iškwāhtem, *a doorway; a door;* Silvy (ca. 1680) "ichk8atem, *carrure de porte ou ouverture*" origin | PA ***eškwāntēmi** (Hewson, 1993) see | *škwāht, *škwāhtaw compare | wēskwāhtēm

***ɩškwē**

INITIAL

— last

evidence | PC iskwēcihcānis, *the little finger;* WC iskwīyānihk, *the last, the end;* Watkins (1865) "Iskwāchan, n.an. *The last child (i.e. the youngest of the family);*" Silvy (ca. 1680) "ichk8eïatch tag8chin8, *il arrive le dernier;*" Fabvre (ca. 1690) "Isk8esitan, ichk8esitan, *le petit doit du pied*" | ANISH ishkwegamaa, *to be the last lake* (Livesay & Nichols, 2021) compare | *ɩškwā

*ɩšp

INITIAL

— high

evidence | PC ispākonakāw, *to be deep snow;* MC išpipaliw, *it ascends;* išpitōhtaneyāw, *to be high-heeled;* SEC išpimihc, *above;* ɩšpahcāw, *to be high ground;* Laure (ca. 1726) "ispatauagau, *terre haute;*" Silvy (ca. 1680) "ispi8, ispagamisgau, *terre haute, terre de cette hauteur*"

*ɩšt[1]

MEDIAL (NOUN INCORPORATION)

— hair

evidence | PC wāpistān, *a marten;* MC māniščāniš, *a sheep;* SEC wāpištān, *marten;* māniščāniš, *a sheep;* Silvy (ca. 1680) "8abichtanich, *fouine, martre*" origin | PA ***eʔt** see | *ēštakay compare | *itišt

*ɩšt[2]

PREFINAL

— pierce see | *ɩštah, *ɩštahw

*ɩšt[3]

FINAL (VERB, TRANSITIVE, INANIMATE, ABSTRACT)

sound change | v + ɩšt → v̄št

— adds a benefactive argument when suffixed to animate intransitive verb stems

evidence | PC apīstam, *to sit near sth; to live near sth;* WC nanīhcīstam, *to fear sth;* MC ayeskawīštam, *to get ready for sth;* ohtiškawikāpawīštam *stand facing sth;* SEC nīkānapištam, *to sit at the front of sth;* NEC nīmīshtim, *to dance in honour of sth;* WI (Uashat) apishtam[u] [pīstəm], *to occupy sth, as a dwelling* | ANISH odabiitaan, *to live in sth, to occupy sth* (Livesay & Nichols, 2021) origin | PA ***ʔt** (Aubin, 1975) paired with | *ɩštaw compare | *tiht[2] discussion | Vowel lengthening of a preceding vowel is inconsistent in SEC and NEC. It appears to have been lost for short o in MC and lost entirely in EI.

*ɩštah

FINAL (VERB, TRANSITIVE, INANIMATE, CONCRETE)

— pierce

evidence | PC kipostahikēw, *to sew shut;* MC akoštaham, *to stitch or pin sth on;* WI (Pessamit) itishtaim[u] [ītəstīm], *to pin sth thus;* Laure (ca. 1726) "pitchetsistahigan, *pli de robe*" see | *ɩšt[2], *ah paired with | *ɩštahw

*ɩštahw

FINAL (VERB, TRANSITIVE, ANIMATE, CONCRETE)

— pierce

evidence | PC itistahwēw, *to sew sth on thus;* MC kipoštahwēw, *to stitch or pin sth closed;* SEC akoštahwew, *to sew sth on* see | *ɩšt[2], *ah paired with | *ɩštah

*ɩštaw

FINAL (VERB, TRANSITIVE, ANIMATE, ABSTRACT)

sound change | v + ɩštaw → v̄štaw

— adds a benefactive argument when suffixed to animate intransitive verb stems

evidence | PC nōkosīstawēw, *to reveal oneself to sb;* WC nanīhcīstawīw, *to fear sb;* MC ohtiškawikāpawīštawew, *stand facing sb;* tipācimoštawew, *to tell sb a story;* AT (Wemotaci, Jeannette Coocoo) atimapictowew [atimapīštawew], *to sit with one's back to sb;* SEC nīkānapištawew, *to sit ahead of sb;* WI (Pessamit) uitapishtueu [wītəpīstwēw], *to sit near sb;* EI (Sheshatshiu) mupishtueu [mūpɨstwēw], *to visit sb;* uitapishtueu [wītəpistwēw], *to sit near sb;* Silvy (ca. 1680) "nit'atochtechta8au, *je travaille pour lui*" | ANISH odanokiitawaan, *to work for sb* (Livesay & Nichols, 2021) **origin** | PA ***ʔtaw** (Aubin, 1975) **paired with** | *ɩšt³ **see** | *ɩšt³, *aw³ **compare** | *tiht¹ **discussion** | Vowel lengthening of a preceding vowel is inconsistent in SEC and NEC. It appears to have been lost for short o in MC and lost entirely in EI.

*ɩšw

FINAL (VERB, TRANSITIVE, ANIMATE, CONCRETE)

— cut

evidence | PC pistiswēw, *to cut sb accidentally;* MC itišwew, *to cut sb thus;* AT ta:škišw-, *to split sb by knife* (Béland, 1978); SEC sehkwešwew, *to cut sth into a flared shape;* EI (Sheshatshiu) matishueu [mātəʃwēw], *to cut sb; to operate on sb* **paired with** | *ɩš

*ɩt¹ (~ *ɩš, *ɩs, *ɩh)

INITIAL

sound change | ɩt + i… → ɩši…; ɩt + p… → ɩsp…; ɩt + t… → ɩht…

— **1** thus

— **2** thither

evidence | [1]PC itaham, *to handle sth so by tool;* MC ispalihow, *to move thus;* AT icinakew [iʒinākēw], *to see others thus;* SEC ihtōtam, *to do sth thus;* NEC ishinākusiu, *to appear thus;* WI (Pessamit) itinamᵘ [ītnəm], *to hold sth in a certain way;* Silvy (ca. 1680) "ichitin8, *il est mis;*" "nit'aïsp8n he isp8t, *je mange de ce qu'il mange*" [2]MC itātakāw, *to swim thither;* AT ispariw, *to move thither spontaneously;* PC ispahtāw, *to run thither;* SEC itohtew, *to walk thither;* itahoyew, *to transport thither by boat;* WI (Pessamit) ishitatshimu [īʃətātʃəmu] *to drag oneself thither* | ANISH inizhige, *to cuts things a certain way;* izhidaabii, *to drag a load to a certain place* (Livesay & Nichols, 2021); MIAMI ilakintam-, *to price sth at a certain amount* (ILDA, 2017) **origin** | PA ***eθ** (Aubin, 1975; Hewson, 1993) **compare** | *ɩt²

*ɩt² (~ *ɩš)

INITIAL

— **1** say thus

— **2** call thus

evidence | PC itēw, *to say sth to sb; to call sb thus;* MC itwew [itwow], *to say thus;* itam, *to say to or about sth; to call sth thus;* SEC iš [īš], *tell h/ (imperative);* WI (Pessamit) iteu [ītēw], *to say to or about sb* | ANISH odinaan, *to say to sb* (Livesay & Nichols, 2021); MIAMI el-, *to say to sb; to call sb sth* (ILDA, 2017) **origin** | PA ***eθ** (Aubin, 1975; Hewson, 1993) **compare** | *ɩt¹

*ɩt³

FINAL (VERB, ANIMATE, INTRANSITIVE, ABSTRACT)

— forms stative verbs

evidence | PC kosikwatiw, *to be heavy;* ESC nāhkacišiw, *be light;* MC ispihtinikotiw, *weigh so much;* AT rakitciciw [rāhkiciššiw], *to be light;* SEC wīhcitiw, *to taste good;* WI (Pessamit) latshitishu [lāstəʃu], *to be lightweight;* EI (Sheshatshiu) uitshitu [wītʃitu], *to be delicious;* Watkins (1865) "Yäkitew, Yäkitisew, *v.i.1. He is light (in weight);*" Laure (ca. 1726) "kussigutiu, *pesant fardeau;*" "Pitchiskatetu uih(i)as, *chair morte, pourrie;*" "pitchiskatitu-names, *poisson pourri;*" "ni-ratsitin, *je suis léger du corps;*" Silvy (ca. 1680) "ni g8ssig8tin, ni k8ssig8tin, *je suis pesant;*" "ni ratchitichihau, *je le rend léger;*" "ratchitichi8ets assamak, *les raquettes sont légères*" | ABEN tekwigwel AI, *to be heavy;* ANISH gozigwani, *be heavy* (Livesay & Nichols, 2021); MENO we·hken AI, *to taste good;* MIAMI naankicii-, *to be light weight* **origin** | PA ***eθ** (***eθe**, Aubin, 1975) **paired with** | *an², *ɩn⁴ **compare** |

*ɩsi **discussion** | In most modern dialects, this root has been regularized as a prefinal followed by the epenthetic vowel ***ɩ**, the latter of which is treated as a verb final without transposition. However, in NEC, as demonstrated by Collette (2021), the Old Cree conjunct indicative flexion for the third-person singular for stems ending in consonants continues to be used, providing evidence for the above form. In western dialects, this final has been reshaped as *-ati-* by analogy with the inanimate form ***an**.

*ɩtā (~ *ɩc, *ɩtw)

FINAL (VERB, ANIMATE, INTRANSITIVE, ABSTRACT)

— forms causative verbs

evidence | MC pāhkwāštitāw, *to dry sth in the wind;* akohtitāw, *soak in water;* pīkihticikew, *to cause turbidity;* otāmihtitowew, *to hit sb with sth;* SEC otāmihtitāw, *to bang sth against sth;* WI (Pessamit) kutitau [kūttāw], *to knock sth down by hitting it against sth* **paired with** | *ɩm³ **discussion** | The ***ɩtw** allomorph surfaces only for further derivation when suffixing either the antipassive ***ā** or the benefactive ***aw**. Its origin predates what is otherwise a loss of morphological distinction in Old Cree between Proto-Algonquian transitive inanimate verb class II and animate intransitive verbs ending in ***ā** (cf. Pentland, 1999). Note that contemporary dialects have all contracted ***ɩtw** + ***aw** to a reflex of ***ɩtow**, but the underlying form is revealed when vowel-lengthening processes occur, resulting in reflexes of ***ɩtwā** as expected.

*ɩtāhs

MEDIAL, FINAL (NOUN INCORPORATION)

— leggings

evidence | PC kikitāsēw, *to wear pants;* Lacombe (1874) "pustitāsahew, *(v.a.) il lui met ses pantalons;*" MC āhcitāsew, *to change one's leggings;* SEC napatetāsew, *to wear only one sock;* WI (Pessamit) kueshkuaputitasheu [kwēʃkwāputətāʃēw], *to wear one's sock on the opposite foot;* EI (Sheshatshiu) pakupeutash [pākupēwtāʃ], *a knee-high rubber boot;* Silvy (ca. 1680) "ni michahitasan 3. -eȣ, *je refais des bas*" | ANISH miskodaase, *to wear red pants* (Livesay & Nichols, 2021); MIAMI -taahsi, *a legging or stocking* (ILDA, 2017) **see** | ***tāhs**

*ɩtāp

INITIAL

— just, simply

evidence | PC itāp, *at a later time, in the future;* Lacombe (1874) "Itāb, *(ad.) voy. tcheskwa, attends un peu, dans un autre temps, encore un moment, viendra un temps; v.g., itāb ki ka miyitin, attends un peu, je te le donnerai; itāb nama ekosi ki ka iteyitten, viendra un temps que tu ne penseras pas comme ça; tcheskwa itāb, ni wi-ituttān, attends encore un peu, je vais y aller;*" AT (Opitciwan, Joey Awashish) itap [itāp], *just, simply, only, e.g. Ekoni itap e kiciwasit. Just for that he is mad. Eko-a ni itap? Is that it?;*" Laure (ca. 1726) "itap egu, *bien assez, considérablement;*" "itapi abatchitaganiuanu, *cela est raisonnablement avantageux;*" Silvy (ca. 1680) "itap, itapi *cum pata aliquido un petit, en effet*" | ANISH Nicholas (ca. 1670) "irap, *un peu*" (Daviault, 1994) **origin** | PA ***eθāp**

*ɩtāpit (~ *ɩtāpic)

INITIAL

— be gone

evidence | ESC (Severn) itāpicīw, *to be gone;* MC itāpicīw, *to be gone;* AT itapitciw [itāpiciw], *to take a long time to arrive, to delay, to be late;* SEC itāpichīu, *to be gone for a certain length of time* (CSB, 2018); Laure (ca. 1726) "nika-itapitchin, *je serai long-temps dans les terres;*" Fabvre (ca. 1690) "itabitchin, *tarder à venir*" **limited to** | *ī¹

*ɪtē

INITIAL

— stir

evidence | PC itēhikew, *to stir;* MC iteham, *to stir sth;* SEC iteyākamaham, *to stir a liquid*

*ɪtēhkē

INITIAL

— at or towards a certain side

evidence | PC itēhkēskamik, *thitherward;* MC itehke, *towards a certain side;* itehkehtin, *to run in a certain direction, speaking of a stream;* SEC itehceškam, *to walk along a particular side of sth;* WI (Pessamit) itetshekam [ītētʃēkām], *at another place on the same side of the river or lake*

*ɪtiš

INITIAL

— to drive or be driven thither

evidence | MC itišimow, *to flee thither;* PC itisinam, *to hold sth thither;* SEC itišahwew, *to send sb thither;* EI (Mamit) itishimeu [itɨhɨmēw], *to flee sb* origin | PA ***eθeš** (Hewson, 1993), likely from ***eθ** and a prefinal ***eš** see | *tišah, *tiši, *tišim, *tišimo, *tišin, *tišisk

*ɪto

FINAL (VERB, ANIMATE, INTRANSITIVE, ABSTRACT)

sound change | ...aw + ɪto → āto

— forms the reciprocal from transitive animate verbs

evidence | PC māyi-tōtātowak, *to do ill to one another;* MC wāpamitowak, *to see one another;* SEC wewacikwenitowac, *to hug one another;* NEC mātinimātuwich, *to share sth among one another;* Laure (ca. 1726) "ni-naskuehimatunan, *nous chantons ensemble*" compare | *to

*ɪw¹ (~ *ɪwi)

FINAL (ABSTRACT)

sound change | vw or vy + ɪw → v̄w

— suffixed to nouns, intransitive verbs, or transitive inanimate verbs to form prenouns, preverbs, or initials for further composition where the following element is either a noun, verb, medial, or final

evidence | PC āhkosīwitāpān, *ambulance;* MC askīwi-pimiy, *kerosene;* opīwāwāskikanew, *to have a hairy chest;* SEC ciševinīwikamikw, *an old age home;* WI (Pessamit) ushkatsheu-miush [uʃkātʃēwmjūʃ] *bag made from the hide of the leg of a caribou or moose*

*ɪw²

FINAL (VERB, TRANSITIVE, ANIMATE, ABSTRACT)

sound change | ē → a

— adds a benefactive argument when suffixed to animate intransitive verb stems ending in *ē

evidence | PC ātayōhkawēw, *to tell sacred stories or legends to sb;* MC nīkānohtawew, *to walk ahead of sb;* asāmihkawew, *to make snowshoes for sb;* SEC atoskawew, *to work for sb;* Silvy (ca. 1680) "ni meskanakaȣau, *je luis fais un chemin*" | MIAMI manehsaw-, *gather wood for sb* (ILDA, 2017) compare | *aw³, *w²

*ɪwan

FINAL (VERB, INANIMATE, INTRANSITIVE, ABSTRACT)

sound change | vw or vy + ɪwan → v̄wan

— forms verbs from noun stems

evidence | PC kōniwan, *to be covered in snow;* MC nipīwan, *to be wet;* SEC šōliyāwan, *to be expensive;* maškošīwan, *to be grassy* paired with | *ɪwi

*ɪwat (~ *ɪwaš)

MEDIAL, FINAL (NOUN INCORPORATION)

— bag, pack

evidence | PC kētiwatēw, *to take off one's burden;* MC itawatew, *to carry bag thither;* SEC šōliyāwat, *a wallet or purse;* WI (Pessamit) massimuteush [məssəmutēwʃ], *bag;* Silvy (ca. 1680) "nit'abikȣniȣatan, *j'ouvre coffre, sac, etc.;*" "8atapi8ach, *panier d'osier*" see | *īwat

*ɩwi

FINAL (VERB, ANIMATE, INTRANSITIVE, ABSTRACT)

sound change | vw or vy + ɩwi → v̄wi

— forms verbs from noun stems

evidence | PC kōniwiw, *to be covered in snow;* MC nipīwiw, *to be wet;* SEC šōliyāwiw, *to be expensive* paired with | *ɩwan

E

*ē

FINAL (VERB, ANIMATE, INTRANSITIVE, ABSTRACT)

— suffixed to certain initials, medials and prefinals to form functional verbs

evidence | PC kāsāpitēw, *to have sharp teeth;* WC ðikwākonīpaðiw, *to get covered in snow from a fall;* MC tewištikwānew, *have a headache;* SEC apišitonešiw, *to have a small mouth;* otāhcew, *to be walking behind;* WI (Pessamit) pitakuneiashtan [pītākunējāstn], *the snow blows in;* Fabvre (ca. 1690) "Tepachitan e8, *aur assez de sapin pr La Cabane;*" Silvy (ca. 1680) "ni patchigatan 3. -e8, *j'ai la jambe enflée*" origin | PA *ē (Aubin, 1975) discussion | Wolfart (1973) distinguishes a post-medial accretion -ē- from the animate intransitive verb final -ē- in Plains Cree, though he admits that "they may well be related historically," also citing Bloomfield's uncertainty regarding this. These forms are treated as one and the same in the above reconstruction.

*ēhēpikw (~ *ēhēpiko)

INITIAL (NOUN, ANIMATE)

— spider

evidence | MC ehepikoskāw, *to be many spiders;* AT ehepikorapi [ēhēpikorapiy], *a spiderweb;* SEC ehepik^w, *a spider;* EI (Sheshatshiu) epik^u [ēpuk^w], *whirligig beetle;* Fabvre (ca. 1690) "hehebigau, *haragnée*"

*ēhs[1]

INITIAL (NOUN, ANIMATE)

— mussel

evidence | PC ēsa, *clam, clamshell;* MC esiskāw, *to be many mussels;* AT (Wemotaci, Jeannette Coocoo) esimakw [ēssimākw], *a clam;* SEC es, *a mussel;* EI (Sheshatshiu) esh [ēʃ], *shell, mollusc with a shell;* Laure (ca. 1726) "ese *pl.* esets *rel.* essa, *coque, coquillage;*" Silvy (ca. 1680) "essai *pl.* essak, *coquille;*" "8tessimi8, *il est vêtu d'écailles*" | ANISH esag, *a clam* (Livesay & Nichols, 2021)

*ēhs[2]

MEDIAL, FINAL (NOUN INCORPORATION)

— mussel

evidence | PC pinahēsēw, *to scale fish;* ESC (Attawapiskat, Bill Louttit) manesānān, *place name, literally 'mussel gathering place;'* MC manesew, *to gather mussels*

*ēhsipan

INITIAL (NOUN, ANIMATE)

— raccoon

evidence | MC esipan, *said to be the name lobsters use when referring to the otter in a well-known folktale, an archaic feature maintained from an earlier version of the story, unattested in Moose Cree, where the animal in question was in fact a raccoon;* AT (Wemotaci, Jeannette Coocoo) essipan [ēsipan], *raccoon;* Laure (ca. 1726) "echipanich, *blaireau, animal sauvage;*" Silvy (ca. 1680) "esseban, *gros animal*" | ANISH esiban, *a raccoon* (Livesay & Nichols, 2021); MENO ɛ·hsepan, *raccoon*

*ēk

MEDIAL (CLASSIFIER)

— sheet-like

evidence | PC ayakaskēkan, *to be a wide cloth;* MC aciwekišam, *to reduce the size of sth sheet-like by cutting;* alakaškekan, *to be a wide sheet;* SEC makwecišin, *for one's shape to be discernible through a sheet;* Laure (ca. 1726) "kaueganu *pl.* -a, *âpre, rude au toucher;*" Silvy (ca. 1680) "p8ta8egachtan, *le vent enfle la voile*"

*ēkinw (~ *ēkino)

FINAL (NOUN, INANIMATE, CLASSIFIER)

— sheet-like

evidence | PC askekin, *raw hide;* MC ayamihewekin[w], *a flag;* SEC akohpecin[w], *dress or skirt-making fabric*

*ēmak

ACCRETION (POST-MEDIAL)

evidence | PC atihkwāpēmak, *birch willow;* MC mihkopemak[w], *red-osier dogwood;* ESC peyakošikanemak, *one pair of socks;* AT masinackwemakitin [mazinaškwēmakihtin], *it is imprinted on paper;* WI (Pessamit) shekuepematshiu [ʃēkwēpēmətʃīw], *to have fan-shaped leaves;* Laure (ca. 1726) "pikuaskuemagu, *gargousse;*" Silvy (ca. 1680) "papag8eratchemak, *onguent d'écorce de pin à flocons, contre la brûlure*" compare | *ak[2] see | *ahrakēmak, *aškwēmak, *pēmak discussion | Despite its post-medial affixation, this root appears to function as a classifier for sheet-like objects.

*ēmihkwān

INITIAL (NOUN, ANIMATE)

— spoon

evidence | MC emihkwānaham, *to spoon sth;* Laure (ca. 1726) "nit-emikuanahen 3. -himu, *je puise avec une cuiller;*" Silvy (ca. 1680) "nit'emik8anahaman; nit'emik8anahiman, *j'en puise, je m'en sers (cuiller) en mangeant*" | ABEN amkwōnham, *to eat with a spoon* (Day, 1995); MENO ɛ·meskwanehsen, *to lie like a spoon, doubled up;* MESK ēmehkwānahikēwa, *to use a spoon;* cf. ANISH emikwaan, *ni spoon; na turtle shell* (Livesay & Nichols, 2021); MIAMI eemihkwaani, *squash* (ILDA, 2017) discussion | The Jesuit Bonaventure Fabvre (ca. 1690) lists the following entry in his manuscript dictionary: "Emik8an 3 e8, *Cuiller S'en seruir, en au(oi)r.*" While this entry supports the reconstruction of the Old Cree verb ***ēmihkwēwa** and the lexical root ***ēm**, no corroborative evidence has been found within Cree or sister languages. This raises the question of accuracy regarding Fabvre's entry, as his dictionary is largely, but not entirely, a transcription of an earlier manscript, possibly that of his fellow Jesuit Antoine Silvy.

*ēn

INITIAL

— **1** (of an open space) on this side

— **2** (of land) flat

— **3** (of elevations of land) at the base

— **4** (of objects) to be placed low against the base, to be placed down flat

evidence | MC enakām, *on this side of a body of water;* SEC enipayiw, *to go to the bottom;* enatin, *at the base of a hill or mountain;* enāmisc, *at the bottom of a body of water;* NEC ānipiu, *to sit at the bottom;* ānāwihch, *at the base of a hill;* WI (Pessamit) enishin [ēnəʃənu], *to lie flat on the ground;* enashkamit [ēnəʃkəmət], *flat against the ground;* Watkins (1865) "Ānow, *v.imp. It is flat;*" "Ānuchow, *v.imp. It is flat land;*" Laure (ca. 1726) "enagam teu, *il est en deçà du fleuve;*" Fabvre (ca. 1690) "Enăgam = mik Enakam, *de ce bord du mesme bord;*" Silvy (ca. 1680) "enagamik, *de ce bord du fleuve*"

*ēr[1]

PREFINAL

— consider, deem, or feel a certain emotion about see | *ērim, *ēriht

*ēr[2]

FINAL

— forms particles when suffixed to certain consonant-final initials

evidence | PC kētahtawē, *suddenly;* WC sīhkīð, *on one's own accord;* MC yālitel, *must, necessarily;* šehkel, *willingly; automatically;* ketahtawel, *suddenly;* AT (Wemotaci,

Jeannette Coocoo) saker [sākēr], *before, first;* SEC māhcitey, *the last one; the last time;* WI (Pessamit) shetshel [ʃētʃēl], *for no reason, for nothing, for free;* EI (Sheshatshiu) mashten [māstēn], *the last one, the last time;* Laure (ca. 1726) "chetcher, nit-akusin, *je suis malade par cas fortuit*" compare | *a, *ci, *i[3], *nē[4]

*ēriht

FINAL (VERB, TRANSITIVE, INANIMATE, CONCRETE)

— consider, deem, or feel a certain emotion about

evidence | PC itēyihtam, *to think thus about sth;* MC milwelihtam, *to like sth;* SEC māyeyihtam, *to insult sth* see | *ēr[1], *ht[4] paired with | *ērim compare | *āt[6]

*ērikw[1] (~ *ēriko)

INITIAL (NOUN, ANIMATE)

— ant

evidence | PC ēyik, *an ant;* WC iðikos, *an ant;* ESC enik, *an ant;* MC elikōš, *an ant;* SEC (coastal) eyik^{w}, *an ant;* SEC (Waswanipi) ocicelikōš, *an ant;* WI (Pessamit) elikutak^{u} [ēlukutuk^{w}], *a stump full of ants;* EI (Sheshatshiu) enik^{u} [ēnuk^{w}], *an ant or spider;* Silvy (ca. 1680) "erigȣ, *fourmi*" | MENO ɛ·nek(ok), *an ant* compare | *ērikw[2], *tērikom

*ērikw[2] (~ *ērikom)

MEDIAL (NOUN INCORPORATION)

— nostrils

evidence | MC kipwelikomew, *to have a stuffy nose;* SEC ohcikaweyikomew, *to have a runny nose;* NEC chipwāyikwāu, *to have a stuffy nose;* WI (Pessamit) miliuelikumeu [məlīwēlukumēw], *to have an abscess in one's nose;* Laure (ca. 1726) "ni-siskauerikumeuatsin, *le froid me rend morveux;*" Silvy (ca. 1680) "ni kipȣerikȣman, *j'ai le nez bouché, je parle du nez*" | ANISH mamaangidenigome, *to have big nostrils* (Livesay & Nichols, 2021) see | *tērikom

*ērim

FINAL (VERB, TRANSITIVE, ANIMATE, CONCRETE)

— consider, deem, or feel a certain emotion about

evidence | PC nahēyimēw, *to be pleased with sb;* MC milwelimew, *to like sb;* SEC māyeyimew, *to insult sb;* Silvy (ca. 1680) "ni peterimau, *je pense qu'il vient en deçà*" see | *ēr[1], *m[1] paired with | *ēriht compare | *āt[7]

*ēriwēhk

INITIAL

— used to add a positive comment about a generally negative situation

evidence | PC ēyiwēhk & kēyiwēhk, *at least; nevertheless; so-so, more or less;* SEC eyiwehc, *at least; anyway, nevertheless;* NEC āyiwāhch, *at least give it a try;* EI (Sheshatshiu) enuet [ēnwēt], *at least;* Silvy (ca. 1680) "eriȣek, *encore que*" | ANISH eniwek, *just so, somewhat* (Livesay & Nichols, 2021) limited to | *i[3]

*ēškam

INITIAL

— gradually, more and more

evidence | AT (Wemotaci, Nicole Petiquay) eškam, *gradually, more and more;* SEC (Waswanipi) eškam, *gradually, more and more* | ANISH eshkam, *gradually; less and less; more and more* (Livesay & Nichols, 2021); MENO ɛ·skam, *now and then;* MESK ēshkami, *gradually, more and more;* ēshkamesiwa, *to get sicker and sicker*

*ēškē

INITIAL (VERB, ANIMATE, INTRANSITIVE)

— chisel through ice (to capture beaver)

evidence | PC ēskan, *antler;* MC eškew, *to chisel through ice to capture beaver;* AT eckatam [eškātam], *to chisel a hole into sth;* SEC eškan, *ice chisel; antler;* NEC āshkihp, *place where one hunts beaver by chiseling into a beaver lodge;* WI (Pessamit) eshkateu [ēʃkātēw], *to chisel through the ice to catch a live beaver;* Isham (1743) "es cu nuck, *the horn of a beast;*" Laure (ca. 1726) "nit-eskan 3. esseu, *je perce la glace pour attraper le castor;*" Silvy (ca. 1680) "nit'echkan, *je me sers de cette tranche*" see | *īwit, *wit[3] discussion | Old Cree ***ēškanaki**, "antlers," appears to have replaced the expected reflexes of ***mīwitaki** in contemporary dialects, as antlers were presumably used for making ice chisels in prehistoric times. However, the medial associated with ***mīwitaki** is attested in various dialects and is reconstructible in Old Cree as ***wit**.

*ēštakay

INITIAL (NOUN, DEPENDENT INANIMATE)

— hair

evidence | PC wēstakāw, *to have lots of hair;* Lacombe (1874) "westakāy, *son cheveu;*" WC mīscakās, *a strand of hair;* WSC (Misipawistik, Ellen Cook) nēstakaya, *my hair* | MENO wɛ·qnan, *body hair, wisps of fur* origin | PA ***ēʔt** + ***ak** + ***ay** see | *ɪšt[1], *ak[2], *ay[2] compare | *ītišt

*ēt (~ *ēš)

INITIAL

— dent, imprint

evidence | PC ayēsihtin, *to leave an imprint;* SEC etāpihkātew, *to be marked by being tied;* Laure (ca. 1726) "etischiu, *les pistes de la bête paraissent;*" "etagunatsinamu, *piste sur la neige*" | ANISH ezhisin, "it leaves a mark" (Livesay & Nichols, 2021) origin | PA ***ēθ**

*ētacin

INITIAL

— front side up, face up

evidence | SEC etacininam, *to hold sth front side up;* WI (Pessamit) etatshinipalu [ētətnəpəlu], *to fall on one's back;* Watkins (1865) "Ātuchinipùkesin, *v.i.7. He falls backwards;*" Laure (ca. 1726) "nit-etatchinichinin, *je couche sur le dos;*" Silvy (ca. 1680) "nit'etatchiniparin, *je tombe à la renverse*" | MENO ɛ·necenehsemɛ·w, *to lay sb face up*

*ētataw

INITIAL

— a little more than expected, a little more than another

evidence | PC ētataw, *barely;* Lacombe (1874) "Etatowisiw, *il vit à peine;*" SEC etatawīš, *a little more;* NEC ātitūsīw, *to be lean, weak;* WI (Pessamit) etatu [ētətu], *more;* EI (Sheshatshiu) etatu [ēttu], *more;* Watkins (1865) "Ātutow, *adv. rather too much, a little more.* Ātutow misow, *it is rather too large.* Ātutow chimasin, *it is rather too short.*" Silvy (ca. 1680) "etatau, etataȣich, *un peu*"

*ēw[1] (~ *ēwak)

MEDIAL

— flesh, meat, muscle

evidence | PC kāhkēwak, *dried meat;* MC paskewew, *to be skinny;* aškewakāw, *to be raw flesh;* SEC wāpewew, *to have white flesh;* Laure (ca. 1726) "ka chipeuatchit, *edurci à la fatigue;*" "tatcheuagau, *viande froide*"

*ēw[2]

MEDIAL

— shoreline

evidence | PC kaskēwēw, *to go across land, to portage;* MC tetipewew, *to walk around a point of land;* SEC yāyew, *along the coast;* NEC sāchāwāu, *to come into view from around the point;* WI (Pessamit) iteueiau [ītēwējāw], *to extend in a certain direction or to have a certain appearance, speaking of a shoreline*

*ēyat (~ *ēyaš)

FINAL (VERB, ANIMATE, INTRANSITIVE)

— group, band, pack

evidence | PC asēyas, *in a group;* osāmēyatiwak, *to be too numerous;* WC māmawīyas, *all together;* MC mekweyaš, *among;* Watkins (1865) "Usāyutewuk, *v.i.1. pl. They herd;*" Laure (ca. 1726) "ni-mamaueiatinan, *nous sommes en troupe*" compare | *ɪt[3] discussion | The evidence demonstrates that this root has long been reanalyzed as a prefinal followed by the epenthetic vowel ***ɪ**, which itself has been reanalyzed as an abstract verb final. However, the root also serves to form particles when followed by the abstract final ***i**, supporting its analysis as a verb final.

H

*h

FINAL (VERB, TRANSITIVE, ANIMATE, ABSTRACT)

— forms causative verbs

evidence | MC kīkehew, *heal somebody;* AT aniskehew, *transmettre quelque chose à quelqu'un;* SEC makošehew, *to feast sb;* Silvy (ca. 1680) "ni ma8atchihit8nan, *nous nous assemblons*" paired with | *htā

*hcikwan[1]

INITIAL (NOUN, DEPENDENT INANIMATE)

— distal thigh, knee joint

evidence | PC mihcikwan, *a knee;* ESC (Severn) mihcikon, *front of the thigh;* MC nihcikwana, *my lap, the front of my thighs;* SEC ohcikwan, *one's knee;* EI (Mamit) uitshikun [wītʃukwan], *one's knee;* Fabvre (ca. 1690) "8tchig8an, *genu*" | ANISH gijiingwan, *NDA your lap; your (front of) thigh* (Livesay & Nichols, 2021); MENO nehci·kwan, *AN my knee* see | *hcikwan[2]

*hcikwan[2]

MEDIAL, FINAL (NOUN INCORPORATION)

— distal thigh, knee joint

evidence | PC wīsakihcikwanēw, *to hurt one's knee;* WC māskihcikwan, *a crippled knee;* MC pihkihcikwaneliw, *to bend one's knee;* SEC aspihcikwanehon, *apron;* EI (Sheshatshiu) utamitshikuneshinu [utāmītʃukunēʃinu], *to bump one's knee;* Silvy (ca. 1680) "nit'aïabitchig8anes8n, *je me chauffe les genoux;*" "ni kin8tchik8anin, *j'ai de longues cuisses*" see | *hcikwan[1]

*hcim

FINAL (VERB, TRANSITIVE, ANIMATE, CONCRETE)

— put in water

evidence | PC akohcimēw, *to soak sb, to put sb in water;* MC akohcimew, *to soak sb;* SEC akohcimew, *to soak sb* origin | PA ***ncim** (Aubin, 1975) limited to | *ako[1] see | *ht[3], *ɪm[3] paired with | *htitā[2]

*hcin

FINAL (VERB, ANIMATE, INTRANSITIVE, CONCRETE)

— be in water

evidence | PC akohcin, *to soak, to be in water;* MC akohcin, *to float in one place;* SEC akohcin, *to float in one place* origin | PA ***ncin** (Hewson, 1993) limited to | *ako[1] see | *ht[3], *n[3] paired with | *htin[2]

*hkomān

MEDIAL, FINAL (NOUN INCORPORATION)

— **1** knife

— **2** metal

evidence | [1]MC nīmihkomānew, *to take a knife along;* SEC pīhcihkomān, *pocket knife;* takohkomān, *a pair of scissors;* Laure (ca. 1726) "paskustuaichigan-ikuman, *rasoir;*" Silvy (ca. 1680) "ita8ikoman, *couteau coupant des deux côtés*" [2]MC aškihkomān, *lead;* Laure (ca. 1726) "astchikuman, *plomb, métal;*" "mikukuman-astiku, *chaudière de cuivre rouge;*" Silvy (ca. 1680) "irinikoman, *fer, métal*" origin | Old Cree ***mōhkomāni**

*hkomē

MEDIAL

— knife

evidence | MC pīhcihkomātam, *to sheath a knife;* NEC ashīhkumāu, *to blunt one's knife*

*hkw

MEDIAL, FINAL (NOUN INCORPORATION)

— face

evidence | PC kāsīhkwew, *to wash one's face;* MC macihkweliw, *to make a grimace;* išihkweliw, *to make such a face;* SEC otāštamihk^{w}, *one's face;* Laure (ca. 1726) "ni-mikukuan, *je rougis du visage*" see | *hkway

*hkwakw

FINAL (NOUN, INANIMATE, CLASSIFIER)

— metal implement

evidence | PC isawēhkwak, *a glover's needle;* WC osāwīhkwak, *copper, brass, yellow metal;* MC nōtimihkok^{w}, *rounded needle;* SEC asinīhkok^{w}, *aluminum foil;* NEC shiwāhkuk^{w}, *leather needle;* Watkins (1865) "Nootimikwuk, *n.in. A round-pointed needle*"

*hkway

INITIAL (NOUN, DEPENDENT INANIMATE)

— face

evidence | PC (Maskwacīs, Louise Wildcar) mīhkwākan, *a face;* WC mīhkwiy, *a face;* ESC (Severn) ohkwākan, *one's face;* Watkins (1865) "Mìkwakun, *n.in. The face*" see | *hkw, *ay[2]

*hkwē (~ *nēhkwē)

FINAL (VERB, ANIMATE, INTRANSITIVE, CONCRETE)

— drink or eat

evidence | PC kisēpānēhkwēw, *to eat breakfast;* MC otākošinehkwew, *to eat an evening meal;* SEC nīpehkwew, *to eat a meal after sunset* | ANISH minikwe, *to drink* (Livesay & Nichols, 2021) origin | PA ***ehkwē** discussion | The allomorph ***nēhkwē** is suffixed to intransitive inanimate verb stems.

*ho

FINAL (VERB, ANIMATE, INTRANSITIVE, CONCRETE)

— make oneself appear (in a specified way)

evidence | PC miyohow, *to be well-dressed;* MC iskwewihow, *to be dressed like a woman;* AT kicoho [kīʒōhow], *to dress warmly;* SEC išihow, *to be dressed thus;* wāpihow, *to be dressed in white;* NEC īshihū, *to be dressed thus;* EI (Sheshatshiu) matshu [mətʃū], *to lack hygiene or be a poor housekeeper;* Laure (ca. 1726) "ka matchihut, *souillon, malpropre;*" "miruhuun, *propreté, netteté;*" Silvy (ca. 1680) "ni matchihȣn, *je suis sale, mal peigné, malpropre*" | ANISH giizhi'o, *to dress oneself* (Livesay & Nichols, 2021) see | *h, *o

*hrē

FINAL (VERB, ANIMATE, INTRANSITIVE, CONCRETE)

— fly

evidence | PC takohāw, *to arrive flying;* MC pimilāw, *to fly along;* AT nitawirew [nihtāwirēw], *to be able to fly (as a fledgling);* SEC pāpihyāw, *to arrive flying;* Laure (ca. 1726) "assirheuets, *bande d'oiseaux;*" Silvy (ca. 1680) "ichpireȣ, *il vole haut*" origin | PA ***ʔrē** (***ʔle:**, Aubin, 1975) see | *hrēw

*hrēw

MEDIAL, FINAL (NOUN INCORPORATION)

— grouse, bird

evidence | WC nāpīhðīw, *male partridge;* MC nāpelew, *a male grouse;* oskanilew, *pine grosbeak;* nānatawilewew, *to look for grouse;* SEC mōhyewew, *to eat grouse;* Silvy (ca. 1680) "pipȣnireu, *espèce d'oiseau*" origin | PA ***ʔrēw** (***ʔle·w**, Hewson, 1993), likely as a contraction of PA ***perēwa** by syncope of the first vowel see | *pirēw

*hši[1]

FINAL (VERB, ANIMATE, INTRANSITIVE, CONCRETE)

— encounter or be in particular weather or season

evidence | PC misponisiw, *to get snowed on;* WC nīpinisiw, *to summer somewhere;* MC kimiwanišiw, *to encounter rainy weather;* AT

(Wemotaci, Nicole Petiquay) kimiwaniciw [kimiwaniššiw], *to encounter rain;* nipiniciw [nīpinišiw], *to summer, to spend summer somewhere;* WI (Pessamit) pipunishu [pupunəʃu], *to spend winter somewhere;* Silvy (ca. 1680) "ni kitchitanichin, *je demeure à cause de la pluie*"

*hši[2]

FINAL (VERB, ANIMATE, INTRANSITIVE, CONCRETE)

— leak, drip

evidence | NEC ahkushiu, *to be leaked on;* Silvy (ca. 1680) "ag8isi8ets mentaminets, *les blés sont mouillés, moisis*" paired with | *štin[1]

*hši[3]

FINAL (VERB, INTRANSITIVE, ABSTRACT, DIMINUTIVE)

— suffixed to animate and inanimate intransitive verb stems to convey a diminutive or attenuated sense or to emphasize a sense of beauty

evidence | PC mīcisosiw, *to eat a little;* MC mišikitišiw, *to be somewhat large;* milošišiw, *to have a nice appearance;* AT (Wemotaci, Jeannette Coocoo) kiceatisiciw [kiʒēyātizišsiw], *to become a young adult;* SEC nipāšiw, *to sleep a little;* (Waswanipi, Mary Jane Kitchen) miywāskokātešiw, *to have nice legs;* NEC apishikimaashiu, *to be a small lake or pond;* WI (Pessamit) miluapiteshu [məlwāpətešu], *to have nice teeth* (Drapeau, 1991); EI (Sheshatshiu) minuashu [minwāʃu], *to be beautiful or nice;* Laure (ca. 1726) "uetachiu, *aisé à endurer, tolérable;*" "uirutichichiu, *il est médiocrement riche*" discussion | Contemporary western dialects, including Atikamekw and Moose Cree, display a distinction between the above root, which forms VAI stems in these dialects, and the variant ***hšin** for VII stems. The earliest records show no such distinction, nor do contemporary eastern dialects.

*hšim

FINAL (VERB, TRANSITIVE, ANIMATE, CONCRETE)

— bring into contact with

evidence | PC pīkosimēw, *to break sth against sth or by dropping;* MC pimišimew, *to lay sb down;* AT a:ccišsim-, *to move s.o. lying down* (Béland, 1978); SEC teštacišimew, *to lie sb down with trunk elevated;* Silvy (ca. 1680) "nit'ab8ta8echchimau, *je le mets à contre poil*" | ANISH izhishim, *to put, lay, or set sb a certain way* (Livesay & Nichols, 2021) origin | PA ***hšim** (Aubin, 1975) see | *ht[2], *ɪm[3] paired with | *htitā[1]

*hšimo

— **1** bring oneself into contact with

— **2** dance

evidence | [1]PC yipātiskiwakisimow, *to muddy or dirty oneself;* SEC kawišimow, *to lay oneself down;* Laure (ca. 1726) "aspichimun, *lit*" [2]PC wāpanisimow, *to dance until dawn;* AT iriniššimo-, *to dance;* išiššimo- *to dance so* (Béland, 1978); SEC miyošimow, *to dance well;* Laure (ca. 1726) "uaskachimuin, *danse en rond*" | [1]ANISH apishimo, *to lie on sth* (Livesay & Nichols, 2021) [2]ANISH babaamishimo, *to dance about* (Livesay & Nichols, 2021)

*hšin

FINAL (VERB, ANIMATE, INTRANSITIVE, CONCRETE)

— be or come into contact with

evidence | PC pimisin, *to be lying down;* MC ātakāmešin, *blocked by a body of water;* AT a:ccišsin-, *to move, change place, lying down* (Béland, 1978); SEC ošāšākonacišin, *to slip on snow;* Fabvre (ca. 1690) "Mat8chtechǐnin 3 n8, *t(om)ber au feu;*" Silvy (ca. 1680) "ni pichtabistichinin, *je me heurte à une pierre, etc.*" origin | PA ***hšin** (Aubin, 1975) see | *ht[2], *n[3] paired with | *htin[1]

*hšip

MEDIAL, FINAL (NOUN INCORPORATION)

— duck

evidence | MC nānatawišipew, *to hunt ducks;* AT (Opitciwan, Monique Awashish) napecip [nāpēššip], *a male duck;* SEC mahkatešip, *black duck;* nāpešip, *a drake;* EI (Mamit) nuaishipeu [nawējhɨpēw], *to pursue ducks by boat;* Silvy (ca. 1680) "irinichip, *canard*" | ANISH ininishib, *a mallard* (Livesay & Nichols, 2021) origin | PA ***ʔšip** (Hewson, 1993) see | *šīhšīp

*hšīm

INITIAL (NOUN, DEPENDENT ANIMATE)

— younger sibling

evidence | MC ošīmimew, *to have sb as a younger sibling;* AT (Wemotaci, Jeannette Coocoo) ocima [oššīma], *one's younger sibling;* SEC ošīmimāw, *a younger sibling;* EI (Sheshatshiu) ushimu [uʃīmu], *to have a younger sibling;* Laure (ca. 1726) "uchima, *son cadet;*" Silvy (ca. 1680) "nichim, nichimai, *mon cadet, mon cousin, fils de mon oncle paternel*"

*ht^{1}

MEDIAL

— doorway

evidence | MC āpihtenam, *to open a tent flap;* SEC yōhtenew, *to open a tent flap;* WI (Pessamit) shiputepalu [ʃəputēpəlu], *tent flaps closes;* Laure (ca. 1726) "puskutekuteu, *à demi ouvert;*" "ni-paschitenen, *j'ouvre porte, fenêtre*" | ANISH baakindesijige, *to leave a lodge door or tent fly open* (Livesay & Nichols, 2021) compare | *htaw

*ht^{2} (~ *hš)

PREFINAL

— be or come into contact with

origin PA ***hθ** (Aubin, 1975) see | *htin^{1}, *htitā^{1}, *hšin, *hšim

*ht^{3} (~ *hc)

PREFINAL

— be in water

origin PA ***nt** (Aubin, 1975) see | *hcin, *hcim, *htin^{2}, *htitā^{2}

*ht^{4} (~ *hc)

FINAL (VERB, TRANSITIVE, INANIMATE)

— **1** conveys the semantic role of stimulus to a participant

— **2** applicative that adds a comitative argument when suffixed to animate intransitive verb stems

evidence | ^{1}MC ošihtam, *to flee sth;* SEC wīhcimāhtam, *to like the scent of sth;* NEC miywāyihtim, *to like sth* ^{2}MC wīhpehtam, *to sleep with sth;* NEC wītipihtim, *to sit with sth* paired with | *m^{1} see | *wīt

*htaw

MEDIAL

— doorway

evidence | PC sāpohtawēyāw, *to have an opening at each end;* MC šāpohtawān, *lodge with doorway on each end;* NEC shāhtiwāyāu, *for a conical lodge to have an opening at the top because the cover is low* compare | *ht^{1}

*htawak

MEDIAL (NOUN INCORPORATION)

— ear(s)

evidence | PC pīmihtawakēnēw, *to twist sb's ear;* MC cīwehtawakew, *to have tinnitus;* SEC māmahcihtawacew, *to have big ears;* Laure (ca. 1726) "nit-apichitauaganich 3. -ich, *j'ai de petites oreilles*" see | *htawakay

*htawakay

INITIAL (NOUN, DEPENDENT INANIMATE)

— ear

evidence | PC mihtawakay, *an ear;* MC ohtawakāw, *to have ears;* SEC (Waswanipi) ohtawakay [uhtawkay], *one's ear;* Laure (ca. 1726) "n-utauagan 3. -gau, *j'ai des oreilles;*" Silvy (ca. 1680) "mitaȣagai, l'oreille" | ANISH gitawag, *your ear* (Livesay & Nichols, 2021); MENO nɛhta·wak, *my ear* see | *htawak, *ay[2]

*htā (~ *hc, *htw)

FINAL (VERB, ANIMATE, INTRANSITIVE, ABSTRACT)

— **1** forms causative verbs that are syntactically transitive

— **2** forms stative verbs that are syntactically intransitive

evidence | [1]PC Lacombe (1874) "Nokuttowew, *il lui fait voir;*" MC iskwāpihkehtāw, *to make a string a certain length;* tetāwihtowew, *to separate sth down the middle for sb;* išihcikew, *to make or do things thus;* SEC miyonākohtāw, *to make sth look nice;* WI manatshitueu [mənāstwēw], *to handle sth carefully for sb* [2]MC kakwākihtāw, *to be wretched;* SEC (Waswanipi) wīsakihtāw, *to be cringy;* NEC mūchikihtāu, *to have fun* paired with | *h discussion | The ***htw** allomorph surfaces only for further derivation when suffixing either the antipassive ***ā** or the benefactive ***aw**. Its origin predates what is otherwise a loss of morphological distinction in Old Cree between Proto-Algonquian transitive inanimate verb class II and animate intransitive verbs ending in ***ā** (cf. Pentland, 1999). Note that contemporary dialects have all contracted ***htw** + ***aw** to a reflex of ***htow**, but the underlying form is revealed when vowel-lengthening processes occur, resulting in reflexes of ***htwā** as expected.

*htāhpiy

INITIAL (NOUN, DEPENDENT INANIMATE)

— nape

evidence | PC Lacombe (1874) "otāppïy, a, *le gros nerf du cou;*" ESC (Weenusk) "nahtāpī, *nape of the neck*" (Michelson, 1936:88) | ANISH Cuoq (1886) "ni tanbing, *à mon chignon;*" MESK nehtāhpi, *my nape;* MIAMI nihtaampi, *the back of my neck* (ILDA, 2017) origin | PA ***htāmpy**

*htin[1]

FINAL (VERB, INANIMATE, INTRANSITIVE, CONCRETE)

— **1** be or come into contact with

— **2** to lie or run, speaking of a river

evidence | [1]PC pimihtin, *to lie along a surface;* MC otāmihtin, *to bang against sth;* SEC pīkohtin, *to break upon impact* Silvy (ca. 1680) "papak8atchitin, *la pièce est ôtée, v.g. l'emplâtre*" [2]PC Lacombe (1874) "nistāwittin, wa, (a.in.) *confluent de deux rivières;*" MC nīšohtinwa, *for two rivers to run parallel;* SEC maščekohtin, *the river runs through muskeg* | [1]MENO na·pa·hkihnɛn, *to have a handle* origin | PA ***hθen** (Aubin, 1975) see | *ht[2], *ɩn[4] paired with | *hšin

*htin[2]

FINAL (VERB, INANIMATE, INTRANSITIVE, CONCRETE)

— be in water

evidence | PC akohtin, *to soak, to be in water;* MC akohtin, *to float in one place;* SEC akohtin, *to float in one place* limited to | *ako[1] see | *ht[3], *ɩn[4] paired with | *hcin

*htitā[1]

FINAL (VERB, ANIMATE, INTRANSITIVE, CONCRETE)

— bring into contact with

evidence | PC āsohtitāw, *to lean sth against sth else;* MC pimihtitāw, *to lie sth down;* SEC otāmihtitāw, *to bang sth against sth* origin | PA ***hθetō** (Aubin, 1975) see | *ht[2], *ɩtā paired with | *hšim

*htitā[2]

FINAL (VERB, ANIMATE, INTRANSITIVE, CONCRETE)

— put in water

evidence | PC akohtitāw, *to soak sth, to put sth in water;* MC akohtitāw, *to soak sth;* SEC akohtitāw, *to soak sth* limited to | *ako[1] see | *ht[3], *ɩtā paired with | *hcim

*htwā

FINAL (VERB, ANIMATE, INTRANSITIVE, CONCRETE)

— have custom, be mannered

evidence | PC miyohtwāw, *to be kind;* MC milohtwāw, *to be well-mannered;* SEC macihtwāw, *to be mean;* Silvy (ca. 1680) "nit'ichitȣan 3. -au, *je fais ainsi, c'est ma coutume*"

I

*i¹

INITIAL (VERB, ANIMATE, INTRANSITIVE)

— to say

evidence | SEC (Eastmain, Sarah Mark-Stewart) īw, *to say;* nisin, *I say;* tān enāniwit? *what is being said?;* ci kaš-īyin? *what are you saying?;* tān yāyin? *what are you saying?;* SEC (inland) īnāniwiw, *to be said;* tān enāniwic? *what is being said?;* NEC iyiu, *to say;* WI (Pessamit, Kim Picard) iu [īw], *to say;* EI (Sheshatshiu) iu [īw], *to say;* nishin, *I say;* Watkins (1865) "Yew, *v.irreg. He says, In some localities this word is not known, but in others it is in constant use;*" "Chekussaiyin? *What do you say?;*" Laure (ca. 1726) "eka itu esku, *ne le dis pas encore;*" Silvy (ca. 1680) "iȣa, *il dit;*" "ni sin, *je dis;*" "ki kachaïen, *que dis-tu?;*" "kachaïȣ, *que dit-il?;*" "ȣ tchigain, *tu diras ainsi*" | ANISH Cuoq (1886) "iwak, *disent-ils;*" MENO ewa·h, *he says so;* nese·m, *I say so;* ɛ·c, *what he says* discussion | This root is obsolete in most contemporary dialects and its use is declining in those that have retained it. It is dysfunctional in certain regions, having been suppleted in most cases by reflexes of the verb stem ***ιtwē**, except for certain conjugations such as the third-person forms of the independent order or reflexes of the impersonal stem ***ināniwi**. In Eastmain, where the dialect displays mixed features of SEC and NEC, the changed form for the first and second persons points to a restructured underlying stem of the shape ***yi** or ***yī**, while the first and second persons of the independent preserve the above Old Cree stem, triggering lenition of ***t** to ***s** in what would underlyingly be ***nit ina** for the first-person singular, resulting in ***nis ina**.

*i²

FINAL (VERB, INTRANSITIVE, ABSTRACT)

— forms both stative and dynamic verbs

evidence | MC tašiwak, *be a certain number;* AT itaciw [itāššiw], *to be swept thither by the wind;* PC tahkikamiw, *to be cold water;* SEC koštāciw, *to be afraid;* Silvy (ca. 1680) "nit'ispichigabaȣin, *je suis de cette grandeur, de cette hauteur*" discussion | As per Collette (2022), this final is not to be mistaken for the epenthetic vowel ***ι**, reanalyzed as an animate intransitive verb final in most modern dialects when suffixed to certain Old Cree finals ending in ***t**. Due to the limited evidence, it is unclear whether certain initials ending in ***p**, such as ***nip**, are fully formed verbs in Old Cree as they are in other Algonquian languages, requiring only the epenthetic vowel to satisfy syllabic restrictions, or whether they require the above verb final to form functional intransitive verbs.

*i³

FINAL (ABSTRACT)

— forms particles when suffixed to certain initials and finals

evidence | PC asici, *in addition;* asēyas_, *in a group;* ESC māmawi, *together;* MC kiki, *with;* AT (Opitciwan, Joey Awashish) wipatci [wīpaci], *soon; early;* SEC pāšic_, *passing over;* Silvy (ca. 1680) "ȣastitchi, *dessus, le dehors de qqch*" compare | *a, *ci, *ēr², *nē⁴

*in¹ (~ *ih)

INITIAL (VERB, INANIMATE, INTRANSITIVE)

— happen, fare

evidence | PC tānēhki (lexicalized form), *why;* MC tānehki (lexicalized form), *why;* SEC in, *to happen;* tān ehc, *what is happening?;*

WI (Pessamit) in [īn], *to be, to happen;* Watkins (1865) "Ayin, *v.imp. It happens. The more common expression is èkin;*" Laure (ca. 1726) "kata inu put, *cela n'est encore que futur;*" Silvy (ca. 1680) "in8, *il est ainsi;*" "eg8 in8sin, *ainsi soit-il*" paired with | *ıht[1] discussion | This inanimate intransitive verb stem is derivationally nonproductive. However, it does feature in a few atypical lexicalized forms. For example, Western dialects have lexicalized ***tāni ēhki** into *tānēhki,* "why," while East Cree dialects have lexicalized ***kī inwi** into *cīhin,* "to function." In western dialects the above root has been replaced by *ihkin,* a stem of unknown origin mentioned in the above quote from Watkins (1865).

*in² (~ *ih)

FINAL (VERB, INANIMATE, INTRANSITIVE, ABSTRACT)

— forms dynamic verbs

evidence | MC ohcikawin, *to leak from;* SEC (Waswanipi) cīwepayin, *to return spontaneously* see | *kawin, *parin

*ī¹

FINAL (VERB, ANIMATE, INTRANSITIVE, ABSTRACT)

— forms dynamic verbs of intentional movement

evidence | PC kotāwīw, *to sink oneself into the ground;* MC āhcīw, *to move;* SEC mācīw, *to leave;* Silvy (ca. 1680) "ni 8anin, *je m'éveille*"

*ī²

FINAL (VERB, INANIMATE, INTRANSITIVE, ABSTRACT)

— forms dynamic and stative verbs

evidence | MC timīw, *to be deep water;* SEC pināscīw, *for leaves to fall from trees;* NEC sāchipichīu, *to be budding season;* āpuwīu, *to thaw in warm weather, speaking of ice;* WI (Pessamit) pinassiu [pənāssīw], *for leaves to fall from trees;* EI (Sheshatshiu) uakatimiu [wākājātɨmīw], *to be a curved channel;* Silvy (ca. 1680) "ispi8, *terre haute*" | MENO ka·wi·w, *to be rough* compare | *yā

*īhk

FINAL (VERB, TRANSITIVE, CONCRETE)

sound change | o + īhk → ōhk

— work on, busy oneself on

evidence | PC isīhkam, *to bother thus with sth;* MC ālimīhkawew, *to work on sth with difficulty;* nīšōhkamwak, *to be two working on sth;* SEC pimīhkam, *to work on sth, to busy oneself with sth;* "ni metatchika8au, *j'arrive à lui trop tard*"

*īhkānihs

INITIAL (NOUN, DEPENDENT ANIMATE)

— brother or male friend of a man

evidence | AT (Wemotaci, Nicole Petiquay) nikanis [nīkkānis], *my godfather or godmother;* NSK wīhkānisa, *one's kin;* WI (Pessamit) uikanisha [wīkānəʃ], *one's relative(s), one's kin;* EI (Sheshatshiu) uikanisha [wīkā:jʃa], *one's parents or close relative;* Laure (ca. 1726) "tchikanis, *ton ami;*" "uikanissimituets, *ils sont amis, frères;*" Silvy (ca. 1680) "nikanis, *ami;*" "ni 8ikanissimau, *je l'ai pour ami, frère*" | ANISH wiikaanisan, *one's brother or male friend, speaking of a man* (Livesay & Nichols, 2021); MENO ne·hka·h(-sak), *my brother, man speaking;* ne·hka·n, *my fellow participant in a ceremony, especially in the Mitewin;* MESK nīhkāna, *my friend; my close male friend, speaking of a man;* MIAMI -iihkaan-, *friend of the same sex* (ILDA, 2017)

*īk

INITIAL (NOUN, DEPENDENT INANIMATE)

— home

evidence | PC wīkiw, *to dwell somewhere;* MC wīki, *one's home;* SEC nīcinān, *our home;* WI (Pessamit) uitshu [wītʃu], *to have one's house or tent somewhere* | MENO ne·k, *my dwelling, my house* compare | *ok

*īkatē

INITIAL

— out of the way

evidence | PC īkatēhtēw, *to walk off to one side;* WC īkatīnam, *to put sth out of the way;* MC (w)īkatepitam, *to pull sth out of the way;* AT (Wemotaci, Nicole Petiquay) ikatectaw [īkatēštāw], *to place sth out of the way;* SEC īceštāw, *to place sth out of the way;* NEC īchāsiu, *to move out of the way;* WI (Pessamit) itshepatau [ītʃēpətāw], *to move aside quickly* | ANISH niigadenan, *to push sth aside* (Lippert & Gambill, 2023) discussion | Eastern dialects display a reflex that appears to descend from ***ītakē** by metathesis. The final form can be explained by palatalization of the ***k** and elision of the short vowel between homorganic consonants: īkatē → ītacē → ītcē → īcē.

*īpihs

INITIAL (NOUN, DEPENDENT INANIMATE)

— pointed stick used as a projectile such as a dart or spear

evidence | PC Lacombe (1874) "wipis, a, *(n.r.) flèche;*" NEC wipis, *stick sharped and used as a spear;* NSK miipis, *short spear, sharpened stick or arrow for killing caribou;* Watkins (1865) "wepisew, *v.i.1. He has a pointed arrow*" | MENO ne·p, *my arrow;* MIAMI niipi, *my arrow* (ILDA, 2017)

*īpit (~ *īpic)

INITIAL (NOUN, DEPENDENT INANIMATE)

— tooth

evidence | PC mīpitihkāna, *false teeth, dentures;* MC wīpita, *one's teeth;* SEC nīpit, *my tooth;* Laure (ca. 1726) "uipitch *pl.* uipita, *dent d'homme;*" Silvy (ca. 1680) "nipit *pl.* nipitai, *ma dent*" origin | PA ***īpit** (Aubin, 1975) see | *āpit

*īskw

INITIAL (NOUN, DEPENDENT ANIMATE)

— co-wife

evidence | PC nīskwa, *my husband's former wife;* EI (Unaman-shipit) uishkuapeu [wīhkwāpēu], *to have a rival, speaking of a man or woman whose partner has a lover;* Watkins (1865) "Weskwa, *n.an. Her fellow-wife (i.e. speaking of the wives of a bigamist);*" Silvy (ca. 1680) "niiskȣ *ma compagne, l'autre femme de mon mari*" compare | *īw, *št[1]

*īšikan

INITIAL

— one half of an object

evidence | NEC īshikin, *half;* īshikinihtākutāu, *to hang half open, speaking of a tent flap;* Laure (ca. 1726) "ichiganich, *partie d'un pain, morceau;*" Fabvre (ca. 1690) "ichiganikȣmănich, *un morceau de fer;*" Silvy (ca. 1680) "ichigan, *partie, morceau;*" "nit'ichiganichen, *j'en coupe un morceau*" | ANISH izhiganezi, *to be a half-moon* (Lippert & Gambill, 2023); MENO e·sekan, *one of two similar sides, one half; on one side*

*īštāw

INITIAL (NOUN, DEPENDENT ANIMATE)

— **1** male cross-cousin of a man

— **2** brother-in-law of a man

evidence | WC nīstāw, *my brother-in-law, man to man; my cousin, the son of my father's sister;* MC wīštāwimāw, *a cross-cousin or sibling-in-law of identical sex;* WI (Pessamit) uishtaua [wīstà:w], *his brother-in-law;* uishtaututueu [wīstāwttwēw], *to treat sb as a brother-in-law in the hope of obtaining favors from one's sister, speaking of a man;* EI (Sheshatshiu) uishtaua [wīstāwa], *one's sibling-in-law of the same gender as oneself;* Laure (ca. 1726) "nichtau, *mon beau-frère qui a épousé ma sœur;*" Silvy (ca. 1680) "nichtau *voc.* nichta, *mon cousin*" | ANISH wiitaan, *his brother-in-law* (Livesay & Nichols, 2021); MESK nīhtāwa, *my brother-in-law, of a man* compare | *ītimohs, *tāhkohs

*īštow

INITIAL (NOUN, DEPENDENT INANIMATE)

— facial hair

evidence | NEC wīshtui, *an animal muzzle;* WI (Pessamit) nishtui [nīstwī], *my beard or moustache hair;* EI (Sheshatshiu) uishtui [wīstwī], *one's beard or moustache hair;* Laure (ca. 1726) "tchichtui, *ta barbe;*" Silvy (ca. 1680) "michtȣi, *barbe d'animal, quel qu'il soit*" see | *štow

*ītakay

INITIAL (NOUN, DEPENDENT INANIMATE)

— penis

evidence | MC wītakay, *one's penis;* SEC wītakay, *one's penis;* NEC wītikī, *one's penis* | ANISH wiinag, *one's penis* (Livesay & Nichols, 2021) origin | PA ***īθakay** (Aubin, 1975) see | *tak compare | *atakay

*ītaw

INITIAL

— both sides

evidence | PC āyītawahēw, *to place them on both sides;* MC ītaw, *on both sides;* ītawiškwāht, *both sides of the doorway;* SEC ītawakām, *on both sides of a body of water;* Silvy (ca. 1680) "itaȣikoman, *couteau coupant des deux côtés*" | ANISH eyiidawoonag, *both sides of the canoe or boat;* MENO e·tawa·hkamek, or a·y-, *at both sides of the place*

*ītimohs

INITIAL (NOUN, DEPENDENT ANIMATE)

— cross-cousin of the opposite gender of the subject

evidence | PC nīcimos, *my sweetheart;* MC wīcimosa, *one's sweetheart or romantic partner;* SEC wītimosiw, *to have a cross-cousin of the opposite sex, a sibling-in-law of the opposite sex, or a romantic partner;* NEC wītimusimāw, *a cross-cousin or sibling-in-law;* WI (Pessamit) uitimushu [wītəmuʃu], *to have a lover;* Laure (ca. 1726) "nitimuch, *la fille de mon oncle maternel;*" Silvy (ca. 1680) "nitimoush, *ma cousine, fille de mon oncle;*" "nitimus, *maîtresse*" | ANISH niinimoshenh, *my cross-cousin of the opposite sex to me* (Livesay & Nichols, 2021); MENO ne·nemo·hsɛw, *my sweetheart* compare | *ītimw, *īštāw discussion | Contemporary and historical evidence strongly suggest cross-cousin marriage as an institution was a cultural norm for speakers of Old Cree. This explains how the root acquired a secondary sense of romantic partner in many contemporary dialects.

*ītimw

INITIAL (NOUN, DEPENDENT ANIMATE)

— sibling-in-law of the opposite gender of the subject

evidence | WC kītim, *your cousin; your sibling-in-law of the opposite sex;* MC wītimwa, *a cross-cousin or sibling-in-law of the opposite sex;* AT witimwa [wītimwa], *one's sibling-in-law of the opposite sex;* EI (Sheshatshiu) uitimua [wītumwa], *one's sister-in-law or brother-in-law;* Laure (ca. 1726) "nitim, *ma belle-sœur, femme de mon frère;*" Silvy (ca. 1680) "nitim, *frère de mon mari;*" "ȣitimȣ, *son beau-frère*" | ABEN -ilem, *sister-in-law of a man* (Day, 1995); ANISH wiinimoon, *her brother-in-law; his sister-in-law* (Livesay & Nichols, 2021); Cuoq (1886) "Ninim, ta ikito ikwe, *mon beau-frère, dira la femme;*" MENO ne·nemok, *my sisters-in-law, of a man speaking; my brothers-in-law, of a woman speaking;* MESK nīnemwa, *my brother-in-law, speaking of a woman; my sister-in-law, speaking of a man* origin | PA ***īθemw** (Aubin, 1975) compare | *ītimohs, *īštāw

*ītišān

INITIAL (NOUN, DEPENDENT ANIMATE)

— sibling

evidence | PC nītisān, *my sibling;* MC wīcišāniskwema, *one's sister(s);* AT (Wemotaci, Nicole Petiquay; Opitciwan, Joey Awashish) witcican [wīciʒān], *a family* member; SEC wīcišānimāw, *a sibling;* NEC wīchishānimāu, *a sibling or parallel cousin;* Laure (ca. 1726) "uitchichanituets, *ils sont frères de père et de mère;*" Silvy (ca. 1680) "nikichan, *mon frère ainé, ma sœur ainée;*" "nichichan, nitichan, *mon ainé, mon germain*" | MENO ni·tesyan, *my brother or sister* see | *wīt, *ıšē compare | *tawēmāw

*ītišt (~ *ītihš)

INITIAL (NOUN, DEPENDENT INANIMATE)

— head hair

evidence | PC wītisiw, *to have long, thick hair;* WSC (Misipawistik, Ellen Cook) wītisiw, *to have long, thick hair;* cf. AT (Opitciwan, Joey Awashish) owirisis [owīrissis], *one's hair* | MENO ne·nɛqnan, *my hair (from the head);* MESK nīnesani, *my hair;* owīnesiwa, *to have hair (on one's head)* origin | PA ***īθeʔθ** see | *ıšt[1] compare | *ēštakay

*īw

INITIAL (NOUN, DEPENDENT ANIMATE)

— wife

evidence | PC wīwiw, *to have a wife;* MC nīwa, *my wife;* NEC wīwiu, *to have a wife;* Laure (ca. 1726) "uiua, uiriua *rel., son épouse*" | ANISH wiiwan, *one's wife* (Livesay & Nichols, 2021) origin | PA ***wīwari** (***wi·wali**, Hewson, 1993) compare | *št[1], *īskw

*īwat (~ *īwaš)

INITIAL (NOUN, DEPENDENT INANIMATE)

— bag, pack

evidence | PC mīwatihkēw, *to make a medicine bag;* MC wīwašiw, *to carry a pack;* SEC wīwat, *one's bag or backpack;* Silvy (ca. 1680) "miȣach, *sac, paquet*" origin | PA ***īwaθ** (Aubin, 1975; Hewson, 1993) see | *ıwat discussion | Compare the Old Cree singular ***mīwaši** with its plural, ***mīwatahi**.

*īwit (~ *īwiš)

INITIAL (NOUN)

— **1** (dependent animate) antler

— **2** (dependent inanimate) chisel

evidence | Isham (1743) "me wiss, *a narrow ice chissell*" | ANISH André (ca. 1690s) "mious, *tranche emoussée; plu.* miouilah;" MENO ne·wen, *my horn;* MIAMI awiiwiila, *a horn, an antler; a braid* (ILDA, 2017) origin | PA ***īwiθ** see | *wit[3] compare | *ēškē discussion | In want of Cree cognates that inform the quality of the stem's final consonant, Rhodes (2021) postulates PA ***wi·wila**.

*īyaw

INITIAL (NOUN, DEPENDENT INANIMATE)

— body

evidence | MC kīyaw, *your body;* AT (Opitciwan, Joey Awashish) niaw [nīyaw], *my body;* WI (Pessamit) uiau [uju], *one's body;* Laure (ca. 1726) "nihiau, *mon corps*" | ANISH niiyaw, *my body* (Livesay & Nichols, 2021) compare | *īyāhs

*īyāhs

INITIAL (NOUN, DEPENDENT INANIMATE)

— flesh

evidence | MC wiyās, *one's flesh;* AT (Opitciwan, Joey Awashish) nias [nīyās], *my flesh;* EI (Sheshatshiu) uiash [wjāʃ], *one's flesh;* Laure (ca. 1726) "nihias, *ma chair*" | ANISH niiyaas, *my flesh* (Livesay & Nichols, 2021) compare | *īyaw

K

*k

PREFINAL

— to cut or chop

evidence | PC napakikaham, *to flatten sth by chopping;* MC pīwikaham, *to chop sth into pieces;* SEC kawikahtam, *to fell sth using one's teeth (speaking of a beaver)* see | *kah, *kaht, *kahw, *kam[2]

*kah

FINAL (VERB, TRANSITIVE, INANIMATE, CONCRETE)

— by chopping

evidence | PC napaki<u>kah</u>am, *to flatten sth by chopping;* MC pīwi<u>kah</u>am, *to chop sth into pieces;* SEC kawi<u>kah</u>am, *to fell sth with an axe* | MENO ce·ke<u>kah</u>am, *to hew sth* see | *k, *ah paired with | *kahw

*kaht

FINAL (VERB, TRANSITIVE, INANIMATE, CONCRETE)

— to cut with one's teeth, to chew

evidence | MC wāše<u>kaht</u>am, *to gnaw sth clean;* SEC kawi<u>kaht</u>am, *to fell sth using one's teeth (speaking of a beaver);* Laure (ca. 1726) "ni-tchimi<u>kat</u>en, *je romps du bois avec les dents*" see | *k, *aht³ paired with | *kam²

*kahtikw

MEDIAL, FINAL (NOUN INCORPORATION)

— forehead

evidence | WC māhki<u>kāhtikw</u>īw, *to have a big forehead;* MC alakaški<u>kahtikw</u>ew, *to have a broad forehead;* SEC tōmi<u>kahtikw</u>enew, *to anoint sb's forehead* see | *skahtikw

*kahw

FINAL (VERB, TRANSITIVE, ANIMATE, CONCRETE)

— by chopping

evidence | PC napaki<u>kahw</u>ew, *to flatten sth by chopping;* MC pīwi<u>kahw</u>ew, *to chop sth into pieces;* SEC kawi<u>kahw</u>ew, *to fell sth with an axe* see | *k, *ahw paired with | *kah

*kakayēr

INITIAL

— deceive, deceitful

evidence | PC <u>kakayēy</u>ihēw, *to deceive sb;* <u>kayēy</u>isiw, *to be sly;* MC <u>kakayel</u>imew, *to deceive sb by speech* | ANISH <u>gagayen</u>izi, *to be crafty* (Lippert & Gambill, 2023); MENO <u>kaka·yɛ·n</u>esew, *to be deceitful, crafty*

*kakāraw

INITIAL

— reliable

evidence | PC <u>kakāyaw</u>ātisiw, *to be diligent, hard-working;* <u>kakāyaw</u>ātan, *to be durable, dependable;* <u>kakāyaw</u>icimēw, *to be a good rower;* WC <u>kakāðaw</u>isīw, *to be industrious;* MC <u>kakālaw</u>, *effortfully;* mōla <u>kakālaw</u>, *hardly, barely;* AT (Wemotaci, Jeannette Coocoo) nama <u>kara</u> [nama kāra], *not often;* NEC <u>kāyuw</u>in, *to be sharp, speaking of a tool;* Laure (ca. 1726) "ni-<u>garau</u>ahugun, *je suis hors de portée du fusil*" origin | Possibly a reduplicated form.

*kam¹ (~ *ākam)

MEDIAL (CLASSIFIER)

— **1** body of water

— **2** liquid

evidence | PC misi<u>kam</u>āw, *to be a big lake;* WC apisc<u>ākam</u>isin, *to be a little quantity of liquid;* māhki<u>kam</u>āw, *to be a large body of water;* MC kino<u>kam</u>āw, *to be a long lake;* wāp<u>ākam</u>inam, *to add milk to a drink;* SEC ciš<u>ākam</u>isow, *to be a hot liquid;* osciskā<u>kam</u>āw, *to be a lake marked by the presence of jack pines;* Silvy (ca. 1680) "michi<u>gam</u>au, *grand, large, fleuve, lac, etc.*" | ANISH ginoo<u>gam</u>aa, *to be a long lake* (Livesay & Nichols, 2021) origin | PA ***kam** (Aubin, 1975; Hewson, 1993)

*kam²

FINAL (VERB, TRANSITIVE, ANIMATE, CONCRETE)

— to cut with one's teeth, to chew

evidence | MC wāše<u>kam</u>ew, *to gnaw sth clean;* SEC kawi<u>kam</u>ew, *to fell sth using one's teeth;* WI (Pessamit) natua<u>kam</u>eu [nātwākəmēw], *to section sth in two with one's teeth* see | *k, *am² paired with | *kaht

*kamik

MEDIAL

— dwelling

evidence | PC nīsokamik, *two buildings;* MC peyakokamikisiw, *to have one dwelling;* SEC nīšokamicisiwac, *to constitute two dwellings;* NEC nishtukimich, *three dwellings* | ANISH jiigigamig, *by a house or lodge* (Livesay & Nichols, 2021); MESK nekotikamiki, *one household, one family* compare | *kamikw

*kamikw (~ *kamiko)

MEDIAL, FINAL (NOUN, INANIMATE)

— room or building

evidence | PC okimāwikamik, *a governor's house;* WC māhkikamikwīw, *to have a large house;* MC patetasikamikohkew, *to build a potato cellar;* AT akosiwikamikw [āhkozīwikamikʷ], *hospital;* SEC cištāpāwacikamikwew, *to mop the floors;* NEC nipāukimikw, *a bedroom;* Silvy (ca. 1680) "assiniȣigamik, *mur, maison de pierre*" | ANISH babaamigamigwe, *to wander around the community visiting* (Livesay & Nichols, 2021); MENO na·wikamek, *at the center of the lodge* see | *kamik, *w[1]

*kamiy (~ *ākamiy)

FINAL (NOUN, INANIMATE, CLASSIFIER)

— **1** body of water

— **2** liquid

evidence | PC kihcikamiy, *sea;* MC kihcikamiy, *sea;* tahkikamiy, *cold water;* SEC Piyekwākamiy, *Lac-St-Jean (place name)*

*kan (~ *kanak)

MEDIAL, FINAL (NOUN INCORPORATION)

— bone

evidence | PC mipwāmikan, *femur;* MC išikanakāw, *to be such a bone;* tewikanew, *to have aching bones;* SEC nātwākanešin, *to break one's bone in half;* WI (Pessamit) tshinikanakau, *to be a pointy bone;* Silvy (ca. 1680) "ni michkȣganehȣau, *je le frappe à l'os en le dardant;*" "ȣstigȣanigan, *crâne*" see | *skan

*kanāt (~ *kanāc)

INITIAL

— in proper place or state

evidence | PC kanātisiw, *to be clean;* kanātan, *to be clean, tidy, or neat;* WC kanātīðihtākwan, *to be considered sacred or pure;* ESC kanātan, *to be holy;* MC kanāciahcāhkʷ, *the Holy Spirit;* NEC kināch, *in a hidden, safe place, not readily available* | MENO kana·taqtaw, *to lay it properly away;* kana·tenam, *to put sth down, to put sth away;* MESK kenāchihtôwa, *to be careful with sth, to go easy on sth*

*kano (~ *kanaw)

INITIAL

— keep

evidence | PC kanawāpamēw, *to look at sb;* MC kanohkew, *to bear in mind, to remember;* kanawiškwāhtawew, *to watch the doorway;* SEC kanaweyihtam, *to keep sth;* EI (Sheshatshiu) kanuasseu [kənwāssēw], *to take care or look after a child temporarily;* Laure (ca. 1726) "ganauipan, *réservoir d'eau*" | ANISH ganawaabi, *to look* (Livesay & Nichols, 2021) origin | PA ***kanaw** (Aubin, 1975)

*kapaštawē

INITIAL

— put into water

evidence | PC pakastawēpayin, *to fall into the water;* WC pakastawīham, *to put sth in water;* ESC kapastawepahtāw, *to run into the water;* MC pakaštawewepinew (obsolete) & kapaštawewepinew, *to throw sb into the water;* SEC pakaštaweham & (Waswanipi, archaic) kapaštaweham, *to put sth in the water;* NSK pikistuwāham, *to put sth in the water;* WI (Pessamit) pakashtueteu [pukustwētēw], *to walk into the water;* Laure (ca. 1726) "ni-pakachtauehen 3. -himu, *je jette l'ancre, je mouille;*" Fabvre (ca. 1690) "nigapastaȣechimau, *Immerger;*" Silvy (ca. 1680) "ni kapastaȣehȣau, *je le jette dans l'eau*" compare | *kapā discussion | A variant obtained by metathesis of the two first syllables is widespread across contemporary dialects. However, the form above is the earliest attested form and continues to be present in Eastern Swampy Cree, Moose Cree, and in the speech of elderly East Cree speakers from Waswanipi.

*kapatē

INITIAL

— unload

evidence | PC kapatēham, *to take sth out of a pot and dish it out;* WC kapatīhtatāw, *to take sth onto shore;* MC kapatenam, *to disembark sth by hand; to take sth off the fire, stovetop, or out of the over;* Watkins (1865) "kuputāwāpinum, *v.t.in.6. He throws it on shore;*" Silvy (ca. 1680) "ni kapatestikȣan 3. -eȣ, *je descends la chaudière de dessus le feu*" see | *kapē

*kapā

INITIAL

— **1** cook in water

— **2** bathe

evidence | PC pakāsimow, *to bathe;* WC pakāsimīw, *to boil sth;* ESC kapāšimow, *to bathe;* MC kapāšimonahew, *to give a bath to sb;* AT kapacimew [kapāššimow], *faire bouillir;* SEC pakāhtāw, *to cook sth in water;* (Waswanipi, archaic) kapāšimow, *to bathe;* Laure (ca. 1726) "ni-kapachimun, *je me baigne;*" Fabvre (ca. 1690) "kapātau, *faire bȣillir;*" Silvy (ca. 1680) "ni kapachimau, *je le fais bouillir*" compare | *kapaštawē discussion | A variant obtained by metathesis is widespread across contemporary dialects. However, the form above is the earliest attested form and continues to be present in Eastern Swampy Cree, Moose Cree, Atikamekw, and in the speech of elderly East Cree speakers from Waswanipi.

*kapē

INITIAL (VERB, ANIMATE, INTRANSITIVE)

— disembark, land

evidence | PC kapēwin, *campsite;* MC kapāw, *to disembark;* kapewin, *a landing;* SEC kapāpahtāw, *to run ashore;* kapatāw, *to portage things;* WI (Pessamit) kapatau [kəpətāw], *to portage;* Watkins (1865) "kupuhāo, *v.t.an. He disembarks him, he puts him on shore;*" Laure (ca. 1726) "ni-kapan, *je saute à terre du canot, je débarque;*" Fabvre (ca. 1690) "Kapan 3 peȣ, *Se desbarquer à terre;*" Silvy (ca. 1680) "kapatagan, *portage*"

*kapēhši

INITIAL (VERB, ANIMATE, INTRANSITIVE)

— camp

evidence | PC kapēsiwin, *a campsite;* AT kapešši-, *to camp* (Béland, 1978); SEC kapešiwin, *a campsite;* Silvy (ca. 1680) "ni kapechin, *je cabane*" | ANISH gabeshiwin, *a campsite, a camp* (Livesay & Nichols, 2021)

*kask[1]

INITIAL

— **1** break, break off

— **2** precipice

evidence | [1]PC kaskitokanēsin, *to have a broken hip from falling;* kaskinam, *to break sth off by hand;* kaskikwēpitēw, *to break sb's neck with one's hands;* kaskatahwēw, *to break sb's bone by shooting;* MC kaskitahkakwanehwew, *to break a bird's wings with a projectile;* SEC kascitihtimanehwew, *to break sb's shoulder with a blow;* kaskatinam, *to break sth off by hand;* NEC kishkichipitāu, *to bend and break sth off cleanly;* Watkins (1865) "kuskipitum, *v.t.in. 6. He breaks* *it by pulling;*" Laure (ca. 1726) "ni-kastigatéchinin, *j'en ai une (jambe) de rompue;*" "ni-kaskaskunan, *je moissonne;*" Fabvre (ca. 1690) "Kaskask8nan e8, *Cueillir bled, d inde v.g.;*" Silvy (ca. 1680) "ni kaskask8nan, *je cueille le ble;*" "ni kaskamau, *je casse avec les dents;*" "ni kachkamau, *je romps, je casse avec les dents*" ²PC kaskatināw, *to be a butte;* MC kaskāmiskāw, *underwater precipice;* kaskāmatināw, *steep banks* SEC kaskatināw, *to be a high-cliffed mountain;* kaškātimīw, *underwater precipice;* NEC kishkitinâu, *high-cliffed mountain;* kishkichâu, *to be steep* | ²ANISH gakijiwan, *to be a waterfall* (Livesay & Nichols, 2021); (Abitibi dialect) kahkāpihkiciwan, *to be a waterfall;* MENO kahka·pɛhkat, *to be a sharply cut-off rock; waterfall* discussion | There is some variation in the data regarding the quality of the sibilant in the consonant cluster, though the majority of cases point to the above reconstruction, which is indirectly supported by Anishinabe and Menominee cognates. Note, however, that despite the retention of the distinction between ***sk** and ***šk** in most dialects around James Bay, the inland dialects of SEC and the NEC dialect spoken at Whapmagoostui lose the distinction in favor of ***šk**. The dictionaries cited for these dialects therefore occasionally display inconsistencies regarding these clusters and sibilants in general.

*kask²

INITIAL

— cut across, take a shortcut

evidence | PC kaskēwēw, *to go across land, to portage;* MC kaskēw, *overland from one body of water to another;* WI (Pessamit) kasseueu [kəssēwēw], *to cross from one body of water to another over land;* Laure (ca. 1726) "kasseuechimu, *chemin coupant droit de pointe en pointe*" see | *ēw² compare | *kaskam

*kaskam

INITIAL

— cut across, take a shortcut

evidence | PC Lacombe (1874) "Kaskamuttew, *il fait chemin droit;*" WC kaskam, *by way of a shortcut;* MC kaskamew, *to take a shortcut;* NEC kiskimishkim, *to take a shortcut on foot;* kiskimâu, *to be a shortcut;* EI (Mamit) kashkam [kahkam], *by a shortcut;* Silvy (ca. 1680) "ni kaskaman 3. -e8, *j'abrège mon chemin*" | ANISH gakamezhimon, *to be a shortcut* (Lippert & Gambill, 2023) compare | *kask² discussion | Although certainly a derivative of ***kask**, a root of the same meaning, this root is nonetheless included due to the unidentified second component ***am**.

*kaskanw (~ *kaskano)

INITIAL (NOUN, ANIMATE)

— wave

evidence | WSC (Misipawistik, Ellen Cook) kaskana, *waves;* MC kaskanak, *waves;* SEC kaskan, *NA a wave;* NSK kiskin, *NA a wave;* WI (Pessamit) & EI (Sheshatshiu) kashkan [kəʃkən], *NA a wave;* Watkins (1865) "Kuskun, *v.imp. or sometimes n.in. A wave;*" Laure (ca. 1726) "kaskanu *pl.* kaskanuets, *flot, vague;*" Silvy (ca. 1680) "kaskan *pl.* kaskan8ek, *vague;*" "kaskani8i8, *la mer est agitée*" | cf. ANISH Cuoq (1886) "Kakanase, *sillonner l'eau, y laisser une vestige de son passage, (se dit surtout des navires, des canots)*" see | *kask¹, *an², *w¹ discussion | Watkins (1865) appears to be the only written source that lists a reflex of the above form as a verb stem. On the contrary, the earliest sources and most contemporary dialectal sources are consistent in listing the basic stem as an animate noun. Despite this, the root does appear to have been derived from an inanimate intransitive verb stem of the form ***kask**, "break off," + ***an**, similar to the English word *breaker* when describing a large wave.

*kaskinaw

INITIAL

— all, every

evidence | AT kaskina, *all;* WI (Pessamit) kassinu [kəssnu], *all;* EI (Sheshatshiu) kassinu [kəssnu], *all;* Laure (ca. 1726) "kassinau, *tous;*" Fabvre (ca. 1690) "Kassinau, *tous*" | ANISH gakina, *all; every* (Livesay & Nichols, 2021)

*kaš

MEDIAL (NOUN INCORPORATION)

— nail, claw, or hoof

evidence | PC kāsikasēw, *sharp nails;* ESC kīškikašehon, *nail clipper;* EI mikukasheu, *red nails;* WI kanukasheu, *long nails;* NEC mihkukishāhusuwin, *nail polish;* SEC chinukashew, *long nails* | ANISH gagaanoganzhii, *to have long nails or claws* (Livesay & Nichols, 2021) origin | Old Cree ***-skašiy*** see | *kašiy, *skašiy compare | *kaškw

*kašiy

FINAL (NOUN, ANIMATE)

— nail, claw, or hoof

evidence | NEC chishāyākukishī, *a bear claw;* Silvy (ca. 1680) "mitchichinigachia, *l'ongle du pouce*" | ANISH makoganzh, *a bear claw* (Livesay & Nichols, 2021) see | *kaš, *skašiy

*kašk[1]

INITIAL

— able

evidence | PC kaskihtāw, *to be able to do sth;* MC kaškipitam, *to be able to pull sth;* AT kackiho [kaškihō], *to free oneself;* SEC kašcihow, *be able;* Watkins (1865) "Kuskimāo, *v.t.an. He persuades him*" | ANISH gashkitoon, *to be able to do sth* (Livesay & Nichols, 2021); MESK kashkenēwa, *to be able to lift or carry sb* origin | PA ***kašk*** (Aubin, 1975)

*kašk[2]

INITIAL

— **1** close an open space or gap

— **2** obscuring, darkening

— **3** dark-colored, black

— **4** sad, depressed

evidence | [1]PC kaskāpiskaham, *to close sth in metal, to can sth;* MC kaškatin, *freeze-up;* kaškahpitam, *to wrap sth in a cloth that is tied at the corners to create a bag;* SEC kaškatāmow, *to suffocate;* kašcikwātam, *to sew sth;* Laure (ca. 1726) "ni-kachkapiten, *je ferme en liant quelque chose;*" Silvy (ca. 1680) "kachkatin, *il est gelé, glacé, le fleuve*" [2]PC kaskāpahtēw, *to be smoky;* WC kaskitipiskāw, *to be a pitch black night;* ESC kaškāpiw, *to be snow-blind;* MC kaškawan, *to be foggy;* NEC kishkāpiu, *to be snow-blind;* Fabvre (ca. 1690) "Kachkaȣan, *Brȣillards*" [3]WC kaskitīwāw, *to be black;* WSC (Misipawistik, Ellen Cook) kaskitēwāw, *to be black;* SEC kascitewahcešiw & kahcitewahcešiw, *a black fox;* EI (Mamit) katshitew [kātʃitēw], *charcoal;* Watkins (1865) "kusketāwa, *n.in. pl. Coal, or coals;*" Laure (ca. 1726) "kassiteu, *tison noir;*" Silvy (ca. 1680) "kachtisȣ attai, *la peau se brûle;*" "kastiteȣ, *charbon noir*" [4]MC kaškelihtam, *to be sad;* AT kackeritakon [kaškerihtākun], *to be sad;* SEC kašceyihtam, *to be sad, to be homesick;* Laure (ca. 1726) "uesam ni-kasseriten 3. -tamu, *j'ai le cœur triste*" | [1]ANISH gashkaabika'an, *to lock sth* (Livesay & Nichols, 2021); gashkigwaade, *to be sewn* (Livesay & Nichols, 2021); gashkadin, *to freeze over* (Livesay & Nichols, 2021); MENO kaska·qnew, *to place sb so as to close an opening;* kaska·pɛhkaham, *to lock sth by key;* MESK kashketiwa, *to be constipated* [2]ANISH gashkaabate, *to be smoky* (Livesay & Nichols, 2021) [3]gashkaaso, *to be sunburned* (Livesay & Nichols, 2021) [4]ANISH gashkendam, *to be lonesome and sad* (Livesay & Nichols, 2021); MENO kaskɛ·nehtam, *to be sad* origin | PA ***kašk*** (Aubin, 1975)

*kašk[3]

INITIAL

— friable, tender, come apart easily

evidence | PC kaskāciwahtēw, *to be boiled tender;* MC kaškāciwasam, *to boil sth tender;*

SEC kaškan, *to be friable;* WI (Pessamit) kassiteu [kəssətēw], *to be cooked tender;* Silvy (ca. 1680) "ni kachtisen 8ïas, *je fais trop cuire la viande*" compare | *kašk²

*kaškitēw

INITIAL (NOUN, INANIMATE)

— **1** charcoal

— **2** black

evidence | [1]Laure (ca. 1726) "kassiteu, *charbon noir;*" Silvy (ca. 1680) "kastite8, *charbon noir*" [2]PC kaskitēwāw, *to be black;* WC kaskitīwaðasit, *a Blackfoot person;* MC kaškitewisiw, *to be black;* SEC kascitewahcešiw, *black fox;* WI (Pessamit) kashteuapu [kəstēwāpu] *to have black eyes;* Laure (ca. 1726) "ni-kasteukuan, *je charbonne, je noircis;*" "ni-kassiteuapitan, *j'ai les dents noires;*" Silvy (ca. 1680) "ni kastite8isin, *je suis noir*" see | *kašk², *tē⁴

*kaškw

MEDIAL

— nail, claw

evidence | MC kispakikaškwew, *thick nails;* NEC kikānukishkwāu, *long nails;* SEC kāšikaškwew, *to have sharp nails or claws;* Laure (ca. 1726) "ni-pinigaskuan, *les ongles me tombent;*" Silvy (ca. 1680) "nit'ag8kachk8echinin, *je me pince à un bois qui s'entrouvrant prend ma chair*" compare | *kaš

*katawat (~ *katawaš)

INITIAL

— beautiful

evidence | PC katawatēyimēw, *to think sb is beautiful;* katawasisiw, *to be beautiful;* Lacombe (1874) "katawa, *(ad. et rac.) bien, beau, correctement, voy. mitoni, kwayask, v.g.* katawa totam, *il fait bien;*" Watkins (1865) "Kutuwusisehāo, *v.t.a. He beautifies him;*" Laure (ca. 1726) "katauatichiu & katauachichiu, *attrayant, charmant, beau, belle;*" "katauachichitasitu, *fais une bonne action;*" "katauatachkuchiu, *bâton droit;*" Fabvre (ca. 1690) "Kata8atibeachi8, *fleuue, r(ivière) belle sans sault, riuiere sans trop de rapide(s);*" Silvy (ca. 1680) "ni kata8atichin, *je suis bon;*" "kata8atachkasi8, *bâton droit;*" "ni kata8achichkag8n, *cela m'est bon*"

*katāštap

INITIAL

— agile, quick

evidence | PC tatāstapīw, *to be quick;* WC tatāstapīw, *to be quick;* WSC (Misipawistik, Ellen Cook) kitāstapīw, *to be quick;* ESC katāštapīw, *to be quick;* MC katāštapowew, *to talk quickly;* SEC katāštapīw, *to be quick or agile;* NEC kichāstipwāu, *to talk quickly;* EI (Mamit) katshashtapiu [katʃāhtapīw], *to be agile;* Watkins (1865) "Kitastupassinùhikāo, *v.i.3. He writes fast;*" Laure (ca. 1726) "ni-katchastapichin 3. -iu, *agile, je suis agile*" | ANISH dadaatabii, *to be quick* (Livesay & Nichols, 2021) discussion | The Plains Cree and Woods Cree forms may represent influence from an Anishinabe dialect or are instances of hypercorrection as pseudo-reduplicated forms.

*katikwan

INITIAL

— spend night away from home

evidence | MC kotikwanīw, *to sleep away from home for the night;* SEC kotikwanīmōswew, *to spend the night away from home to hunt moose;* SEC (Waswanipi) katikoni-mōsʷ, *moose aged two years or older, but not yet fully mature;* WI (Pessamit) kutikunitikueu [kutukunītəkwēw], *to spend the night away from camp to hunt caribou;* EI (Mamit) kutikuniu [kutukwanīw], *to camp;* Watkins (1865) "Kutikwunew, *v.i.1. He stops out a night (i.e. sleeps away from his dwelling);*" & "Kootikwunew, *v.i.1. He stops out a night;*" Silvy (ca. 1680) "ni katig8nin 3. i8, *je couche dehors en chassant*"

*kato

INITIAL

— **1** be affected by

— **2** affect by, cause to be

evidence | PC Lacombe (1874) "katoppinew, ok, *(a.a.) il a une maladie intérieure, comme celui qui aurait du sang caillé dans le corps;*" WI (Pessamit) katunateu [kətəntēw], *to set a trap, snare, or hook to catch sth;* Laure (ca. 1726) "katuneu, *il est infirme;*" "ni-katunatau, *je l'ensorcelle;*" Fabvre (ca. 1690) "ki kat8nāchin, *tu me fais m8rir ainsy par sort;*" Silvy (ca. 1680) "ni kat8tchem8n, *j'invite au festin*" | ANISH Cuoq (1886) "katonewi, *il est en langueur, il est toujours malade;*" "katonesi, *il est retombé malade;*" MENO kato·nacekan, *trap, deadfall;* MESK katawinēwa, *to almost die;* MIAMI katonkwaam-, *be sleepy;* katoopii-, *be thirsty* (ILDA, 2017) origin | PA ***kato**, likely alternating with ***kataw**, from which the Old Cree future tense marker ***kata** would be derived. compare | *nato

*kaw[1]

INITIAL

— go from a vertical to a horizontal position

evidence | PC kawisimow, *to lie down for bed;* MC kawipaliw, *to fall over;* SEC kawikahtam, *to fell sth using one's teeth;* Silvy (ca. 1680) "ni ka8achin, *le vent me renverse*" | ABEN gawhakwa, *to cut down a tree* (Day, 1994); ANISH gawaapi, *to fall over from laughing so hard* (Livesay & Nichols, 2021) origin | PA ***kaw** (Aubin, 1975)

*kaw[2]

PREFINAL

— drain, drip, leak

evidence | Silvy (ca. 1680) "ni papatchiga8ab8an 3 -e8, *je fais tomber la graisse, rôtissant*" see | *kawi, *kawin, *sīskaw

*kawi

FINAL (VERB, ANIMATE, INTRANSITIVE, CONCRETE)

— leak, drip, drain

evidence | PC pahkikawiw, *to drip;* MC ohcikawiw, *to leak from;* SEC pāhpahcikawiw, *to drip* paired with | *kawin see | *kaw[2], *i[2]

*kawin

FINAL (VERB, INANIMATE, INTRANSITIVE, CONCRETE)

— leak, drip, drain

evidence | PC pahkikawin, *to drip;* MC ohcikawin, *to leak from;* SEC pāhpahcikawin, *to drip* paired with | *kawi see | *kaw[2], *in[2]

*kā

INITIAL

— hide

evidence | PC kātēw, *to be hidden;* MC kālew, *to hide sb;* AT (Wemotaci, Jeannette Coocoo) kaso [kāzow], *to hide;* SEC kāsow, *to hide oneself* | ANISH gaazo, *to hide oneself* (Livesay & Nichols, 2021) limited to | *r, *so[1], *tā, *tē[2] see | *kāt

*kāhcit (~ *kāhcic)

INITIAL

— catch

evidence | PC kāhcitinam, *to catch sth;* MC kāhcicipitam, *to grab sth as it goes by;* SEC kāhcitahwew, *to just barely hit sb*

*kāhk

INITIAL

— spread apart

evidence | MC kāhkapeštāw, *to part thighs;* SEC kāhkapeyiw, *to part thighs;* Fabvre (ca. 1690) "Kakapērin," *(no translation)* limited to | *ap[2]

*kāhkākiw

INITIAL (NOUN, ANIMATE)

— raven

evidence | PC kāhkākiw, *a raven;* MC kāhkākiw, *a raven or crow;* SEC kāhkāciw, *a raven;* kāhkācīšip, *a cormorant;* kāhkācīwāhtik^{w}, *a juniper bush;* EI (Sheshatshiu) kakatshu [kākātʃu], *a raven;* Silvy (ca. 1680) "kakatchi8, *corbeau*" | ANISH gaagaagiwag, *ravens* (Livesay & Nichols, 2021)

*kāhkw

INITIAL

— jealous

evidence | PC kāhkwēyihtowak, *to be jealous of one another;* MC kāhkwelimew, *to be jealous of sb;* Laure (ca. 1726) "ni-kakuerimau, *jalous (entre époux)*"

*kāhsī

INITIAL

— wipe clean

evidence | PC kāsīyāpiskaham, *to wipe sth metallic;* MC kāsīnam, *to wipe sth clean;* AT (Wemotaci, Jeannette Coocoo) kasinam [kāssīnam], *to wipe sth with one's hand;* SEC kāsītihcew, *to wipe one's hands clean* | ANISH gaasii'igan, *an eraser* (Livesay & Nichols, 2021)

*kāhš

INITIAL

— sharp

evidence | PC kāsāpitēw, *to have sharp teeth;* MC kāšāw, *to be sharp;* AT (Wemotaci, Jeannette Coocoo) kacaw [kāššāw], *to be sharp;* SEC kāšikaškwew, *to have sharp nails or claws* | ANISH gaashaabikizi, *to be sharp, speaking of a rock or metal* (Livesay & Nichols, 2021)

*kāhšispo (~ kāhšispw)

INITIAL

— go beyond

evidence | PC kāsispōw, *to reach beyond, to exceed; to survive into another generation;* kāsispohtin, *to be too long;* Lacombe (1874) "Kāsisposiw, ok, *(a.a.) il est trop long, il dépasse;*" "kāsispopayiw, ok, a, *(a.a. et. in) il passe tout droit, étant à cheval, ça dépasse, ça arrive trop vite;*" WC kāsispowiðīw, *to evade sb;* Watkins (1865) "Kasispoomāo, *v.t.an. He breaks his promise towards him;*" Laure (ca. 1726) "ni-kachispu-iriniuin, *survivre, je survis, je vis après*" | ANISH gaashipoobizo, *to drive past* (Lippert & Gambill, 2023) discussion | In the absence of an Atikamekw cognate, the preaspirate in this reconstruction is indirectly supported by Anishinabe.

*kāht (~ *kāhc)

INITIAL

— push

evidence | MC kāhciwepinew, *to shove sb;* kāhtāšiw, *to be pushed by the wind;* ESC kāhtinam, *to push sth* | ANISH gaanda', *to push sb using sth* (Livesay & Nichols, 2021); (Abitibi dialect) okātinān, *to push sb;* MENO ka·htenɛw, *to push sb;* MESK kāchimēw, *to persuade sb;* kātenēwa, *to push sb* origin | PA ***kānt** (Aubin, 1975) discussion | Cognates for this lexical root have only been found in Moose Cree and Eastern Swampy Cree, dialects in which the root is productive. However, the existence of cognates in Anishinabe, Menominee, and Meskwaki strongly suggest it is inherited from Proto-Algonquian.

*kāhtap

INITIAL

— different size, shape, or place

evidence | PC kāhtapastāw, *to place things here and there or at intervals;* Lacombe (1874) "kāttap, *(ad.) de différentes proportions, en différentes places, v.g.* kāttap *iskusiwok, ils sont de différentes longueurs,* kākāttap iskwāwa mokkumāna, *couteaux de différentes longueres,* kākāttap nakatam, *il en laisse en différentes places, voy. nanāhwäy;*" NEC kāhtipāpiskāu, *to be a ledge in the rock;* WI (Pessamit) katipau [kātəpāw], *to be in the shape of a terrace or platform;* Fabvre (ca. 1690) "Kakatap? *L'un apres l(')autre*"

*kākikē

INITIAL

— forever

evidence | WC kākikīsikwāw, *ice does not melt during the summer;* MC kākikēpak^{w}, *Labrador tea;* NEC kāchichāsikw, *iceberg;* WI (Pessamit) katshitshepu [kātʃətʃēpu], *to be always seated;* Laure (ca. 1726) "ka katchitchekasut, *victime de flammes de l'enfer*" | ANISH gaagige-, *forever* (Livesay & Nichols, 2021); MENO ka·kekɛ·hkamek, *forever*

*kākīt (~ *kākīc, *kākīs)

INITIAL

— appease

evidence | PC kākīcimēw, *to comfort sb with one's words;* MC kākīcihew, *to comfort sb;* kākīsomew, *to comfort or console sb;* WI (Pessamit) katshitshieu [kātʃītʃjēw], *to mollify sb;* Laure (ca. 1726) "ni-katchitchihau 3. -heu, *amadouer, flatter*"

*kākw (~ *kāko)

INITIAL (NOUN, ANIMATE)

— porcupine

evidence | PC kākosis, *a baby porcupine;* MC kāko, *porcupine;* SEC kwākwāyow, *a porcupine tail;* Silvy (ca. 1680) "kak8, kak8a *pl.* 8ek, *porc-épic*" | ANISH gaagowi, *to be a porcupine* (Livesay & Nichols, 2021); MESK akākwa, *a porcupine* see | *ākw

*kāmo

FINAL (VERB, ANIMATE, INTRANSITIVE, CONCRETE)

— corpulent, fat

evidence | PC miyokāmow, *to be well-fattened;* MC milokāmow, *to be well-fattened;* WI (Pessamit) ishikamu, *avoir telle corpulence;* Silvy (ca. 1680) "ni ristigam8tan 3. -tau, *mon nez ne paraît pas, tant je suis gras*" | ABEN ginigōmo, *to be very fat* (Day, 1994); ANISH apiichigaamo, *to be so fat* (Livesay & Nichols, 2021) origin | PA ***kāmo**

*kāmwāt (~ *kāmwāc)

INITIAL

— solemn, somber, grave

evidence | PC kāmwātan, *to be quiet, depressing, or sad;* WC kāmwātīðihtam, *to brood;* Laure (ca. 1726) "ka kamuatichit, *grave, sérieux, qui ne rit pas;*" Fabvre (ca. 1690) "Kam8atsirini8, *graue, sage, parler peu;*" "Kam8atibeiau, *fl(euu)e qui n(')a pas beauc(ou)p d(')eau, Lac qui n(')a pas d(')eau;*" Silvy (ca. 1680) "ni kam8atisin, *je suis sage, grave, parlant peu*"

*kāpawi

FINAL (VERB, ANIMATE, INTRANSITIVE, CONCRETE)

— stand

evidence | PC āhcikāpawiw, *to stand elsewhere;* MC ohtiškawikāpawīštawew, *stand facing sb;* Laure (ca. 1726) "ni-napatékategabauin, *je me tiens sur un pied;*" Silvy (ca. 1680) "nit'ispichigaba8in, *je suis de cette grandeur, de cette hauteur*" | ANISH azhegaabawi, *to stand back* (Livesay & Nichols, 2021) see | *i²

*kārahkonāw

INITIAL (NOUN, ANIMATE)

— unleavened bread

evidence | ESC (Severn) ānahkonāw, *bannock;* MC ālahkonāw, *bannock;* AT (Opitciwan, Joey Awashish) karkonaw [kārhkonāw], *a scone; a cookie;* SEC āyahkonāhcew, *to make bannock;* NEC āihkunāu, *bannock; cake;* NSK kwaayihkunaas, *a cookie;* WI (Pessamit) kalakunass [kālukunāss], *a cookie, a cracker;* EI (Sheshatshiu) kanakunau [kānākunāw], *pilot biscuit, hardtack;* Faries (1938) "Ayùkoono'wikumik, *n.in. A baking house, an oven;*" Isham (1743) "ha ra ca naw u'komick, *an oven;*" Laure (ca. 1726) "karakunau, *pl. -ets, biscuit;*" Fabvre (ca. 1690) "karak8na, *galette, biscuit de mer;*" Silvy (ca. 1680) "karak8na8ek, *galette;*" Le Jeune (1633) "carocana, *pain*" | ANISH Cuoq (1886) "anakona, *biscuit*" origin | St. Lawrence Iroquoian *karahkō·ni* (Pentland, 1979)

*kārk

INITIAL

— superficially cured

evidence | PC kāhkēwak, *dried meat;* WC kāðkīwak, *dried meat;* MC kāhkāpahtew, *cured superficially by smoking;* kāhkitew, *to be cured superficially by heat* | ANISH gaaskamik, *smoked beaver* (Livesay & Nichols, 2021)

*kāsk

INITIAL

— crunchy, crispy

evidence | MC kāskāskahtowān, *cartilage;* AT kaskaskiso [kāskāskizow], *to be burned or grilled;* SEC kāskāschihkasū, *to be cooked crispy* (CSB, 2018) | MENO ka·ketowɛ·tɛ·w, *to cook noisily, to sizzle, sputter, or crackle*

*kāsp

INITIAL

— brittle

evidence | PC kāspihkasow, *to be cooked until crisp;* MC kāspāhkatosow, *be brittle and dry;* SEC kāspan, *to be brittle from the cold* | ANISH gaapan, *to be brittle*

*kāšak

INITIAL (NOUN, ANIMATE)

— tapeworm

evidence | PC kāsak, *a tapeworm;* kāsakēw, *to be gluttonous;* MC kāšakātisīw, *to be greedy;* AT okācikimiw [okāʒikimiw], *to be gluttonous;* SEC okāšacimiw, *to be gluttonous;* okāšacimeyāpiy, *a tapeworm;* WI (Uashat) ukashatshimikatam[u] [ukāʃətʃimīkətəm], *to eat sth voraciously;* EI (Unaman-shipit) ukashatshim [ukāhatʃim], *a tapeworm;* Laure (ca. 1726) "ukachatchimiu, *on ne peut le rassasier;*" Silvy (ca. 1680) "kachatchichich, *chat*" | ANISH gaazhage, *to be gluttonous;* gaazhagens, *a cat* (Livesay & Nichols, 2021); MENO ka·sakeh, *cat*

*kāšk

INITIAL

— scrape, scratch

evidence | PC kāskipitēw, *to scratch sb;* MC kāškaham, *to scrape sth;* SEC kāšcipāsow, *to shave;* Silvy (ca. 1680) "ni kachkachkahȣau, *je l'égratigne, je le racle avec, etc.*" | MENO ka·skapenɛ·w, *to scratch sb in the eye*

*kāt[1] (~ *kāc)

INITIAL

— hide

evidence | MC kāciwepinam, *to hide sth in a hurry;* SEC kātinam, *to hide sth with one's hand;* Laure (ca. 1726) "ni-katchipun, *je mange en cachette*" | ANISH gaadawinzo, *to hide berries being picked* (Livesay & Nichols, 2021) see | *kā, *tā

*kāt[2] (~ *kāc)

MEDIAL, FINAL (NOUN INCORPORATION)

— leg; (of a quadruped) hind leg

evidence | PC māskikātēw, *to have a lame leg;* MC kakānokātew, *to have long legs;* SEC otāmikātehwew, *to strike sb's leg;* WI (Pessamit) napatekat [nəpətēkāt], *using only one leg;* Laure (ca. 1726) "ni-napatékategabauin, *je me tiens sur un pied;*" Silvy (ca. 1680) "ni patchigatan 3. -eȣ, *j'ai la jambe enflée;*" Le Jeune (1634) *"Ie sçeu seulement qu'ils l'appelloient Manitoukathi, c'est à dire, jambe du Manitou, ou du Diable; elle fut long temps penduë dans la Cabane au lieu où s'asseoit le Sorcier"* | ANISH baagigaade, *to have a swollen leg(s)* (Livesay & Nichols, 2021) origin | PA ***kāt** (Aubin, 1975) see | *skāt

*kāw[1]

INITIAL

— rough

evidence | MC kāwāštakāw, *rough or prickly conifer bough flooring;* SEC kāwihtakāw, *to be rough wood or floor;* Laure (ca. 1726) "kaueganu *pl.* -a, *âpre, rude au toucher;*" Silvy (ca. 1680) "kaȣau, *rude, âpre au toucher*" | ANISH gaawaa, *to be rough* (Livesay & Nichols, 2021); MENO ka·wi·w, *to be rough* compare | *kāwiy[2]

*kāw[2]

INITIAL

— once again, back, in return

evidence | PC kāwi, *again; back, in return;* SEC kāw, *again, in return;* Silvy (ca. 1680) "kaȣi, *derechef*" limited to | *i[3]

***kāwiy[1] (~ *kāwī)**

INITIAL (NOUN, DEPENDENT ANIMATE)

— mother

evidence | PC okāwīw, *to have a mother;* MC okāwiya, *one's mother;* SEC nikāwīnān, *our mother;* Silvy (ca. 1680) "n'8ga8ima8in, *je suis mère*"

***kāwiy[2] (~ *kāwī)**

INITIAL (NOUN, ANIMATE)

— porcupine quill

evidence | PC kāwiyātam, *to put quills on sth;* WC kāwiyaham, *to put quills on sth;* WI (Pessamit) kaui [kāwī], *porcupine quill;* Laure (ca. 1726) "kauiets, *poil ou brin de porc-épic;*" Silvy (ca. 1680) "ka8ïak, *brins de porc-épic*" | MENO ka·wey, *a quill of a porcupine* see | *āwiy compare | *kāw[1]

***kē[1]**

FINAL (VERB, ANIMATE, INTRANSITIVE, CONCRETE)

sound change | ē → ā, i → iwā, o → owā

— applicative that adds an instrumental argument when suffixed to animate intransitive verb stems or transitive inanimate verb stems, resulting in a syntactically transitive verb requiring two arguments

evidence | MC mīcisowākew, *to eat using sth;* āšokanihkākew, *to make a bridge out of sth;* SEC minihkwācew, *to use sth as a drinking vessel;* natohtamowācew, *to use sth to listen, as a stethoscope;* EI (Unaman-shipit) atsheuatsheu [ātʃēwātʃēw], *to use sth to grind caribou bones*

***kē[2]**

FINAL (VERB, INTRANSITIVE, ABSTRACT)

sound change | m + kē → hkē; t (PA *θ) + kē → skē

— forms the antipassive when suffixed to transitive inanimate (and certain transitive animate) verb stems or animate intransitive verb stems that syntactically require an object

evidence | PC wāpahkēw, *to watch things or people;* MC mākohcikew, *bite;* atoskew, *work;* SEC māyeyihcicew, *insult;* wāpāsicew, *sun shines white;* WI nipatatsheu, *kill;* Silvy (ca. 1680) "nit'achakan, *je donne à manger*" | ANISH aabajichige, *to use sth* (Livesay & Nichols, 2021); waabange, *to observe people* (Livesay & Nichols, 2021); MENO se·wahcekɛ·w, *to eat sweet things* origin | PA ***kē** (Aubin, 1975) compare | *ā[2], *ıkē, *kēmo, *wē[2]

***kēhciko (~ *kēhcikw)**

INITIAL (VERB, ANIMATE, INTRANSITIVE)

— slide something off or out of something else

evidence | PC kēcikopitam, *to pull sth off or out;* MC kehcikonam, *to slide sth off;* kehcikow, *to get loose from a trap; to moult, speaking of a snake;* SEC (Waswanipi) cehcikosāmew, *to slide off one's snowshoes;* Silvy (ca. 1680) "ni ketchig8ask8titan 3. tau, *j'ôte le manche*" | ANISH giichigobidoon, *to pull sth off* (Livesay & Nichols, 2021) compare | *kēšt[1]

***kēhkēhkw (~ *kēhkēhko)**

INITIAL (NOUN, ANIMATE)

— hawk

evidence | PC kēhkēhk, *hawk, falcon;* MC kehkehk^{w}, *general term for diurnal raptors excluding eagles and buzzards;* SEC kehkehk^{w} & cehcehk^{w}, *general term for diurnal raptors excluding eagles and buzzards;* NEC chāhchāhkw, *a goshawk;* WI (Pessamit) tshetshek^{u} [tʃētʃēk^{w}], *northern harrier hawk;* EI (Sheshatshiu) tshetshek^{u} [tʃētʃēk^{w}], *northern harrier hawk;* Watkins (1865) "Kākāk, *n.an. A hawk;*" Laure (ca. 1726) "tchetcheku, *épervier, oiseau de proie*" | ANISH gekekwag, *hawks* (Livesay & Nichols, 2021); MENO kɛ·hkɛ·hkok, *hawks;* MESK kēhkēhkwa, *duck hawk, peregrine falcon* origin | PA ***kēhkēhkwa** (Aubin, 1975)

*kēhtē

INITIAL

— old

evidence | PC kēhtēstim, *old dog or horse;* MC kehteyātisīw, *to be elderly;* AT keteaw, *to be old;* Watkins (1865) "Kātāyatisew, *v.i.1. He is of good age (i.e. past the prime of life)*" | ANISH getenaagozi, *to look old* (Livesay & Nichols, 2021) origin | PA ***kēhtē** (Aubin, 1975)

*kēk

INITIAL

— by and by, eventually

evidence | ESC (Severn) keka, *finally;* MC kekakeka, *gradually;* SEC cek, *finally, eventually;* EI tshek [tʃēk], *at a certain moment; suddenly, all of a sudden* | ANISH Nicholas (ca. 1670) "keg, *enfin*" (Daviault, 1994) limited to | *a

*kēkāt (~ *kēkāc)

INITIAL

— almost

evidence | PC kēkā, *almost;* WC kīkāc, *almost;* ESC (Severn) kekāt, *almost;* SEC cekāt, *almost;* Silvy (ca. 1680) "kegat, *presque*"

*kēkišēp

INITIAL

— morning

evidence | PC kēkisēp, *this morning;* WC kīkisīpāyāw, *to be morning;* MC kekišepānehkwew, *to eat breakfast;* AT kekicep [kēkiʒēp], *this morning;* SEC cecišepāyāw, *to be morning;* Silvy (ca. 1680) "ketchicheba8atin, *il fait froid le matin*"

*kēko (~ *kēkw)

INITIAL

— which

evidence | PC kēkwāy, *what;* WC kīkway, what; something; kīkwās, *something small;* ESC keko, *which one;* MC kekwān, *what;* kekwāhtikʷ, *which tree;* SEC cēkʷ, *which;* cekwān, *what;* EI tshekuen [tʃēkwēn], *which person;* Laure (ca. 1726) "tcheguan, tchekuariu, *pourquoi;*" Silvy (ca. 1680) "kek8? *qu'est-ce?;*" "tchek8 irini8? *quel homme est-ce?;*" "keg8eïa, *qqch*"

*kēmo

FINAL (VERB, ANIMATE, INTRANSITIVE)

sound change | m → h

— forms the antipassive when suffixed to transitive animate verb stems ending in speech finals

evidence | PC misihkēmow, *to tattle, to tell on;* MC šīhkihkemow, *to urge people;* SEC kakwecihcemow, *to ask a question;* Fabvre (ca. 1690) "nat8kēm8n m8, *Inuiter au festin, faire les inuit(at)ions*" compare | *ā², *kē², *ıkē, *wē²

*kēšt¹ (~ *kēhc)

INITIAL

— remove article of clothing

evidence | PC kētastisēw, *to take off one's mitts;* WC kītaskisinīw, *to take off one's shoes;* ESC kehtaskisinew, *to take off shoes;* MC keštasākew, *to take off one's clothes;* kakehcīw, *to remove one's clothes;* AT ketcikapotowanew [kehcikāpōtowānew], *to take off one's coat;* SEC ceštasāmew, *to take one's snowshoes off;* Laure (ca. 1726) "ni-tchestassianan 3. -eu, *je quitte mon brayet;*" Silvy (ca. 1680) "ni kechtanag8an 3. -e8, *je dévêts mes manches*" | ANISH giitaagime, *to take off one's snowshoes;* gagiichii, *to take off one's shoes* (Livesay & Nichols, 2021) origin | PA ***kyēʔt** compare | *kēhciko

*kēšt² (~ *kēhs)

INITIAL

— catch just in time

evidence | PC kēsiskam, *to come in time for sth;* kēstinam, *to catch sth in time;* MC keštahtam, *to arrive in time to eat sth;* SEC ceštiškawew, *to catch sb in the act;* NEC chāsiskiwāu, *to catch sb in the act;* WI (Pessamit) tsheshtineu [tʃēstnēw], *to catch sth in time*

*kēštinā

INITIAL

— certain

evidence | PC kēhcināhow, *to be sure;* WC kīhcināc, *certainly;* MC kehcināhew, *to assure sb;* SEC ceštināhow, *to be certain;* WI (Pessamit) tsheshtinatelitakuan [tʃēsnātēltāwn], *to be certain* | ANISH gechinaawendam, *to be sure* (Livesay & Nichols, 2021)

*kēyāpit (~ *kēyāpic)

INITIAL

— from the present time into the future, continuously, yet

evidence | PC kēyāpic, *still, yet;* MC kēyāpac, *still, yet; nevertheless;* AT (Opitciwan, Joey Awashish) keapatci [kēyāpaci], *still;* NEC ayāpich, *still; nevertheless;* EI (Sheshatshiu) iapit [jāpit], *anyway, even so; also, too;* Laure (ca. 1726) "eiapitch, *sans cesser, toujours*" | ANISH geyaabi, *still, yet* (Livesay & Nichols, 2021); Nicholas (ca. 1670) "eiapitch, *tousjours*" (Daviault, 1994) limited to | *i[3]

*ki

FINAL (VERB, ANIMATE, INTRANSITIVE, CONCRETE)

— grow

evidence | PC ohpikiw, *to grow up;* MC lahkikiw, *to grow in size;* SEC ciyipiciw, *to grow fast;* Laure (ca. 1726) "ni-punitchin, *je cesse de croître*" | ABEN minawigo, *to grow again* (Day, 1994); ANISH agogi, *to grow attached to sth* (Livesay & Nichols, 2021); MENO sa·kekew, *to grow up through the soil* paired with | *kin

*kicišt (~ *kicihc)

INITIAL

— clean

evidence | WC kicistinam, *to clean sth;* MC kicištāpāwatāw, *to wash sth;* kiciščišimew, *to clean sth by wiping it against sth;* SEC cištāpāwatāw, *to wash sth;* Watkins (1865) "Kichistākùham, *v.t.in.6. He cleans it (as a garment, a blanket, &c.);*" Laure (ca. 1726) "ni-tchichistabauatchitunan, *je me lave la bouche;*" "ni-tchichistetsinen, *je frotte du linge*"

*kicīšk

INITIAL

— grate, creak

evidence | PC cīskāpitēw, *to grind one's teeth;* WC kicīskipaðiw, *to creak;* MC kicīškahtam, *to cause sth to make a grating sound by biting;* Watkins (1865) "Kicheskipuyew, *it creaks;*" Laure (ca. 1726) "ni-tchitchiskabitan, *je grince des dents*"

*kihcit (~ *kihcic)

INITIAL

— drive in

evidence | PC kīhcitahāskwān, *a hitching post;* WC kīhcitaham, *to drive sth in by hitting it;* MC kihciciwepahwew, *to knock or thrust sth straight in;* kihcicipaliw, *to migrate inwards, to go straight in;* Watkins (1865) "Kichìchewāpuhum, *v.t.in.6. He knocks it in;*" Laure (ca. 1726) "ni-tchitchitahen tchistaskuan, *j'enfonce un clou dans la muraille*" | ANISH ginjida'an, *to tap sth in, to pound sth in* (Livesay & Nichols, 2021)

*kihkā

INITIAL (VERB, ANIMATE, INTRANSITIVE)

— be elderly

evidence | PC Lacombe (1874) "kāwikikkaw, *il est accablé sous le poids de la vieillesse;*" MC šīpi-kihkāw, *to be vigorous in old age;* SEC nama cihkāwātisīw, *he is irresponsible;* Fabvre (ca. 1690s) "kikan 3 au, *estre uieil uieux*" | ANISH gikaa, *to be elderly;* MESK kehkyēwa, *to be or get old* see | *ā[2]

*kihr

INITIAL

— slippery

evidence | MC kilaskamikāw, *slippery ground;* SEC cihīšin, *to slip;* NEC chihyāpiskāu, *to be slippery rock;* Fabvre (ca. 1690) "kirau, *cela e(st) glissant;*" Silvy (ca. 1680) "kirisi8, kihisi8, *il est glissant ut pisces*"

*kihriw

INITIAL (NOUN, ANIMATE)

— golden eagle (Aquila chrysaetos)

evidence | PC kihīw, *a golden eagle* | ANISH giniw, *a golden eagle* (Livesay & Nichols, 2021); MENO kene·w, *an eagle*

*kihsin

INITIAL (VERB, INANIMATE, INTRANSITIVE)

— be frigid weather, be bitterly cold weather

evidence | PC kisin, *to be very cold weather;* MC kisināw, *to be cold winter weather;* AT (Wemotaci, Jeannette Coocoo) kisinaw [kissināw], *to be cold weather;* SEC cisinipeyāw, *to be cold, wet weather;* NEC chisināpin, *to be a cold morning;* WI (Pessamit) tshishinapatshu [tʃʃənāpətʃu], *to have tired eyes because of the cold;* EI (Sheshatshiu) tshishin [tʃʃɨn], *to be freezing cold weather;* Silvy (ca. 1680) "kisin, *il fait froid*" | ANISH gisinaa, *to be cold weather* (Livesay & Nichols, 2021)

*kiht (~ *kihc)

INITIAL

— start

evidence | MC kihtohtew, *to start off on foot;* AT kitciparin [kihciparin], *to start;* SEC cihcipayihtāw, *to start sth such as a motor*

*kihtāw[1] (~ *kihtā)

INITIAL

— discrete, wise, mature

evidence | PC kakēhtawātisiw, *mature;* MC kakehtāsīw, *discrete;* AT kitaweritam, *mature, intellgent;* SEC kacehtāwew, *speak wisely;* NEC kichāhtāwināu, *hold or manipulate skillfully;* Fabvre (ca. 1690) "Kita8eriten, *scau(oi)r bien, s'expliq(ue)r, disc8rir bien*"

*kihtāw[2] (~ *kihtā)

INITIAL

— submerge

evidence | PC kihtāpayiw, *to go underwater;* MC kihtānam, *to dip sth;* kihtāpekiškam, *to weigh down a canoe;* SEC cihtāwīw, *to sink;* Laure (ca. 1726) "ni-tchitabetchissen, *j'enfonce avec le pied*" | MENO kɛhta·pi·qtaw, *to immerse oneself*

*kihtim

INITIAL

— lazy

evidence | PC kihtimiw, *to be lazy;* MC kihtimohtew, *to walk lazily;* SEC cihtimikanew, *to be a lazybones;* Laure (ca. 1726) "tchitimiuin, *paresse*"

*kik

INITIAL

— with

evidence | PC kiki, *with;* kikinam, *to include sth, to add sth;* kakēkinam, *to pick sth from a group of things;* MC kikasāmohtew, *walk with snowshoes;* SEC cikamohtāw, *to stick sth onto;* NEC chichishkim, *to wear sth;* Fabvre (ca. 1690) "Kiki, *auec, uel Auprès, ny v.g.* Kiki 8i8a nama tagochin8, *ny Luy ni sa femme ne reuient;*" Silvy (ca. 1680) "kikam8, *cela tient, cela est attaché*" origin | PA ***kek** (Aubin, 1975)

*kimisā

INITIAL (VERB, ANIMATE, INTRANSITIVE)

— to clean the anus after a bowel movement

evidence | PC kimisāhēw, *to wipe sb's anus;* AT kimisaho [kimizāhow], *to wipe one's anus after a bowel movement;* SEC cimisāhow, *to wipe one's anus clean after a bowel movement;* NEC cimisāhun, *anything used to wipe one's anus after a bowel movement, such as toilet paper;* Laure (ca. 1726) "ni-tchimichahau auachich, *je torche l'enfant, j'essuie l'enfant*"

*kimiwan (~ *kimiwah)

INITIAL (VERB, INANIMATE, INTRANSITIVE)

— rain

evidence | PC kimiwanēyāpiy, *rainbow;* WC kimowan, *to rain;* MC kimiwanišiw, *to encounter rainy weather;* AT (Wemotaci, Jeannette Coocoo) kimiwocin [kimiwaššin], *to rain a little;* Laure (ca. 1726) "tchimiuanu, *il pleut*" | ANISH gimiwanishi, *to get caught in the rain* (Livesay & Nichols, 2021); MENO keme·wanapoh, *rain water* origin | PA ***kemiwan** (Aubin, 1975), with the allomorph ***kimiwah** triggered by the suffixation of consonant-initial verb finals. discussion | Although the final ***an** is likely a component in this root, the above form is proposed until evidence of the remainder in composition with other roots can be identified.

*kimot (~ *kimoc)

INITIAL (VERB, ANIMATE, INTRANSITIVE)

— steal

evidence | PC kimotiw, *to steal;* MC kakemotāpošwew, *to steal hares;* kimocimīcimew, *to steal food;* SEC cimotisk, *thief;* NEC kichāmuchipāu, *to steal a drink* | ABEN gemodenawōgan, *theft* (Day, 1994); ANISH gimoojinaabeme, *to steal sb's husband* (Livesay & Nichols, 2021)

*kin

FINAL (VERB, INANIMATE, INTRANSITIVE, CONCRETE)

— grow

evidence | PC māskikin, *to grow deformed;* MC kipokin, *to grow shut;* SEC nihtāwicin, *to grow* | ANISH agogin, *to grow attached to sth* (Livesay & Nichols, 2021); MENO sa·kekɛn, *to grow up through the soil* paired with | *ki

*kino (~ *kinw)

INITIAL

— long

evidence | MC kinwātakan, *long burrow, tunnel, hole or bore;* kakānopitonew, *to have long arms;* SEC cinwāw, *to be long;* EI (Unaman-shipit) tshinuaukanu [tnwāwkanu], *to have a long back;* Laure (ca. 1726) "tchinuarueu, *l'animal a la queue longue*" | ANISH ginokoozhe, *to have a long bill* (Livesay & Nichols, 2021) origin | PA ***keno** (***kenw,** Aubin, 1975)

*kinošēw

INITIAL (NOUN, ANIMATE)

— pike, jackfish

evidence | PC kinosēw, *a fish;* kinosēwāpoy, *fish broth;* WC kinosīskāw, *to be many fish;* ESC kinošew, *a pike;* MC kinošew, *a pike;* AT kinošew, *pike* (Béland, 1978); SEC cinošew, *a pike;* EI (Sheshatshiu) tshinusheu [tʃinuʃēw], *a northern pike;* Silvy (ca. 1680) "kin8che8, *brochet*" | ANISH ginoozhe, *a northern pike* (Livesay & Nichols, 2021) origin | PA ***kenwešyēwa** (Aubin, 1975)

*kip

INITIAL

— close

evidence | PC kipahwēw, *to close sb in;* MC kipaham, *to close sth;* SEC cipihtew, *to be deaf;* WI (Pessamit) tshipishkuatuepu [tʃəpəʃkwātwēpu], *to be seated in front of the entrance;* Silvy (ca. 1680) "ni kipit8nenau, *je l'étrangle avec la main*" | ABEN gebaden, *to be frozen shut, to be frozen over* (Day, 1994); ANISH giba'on, *a diaphragm* (Livesay & Nichols, 2021) origin | PA ***kep** (Aubin, 1975)

*kipiht (~ *kipihc)

INITIAL

— stop

evidence | PC kipihtinēw, *to stop sb by hand;* MC kipihcīw, *to stop;* SEC cipihcipayihtāw, *to stop a vehicle* | ANISH gibitanaamo, *to stop breathing* (Livesay & Nichols, 2021)

*kipo (~ *kipw)

INITIAL

— block, plug up

evidence | PC kipwatāmow, *to suffocate;* MC kipwāw, *be blocked;* SEC cipotāmow, *to suffocate;* Silvy (ca. 1680) "kip8chkau, *il est bouché*" origin | PA ***kepo** (***kepw,** Aubin, 1975)

*kirak

INITIAL

— itch

evidence | PC kiyakinēw, _to tickle sb;_ kiyakasēw, _to have itchy skin;_ WSC (Misipawistik, Ellen Cook) kinakisiw, _to be itchy;_ kinakinēw, _to tickle sb;_ MC kalakašew, _have itchy skin;_ SEC ciyakāpitew, _for one's gums to itch when teething;_ Silvy (ca. 1680) "ni kiragamigȣets papikȣets, _les puces me laissesnt des marques_" | ANISH ginaginike, _one's arm itches_ (Livesay & Nichols, 2021)

*kiraw

INITIAL

— lie, tell an untruth

evidence | PC kiyāskihēw, _to make sb lie;_ MC kilāskiw, _to lie;_ WI (Pessamit) katshilau [kətlāw], _to lie;_ EI (Mamit) katshinau [katnāw], _to lie;_ Laure (ca. 1726) "ni-tchirassin, _je mens;_" Fabvre (ca. 1690) "Kiraȣitaȣau, kirassikaȣau, _mentir à qlqn_" | ANISH ggiinwi, _to tell a lie_ (O&OE, 2022); gagiinawishki, _to be a habitual liar_ (Livesay & Nichols, 2021) origin | PA ***keraw** (***kelaw**, Aubin, 1975) discussion | In most dialects this root has been lexicalized as a reflex of ***kirāski-** (***kiraw** + ***ɩski**).

*kirā

INITIAL

— finish or arrive before, anticipate

evidence | MC kilāhew, _to finish or arrive before sb;_ SEC ciyāhew, _to finish or arrive before sb_ compare | *rā

*kirikaw

INITIAL

— mix

evidence | MC kilikawaštāw, _to mix sth in;_ SEC ciyikawipeštān, _to be a mix of rain and snow;_ WI (Pessamit) tshilikushtau [tʃələkūstāw], _to mix two different things_ origin | PA ***kerek** (***kelek**, Aubin, 1975; Hewson, 1993)

*kirip

INITIAL

— quickly

evidence | WC kiðipa, _hurry;_ MC kilipīw, _to be fast;_ SEC ciyipiciw, _to grow fast;_ Laure (ca. 1726) "ni-tchiripuan, _je parle vite;_" Silvy (ca. 1680) "katcheribacha, _en peu, bientôt_" | ANISH ginibanjige, _to eat quickly_ (Livesay & Nichols, 2021)

*kisiskā

INITIAL

— quickly

evidence | PC kisiskāciwan, _swift current;_ MC kisiskāhtew, _to walk quickly;_ AT (Wemotaci, Nicole Petiquay) kisiskatew [kiziskāhtēw], _to walk fast;_ Laure (ca. 1726) "ni-tchichiskahiabukunan, _le courant est renvoyé, il nous emporte [rapidement];_" Fabvre (ca. 1690) "Kisiskatchĭman eȣ, _aller uiste par eau_"

*kisī

INITIAL

— clean

evidence | PC kisīpēkīw, _to bathe;_ MC kisīpekinam, _to wash sth;_ AT kisikwew [kizīhkwēw], _to wash one's face;_ kisi:hikan, _a car wiper, instrument used to wipe_ (Béland, 1978); SEC cisīnam, _to wipe sth clean;_ Silvy (ca. 1680) "ni kisihen, _je torche, frotte, essuie_" | ABEN gezilja, _to wash one's hands_ (Day, 1994); ANISH giziibiigii, _to wash up_ (Livesay & Nichols, 2021); MESK kesīnechēwa, _to wash one's hands_ origin | PA ***kesī** (Aubin, 1975)

*kisīp

INITIAL

— squeak

evidence | MC kisīpihtākwan, _to sound squeaky;_ SEC cisīpāskʷ, _a squeaky tree (one that rubs against another one);_ WI (Pessamit) tshishipashkᵘ [təʃəpāʃkʷ], _idem;_ Silvy (ca. 1680) "kisipaskȣtȣ, _les arbres bruissent, sifflent, en se frottant_" |

ABEN gezibanakw, *a tree squeak* (Day, 1994); ANISH giziibanaamo, *to wheeze;* giziibweweshkaa, *to squeak in motion* (Livesay & Nichols, 2021) origin | PA ***kesīp**

*kisk

INITIAL

— be aware of, know

evidence | PC kiskēyihtam, *to know sth;* MC kiskisiw, *to remember;* SEC cisceyihtam, *to know sth;* NEC kichāschimāu, *to offer advice or instruction to sb; to preach to sb;* Watkins (1865) "Kiskimāo, *v.t.an. He comes to an understanding with him, he is under an engagement to him*" | ANISH gikendam, *to know* (Livesay & Nichols, 2021) origin | PA ***kesk** (***kexk**, Hewson, 1993) compare | *kiskino, *kiskinawāt

*kiskinawāt (~ *kiskinawāc, *kiskinawās)

INITIAL

— mark for identification

evidence | PC kiskinawācihtāw, *to mark sth;* MC kiskinawācihcikan, *an identifying mark or sign;* SEC ciscinawātišam, *to cut an identifying mark into sth;* SEC chischinuwāsinākun, *to be used for a sign* (CSB, 2018) compare | *kisk, *kiskino

*kiskino (~ *kiskinaw)

INITIAL

— teach, learn

evidence | PC kiskinohtahēw, *to guide sb on foot;* MC kiskinawāpamew, *to learn by watching sb;* SEC (Waswanipi) ciscinohamawew, *to teach sb* | ABEN gikinōzo, *to be observed* (Day, 1994); ANISH gikinoo'amaage, *to teach* (Livesay & Nichols, 2021); MESK kehkinawāpiwa, *to learn by looking* origin | PA ***keskinaw** (***kexkinaw**, Hewson, 1993) compare | *kisk, *kiskinawāt

*kispak

INITIAL

— thick

evidence | WC kispakasākīw, *to be wearing a thick coat;* MC kispakāw, *to be thick;* SEC cispacekan, *to be a thick sheet-like object* | ANISH gipagaa, *to be thick* origin | PA ***kespak** (***kexpak**, Hewson, 1993)

*kispēw

INITIAL

— defend, take sides

evidence | PC kispēwēwin, *defence;* Lacombe (1874) "kispew, *(ad.) si peu que, au moins, tant bien que mal; v.g.* kispew *ki ka miyitin, si peu que j'en ai, je vais te le donner;* kispew *miyo kijikaw anotch, au moins il fait beau temps aujourd'hui;*" WSC (Misipawistik, Ellen Cook) "kispēwātēw okosisa ēkwa ē-nōtinikēskinit. *He defends his son even though he's always getting into fights.;*" MC kispewātew, *to be protective of sb;* SEC cispew, *what a waste;* cispewew, *to be protective;* cispewāwasow, *to spoil one's child by being overly protective;* NEC chispāwāusū, *to spoil one's child, to defend one's child;* WI (Pessamit) tshishpeuaushu [tʃəʃpēwāwʃu], *to defend a child;* Laure (ca. 1726) "tchispeu, *trop comble en sorte qu'il s'en perd;*" "kispeu, *dommage;*" "ni-tchispeuuauasun, *je perds, gâte mes enfants;*" "ni-tchispeu-uau, *je lui donne trop de pied, trop de liberté*" | ANISH Cuoq (1886) "Ni kipiwa, *je le defends;*" MENO kɛhpiawɛ·w, *to join him, to stay overnight at sb's house*

*kiš

INITIAL

— hot

evidence | ESC kišahkonew, *to be hot flame;* MC kišitew, *be hot;* AT (Opitciwan, Joey Awashish) kicekiswew [kiʒēkizwēw], *to heat sth sheet-like;* SEC cišākamisow, *to be a hot liquid;* Laure (ca. 1726) "tchichachteu, *âpre, en parlant de feu, du soleil;*" Silvy (ca. 1680) "ni kichis8n, *je fais cuire, j'échauffe*" | ANISH gizhaawangide, *to be hot sand* (Livesay & Nichols, 2021) origin | PA ***kešy** (Aubin, 1975; Hewson, 1993)

*kišā

INITIAL

— refuse to abandon

evidence | PC kisātew, *to refuse to leave sb;* MC kišātinew, *to prevent sb from leaving;* AT (Wemotaci, Nicole Petiquay) kicatinew [kiʒātinēw], *to prevent sb from leaving;* NEC chishātim, *to regret parting with sth; to miss sth;* WI (Uashat) tshishateu [tʃʃātēw], *to be very attached to sb;* Silvy (ca. 1680) "ni kichatiban, *la boisson m'arrête;*" "ni kichap8n, *le manger m'arrête*" | ANISH gizhaadaawaso, *to babysit* (Livesay & Nichols, 2021) limited to | *t³, *t⁴

*kišē

INITIAL

— **1** great, large

— **2** adult or full-grown, speaking of animals or trees

— **3** elderly, speaking of people

evidence | MC kiše-cīmān, *a ship;* kišeštimʷ, *an adult dog;* kišeliliw, *an elderly man;* AT kiceatisiw [kiʒēyātiziw], *to be aged;* kicemiskw [kišēmiskʷ], *an adult beaver;* SEC Cišesīpiy, *Chisasibi, literally 'great river' (place name);* NEC chishāwīnipākw, *ocean;* chishāyāhtikw, *a full-grown tree;* WI (Uashat) Tshishe-shatshu [tʃʃēʃātʃu], *Sheshatshiu, literally 'great outlet' (place name);* (Pessamit) tshisheiakᵘ [tʃʃējākʷ], *an adult porcupine;* tshisheiapeu [tʃʃējāpēu], *to be an elderly man;* Silvy (ca. 1680) "kichere8, *grosse perdrix;*" "kiches8, *gros orignal*" | ANISH gizhenaabe, *a middle-aged man* (Livesay & Nichols, 2021)

*kišēwāt

INITIAL

— kind

evidence | PC kisēwātēyimēw, *to think of sb in a kindly way;* AT kicewatisiwin [kiʒēwātiziwin], *goodness, kindness;* MC kišewātotātowak, *to be kind to one another;* SEC cišewātisīw, *to be kind* see | *kišē, *āt⁵

*kišip

INITIAL

— end, extremity

evidence | PC kisipisiw, *to end;* MC kišipāw, *to be the end;* AT (Wemotaci, Nicole Petiquay) kicipitakaw [kiʒipihtakāw], *to be the end of a piece of wood or surface made of wood;* SEC cišipisikwāw, *to be the end of an expanse of ice* | ANISH gizhibizhan, *to cut off a projecting part or limb of sth* (Livesay & Nichols, 2021)

*kišiw (~ *kišiwā)

INITIAL

— angry, anger

evidence | PC kisiwāsiw, *to be angry;* WC kisiwīðimow, *to feel angry;* ESC (Severn) kishiwenihtam, *to be angry about sth;* AT kiciwasiw [kiʒiwāziw], *to be angry;* MC kišiwāhew, *to anger sb;* SEC cišiwāpamew, *to be angered at the sight of sb;* WI (Pessamit) tshishukateu [tʃʃūkətēw], *to be angry from hunger;* Laure (ca. 1726) "tchichiuaganiu, *animé, irrité, fâché*" compare | *rišk

*kišī

INITIAL

— fast

evidence | PC kisīyāsiw, *to sail fast;* WC kisīcimīw, *to paddle fast;* AT kicipataw [kiʒīpahtāw], *to run fast;* MC kišīpaliw, *to move fast;* SEC (Waswanipi) cišipayin, *to move fast;* WI (Pessamit) tshishipalu [tʃʃəpəlu], *to move fast* | ANISH gizhiiyoode, to crawl fast (Livesay & Nichols, 2021) origin | Variously reconstructed in PA as ***kešy** (Aubin, 1975), ***kešyī** (Aubin, 1975), and ***kešyiw** (Hewson, 1993)

*kišk

INITIAL (NOUN, ANIMATE)

— female dog

evidence | PC kiskisis, *a female animal;* WC kiskānakos, *a female dog;* Watkins (1865) "kiskisis, *n.an. a mare;*" Silvy (ca. 1680) "kistchich, *chienne*" | ANISH gishkishenh, *a female dog or mare* (Livesay & Nichols, 2021)

*kišt (~ *kihc)

INITIAL

— **1** great

— **2** solid, firm, packed down

evidence | [1]MC kištelihtākosiw, *to be esteemed;* PC kihcinawēw, *to look at sb with admiration;* SEC cišteyimew, *to esteem sb* [2]PC kistaskisow, *to stand solidly, as a tree;* MC kištaskamikāw, *to be firm ground;* kištāpiskʷ, *rock;* SEC cištamow, *to be hard-packed;* EI (Unaman-shipit) tshishtashkamikᵘ [tʃɨstahkamukʷ], *"continent across the ocean (mentioned in stories);"* Laure (ca. 1726) "tchistamu, *chemin battu*" | [1]ABEN gitōgama, *a big lake;* gichitegw, *a big river* (Day, 1995); ANISH gitenim, *to think highly of sb* [2]ABEN kitakamigw, *the land as opposed to water, the mainland* (Day, 1994) origin | PA ***keʔt*** (Aubin, 1975; Hewson, 1993)

*kištākan

INITIAL (NOUN, INANIMATE)

— post, stake

evidence | MC kištākan, *a stake;* WI (Pessamit) tshishtakanashkᵘ [tʃəstākənāʃkʷ], *stick used to block the underwater exit of a beaver lodge;* EI (Sheshatshiu) tshishtakanashkᵘ [tʃɨstākənāʃkʷ], *stick used to block the underwater exit of a beaver lodge;* Silvy (ca. 1680) "tistagan, *clôture de pieux;*" "ni tistaganikan 3. -e8, *j'en fais une;*" "tchitaganask8, *pieu de palissade*" | MESK ketākana, *one of the large central posts holding up the roof of a traditional Meskwaki house* see | *kišt, *ākan² discussion | The noun derived from this initial is treated as animate in Eastern Innu but inanimate in Western Innu and Moose Cree.

*kištikē

INITIAL (VERB, ABSTRACT, INTRANSITIVE)

— grow crops

evidence | PC okistikēw, *a farmer;* WC kistikātam, *to plant sth;* Watkins (1865) "kistikachikun, *n.in. a plant, a seed;*" Laure (ca. 1726) "tchistigan, *jardin;*" Silvy (ca. 1680) "ni kistigan, *je travaille à la terre, je travaille mon champ*" | ANISH gitige, *to plant, garden, farm* (Livesay & Nichols, 2021) origin | PA **keʔtwikē** (Hewson, 1993)

*kištohkan

INITIAL (NOUN, INANIMATE)

— door

evidence | PC kistohkan, *door, tent flap;* MC kištohkan, *tent flap;* EI (Sheshatshiu) tshishtukan [tʃɨstūkən], a door; Silvy (ca. 1680) "kicht8kan, *la porte*"

*kit

INITIAL

— forbid

evidence | PC kitahamawēw, *to warn sb against sth; to forbid sb;* MC kitahamākew, *to admonish;* SEC citahamawew, *to admonish sb;* WI (Pessamit) tshitaimatishu [stīmātīʃu], *to refrain, to stop oneself from acting* | ABEN ogelahamawō, *to forbid sb;* gelahigan, *a deadfall trap;* gelapskwaha, *to anchor sth* (Day, 1994); ANISH gina'amaadiwin, *a prohibition;* ginaa'ogo, *to be stranded in a boat* (Livesay & Nichols, 2021); MESK kenahamawāwa, *to forbid or dissuade sb;* kenahōchikani, *a braided strap for securing war captives* origin | PA ***keθ***, "restrain, hold back" (Aubin, 1975; Hewson, 1993)

*kitak

INITIAL

— spotted

evidence | MC kicakālowew, *to have a spotted tail;* Laure (ca. 1726) "tchirigaui-tchitagu [*sic*], *taché de différentes marques*" | ANISH gidagaakoons, *a fawn* (Livesay & Nichols,

2021); MENO keta·kaqnεm(-ok), *spotted dog;* MESK ketakesiwa, *to be spotted* origin | PA ***ketak** (Aubin, 1975; Hewson, 1993)

*kitamw

INITIAL (VERB, TRANSITIVE, ANIMATE)

— consume completely

evidence | PC kitamwew, *to eat all of sth, to smoke all of sth;* SEC citamwew, *to eat or drink all of sth;* EI (Sheshatshiu) tshitamueu [tʃɨtəmwēw], *to have eaten or drunk all of sth* | ANISH ogidamwaan, *to eat all of sth* (Livesay & Nichols, 2021) paired with | *kitā

*kitā

INITIAL (VERB, ANIMATE, INTRANSITIVE)

— consume completely

evidence | PC kitāw, *to consume sth entirely;* SEC citāw, *to eat or drink all of sth;* Silvy (ca. 1680) "ni kitan 3. -tau, *je mange tout, je bois tout*" | ANISH ogidaan, *to eat all of sth* (Livesay & Nichols, 2021) paired with | *kitamw

*kitikw[1] (~ *kitiko)

INITIAL (NOUN, DEPENDENT INANIMATE)

— anterior knee, kneecap

evidence | PC mikitik, *a kneecap; a knee;* MC okitikokekan, *a kneecap;* AT nikitikw, *my knee;* EI (Sheshatshiu) utshitikua [utʃɨtukwa], *one's kneecap;* Laure (ca. 1726) "tchitigukan, *os du genou;*" Silvy (ca. 1680) "kitig8, *genou*" | MENO nekε·tek, *my knee* see | *kitikw[2]

*kitikw[2]

MEDIAL, FINAL (NOUN INCORPORATION)

— anterior knee, kneecap

evidence | MC kisīpikitikwew, *for one's knee(s) to crack;* AT (Opitciwan, Joey Awashish) akosikitikwew [āhkozikitikwēw], *to feel a pain in one's knee(s)* | ANISH babaagigidigwe, *to have swollen knees* (Livesay & Nichols, 2021) see | *kitikw[1]

*kitim

INITIAL

— **1** make pitiable

— **2** impoverish

evidence | PC kitimahēw, *to treat sb badly;* MC kitimahew, *to impoverish sb; to mistreat sb or be cruel to sb;* SEC citimahew, *to mistreat sb or be cruel to sb;* WI (Pessamit) tshitimaiueu [stəmīwēw], *to impoverish;* Watkins (1865) "kitemahāo, *v.t.an. He injures him, he harms him, he impoverishes him;*" Laure (ca. 1726) "ni-tchitimahau, *je le mets en pitoyable état*" | MENO ketε·mahεw, *to make sb miserable or bring sb to ruin* origin | PA ***ketem** (Aubin, 1975; Hewson, 1993) see | *kitimāk

*kitimāk

INITIAL

— **1** pitiable

— **2** poor

evidence | PC kitimākan, *it is pitiable or a poor area;* MC kitimākinākosiw, *to look pitiful;* SEC citimāceyimew, *to have sympathy for sb* | ABEN gedemōgiha, *to make miserable, poor, or pathetic* (Day, 1994); ANISH gidimaaginaagwad, *to look poor* (Livesay & Nichols, 2021); MENO ketε·ma·kesew, *to be in a miserable or piteous state; to be poor; to be emaciated* origin | PA ***ketemāk** (Aubin, 1975; Hewson, 1993) see | *kitim

*kitišk

INITIAL

— drop

evidence | PC kitiskipayiw, *to drop;* MC kitiškinam/kiciškinam, *to drop sth from one's hands;* AT kitcickinew [kiciškinēw], *to drop sb from one's hands;* SEC ticiščinam [titsnam] *to drop sth from one's hands;* WI (Pessamit) tshitissineu [tətəssnēw], *to drop sb;* EI (Sheshatshiu) tshitissineu [tʃɨtɨssinēw], *to drop sb;* Watkins (1865) "Kuchistinum, *v.t.in.6. He drops it;*" Laure (ca. 1726) "ni-tchitissinau, *je lâche la bête*" | MESK keteshkenamwa, *to release sth from one's* *hands* origin | PA ***ketešk** (Aubin, 1975; Hewson, 1993)

*kito

INITIAL (VERB, ANIMATE, INTRANSITIVE)

— vocalize

evidence | PC kitowēhkwāmiw, *to snore;* MC kitow, *to vocalize;* SEC citohew, *to call an animal or bird;* WI (Pessamit) tshitu [tʃətu], *to vocalize; to rumble, speaking of the thunder;* Laure (ca. 1726) "ni-tchittun, *je parle [émettre un son]*" | ANISH gidotoon, *to play a musical instrument or radio* (Livesay & Nichols, 2021)

*kiwāhp

MEDIAL, FINAL (NOUN INCORPORATION)

— dwelling, lodge

evidence | PC mihtikiwāhp, *a wooden lodge;* WC mīhtokiwāhp [*sic*], *teepee made from dry wood;* ESC mihtikiwāhp, *a sod house;* NEC wīshkichānichiwāhp, *oblong-shaped dwelling;* WI (Pessamit) mititshuap [məttətʃwāp], *a woodshed;* atimutshuap [təmutʃwāp], *a doghouse;* EI (Sheshatshiu) mishiutshuap [mīʃīwtʃwāp], *a bathroom;* Watkins (1865) "Mìtekewap, *n.in. A wooden tent;*" Laure (ca. 1726) "takutchitchiuapitch, *au faite de la maison;*" "atatchitchiuapi, *appartement;*" Silvy (ca. 1680) "ni mir8tchi8apan, *je demeure en bonne cabane*" | ANISH enigoonsigiwaam, *an anthill* (Livesay & Nichols, 2021) origin | Old Cree ***mīkiwāhpi** see | *mīkiwāhp discussion | The alternative reconstruction ***ɩkiwāhp** is specious as its evidence is limited to forms beginning with the various contemporary reflexes of ***miht**, a root that is now invariable in these dialects, thus masking the phonemic identity of the following vowel. While in Old Cree this root did in fact alternate with its allomorph, ***mihš**, we could find no evidence to support the alternative construction ***mihšikiwāhpi**. Laure (ca. 1726) provides two examples that clearly demonstrate the lenition of a preceding /t/ at the morpheme boundary, supporting instead ***kiwāhp** as the correct reconstruction.

*kiyām

INITIAL

— still, tranquil

evidence | PC kiyāmēwan, *to be a peaceful area;* MC kayāmapiw, *to sit still;* SEC ciyāmeyihtam, *to be serene;* Silvy (ca. 1680) "ni kiamapin, *je suis en repos*"

*kiyāš

INITIAL

— old

evidence | PC kayāsipakwa, *withered leaves;* WSC (Misipawistik, Ellen Cook) kayāsicīmān, *an old canoe;* MC kayāšinākwan, *to look old;* SEC ciyāšinākwan, *to look old;* EI (Sheshatshiu) tshiashassin [tʃjāʃəssɨn], *old shoe;* Laure (ca. 1726) "tchiachinagusiu, *qui a perdu sa couleur (parlant d'une personne);*" Fabvre (ca. 1690) "Keach assam *pl.* mak, *uielles raq(uettes);*" Silvy (ca. 1680) "ni keachag8pan, *j'ai une vieille robe*" | ANISH Nicholas (ca. 1670) "keach, *vieux*" (Daviault, 1994); MENO kɛ·yas, *long ago, ever since long ago, old*

*kiyāškw (~ *kiyāško)

INITIAL (NOUN, ANIMATE)

— gull

evidence | PC kiyāsk, *a seagull;* MC kiyāškoskāw, *to be many gulls;* SEC ciyāšk[w], *a gull;* Fabvre (ca. 1690) "tchiachk8, *maue, g8alan, oyseau*" | ANISH gayaashkwag, *a seagull* (Livesay & Nichols, 2021)

*kī

INITIAL

— escape

evidence | WC kīhīw, *to get away from sb;* MC kīhiwew, *to escape;* WI (Pessamit) tshieu [tʃījēw], *to escape sb;* Watkins (1865) "kèhâo, *he escapes him;*" Silvy (ca. 1680) "ni kihig8n, *l'animal poursuivi m'échappe"* | ANISH gii', *to escape sb* (Livesay & Nichols, 2021) origin | PA ***kī** (Aubin, 1975; Hewson, 1993)

*kīhikohšim

INITIAL (VERB, TRANSITIVE, ANIMATE)

— make sb abstain from food and drink, make sb fast

evidence | Laure (ca. 1726) "nit-aiamihe-tchigusimau, *je le fais jeûner selon la prière"*
see | *kī, *hšim

*kīhikohšimo

INITIAL (VERB, ANIMATE, INTRANSITIVE)

— abstain from food and drink, fast

evidence | PC kīhikosimowin, *fasting;* Lacombe (1874) "kihikusimow, ok, *(v.n.) il jeûne, il se prive de manger; voy. iyewanisihisuw. N.B. C'est aussi l'expression dont on se sert pour désigner les jeûnes dans [*sic*] le manger et le boire que s'imposent les infidèles, allant passer des deux ou trois jours, sur unr haute colline, sans manger, tâchant d'y dormir, afin d'obtenir de leurs génies des rêves mystérieux;"* Laure (ca. 1726) "nit-aiamiheutchigusimun, *je jeûne selon la prière;"* Silvy (ca. 1680) "ni kihig8chim8n, *je jeûne"* | ANISH gii'igoshimo, *to fast for a vision* (Livesay & Nichols, 2021) see | *kī, *hšimo

*kīhk

INITIAL

— persist

evidence | PC kīhkīhk, *in spite, nevertheless;* kīhkihēw, *to trouble sb, to make sb nervous;* kīhkīhkimēw, *to persuade sb against their will;* Lacombe (1874) "Kikkimew, *(v.a.)* ttam, miwew, tchikew, *il s'obstine auprès de lui par ses paroles, il veut le persuader;"* WSC (Misipawistik, Ellen Cook) kīhkimēw, *to scold sb;* AT (Wemotaci, Nicole Petiquay) kikimow [kīhkimow], *to sob incessantly* | MESK kīhkihēwa, *to prolong sb's life;* kīhkīhkihēwa, *to force sb against their will;* kīhkīhkikenwi, *to grow on an on*

*kīhkā

INITIAL

— conspicuous, pronounced

evidence | PC kīhkāmāswēw, *to burn sth with a strong odor;* kīhkāhtowak, *to argue or quarrel with one another;* MC kīhkāhtākosiw, *to be heard discernibly;* SEC cīhkāyeyihtākosiw, *to be famous;* NEC chīhkānākusiu, *to be in full view;* WI (Pessamit) tshikaiashteu [tʃīkājāstēw], *to shine brightly;* Laure (ca. 1726) "ni-tchikamau, *je le querelle;"* Silvy (ca. 1680) "kikamag8an, *cela sent fort"*

*kīhkē

INITIAL

— angled

evidence | PC kīhkēhtakāhk, *in the corner;* MC kīhkeyāw, *to be angled;* SEC kacīhcepotāw, *to file or saw it square;* Laure (ca. 1726) "tchitcheiau *pl.* -a, *angle d'une maison"*

*kīhtwām

INITIAL

— anew

evidence | PC kīhtwāmēyihtam, *to think of sth again, to recall sth;* WC kāhkīhtwām, *over and over again;* MC kīhtwām, *afresh, once more;* SEC cīhtwām, *over again;* Watkins (1865) "Ketwam, *adv. Afresh, again, over again.* Mena ketwam, *once again"*

*kīkē

INITIAL (VERB, ANIMATE, INTRANSITIVE)

— heal (a wound or sore)

evidence | PC kīkēw, *to heal from a sore;* MC kīkēhew, *to heal sb;* SEC cīcesikan, *salve;* Laure (ca. 1726) "ka tchitchehaganit, *réchappé d'une maladie;"* Fabvre (ca. 1690) "Kikan e8, tchikan e8, *estre guery"*

*kīm

INITIAL

— furtively, secretly

evidence | PC kīmīw, *to sneak away;* kīmwēw, *to whisper;* WC kīmāpimīw, *to spy on sb;* Laure (ca. 1726) "ni-tchiminatau *je tue en cachette, id est, je trame sa mort en secret;*" "ni-tchiminau he nepat, *illum vel illam invere [cunde] tango*" | ABEN gimosa, *to walk secretly or quietly* (Day, 1994); ANISH giimaabi, *to spy or peep* (Livesay & Nichols, 2021) compare | *kīmōt

*kīman

INITIAL (NOUN, INANIMATE)

— tinder

evidence | PC Lacombe (1874) "Kimana, *(n.r.) foin écrasé, frotté, qu'on prépare pour allumer le feu au campement, d'ou, manikimanew, il prend du foin pour fair du feu;*" SEC cīman, *a match;* WI (Pessamit) tshiman [tsimən] *sulphur; match* (Drapeau, 1991); Silvy (ca. 1680) "Kiman, tchiman, *bois bien sec, s8ffre, p8dre à canon*" | ANISH Cuoq (1886) "Kiman, *tout ce dont on se sert pour allumer le feu*"

*kīmōt (~ *kīmōc, *kīmōs)

INITIAL

— furtively, secretly

evidence | PC kīmōciyawesiw, *to be secretly angry*; kīmōtan, *to be a secret;* MC kīmōsāpamew, *to spy sb;* AT (Wemotaci, Jeannette Coocoo) kimosapiw [kīmōzāpiw], *to spy;* SEC cīmōtisīw, *to be secretive;* WI (Pessamit) tshimushapu [tʃīmūtāpu], *to spy* compare | *kīm

*kīn

INITIAL

— sharp point

evidence | PC kīnipocikēw, *to sharpen things;* WC kīnipocikan, *file;* MC kīnipotāw, *to file or saw sth into a point;* AT kinipotcikewakew [kīnipocikēwākēw], *to use sth for sharpening;* SEC cīnāw, *to be pointy;* NEC chīnishim, *to cut sth into a point;* WI (Pessamit) tshinikanakau, *to be a pointy bone;* EI (Sheshatshiu) tshinau [tʃīnāw], *to have a sharp edge;* Laure (ca. 1726) "tchinau, *aigu, pointu, qui a une pointe;*" Silvy (ca. 1680) "kinik8te8, *il a le bec pointu;*" cf. PC kīnikatos, *pointed arrow;* WC kīnikisiw, *to be sharp and pointy;* ESC kīnikisiw, *to be pointy;* MC kīnikāw, *be pointy* | ANISH giinaa, *to be sharp* (Livesay & Nichols, 2021) discussion | This form is unproductive in contemporary nonpalatalizing dialects spoken west of Western Innu and Southern East Cree but is nonetheless attested as lexicalized forms in words containing the finals for filing or sawing. In these dialects, with the exception of Atikamekw, the productive form is now **kīnik**, likely a combination of Old Cree ***kīn** and the prefinal ***k**, as in ***kīnikahamwa,** *to chop sth into a point.* Atikamekw instead uses *kīnihko-*, a form it shares with the neighbouring Anishinabe dialect.

*kīnānihš

INITIAL (NOUN, DEPENDENT INANIMATE)

— rump

evidence | WC okīnānis, *the lower part of an animal's backbone; Seven stars;* MC okīnānišak, *Pleiades, a cluster of stars whose mythological origin is ascribed to the rump of a dead woman;* NEC uchīnānish, *Pleiades;* WI (Pessamit) Utshinanish [ūtʃīnānəʃ], *Cepheus;* Watkins (1865) "ookenanis, *n.an. The seven stars;*" Fabvre (ca. 1690) "8kinanich, *son cr8pion d a(nim)al, uel oyseau;*" Silvy (ca. 1680) "8tchinanich, *la poussinière, proprie son croupion*" discussion | The Old Cree name for the cluster of stars known as the Seven Sisters or Pleiades, ***wikīnānihša**, is derived from this root.

*kīnikwān

INITIAL

— be or move round

evidence | PC kīnikwānipayiw, *to revolve or spin;* MC kīnikwānāpihkehtin, *be coiled;* SEC cīnikwānipayiw, *to go around by vehicle;* WI (Pessamit) tshinikuanuteu [tʃīnəkwāntēw], *to walk in a circle*

*kīp

INITIAL

— topple

evidence | PC kīpipayiw, *to fall over, to tumble over;* Silvy (ca. 1680) "ni kibichinin, *je tombe à la renverse*" compare | *kīpat

*kīpat (~ *kīpac)

INITIAL

— topple

evidence | MC kīpaciwepinam, *to topple sth by hand;* NEC chīpichipiyiu, *to topple over;* chīpitinim, *to pull sth back from an erect position* compare | *kīp

*kīskim

INITIAL

— numb

evidence | PC kīskimisitēw, *to have numb feet;* MC kīskimisiw, *to be numb;* SEC cīscimikātew, *for one's leg(s) to be numb* | MIAMI "Nikikimineki, *j ay la main engourdie*" (Largillier - ILDA, 2017)

*kīsp

INITIAL

— chapped

evidence | PC kīspisiw, *to be chapped;* Silvy (ca. 1680) "ni kihispit8nin, *j'ai les lèvres fendues, sèches*" | ANISH giipininjii, *to have a chapped hand(s)* (Livesay & Nichols, 2021)

*kīš

INITIAL

— complete, finish

evidence | PC kīsikwātēw, *to finish sewing sth;* MC kīšakwew, *to finish erecting a dwelling;* AT kicihew [kīʒihēw], *to finish sth;* SEC cīšihtāw, *to finish sth* | ANISH giizhigin, *to be full grown or ripe* (Livesay & Nichols, 2021); MENO ke·sa·hpenɛw, *to come to the fatal end of one's sickness or suffering anticipation of; immediately;* EI (Sheshatshiu) tshishat [tʃīʃāt], *immediately, before anything else;* Silvy (ca. 1680) "kichats, *devant, auparavant*"

*kīšāt (~ *kīšāc)

INITIAL

— beforehand

evidence | PC kīsāc, *in advance, in preparation; at once, immediately;* AT kicatc [kīʒāc], *ahead of time, first;* MC kīšāc, *in*

*kīšik

INITIAL

— bright sky, day

evidence | PC kīsikāsiw, *to be a bit of daylight left;* MC kīšikāw, *to be day;* kīšikʷ, *sky;* AT (Opitciwan, Joey Awashish) kicikaw [kīʒikāw], *to be day;* SEC cīšikāštew, *moonlight;* NEC chīshikw, *sky;* WI (Mashteuiatsh) tshishikᵘ, *sky;* Fabvre (ca. 1690) "Kichik8, *L air, Le tems, Le I8r;*" Silvy (ca. 1680) "kichigaste8, *la lune luit*" | ANISH giizhigad, *to be day* (Livesay & Nichols, 2021); MENO ki·seku·hkiw, woman's name "Sky-woman" compare | *wāskw

*kīšikan

INITIAL

— bright sky, day

evidence | PC kīsikanisiw, *to spend one's day, to live through the day;* māyi-kīsikanisiw, *to have a bad day;* MC kīšikanihkwāmiw, *to sleep during the day;* SEC miyo-makošecīšikanihtāw, *to experience a good Christmas day;* WI (Pessamit) matshitshishikanishu [mətʃʃīʃəkənəʃu], *to run into bad weather* see | *kīšik

*kīšināt (~ *kīšināc, *kīšinās)

INITIAL

— grief, sorrow

evidence | PC kīsināc, *unfortunately;* kīsinācipayiw, *to fall into unfortunate circumstances;* kīsinātēyimēw, *to feel sorry for sb;* MC kīšinātelihtākwan, *to arouse grief or sorrow;* AT (Wemotaci, Jeannette Coocoo) kicinaterimew [kīʒinātērimēw], *to feel sorry for sb* discussion | Despite the broad geographic distribution of this root, cognates have not been identified in dialects spoken east of Moose Cree and Atikamekw. Its inclusion here is therefore tentative.

*kīšk

INITIAL

— **1** sever

— **2** abrupt rise or fall in terrain

evidence | [1]PC kīskāw, *to be severed;* MC kīškišam, *to cut sth off;* SEC cīšcipotāw, *to saw sth off* [2]PC kīskāyawāw, *to be deep (underwater);* MC kīškāskweyāw, *sudden change in the height of trees;* SEC ciškāyawāw, *underwater precipice;* EI (Sheshatshiu) tshishkakamau [tʃīʃkākəmāw], *to be a lake with a steep bank* | [1]MENO ke·skɛhtɛsosow, *to cut off one's own ear* origin | PA ***kīšk** (Hewson, 1993)

*kīškwē

INITIAL (VERB, ANIMATE, INTRANSITIVE)

— out of one's wits, stunned, dizzy

evidence | PC kīskwēpēw, *to be drunk;* MC kīškweyāpamow, *to be dizzy;* SEC cīškwew, *to be crazy;* WI (Pessamit) tshishkueueu [tʃīʃkwēwēw], *to knock sb out*

*kīšopwē

INITIAL (VERB, INANIMATE, INTRANSITIVE)

— be mild winter weather

evidence | PC kīsapwēyāw, *to be warm weather;* Lacombe (1874) "Kisopwekkattew, a, *(a.in) c'est chaud, v.g., une maison où il y a grand feu;*" NEC chīshipwāyāu, *to be mild weather in the winter;* WI (Pessamit) tshishipueu [tʃīʃəpwēw], *to be warm weather, to be a winter thaw;* Watkins (1865) "Kesoopwāo, *v.imp. It is mild weather;*" Laure (ca. 1726) "kichupuesiu, *le temps, le froid s'adoucit*"; Silvy (ca, 1680) "kichab8e8, kichib8echi8, *temps doux;*" "kich8b8eu, *temps étouffé, doux*" compare | *kīšō

*kīšō (~ *kīšow)

INITIAL

— warm

evidence | PC kīsōnēw, *to warm sb with one's hands;* MC kīšōškawew, *to warm sb up with one's body;* AT kicoho [kīʒōhow], *to dress warmly;* NEC cīshuwāyāu, *to be warm weather;* EI (Sheshatshiu) tshishukuniu [tʃīʃūkunīw], *to cover oneself warmly;* Laure (ca. 1726) "tchichugamiu, *boisson tiède*" compare | *šō compare | *kīšopwē

*kīštin

INITIAL (VERB, INANIMATE, INTRANSITIVE)

— windstorm

evidence | PC kīstin, *to be a tempest;* MC kīštinišiw, *to encounter a windstorm;* NEC chīshtinipiyiu, *to be a sudden gust of strong wind;* Laure (ca. 1726) "tchistinu, *bouffée de vent;*" Silvy (ca. 1680) "kichtin8, *il fait tempête*" compare | *štin[3], *tin

*kīšwē

FINAL (VERB, ANIMATE, INTRANSITIVE, CONCRETE)

— speak

evidence | MC išikīšwew, *to speak thus;* SEC macicīšwew, *to speak badly;* WI (Pessamit) issishueu [īssīʃwēw], *to say;* Laure (ca. 1726) "tchi-uanatchichuan, *tu parles en étourdi;*" Silvy (ca. 1680) "echitchich8an, *un mot*" | ANISH majigiizhwe, *to swear* (Livesay & Nichols, 2021)

*kīw

INITIAL

— go or move about

evidence | PC Lacombe (1874) "kiyutew, *visiter à une distance;*" WC kiyokīw, *to visit;* MC kīwāhpihitowak, *to frolic with one another, speaking of animals;* SEC cīwotew, *to visit;* cīwāhpiw, *to frolic, speaking of an animal;* NEC chīupiyiu, *to be loose or slack;* chīuwihtāu, *the caribou leaves the area after losing velvet on antlers and goes in search of a mate;* WI (Pessamit) tshiuapishtueu [tʃīwāpīstwēw], *to want to play with sb, speaking of a dog;* Laure (ca. 1726) "tchiuipariu, *l'oiseau voltige;*" "ni-tchiutan, *je voyage;*" Silvy (ca. 1680) "ni kih8tan 3. -8, ni ki8tan, *je vais à la chasse;*" "ki8aste8, *chose délaissée;*" "ni ki8amisk8tan, *je vais sur le bord de l'eau, sur le sable*" | ANISH giiwose, *to hunt* (Livesay & Nichols, 2021); MENO ke·wohnεw, *to walk about*

*kīwahš

INITIAL

— forlorn, forsaken

evidence | ESC (Severn) kīwashishān, *an orphan;* MC kīwašelimew, *to long for sb;* kīwašišān, *an orphan;* AT (Wemotaci, Nicole Petiquay) kiwocican [kīwaššiʒān], *an orphan;* SEC chīusheyihtam, *to be forlorn with sb* (CSB, 2018); NEC chīwishishānishish, *an orphan;* chīushāyihtim, *to be homesick;* NSK chiiusaawaas, *an orphan;* EI (Unamanshipit) tshiussan [tʃīwassān], *an orphan;* Watkins (1865) "kewusāyimāo, *v.t.an. He longs for him, he grieves about him;*" "kewusehāo, *v.t.an. he makes him an orphan;*" Laure (ca. 1726) "ni-tchiuasseritamihau, *je lui donne de l'inquiétude;*" Silvy (ca. 1680) "kiȣachichan, *orphelin*" | ANISH giiwashizi, *to be orphaned;* giiwashizhaan, *an orphan* (Lippert & Gambill, 2023); Cuoq (1886) "Kiwac-ikwesens, *une petite orpheline*" compare | *kīwāt see | *kīw

*kīwāt (~ *kīwāc)

INITIAL

— forlorn, forsaken

evidence | PC kīwātan, *to be a lonely, desolate area;* kīwātēyimow, *to feel lonely and depressed;* WC kīwātīðihtam, *to be lonely or forlorn;* kīwācihīw, *to be an orphan;* kīwātis, *a person who is alone in the world; an orphan;* ESC (Severn) kīwācipaniw, *be one missing of a pair;* MC kīwātan, *to be uninhabited, desolate;* kīwātohtew, *to walk solitarily;* kīwātisiw, *to be alone from a loss, to be a widow or orphan* | MENO ke·wa·tesew, *to stay about here and there;* MESK kīwātesiwa, *to be lonely* compare | *kīwahš see | *kīw, *āt[5]

*kīwē

INITIAL (VERB, ANIMATE, INTRANSITIVE)

— return

evidence | PC kīwēpahtāw, *to run home;* MC kīwehow, *to return by canoe;* kāhkīwetācimow, *to crawl back and forth;* SEC cīwew, *to return or to go home* | MENO ke·wε·w, *to go back, to go home* origin | PA ***kīwē** (Aubin, 1975; Hewson, 1993)

*koh

INITIAL

— swallow

evidence | PC kohcipayihtāw, *to swallow sth;* MC kolew, *to swallow sth (speaking of a fish);* SEC kohtam, *to swallow sth (speaking of a fish)* | ANISH gondan, *to swallow sth* (Livesay & Nichols, 2021) origin | PA ***kwen** (Hewson, 1993; cf. ***kwan**, Aubin, 1975), via debuccalization of the final PA ***n** when followed by consonant-initial verb finals, satisfying the morphophonological constraint on preconsonantal nasals. limited to | *r, *t[6] compare | *wīh

*kohpit

INITIAL

— outlet of a lake

evidence | SEC (Waswanipi) e kohpitahc sīpiy, *place name* (Bishop, 2022); NEC kuhpitiniwāchiwin, *to flow out from a lake, speaking of water;* WI (Uashat) kupitan [kupɨtən], *to be the outlet of a lake;* EI (Sheshatshiu) kupitan [kūpɨtən], *to be the outlet of a lake;* Laure (ca. 1726) "kupitanu, *embouchure de rivière;*" Laure (ca. 1726) "tante he kupitatch sakahigan, *où est l'embouchure du lac*" limited to | *an[2]

*kohs

INITIAL (NOUN, DEPENDENT ANIMATE)

— son

evidence | PC Lacombe (1874) "nikose! *mon fils!;*" AT (Opitciwan, Joey Awashish) nikosa [nikossa], *my son;* nikosak [nikossak], *my sons;* nikose [nikossē], *son!* (Wemotaci, Nicole Petiquay) nikositokw! [nikossitokw], *sons!;* NEC nikusā, *son!;* Watkins (1865) "nekoosā, *son!*" | ANISH Cuoq (1886) "Ningwise, *fili mi;*" MESK nekwisa, *my son; (of a man) the son of my brother; (of a woman) the son of my sister;* MIAMI kikwihsa, *your son* (ILDA, 2017); MENO neki·qs, *my son* origin | PA ***kwiʔs** (Aubin, 1975; Hewson, 1993) compare | *kosihs

*kohsikē

INITIAL (VERB, ANIMATE, INTRANSITIVE)

— divine by use of fire

evidence | Laure (ca. 1726) "ni-kusigan 3. -tseu, *je devine par le feu, par le manger;*" Silvy (ca. 1680) "ni k8sigan 3. -tgeu, *je divine par le feu*" | ANISH André (ca. 1690s) "goussikeouin, *divination par le feu;*" MESK kosikēwa, *to play bowl-and-dice;* MIGM wesigen, *"you are a fortune-teller who prophesizes, usually with the help of cards;"* PASS 'qosikatun, *to predict what will happen to sth* origin | Likely PA ***kweʔsikē**, from ***kwet** + ***s** + ***kē**. see | *kot[1], *s, *kē[2] discussion | In the absence of an Atikamekw cognate, the preaspirate in the above form is presumed etymologically.

*kohtākan[1]

INITIAL (NOUN, INANIMATE)

— a throat, as in the front part of the neck

evidence | PC kohtākan, *a windpipe; a throat;* mikohtākan, *a throat;* WC okohtākan, *one's windpipe;* MC okohtākan, *a trachea; a pipe; a chimney;* SEC okohtākan, *one's throat; a stovepipe;* EI (Sheshatshiu) ukutakan [ukūtākən], *one's throat;* Laure (ca. 1726) "kutagan, *gosier;*" "ukutaganiu-chipiu, *la rivière des Prairies;*" Fabvre (ca. 1690) "8ek8tagani8i8, *Riu(ier)e de Iac(ques) Cartier*" | MENO ko·htakan, *throat* see | *koh, *kohtākan[2]

*kohtākan[2]

MEDIAL, FINAL (NOUN INCORPORATION)

— a throat, as in the front part of the neck

evidence | PC wīsakikohtākanēw, *to have a sore throat;* MC pākikohtākanepaliw, *to have swelling around the windpipe;* SEC wīsacikohtākanēw, *to have a sore throat;* WI (Pessamit) massikutakanu [māssəkutākənu], *to have a hoarse voice;* Fabvre (ca. 1690) "Kip8k8tagănin, *au(oi)r Le gozier b8ché, etre enr8é;*" Silvy (ca. 1680) "pisk8k8tagan, *os du gosier*" see | *kohtākan[1]

*konēw

MEDIAL

— oral cavity

evidence | PC ispīhcikonēwēw, *to have a mouth of such a capacity;* MC pīhcikonew, *inside a mouth;* SEC wīnikonewew, *to have bad breath;* WI (Pessamit) shatshikuneueshinu [ʃātʃəkunēwēʃənu], *to have sth come out of one's mouth;* Laure (ca. 1726) "peiokuguneu, *une gorgée d'eau*"

*kop

MEDIAL (NOUN INCORPORATION)

— bark used for making cordage

evidence | NEC ashpichikupānh, *strings for net sinkers and floats* | ANISH asigobaan, *processed basswood bark fiber* (Livesay & Nichols, 2021) see | *wīkopiy

*kopiy

FINAL (NOUN INCORPORATION)

— bark used for making cordage

evidence | Fabvre (ca. 1690) "8chachig8bi *pl.* ia, *ormes, ulm(us), arbre*" | ANISH ozhaashigob, *a slippery elm* (Livesay & Nichols, 2021) see | *wīkopiy

*kosā

INITIAL

— sink

evidence | PC kosāpēw, *to sink into the water;* MC kosāpeškam, *to make sth sink under one's weight;* AT kosapenew [kozāpēnēw], *to submerge sb with one's hands;* SEC kosāpecipitam, *to pull sth underwater;* Silvy (ca. 1680) "ni k8essaban, *je vais à fond*" | ANISH gonzaabii, *to sink in the water* (Livesay & Nichols, 2021); Cuoq (1886) "Konzabi, *enfoncer dans l'eau, sombrer*" origin | PA ***kwesaw** (Hewson, 1993) limited to | *ɪp compare | *kotāw

*kosihs

INITIAL (NOUN, DEPENDENT ANIMATE)

— son

evidence | PC okosisiw, *to have a son;* Lacombe (1874) "okosissa, *son fils;*" MC nikosis, *my son;* AT (Wemotaci, Nicole Petiquay) nikosis [nikozis], *my son;* o:kosissa, *his son* (Béland, 1978); NEC nikusis, *my son;* WI (Pessamit) ukussa [ukussē], *one's son;* Watkins (1865) "ookoosisimow, *son;*" Laure (ca. 1726) "nikussis, *mon fils;*" "ukussisa, *son fils;*" Fabvre (ca. 1690) "nik8chich, *mon fils;*" "n 8k8sisin i8, *au(oi)r enf(an)t, etre pere d enf(an)t;*" "he 8k8shisima8ian, *etre fils unique;*" Silvy (ca. 1680) "n'8k8chisimau, *je l'ai pour fils*" | ANISH Cuoq (1886) "Ningwisis, *filius meus;*" ogozisan, *one's son* (Livesay & Nichols, 2021) compare | *kohs discussion | The comparative evidence is insufficient to reconstruct a semantic distinction, if any, between ***kohs** and ***kosihs**. Though both can be reconstructed in Old Cree, the former appears much more widespread across the Algonquian language family. It is therefore possible that the latter was inherited as an early loan from Anishinabe.

*kosiko (~ *kosikw)

INITIAL

— heavy

evidence | PC kosikohtāw, *to make sth heavy;* WC kosikwamahcihtāw, *to feel sth is heavy;* MC kosikwan, *to be heavy;* AT kosikotiw [kozikotiw], *to be heavy;* SEC kosikwāpiskāw, *to be a heavy object of mineral composition* | ANISH gozigwan, *to be heavy* (Livesay & Nichols, 2021); MENO koseˑkwan, *to be heavy* origin | PA ***kwesekw** (Hewson, 1993)

*koskē[1]

INITIAL (VERB, ANIMATE, INTRANSITIVE)

— to set a fishing line

evidence | MC okoskew, *to set a night-line;* SEC koscew, *to set a night-line;* koskanāpiy, *a fishing line attached to an unmanned fishing pole;* NEC kuschāyiu, *bait;* WI (Pessamit) kusseu [kussēw], *to fish with a line;* Silvy (ca. 1680) "ni k8skan, *je pêche à la ligne;*" "ni k8skatau, *je l'ai pêché à la ligne*" | ANISH Cuoq (1886) "Koke, *pêcher à la ligne;*" MENO kohkɛˑw, *to fish with hook and line*

*koskē[2]

INITIAL

— tilt

evidence | MC koskeškam, *to make sth tilt under one's weight;* koskoskeyāhotew, *to be rocked by the waves;* SEC koskoscēpayihtāw, *to rock sth, typically speaking of a boat;* NEC kuskuschāpiyihtāu, *to rock sth, typically speaking of a boat;* WI (Pessamit) kussepalu [kūssēpəlu], *to be off balance, speaking of a boat*

*koskosk

INITIAL (NOUN, INANIMATE)

— crossbar of a snowshoe

evidence | MC koskosk, *snowshoe crossbar;* SEC koskosc, *snowshoe crossbar;* koskoskāhtik^w, *snowshoe crossbar;* EI (Sheshatshiu) kushkuss [kuʃkuss], *crossbar of a snowshoe;* Silvy (ca. 1680) "k8sk8st, *les barres des raquettes*" | ANISH okwik *small crossbars of a snowshoe* (Lippert & Gambill, 2023)

*kosp

INITIAL

— go inland

evidence | PC kospamow, *road leads into the bush or uphill;* MC kospaham, *to paddle inland;* SEC kospipahtāw, *to run up from the shore* | MENO kohpeˑw, *to go upload or inland, to go up from the water to the wooded land* origin | PA ***kwesp** (***kwexp**, Hewson, 1993)

*kospan

INITIAL

— anticipate with uneasiness, feel apprehension

evidence | PC kakwēspanēyihtākwan, *to be considered dangerous;* MC kospanīw, *to be apprehensive;* WI (Pessamit) kushpanelimu [kuʃpənēləmu], *to feel apprehension or anxiety;* Laure (ca. 1726) "ni-kuskuspanin 3. -iu, *je crains les ennemis*"

*koš (~ *koh)

INITIAL

— fear

evidence | PC kostākan, *enemy;* MC koštāciw, *to be afraid;* SEC koštew, *to be afraid of sb;* ci košin, *you are afraid of me;* Laure (ca. 1726) "ni-kustau, *j'ai peur de lui;*" Silvy (ca. 1680) "ni k8chten, *je crains*" | ANISH ogosaan, *to be afraid of sb;* ogotaan, *to be afraid of sth* (Livesay & Nichols, 2021); MENO koqnew, *to fear sb;* koqtam, *to fear sth;* koqsewɛ·w, *to fear people;* MIAMI kohs-, *to be afraid of sb* (ILDA, 2017) origin | PA ***kweʔθ** & ***kweʔt** (Hewson, 1993) limited to | *t[5], *t[6]

*košāwē

INITIAL

— hang

evidence | PC kosāwēkotēw, *to be suspended;* kosāwēnam, *to pack sth hanging down;* AT (Opitciwan, Joey Awashish) kocawekotew [koʒāwēkotēw], *to hang from sth, to be suspended;* SEC kushāweyāpihkāteu, *to dangle by a string* (CSB, 2018); EI (Ekuanitshit) kushaueshkutatshikan [kuhāwēhkutātʃikan], *a lead sinker for a fishing line;* Silvy (ca. 1680) "k8cha8eg8te8, *ign. cela est pendu*"

*koško (~ *koškw)

INITIAL (VERB, ANIMATE, INTRANSITIVE)

— **1** jerk, stir

— **2** awaken

evidence | PC koskopayiw, *to wake up or to shake;* MC koškonew, *to wake sb up;* koškow, *to stir;* AT (Wemotaci, Nicole Petiquay) kockosiw [koškoziw], *to wake up;* SEC koškoškopitam, *to shake sb;* Laure (ca. 1726) "ni-kuchkunen, *je fais trembler, je remue quelque chose*" | ANISH goshkozi, *to wake up* (Livesay & Nichols, 2021); MENO kosko·sew, *to wake up*

*koškwāwāt (~ *koškwāwāc, *koškwāwās)

INITIAL

— quiet and somber

evidence | PC koskwāwātapiw, *to sit quietly;* MC koškwāwāsinākosiw, *to appear somber;* SEC koškwāwāteyihtam, *to be quietly preoccupied;* NEC kushkwāwātisīu, *to be still and quiet;* WI (Pessamit) kushkuauatapu [kuʃkwāwātəpu], *to sit quietly because of a preoccupation;* Watkins (1865) "Kooskwawachegapowew, *v.i.1. He stands quietly*" | ANISH goshkwaawaajishin, *to lie still;* goshkwaawaazom, *to make sb still and quiet by what one says* (Livesay & Nichols, 2021)

*kot[1] (~ *koc, *koh, *kos)

INITIAL

— **1** try

— **2** try to see or know supernaturally, divine

evidence | [1]PC kakwēcimēw, *to ask sb a question;* WC kocispitam, *to taste sth;* ESC kotinam, *to test sth by hand;* SEC kotāskoham, *to test sth using a stick-like tool;* WI (Pessamit) kukuetshipueu [kukwētʃəpwēw], *to taste each one;* kutamishkaitsheu [kutāməʃkītʃēw], *to test the depth of the water;* Silvy (ca. 1680) "ni k8tchiparihau, *j'éprouve, v.g. raquettes*" [2]PC kosāpamew, *to find out about sb through the spirits;* Lacombe (1874) "kutchiw, ok, *(v.n.) Ce mot s'entend des supersititions; v.g. quand les sauvages essaient de faire des choses merveilleuses pour en imposer;*" MC kosāpahtam, *to divine sth by use of the shaking tent;* EI (Sheshatshiu), kushapatam[u] [kuʃāpātəm], *to perform a shaking tent;* Silvy (ca. 1680) "ni k8sigan 3. -tgeu, *je divine par le feu*"

*kot[2] (~ *koš)

MEDIAL, FINAL (NOUN INCORPORATION)

— **1** nose

— **2** beak

evidence | PC mahkikotēw, *to have a large nose or beak;* MC kinokotew, *to have a long nose or beak;* SEC mahcikotew, *to have a big nose or beak;* Silvy (ca. 1680) "kinikȣteȣ, *il a le bec pointu*" see | *skot

*kotak

INITIAL

— wretched, miserable

evidence | PC kakwātakatāmow, *to have a difficult time breathing;* WC kakwātakihīw, *to torment sb;* MC kakwātakamahcihow, *to feel miserable;* Laure (ca. 1726) "kutatchittau, *chétif, misérable;*" "kokuatchittaian suka! *ha! que je suis malheureux!;*" Silvy (ca. 1680) "ni kȣtatchihau, *je lui suis cruel, je le fais souffrir*" | ANISH godagitoo, *to suffer* (Livesay & Nichols, 2021)

*kotawē

INITIAL

— build fire

evidence | PC kotawēw, *to build a fire;* MC kotawatew, *to build a fire for sb;* NEC kutiwākin, *kindling;* Silvy (ca. 1680) "ni kȣttaȣan 3 -eȣ, *je fais du feu*" | MENO kota·wa·n, *piece of firewood*

*kotāw

INITIAL

— sink

evidence | PC kotāwīw, *to sink oneself into the ground;* MC kotāwākonenam, *to sink in the snow as one walks;* SEC kotāwipayiw, *to sink* compare | *kosā

*kotiko (~ *kotikw)

INITIAL

— dislocate

evidence | PC kotikoswēw, *to cut a limb from sb;* WC kotikonikan, *a breech-loading shotgun;* MC kotikohkwanešin, *to sprain or dislocate one's ankle;* WI (Pessamit) kutikupitam[u] [kutukupətəm], *to dislocate sth by pulling*

*kōhpāt (~ *kōhpāc, *kōhpās)

INITIAL

— degraded, wretched

evidence | PC kohpātēyihtākwan, *to be considered contemptible;* Lacombe (1874) "Koppātan, wa, *(a.in.), il est sale, vil;*" WC kōhpātīðimowin, *misery, sorrow;* MC kōhpātelimew, *to feel sorrow for sb;* kōhpāsinākosiw, *to look worthless, contemptible;* SEC kōhpātisīwin, *misery;* kōhpāchihew, *to make sb miserable;* NEC kūhpātāyimū, *to be miserable from always being sick* | ANISH ogoopadenimaan, *to think sb is worthless; to feel pity for sb, to feel sorry about sb* (Livesay & Nichols, 2021); MENO ko·hpatɛsew, *to be desolate, hopeless, unusable*

*kōk

INITIAL

— submerge

evidence | PC kōkīw, *to dive;* ESC kōkīhonew, *to take sb underwater as one dives;* MC kōkaham, *to dive after surfacing, speaking of a fish;* AT kokiw [kōkīw], *to dive;* SEC kōcīw, *to dive;* WI (Pessamit) kukaim [kūkīm], *to dive and disappear underwater;* Laure (ca. 1726) "ni-kutchituten 3. -tamu, *je cherche au fond de l'eau;*" Silvy (ca. 1680) "ni kȣtchitichinau, *je le plonge*" | ANISH googiikweni, *to put one's head underwater* (Livesay & Nichols, 2021); MENO ko·ke·hsen, *to fall into deep water;* MESK kōkenamwa, *to wash sth* origin | PA ***kōk** (Aubin, 1975; Hewson, 1993)

*kōn

INITIAL (NOUN, ANIMATE)

— snow

evidence | PC kōna, *snow;* WC kōnikamik, *a dwelling made of snow;* MC kōnipiy, *snowmelt;* SEC kōnīštihcew, *to insulate one's lodge with a mix of snow, mud, and sticks, speaking of a* *beaver;* Laure (ca. 1726) "guniuanu, *il y a de la neige;*" Silvy (ca. 1680) "k8n, *neige*" see | *ākon

*kw

MEDIAL (NOUN INCORPORATION)

— neck

evidence | PC kaskikwēpitēw, *to break sb's neck with one's hands;* MC pīmikwenew, *to wring sb's neck;* SEC wewacikwenitowac, *to hug one another;* NEC sichikwāpitāu, *to grab sb by the neck* | MESK sakikwēnēwa, *to take or hold sb by the neck* see | *kwayaw[1]

*kwahko

INITIAL

— push forward

evidence | WC kwāhkonīw, *to thrust sb;* MC kwahkosow, *to pole;* SEC kohkonew, *to push sb forward* | ABEN gwagweniga, *to push* (Day, 1995)

*kwakwārak

INITIAL

— tickle

evidence | PC kakwēyakinam, *to tickle sth;* Lacombe (1874) "kakwāyakisiw, ok, *(a.a.) il est chatouilleux;*" "kakwāyakan, wa, *(a.in.) c'est répugnant;*" "kakwāyakinawew, *(v.a.)* nam, nākew, nātchikew, *il en est effrayé en le voyant;*" WSC (Misipawistik, Ellen Cook) kakwānakinēw, *to tickle sb;* SEC kwākwāyacisiw, *to be ticklish;* WI (Pessamit) kualatshishiteneu [kwāltʃʃətēnēw], *to ticle sb's feet;* EI (Sheshatshiu) kukuanatshineu [kukwānətnēw], *to tickle sb;* Watkins (1865) "*Tickle, v.t.* Kăkwayukināo;" Laure (ca. 1726) "ni-kokuaratichin, *je suis chatouilleux;*" "ni-kokuaratichitan 3. -teu, *chatouilleux à la plante des pieds;*" Fabvre (ca. 1690) "k8ak88atĭnen n. nau, *chat8iller, exciter à rire qlqn*" discussion | Lacombe (1874:365) glosses this root as "*avoir horreur, trouver terrible, redouter,*" without nonetheless omitting entries built on this root that refer to tickling. While his gloss points to a more general sense, the possibility that it represents a local innovation, in the absence of corroborative data, cannot be excluded.

*kwam

MEDIAL

— canoe bark

evidence | Watkins (1865) "munikoomew *v.i.1.*, munikoomoo, *v.i.4. He is gathering birch bark (for canoes);*" Laure (ca. 1726) "ni-manikuamin, *je l'arrache de l'arbre (écorce pour canots);*" Fabvre (ca. 1690) "misk8k8ămin i8, *tr8uer ecorce p(ou)r en fair canot, 8ragan;*" "nat8k8amin i8 m8n 3 8, *aller chercher ecorce à canots;*" Silvy (ca. 1680) "ni ma8ik8amin, *je vais arracher des écorces à canots*" | ANISH Cuoq (1886) "manikwam, *lever des écorces*" compare | *wašikway

*kwan

MEDIAL, FINAL (NOUN INCORPORATION)

— flight feather

evidence | PC kinokwanēw, *to have long feathers;* SEC manikwanepitew, *to pluck the flight feathers from a bird;* Laure (ca. 1726) "satchikuaneu, *se remplumer (l'oiseau);*" "nistchiguanets, *plume d'outarde*" origin | Old Cree ***mīkwana*** see | *mīkwan

*kwarako (~ *kwarakw)

INITIAL (VERB, ANIMATE, INTRANSITIVE)

— come out or take out of container or enclosed space

evidence | PC kwayakow, *to crawl out of an enclosed space;* Lacombe (1874) "Kakweyakunew, *(v.a.)* nam, niwew, nikew, *il tâche de le vider en le secouant, v.g. un sac ou un baril, en se servant de ses mains;*" WC kwaðakospwākanīw, *to empty out one's pipe;* MC kwalakohtin, *to spill out;* WI (Pessamit) kulakunam [kulukunəm], *to empty sth out*

*kwarasitē

INITIAL (VERB, ANIMATE, INTRANSITIVE)

— go into a hollow in the ground

evidence | PC kwayasitēyāmow, *to flee into a hole;* WC kwaðasitīw, *to go into a den or hole;* MC kwalasitēpahtāw, *to run into a hollow in the ground;* (Wemotaci, Nicole Petiquay) korositew [korozitēw], *to go into a hole;* WI (Pessamit) kulashteu [kuləstēw], *to enter an underground hole;* Watkins (1865) "kwayusitāo, *v.i.3. He gets his foot into a hole, he slips into a hole;*" Laure (ca. 1726) "kurassiteu, *fourré dans un trou;*" "ni-kurasitetichinen, *je fais couler, je glisse quelque chose dans un lieu;*" Silvy (ca. 1680) "ni k8arassitebatan, *je descends en courant en lieu bas*"

*kwatap

INITIAL

— fall out or cause to fall out by upsetting container

evidence | PC kwatapīw, *to capsize;* Lacombe (1874) "kwatapinew, *(v.a.)*, nam, niwew, nikew, *il le tourne en sense contraire;*" MC kotapinam, *to spill sth out by knocking its container;* SEC kotapihtitāw, *to spill sth by knocking its container against sth;* WI (Pessamit) kutapishkam[u], *to spill sth by overturning the container with one's body or feet;* Watkins (1865) "Kootupipuyew, *v.imp. It capsizes;*" Laure (ca. 1726) "ni-kutapistchen 3. -kamu, *je fais tourner le canot;*" Silvy (ca. 1680) "ni k8tabah8g8n, *je renverse par la marée*" | ANISH gwanabise, *to tip or capsize* (Livesay & Nichols, 2021); Cuoq (1886) "Kwanabika, *chavirer*" origin | PA ***kwaθap** (***kweθap**, Hewson, 1993)

*kway

FINAL (NOUN)

— **1** (inanimate) bark

— **2** (animate) tree with useful bark

evidence | MC cīmānišikway, *canoe bark;* SEC iyihkway, *eastern paper birch (Betula cordifolia);* EI (Ekuanitshit) innikuai [*sic*] [īnīkwēj], *eastern paper birch; bark of eastern paper birch;* Laure (ca. 1726) "uchikuai *pl.* uchikuéia, *écorce à canot;*" Silvy (ca. 1680) "8achig8ai, *écorce à faire canot*" see | *wašikway compare | *kwam, *waškway

*kwayasko (~ *kwayaskw)

INITIAL

— **1** straight

— **2** correct

evidence | [1]PC kwayaskonam, *to straighten sth by hand;* MC kwayaskohtāw, *make sth straight;* WI (Pessamit) kuishkukuteu [kwīʃkukutēw], *to hang straight;* NSK kuiiskukuyaaw, *to hang sb straight* [2]PC kwayaskowēw, *to express oneself correctly;* MC kwayaskosinaham, *to write sth correctly;* WI (Pessamit) kuishkuteieu [kwīʃkutējēw], *to be honest*

*kwayaw[1]

INITIAL (NOUN, DEPENDENT INANIMATE)

— neck

evidence | PC mikwayaw, *a neck;* SEC okwayaw, *one's neck;* EI (Sheshatshiu) ukueiau [ukuju], *one's neck;* Laure (ca. 1726) "tchikuéiau, *ton cou*" see | *kw[1], *kwayaw[2]

*kwayaw[2]

MEDIAL, FINAL (NOUN INCORPORATION)

— neck

evidence | PC cimikwayawēw, *to have a short neck;* MC āhcikwayaweliw & āhcikwayeliw, *to move one's neck;* SEC āpišāpecikwayawešiw, *to have a skinny neck* see | *kwayaw[1]

*kwayāt (~ *kwayāc)

INITIAL

— ready

evidence | PC kwayāc, *ready, prepared in advance;* WC kwayātapiw, *to be ready to be picked up;* WSC (Misipawistik, Ellen Cook) kwayācīw, *to prepare oneself;* ESC (Severn) kwayātan, *to be ready;* Watkins (1865) "Kwayachēw, *v.i.5. He is ready*" discussion |

Despite the broad geographic distribution of this root, cognates have not been identified in dialects spoken east of Eastern Swampy Cree. Its inclusion here is therefore tentative.

*kwāhko

INITIAL

— flame

evidence | PC kwāhkosow, *to be on fire;* Lacombe (1874) "kwākkotew, a, *(a. in.) c'est en flamme;*" WC kwāhkotīw, *to be blazing;* Watkins (1865) "Kwàkootāo, *v.imp. It blazes, it burns, it flames;*" NEC kwāhkutānim, *to build up the fire;* Fabvre (ca. 1690) "K8ak8te8, k8ak8ak8te8, *Il y a bon gr(an)d feu, Le feu e(st) gr(an)d et apre*"

*kwāhso

FINAL (VERB, ANIMATE, INTRANSITIVE, CONCRETE)

— **1** be sewn

— **2** sew

evidence | [1]PC pīmikwāsow, *to be sewn crooked;* MC kipokwāsow, *to be sewn closed;* AT (Wemotaci, Nicole Petiquay) icikwaso [iʒikwāssow], *to sew thus;* WI (Pessamit) kuishkukuashu [kwīʃkukwāʃu], *to be sewn straight* [2]PC mācikwāsow, *to start sewing;* MC išikwāsow, *to sew or be sewn thus;* SEC kaščikwāsow, *to sew* | ANISH nitaawigwaaso, *to be good at sewing* (Livesay & Nichols, 2021) paired with | *kwātē

*kwām

PREFINAL

— jump

evidence | PA āpocikwānīw, *to somersault;* WC āpocikwānīw, *to somersault;* MC kweskāpocikwānipalihow, *to somersault;* Silvy (ca. 1680) "nit'ab8tchig8am8n, *je fais un sursaut*" | ANISH "aabijigwaanii, aabijigwaanise, & aaboojigwaame, *to somersault*" (Lippert & Gambill, 2023); Cuoq (1886) "Abodjikwamese, *faire la culbute (par accident et sans le vouloir)*" discussion | Though clearly descended from a single source that is likely a verb final, the cognates have diverged such that a degree of uncertainty remains regarding the above reconstruction. A similar divergence can be observed in Anishinabe, which suggests the variants may have been present in Proto-Algonquian.

*kwāp

INITIAL

— scoop

evidence | PC kwāpaham, *to scoop sth up;* MC kwāpahtam, *take sip of sth;* SEC kwāpahipān, *a dipper* | MENO kuapahekan, *scoop, dipper*

*kwāro

INITIAL

— assault, assail

evidence | WSC (Misipawistik, Ellen Cook) kwānototawēw, *to assault sb;* ESC (Attawapiskat, Bill Louttit) kwānotawew, *to assault sb;* MC kwālototawew, *to assault sb;* Watkins (1865) "Kwayootakāo, *v.i.3. He fights*" | ABEN gwalōm, *war club; bat* (Day, 1994); ANISH kwānozo, *attack;* kwānodawā-n, *attack sb* (McGregor, 2004) origin | PA ***kwāro**

*kwāskonēw

INITIAL (NOUN, DEPENDENT)

— fleshy part of the face from the lower lip to the chin

evidence | PC mikwāskonēw, *a chin;* WC mikwāskoniy, *a chin;* MC okwāhkon, *a chin, speaking of animals;* AT okwakonew [okwāhkonēw], *a chin;* SEC okwāhkonew, *a chin;* NEC ukwāhkunāuh, *one chin;* NSK ukwaaskunaaw, *one's chin;* WI (Pessamit) ukuashkuneua [ukwāʃkunēw], *one's chin;* EI ukuashkuneua [ukwāʃkunēwa], *one's chin;* Fabvre (ca. 1690) "K8achk8nēh8n, *menton, machoire d'en bas qui saute;*" cf. Laure (ca. 1726) "ni-tchinaskuneuanach, *j'ai le menton affilé, pointu*" | ANISH Cuoq (1886) "kwakun, *menton, ce mot ne s'applique guère à présent qu'au chevreuil, à l'orignal et à quelques autres animaux*" compare |

*škišay **discussion** | The grammatical gender of the basic noun derived from this stem is ambiguous as it is animate only in dialects east of MC and AT. There is also some variation regarding the consonant cluster, but the preaspirated form found in central dialects likely represents influence from a neighbouring Anishinabe dialect. Medial and final forms are uncertain as contemporary dialects incorporate the entire root, in contrast to a single example in Laure (ca. 1726) that supports the shortened form ***āskonēw**. In the regions where SEC and NEC are spoken, this part of a black bear is traditionally decorated and kept as a token of a successful hunt.

*kwāškoht

INITIAL (VERB, ANIMATE, INTRANSITIVE)

— jump

evidence | MC kwāškohtotawew, *to jump at sb;* AT kwackotimakan, *to jump;* PC kwāskohtisimow, *to dance the Ghost Dance;* WSC kwāskohtiw, *to jump;* ESC kwāškohcipanihow, *to suddenly jump;* SEC kwāškwāškohtiw, *to jump repeatedly;* EI (Mamit) kuashkutu [kwāhkūtu], *to jump;* Watkins (1865) "kwaskootootum, *He jumps or leaps at it;*" Laure (ca. 1726) "ni-kuakuaskutin, *je saute, je bondis;*" Fabvre (ca. 1690) "k8achk8tĭban e8, *saulter en l'eau, s'y ietter*" | ANISH gwaashkwani, *to jump* (Livesay & Nichols, 2021) **origin** | PA ***kwāškwaθ** has been proposed by Hewson (1993), but Cree data from historical and contemporary sources strongly support ***kwāškonθ** **compare** | *kwāškwē **discussion** | This root forms a fully functional animate intransitive verb, likely due to a Proto-Algonquian final that is opaque in Old Cree. Evidence supporting this can be gleaned from NEC & WI, as demonstrated by Collette (2022), in which the Old Cree conjunct indicative flexion for the third-person singular for stems ending in consonants continues to be used. However, in most contemporary dialects the epenthetic vowel ***ɩ** has been reanalyzed as a verb final without transposition, changing the conjunct indicative third-person flexion as expected.

*kwāškwē

INITIAL

— bounce

evidence | PC kwāskwēpayiw, *to bounce;* MC kwāškwehtin, *to bounce;* SEC kwāškwehtitāw, *to bounce sth off a surface* **compare** | *kwāškoht

*kwāštiko (~ *kwāštikw)

INITIAL

— sip

evidence | SEC kwāštikohtam, *to take a sip of =sth;* Laure (ca. 1726) "ni-kuachtiguaten pimi, *j'avale de la graisse;*" Silvy (ca. 1680) "ni k8achtig8atam8rau, *je lui en fais boire une (médecine)*"

*kwāt[1] (~ *kwāc)

FINAL (VERB, TRANSITIVE, INANIMATE, CONCRETE)

— sew

evidence | PC isikwātam, *to sew sth thus;* MC sihpokwātam, *stitch sth up;* SEC kašcikwātam, *to sew sth;* Laure (ca. 1726) "ni-mamaukuaten, *je relie un livre*" **paired with** | *kwāt[2]

*kwāt[2] (~ *kwāš)

FINAL (VERB, TRANSITIVE, ANIMATE, CONCRETE)

— sew

evidence | PC kīsikwātēw, *to finish sewing sth;* MC išikwātew, *to sew sth thus;* SEC kašcikwātew, *to sew sth* **paired with** | *kwāt[1]

*kwātē

FINAL (VERB, INANIMATE, INTRANSITIVE, CONCRETE)

— sewn

evidence | PC pīmikwātēw, *to be sewn crooked;* MC išikwātew, *be sewn thus;* WI

(Pessamit) kuishkukuateu [kwīʃkukwātēw], *to be sewn straight* paired with | *kwāhso

*kwātištak

INITIAL

— arousing a repulsive feeling

evidence | WC kwācistakāc, *exclamation of wonder;* ESC kwācistak, *oh my!;* MC kwācištak, *expression of surprise or disappointment;* SEC (Waswanipi) kwātištakeyimew [kwātstakēymēw], *to shudder at the thought of sb;* Watkins (1865) "Kwachistuka, *interj. Alas! what a pity!;*" Fabvre (ca. 1690) "K8atistăgach, *Ah ch(os)e ep8u(en)table*" | ANISH gagwaanisagad, *to be terrible* (Livesay & Nichols, 2021); MENO kakuanɛqnakɛ·nehtam, *to think sth frightful* origin | PA ***kwāθeʔθak** discussion | While the Anishinabe and Menominee cognates suggests PA ***kakwāθeʔθak**, extant contemporary and historical Cree sources provide evidence only for the shorter form presented here. Additionally, Cuoq (1886) was of the opinion that the shorter Anishinabe form **kwānisak** was in fact an obsolete form replaced by the reduplicated form **kakwānisak**, cf. "KOKWANISAK-, *altération de kakwanisak qui n'est que le fréquentatif de* KWANISAK, *maintenant hors d'usage.*"

*kwēsk

INITIAL

— turn around, turn over

evidence | PC kweskaham, *to turn sth around using sth;* MC kweskapiw, *to turn around while sitting;* SEC kwescišin, *to turn around while lying* | ANISH gwekinige, *to turn things by hand* (Livesay & Nichols, 2021)

*kwēšwān

INITIAL

— by chance

evidence | PC Lacombe (1874) "Keswān, *(ad.) voy. miskawi; nahitāk, par hasard, par chance. v.g., keswān nakiskutātuwok, par hasard ils se rencontrent; keswān takusin, par une chance, il arrive; tāpwe mitoni keswān ispayiw, en vérité ça arrive bien par hasard; keswān tābiskotch iteyittamok, il arrive par hasard qu'ils ont la même penser; namawiya keswān ki ka ki miskawaw, tu n'auras pas la chance de le trouver;*" AT (Wemotaci, Jeannette Coocoo) kwecwan [kwēʒwān], *possiblement, probablement;* SEC kweśwān & NEC kwāśwān, *as a precaution, just in case, e.g., kweśwān ekā pāpayite, in case he does not arrive; to be a good thing that, luckily, e.g. kweśwān wīpac e cī pāpayit, fortunately he arrived early;* WI (Pessamit) kueshunat [kwēʃūn], *at the very least;* Silvy (ca. 1680) "k8ech8ana, k8ech8ania, *voila bien de quoi*"

*kwētip

INITIAL

— turn over

evidence | PC kwētipāhotēw, *to be tipped over by the waves;* MC kwetipipaliw, *to overturn;* Fabvre (ca. 1690) "K8etipinen n. nau, *t8r(ner) uirer mettre d(')autre façon, sense*" | ANISH Cuoq (1886) "Kwenibise, *se renverser, verser, chavirer*" origin | PA ***kwēθep**

*kwīhko (~ *kwīhkw)

INITIAL

— quake

evidence | WC kīhkwan, *to be an earthquake;* MC kīhkopaliw, *quake;* SEC kwīhkwan, *to be an earthquake;* WI (Pessamit) kuikuikuaimᵘ [kwīkwīkwīm], *to beat one's wings noisily, speaking of a grouse;* Laure (ca. 1726) "ni-kuikuikutehan, *le cœur me palpite*" | ANISH Cuoq (1886) "Kwingwan, *tremblement de terre*" origin | PA ***kwīnko**

*kwīhkwahākēw

INITIAL (NOUN, ANIMATE)

— wolverine

evidence | PC kīhkwahāhkēw, *wolverine;* MC kīhkohākew, *a wolverine;* SEC kwīhkohācew, *a wolverine;* Laure (ca. 1726) "kuikuahatcheu *pl.* -ets, *carcajou (enfant du diable), animal sauvage très malfaisant*" |

ANISH gwiingwa'aage, *a wolverine* (Livesay & Nichols, 2021) compare | *kwīhko see | *wīhsahkēcāhkw

*kwīškohš

INITIAL

— whistle

evidence | WC kwīskosimīw, *to whistle at sb;* WSC (Misipawistik, Ellen Cook) ni kwēskosīn, *I whistle;* MC kweškošīw, *to whistle;* kīškošīw, *to whistle;* AT (Wemotaci, Nicole Petiquay) kweckociw [kwēškoššiw], *to whistle;* SEC kwīškošiw, *to whistle;* (Waswanipi) kweškošipātam^{w}, *a black scoter;* NEC kuishkushīmāu, *to whistle at sb;* WI (Pessamit) kuishkushu [kwīʃkuʃu], *to whistle;* EI (Mamit) kuishkushu [kwēhkuhu], *to whistle;* Laure (ca. 1726) "kuiskuchiuin, *sifflement d'homme;*" Silvy (ca. 1680) "ni k8ichk8chi8agan, *sifflet*" | ANISH gwiishkoshim, *to whistle to sb* (Livesay & Nichols, 2021) origin | PA ***kwīškwihš** (Hewson, 1993)

*kwītamā

INITIAL (VERB, ANIMATE, INTRANSITIVE)

— be in need

evidence | PC kwētamāw, *to be in need, to be short of provisions;* MC kwītamāw, *to be in need;* SEC kwītamāw, *to be in need* compare | *kwītaw discussion | This root appears to be an antipassive built on the unattested transitive inanimate theme ***kwītam**, paired with what is likely the corresponding transitive animate verb stem ***kwītaw**. However, neither ***kwītamwa** or ***kwītawēwa** are attested in the cross-dialectal or historical data, leading to the reconstruction of what are likely derivatives of the unattested root ***kwīt**.

*kwītaw (~ *kwīto)

INITIAL

— be at a loss

evidence | PC kwētawēyihtam, *to be at a loss for what to do about sth;* MC kītawāpahtam, *to look for sth in vain;* WI (Pessamit) kuetu [kwētu], *at the end of one's resources;* EI (Unaman-shipit) kuetuenimeu [kwētwēnimēw], *to wonder about sb;* Silvy (ca. 1680) "ni k8it8ban, *je suis en peine de boire*" compare | *kwītamā

M

*m^{1}

FINAL (VERB, TRANSITIVE, ANIMATE, ABSTRACT)

— **1** conveys the semantic role of stimulus to a participant

— **2** applicative that adds a comitative argument when suffixed to animate intransitive verb stems

evidence | ^{1}SEC ošimew, *to flee sb;* NEC miywāyimāu, *to like sb* ^{2}WC wītokīmīw, *to live with sb;* MC wīci-metawemew, *play with sb;* SEC wītapimew, *to sit with sb* paired with | *ht^{4} see | *wīt

*m^{2}

FINAL (VERB, TRANSITIVE, ANIMATE, ABSTRACT)

sound change | ē → ā

— conveys the semantic role of patient to a participant

evidence | MC matāpewatāmew, *to reach a body of water while carrying sb on one's back;* pawāmew, *to dream about sb;* WI (Pessamit) nunamew [nūnāmēw], *to suckle from her;* EI (Sheshatshiu) ituatameu [itwətāmēw], *to go somewhere on foot carrying sb on one's back* paired with | *t^{4}

*m^{3} (~ *om)

FINAL (VERB, TRANSITIVE, ANIMATE, CONCRETE)

sound change | ...t_1 + om → som

— to vocalize about or do to or affect by vocalizing

evidence | PC ācimew, *to give an account of sb;* MC manāsomēw, *speak politely to sb;* kākīsomew, *to comfort or console sb;* wayešimew, *to deceive sb by speech;* SEC āyimōmew, *to talk about sb;* Laure (ca. 1726) "ni-pagunumuan, *je suis médisant;*" Fabvre (ca. 1690) "Amamau, *faire fuir a(nim)al en parlant;*" Silvy (ca. 1680) "n'8tamimau, *je lui nuis en parlant*" paired with | *t²

*mac

INITIAL

— bad

evidence | WC macāspinīw, *to have a venereal disease;* MC macinākwan, *to look bad;* SEC macisiw, *to be dirty;* macimāhtam, *to dislike the smell of sth;* WI (Pessamit) macelihtam [mətʃēltəm], *to be in a bad mood;* Fabvre (ca. 1690) "ni matchib8rau, *donner à qlqn mauuaise portion*" | ANISH majigiizhwe, *to swear* (Livesay & Nichols, 2021); MENO mata·cemi·qtawɛw, *to tell sb bad news* origin | PA ***mat**

*macitēw

INITIAL (NOUN, INANIMATE)

— cape, point

evidence | ESC maciteweyāskweyāw, *to be a wooded point;* MC macitewehkopāw, *to be a bushy cape or point;* WI (Mashteuiatsh) Mashteuiatsh [məstēwjāhts], *at the point, place name;* Laure (ca. 1726) "matchiteu, *pointe de terre;*" Silvy (ca. 1680) "matchite8etinau, *cap haut, élevé*" see | *ēw²

*mahīhkan

INITIAL (NOUN, ANIMATE)

— wolf

evidence | WC mahīhkan, *a wolf;* MC mahīhkaniwiw, *to be a wolf; to be angry;* SEC mahīhkaniskāw, *to be many wolves;* NEC mihīhkininākusiu, *to look like a wolf;* WI (Pessamit) maikanapit [mājkənāpət], *bone in joint of rear leg of caribou or moose;* Silvy (ca. 1680) "mahikan, *loup*"

*mahk

INITIAL

— large

evidence | PC mahkāpitēw, *to have large teeth;* WC māhkikāhtikwīw, *to have a big forehead;* MC mahkāpiskisiw, *large stone;* mahkitonew, *to have a big mouth;* SEC māmahciminakāw(a)h, *for there to be large berries;* Watkins (1865) "mùkusakāo, *v.i.3. he wears a large coat;*" Laure (ca. 1726) "mamatchipestanu, *la pluie tombe dur;*" Silvy (ca. 1680) "ni mamatchichen, *je coupe à gros morceaux,*" "ni mamakabin, *j'ai de grands yeux*" | ANISH mamaangizhigwane, *to have big tail fins;* mangadinaa, *big hill* (Livesay & Nichols, 2021); MENO mama·hkesetɛ·w, *to have big feet* origin | PA ***mank** (Hewson, 1993)

*mahkēhšiw

INITIAL (NOUN, ANIMATE)

— fox

evidence | PC mahkēsīs, *fox;* MC mahkešīwimākosiw, *to smell like fox;* AT mikkeššiw, *a fox* (Béland, 1978); SEC mahcešiw, *fox;* EI (Sheshatshiu) matsheshu [mātʃēʃu], *a fox;* Laure (ca. 1726) "matchechiu, *renard;*" Fabvre (ca. 1690) "makesi8, *renard;*" "makechi8eïan, *peau de renard;*" Silvy (ca. 1680) "matchesi8, *renard*" see | *ahkēhšiw

*mahkwatoy

INITIAL (NOUN, ANIMATE)

— bear paw snowshoe

evidence | AT (Opitciwan, Joey Awashish) makotosam [mhkotōssām], *bearpaw snowshoe;* SEC (Oujé-Bougoumou, Alice Bosum) mahkotow, *bear paw snowshoe;* WI (Pessamit) mukutui [mukutwī], *bear paw snowshoe;* Laure (ca. 1726) "makuatum *pl.* -ets -ats, *raquettes rondes;*" Silvy (ca. 1680) "mak8at8m, *pl.* -t8mak, *raquettes rondes*" | ANISH makwasaagim, *bear paw snowshoe* (Livesay & Nichols, 2021) compare | *ahsām¹, *ākim¹, *miskwahtoy see | *ɪm²

*mahrako (~ *mahrakw)

INITIAL

— bad luck

evidence | PC māyakwan, *to be unlucky;* WC maðakosiw, *to be unluck in trapping;* MC malakosiw, *to be unlucky;* NEC mihīkumāu, *to bring bad luck to sb by what one says;* Watkins (1865) "mayukoomāo, *v.t.an. he brings bad luck on him*" | MENO maqnakosew, *to have bad luck*

*maht (~ *mahs)

INITIAL

— perceive

evidence | NEC mihtāyimāu, *to be aware or have a feeling of what sb is doing;* WI (Pessamit) mashpitamuᵘ [məʃpətəm], *to discern the taste of sth;* EI (Sheshatshiu) matenitakuan [mātēntākwən], *to be felt, to have an effect;* Watkins (1865) "mutāyètum, *v.t.in.6. he feels it (mentally), he perceives it;*" Fabvre (ca. 1690) "massǐten 3 tamȣ, *entendre du bruit*"

*mahtonē

INITIAL

— cause something or someone to suffer for one's own dissatisfaction, take one's temper out on something or someone

evidence | PC Lacombe (1874) "mattonehew, *(v.a.)* ttaw, hiwew, tchikew, *il s'en prend à lui sans raison;*" "mattonewokeyimew, *(v.a.)* ttam, miwew, tchikew, *v.g.* Kijemanitowa mattonewokeyimew, *il s'en prend à Dieu du mal qui lui arrive,* mattonewokeyitam ayamihāwin, *il en accuse la religion;*" SEC mihtunehtāu, *to take out one's temper on sth* (CSB, 2018); NEC mihtunāhtāu, *to take it out on sth else;* Silvy (ca. 1680) "ni matȣnehen; ni matȣnehau, nob., *je décharge ma colère sur, etc.*" see | *nē³

*mahtāko (~ *mahtākw)

INITIAL

— esteem, praise

evidence | PC mamāhtākwan, *to be glorious;* mamāhtākomēw, *to glorify sb;* MC mamāhtākosīw, *to be boastful or proud;* mamāhtakomew, *to praise sb;* SEC māmahtākomow, *to brag;* NEC mimihtākumū, *to brag* | MESK matākwēnemēwa, *to enjoy sb, to think sb is interesting, fascinating, or curious*

*mahtāw

INITIAL

— wondrous, marvelous

evidence | PC mamāhtāwan, *to be amazing or wondrous; to be spiritually powerful;* MC mamāhtāwelihtākwan, *to be considered marvelous or wondrous;* mamāhtāwasinātew, *to be decorated with fancy motifs, to be fancily marked;* SEC māmāhtāwātisīw, *to have supernatural powers;* NEC mimāhtāusīu, *to be amazing, to do amazing things;* mimāhtāunākun, *to be decorated, to look fancy;* WI (Pessamit) matauapeu [mātāwāpēw], *to weave designs into the snowshoe netting;* Watkins (1865) "Mútaminuk, *n.an. pl. Indian corn, maize;*" Laure (ca. 1726) "tchi-mamatauassinaten, *tu chamarres, tu couvres de différentes couleurs, ton habit, ton bonnet;*" "matamin -ets, *blé d'inde;*" Silvy (ca. 1680) "ni mamataȣeriten, *je m'étonne, je crains*" | ANISH mamaandaawizi, *to perform wonders;* mandaamin, *a kernel of corn* (Livesay & Nichols, 2021) compare | *manitow

discussion | Other than the Old Cree name for "maize," ***mahtāmina**, corroborative evidence in the contemporary and history record overwhelmingly supports the reconstruction of the reduplicated form ***mamāhtāw**. See Pentland (1981) for a discussion on the relation between this root and the PA word ***manetōwa**.

*makan

FINAL (VERB, INANIMATE, INTRANSITIVE, ABSTRACT)

sound change | i → ī, o → ō

— derives inanimate verbs from animate intransitive and transitive inanimate verb stems

evidence | PC twēhōmakan, *to land;* MC pimilāmakan, *it flies;* SEC miyweyihtamōmakan, *to be happy* see | *an²

*makār

INITIAL

— shovel

evidence | AT makaripakan [makāripākan], *a shovel;* SEC makāhikan, *a snow shovel;* NEC mikāyiskuham, *to scoop ice out from a hole;* WI (Pessamit) makalitam [məkāltəm], *to shovel snow from sth;* EI (Sheshatshiu) makanipu [məkānipu], *to shovel;* Watkins (1865) "Mukanipan, n.an. *A wooden shovel;*" Silvy (ca. 1680) "magariteȣ, *cela est nettoyé avec la pelle*" | ANISH mangaanibaajige, *to shovel things* (Livesay & Nichols, 2021); MENO maka·nahekɛ·w, *to remove the snow* origin | PA ***makār** (cf. **maka·lipiwa**, Hewson, 1993) discussion | South East Cree forms have been hypercorrected as **makāh**, presumably by analogy with the final ***ah**.

*mako

INITIAL

— discernible through

evidence | MC makohtin, *for one's shape to be discernible through sth;* SEC makwecišin, *for one's shape to be discernible through a sheet;* NEC mikwākunāshtāu, *to create a mound by sitting under the snow;* cf. PC makwahcāw, *a knoll* | ANISH magwaagoneshin, *to lie covered with snow so only one's shape or contour can be seen* (Livesay & Nichols, 2021); MENO makuamɛhke·hsen, *to lie under the earth, sand, or ashes forming a lump* origin | PA ***mako**

*makohšē

INITIAL

— feast

evidence | PC makosēw, *to feast;* MC makošehew, *to feast sb;* AT (Wemotaci, Nicole Petiquay) makocan [makoššān], *a feast;* SEC makošān, *a feast;* EI (Sheshatshiu) makushesseu [mukuʃēssēw], *to take part in a goose feast;* Silvy (ca. 1680) "ni magȣchan, *je fais festin*"

*man

INITIAL

— remove, detach

evidence | PC manīw, *to harvest, to pick plants;* MC manipitam, *to pull sth off;* SEC (Waswanipi) manahapew, *to remove one's fishing net;* WI (Pessamit) manakueu [mənəkwēw], *to remove a snare;* Watkins (1865) "munowikun'ātin, *v.imp. the keel gets broken off;*" Silvy (ca. 1680) "ni manahipiman, *j'amasse la graisse*"

*manāt (~ *manāc, *manās)

INITIAL

— to spare, to treat or use in a way that refrains from damaging, wasting, or distressing

evidence | PC manātisiw, *to be respectful or polite;* MC manāsomew, *to speak politely to sb;* SEC manācihew, *to spare sb;* WI manatshitueu [mənāstwēw], *to handle sth carefully for sb;* EI (Unaman-shipit) manatshitau [mināt∫ītāw], *to use sparingly, to conserve;* Silvy (ca. 1680) "ni manatchihitisȣn, *je me respecte, je ne fais ni ne mange rien de nuisible*" | ANISH manaajitoon, *to spare, respect, or go easy on sth* (Livesay & Nichols, 2021)

*manēw

INITIAL

— be poor, be short of

evidence | PC manēsiw, *to be poor or in need of sth;* MC manehew, *to impoverish sb;* SEC manewan, *to be scarce;* WI (Pessamit) maneshimakan [mənē∫īməkən], *to be scarce;* Fabvre (ca. 1690) "manēsin iȣ, *estre pauure*" | ANISH manepwaa, *to be short of tobacco* (Livesay & Nichols, 2021)

*manitow

INITIAL (NOUN, ANIMATE)

— **1** a type of aquatic divinity

— **2** possess extraordinary powers

— **3** be extraordinary

evidence | PC manitōwihēw, *to grant sb supernatural power;* manitōmin, *black* *currant;* WC manitōhkān, *an idol;* MC manitow, *a god; a lake monster;* manitōhkew, *to conjure;* manitōwi-pīwāpisk^{w}, *a barometer;* manitōwekin^{w}, *cloth;* SEC manitow, *an aquatic divinity associated with storms to whom offerings of tobacco are made;* manitōnak^{w}, *an island associated with an aquatic divinity towards which one should not point lest a storm arise;* manicōš, *any small animal traditionally considered inedible such as an amphibian, reptile, or invertebrate;* WI (Pessamit) manituian [məntūjān], *woolen cloth;* EI (Sheshatshiu) manitushiu [məntūʃīw], *to use one's mental and spiritual power;* Watkins (1865) "Munito, *n.an. God;*" "Munitoatisew, *v.i.1., He is devout, godly;*" "Munitooākin, *n.in. Cloth;*" "Munitooweskatask, *n.an. The poisonous carrot;*" Laure (ca. 1726) "ni-manituuin 3. manituiu, *je suis un esprit, génie;*" "manituch, *insecte;*" "manituian *pl.* -a, *couverture de lit;*" "*il ne faut pas prendre ici le change; pour qu'une chose est très dangereuse ou difficile, le Montagnais se sert très souvent de manitu comme; cette roche est à craindre, ils disent ordinairement, tapue manituu assini;*" Fabvre (ca. 1690) "mantȣmēgȣch, *ep(er)lan, poisson plat de mer;*" Silvy (ca. 1680) "manitȣ, *esprit, chose admirable, extra-ordinaire;*" "ni manitȣisin, *je suis sorcier, médecin;*" "ni manitȣkassȣn, *je suis un esprit;*" "manitȣchich, *bestioles, comme des fourmis, etc.;*" "manitȣmin, *rassade;*" Le Jeune (1634) "Manitousiouets, *sorciers ou iongleurs*" origin | PA ***manetōwa*** (Aubin, 1975; Hewson, 1993) compare | *mahtāw discussion | Evidence from WC, MC, AT, SEC, WI, and EI regions corroborate the notion that a ***manitowa*** was believed to be a type of aquatic divinity, typically associated with storms. Though rarely discussed in ethnographic literature, folklore is rich with stories of lakes and islands associated with this belief and toponyms attesting to it are widespread. Skinner (1911) recorded this belief and the association with tobacco offerings, writing: "Tobacco is always thrown in the fire before a feast, to propitiate the spirits in general, and when reaching a rapid the Cree voyageurs invariably cast tobacco into it to conciliate the resident manitou or demon, half woman and half fish." The aquatic nature of this being is referenced by Flannery (1995) in her biography of Ellen Smallboy, a woman born in the mid-1800s, where she provides a diminutive form of the word and a brief description of a harrowing encounter. Curiously, invertebrates are cross-dialectally referred to as "small ***manitowa**." A detailed discussion of idols made in the likeness of these divinities can be read in Brightman (1993). When serving as an initial for verbal derivation, this root extends to the verb the sense of possessing extraordinary powers. With the arrival of Europeans, trade goods exchanged during early contact occasionally came to be described with this root, likely as a result of the strong impression these objects made on the people. These objects included glass beads, cloth, and the barometer. With ongoing contact came evangelization and a need to translate Christian beliefs, resulting in the appropriation of this root for these purposes. Words such as "god," "godly," "godliness," and "piety" came to be built on this root, as did words relating to what came to be translated as the "bad ***manitowa**," namely "Satan" and "devil." For a discussion of the root word being applied on the west coast of James Bay to a supreme being, likely as a result of religious syncretism, see Cooper (1933). For a study on this concept along the east coast of James Bay, see Long *et al.* (2006). Unfortunately, both studies ignore toponymy, and neither report on the common belief regarding the aquatic divinity. However, Cooper (1933) does cite an account of a visit to York Factory in 1697 by La Potherie, who documented the practice of offering tobacco to this divinity when caught in a storm on the water. This practice remains common in the region where East Cree is spoken. Long *et al.* (2006) also mention an account written in 1969 by Walton, a missionary posted at Fort George, who reported the belief that "manitu" referred to a "mythical man-animal of the sea."

*marōk

INITIAL

— soft, yielding

evidence | MC malōkahcāw, *the ground is soft;* SEC mayōkāw, *to be soft;* Fabvre (ca. 1690) "Marȣkistiȣăgau, *terre molle, uase, on y enf(on)ce;*" Silvy (ca. 1680) "ni marȣgachan 3. -eȣ, *j'ai la peau molle, délicate*"

*masān

INITIAL (NOUN, ANIMATE)

— nettle

evidence | PC masāniwiw, *to be a nettle or thistle;* AT (Wemotaci, Jeannette Coocoo) masan [mazān], *thorn;* SEC masānišin, *to fall in nettles;* Fabvre (ca. 1690) "Massan *pl.* nak, *Hortie, ch(an)ure Huron;*" Silvy (ca. 1680) "massanaȣeȣ, *cela pique, l'ortie*" | ABEN mazōnibagw, *nettle leaf* (Day, 1994); ANISH mazaanaatig, *nettle, thistle, thorn* (Livesay & Nichols, 2021); MENO masa·n, *thistle*

*masin

INITIAL

— geometric design

evidence | PC masinisin, *to be pictured; to be drawn; to be represented in embroidery;* WC masinipīham, *to paint sth;* MC masinikwātam, *to embroider sth;* AT (Wemotaci, Jeannette Coocoo) masinahikan [mazinahikan], *a book;* SEC masinaham, *to write sth;* NEC misinihāpāu, *to weave a design;* Silvy (ca. 1680) "ni massinatan, *je fais une marque sur, etc.*" see | *masināw

*masināw

INITIAL

— imprint, impress

evidence | MC masināwihtin, *to leave an imprint or impression on impact;* WI (Pessamit) mashinauatikueu, *to put a mark on wood;* EI (Sheshatshiu) mashinaukutatsheu [məʃināwkutātʃēw], *to carve designs with a crooked knife;* Laure (ca. 1726) "ni-massinauabiskahen 3. -himu, *je burine*" see | *masin

*masisko (~ *masiskw)

INITIAL

— remove or take away everything, strip, dispossess

evidence | PC masaskoyawēw, *to deprive sb of everything in a game;* masaskonam, *to grab or gather sth all up;* Lacombe (1874) "masaskukkasuw, ok, *(a.a) il est tout brûlé;*" WC masisko, *wholly, left destitute;* masiskonīw, *to take away all of sb's possessions;* Laure (ca. 1726) "ni-masiskupiten 3. -tamu, *j'arrache des herbes, du foin*" discussion | The absence of a preaspiration on the first sibilant cannot be confirmed due to the lack of an Atikamekw cognate.

*mask

INITIAL

— rob

evidence | PC maskamēw, *to rob sb of sth;* MC maskahtowak, *to rob one another of things;* SEC maskahtwew, *to rob sth* | ANISH makandwe, *to rob sth* (Livesay & Nichols, 2021); MENO mahka·mɛ·w, *to rob sb* see | *m[1]

*maskatēw (~ *maskatē)

INITIAL

— charcoal

evidence | PC maskatēpwēw, *to roast on coals;* MC maskatepwew, *to cook fish or meat directly on embers;* WI (Pessamit) mashkatepueu [məʃkətēpwēw], *faire cuire de la viande en la mettant directement sur la braise;* Laure (ca. 1726) "ni-maskatepuan 3. -pueu, *j'en rôtis;*" "ni-maskatéuikuan, *je charbonne, je noircis;*" Silvy (ca. 1680) "ni maskatepȣan ȣias, *je cuis la chair à la hâte, sur les charbons*" | ANISH makadewizi, *to be black;* makade, *black gunpowder* (Livesay & Nichols, 2021); MESK mahkatēwānehkwēwa, *to have black hair;* mahkatēwi, *gunpowder;* MIAMI mahkateewi, *charcoal or gunpowder* (ILDA, 2017)

*maskāt (~ *maskāc, *maskās)

INITIAL

— amaze

evidence | PC māmaskātam, *to find sth strange or amazing;* MC māmaskātelihtākwan, *to be amazing;* māmaskācihew, *to amaze sb;* SEC māmaskāsinam, *to be amazed at the sight of sth;* WI (Pessamit) mashkashinakuan [məʃkāʃənākwən], *to be a surprising quantity of sth;* Laure (ca. 1726) "maskateritamuin, *étonnement, admiration;*" Silvy (ca. 1680) "ni maskassitagȣsin, *je discours admirablement*" | ANISH maamakaazitaw, *to be amazed at what sb says;* maamakaajichige, *to do amazing things* (Livesay & Nichols, 2021) origin | Derived forms suggest the underlying root may be ***mask**, a form that remains unattested without the referenced finals. see | *āt[6], *at[7]

*maskisin

INITIAL (NOUN, INANIMATE)

— moccasin

evidence | PC maskisinēyāpiy, *a moccasin string; a shoelace;* AT (Opitciwan, Joey Awashish) maskisinikew [maskizinihkēw], *to make moccasins;* SEC mascisin, *a moccasin, a shoe;* Laure (ca. 1726) "ka mastisinitchechit, *cordonnier, qui fait des souliers;*" Silvy (ca. 1680) "mastisin, *soulier*" | ABEN makezen, *a moccasin, a shoe* (Day, 1994); ANISH makizin, *a moccasin, a shoe* (Livesay & Nichols, 2021); MENO mahkɛ·sen, *a moccasin, a shoe;* MESK mahkesenehkēwa, *to make moccasins* origin | PA ***maskeseni** (***maxkeseni**, Hewson, 1993) see | *askisin compare | *ašēsin

*maskw (~ *masko)

INITIAL (NOUN, ANIMATE)

— bear

evidence | PC maskoskāw, *bears abound;* MC masko, *a black bear;* maskwāpit, *a bear tooth;* SEC mask^w, *a black bear;* WI (Pessamit) mashkuss [muʃkūss], *bear under one year old;* Laure (ca. 1726) "maskuach *pl.* maskuata, *ours, caverne à ours, antre;*" Silvy (ca. 1680) "maskȣa, *ours*" | ANISH makoganzh, *a bear claw* (Livesay & Nichols, 2021) origin | PA ***maθkwa** (Hewson, 1993) see | *askw[2]

*maškaw

INITIAL

— **1** hard

— **2** strong

evidence | PC maskawatin, *to be frozen hard;* maskawisīw, *to be strong;* MC maškawāw, *to be hard;* AT mackowakamin [maškowākamin], *to be strong, speaking of a drink;* SEC maškawipayin, *to become hard;* maškawīw, *to be strong;* EI (Sheshatshiu) mashkuau [məʃkwāw], *to be hard;* Laure (ca. 1726) "ni-maskauisin, *je suis dur, robuste;*" Silvy (ca. 1680) "ni maskaȣachan, 3. -au, *j'ai la peau dure*" | ANISH mashkawaa, *to be strong, hard, or dense* (Livesay & Nichols, 2021)

*maškēkw (~ *maškēko)

INITIAL (NOUN, INANIMATE)

— muskeg

evidence | PC maskēkomināna, *cranberries;* MC maškēkohk, *in the muskeg;* SEC maščekwāhtik^w, *a stunted black spruce growing in muskeg;* Silvy (ca. 1680) "machtekȣ, *prairie, marécage*" | ANISH mashkiigong, *in the muskeg* (Livesay & Nichols, 2021); MENO maski·k(on), *swamp* origin | PA ***maškyēkwi** (Hewson, 1993) see | *aškēk

*maškimotay

INITIAL (NOUN, INANIMATE)

— bag

evidence | PC maskimot, *a bag or sack;* MC wāskāmotiy (as an alteration via a folk etymology of the above root, obsolete in the said dialect), *ace of spades;* AT mackimotai [maškimotay], *a backpack; a pocket;* mackimotacic [maškimotāʒiš], *a small bag;* EI (Sheshatshiu) massimuteush [məssimutēwʃ], *bag, sack, pocket; scrotum;* Silvy (ca. 1680) "massim8te8ach, *sac*" | ANISH mashkimodaang, *in a bag or sack* (Livesay & Nichols, 2021)

*maškohsiw

INITIAL (NOUN, INANIMATE)

— herbaceous vegetation, grass

evidence | PC maskosīs, *a blade of grass;* MC maškošiya, *grass;* maškošīskāw, *to be lots of grass;* AT maškoššiy, *grass, hay* (Béland, 1978); NEC mishkushiuh, *grass;* mishkushīwākimāu, *to be a grassy body of water;* WI (Pessamit) mashkushu [məʃkuʃu], *blade of grass or hay;* mashkushitsheu [məʃkuʃītʃēw], *to make hay;* Laure (ca. 1726) "maskuchiu, *chaume;*" "maskuchiuitchuap, *chaumière, cabane française;*" Silvy (ca. 1680) "machk8si8, *paille, foin, herbe;*" "machk8chi8ach, *panier de paille, de jonc*" | ANISH mashkosiw, *grass, hay, a blade of grass* (Livesay & Nichols, 2021); Cuoq (1886) "mackosi, *prairie naturelle*" see | *aškw[1], *aškohsiw compare | *maškotē

*maškotē

INITIAL

— grassy clearing after a fire

evidence | AT iškoterew [škotērēw], *a spruce grouse;* SEC (Washaw-Sipi) maškutenak^w, *place name, literally 'grassy island;'* (Waskaganish) meškotenakāšiy, *place name, literally 'grassy island'* (Bishop, 2022); NEC (Whapmagoostui) kā miškotānikāw *place name, literally 'grassy island'* (Bishop, 2022) | ANISH mashkodese, *a spruce grouse* (Livesay & Nichols, 2021); MENO masko·tɛ·mas(kon), *prairie weed* see | *maškotēw, *aškotē[2] compare | *maškohsiw discussion | The Atikamekw name for "spruce grouse" is a calque from the neighbouring Anishinabe dialect that was reanalyzed as "fire grouse."

*maškotēw

INITIAL (NOUN, INANIMATE)

— grassy clearing after a fire

evidence | PC maskotēw, *a prairie;* maskotēwan, *to be a prairie;* Watkins (1865) "Muskootāo, *n.in. A plain*" | ANISH mashkode, *a prairie, a plain, a natural clearing* (Livesay & Nichols, 2021); Cuoq (1886) "mackote, *plaine, et dans le dialecte des Sauteux, prairie naturelle;*" MENO masko·tɛ·w, *prairie* origin | PA ***maškwitēwi** (Hewson, 1993) see | *maškotē, *w[1], *aškotē[1], *aškotēw

*maštaw

INITIAL

— anew, newly

evidence | PC mastaw, *newly, recently;* mastahtēw, *to track over sb's footprints;* WI (Pessamit) mashtu [məstu], *new, again;* EI (Ekuanitshit) mashtu [mahtaw], *new, again*

*mat (~ *mac, *mas)

INITIAL

— make, made

evidence | PC matokahp, *empty camp, messy campsite;* macēkin, *tipi, lodge;* WC matot, *an old canoe or boat;* MC matokahp, *a deserted camp;* masililiw, *idol, graven image;* NEC musinākun, musinākusiu, *to be done, completed, made; to be fully developed (speaking of an animal);* Watkins (1865) "Mutookùp, *n.in. An old tent (i.e. one deserted);*" Fabvre (ca. 1690) "matitchin i8, *trauailler bien, artistem(en)t elab8ré;*" "matitchinani8i8, *faict artificiellem(en)t;*" "matitchihau, *hig8, artistem(en)t élab8ré;*" "matătas, *belle robe de castor passé, rayé;*" "Mat8tisch, *meschant petit canot;*" Silvy (ca. 1680) "matatas, *robe de castor;*" "mat8gap, *cabane délaissée;*" "mat8tich, *petit méchant canot*" | ANISH majigoodenh, *a dress* (Livesay

& Nichols, 2021); madogaan, *a cone-shaped lodge;* mazininiig, *statues* (Lippert & Gambill, 2023); Nicholas (ca. 1670) "matchioueian, *robbe de castor*" (Daviault, 1994); MENO masi·neni·hsεh, *statue, human image, doll* see | *matwē

*matin

INITIAL

— mark

evidence | MC matinisāwew, *to perform pyromantic scapulimancy;* AT (Wemotaci, Nicole Petiquay) matinasowew [matināzowēw], *to perform pyromantic scapulimancy;* SEC matinisāwew, *to perform pyromantic scapulimancy;* NEC mitinisāwāu, *to hold the shoulderblade or breastbone of an animal close to the fire to see where it scorches to foretell events;* WI (Pessamit) mitunishaueu [mətnəʃāwēw], *to foretell the future with animal bones* | MIAMI "Nimareniha, *je le peins, fais son portrait sur un arbre, ou casse teste*" (Largillier - ILDA, 2017) origin | PA *maθen discussion | Evidence for this root in Old Cree is limited to the verb ***matinisāwēwa**, "to divine by producing scorch marks on animal bones."

*matāw

INITIAL

— to reach an open space coming from the bush or inland

evidence | WC matāwisiw, *to come to a lake or clearing from the bush;* ESC matāpew, *to come out of the bush into an open space;* MC matāskow, *to reach a frozen body of water;* AT matapew [matāpēw], *to reach a body of water or clearing;* NEC mitāskupichiu, *to travel onto a body of water while moving winter camp;* EI (Sheshatshiu) matapeu [mətāpēw], *to arrive at the water's edge, to come out of the bush;* Silvy (ca. 1680) "ni matabebarin, *je viens des terres au bord, etc;*" "ni mataȣahen, *je reviens des terres en canot*" | ANISH madaabii, *to go down to shore or an open place;* madaako, *to get out on or go on the ice* (Livesay & Nichols, 2021); MENO mata·pi·nesemow, *to flee down to the water's edge*

*matonisk

INITIAL (NOUN, ANIMATE)

— clay

evidence | EI (Sheshatshiu) Mitinissiu-shipu [mətnəssīwʃīpu], *place name, Beaver River; literally, muddy river;* EI (Sheshatshiu) Kamitinishkau-shipiss [kāmətnəʃkāw-ʃīpīs], *place name, literally 'muddy place river'* (Armitage, 2008) | MENO mano·nεh, *red or yellow earth; clay; chalk;* MIAMI "marȣniki, *terre forte, p̄p̄re a boucher des canots qui prennent de l eau*" (Largillier - ILDA, 2017) see | *atonisk, *wāpatonisk

*matoštē

INITIAL

— put in fire

evidence | PC macostēpayiw, *to fall into the fire;* WC macostīham, *to throw sth in the fire;* MC macoštewepinam, *to throw sth into the fire;* SEC macošteham, *to put sth into the fire;* Laure (ca. 1726) "ni-matuchteuau, *je le jette dans le feu;*" Fabvre (ca. 1690) "Matȣchtechǐnin 3 nȣ, *t(om)ber au feu*"

*matot

INITIAL

— do steam bath

evidence | PC matotisahēw, *to have sb hold a sweat lodge;* MC matotisiw, *to take a steam bath;* SEC matotisān, *sweat lodge;* Laure (ca. 1726) "ni-matutichin, *je sue, sur une chaudière ou sur des pierres chaudes;*" Silvy (ca. 1680) "matȣtisan, *suerie*" | ANISH madoodoo, *to takes a sweat bath;* madoodison, *a sweat lodge* (Livesay & Nichols, 2021)

*matwē

INITIAL

— make sound, be audible

evidence | PC matwēsin, *to fall or walk audibly in the distance;* MC matwelawew, *wind blows audibly;* SEC matwehkoyew, *fire burns audibly;* WI (Pessamit) matueshtin [məttwēstən], *wind makes rustling sound through branches* | ANISH madwezhaazo, *to be heard urinating* (Livesay & Nichols, 2021) see | *mat, *wē¹

*maw

INITIAL

— go to

evidence | PC mawimow, *to cry out;* MC mawinēhwew, *to go after sb with the intention of harming;* SEC mawatišiwew, *to visit;* EI (Sheshatshiu) mupu [mūpu], *to be visiting;* Fabvre (ca. 1690) "Maȣachtȣrin iȣ, *aller faire, bastir canots;*" Silvy (ca. 1680) "ni maȣabamau, *je vais, je viens le voir*" | ANISH mawinadan, *to run at, rush at, or charge sth* (Livesay & Nichols, 2021); MESK mawīhkawēwa, *to go deal with sb* origin | PA ***maw*** (Hewson, 1993)

*mawihso

INITIAL (VERB, ANIMATE, INTRANSITIVE)

— gather fruit, pick berries

evidence | PC mawisow, *to pick berries;* AT (Wemotaci, Nicole Petiquay) mawiso [mawissow], *to pick berries;* SEC māwisow, *to pick berries;* NEC muwisū, *to pick berries;* EI (Sheshatshiu) maushu [mūʃu], *to pick berries;* Laure (ca. 1726) "ni-mauisun, *cueillir des fruits;*" Silvy (ca. 1680) "ni maȣisȣn, *he cueille des fruits*" | ANISH mawinzo, *to pick berries* (Livesay & Nichols, 2021); MENO mawe·hsow, *to gather acorns, speaking of a bear* see | awihso

*mayak

INITIAL

— strange, foreign

evidence | PC mayakāw, *to be different, surprising;* MC mayakelimew, *to be suspicious of sb;* Laure (ca. 1726) "ni-miakuan, ni-meiakuan, *je parle une langue étrangère*" | ANISH mayagendam, *to feel strange, feels out of place* (Livesay & Nichols, 2021); MENO maya·kat, *to be strange, unfamiliar, changed*

*mā¹

INITIAL

— downriver

evidence | ESC māhāponow, *to drift downriver;* MC māham, *to paddle downriver;* SEC māmihc, *downriver;* Silvy (ca. 1680) "ni mahen, *je descend la rivière par eau*"

*mā²

PREFINAL

— smell

evidence | PC isimāmēw, *to smell sb thus;* MC macimākwan, *to smell bad;* SEC wīhcimāhtam, *to like the scent of sth* origin | Contraction of PA ***myaw*** + ***e*** (Hewson, 1993). see | *māht, *māko², *mām, *māhs, *māhso, *māštē

*māhciko (~ *māhcikw)

INITIAL

— restrain

evidence | PC māhcikwahpitam, *to tie sth down;* MC māmāhcikositehpisow, *to be tied down by one's feet;* NEC mimaahchikuham, *to keep sth from moving by putting a weight on it;* WI (Pessamit) matshikupalu [mātʃəkupəlu], *to be held back or paralysed;* Silvy (ca. 1680) "ni mamachigȣapikatau, *je le lie fort, je le garrotte*" | ANISH omamaanjigonaan, *to hold sb so they cannot move, to restrain sb* (Livesay & Nichols, 2021)

*māhcit (~ *māhcic)

INITIAL

— last

evidence | MC māhcic, *the last one; the last time;* māhcitōšān, *a last-born;* SEC māhcitey, *the last one; the last time;* māhcitōšān, *a last-born;* NEC māhcic, *last;* WI (Pessamit) mashtelu [māstēlu], *to make love for the last time before leaving;* EI (Sheshatshiu) mashten [māstēn], *the last one, the last time*

*māhs

FINAL (VERB, TRANSITIVE, INANIMATE, CONCRETE)

— to create a smell while cooking sth

evidence | PC kīhkāmāsam, *to burn sth with a strong odor;* MC wīhkimāsam, *to create a pleasant aroma while cooking sth;* AT (Wemotaci, Nicole Petiquay) wikimasam [wīhkimāssam], *to create a pleasant aroma while cooking sth;* (Opitciwan, Joey Awashish) icimasam [iʒimāssam], *to create such an odor while cooking;* SEC sōhcimāsam, *to produce a strong smell while burning or cooking sth* see | *māko², *s paired with | *māhsw

*māhso

FINAL (VERB, ANIMATE, INTRANSITIVE, CONCRETE)

— to give off a smell while cooking

evidence | MC wīhkimāsow, *to give off a pleasant aroma while cooking;* SEC sōhcimāsow, *to smell strong while burning or cooking* see | *māko², *so² paired with | *māštē

*māhsw

FINAL (VERB, TRANSITIVE, ANIMATE, CONCRETE)

— to create a smell while cooking sth

evidence | PC kīhkāmāswēw, *to burn sth with a strong odor;* MC wīhkimāswew, *to create a pleasant aroma while cooking sth;* SEC sōhcimāswew, *to produce a strong smell while burning or cooking sth* see | *māko², *sw paired with | *māhs

*māht

FINAL (VERB, TRANSITIVE, INANIMATE, CONCRETE)

— smell sth

evidence | PC miyomāhtam, *to like the smell of sth;* MC nānatomāhtam, *to search for sth by scent;* SEC wīhcimāhtam, *to like the scent of sth;* Laure (ca. 1726) "ni-nichitumaten 3. -tamu, *je connais par le sentir*" see | *mā², *ht⁴ paired with | *mām

*māhtako (~ *māhtakw)

INITIAL

— weigh down

evidence | PC māhtakoskawēw, *to step, sit, or lie on sb;* WC pāhtakoskam, *to keep sth down by sitting on it;* ESC (Severn) pāhtakoskocikan, *weighting pole for outside of tent;* ESC (Peawanuck) pāhtakomān, *a sort of enclosure used to funnel caribou towards a killing zone;* MC pāhtakopicikew, *to catch birds using a framed net;* māhtakoskātam, *to step onto sth;* SEC māhtakoham, *to place a weight on sth;* opāhtakomān, *Obatogamau Lake, earlier Obatigoman, place name, literally "caribou enclosure;"* EI (Sheshatshiu) matakushkueu [mātəkuʃkwēw], *to put one's weight on sb;* Silvy (ca. 1680) "ni matag8(e)chtam, 3. -kam, *je foule aux pieds, je marche dessus, j'acravante*" | ANISH maatagwa'an, *to crush sth* (Lippert & Gambill, 2023) compare | *patako discussion | The initial consonant of this root alternates cross-dialectally between ***m** and ***p**, possibly under the influence of ***patako**. The alternative reconstruction, ***pāhtako**, may therefore be valid.

*māko¹ (~ *mākw)

INITIAL

— **1** press, compress

— **2** oppress, overwhelm

evidence | ¹PC māmākwahtam, *to chew sth;* MC mākotinam, *to press sth soft;* SEC mākoham, *to press sth using a tool;* Silvy (ca. 1680) "ni mamag8nen, *je tâte, je manie, je serre avec la main*" ²PC mākwēyimow, *to feel troubled, to feel oppressed;* WSC (Misipawistik, Ellen Cook) mākwaciw, *to be intolerant to the cold;* MC mākohikow, *to be overwhelmed emotionally by sth;* SEC (Oujé-Bougoumou) mākociw, *to be intolerant to the cold;* NEC mākuhāu, *to defeat sb*

*māko[2] (~ *mākw, *māh, *māš)

PREFINAL

— smell

evidence | PC wīhkimākohow, *to perfume oneself;* MC macimākwāciwasow, *to smell bad while boiling;* wīhkimāštew, *to give off a pleasant aroma while cooking;* SEC miyomākosiw, *to smell good* origin | Contraction of PA ***myaw** + ***ekw** (Hewson, 1993). The allomorphs ***māh** and ***māš** result from PA ***myākʷ** contracting to ***myāʔ** when followed by consonant-initial finals. see | *mā², *ıko see | *māhs, *māhso, *māhsw, *māštē

*mām

FINAL (VERB, TRANSITIVE, ANIMATE, CONCRETE)

— smell sb

evidence | PC kīhkāmāmēw, *to smell sb clearly, to smell a strong odor from sb;* MC nānatomāmew, *to search for sb by scent;* SEC wīhcimāmew, *to like the scent of sb* see | *mā², *m¹ paired with | *māht

*māmaw

INITIAL

— together

evidence | PC māmawastāw, *to place things together;* MC māmawāpihkātam, *to tie them together;* SEC māmawīwac, *to gather together;* Laure (ca. 1726) "ni-mamaukuaten, *je relie un livre;*" Silvy (ca. 1680) "ni mama8inen, *j'assemble*"

*māmāw[1]

INITIAL (NOUN, ANIMATE)

— eyebrow

evidence | SEC ni māmāmac, *my eyebrows;* NSK umaamaam, *one's eyebrow;* EI (Sheshatshiu) umamama [umāmāma], *one's eyebrows;* Isham (1743) "maw maw wuck, *the eye brow*" see | *māmāw²

*māmāw[2]

MEDIAL (NOUN INCORPORATION)

— eyebrow

evidence | SEC cispacimāmāwew, *to have thick eyebrows* | ANISH Cuoq (1886) "Naniskimamawe, *avoir les sourcils hérissés*" see | *māmāw¹

*mān[1]

INITIAL

— usually, often

evidence | PC māna, *usually, habitually, generally;* MC māna, *usually, typically; seemingly;* SEC māna [mānh], *often, usually;* EI (Sheshatshiu) mani [mà:n], *regularly* compare | *mān²

*mān[2]

INITIAL

— to finish a task or journey

evidence | MC mānokew, *to erect a dwelling;* māntew, *a stranger;* AT mantew [māntēw] *visitor, stranger;* SEC mānokāsow, *to build a shelter for oneself;* WI (Pessamit) manutsheu [māntʃēw], *to build a house;* Watkins (1865) "Manookāo, *v.i.3. He is making a tent;*" "Mantāo, *n.an. A stranger;*" Laure (ca. 1726) "manuteu *pl. -ets, un nouvel arrivé;*" Fabvre (ca. 1690) "man8kan e8, *faire cabane, maison;*" "man8tan e8, *arriuer d'un autre pays, en apporter n8uelles;*" "mante8 pl 8ek, *n8ueaux uenus, etr(an)gers;*" Silvy (ca. 1680) "ni man8tan, *j'arrive, et je porte des nouvelles;*" "ni man8tekaBau, *j'arrive en son quartier*" discussion | As this root seemingly appears in two basic constructions only, its sense is elusive. The above is therefore an attempt to reconcile the sense of both constructions, "arriving from a foreign place" and "building a dwelling." Any relationship with the particle ***māna** is unclear. Note that the verb ***mānotēwa** produces a noun of the same form meaning "foreigner" or "stranger" and is used productively in most dialects as an initial referring to "foreign."

*mān[3]

INITIAL

— a little quantity

evidence | MC mānišīš, *a little;* AT (Wemotaci) memantcic [mēmānciš], *a little;* Watkins (1865) "Manshesh, *n.in. A little, a bit;*" Fabvre (ca. 1690) "Emanik8nich, *il y a peu de neige;*" Silvy (ca. 1680) "emanichich, *un peu, un petit*" | ANISH Cuoq (1886) "Memandjic, *un peu, tant soit peu;*" ANISH Nicholas (ca. 1670) "memanchich & emanchich, *tant soit peu, un peu*" (Daviault, 1994) discussion | The form cited for AT is likely a loanword from the neighbouring Anishinabe dialect.

*mār

INITIAL

— bad

evidence | PC māyinawēw, *to find sb ugly;* MC mālātan, *to be bad or ugly;* SEC māyisīw, *to be stingy;* Silvy (ca. 1680) "ni maratchimau, *je lui dis de sales paroles*" | ANISH maanakamigaa, *to be poor ground* (Livesay & Nichols, 2021); MIAMI myaalameekwa, *catfish* (ILDA, 2017) origin | PA ***myār** (***mya·l**, Hewson, 1993)

*māsk

INITIAL

— deformed

evidence | PC māskāwikanēw, *to have a deformed back;* ESC māskitōhtanew, *to have a lame heel;* MC māskikin, *to grow in a mishapenly;* SEC māscikātew, *to have a deformed leg* | MENO ma·hkekate·w, *to have a crippled leg*

*māš

INITIAL

— **1** be imperfect or ill-formed, do in an imperfect manner, do poorly

— **2** fight, wrestle

evidence | [1]PC māmāsīs, *poorly done; without care;* māsamēkos, *a speckled trout;* ESC māši, *sort of;* MC māmāš, *haphazardly, carelessly;* AT (Wemotaci, Jeannette Coocoo) macamekos [māʒamēkos], *a speckled trout;* SEC māši-mītosʷ, *a balsam poplar;* WI (Pessamit) mashi-mitush [māʃəmītuʃ], *a balsam poplar;* EI (Uashat) mashinnu [māʃɨnnu], *person of mixed race who has one First Nations parent;* mamashiputau [māmāʃəputāw], *to saw or file sth roughly;* Laure (ca. 1726) "machameguch, *petite truite;*" "machimituch -ats -ets, *tremble, bois;*" "ni-machirinikan, *je suis avare*" [2]PC māsihitowak, *to wrestle one another;* MC māšihkew, *to fight;* AT (Wemotaci, Jeannette Coocoo) macihiwewin [māʒihiwēwin], *violence;* SEC māšihew, *to fight sb;* WI (Pessamit) mashikam [māʃīkəm], *to fight sth;* Silvy (ca. 1680) "machihit8in, *lute*" | [1]ANISH maazhigwaade, *to be poorly sewn* (Livesay & Nichols, 2021) [2]ANISH maazhi', *to overpower sb* (Livesay & Nichols, 2021) origin | PA ***myāš** (Hewson, 1993) see | *māšikīsk discussion | The Old Cree name for the white cedar, ***māšikīska**, is based on this root, likely due to the furrowed appearance of its bark. The root is also used in the name for the balsam poplar in contemporary eastern dialects, likely for the same reason.

*māšikīsk

INITIAL (NOUN, ANIMATE)

— cedar

evidence | PC Lacombe (1874) *Cèdre,* mānsikiska, k; MC māsikīsk, *a white cedar;* māsikīskāhtikʷ, *a white cedar;* SEC māsicīsk, *white cedar;* NEC māschīsk, *white cedar;* WI (Pessamit) massishk [māssīʃk], *white cedar;* EI (Ekuanitshit) massishk [māhtʃīhk], *white cedar;* La Brosse (1766) "Mashitshish, *cedrus;*" "Mashitshishgau, *cedretum;*" Silvy (ca. 1680) "machitchiskau, *cèdrière*" see | *māš

*māškot (~ *māškoc)

INITIAL

— maybe

evidence | PC māskōc, *maybe;* MC māškoc, *maybe;* SEC māškoc, *maybe;* NEC māshkuch, *maybe* limited to | *i³

*māštē

FINAL (VERB, INANIMATE, INTRANSITIVE, CONCRETE)

— to give off a smell while cooking

evidence | MC wīhkimāštew, *to give off a pleasant aroma while cooking;* SEC sōhcimāštew, *to smell strong while burning or cooking* see | *māko², *tē⁴ paired with | *māhso

*māt¹ (~ *māc)

INITIAL

— start

evidence | PC mātamahcihow, *to start experiencing pain;* MC mācištan, *break-up season;* SEC māciw, *depart;* Silvy (ca. 1680) "matchipariȣ, *cela se remue*" | ANISH maadademo, *to start to cry* (Livesay & Nichols, 2021); MIAMI maacaamwi-, *to run away* (ILDA, 2017) compare | *māt²

*māt² (~ *māc)

INITIAL

— divide, sunder

evidence | PC mācisam, *to cut sth;* ESC mātahikew, *to scrape a frozen hide;* MC mātinamākew, *to apportion manually;* AT maticam [mātiʒam], *to cut sth;* NEC mātihwāu, *to scrape a frozen hide;* WI (Pessamit) matish [mātəʃ], *knife used for bloodletting;* Laure (ca. 1726) "ni-matichusun, *je me coupe;*" "ni-matauau, *je gratte une peau;*" Silvy (ca. 1680) "ni matinaȣan, *je distribue, v.g. le potage, le manger*" | ANISH maada'ige, to scrape hides (Livesay & Nichols, 2021); MESK mātesi, *a knife* compare | *māt¹

*mātāw

INITIAL

— **1** junction (of two rivers)

— **2** junction (of two paths)

evidence | [1]MC mātāwāw, *to be a confluence;* mātāhtin, *it (stream) flows into another;* SEC mātākamiy, *confluence lake;* NEC mātāshtikwāpiyiu-h, *confluence of rivers* [2]PC Lacombe (1874) "Mātāmew, *il arrive sur ses pistes;*" MC mātāhew, *to reach sb's path;* SEC mātāmew, *to reach a path;* Fabvre (ca. 1690) "Mataȣan, *fȣrche de 2x riuieres qui se reioignent*" | [1]MESK mātāyāwi, *for a river to join another river* [2]MESK mātāshkamwa, *to come to a larger road or path*

*mātāpo

INITIAL

— abreast

evidence | PC mātāposinwak, *to lie side by side;* WC mātāpohtīwak, *to walk side by side, abreast;* SEC mātāpohtewac, *to walk side by side;* NEC mātāpuhtāwich, *to walk side by side;* Watkins (1865) "Matapoogapowewuk, *They stand abreast, they stand in a row;*" Laure (ca. 1726) "ni-matabutan, *je vais par ordre, rang;*" Silvy (ca. 1680) "ni matabitachiparin, *je vais côte à côte d'un canot*"

*māto

INITIAL (VERB, ANIMATE, INTRANSITIVE)

— cry

evidence | PC mātow, *to cry;* MC mātohew, *to make sb cry;* SEC mātototawew, *to cry about sb;* WI (Mashteuiatsh) matu [mātū], *to cry* compare | *mē, *mō¹, *mōsko

*māw

INITIAL (NOUN, DEPENDENT ANIMATE)

— omasum, psalterium

evidence | PC Lacombe (1874) "omāw, ok, nimāw, ok, *feuillet, troisième estomac;*" MC omāw, *omasum; pulley;* WI (Pessamit) umau [umāw], *third stomach*

*māwahtō

INITIAL

— gather

evidence | ESC māwahtōpahew, *to gather people on the run;* MC māwahtōnam, *to gather things up;* SEC māwahtōnam, *to gather things up;* Watkins (1865) "Mowutoopuyew, *v.imp. It gathers, it collects;*" Laure (ca. 1726) "ni-mauatunen, *rassembler, assembler;*" Silvy (ca. 1680) "ni maȣatȣtichahen, *je balaye, j'assemble les ordures*" | ANISH maawandoobiwag, *to sit together* (Livesay & Nichols, 2021); MENO ma·watonam, *to gather sth by hand* compare | *māwasako, *māwat

*māwasako (~ *māwasakw)

INITIAL

— gather together

evidence | PC māwasakōw, *to gather;* MC māwasakohpitam, *to tie things together;* NEC māwisikwāpihkātim, *to tie things together;* EI (Sheshatshiu) maushakunam^u [māwʃukunəm], *to piles things around oneself;* Laure (ca. 1726) "ni-mauachagunauets iriniuets, *je rassemble les hommes;*" Silvy (ca. 1680) "ni maȣasagopiaȣak, ni maȣisagopiaȣak, *j'assemble le conseil*" compare | *māwahtō, *māwat discussion | The absence of a preaspiration on the sibilant cannot be confirmed due to the lack of an Atikamekw cognate.

*māwat (~ *māwac)

INITIAL

— **1** gather

— **2** superlative

evidence | [1]PC māwatastāw, *to place things in a pile;* WC māwacihtāw, *to collect sth;* ESC māwacihew, *to gather things;* MC māwacihcikew, *to harvest;* SEC māwacihtāw, *to gather things;* EI (Mamit) mautshieu [māwatʃjēw], *to gather things;* EI (Sheshatshiu) mautshishikueu [māwtʃīkwēw], *to gather one's saliva;* Watkins (1865) "Mowuchetow, *v.t.in.2. He collects it, he gathers it, he accumulates it;*" Laure (ca. 1726) "ni-mauatchichuriauan, *je quête, mendiant;*" Silvy (ca. 1680) "ni maȣatchihitȣnan, *nous nous assemblons*" [2]PC māmāwacēyas, *beyond others, most;* MC māwac, *the most;* NEC māuch, *the most;* NSK maauch, *the most* | [1]ANISH maawanjitoon, *to collect sth* (Livesay & Nichols, 2021); MENO ma·wacehɛ·w, *to gather or collect things;* māwachi, *gathering;* [2]ANISH (Oji-Cree) maawach, *the most* (Lippert & Gambill, 2023); MESK māwachi, *most of all, among all, only one of all* compare | *māwahtō, *māwasako discussion | The Anishinabe cognate and the similarity with the root ***māwahtō** favor the alternative reconstruction ***māwaht**. However, comparative evidence from contemporary sources do not support the presence of the preaspirate.

*mē

INITIAL

— **1** moan, weep

— **2** have sex

evidence | [1]WC mamāhpinīw, *to groan in pain;* PC māhpinēw, *to moan or cry in pain;* WI mau [mēw], *to cry;* EI mau [māw], *to cry;* EI (Unaman-shipit) matutam^u [māhtam], *to cry because of sth;* Lemoine (1901) "man, meu, *to cry, weep;*" Laure (ca. 1726) "ni-man 3. meu, *pleurer, je pleure, je jette des larmes;*" Fabvre (ca. 1690) "Man 3 maȣ, *pleurer, crier;*" Silvy (ca. 1680) "ni mekasȣn, *je fais semblant de pleurer*" [2]PC matēw, *to have sex with sb;* Lacombe (1874) "masiwewin, a, (n.f.) *copulatio, fornicatio;*" MC omašiwew, *promiscuous person;* mašiwātew, *to have sex with sb* | [1]MENO ma·w, *to weep;* cf. nemo·m; mo·k [2]ANISH mazhi, *to have sexual intercourse with sb;* mazhiwe, *to have sexual intercourse* (Livesay & Nichols, 2021); MENO ma·manɛw, ma·matam, *to copulate with sb,* *sth;* MESK manēwa, *to copulate with sb;* manetīwaki, *they copulate;* MIAMI mal-, *to have sexual intercourse with sb* (ILDA, 2017) compare | *māto, *mō¹, *mōsko

*mēciy

INITIAL (NOUN, INANIMATE)

— contents of a digestive tract

evidence | ESC (Severn) omeciy, *partially digested contents of an animal or fish stomach, dirty laundry;* EI (Sheshatshiu) umetshi [umētʃī], *partially digested food in the paunch of a caribou or moose;* Silvy (ca. 1680) "n'8metchi8in, *je me fiente*" see | *mēy

*mēhtāt (~ *mēhtāc, *mēhtās)

INITIAL

— beyond what is intended, too

evidence | MC mehtātaham, *to paddle farther than intended;* SEC mehtāspow, *to is unsated despite having eaten;* Laure (ca. 1726) "ni-metatichen, *je coupe trop fort en dolant;*" Fabvre (ca. 1690) "metasp8n 8, *ne pas etre rasasie de m(an)ger;*" Silvy (ca. 1680) "ni metatichen, *je ne dole pas bien, j'en ôte trop;*" "ni metatchika8au, *j'arrive à lui trop tard*"

*mēk

INITIAL

— give

evidence | PC mēkiw, *to give sth away, to donate;* WC mīkiwin, *a gift;* WSC (Misipawistik, Ellen Cook) mēkiw, *to give sth away* | ABEN maga, *to give away* (Day, 1995); ANISH miigiwe, *to give sth away;* MENO me·kow, *to give sth to sb; to make a gift or payment* origin | PA ***myēk**

*mēkwā

INITIAL

— **1** while, during

— **2** encounter

evidence | PC Lacombe (1874) "Mekwāskawew, il arrive qu'il est encore là;" MC mekwāhwew, *to encounter sb by vehicle;* mekwāškawew, *to encounter sb on foot;* mekwāc, *during, while;* SEC mekwā-nīpin, *during the summer;* WI & EI mekuat [mēkwāt], *meanwhile, while, during;* Laure (ca. 1726) "megua tchighigatgs, *en plein jour;*" Silvy (ca. 1680) "ni meg8ah8au, *je le rencontre par eau*" | ANISH megwaa, *while, during, right now* (Livesay & Nichols, 2021) compare | *mēkwē

*mēkwē

INITIAL

— among, amidst

evidence | PC mēkwayāhtik, *among the trees;* ESC (Severn) mekwehkp, *among the willows;* MC mekweyaš, *among;* mekweyāpisk, *among the rocks;* mekweskamik, *in the midst of a mossy area; in the midst of the bush, out on the land;* SEC mekweyāhtikʷ, *among the trees;* NEC mākwāyānich, *in the middle of the island* | ANISH megwekob, *in the brush, in a thicket* (Livesay & Nichols, 2021) compare | *mēkwā

*mēmēkwēhšiw

INITIAL (NOUN, ANIMATE)

— a thievish simian-like creature believed to inhabit rocky banks

evidence | PC Lacombe (1874) "memekwesiw, ok, *(n.r.) petits êtres, nains, génies qui demeurent dans l'eau et dans la terre;*" MC memekwešīwasiniy, *a round, black stone typically found near rapids and occasionally kept as an ornament;* AT (Wemotaci, Nicole Petiquay) memekweciw [mēmēkweššiw], *mi-homme mi-poisson, protecteur de son territoire;* SEC memekwešiw, *a thievish simian-like creature believed to inhabit rocky banks;* NEC māmākwāshiu, *a mythical being who resembles monkeys or gorillas;* WI (Pessamit) Memekueshu [mēmēkwēʃu], *creature living in the cliffs (character in stories);* EI (Unaman-shipit) Memekueshu [mēmēkwēhu], *creature living in the cliffs (character in stories);* Watkins (1865) "Māmākāsew, *n.an. a spirit dwelling in the water or on the rocks, a sea nymph;"* Silvy (ca. 1680) "memeg8echi8, *génies des rochers, qui sont à l'eau"* | ANISH memegwesi, *a hairy-faced bank-dwelling dwarf spirit* (Livesay & Nichols, 2021); Cuoq (1886) "memegwesi, ...wak, *sorte de triton, de sirène, ou de nymphe que la mythologie américaine suppose vivre, dans l'eau et dans le creux des rochers. On dit qu'ils nasillent, qu'ils sont pillards"*

*mēmēw

INITIAL (NOUN, ANIMATE)

— pileated woodpecker (Dryocopus pileatus)

evidence | AT (Opitciwan) omemew, *a pileated woodpecker;* SEC mēmēw, *a pileated woodpecker;* WI (Pessamit) umemeu [umēmēw], *a pileated woodpecker;* Laure (ca. 1726) "memeu, *pivert;"* Silvy (ca. 1680) "meme8, *gros pic-bois à la tête rouge"* | ANISH meme, *a pileated woodpecker* (Livesay & Nichols, 2021); MENO mɛ·mɛ·w, *woodpecker;* MESK mēmēwa, *pileated woodpecker* origin | PA ***mēmēwa** (Aubin, 1975; Hewson, 1993) compare | *pāhpāštēw, *wirikwanēw

*mēnisk

INITIAL (NOUN, INANIMATE)

— fortification, palisade

evidence | PC mēnisk, *trench, earthwork, fortification;* MC meniskew, *to build a fence or palisade;* SEC meniskāhtikʷ, *a fence;* WI (Pessamit) meniss [mēnəss], *a fort, a fortress;* Laure (ca. 1726) "meniskasku, *fort, palissade, petit fort"*

*mēskanaw

INITIAL (NOUN, INANIMATE)

— path

evidence | PC mēskanaw, *a path, a road;* MC meskanāwan, *to be a path or road;* SEC meskanāhcew, *to build a road;* Silvy (ca. 1680) "meskanau, *chemin;"* "ni meskanaka8au, *je lui fais un chemin"* see | *mēw, *ıskanaw

*mēšakwam

INITIAL

— **1** everyday

— **2** every, speaking of periods of time

evidence | PC mēsakwanipipon, *every winter;* MC mešakʷ, *every day;* mešakwani- & mešakwami-, *every, speaking of periods of time;* NEC māshikumichīshikāuh, *every day;* EI (Sheshatshiu) eshakuma [ēʃəkuma], *every time, each time;* Laure (ca. 1726) "mechaguam tchighigua, *chaque jour;"* "mechagua *adv.* mechaguana, *ordinaire, ordinairement;"* Silvy (ca. 1680) "mechag8an, *ordinairement"* | ANISH Nicholas (ca. 1670) "mechagouam, *ordinairement"* (Daviault, 1994) discussion | The absence of a preaspiration on the sibilant cannot be confirmed due to the lack of an Atikamekw cognate.

*mēšt (~ *mehc)

INITIAL

— consume, use up

evidence | PC mēstāskitēw, *to be burnt out;* WC mīstihkasow, *to be burnt up;* MC meštāciwahtew, *to boil away;* SEC mehcipayiw, *to be used up;* Laure (ca. 1726) "etaian mechtauakahanu, *la marée dégrade ma maison;"* Silvy (ca. 1680) "mestite8, *cela brûle;"* "ni metchiau, *je le fais fuir"* | MENO mɛ·qtenam, *to use sth all up* origin | PA ***mēʔt** (Hewson, 1993)

*mētawē

INITIAL (VERB, ANIMATE, INTRANSITIVE)

— play

evidence | PC mētawēhēw, *to make sb play;* MC metawew, *to play;* SEC metawācew, *to play with sth;* Laure (ca. 1726) "metauagan *pl.* -a, *jouets d'enfants;"* Silvy (ca. 1680) "ni meta8an 3. -e8, *je joue, je m'ébats"*

*mētinaw

INITIAL

— slowly, gently

evidence | NEC mātiniu, *slowly;* WI (Pessamit) metinupalu, *to move, function slowly or gently;* EI metinu [mētnu], *slowly, gently;* Laure (ca. 1726) "ni-metinauipun, *je mange lentement, étant déjà à demi rassasié*"

*mēw

FINAL (NOUN, INANIMATE)

— path

evidence | NEC utimiskumāu, *a beaver trail;* SEC wāpošomew, *a hare trail;* WI (Pessamit) umashkumeu [ūmuʃkumēw], *a bear path;* EI (Mushuau) atikumeu [ətīkumēw], *a caribou path;* Laure (ca. 1726) "uabuchumeu, *piste de lièvre;*" Silvy (ca. 1680) "m8s8me8, *piste d'orignal*" | ANISH moozomii, *moose trail* (Lippert & Gambill, 2023) origin | PA ***myēw*** (Aubin, 1975) see | *ām², *ɪm¹, *mēskanaw

*mēy

INITIAL (NOUN, INANIMATE)

— excrement, feces

evidence | PC mēyi, *excrement;* SEC mey, *stool;* omeyāwikanān, *a fish kidney;* EI (Sheshatshiu) meiapui [mējāpwī], *sewer water;* Silvy (ca. 1680) "meï, *excrément;*" "ni meï8itan 3. -tau, *je fiante qqch*"

*mēyāw

INITIAL

— put right

evidence | WSC (Misipawistik, Ellen Cook) mēyāw, *serves one right;* SEC mēyāw, *as deserved, serves one right;* NEC maayaauchaayimaau, *to think sth serves sb right;* NSK maayaauchaayimaaw, *to think sth serves sb right, to think sb derves the disrespect or misfortune;* Watkins (1865) "Māyow, *part. indec. This is a local word, and seldom used except in the expression ākoo māyow, it serves him right;*" Laure (ca. 1726) "ni-meiauabauarau namesh, *je dessale du poisson*" | MENO mɛ·yaw, *correct, correctly; as the main thing, in the main;* meya·wenam, nemɛ·yawɛna·n, *to straighten sth out by hand; to guide sth or correct sth*

*micihcin

INITIAL (NOUN, INANIMATE)

— thumb

evidence | WC micīhcin, *a thumb;* MC ki micihcin, *your thumb;* SEC micihcin, *a thumb;* Laure (ca. 1726) "nimitchitsin, *mon pouce;*" "mitchitchinichitan, *gros orteil;*" Silvy (ca. 1680) "mitchichinigachia, *l'ongle du pouce*"

*micim

INITIAL

— restrain

evidence | PC mamēciminēw, *to hold sb fast;* MC miciminam, *to hold onto or hold sth back;* SEC micimīw, *to hold on;* Silvy (ca. 1680) "ni mitchiminen, *je retiens, je soutiens*"

*micimo (~ *micimw)

INITIAL

— be stuck

evidence | PC micimoskiwēw, *to be stuck in the mud;* MC micimwākonešin, *be stuck in the snow;* SEC micimohtin, *to be stuck*

*miciskē

INITIAL (VERB, ANIMATE, INTRANSITIVE)

— build a fish weir

evidence | PC Mandelbaum (1979) "*The weir was called mitcskan in the old days. Now it is called askonan.*" ESC (Attawapiskat, Bill Louttit) miciskew, *to build a fish weir;* MC miciskan, *a fish weir;* AT (Opitciwan, Joey Awashish) mitciskan [miciskan], *place name, Fort Migiskan, also written as Mechiskan and Michiskun, site of a Hudson's Bay Company post that closed around the year 1890;* Faries & Mackay (1938) "michiskun, *fish-weir*" | ANISH michikan, *fence* (McGregor, 2004); micihkan & mihcihkan, *a fish weir* (Oji-Cree, 2024)

*mihcikiw

INITIAL (NOUN, ANIMATE)

— harpoon, barbed spear

evidence | PC Lacombe (1874) "mitchikiw, ok, *dard;*" WC mīhcikiw, *a spear; sharp dorsal fin of a walleye;* MC mihcikiw, NA *a pointed or barbed missile that can be thrown or fired* | ANISH Cuoq (1886) "mitcikiw, *dard à une seule branche avec trois barbillons;" "Au lieu de* mitcikiw, *on dit plus souvent aujourd'hui cimagan, pajipaigan;"* "Name-mitcikiw, *dard à esturgeon, dard à un seul barbillon;"* "Amik-mitcikiw, *dard à castor (ayant deux barbillons);" "Ces différents dards se fabriquent avec les cornes des animaux tués à la chasse"*

*mihs

INITIAL (NOUN, DEPENDENT ANIMATE)

— elder sister

evidence | MC omisimew, *to have sb as an elder sister;* AT (Wemotaci, Jeannette Coocoo) omisa [omissa], *one's older sister;* SEC nimis, *my elder sister;* EI (Sheshatshiu) umishu [uməʃu], *to have an elder sister;* Silvy (ca. 1680) "nimis, nimisai, *ma sœur"* | ANISH gimisenh, *your older sister* (Livesay & Nichols, 2021); MENO neme·hsak, *my elder sisters* origin | PA ***mihs** (Hewson, 1993)

*mihsaw

INITIAL

— disappoint, dissatisfy

evidence | PC misawīw, *to be disappointed, to experience defeat;* misawihēw, *to leave sb disappointed, to defeat sb;* WC misawīhīw, *to cause sb to be fed up;* AT (Opitciwan, Joey Awashish) nama moci misawiw [nama moššі missawiw], *he is not yet mature;* misaweritam [missawerihtam], *to desire sth;* SEC misūheu, *to treat sb such that they have enough of the situation and want to avoid it* (CSB, 2018); WI (Pessamit) mishushu [məʃūʃu], *to be wary or on guard because of a previous experience;* Faries (1938) "Miso'wehāo, *v.t.an. He treats him so that he has had enough;"* Laure (ca. 1726) "ni-michauihau, *j'abats, j'affaiblis;"* Silvy (ca. 1680) "ni missa8ihig8n, *ce lieu m'a mal traité, ne me donnant pas à manger;"* "ni missa8ihau, *je le traite, je le reçois mal"* | ANISH misawendan, *to want or desire sth* (Livesay & Nichols, 2021); MESK mesawinākosiwa, *to look tempting, to be coveted as a meal* see | *mihsawāt

*mihsawāt (~ *mihsawāc)

INITIAL

— anyway, even if, even though

evidence | PC misawāc, *anyway, in spite of;* MC misawāc, *anyway, at any rate;* AT (Wemotaci, Jeannette Coocoo) misawatc [missawāc], *even if;* NEC mishiwāch, *at any rate, anyway, nonetheless* | ANISH misawaa, *even though; no matter what; even if* (Livesay & Nichols, 2021) see | *mihsaw, *āt[5] limited to | *i[3]

*miht[1] (~ *mihc)

INITIAL

— regret

evidence | PC mihtawēw, *to grumble, to be dissatisfied;* MC mihtātam, *to regret sth;* SEC mihciyawesiw, *to be sorry*

*miht[2] (~ *mihš)

INITIAL (NOUN, INANIMATE)

— firewood, log

evidence | PC mihtikiwāhp, *a wooden lodge;* MC mihtokān, *a winter lodge built of logs;* WI (Pessamit) umitimu [umətəmu], *to have firewood;* Watkins (1865) "Mìtikan, *n.in. A wood-pile;"* Laure (ca. 1726) "uepahanua nimittima, *la marée emporte mon bois de chauffage;"* Fabvre (ca. 1690) "Mit8ch, *Caieux de bois liés p(ou)r porter co(mm)e canots;"* Silvy (ca. 1680) "michi, *pl* mita, *bûche de bois"* origin | PA ***mehθ-**, *firewood* (Aubin, 1975; Hewson, 1993) see | *ɩht[4]

*mik

INITIAL

— bark

evidence | PC mikitēw, *to bark at sb;* mikiw, *to bark;* MC mikisimow, *to bark;* SEC micitam, *to bark at sth* | ABEN megika, *to bark* (Day, 1994); ANISH migi, *to bark*

(Livesay & Nichols, 2021) origin | PA ***mek** (Aubin, 1975; Hewson, 1993) compare | *wihkē

*mikirkan

INITIAL (NOUN, INANIMATE)

— fishhook

evidence | AT mikikan [mikihkan], *a fish hook;* WI (Pessamit) mitshikan [mətʃəkən], *fish hook;* Laure (ca. 1726) "mitchikan *pl.* -a, *hameçon;*" "ni-mitchiganikan 3. -tseu, *je fais un hameçon;*" Fabvre (ca. 1690) "mikikan *pl.* na, *hain, hameçon*" | ANISH migiskan, *a fish hook* (Livesay & Nichols, 2021) discussion | In the absence of a Woods Cree cognate, the reconstruction of the consonant cluster is indirectly supported by an Anishinabe cognate.

*mikisiw

INITIAL (NOUN, ANIMATE)

— bald eagle (Haliaeetus leucocephalus)

evidence | PC mikisiw, *a bald eagle;* MC mikisiw, *an eagle;* AT (Opitciwan, Patrick Awashish) mikisiw [mikiziw], *a bald eagle;* SEC micisiw, *an eagle;* Silvy (ca. 1680) "mitchisiȣ, *aigle*" | ABEN megezo, *an eagle* (Day, 1994); ANISH migizi, *a bald eagle* (Livesay & Nichols, 2021); MESK mekesiwa, *bald eagle* origin | PA ***mekesiwa** (Hewson, 1993) compare | *mik

*mikisk

INITIAL

— period of transition between fall and winter

evidence | PC mikiskāw, *to be late fall or freeze-up;* WC mikiskāw, *to be late fall or early winter;* MC mikiskāw, *to be the time of the first frosts, late fall or early winter;* Watkins (1865) "Mikiskow, *v.imp. The late autumn or early winter, the time of the first frosts;*" Isham (1743) "me kis coak, *the first of the winter*" discussion | Despite the broad geographic distribution of this root, cognates have not been identified in dialects spoken east of Moose Cree. Its inclusion here is therefore tentative.

*mikiy

INITIAL (NOUN, INANIMATE)

— scab

evidence | PC mikiy, *scab;* MC mikiy, *scab;* SEC omicīw, *to be scabby;* EI (Sheshatshiu) mitshi [mətʃĩ], *wound, sore on the skin;* Silvy (ca. 1680) "mikhii, *plaie, ronge, galle*" origin | PA ***mekyi** (Hewson, 1993) see | *wimik

*miko (~ *mikw)

INITIAL

— to move back and forth vigorously, to shake

evidence | PC mimikopitam, *to shake sth briskly;* MC mamikonam, *to rub sth against itself manually;* Laure (ca. 1726) "ni-mimigunen, *je broie en poussière;*" "ni-mimikuetsinen, *je frotte du linge*" | ANISH mamigoshkam, to thresh sth under one's feet (Livesay & Nichols, 2021); MENO memɛ·konam, *to shake sth*

*mikoškāt (~ *mikoškāc, *mikoškās)

INITIAL

— bother

evidence | PC mikoskātisiw, *to be bothersome;* mikoskāsihtākwan, *to make a bothersome sound;* MC mikoškācihew, *to bother sb;* SEC mikoškāteyihtam, *to be bothered by the thought of sth;* Laure (ca. 1726) "ni-mikuskatchihau, *je le fais devenir fou (dans le sens figuré)*" origin | PA ***mekweškāt** (Hewson, 1993)

*min[1]

INITIAL (VERB, ANIMATE, INTRANSITIVE)

— drink

evidence | MC minahew, *to give sb sth to drink;* SEC minahiwew, *to provide drinks;* WI (Pessamit) minu [mənu], *to drink;* Silvy (ca. 1680) "ni minin, *je bois;*" "minagan, *tasse, instrument à boire*" | MESK menowa, *to drink;* MIAMI men-, *to drink sth* (ILDA, 2017) origin | PA ***men** (Hewson, 1993) compare | *min², *min³

*min²

INITIAL

— have a successful hunt

evidence | PC minahow, *to have a successful hunt, to kill game;* MC minahow, *to have a successful hunt;* SEC ošci-minahow, *to have one's first successful hunt;* Laure (ca. 1726) "minahuin, *proie d'oiseau*" | ANISH Cuoq (1886) "Minah,o, *avoir réussi à la chasse, revenir avec beaucoup de pelleteries*" compare | *min¹, *min³

*min³

INITIAL

— **1** island

— **2** an instance of

evidence | ¹MC miništikw, *island;* PC ministik, *island;* NEC minisākw, *rock island* ²MC mināskwēyāw, *patch of trees;* SC mamenipestāw, *rain intermitently;* SEC mamenihkopāw, *clumps of willows here and there;* WI minashteu, *cord of firewood;* Laure (ca. 1726) "minauatanu, *une pluie soudaine;*" Silvy (ca. 1680) "ni mamen8ganan, *nous demeurons çà et là*" | ¹ABEN menahan, *an island* (Day, 1994) ²ABEN menasokwad, *to be clouds here and there;* menadena, *to be mountains here and there* (Day, 1994) origin | PA ***men**, the root of PA ***menehsyi**, ***menehš-**, and ***mene?tekwi** (Hewson, 1993) see | *ɪn¹, *ɪnak

*min⁴ (~ *minak)

MEDIAL, FINAL (NOUN INCORPORATION)

— fruit, berry

evidence | PC apisiminakāsin, *to have small berries, speaking of a bush;* MC ililimin, *blueberry;* SEC māmahciminakāw(a)h, *for there to be large berries;* Laure (ca. 1726) "ni-passiminan, *je sèche du blé d'inde ou des graines*" origin | PA ***min** (Aubin, 1975) see | *mīn

*minahikw (~ *minahiko)

INITIAL (NOUN, ANIMATE)

— white spruce

evidence | WC minahikwāsiht, *a spruce bough;* SEC minahikoskatināw, *to be a hill or mountain with many white spruce;* Silvy (ca. 1680) "minahig8, *sapin*" | ANISH mina'igwaandag, *a white spruce bough* (Livesay & Nichols, 2021)

*miramaw

INITIAL

— damp

evidence | MC milamawāw, *to be damp;* NEC miyimiwākunikāu, *damp expanse of snow;* Laure (ca. 1726) "miramauipikuagan, *poudre éventée*"

*miray

INITIAL (NOUN, ANIMATE)

— burbot

evidence | PC miyay, *a mariah, a burbot;* MC milay, *a cod or cod-like fish such as the burbot or Atlantic cod;* EI (Mamit) minai [mɨnnēj], *a burbot;* Fabvre (ca. 1690) "Mirai, *Loche, poisson à La queüe d'anguille*"

*mirā

INITIAL

— smell

evidence | MC milākwan, *to be smelly;* SEC miyāštew, *to give off a scent while cooking;* Laure (ca. 1726) "ni-miraten 3. -tamu, *je sens par le nez*" | ABEN melōdam, *to smell sth* (Day, 1994); ANISH ominaamaan, *to smell sb* (Livesay & Nichols, 2021) origin | PA ***meraw** (***melaw**, Hewson, 1993)

*mirēk

MEDIAL (NOUN INCORPORATION)

— pus

evidence | ESC wāšteminekipaliwin, *suppuration;* MC wāštemilekan, *to suppurate;* WI (Pessamit) uashtemilekan [wāstēməlēkən], *to be an infected wound;* Laure (ca. 1726) "piskumireganuch, *pustule*" origin | from PA ***meryi**, *pus* (***melyi**, Hewson, 1993) + ***ak** see | *miriy, *ak²

*miriy (~ *mirī)

INITIAL (NOUN, INANIMATE)

— pus

evidence | PC miyi, *pus; abscess;* WC miðiy *pus;* MC milīwatāmowin, *tuberculosis;* WI (Pessamit) miliutushkunu [məlīwtūʃkwənu], *to have an abscess at the elbow;* Silvy (ca. 1680) "miri, *pus;*" "miri8an, *il jette du pus*" | ANISH mini, *pus;* miniiwan, *to have pus, to be inflected* (Livesay & Nichols, 2021) origin | PA ***meryi** (***melyi**, Hewson, 1993) see | *mirēk

*mirk

INITIAL

— flesh a hide

evidence | PC mihkiw, *to flesh a hide;* WC miðkitīw, *to flesh a hide;* MC mihkicikew, *to flesh a hide;* SEC mihcitew, *to flesh sth;* NEC mihchiu, *to flesh a hide;* EI (Sheshatshiu) mitshitakanashkᵘ [mītʃitākənāʃkʷ], *a fleshing pole;* Fabvre (ca. 1690) "mikin i8, *se seruir de cet os p(ou)r c8royer passer peau*" see | *mirkihkwan

*mirkihkwan

INITIAL (NOUN, INANIMATE)

— bone flesher

evidence | PC mihkihkwan, *a hide scraper;* WC miskīhkwan, *a flesher;* MC mihkihkwan, *a bone flesher;* SEC mihcihkwan, *a bone flesher;* WI (Pessamit) mitshikunikatueu [mətʃəkunəkətwēw], *to flesh a hide with a bone flesher;* Fabvre (ca. 1690) "mikik8an v. mitchik8an pl na, *os à c8royer passer peaux*" see | *mirk

*mirko (~ *mirkw)

INITIAL (NOUN, INANIMATE)

— **1** blood

— **2** red

evidence | PC mihkwāpoy, *blood soup;* mihkwāw, *to be red;* WC miðkwāskwan, *to be red, speaking of a stick-like object;* MC mihkonawew, *have red cheeks;* SEC mihkwāyihkwew, *to have red hair;* NEC mihkwāyāpī, *a blood vessel;* Isham (1743) "mirth co, *blood;*" Laure (ca. 1726) "ni-mikukuan, *je rougis du visage;*" Silvy (ca. 1680) "ni mamik8an8an, *j'ai les joues rouges*" | ABEN mkwibaga, *to be red leaves* (Day, 1994); ANISH miskwaa, *to be red* (Livesay & Nichols, 2021); MESK meshkwēkenwi, *red woolen broadcloth blanket* see | *rkw

*miro (~ *miraw)

INITIAL

— good, well

evidence | PC miyawātikwan, *to be pleasant;* WC miðohtākwan, *to sound nice;* MC milawātew, *to like sb;* AT mirocakew [miroʒakew], *avoir une belle peau;* SEC miyonākwan, *to look good;* Silvy (ca. 1680) "ni mir8sin, *je suis bon, brave, bienfaisant, bienveillant*" | MESK menwāchimowa, *to speak well* origin | PA ***mero** (***melw**, Aubin, 1975)

*mis

INITIAL

— all of, whole

evidence | MC misite, *everywhere;* NEC misihtikw, *a whole log;* SEC misi-pakāheu, *to boil sth whole* (CSB, 2018); WI (Pessamit) mishitue [məʃətwē], *everywhere;* Watkins (1865) "Misepuyehāo, *v.t.an. He swallows him whole;*" Laure (ca. 1726) "missi tchekuan ni-naheriten, *je prends tout en bonne part;*" Silvy (ca. 1680) "missi missi, *partout, de tous côtés;*" "ni missig8ten, *j'avale tout sans mâcher*" | ABEN mezi, *all* (Day, 1994); MENO mesahkamek, *all the world* see | *misiwē, *misihtaw

*misihtaw

INITIAL

— all of, whole

evidence | PC misīhtawikāpawiwak, *to stand in numbers;* MC misihtawāw, *to be clumped together;* NEC misihtiwāu, *to be one whole piece;* WI (Pessamit) mishitue [məʃətwē], *everywhere;* EI (Sheshatshiu) mishitueiekan [məʃītwējēkən], *to be a single, whole piece, speaking of sth sheet-like;* Watkins (1865) "misètowināo, *v.t.an. She kneads him (i.e. the dough)*" see | *mis compare | *misiwē

*misik

INITIAL

— freezing rain

evidence | MC misikan, *to be freezing rain;* NEC misikin, *to be freezing rain;* Fabvre (ca. 1690) "Misigan, *uerglas, pluye menue qui se gele*" | MENO mese·kahnan, *to hail*

*misisāhkw

INITIAL (NOUN, ANIMATE)

— horsefly

evidence | PC misisāhk, *horsefly;* MC misisāhkʷ, *horsefly;* AT (Opitciwan, Patrick Awashish) misisakw [mizizāhkw], *horsefly;* NEC misisāhkw, *horsefly;* EI (Ekuanitshit) missakᵘ [mɨssākʷ], *horsefly* | ABEN masezakwa, *deerfly* (Day, 1995); ANISH mizizaak, *horsefly* (Livesay & Nichols, 2021); MENO mesa·sa·hkok, *horseflies*

*misiwē

INITIAL

— **1** everywhere

— **2** all of, whole

evidence | PC misiwēpayiw, *to congeal, coagulate, or form a whole;* MC misiweskamik, *all over the world;* AT (Wemotaci, Jeannette Coocoo) misiwe [miziwē], *all;* SEC misiwesiw, *to be whole;* NEC misiwāpiyihtāu, *to swallow sth whole;* WI (Pessamit) mishue [məʃwē], *everywhere;* Watkins (1865) "Misewātuk, *n.in. Round wood, whole wood (i.e. not chopped into billets);*" Laure (ca. 1726) "missiué, *partout*" | ANISH miziwekamig, *all over the world* (Livesay & Nichols, 2021); MENO mese·wɛ·pi·w, *to be brimful of liquid* see | *mis, *wē³ compare | *misihtaw

*misk[1]

INITIAL (VERB, TRANSITIVE, INANIMATE)

— find

evidence | PC miskam, *to find sth;* WC miskam, *to find sth;* MC miskikātew, *to be found;* SEC miskam, *to find sth;* EI (Sheshatshiu) mishkamᵘ [mɨʃkəm], *to find sth* | ABEN meskam, *to find sth* (Day, 1994); ANISH mikige, *to find things* (Livesay & Nichols, 2021) paired with | *miskaw discussion | Further derivation is built directly on the transitive animate stem ***miskaw**.

*misk[2] (~ *āmisk)

MEDIAL

— bed of a body of water

evidence | MC kaškāmiskāw, *underwater precipice;* SEC akwāmisciw, *to move along the bed;* opimiskāw, *narrow bed (place name);* WI (Pessamit) mashkuamishkau [məʃkwāməʃkāw], *to be a hard bed of a body of water;* EI Nemishkau, *Longue-Pointe-de-Mingan (place name);* Silvy (ca. 1680) "ni ki8amisk8tan, *je vais sur le bord de l'eau, sur le sable* | ANISH asiniiwaamikaa, *to have a rocky bottom* (Livesay & Nichols, 2021); MESK ahkwēyāmihkiwi, *tract of wooded bottomland*

*miskaw (~ *misko)

INITIAL (VERB, TRANSITIVE, ANIMATE)

— find

evidence | PC miskawastimwēw, *to find a horse;* miskonam, *to find sth with one's hands;* WC miskawīw, *to find sb;* miskawāsomīw, *to remind sb;* MC miskawew, *to find sb;* miskonam, *to find sth manually;* miskohtam, *to find sth in a morsel;* SEC miskonam, *to find sth manually;* NEC miskiwāhtāu, *to discover sth;* Laure (ca. 1726) "ni-miskaueriten, *je déterre, je trouve;*" Silvy (ca. 1680) "ni miska8au, *je le trouve, je le rencontre*" see | *misk[1], *aw[3] paired with | *misk[1] discussion | The allomorph ***misko** is limited to lexical derivations.

*miskināhkw (~ *miskināhko)

INITIAL (NOUN, ANIMATE)

— turtle

evidence | PC miskināhk, *a turtle or tortoise;* WC miskināhk, *turtle;* SEC miscināhkʷ, *a turtle; the deity who presides over aquatic life;* EI (Sheshatshiu) missinakᵘ [məssɨnākʷ], *a turtle or tortoise; master of water animals;* Laure (ca. 1726) "mistinaku, *tortue (coquillage);*" Silvy (ca. 1680) "mistinak8, *tortue*" | ABEN mikinakw, *a tortoise, a turtle shell* (Day, 1994); ANISH mikinaak, *a snapping turtle* (Livesay & Nichols, 2021) origin | PA ***meskenāhkwa** (***mexkena:hkwa**, Aubin, 1975)

*miskwahtoy

INITIAL (NOUN, INANIMATE)

— circular frame

evidence | WC miskōhtōhkān, *frame for stretching hides;* MC maskohtow & amiskohtoy, *circular frame used for stretching and drying pelts;* NEC amiskuhtui, *wooden frame for stretching seal and beaver pelts;* WI (Pessamit) mishkutui [məʃkutwī], *a wooden hoop; a round frame for stretching a beaver pelt;* EI (Ekuanitshit) mishkutui [miskwātwī], *a wooden hoop; a round frame for stretching a beaver pelt;* Laure (ca. 1726) "miskutui -a, miskutuai -a, *cercle, rond pour attacher quelque peau;*" Silvy (ca. 1680) "misk8t8i, *cercle*" | ANISH Cuoq (1886) "Mikwind, *ce mot se dit du cercle qui est au haut d'un panier, du tour qui est au haut d'un casseau, d'un macaque, et en général, de tout ce qui sert à soutenir, à tenir tendu ou debout ce qui de soi-même n'a pas assez de consistance pour cela*" compare | *mahkwatoy

*miskwamiy

INITIAL (NOUN, ANIMATE)

— ice

evidence | PC miskwamiy, *ice;* WC miskwamīwikamik, *ice house;* MC maskwamiy, *ice;* EI (Sheshatshiu) mishkumi [miʃkumī], *ice;* Silvy (ca. 1680) "misk8ami8an, *cela est glacé*" | ABEN pkwami, *ice, icicle;* MENO mɛhkuam(-yak), *ice, piece or block of ice; expanse of ice;* MESK mehkwami, *the ice surface* origin | PA ***meskwamya** (***mexkwamya**, Hewson, 1993) see | *ɩskwam

*mispo

INITIAL

— snow

evidence | PC misposkin, *to snow often;* WC misposin, *to snow a little;* SEC mispon, *to snow;* Silvy (ca. 1680) "misp8n, *il neige*" | ANISH Nicholas (ca. 1670) "mipoun, *il neige*" (Daviault, 1994); MESK mehpowi, *to snow* see | *spon

*miš

INITIAL

— **1** reach

— **2** depend, rely

— **3** tell on, inform against

evidence | [1]PC miswēw, *to wound sb;* MC misaskeham, *run aground;* mišwew, *to hit sb on target;* AT (Opitciwan, Joey Awashish) micakaw [miʒakāw], *arrive by boat;* micakamepariw [miʒakāmepariw], *arriver à destination au moyen d'un canot;* SEC mišakāw, *arrive by boat;* Silvy (ca. 1680) "michastetin sipi8, *la rivière, l'eau a fond*" [2]PC mamisīw, *to rely on;* MC mamišītotawew, *to rely on sb;* SEC māmishītutam, *to be hopeful of sth* (CSB, 2018); NEC mimishīu, *to count on sth* [3]PC misimēw, *to tell on sb;* MC mišihew, *to incriminate sb;* WI (Pessamit) mamishieu [māməʃjēw], *to denounce sb;* Laure (ca. 1726) "niui-mamichimau, niui-michimau, *je parle à son désavantage*" | [1]ANISH mizhagaako, *to land coming off the ice;* mizhine, *to catch an illness* (Livesay & Nichols, 2021); MENO mesɛ·nam, nemɛ·senan, *to get one's hand on sth, to catch sth* [3]ANISH mamizhinge, *to inform on, tell on, tattle on people* (Livesay & Nichols, 2021) compare | *mišo

*mišo (~ *mišw)

INITIAL (VERB, TRANSITIVE, ANIMATE)

— hit and wound target

evidence | PC miswēw, *to wound sb with a missile;* MC mišwew, *to hit sb on target;* SEC mišwākan, *a wounded person or animal;* Silvy (ca. 1680) "ni mich8au, *je le frappe en mirant, en visant;*" "ni mich8ten, *je frappe où je vise*" | MENO mesi·w, neme·suaw, *to hit sb with a missile* see | *miš, *w²

*mišt (~ *mihš, *mihc)

INITIAL

— big

evidence | PC mistatim, *horse;* misikamāw, *to be a big lake;* WC mihcākamiw, *to be a large volume of liquid;* MC mišāw, *to be large;* AT miššaːpišiw, *lion, tiger* (Béland, 1993); SEC mištāpiskāw, *to be a large rock;* WI (Pessamit) mishtamekᵘ [məstəmeēkʷ], *whale;* mitshashkulueu [mətʃāʃkulwēw], *to have a large waist;* EI (Sheshatshiu) mishitunu [məʃitunu], *to have a big mouth;* Laure (ca. 1726) "ni-michikuan, *je suis gros de visage;*" Silvy (ca. 1680) "ni michtatchigan 3. -e8, *j'ai beaucoup mangé;*" "michigamau, *grand, large, fleuve, lac, etc.*" | ANISH misaabooz, *a jack rabbit* (Livesay & Nichols, 2021); MENO mɛqnapɛ·w, *a giant* origin | PA ***meʔθ** (Hewson, 1993) compare | *mištē discussion | The allomorph ***mihš** is inherited directly from PA as a lenited form of ***meʔθ**, while the secondary allomorph ***mihc** represents a later form derived directly from Old Cree ***mišt** that may have only arisen after the breakup of the protolanguage.

*mištē (~ *mihšē, *mihcē)

INITIAL

— much, many

evidence | PC mihcētwāw, *many times;* WC mihcītinwa, *to be plentiful;* MC mištetiwak, *to be many;* mištetōšew, *to give birth to many children;* AT mitcen [mihcēn], *to be a large quantity; to be many;* SEC mihcetiwac, *to be many;* NEC mihchānh, *to be many;* WI (Pessamit) mitshetu [mətʃētu], *to be plentiful;* EI (Sheshatshiu) mitshena [mītʃēna], *to be many things;* Watkins (1865) "Mèchātin, *v.imp. It is plenteous.* Mèchātinwa, *pl. they are many, they are numerous;*" Laure (ca. 1726) "mitchenua mina Chekutimitch, *Chekutimi abonde de bleuets;*" "mitchetuets puachinauets, *armée nombreuse;*" "missetiuets, missenua, *multitude, plusieurs;*" Silvy (ca. 1680) "michen8, *pl.* michen8ai, *ign. plusiers, beacoup*" limited to | *ɪt³, *ɪn⁴ compare | *mišt, *ēyat see | *w¹ discussion | Derivations beyond the basic VAI and VII forms are built on the numeral stem ***mištētw**, itself built on the VAI stem ***mištēt**. With regard to the form of the above reconstruction, note that all corroborative evidence, except for the contemporary MC form, exhibit a process of lenition, suggesting the latter may be an innovation based on the analogy of what is undoubtedly the underlying root, ***mišt**, ultimately from PA ***meʔθ**. The latter provides strong evidence for the historical form ***mihšē**, corroborated by both Silvy (ca. 1680) and Laure (ca. 1726).

*mištikw (~ *mištiko)

INITIAL (NOUN)

— **1** tree

— **2** stick

evidence | PC mistik, *a tree; a stick;* MC mištikohkān, *a mast;* AT mictikoskaw [mištikoskāw], *to be many trees;* SEC mištikʷ, *tree; stick;* Laure (ca. 1726) "mistiku *pl.* -ets, *arbre;*" Silvy (ca. 1680) "ni michtig8astisinikan, *je fais des souliers de bois*" | ANISH mitigokaa, *to be many trees* (Livesay & Nichols, 2021) origin | PA ***meʔtekw-**

*mit

INITIAL

— track

evidence | PC mitihtam, *to track sth;* MC mitimew, *to follow a path;* NEC mitihtāu, *to track sb;* Watkins (1865) "Mitìtāo, *v.t.an. He tracks him;*" "Mitimāo, *v.i.3. He follows (as in a track or path);*" Laure (ca. 1726) "ni-mititau, *je suis la piste;*" Silvy (ca. 1680) "ni mitiman meskanau, *je suis le chemin*" | ANISH Nicholas (ca. 1670) "nimitira, *je le suis*" (Daviault, 1994); MENO metɛ·hnɛw, *to track sb;* metɛ·mow, nemɛ·temin, *to follow a path or trail* limited to | *ɪm[1]

*mitē

INITIAL

— stay behind

evidence | PC Lacombe (1874) "Mitepiw, ok, *(v.n.) il reste, il demeure là, les autres étant partis;*" "Mitewikiw, ok, *(v.n.) il reste campé seul, sa loge reste là;*" MC miteškāw, *to stay behind when others leave;* NEC mitāpiu, *to stay behind as others leave;* WI (Pessamit) miteshkateu [mətēʃkətēw], *to depart and leave sb behind* compare | *mitēw[1]

*mitēw[1]

INITIAL (NOUN, ANIMATE)

— conjuror, sorcerer

evidence | PC mitēwikamik, *medicine lodge;* WC mitīw, *witch doctor;* ESC mitewiw, *to be a shaman or conjuror;* MC mitehkew, *to invoke supernatural powers;* AT (Opitciwan, Joey Awashish) mitew, *sorcerer;* SEC mitehkahtātowac, *to curse each other;* NEC mitāwātisīu, *to practice conjuring;* Watkins (1865) "Mitāwew, *v.i.1. He is a conjuror;*" La Brosse (1766) "Miteunimin, *Salto superstitiose*" | ANISH midewigaan, *a Mide lodge* (Livesay & Nichols, 2021); MENO metɛ·w, *participant in the Mystic Rite;* MESK metēwa, *member of the Midewiwin* origin | PA ***metēwa** (Hewson, 1993) see | *mitēw[2] compare | *mitē

*mitēw[2]

MEDIAL (NOUN INCORPORATION)

— conjuror, sorcerer

evidence | Laure (ca. 1726) "ni-nutchimiteuatau, *je le menace par la jonglerie*" see | *mitēw[1]

*miton

INITIAL

— thoroughly

evidence | PC mitoni, *completely;* MC mitonelihcikan, *a mind;* SEC māmitoneyihtam, *to think about sth* | ANISH maaminonenim, *to think about sb* (Livesay & Nichols, 2021); MIAMI meloniteehee-, *ponder, reflect, study* (ILDA, 2017) origin | PA ***meθon**

*miyāw

INITIAL

— pass by

evidence | PC miyāskawēw, *to pass sb on foot;* MC mayāškam (modern) & miyāškam (Moose Cree Bible, 1876), *to pass sth on foot;* SEC miyāwipayiw, *to go past by vehicle;* miyānam, *to leave tracks as one goes by;* WI (Pessamit) mienam[u] [mījēnəm], *to be found by the tracks left behind;* Laure (ca. 1726) "ni-miauauauets, *je les visite en passant chemin en canot;*" Silvy (ca. 1680) "ni meïachkaȣau, *je l'ai vu en passant chemin*"

*mīci

INITIAL (VERB, ANIMATE, INTRANSITIVE)

— eat sth

evidence | PC mīciwin, *food;* MC mīciw, *to eat sth;* WI mitshu [mītʃu], *to eat sth;* Laure (ca. 1726) "ni-mitchin uihias, *je mange de la chair*" | ANISH omiijin, *to eat sth* (Livesay & Nichols, 2021); MESK mīchiwa, *to eat sth;* mīchiweni, *food* compare | *mīcihso, *mō[2]

*mīcihso

INITIAL (VERB, ANIMATE, INTRANSITIVE)

— eat

evidence | PC mīcisowin, *food, a meal;* WC mīcisoskiw, *to eat often;* MC mīcisow, *to eat;*

mīcisowināhtikʷ, *a table;* AT (Wemotaci, Jeannette Coocoo) mitciso [mīcissow], *to eat;* SEC mīcisow, *to eat;* WI (Pessamit) mitshishumatshu [mītʃʃūmətʃū], *to feel well-nourished;* Laure (ca. 1726) "ni-maninen mitchisuagan, *je dessers, j'ôte les mets;*" Silvy (ca. 1680) "ni mitchisȣn, *je mange;*" "ni mitchisȣhau, *je lui donne à manger*" | MENO me·cehsow, *to eat* see | *mīci

*mīcim

INITIAL (NOUN, INANIMATE)

— food

evidence | PC mīcim, *food;* mīcimihkēw, *to prepare food* WC mīcimāpoy, *soup;* MC mīcimihkahtam, *to bait sth;* NEC mīchim, *food;* SEC mīcimāhtikʷ, *a stick used as food by a beaver; a stick put on either side of a snare to close a gap and serve as bait;* WI (Pessamit) mitshim [mītʃəm], *food;* EI mitshim [mītʃɨm], *food; social assistance allowance;* Watkins (1865) "Mechimikumik, *n.in. A provision-store;*" Laure (ca. 1726) "mitchim, *nourriture;*" Silvy (ca. 1680) "mitchim, *aliment;*" Le Jeune (1634) "Khimitchimi, *ton mets*" | ANISH miijim, *food* (Livesay & Nichols, 2021); MENO me·cem, *food, fodder* see | *mīci discussion | Although reconstructed in PA as ***mīcimi** by Hewson (1993), Pentland (1982) postulated ***mīcyeʔmi** and argued that the Cree form would have ultimately been a loanword, likely from an early Anishinabe dialect.

*mīhr

INITIAL

— hairy, fuzzy

evidence | WC mīðāmō, *bumble bee;* MC mīlāškoštowew, *to have facial hair;* SEC mīhyāpāhkwan, *tree moss;* Fabvre (ca. 1690) "mirau mihau, *velu*" | ANISH miishaa, *to be hairy or fuzzy* (Livesay & Nichols, 2021); MENO me·qnamow, *wasp;* MIAMI miihsilookiaakan-, *body hair* (ILDA, 2017)

*mīkē

INITIAL

— fight

evidence | AT (Opitciwan, Joey Awashish) mikaso [mīkāzow], *to fight;* SEC (Waswanipi, Ella Neeposh) mīkātew, *to fight sb* | ABEN migaka, *to fight or make war* (Day, 1994); ANISH omiigaanaan, *to fight sb* (Livesay & Nichols, 2021); MENO mi·ka·twan, *fighting, war* compare | *māš[1] discussion | This root is undocumented in most contemporary dialects and is absent from the historical record. However, its presence in various branches of the Algonquian family supports a Proto-Algonquian reconstruction, as well as evidence that the root was likely inherited rather than borrowed from a neighbouring language.

*mīkihs[1]

INITIAL (NOUN, ANIMATE)

— shell bead

evidence | PC mīkis, *a bead;* mīkisistikwānēw, *to have beads on one's head;* WC mīkisiðākan, *a porcelain dish;* mīkisaskisin, *a beaded moccasin;* MC mīkisikwāsow, *to do beadwork;* AT (Wemotaci, Jeannette Coocoo) mikisikwason [mīkissikwāsson], *beadwork;* SEC mīcisištahicew, *to do beadwork;* Watkins (1865) "Mekisikàtum, *v.t.in.6. She works it with beads;*" Silvy (ca. 1680) "mitis, mitchis, *porcelaine*" | ANISH miigis, *a Mide shell, a pearl* (Livesay & Nichols, 2021); me·kɛhsak, *cowrie shells* origin | PA ***mīkehsa** (Hewson, 1993) see | *mīkihs[2]

*mīkihs[2]

MEDIAL (NOUN INCORPORATION)

— shell bead

evidence | MC tāpisikohimīkisew, *to thread beads;* SEC (Waswanipi) nōcimīkisew, *to bead;* Silvy (ca. 1680) "nit'abikȣahimitisan, *j'enfile des porcelaines*" see | *mīkihs[1]

*mīkiwāhp

INITIAL (NOUN, INANIMATE)

— lodge

evidence | PC mīkiwāhp, *a tipi;* SEC mīciwāhp, *a conical lodge;* NEC mīchiwāhp, *a tipi, a dwelling;* EI (Sheshatshiu) mitshuap [mītʃwāp], *a house, a dwelling;* Silvy (ca. 1680) "mitchiȣap, *cabane*" see | *kiwāhp, *īk, *ihp

*mīkwan

INITIAL (NOUN, ANIMATE)

— flight feather

evidence | PC mīkwanak, *feathers;* SEC mīkwan, *a flight feather; snare made from a quill feather shaft and strung across a drumhead;* WI (Pessamit) mikun [mīkwən], *feather; quill pen; drum snare make from a quill feather shaft;* Laure (ca. 1726) "ni-mikuan-aspichimunikan, *je fais un lit de plume*" | ABEN migwen, *a feather, quill, or pen* (Day, 1994); ANISH miigwan, *a feather* (Livesay & Nichols, 2021) see | *kwan

*mīkwanākway

INITIAL (NOUN, INANIMATE)

— bark container for collecting or storing liquids

evidence | SEC mīkwanākway, *birch bark container for storing liquids;* WI (Pessamit) mikunakuai [mīkunākwī], *waterproof container made of birchbark;* Watkins (1865) "Mekoonakwi, *n.in.* A roggin;" Fabvre (ca. 1690) "mikȣanagȣe *pl.* eïa, *coffin, cassot d'ecorce*"

*mīn

INITIAL (NOUN)

— **1** (inanimate) fruit, berry

— **2** (animate) mole, beauty mark, hemangioma, cherry angioma

evidence | [1]WC mīnis, *a berry;* MC mīnišiwan, *to bear fruit;* SEC mīniskāw, *to be many berries;* miniš, *a berry; a blueberry;* EI (Sheshatshiu) minaputsheu [mīnāpūtʃēw], *to make jam;* Silvy (ca. 1680) "mini *pl.* minai, *bleuets*" [2]ESC omīnimipitonew, *to have moles on one's arms;* MC omīnima, *one's mole, beauty mark, or birth mark;* AT (Opitciwan, Joey Awashish) niminimak [nimīnimak], *my cherry angiomas;* SEC nimīnimac, *my beauty marks or moles;* WI (Pessamit) min [mīn], *a beauty mark, birthmark, or Mongolian spot;* EI (Sheshatshiu) uminimu [umīnɨmu], *to have a dark birthmark or a mole or a Mongolian spot;* Laure (ca. 1726) "uminimikueuin, *marque au visage*" | ANISH miinikaa, *to be many blueberries* (Livesay & Nichols, 2021); MENO me·nan, *blueberries* origin | PA ***mīni** (Hewson, 1993) see | *min⁴ compare | *pāhpāhtēw

*mīno (~ *mīnaw)

INITIAL

— **1** rectify

— **2** again

evidence | [1]WC mīnoskam, *to balance sth under one's weight;* MC mīnoham, *to rectify the course of a canoe;* SEC mīnawācihew, *to make sb well again;* Watkins (1865) "Menoosinùhum, *v.t.in.6. He corrects it (as a writing);*" Laure (ca. 1726) "ni-minauatamun, *je reprends haleine;*" Fabvre (ca. 1690) "Minȣnen, nau, *releuer, redresser;*" Silvy (ca. 1680) "minaȣaȣatchipariȣ, *on ne voit plus la piste*" [2]PC mīna, *and; again;* MC mīna, *again; more;* EI (Mushuau) minuat [mīnwātʃ], *again;* Silvy (ca. 1680) "mina, *encore, de plus, advantage*" | [1]ANISH miinon, *to put sb right* (Livesay & Nichols, 2021) [2]ABEN minawigo, *to grow again* (Day, 1994); ANISH miinawaa, *also; and; again* (Livesay & Nichols, 2021)

*mīr

INITIAL (VERB, TRANSITIVE, ANIMATE)

— to give

evidence | WC mīðīw, *to give sth to sb;* MC mīlew, *to give sth to sb;* SEC mīyiwewin, *a gift;* WI (Uashat) minishkueueu [mīniʃkwēwēw], *to give sth to a woman;* Laure (ca. 1726) "ni-miritunan, *nous nous entredonnons*" | ABEN mila, *to give sth to sb* (Day, 1994); ANISH miinidiwag, *to give each other things* (Livesay & Nichols, 2021); MENO me·nɛ·w, *to give sth ro sb* origin | PA ***mīr** (***mi·l**, Hewson, 1993)

*mīskaw

INITIAL

— **1** by chance, fortuitously

— **2** good, better

evidence | PC mīskaw, *occasionally;* WC mīskwa, *by chance; accidentally;* ESC (Severn) mīskawās, *once in a while;* MC mīskaw, *by chance; seldomly, rarely;* SEC mīskaw itamahcihow, *to feel better;* EI (Ekuanitshit) mishku [mīhkaw], *by chance; it is lucky that;* Laure (ca. 1726) "miskau-, *casuel, casuellement, fortuitement;*" Silvy (ca. 1680) "miskau, *cela est par hasard;*" "miskau ichinag8an, *admirable*" | ANISH miikawinaagozi, *to be good-looking* (Livesay & Nichols, 2021); MENO me·hkawatɛsew, *to be handsome;* MESK mīhkwi, *happen by chance* compare | *mīsko

*mīsko (~ *mīskw)

INITIAL

— hit target

evidence | WC mīskonam, *to feel sth by hand;* ESC mīskoškātowak, *to run into one another;* MC mīskohwew, *to hit sb on target;* SEC mīskoham, *to hit sth on target;* Silvy (ca. 1680) "ni michk8ganeh8au, *je le frappe à l'os en le dardant*" | ANISH miikoshkaw, *to bump in to sb* (Livesay & Nichols, 2021) compare | *mīskaw

*mīš

INITIAL

— mend, patch

evidence | WC mīsahaðapīw, *to mend a net;* MC mīšahanakwew, *patch a sleeve;* SEC mīšahwew, *to patch sth;* Laure (ca. 1726) "michahigan, *pièce à boucher un trou;*" Silvy (ca. 1680) "ni michahitasan 3. -e8, *je refais des bas*" | ABEN mishigan, *a patch* (Day, 1994); MENO mi·sekwatam, *to sew sth*

*mīšak

INITIAL

— rich, plentiful

evidence | ESC (Severn) mīsikisīw, *to be rich;* MC mīšakisīw, *to be rich;* mīšakāskweyāw, *to be richly wooded;* AT mi:šakitta:-, *to be rich, wealthy* (Béland, 1978); (Wemotaci, Jeannette Coocoo) micikitawin [mīʒikihtāwin], *wealth;* SEC mīšacisīw, *to be rich*

*mīškot (~ *mīškoc)

INITIAL

— in exchange, in turn

evidence | PC mīskotinam, *to change or replace sth;* MC mīškocipaliw, *to change from one to another;* SEC māmīškoc, *alternately;* Silvy (ca. 1680) "ni michk8tichkagan, *je supplée*" | ANISH meshkwad, *in turn, in exchange* (Livesay & Nichols, 2021) compare | *mīškotō

*mīškotō

INITIAL

— in exchange

evidence | PC mīskotōnam, *to exchange sth;* MC mīškotōnam, *to exchange sth;* SEC mīškotōnamawew, *to exchange sth with sb;* EI (Sheshatshiu) mamishkutunam[u] [māmīʃkutūnəm], *to exchange sth repeatedly;* Silvy (ca. 1680) "ni michk8t8nen, *je change de place*" compare | *mīškot

*mīt (~ *mīc, *mīs)

INITIAL

— **1** defecate

— **2** spray, speaking of a skunk

evidence | PC mītihkwāmiw, *to defecate in one's sleep;* MC mīcipaliw, *to defecate spontaneously;* mīsīw, *to defecate; to spray;* AT (Wemotaci, Jeannette Coocoo) misiworakan [mīzīworākan], *a toilet bowl;*

SEC mīsīw, *to defecate;* māmītahikow, *to defecate because of sth;* WI (Pessamit) mitshiteu [mītʃətēw], *to shit on sb; to spray sb;* Fabvre (ca. 1690) "mitchiten 3 ta(m), *gaster auec fiante;*" Silvy (ca. 1680) "ni missin, *je vais à la selle*" | ANISH miijidan, *to shit on sth* (Livesay & Nichols, 2021); MENO me·ceqtaw, *to defecate as one moves or works;* MESK mīchinēwa, *to defecate on sb*

*mītākwē

INITIAL

— off in the distance

evidence | ESC mītākwekāpawiw, *to stand in the distance, to be standing while keeping one's distance;* MC mītākwenam, *to put sth at a distance;* WI (Pessamit) mitakuepu [mītākwēpu], *être assis en retrait*

*mītohs

INITIAL (NOUN, ANIMATE)

— aspen, poplar

evidence | PC mītos, *trembling aspen;* mītosiskāw, *to be many aspens;* WC mītosiskāw, *to be many poplars or aspens;* SEC mītososkāw, *to be many trembling aspens;* EI (Sheshatshiu) mitushitak[u] [mītuʃītuk[w]], *wood of a quaking aspen;* Laure (ca. 1726) "machimituch -ats - ets, *tremble, bois*" origin | PA ***mītohsa** (cf. nondiminutive ***mītwiya**, Hewson, 1993)

*mīw

INITIAL

— to get away from (a negative experience), to seek to avoid

evidence | AT mīwaciw, *to get away from the cold;* SEC mīweheu, *to drive sb away;* WI (Pessamit) miutshu [mīwtʃu], *to avoid the cold;* Laure (ca. 1726) "ni-miuitissauauets, *je brouille ensemble les amis;*" "ni-miuihau, *je chasse quelqu'un, je l'oblige à se retirer;*" Fabvre (ca. 1690) "mi8ihau, *rebutter, chasser, renuoyer de chez soy*" | ANISH miiwinan, *to push sth away or reject* (Livesay & Nichols, 2021); MENO me·wehɛw, *to drive sb off*

*mohšaw

INITIAL

— barren

evidence | PC mosawaham, *to bare sth using a tool;* MC mošawānakāw, *to be a barren island;* NEC mushiwāu, *to be barren;* WI mushutinau [mūʃutnāw], *to be a barren mountain;* Fabvre (ca. 1690) "M8cha8ask8te8, *ou le feu a brulé Les arbres;*" Silvy (ca. 1680) "ni m8cha8ahigan 3. -e8, *je coupe les bois, les arbres, les broussailles*"

compare | *mohšē

*mohšē

INITIAL

— bare

evidence | PC mosēpitēw, *to uncover sb;* MC mošecihcew, *to be barehanded;* AT (Opitciwan, Joey Awashish) moceiaw [moššēyāw], *to be bare;* SEC mošeškatew, *to be naked;* WI musheiau [mūʃējāw], *to be bare* compare | *mohšaw

*mohšōm

INITIAL (NOUN, DEPENDENT ANIMATE)

— grandfather

evidence | PC omosōmiw, *to have a grandfather;* WSC (Misipawistik, Ellen Cook) nimosōm, *my grandfather;* MC omošōmimāw, *a grandfather;* AT (Opitciwan, Jeannette Coocoo) omocoma [omoššōma], *one's grandfather(s);* SEC nimošōm, *my grandfather;* EI (Sheshatshiu) umushuma [umuʃūma], *one's grandfather(s);* Silvy (ca. 1680) "nim8ch8m, *mon grand-père*"

*mošt (~ *mohc)

INITIAL

— **1** on a bare surface, on nothing but, directly on

— **2** with no equipment, with nothing but, just

evidence | [1]PC mostaskamik, *on the surface of the ground;* mohcihk, *on the bare ground;*

MC moštākonehkwāmiw, *to sleep directly on the snow;* mohcihtak, *on the floor;* WI (Pessamit) mushtashtat [mūstāstət], *on the conifer bough flooring;*" Laure (ca. 1726) "muchtachkamitch, *à platte terre*" ²PC mostinam, *to take with bare hands;* MC moštohtew, *to go on foot;* SEC moštahtam, *to eat sth on its own, with nothing else* | MENO moqto·hnɛw, *to walk afoot, having no mount or vehicle* **origin** | PA ***mweʔt*** (Hewson, 1993)

*moštaw

INITIAL

— desire

evidence | PC Lacombe (1874) "mustaweyittamāwew, etc., *(v.a.) il lui désire;*" EI (Sheshatshiu) mushtuenimeu [mūstwēnɨmēw], *to desire sb;* Watkins (1865) "Moostowināo, *v.t.an. He covets him, he longs for him;*" Laure (ca. 1726) "muchtaueritaguanu, *désirable, souhaitable;*" Silvy (ca. 1680) "ni m8chta8inen; ni m8chta8inan, *je désire qqch*" | ANISH misawenjige, *to desire things* (Livesay & Nichols, 2021) **origin** | PA ***mweʔθaw*** (Hewson, 1993) **compare** | *moštē **discussion** | This root is possibly derived from a transitive animate stem, as suggested by Silvy (ca. 1680) "ni m8chta8au, *je m'en vais le trouver, le sonder.*" In the absence of corroborative evidence for this verb stem or its transitive inanimate counterpart, we reconstruct the root as above.

*moštē

INITIAL

— desire

evidence | MC mošteyelihtākwan, *to be desirable;* AT moctenam [moštenam], *to find sth appealing;* SEC moštenawew, *to desire sb;* WI (Pessamit) mushtenakushu [mūstēnākuʃu], *to be visually tempting;* Laure (ca. 1726) "ni-muchtenamauau, *je désire le bien d'autrui*" **compare** | *moštaw

*moyaw

INITIAL

— thank

evidence | Fabvre (ca. 1690) "M8ïa8atis8n, 8, *Remercier en festin, ch(an)tant, en har(a)g(nan)t;*" Silvy (ca. 1680) "ni m8ia8atis8n, *je remercie en festin, en chantant, en haranguant*" | ANISH Cuoq (1886) "Ki mamoiawamin, *je vous remercie;*" "mamoiawandis,o, *se féliciter, se remercier soi-même, s'applaudir, se réjouir d'avoir fait ceci ou cela;*" "mamoiawe, *remercier, dire merci;*" MENO mami·yawamɛ·w, *to give thanks to sb* **discussion** | This root is obsolete in contemporary dialects and its reconstruction depends on cognates from Anishinabe and Menominee.

*mō¹

INITIAL

— cry

evidence | PC mōhiwēw, *to make people cry;* MC mōhew, *to make sb cry;* SEC mōhew, *to make sb cry;* Laure (ca. 1726) "ni-muhau, *je le fais pleurer*" | MENO ma·w, *to weep;* cf. nemo·m; mo·k; mo·hɛ·w, *to make sb weep* **compare** | *māto, *mē, *mōsko

*mō² (~ *mow)

INITIAL

— eat sth

evidence | PC mowēw, *to eat sb;* MC mōmesew, *eat fish;* SEC mōminew, *eat berries;* mōhtew, *a woodworm;* Laure (ca. 1726) "niui-mugusin, *je veux être mangé;*" Silvy (ca. 1680) "ni m8au, *je le mange;*" "ni m8t8nan, *nous nous entre-mangeons*" **compare** | *mīci, *mīcihso

*mōcik

INITIAL

— merry, fun

evidence | PC mōcikihtāw, *to have fun;* MC mōcikelihtākwan, *to be fun;* SEC mōcikan, *to be fun*

*mōhkit (~ *mōhkic)

INITIAL

— back end elevated

evidence | PC mōhkicīw, *to expose oneself indecently;* MC mōhkicišin, *to lie with one's bum elevated;* SEC mōhcitaštew, *to sit with the back elevated, as a car in the ditch;* WI (Pessamit) mutshitshipalu [mūtʃətʃəpəlu], *to fall head first with one's rear end in the air* compare | *cāhk discussion | In the absence of a Woods Cree cognate, the status of the preaspiration cannot be confirmed.

*mōhko

INITIAL

— shave wood, carve

evidence | PC mōhkomān, *a knife;* MC mōhkocikew, *to carve or plane;* SEC mōhkotam, *to carve or plane sth;* Silvy (ca. 1680) "ni m8k8ten, ni m8k8tau, *nob. je le dole*" | ANISH mookodan, *to carve or plane sth* (Livesay & Nichols, 2021); MENO mo·hkotam, *to whittle sth, to do woodcarving on sth* origin | PA ***mōhko** compare | *mōhš

*mōhš

INITIAL

— shave scalp, shear

evidence | PC mōswēw, *to shear sb;* MC mōšotowin, *hair-cutting shears;* Watkins (1865) "Moosoo, *v.i.4. He cuts his hair;*" Silvy (ca. 1680) "ni m8ch8au, *je tonds*" | ANISH Cuoq (1886) "Ni monjwa, *je lui coupe les cheveux;*" MENO mo·hsokan, *scissors* origin | PA ***mōnš** (Hewson, 1993) compare | *mōhko discussion | In the absence of an Atikamekw cognate, the preaspirate in this reconstruction is indirectly supported by Anishinabe and Menominee.

*mōn

INITIAL

— dig up

evidence | PC mōnaham, *to dig sth up (using sth);* MC mōnipicikew, *to dig with one's hands or paws;* NEC mūnitipāu, *to dig up roots* | ANISH moona'asinii, *to dig up rocks or mine ore* (Livesay & Nichols, 2021)

*mōr

INITIAL

— premonition, presentiment

evidence | PC Lacombe (1874) "Moyeyimew, *il a des soupçcons sur lui;*" MC mōlisīw, *to have a presentiment;* SEC mōyisīw, *to have a presentiment;* EI (Sheshatshiu) munenitamᵘ [mūnēntəm], *to suspect sth* | ANISH moonenim, *to suspect or blame sb* (Livesay & Nichols, 2021); MENO mo·nesew, *to have a premonition* origin | PA ***mōr** (***mo·l**, Hewson, 1993)

*mōrkahōhsiw

INITIAL (NOUN, ANIMATE)

— American bittern (Botaurus lentiginosus)

evidence | WC (Stanley Mission, Solomon Ratt) mōðkahosiw, *a night heron;* MC mōhkahōsiw, *American bittern; great blue heron;* AT (Opitciwan, Patrick Awashish) mokohosiw [mōhkohōssiw], *a heron;* SEC mōhkahōsiw, *American bittern; great blue heron;* NEC mūhkiwisiw, *a heron* | ANISH mooshka'osi, *a bittern, a shypoke* (Livesay & Nichols, 2021)

*mōsk

INITIAL

— emerge from under a surface

evidence | WC mōskinam, *to uncover sth;* MC mōskākonakīw, *to surface from under the snow;* WI (Pessamit) mussipitamᵘ [mūssəpətəm], *to pull sth to the surface;* Watkins (1865) "Mooskitāo, *v.imp. The smoke rises*" | ABEN moskenem, *to make sth emerge, to bring sth out* (Day, 1994); ANISH mookibii, *to emerge from the water* (Livesay & Nichols, 2021) origin | PA ***mōθk** (Hewson, 1993)

*mōsko (~ *mōskw, *mōskaw)

INITIAL

— cry because of

evidence | PC mōskomēw, *to make sb cry by weeping or speaking;* MC mōskawātew, *to cry for sb;* mōskwāpākwew, *to cry of thirst;* EI (Mamit) mushkuapineu [mūhkwāpɨnēw], *to cry because of pain* | ANISH mookwaakizo, *to cry from being burned* (Livesay & Nichols, 2021) origin | PA ***mōθko** compare | *māto, *mē, *mō[1]

*mōsw (~ *mōso)

INITIAL (NOUN, ANIMATE)

— moose

evidence | PC mōswa, *a moose;* MC mōsoskāw, *to be many moose;* AT (Opitciwan, Joey Awashish) ni mōsom [ni mōzom], *my moose;* SEC mōsʷ, *a moose;* Silvy (ca. 1680) "m8s8me8, *piste d'orignal;*" Le Jeune (1634) "mousouakhi, *elans*" see | *osw

*mōš[1]

INITIAL

— having a physical feeling or intuition

evidence | PC mōsihow, *to have a premonition or physical feeling;* MC mōšihtāw, *to have a feeling or intuition about sth;* AT (Wemotaci, Nicole Petiquay) mociho [¿mōʒihow], *to have a feeling or intuition;* WI (Pessamit) mushieu [mūʃjēw], *to feel sb physically* | ANISH moozhi'o, *to feel sth* (Livesay & Nichols, 2021); MENO mo·sehɛw, *to perceive sb's coming or presence* origin | PA ***mōš** (Hewson, 1993)

*mōš[2]

INITIAL

— nothing but, merely

evidence | PC mōsak, *always;* mōsākamin, *to be weak, speaking of a liquid;* WC mōsāpīw, *a bachelor;* MC mōšak, *always;* mōškamiy, *broth;* AT (Wemotaci, Nicole Petiquay) mōšak [mōʒak], *always;* (Wemotaci, Nicole Petiquay) mocakamin [mōʒākamin], *to be thin liquid;* SEC mōš, *always;* mōšākamihkwew, *to have thin blood;* NEC mūsh, *always;* mūshkimī, *broth;* mūshākimisiu, *to be thin liquid;* WI (Pessamit) mush [mūʃ], *often, regularly;* WI (Uashat) mushapeu [mūʃāpēw], *a solitary man;* Silvy (ca. 1680) "ni m8chabe8in 3. -i8, *je suis garçon;*" "m8chask8au, *il fai beau temps, serein;*" Fabvre (ca. 1690) "m8skami v. m8chkami, *b8illon de chair ou poisson*" | MESK mōshaki, *no one else but, nothing else but;* MIAMI moošaki, *always* (ILDA, 2017)

*mōšahk

INITIAL

— gather up

evidence | PC mōsāhkipitam, *to gather sth up quickly;* MC mōšahkinam, *to gather sth up with one's hands;* AT (Wemotaci, Nicole Petiquay) mockinaso [mōškināssow], *to pick things up;* WI (Pessamit) mamushatshineu [māmūssnēw], *to gather things, to put things together;* Silvy (ca. 1680) "ni mam8chatchinen, ni m8chatchinen, *je ramasse, v.g. des pois*" discussion | The absence of a preaspiration on the sibilant cannot be confirmed due to the contracted form of the Atikamekw cognate.

*mōšāw (~ *mōšawē)

INITIAL

— towards open water, offshore

evidence | SEC (coastal) mushāwehyāu, *to fly out over the water* (CSB, 2018); NEC mushāwātin, *to be an offshore wind;* WI (Pessamit) mushauetin [mūʃāwētn], *to start freezing over, speaking of open water;* EI (Sheshatshiu) mushauetakaimᵘ [mūʃāwētəkējm], *to head towards the end of the wharf on foot;* Watkins (1865) "moosowuhum, *v.i.6. He goes out to sea;*" "moosowāapootāo, *v.imp. It floats out with the current (i.e., into the sea or lake)*" compare | *nimitāw discussion | The absence of a preaspiration on the sibilant cannot be confirmed due to the lack of an Atikamekw cognate.

*mōšk

INITIAL

— fill with water, flood

evidence | MC mōškahan, *to flood, speaking of a body of water;* AT mockahan [mōškahan], *to flood, speaking of a body of water;* Watkins (1865) "Mooskuhipāo, *v.pass. It is flooded*" | ANISH mooshka'ogo, *to have one's place flooded;* mooshka'oodoon, *to add water or other liquid to sth* (Livesay & Nichols, 2021); MENO mo·skeqnɛn, *to be full of liquid, to be flooded;* MESK mōshkahanwi, *to be flooded;* mōshkāpowēwa, *to add water to the cooking* compare | *mōškinē

*mōškinē

INITIAL (VERB, INTRANSITIVE)

— full

evidence | PC mōskinēw, *to be full;* Lacombe (1874) "moskinattaw, *il le remplit jusqu'au faite;*" MC mōškin, *full;* mōškinahtāw, *to fill sth;* AT mockinepew [mōškinēpēw], *to be full of liquid;* Silvy (ca. 1680) "m8chtine8, m8chtinebe8, *cela est plein*" | ANISH mooshkine, *to be full* (Livesay & Nichols, 2021) origin | Query obscure noun incorporation. see | *aškinē compare | *mōšk

*mōtā

INITIAL

— deep

evidence | MC mōtāyāw, *to be deep;* SEC mōtāhtin, *to be a deep stream;* EI (Sheshatshiu) [mūtātəkāw], *to be a deep canoe;* Laure (ca. 1726) "ni-mutaskamigahen, *enfoncer bien avant dans la terre*" | ABEN molōjoan, *to be a deep current* (Day, 1994); ANISH Cuoq (1886) "moneia, *to be deep*" origin | PA ***mōθā**

*mwākw (~ *mwāko)

INITIAL (NOUN, ANIMATE)

— loon

evidence | WC mwākwa, *a loon;* MC mwākokan, *bone of a loon;* NEC mwākwāpui, *broth obtained from cooking a loon;* Silvy (ca. 1680) "m8ag8a, *huard*"

*mwēšt (~ *mwēhc, mwēhs)

INITIAL

— be too late for, just miss

evidence | PC mwēsiskawēw, *to arrive too late for sb;* mwēhci, *just after; just like;* MC mweštahwew, *to fail to hit the target by being too late;* mwehciškam, *to arrive too late to catch sth;* SEC mweštinam, *to be too late to catch sth;* mwehc, *just now, very recently; just, exactly; just like, alike;* WI (Pessamit) mueshishkam [mwēʃəʃkəm], *to arrive too late for an event;* mueshtash [mwēstəʃ], *too late;* Fabvre (ca. 1690) "M8echtah8au, *uenir arriuer trop tard à qlqn qui e(st) mort ou parti;*" "M8esiskāgan 3 ke8, *uenir tard, Le dernier*" | ANISH memwech, *just that, exactly, it is so* (Livesay & Nichols, 2021)

*mwēštāt (~ *mwēštāc, *mwēštās)

INITIAL

— weary

evidence | PC mwēstāsihtam, *to tire to listen to sth;* SEC mweštāteyihtākwan, *to be wearisome, annoying;* WI (Pessamit) mueshtatshiu [mwēstātʃīw], *to be tired of, annoyed;* Laure (ca. 1726) "ni-muechtatchimun, *je m'ennuie de parler;*" Silvy (ca. 1680) "ni m8echtatapin, *je suis las d'être assis*"

N

*n[1]

FINAL (NOUN, ABSTRACT)

sound change | ē → ā

— suffixed to animate intransitive verbs and forms nouns that generally refer to objects or places where particular activities are performed

evidence | PC sīpīhkān, *canal;* AT manāwān, *egg gathering place;* MC ihkahipān, *a bilge pump;* likohaskān, *grave;* SEC apwān, *roast* *meat on a stick;* EI utaipan, *a well;* Silvy (ca. 1680) "8taban, *traîne*" compare | *ıhp, *ın², *win

*n²

FINAL (VERB, TRANSITIVE, INANIMATE, CONCRETE)

— see

evidence | PC māyinam, *to find sth ugly;* MC išinam, *to see sth thus;* nisitawinam, *to recognize sth;* SEC miyonam, *to find sth good-looking* paired with | *naw²

*n³

FINAL (VERB, ANIMATE, INTRANSITIVE, ABSTRACT)

— forms stative verbs

evidence | PC pimišin, *to lie;* MC akocin, *to hang;* SEC takošino, *to arrive;* NEC akuhchin, *to soak* see | *cin, *hcin, *hšin

*nah

INITIAL

— convenient, favorable, proper

evidence | PC nahapiw, *to sit down;* MC nahilawew, *favorable wind;* SEC nahīw, *to be right-handed;* Silvy (ca. 1680) "ni naheriten, *j'accomode ma pensée, je me console étant triste*" | ANISH na'abi, *to move to get seated comfortably* (Livesay & Nichols, 2021)

*nahāhk

INITIAL (NOUN, ANIMATE)

— person living among spouse's social group

evidence | PC onahāhkimiw, *to have a son-in-law;* MC onahāhkišīma, *to have a son-in-law;* AT (Wemotaci) nahakic [nahāhkiš], *a son-in-law;* SEC cinahāhchim, *your son-in-law;* WI (Pessamit) unatshishkuema [unātʃəʃkwèːm], *one's daughter-in-law;* EI (Sheshatshiu) unatshima [unātʃima], *one's son-in-law;* Fabvre (ca. 1690) "Nahakich, *femme etr(an)gere mariée en ce paÿs;*" Silvy (ca. 1680) "ni nahatchichi8in, *je suis mariés hors du pays, en autre nation*" | ANISH na'aangish, *a son-in-law;* na'aangabi, *to live with one's wife's parents, speaking of a man* (Livesay & Nichols, 2021); MENO noha·hkapew, *to live with one's wife's parents* see | *nahākan

*nahākan

INITIAL (NOUN, ANIMATE)

— person living among spouse's social group

evidence | WC kinahākaniskwīm, *your daughter-in-law;* MC onahākaniskwema, *one's daughter-in-law;* AT kinahakaniskwem [kinahākaniskwēm], *your daughter-in-law;* SEC cinahākaniskwem, *your daughter-in-law;* EI (Sheshatshiu) unakanishkuema [unākəniʃkwēma], *one's daughter-in-law;* Laure (ca. 1726) "uhuhaganiskuema [*sic*], *sa bru*" | ANISH na'aanganikwe, *a daughter-in-law* (Livesay & Nichols, 2021) see | *nahāhk

*nahāw

INITIAL

— orderly

evidence | PC nahāwēkinam, *to fold sth neatly;* MC nahāwaštāsow, *to tidy up;* EI (Mamit) naunamᵘ [nāwnam], *to put things in order* | Silvy (ca. 1680) "naha8au; naha8an, *cela est aisé, facile; voilà bien de quoi*"

*nak

INITIAL

— stop, prevent from proceeding

evidence | PC nakipayiw, *to stop driving, to stop working, to stop suddenly;* WC nakiskawīw, *to meet sb;* MC nakipiponew, *to be stopped by the winter;* SEC nacimew, *to stop sb with one's voice;* Fabvre (ca. 1690) "nit Achenakinau, *ie rep8sse celuy qui veut entrer*" | ANISH nagishkaage, *to meet people* (Livesay & Nichols, 2021) compare | *nakā

*nakarā (~ *nakaram)

INITIAL

— habituated, used to

evidence | PC nakayāskam, *to be accustomed to sth;* AT nakarawiw [nakarāwīw], *to be used to;* SEC nakayāwīw, *to have a habit of, to be used to;* nakayamihtāw, *to be used to sth;* WI (Pessamit) nakalamieu [nəkələmjēw], *to be used to sb;* nakalatueu [nəkəlātwēw], *to be used to hearing sb;* Laure (ca. 1726) "nema nagara ni-uabamau, *je n'en ai point avec cet homme;*" "ni-nagara-mihau 3. miheu, nagara-mihigu, *je m'accoutume à lui;*" Silvy (ca. 1680) "nagara, *in compositione, accoutumance*" discussion | The Moose Cree and Eastern Swampy Cree equivalent *nakat-* is in fact a loan from the neighbouring Anishinabe dialect.

*nakā

INITIAL

— stop, prevent from proceeding

evidence | PC nakāham, *to stop sth;* MC nakānew, *to stop sth manually;* WI (Pessamit) nakapalu [nəkāpəlu], *to come to a standstill, to stop;* Silvy (ca. 1680) "ni naganau, *je l'arrête*" | ANISH nagaashkaa, *to stop moving* (Livesay & Nichols, 2021) compare | *nak

*nakē¹

INITIAL

— leave behind

evidence | PC nakacipahēw, *to leave sb behind as one runs away;* MC nakatam, *to leave sth behind;* SEC cicī nakašin, *you left me behind;* Laure (ca. 1726) "ni-nakatahunan, *nous nous entre-quittons (par eau);*" Silvy (ca. 1680) "ni nagat8gan 3. -ge8, *je quitte ma cabane, ma maison*" | ANISH nagadan, *to leave sth behind* (Livesay & Nichols, 2021) limited to | *t⁵, *t⁶ discussion | Derivations beyond the basic VTA and VTI forms are built onto the VTI stem ***nakat**.

*nakē²

INITIAL

— slope, slant

evidence | MC nakeyāw, *to slope;* nakeyāštan, *to accumulate to one side from the wind, such as sand;* WI (Pessamit) natsheiau [ntʃējāw], *to be crosswise;* EI (Mamit) natshe [natshe], *crosswise*

*nakiskaw

INITIAL

— a little while

evidence | ESC nakiskaw, *a little while;* MC nakiskaw, *a little while, a short period;* Silvy (ca. 1680) "natiska8ich, natchiska8ich, *bientôt*" | ANISH Cuoq (1886) "Nakikawis,i, *être de peu de valeur;*" Nicholas (ca. 1670) "nakika, *pour un peu de temps*" (Daviault, 1994)

*nakwē

INITIAL

— snare

evidence | PC nakwāsiwēw, *to snare animals;* MC nakwātamāw, *to catch game in a snare;* SEC nakwātahoyew, *to catch sth with a snare tied at the end of a stick;* Laure (ca. 1726) "ni-nakuasun, *je tombe dans le piège;*" Fabvre (ca. 1690) "nak8āgan *pl.* găna, *colets, lacets, piege;*" Silvy (ca. 1680) "ni nag8atau, *je l'ai pris au collet*" limited to | *kē¹, *so¹, *t³, *t⁴, *tē² see | *akwē

*nam¹

INITIAL

— tremble, quiver

evidence | PC namipayiw, *to shake;* MC nanamaciw, *to shiver from the cold;* SEC nanamitāmihkanewaciw, *to chatter from the cold;* Silvy (ca. 1680) "ni nanaman8ebarin, *la joue me frémit*"

*nam²

INITIAL

— no

evidence | PC mōya, namōya, nama, *no, not;* namayēw, *to not occur in time;* MC mōla, namōla, namawīla, *no;* matakwan, *to be none;* SEC nama, *no;* NEC nimiyāu, *to not be;* WI & EI mauat [māwāt], *no;* Silvy (ca. 1680) "nama, *non;*" "namaïau, *ce n'est pas cela*"

*namaht (~ *namahc)

INITIAL

— left

evidence | PC namahcīwin, *left-handedness;* WC namāhcīw, *to be left-handed;* MC namahtiniskīhk, *to the left;* SEC namahcīw, *to be left-handed* | ANISH namanjii, *to be left-handed* (Livesay & Nichols, 2021)

*namē

INITIAL

— to leave traces of one's presence

evidence | PC namēhēw, *to find traces of sb's presence;* WC namīhīw, *to find traces of sb's presence;* MC namehcikew, *to leave bite marks;* SEC namehtāw, *to leave traces of one's presence* | ANISH nametoo, *to leave signs of one's presence* (Livesay & Nichols, 2021)

*namēhs

INITIAL (NOUN, ANIMATE)

— fish

evidence | ESC names, *a fish;* MC namesakan, *to smell like fish;* AT namess, *fish* (Béland, 1978); SEC names, *a fish;* EI (Sheshatshiu) nameshapui [nəmēʃāpwī], *fish broth;* Silvy (ca. 1680) "names *pl.* namesak, *poisson*" origin | PA ***namēʔsa** (Aubin, 1975; Hewson, 1993) see | *amēhs

*namēkohs

INITIAL (NOUN, ANIMATE)

— lake trout

evidence | PC namēkos, *a lake trout;* ESC namekos, *a lake trout;* AT (Opitciwan, Nadia Awashish) namekosa [namēkossa], *a lake trout;* SEC namekos, *a lake trout;* Laure (ca. 1726) "nameguch, *truite, grosse truite (il y en a aux Mistassins)*" | ANISH namegosikaa, *to be many lake trout* (Livesay & Nichols, 2021) origin | PA ***namēkwehsa** (Hewson, 1993) see | *amēkohs, *amēkw

*namēpir

INITIAL (NOUN, ANIMATE)

— sucker

evidence | PC namēpiy, *a sucker;* MC namepiliskāw, *to be many suckers;* SEC namepiy, *a sucker;* WI (Pessamit) namepil [nəmēpəl], *white sucker;* Silvy (ca. 1680) "namepira, *carpe*" | ANISH namebin, *a sucker* (Livesay & Nichols, 2021) origin | PA ***namēpira** (***name:pila**, Aubin, 1975)

*namēw

INITIAL (NOUN, ANIMATE)

— sturgeon

evidence | PC namēw, *a sturgeon;* MC namewāpew, *to set a night-line for sturgeon;* SEC (Waswanipi) namewahāw, *to set a net for sturgeon;* Silvy (ca. 1680) "nameȣ, *gros esturgeon*" | ANISH name, *a sturgeon* (Livesay & Nichols, 2021) origin | PA ***namēwa** (Aubin, 1975; Hewson, 1993)

*nanāhkaw

INITIAL

— various

evidence | ESC nanāhkawinākosiw, *to have various appearances;* MC nanāhkawasināsow, *to be marked with various colors;* SEC nanāhkawinākwan, *to looks variegated;* NEC nanāhkiu, *various, different;* Laure (ca. 1726) "ni-nanakauitan, *diversifier, je diversifie, je varie mes couleurs*" discussion | The above reconstruction is suggestive of reduplication, but evidence of the presumed nonreduplicated form ***nahkaw** has yet to be identified.

*nanāništ (~ *nanānihš)

INITIAL

— in various places or directions

evidence | PC nanānis, *in various places or directions;* WC nanānistinam, *to separate things;* NEC ninānish, *in all directions, all apart;* ninānishtinim, *to take sth apart;* ninānishipiyiu, *to break and scatter in all directions;* Silvy (ca. 1680) "nananich, *en divers endroits, deçà et delà*"

*nanēhkāt (~ *nanēhkāc, *nanēhkās)

INITIAL

— suffer, torment

evidence | PC Lacombe (1874) "Nanekkātisiw, *il est languissant, souffrant;*" MC nanehkātahpinew, *to be anguished from* *pain;* AT nekatewotam [nēhkātēwotam], *to moan from pain;* nanehkāsihtākosiw, *to sound wretched;* SEC nanehkācihew, *to torment sb;* WI (Pessamit) nekatikushu [nēkātəkuʃu], *to suffer from insomnia;* Silvy (ca. 1680) "ni nanekaterimau, *je suis fâché de le voir souffrir*" discussion | The above reconstruction is suggestive of reduplication, but evidence of the presumed non-reduplicated form ***nihkāt** has yet to be identified.

*naniht (~ *nanihc)

INITIAL

— dread

evidence | ESC nanihcīstawew, *to dread sb;* MC nanihcīštawew, *to dread sb;* nanihtelimew, *to be apprehensive about sb;* AT nitcictam [nihcīštam], *to have a bad feeling about a danger;* SEC nanihcīw, *to dread* origin | Possibly a reduplicated form.

*nanīsān

INITIAL

— dangerous, perilous

evidence | PC nanīsānan, *to be difficult;* ESC (Severn) nanīsānenihtākwan, *to appear dangerous;* MC nanīsānihew, *to endanger sb;* Watkins (1865) "Nunesanisew, *v.i.1. He is in danger*" | ANISH naniizaanizi, *to be dangerous;* MENO ni·sa·nat, *to be dangerous* discussion | The above reconstruction is suggestive of reduplication, but evidence of the presumed nonreduplicated form ***nīsān** has yet to be identified in CINA.

*napak

INITIAL

— flat

evidence | PC napakihtakāw, *to be a flat floor;* MC napakāw, *to be flat;* SEC napacisiw, *to be flat* origin | PA ***napak** (Hewson, 1993)

*napatē

INITIAL

— one only (when speaking of a pair), only one side

evidence | PC napatēkātēw, *to have only one leg as opposed to two;* MC napatecāpiw, *to only have one eye;* SEC napatemew, *to eat one half of sth;* Laure (ca. 1726) "ni-napatékategabauin, *je me tiens sur un pied*" | ANISH nabanekizine, *to only have one shoe on* (Livesay & Nichols, 2021) origin | PA ***napaθē**

*napāt (~ *napāc, *napās)

INITIAL

— mediocre, so-so

evidence | PC napācihtāw, *to repair sth;* WC nānapācihtāw, *to clean sth up;* MC nānapāc, *so-so, mediocrely;* SEC napāc, *so-so, mediocrely*

*napo (~ *napw)

INITIAL

— double, pair, join together as a pair

evidence | PC nānaponam, *to fold two of sth together;* WC naposinwak, *to lie together;* napotokanīw, *to be knock-kneed;* MC napoštaham, *to stitch or pin sth folded over on itself;* napokātepiw, *to sit with one's legs together;* SEC napokātehpitew, *to catch sb by both legs in a snare;* NEC nipwāchinim, *to fold sth sheet-like;* WI (Uashat) napuetshinashu [nəpwētnāʃu], *to fold clothes;* Laure (ca. 1726) "ni-napuchitéuatsin, *les deux pieds gelés*" | ANISH nabobizo, *to drive making a return trip;* nabogaadeshkoozo, *to be caught with one's legs doubled up* (Livesay & Nichols, 2021)

*narim

INITIAL

— against the wind, upwind

evidence | PC nayimohtēw, *walk against the wind;* MC lalimikāpawiw, *stand facing the wind;* SEC nayimakocin, *to fly against the* *wind;* WI (Pessamit) lalimaim [ləlǝmīm], *to paddle against the wind* compare | *nāmiwan

*naskawē

INITIAL

— along the way

evidence | PC naskwēnam, *to pick sth up along the way;* MC naskawēhkwāmiw, *to doze off along the way;* WI (Pessamit) nashkueshinu [nəʃkwēʃənu], *to brush lightly against sth as one falls;* Fabvre (ca. 1690) "Naska8etahau, *pr(en)dre qlqn. en chemin par terre*" | ANISH Nicholas (ca. 1670) "nakaoué, *en passant*" (Daviault, 1994)

*nasko[1] (~ *naskw)

INITIAL

— respond

evidence | PC naskwaham, *to respond in song;* WC naskwāstāmāsow, *to fight for one's rights;* MC naskōštawew, *to resist sb;* SEC naskowehamawew, *to respond in song;* nanāskomēw, *to thank sb;* Fabvre (ca. 1690) "Nask8m8n 8, *accorder, dire ouy, c(on)s(en)tir*" | ANISH nanaakwii, *to fight back or defend* (Livesay & Nichols, 2021); MENO nana·hkomewɛ·w, *to talk back, to retort*

*nasko[2] (~ *naskw)

INITIAL

— be covered by

evidence | MC naskotin, *to be coated with a thin layer of ice; to be a silver thaw;* NEC niskuchū, *to be iced up* (CSB, 2018) | ANISH nakwadin, *to be frozen or frosted from frozen breath* (Livesay & Nichols, 2021); MENO nahkuahkonɛw, *to catch fire* limited to | *aci, *atin[2]

*nasp

INITIAL

— similar, alike

evidence | PC naspasinaham, *to reproduce sth in writing; to draw sth;* SEC iši-naspi-wīhyew, *to surnames sb thus;* Watkins (1865) "Nuspimoo, *v.i.4. He answers;*" Laure (ca. 1726) "ni-naspimau, *je le remercie de paroles;*" Silvy (ca. 1680) "ni naspinikass8n, *je tire mon nom de, etc.*" see | *naspit, *naspitaw

*naspāt (~ *naspāc, *naspās)

INITIAL

— wrong

evidence | PC naspātinēw, *to hold sb the wrong way;* MC nanāspātaskisinew, *to have one's shoes on the wrong feet;* SEC naspācinākwan, *to look wrong or false;* Watkins (1865) "Nuspasinakwun, *v.imp. It looks wrong;*" Silvy (ca. 1680) "ni naspatchin, *je suis gaucher*" | ANISH napaajigaabawi, *to stand the wrong way* (Livesay & Nichols, 2021)

*naspit (~ *naspic)

INITIAL (VERB, TRANSITIVE, INANIMATE)

— resemble

evidence | PC naspitam, *to resemble sth;* MC naspitam, *to resemble sth;* SEC naspitam, *to resemble sth;* Fabvre (ca. 1690) "Naspitinikas8n 8, *tirer son nom d'une ch(os)e;*" Silvy (ca. 1680) "ni naspiten, *j'imite*" see | *nasp paired with | *naspitaw

*naspitaw (~ *naspito)

INITIAL (VERB, TRANSITIVE, ANIMATE)

— resemble

evidence | PC naspitawew, *to resemble sb;* naspitohtawēw, *to imitate sb vocally;* MC naspitātowak, *to resemble one another;* naspitohtam, *to imitate sth vocally;* NEC nispitiwāu, *to resemble sb;* WI (Pessamit) nashpitueu [nəʃpətwēw], *to resemble sb;* Silvy (ca. 1680) "ni nanaspit8ta8au, *je répète ce qu'il a dit, sérieusement ou en riant, en me moquant*" see | *nasp, *naspit, *aw[3] paired with | *naspit discussion | The allomorph ***naspito** is limited to lexical derivations.

*nat[1]

INITIAL

— upriver

evidence | PC natimihk, *upriver;* MC nataham, *to paddle upstream;* SEC natahipahtāw, *to run upriver;* Silvy (ca. 1680) "natimitch, *amont, en haut de la rivière*"

*nat[2] (~ *naš)

FINAL (VERB, TRANSITIVE, ANIMATE, CONCRETE)

— harm, kill

evidence | PC paspinatēw, *to nearly kill sb;* MC paspinatew, *to nearly kill sb;* Laure (ca. 1726) "ni-tchiminatau *je tue en cachette, id est, je trame sa mort en secret;*" Silvy (ca. 1680) "ni nitaȣinatagan 3. -eȣ, *je suis heureux chasseur*" | ANISH onjinazh, *to injure or kill sb for a certain reason* origin | PA ***naθ** (Aubin, 1975) see | *nē[3], *t[5] compare | *ahpinat, *pinat

*natamā

INITIAL

— in spite of, notwithstanding, nevertheless

evidence | MC natamā, *used to express a hope or desire, would that, I wish;* Laure (ca. 1726) "natama, *nonobstant, néanmoins;*" Silvy (ca. 1680) "natama, *cela n'est rien;*" "nata, natama, *en riant, sans dessein*" | Nicholas (ca. 1670) "narama, *néanmoins, mais, parce que* (Daviault, 1994) origin | PA ***naθamā** compare | *nataw

*nataw

INITIAL

— any, aught

evidence | PC nānitaw, *something; somewhere; anyhow;* Lacombe (1874) "pikonata, *(adv.) sans dessein, sans raison, gratis;*" MC nāntaw, *approximately;* pakwantaw, *any; anywhere; trivially, vainly; wrongly, inappropriately;* SEC natamik^{w}, *any; anywhere;* SEC (Eastmain) nāntaw, *maybe;* EI (Ekuanitshit) nantu [nāntaw], *approximately;* Watkins (1865) "n'tumik, *adv. without cause;*" "nantow, *adv. about, nearly, thereabout.* Nantow kākwi, *aught, any thing.* Nantow isse, *by any means.* Nantow ita, *somewhere;*" Silvy (ca. 1680) "nataȣich, *quelque chose;*" "nata, natama, *en riant, sans dessein*" | ANISH nanawizi, *to get nothing in the hunt, to be disappointed in hunting or gathering* (Livesay & Nichols, 2021); Nicholas (ca. 1670) "nara, *en vain, sans dessain, rien; parce que; voilà bien*" (Daviault, 1994) origin | PA ***naθaw** compare | *natamā

*nato (~ *nataw)

INITIAL

— desire or seek (the presence, possession, or fulfillment of)

evidence | PC nitawaskēw, *to explore for land;* Lacombe (1874) "N'tawi, N'taw, N'ta, *racine, ou plutôt préposition qui devrait s'écrire natawi, mais que j'écris n'tawi, parce que le premier a n'est pas sensible, c'est un auxiliaire qui signifie: aller vers;*" ESC natawāpahtam, *to go see sth;*" MC nānatawišipew, *to hunt ducks;* SEC nataweyihtam, *to want or need sth;* NEC nānitunim, *to feel around for sth;* Watkins (1865) "Nutoomāo, *v.t.an. He bids him, he invites him, he calls him, he sends for him;*" WI (Pessamit) nanatuakueu [nāntwākwēw], *to look for porcupine;* Laure (ca. 1726) "ni-nanatunen, *je tâte sans voir;*" Silvy (ca. 1680) "ni nataȣastikȣan, *je vais au loup-marin*" | ANISH nandawasimwe, *to look for horses* (Livesay & Nichols, 2021); MENO nata·wɛ·nemɛw, *to desire sb;* MIAMI natawaapam-, *to look for sb* (ILDA, 2017) origin | PA ***nato, *natw, *nataw** (Hewson, 1993) compare | *kato, *natohko

*natohko (~ *natohkw)

INITIAL (NOUN, INANIMATE)

— **1** thing, something

— **2** treat with something medical

— **3** when reduplicated, variety of things, variety, various

— **4** when reduplicated, do various things, tease

evidence | [1]Silvy (ca. 1680) "nat8k8ch, *hardes, meubles, marchandises, etc.*" [2]ESC natohkonon, *medicine; doctor;* MC natohkoliy, *medicine;* AT natokohew [natohkohēw], *traiter, soigner, guérir quelqu'un;* SEC natohkohew, *to treat sb with medicine;* EI (Sheshatshiu) natukuitishu [ntūkwītīʃu], *to cure or heal oneself;* Isham (1743) "en to ko thi, *a surgeon;*" Laure (ca. 1726) "natukurun, *drogue, médecine;*" Fabvre (ca. 1690) "nat8k8tan tau, *pancer ulcere, y appliq(ue)r remede;*" Silvy (ca. 1680) "nat8k8r8nab8i, *médecine, potion*" [3]PC nanātohkonākwan, *to be a variety of colors or appearances;* WC nanātohk, *various, several kinds;* MC nanātohkʷ, *various, variously;* Laure (ca. 1726) "ka narauatgsi nanatukucha, *biens dissipés;*" Silvy (ca. 1680) "nanat8k8rini8, *gueux, demandeur*" [4]PC nanātohkomēw, *to tease sb;* MC nanātohkosīw, *to tease;* SEC nanātohkohew, *to tease sb* compare | *nato

*naw[1]

INITIAL

— pursue

evidence | PC nawahwew, *to chase sb by canoe;* MC nawahāmew, *to follow a path;* SEC nawimōswew, *to pursue a moose;* EI (Mamit) nuaishipeu [nawējhipēw], *to pursue ducks by boat;* Silvy (ca. 1680) "ni na8achtim8an, *je cours après les chiens*"

*naw[2] (~ *nā)

FINAL (VERB, TRANSITIVE, ANIMATE, CONCRETE)

— see

evidence | PC māyinawēw, *to find sb ugly;* WC kitimākinākīw, *to be compassionate;* MC lāwinākwan, *to be far;* nisitawinawew, *to recognize sb;* SEC miyonawew, *to find sb good-looking;* Silvy (ca. 1680) "ni maskassina8au, *j'admire son courage*" see | *n[2], *aw[3] paired with | *n[2]

*nawahšō (~ *nawahšaw)

INITIAL

— the best, choose the best

evidence | PC nawasawāpahtam, *to choose sth by sight;* WC nawasō, *the best in anything;* MC nawasōnam, *to choose sth;* WI (Pessamit) naushushkamᵘ [nāwʃūʃkəm], *to be careful about where one sets one's foot down;* Fabvre (ca. 1690) "Na8ach8nen *v.* nan8ach8nen, *n.* nau, *choisir q(ue)lq(ue) ch(os)e;*" Silvy (ca. 1680) "ni na8acha8eriten, *je le choisis*" | ANISH Cuoq (1886) "Ni nawanjojwa piciki, *je coupe le meilleur morceau du buffle;*" MIAMI "Na8ancha8itehe8a, *bien né, brave, genereux, sage, modeste*" (Largillier - ILDA, 2017) discussion | In the absence of an Atikamekw cognate, the preaspirate in this reconstruction is indirectly supported by Anishinabe and Miami-Illinois.

*nawak

INITIAL

— bend forward

evidence | PC nawakiskwēnēw, *to bend down sb's head by hand;* MC nawakīštawew, *to bow to sb or to worship sb;* WI (Pessamit) nutshikapau [nūtʃəkāpū], *to lean forward;* Laure (ca. 1726) "ni-nauakapin, *je me courbe étant assis;*" Silvy (ca. 1680) "ni na8atchinau, *je le penche, le courbe, l'abaisse*" | ANISH nawagikwebi, *to sit with one's head down* (Livesay & Nichols, 2021) compare | *nawē

*nawat (~ *nawac, *nawas)

INITIAL

— **1** along the way (before reaching the destination)

— **2** to a great extent (but not fully) (e.g., rather, quite, fairly, etc.)

evidence | PC nawatinam, *to catch sth in mid-air;* nawac, *somewhat, more;* WC nawac, *rather;* MC nawatinam, *to catch sth manually as it goes by;* nawaciw, *to stop for a meal;* nawac, *rather, quite, more;* SEC (Waswanipi) nawacipitam, *to grab it as it goes by;* nawac, *very;* NEC niwitiham, *to hit sth as it goes by;* WI (Pessamit) nutameu [nūtəmēw], *to catch sb with one's jaws as they fly or move;* Laure (ca. 1726) "nauatch, *en chemin;*" Fabvre (ca. 1690) "ni naȣatchin, *m(an)ger v.g. desieuner p(ou)r uoyage;*" Silvy (ca. 1680) "ni naȣaspȣrau, *je lui donne des vivre pour le voyage;*" "ni naȣatisȣn, *je fait chaudière en chemin;*" "naȣatch, *en chemin*" | ANISH nawajibidoon, *grab or seize sth;* nawajii, *to eat a light meal or lunch;* nawaj, *more* (Livesay & Nichols, 2021); MENO nawa·tenam, *to pick sth up on the way or preliminary to other action;* nawa·sa·pahtam, *to look at sth before going or acting;* naw·c, *beforehand, before other action, first*

*nawē

INITIAL

— stoop, hunch, bend over

evidence | MC naweskweliw, *to bend one's neck forward;* SEC nawepiw, *to sit stooped forward;* EI (Unaman-shipit) nawekapau [nawēkāpaw], *to stand leaning* | ANISH nawetaa, *to bend over* (Livesay & Nichols, 2021) compare | *nawak

*nay

INITIAL (VERB, TRANSITIVE, ANIMATE)

— carry on one's back

evidence | PC nayēw, *to pack sb on one's back;* WC nayāhtam, *to pack sth on one's back;* MC nayahcikan, *a burden;* Fabvre (ca. 1690) "ki Nain 2 naïtin, *tu me porte(s) Ie te porte ainsy*" | MENO naya·hɛw TA, *to take or carry sb on one's back;* nena·yahok

*nayēhtāw

INITIAL

— vexatious

evidence | PC nayēhtāwisiw, *to be hard to get along with;* WC nayīhtāwan, *to be difficult;* MC nayehtāwelihtākwan, *to be vexatious*

*nayēwat (~ *nayēwac)

INITIAL

— part way, at some distance (on the ground or in the air)

evidence | PC nayēwacimow, *to speak along the way;* Lacombe (1874) "nayewatch, *(adv.) entre, dans l'espace, v.g.* nayewatch pimiyaw, *il voles dans les airs,* nayewatch akotchin pisim, *le soleil des suspendu dans l'espace,* nayewatch nakatam, *il laisse cela à une certain distance;*" WC nayīwac, *part way;* NEC niyāutāuhch, *halfway up a mountain;* Watkins (1865) "Nayāwuch, *Afloat, floating in the air*"

*nā

INITIAL

— **1** fetch

— **2** go to

evidence | PC nātam, *to approach sth; to fetch sth;* WC nātam, *to go get sth;* SEC nātew, *to fetch sb* limited to | *t³, *t⁴ see | *nāt

*nāhtē

INITIAL

— heat haze

evidence | PC nānāhtēw, *to be a mirage, to be dazzling sunlight;* MC nānāhtepaliw, *to be a heat haze;* AT (Opitciwan, Joey Awashish) nanatewiparin [nānāhtēwiparin], *to be a heat haze;* SEC nanāhtepayū, *to be heat waves rising off the snow or ice in the spring* (CSB, 2018) see | tē⁴

*nākat (~ *nākac, *nākas, *nākataw)

INITIAL

— observe, watch

evidence | PC nākacihtāw, *to look after sth; to observe sth;* WC nānākasīhtam, *to listen closely to what is said;* MC nākatawāpamew, *to observe sb;* SEC nānākacihew, *to watch sb or watch for sb;* WI (Pessamit) nakatuelimeu [nākətwēləmēw], *to watch or pay attention to sb*

*nākē

INITIAL

— in a while, later

evidence | PC nākē, *later on;* MC nākē, *later;* SEC nāce, *later;* EI (Sheshatshiu) natshe [nātʃē], *later* | ANISH naage, *later, after a while, eventually; further* (Livesay & Nichols, 2021)

*nāko (~ *nākw)

PREFINAL

— appear, look

evidence | PC oskinākwan, *to look new;* MC išinākosiw, *to look thus;* SEC miyonākohtāw, *to make sth look nice;* Silvy (ca. 1680) "ni 8itchinag8simau, *je lui ressemble*" see | *naw², *ɩko

*nām

INITIAL

— move up and down, bob

evidence | PC Lacombe (1874) "Nāmiw, ok, *(v.n.) il se balance, il se dodine;*" WC nāmiskwīstawīw, *to nod one's head to sb;* MC nānāmiskwešimow, *to bob one's head while dancing;* SEC nāmiskweyiw, *to nod one's head;* WI (Pessamit) nanamipalu [nānāmpəlu], *to make a springlike movement*

*nāmiwan

INITIAL

— with the wind, downwind

evidence | PC nāmiwanāw, *to be a wind from the rear;* MC nāmowaniškāw, *to walk leeward;* Watkins (1865) "Namoowunasew, *v.i.1., He goes with the wind (on the water);*" Laure (ca. 1726) "ni-namiuanachin, *j'ai du vent arrière*" | MENO na·miah, *with the wind, on the side towards which the wind is blowing* compare | *narim

*nāpē

INITIAL

— male

evidence | MC nāpelew, *a male grouse;* SEC nāpešip, *a drake;* Laure (ca. 1726) "napechtimu, *chien mâle;*" Fabvre (ca. 1690), "Nape8chan, e8, *acc8cher d'un garçon;*" Silvy (ca. 1680) "napesk8, *ours mâle*" see | *nāpēw¹

*nāpēw¹

INITIAL (NOUN, ANIMATE)

— man

evidence | PC nāpēw, *a man;* nāpēwakēyimow, *to think of oneself as a man;* MC nāpewapiw, *to sit like a man;* SEC nāpewihow, *to be dressed like a man;* Fabvre (ca. 1690) "Nape8 *pl.* 8ek, *masles, ho(mm)es, viri;*" Silvy (ca. 1680) "ni nape8in, *je suis garçon*" see | *nāpē, *w¹, *nāpēw², *āpēw

*nāpēw²

MEDIAL, FINAL (NOUN INCORPORATION)

— man (typically in the context of interaction with a woman), male sexual or romantic partner

evidence | MC oškināpewew, *to have a new husband;* mištikonāpew, *a carpenter;* SEC wīhcināpewew, *to be fond of men;* EI mininapeueu [minīnāpēwēw], *to give sth to drink to a man;* Laure (ca. 1726) "ka missetunapeuet, *prostituée, qui a plusieurs maris*" see | *nāpēw¹ compare | *āpēw

*nāraw

INITIAL

— ruin

evidence | SEC (inland) nāyawihtāw, *to ruin sth;* WI (Pessamit) laluapaueu [lālūwāpwēwēw], *to be spoiled from being wet;* EI nanuapaueu [nanwāpāwēw], *to be spoiled from being wet;* Lemoine (1901) "nalutan -tau, *to damage;*" Watkins (1865) "Yayoohoo, *v.i.4. He perished;*" Laure (ca. 1726) "narauaskamitchitau, *l'ennemi ravage la terre;*" Fabvre (ca. 1690) "Nara8ihau, *gaster une chose noble*"

*nāspit (~ *nāspic)

INITIAL

— **1** definitively, for good

— **2** to lose consciousness for good, never come to, die

evidence | PC nāspic, *for good, forever;* nāspitahwēw, *to club sb to death;* MC nāspic, *very;* nāspitāpicīw, *to be gone for good;* nāspicišin, *to die in a collision;* SEC nāspitanihow, *to be gone and not return as expected;* nāspitawahtān, *to rain incessantly;* nāspitihkwāmiw, *to sleep and never wake up, to die in one's sleep;* EI (Sheshatshiu) nashpit [nāʃpɨt], *for good, irremediably, irreparably;* Silvy (ca. 1680) "ni naspitchichiman, *je m'embarque pour ne pas revenir*"

*nāšit (~ *nāšic)

INITIAL

— to a great degree, very

evidence | PC nāsic, *very much;* MC nāšic, *very;* SEC nāšc, *very;* WI (Pessamit) nasht [nāss], *quite, really;* EI (Mamit) nasht [nāht], *quite, really* limited to | *i³ discussion | The absence of a preaspiration on the sibilant cannot be confirmed due to the lack of an Atikamekw cognate.

*nāt (~ *nāc, *nās)

INITIAL

— **1** fetch

— **2** go to

evidence | PC nātakohpēw, *to fetch a blanket(s);* MC nācipew, *to fetch a drink of alcohol;* AT (Wemotaci, Jeannette Coocoo) nasiperew [nāzipērēw], *to fly to the shore from land;* SEC nātahwew, *to pick sb up by vehicle;* nāspinatew, *to chase sb;* EI (Sheshatshiu) natakamipiteu [nātəkāmpɨtēw], *to pull sb towards the shore (from the water);* Silvy (ca. 1680) "ni nassibe8tan 3. -e8, *je vais vers l'eau, v.g. retournant des terres*" | ANISH naazibiimon, *to lead to the water, speaking of a path* see | *nā, *t⁴

*nātowēw

INITIAL (NOUN, ANIMATE)

— Iroquois

evidence | WC nātowīw, *an Iroquois;* MC nātoweskwew, *an Iroquois woman;* SEC nātowew & nācowew, *Iroquois person; generally, a non-Cree Native American;* NSK naatuwaaw, *an Iroquois, a Mohawk* | ANISH Nicholas (ca. 1670) "nadoué, *ennemi*" (Daviault, 1994)

*nātwā

INITIAL

— break in two

evidence | PC nātwāpayiw, *to break in two;* MC nātwākātešin, *to break one's leg on impact;* SEC nātwākanešin, *to break one's bone in half;* WI (Pessamit) natuapuieu [nātwāpujēw], *to have a paddle broken in two*

*nē¹

INITIAL

— point

evidence | PC nēyāw, *to be a point or cape;* MC nehkopāw, *to be a bushy point;* SEC neyāpiskāw, *rocky point;* Fabvre (ca. 1690) "Neïau, *pointe de terre, ce qui passe, auance*" | ANISH nekobaa, *to be a point of brush* (Livesay & Nichols, 2021)

*nē²

INITIAL

— growl

evidence | PC nēmow, *to growl;* WC nīmow, *to growl;* SEC nemototam, *to growl at sth;* NEC nāmū, *to growl;* WI (Pessamit) nemututueu [nēmuttwēw], *to growl at sb;* Silvy (ca. 1680) "nem8 attim8, *le chien gronde*" limited to | *ımo

*nē³

FINAL (VERB, ANIMATE, INTRANSITIVE, CONCRETE)

— suffer pain

evidence | PC tēpinēham, *to have enough money for sth;* Lacombe (1874) "SIPINEW, ok, *(a. a.) il est fort contre le mal, il résiste à la maladie, il la supporte courageusement;*" MC mawinehwew, *to go after sb with the intention of harming;* šīpinew, *resistent to pain;* SEC šewinew, *to have a low tolerance for pain;* Laure (ca. 1726) "ni-tchiripinan 3. -neu, *je meurs soudainement*" | ANISH amajine, *awakened by pain* (Livesay & Nichols, 2021) compare | *ahpinē, *āspinē, *nēsi, *pinē[2]

*nē[4]

FINAL

— forms aspectual particles

evidence | PC tahkine, *always, forever;* MC tahkine, *continually;* tašine, *incessantly, continuously;* SEC tašine, *constantly, continuously;* WI (Pessamit) aishine [jājʃənē], *taking one's time, in no hurry* compare | *a, *ci, *i[3], *ēr[2]

*nēhiraw

INITIAL

— **1** by oneself, in person

— **2** of or allied to the local people

evidence | PC nēhiyawiskwēw, *a native woman;* nēhiyawipwātak, *Piapot Band, band of mixed Cree and Dakota;* WC nīhiðaw, *a Cree person;* AT nehirowimo, *to speak the native language;* NEC nāhiyiu, *in person;* NSK nāyiyuw, *in person;* WI (Mashteuiatch) nehlueu [nēhlwēw], *to speak the native language;* WI (Pessamit) lelushtau [lēlūstāw], *to write sth in the native language;* Watkins (1865) "Nāeyoweyeyinew, *a Cree Indian;*" Laure (ca. 1726) "nehiro-iriniuets, *Montagnais;*" "nehiro-aitchimeu *pl.* -ets, *mikmaks incorporés parmi les Montagnais;*" Fabvre (ca. 1690) "Neïraȣikȣetatchiȣ, *Hurons;*" Silvy (ca. 1680) "ni nehiraȣan, *je parle montagnais*" | ABEN nihlōji, *by self* (Day, 1994); ANISH Cuoq (1886) "Niina natowek, *les Hurons, c-à-d. les Iroquois neutres, qui sont nous, avec nous, pour nous, qui sont nos allies;*" André (ca. 1690) "nihiraoue, *il parle la langue de sa nation*" origin | PA ***nyēhiraw**

*nēhpēm

INITIAL

— in plain view, at the ready

evidence | PC nēhpēmapiw, *to sit at the ready;* WC nīhpīmīw, *to stand ready;* MC nehpemaštew, *it sits in plain sight, at the ready;* WI (Pessamit) nepemakutau [nēpēməkutāw], *to hang it within hand's reach*

*nēhsitām

INITIAL

— awkward

evidence | WSC (Misipawistik, Ellen Cook) nēsitāmipaniw, *to turn out awkwardly, to come out wrong;* MC nesitāmotakāw, *to be an awkward canoe to manœuvre;* AT (Opitciwan, Joey Awashish) nesitāmatatam [nēssitāmatāhtam], *to breathe awkwardly;* SEC neshtāmipayū, *to be a serious disturbance at the meeting or party* (CSB, 2018); WI (Pessamit) nashtaminakushu [nəstāmənākuʃu], *to appear vexed, spiteful, bitter;* Laure (ca. 1726) "ni-nassitamichinin, *je me couche mal à mon aise;*" Fabvre (ca. 1690) "Nassitaminen, *au(oi)r peine à marcher par chemin facheux;*" Silvy (ca. 1680) "ni nassitamatemau, *je tiens mal le calumet à la bouche*" | ANISH Nicholas (ca. 1670) "nassitamissé, *incommodément*" (Daviault, 1994); Cuoq (1886) "Nesitamenindam, *être affligé, être dans la peine*" compare | *wašištaw discussion | The above reconstruction is favored over the alternative ***nahsitām** as the latter appears to be a regional innovation limited to Western Innu and the dialects historically spoken in the Saguenay region.

*nēsi

FINAL (VERB, ANIMATE, INTRANSITIVE, CONCRETE)

— suffer from pain or sickness

evidence | MC cīhcīšinesiw, *to experience an intermittent stabbing pain;* neštonesiw, *to be wearied by sickness or pain;* AT (Opitciwan, Nadia Awashish) niponesiw [niponēziw], *to be paralysed;* SEC āyiyikānesiw, *to suffer from an infection;* WI (Pessamit) ailikaneshu [jājləkānēʃu], *to have an infected or inflamed wound;* Laure (ca. 1726) "tchiskuenesiu, *il est fou de maladie;*" "ni-tchichiuinésin, *je le suis dans ma maladie;*" Fabvre (ca. 1690) "Aïats iriganēsin i8, *deuenir plus mal, desesperé*" compare | *nē³

*nēšto (~ *nēštw)

INITIAL

— exhaust, fatigue

evidence | PC nēstohtēw, *to be tired from walking;* Lacombe (1874) "Nestusiw, *il est fatigué, accablé;*" MC neštwelimow, *to be wearied by an emotion or thought;* SEC neštwāmīw, *to be weak after spawning, speaking of a fish;* WI (Pessamit) neshtumu [nēstəmu], *to be exhausted from talking or crying;* Laure (ca. 1726) "ni-nechtutaten, *j'en suis hors d'haleine*"

*nēw

INITIAL

— four

evidence | PC nēwo, *four;* MC newinwa, *to be four;* Watkins (1865) "Nanāo, *adv. By fours, four apiece;*" Fabvre (ca. 1690) "Ne8, *quatre;*" Silvy (ca. 1680) "ni ne8inan, *nous sommes 4*"

*nihcik

INITIAL

— silhouette

evidence | PC nihcikisiw, *to be a dark outline in the distance;* MC nihcikānaskwan, *to be dark clouds;* NEC nihcikāu, *to be visible as an outline*

*nihk

INITIAL

— hurry

evidence | PC nānihkihtāw, *to hurry sth up;* WC nanīhkisiw, *to be in a hurry;* ESC ninihkipaniw, *to tremble;* MC nanihkaciw, *to shiver;* nanihkelimow, *to be tense or nervous;* NEC ninihcipow, *to eat hastily;* Watkins (1865) "ninìkisew, *v.i.1. He is in haste;*" Laure (ca. 1726) "ni-ninitchimau, *je le dépêche, je le hâte;*" "ni-nitchipun, *dévorer, je dévore, je mange avec avidité;*" Silvy (ca. 1680) "ni nitchit8an 3. -t8au, *je me hâte, je suis pressé*" | MESK nenekesiwa, *to tremble*

*nihkāso

FINAL (VERB, ANIMATE, INTRANSITIVE, CONCRETE)

— be named

evidence | MC ililiwinihkāsow, *to have a Cree name;* AT nehirowinikaso [nēhirowinihkāzow], *avoir un nom amérindien;* SEC miyonihkāsow, *to have a good name;* Laure (ca. 1726) "nit-atchinikasun, *je change de nom*" see | *nihkē, *so¹

*nihkāt¹ (~ *nihkāš)

FINAL (VERB, TRANSITIVE, ANIMATE, CONCRETE)

— name

evidence | MC išinihkātew, *to name sb thus;* AT ariminikatew, *donner un nom difficile à quelqu'un;* SEC miyonihkātew, *to give sb a good name* see | *nihkē, *t³

*nihkāt² (~ *nihkāc)

FINAL (VERB, TRANSITIVE, INANIMATE, CONCRETE)

— name

evidence | MC milonihkātam, *to give sth a nice name;* SEC išinihkātam, *to name sth thus;* Laure (ca. 1726) "nit-ichinikaten 3. -tamu, *appeler, nommer, je l'appelle*" see | *nihkē, *t⁴

*nihkātē

FINAL (VERB, INANIMATE, INTRANSITIVE, CONCRETE)

— be named

evidence | MC išinihkātew, *to be named thus;* SEC miyonihkātew, *to have a good name* see | *nihkē, *tē²

*nihkē

FINAL (VERB, INTRANSITIVE, CONCRETE)

— be named

evidence | Silvy (ca. 1680) "ichinitcheu, *ign. il est nommé*" see | *nihkāso, *nihkāt¹, *nihkāt², *nihkātē

*nihkinākō

INITIAL (VERB, ANIMATE, INTRANSITIVE)

— put on one's moccasins

evidence | AT (Opitciwan, Joey Awashish) ni nikinakon [ni nihkinākōn], *I put on my shoes or moccasins;* SEC nihcinākōw, *to put on one's moccasins;* NEC nihchinākunāu, *to put clothes and shoes on sb;* WI (Pessamit) nitshinakuneu [ntʃənākūnēw], *to put shoes on sb;* EI (Sheshatshiu) nitshinaku [nītnāku], *to put on one's footwear;* Fabvre (ca. 1690) "Nisinăg8an e8, *se uestir, s'aprester à partir;*" "Nitsinag8n 8, *se disposer mettant hardes*" discussion | In the absence of a Woods Cree cognate, the status of the preaspiration cannot be confirmed.

*nihsito (~ *nihsitaw)

INITIAL

— recognize, understand

evidence | PC nisitohtam, *to understand sth;* MC nisitawinawew, *to recognize sb;* AT nissitawin-, *to recognize sth* (Béland, 1978); SEC nisitomahcihtāw, *to recognize the feeling of sth;* Laure (ca. 1726) "ni-nichitumaten 3. -tamu, *je connais par le sentir*" | ANISH nisidawinan, *to recognize sth by sight* (Livesay & Nichols, 2021)

*nihš

INITIAL

— alone

evidence | ESC (Attawapiskat, Angela Sheesheesh), niši-peyakow, *to be alone;* Laure (ca. 1726) "nichichiu, *castor seul dans sa cabane;*" Silvy (ca. 1680) "nichisi8 amisk8, nisisi8 amisk8, *le castor fait une cabane pour lui seul*" | MESK neshi, *alone* compare | *nihšihkēw, *nihšihkato

*nihšihkato (~ *nihšihkataw)

INITIAL

— alone

evidence | PC nisikatanohk, *in an isolated place;* "nisikkatisiw, ok, *(a.a.) il est seul à l'écart, avec sa famille*" (Lacombe, 1874); MC nišihkatowelihtākwan, *to be solitary;* Watkins (1865) "Nisikutoo, *adv. Alone, secretly;*" Fabvre (ca. 1690) "Nichikat8chi8 v. peïk8nachi8, *être seul, seulet*" compare | *nihš, *nihšihkēw

*nihšihkēw

INITIAL

— alone

evidence | MC nišihkewisiw, *to be alone;* AT (Wemotaci, Nicole Petiquay) nicikewisiw [niššihkēwiziw] *to be alone;* Watkins (1865) "Nisikāpew, *v.i.1. He sits alone, he sits solitary, he sits deserted;*" "Nisikāwisew, *v.i.1. He is alone, he is solitary*" | ANISH nishikewiz-i, *to be alone* (McGregor, 2004); nazhikewabi, *to live alone, to be home alone, to sit alone;* nishikewige, *to live alone* (Livesay & Nichols, 2021); MESK "neshihkēwēnemēwa, *to think only of sb*" compare | *nihš, *nihšihkato

*nihšiwanāt (~ *nihšiwanāc, *nihšiwanās)

INITIAL

— spoil, destroy

evidence | PC nisiwanācihtāw, *to ruin or destroy sth;* MC nišiwanātan, *to be spoiled or rotten; to be ruined or destroyed;* AT (Opitciwan, Nadia Awashish) niciwonasinakosiw [niššiwanāzinākoziw], *to look pitiful;* NEC nishiwinātisīu, *to be destroyed* | ANISH nishiwanaadad, *to be spoiled, ruined, destroyed* (Livesay & Nichols, 2021); MENO nɛqswana·ceqtaw, *to make a mess of sth* origin | PA **neʔšiwanāt** (Hewson, 1993) see | *ništ², *wanāt

*nihtāw

INITIAL

— to acquire an expected ability (such as the ability to walk or talk) or to be proficient at

evidence | PC nihtāwikin, *to grow;* MC nihtāwew, *to be able to speak (as a child);* nihtāwikiw, *to grow; to be born;* AT nitawirew [nihtāwirēw], *to be able to fly (as a fledgling);* SEC nihtāwōšew, *to be able to bear children;* nihtāwācimow, *to be proficient at telling stories;* Silvy (ca. 1680) "ni nita8inatagan 3. -e8, *je suis heureux chasseur*" origin | PA ***nehtāw** (Hewson, 1993)

*nikamo

INITIAL (VERB, ANIMATE, INTRANSITIVE)

— sing

evidence | PC nikamow, *to sing;* SEC nikamohew, *to sing about sb;* Silvy (ca. 1680) "nigam8in, *chanson*"

*nikān

INITIAL

— antiquated, old

evidence | SEC (Oujé-Bougoumou, Jean-Pierre Bosum) nikāninākwan, *to look antiquated;* NEC nikānim, *to have old tracks;* WI (Pessamit) nakanamᵘ [nəkānəm], *to be hard to locate due to one's old tracks;* EI (Sheshatshiu) nakanamᵘ [nəkānəm], *to be hard to locate due to one's old tracks;* Watkins (1865) "Nukanum, v.imp. *It is an old track*" | ABEN negōninōgwad, *to look old* (Day, 1995); MIAMI nakaaniwi, *to be old;* nakaanihsen-, *to be an old path* (ILDA, 2017); PASS 'kaney, *sth old, antiquated, archaic* discussion | The cognates identified in Watkins (1865) and three eastern dialects likely represent a contraction or hyper-correction of Old Cree ***nikānınamwa**.

*nikē

FINAL (VERB, ANIMATE, INTRANSITIVE, DERIVED)

— carry on one's shoulder(s)

evidence | MC ohcinikew, *to carry sth or sb on one's shoulder from a certain place;* SEC piminikātaham, *to carry sth along on one's shoulder;* Silvy (ca. 1680) "ni petchinikaten, *je porte sur le dos*" | ANISH onaajinigaadaan, *to go get sth on the shoulder* (Livesay & Nichols, 2021) see | *winikē

*nikikw (~ *nikiko)

INITIAL (NOUN, ANIMATE)

— otter

evidence | PC nikikomina, *a variety of blueberries;* MC nikikošiš, *a baby otter;* SEC nicikʷ, *an otter;* Fabvre (ca. 1690) "nikik8 *pl.* 8ek, nitsik8 *pl.* 8ek, *L8tres, a(nim)al anphibie*" | ABEN onegigw, *otter* (Day, 1995); ANISH nigigwag, *otters* (Livesay & Nichols, 2021) origin | PA ***nekikwa** (Hewson, 1993)

*niko¹ (~ *nikw)

INITIAL

— fetch

evidence | PC nikwatisow, *to fetch meat from the kill site;* AT nikotiso [nikotissō], *to fetch the moose meat from the bush;* MC nikohtew, *to chop firewood;* WI (Pessamit) nikuteu [nəkutēw], *to chop firewood;* Silvy (ca. 1680) "ni nik8tis8n, *je vais quérir l'orignal tué*" | ANISH ningwaniso, *to go get the meat from killed game* (Livesay & Nichols, 2021) discussion | Evidence for this initial is found in all Cree dialects, but only in two words, one for obtaining firewood and another for meat.

*niko² (~ *nikw)

INITIAL

— curl

evidence | MC nanikoweyāškoštowew, *to have a curly moustache;* SEC nanikoweyāhtaciskwew, *to have curly hair;* Fabvre (ca. 1690) "Nig8ekichkau, *cela e(st) froissé v.g. poil de castor;*" Laure (ca. 1726) "ni-nikustiguanikasun, *je me frise;*" Silvy (ca. 1680) "ni nig8stig8aneh8au, *je le frise*"

*nikoto (~ *nikotw)

INITIAL

— one

evidence | PC nikotwāw, *anytime;* WC nikotwāsik, *six;* MC niyānikotanīka, *sometimes;* nikotwās^{w}, *six;* SEC niyānikoton & niyānikotehc, *sometimes;* NEC nikutun, *one of these days;* EI (Unaman-shipit) nanikutini [nānukutnī], *sometimes;* Laure (ca. 1726) "nianikutun, *quelquefois;*" "nikuturiniu, *dix;*" Silvy (ca. 1680) "nig8t, nig8t8, *quelque chose, un;* namanig8t, *rien;*" "nig8t8astisin, *paire de souliers*" | ANISH ningodwaak, *one hundred* (Livesay & Nichols, 2021); MIAMI nkoti aantapita, *one hour* origin | PA ***nekwetwi*** (Hewson, 1993) compare | *pēyako

*nim

INITIAL

— brandish fist

evidence | PC nimaham, *to shake one's fist at sth;* MC nanemahwew, *to shake one's fist at sb;* SEC nimahwew, *to shake one's fist at sb*

*nimit

INITIAL

— rub antlers against trees or brush

evidence | PC nimitaham, *to rub one's antlers against wood;* MC nimitaham, *to rub one's antlers against a tree;* SEC nimitahicewāhtik^{w}, *a tree on which a moose has rubbed its antlers*

*nimitāw (~ *nimitāwē)

INITIAL

— move into an open space and away from the shore, forest, or wall

evidence | PC nimitāsiw, *to walk out onto a lake;* MC nimitāwelāw, *to fly away from the shore;* SEC nimitāwaham, *to paddle away from the shore;* WI (Pessamit) nimitaueiapateu [nəmətāwījāpətēw], *smoke travels towards away from shore;* Laure (ca. 1726) "nimitauiabuteu, *le canot est seul (sans homme)*" | ANISH niminaawa'o, *paddles out from shore* (Livesay & Nichols, 2021) compare | *mōšāw

*ninimiskiw

INITIAL (NOUN, ANIMATE)

— thunderbird

evidence | MC onimiskiw & ominiskiw, *thunderer, thunderbird; a battery; a spark plug;* AT onimiskiskaw [onimiskīskāw], *to thunder;* SEC nimiscīskāw, *to be a thunderstorm;* NEC nimischīuskwāu, *to be thunderclouds;* NSK nimischuuch, *thunder;* WI (Pessamit) nanimissuat [nənəməssūt], *thunder;* EI (Sheshatshiu) nanimissuat [nənimissūt], *thunder;* Watkins (1865) "Oonimiskewuk, *n.an. pl. An imaginary kind of birds [*sic*], supposed to dwell in the clouds. Oonimiskewuk kitoowuk, it thunders, lit. the oonimskewuk call out;*" Laure (ca. 1726) "nimissiuets tchittuets, *il tonne;*" Silvy (ca. 1680) "ninimisti8, *tonnerre;*" "tit8ets nimisti8ek, *il tonne, oiseau du tonnerre*" | ANISH Cuoq (1886) "Onimiki, *ce mot ne s'emploie qu'au pluriel; on dit onimikik, les tonnerres, et jamais onimiki, le tonnerre;*" MESK nenemehkiwaki, *thunderers*

*nip[1]

INITIAL (VERB, ANIMATE, INTRANSITIVE)

— die

evidence | PC nipōstamawēw, *to die for sb;* MC nipahew, *to kill sb;* SEC nipiw, *to die;* Silvy (ca. 1680) "tetabisk8ch nip8ets, *ils meurent ensemble, en même temps*" | ANISH nibo, *to die* (Livesay & Nichols, 2021); MESK nepwa, *to die* origin | PA ***nep*** (Hewson, 1993) compare | *nipē

*nip[2]

INITIAL

— to heal supernaturally

evidence | PC nipiskēw, *to doctor using traditional rites;* Lacombe (1874) "Nipiskew, ok, *(v.n.) il souffle; C'est une des magies des jongleurs qui soufflent les malades, et font croire qu'ils arrachent du corps toutes sortes d'objets, fer, os, etc.;*" Watkins (1865) "Nepiskāo, *v.i.3. He conjures (for the removal of diseases);*" Laure (ca. 1726) "nipiskatigu ka iagusit, *le jongleur chante un malade;*" Fabvre (ca. 1690) "ki nipichin = nipiskāchin, *tu me pense(s) à l(eu)r mode;*" Silvy (ca. 1680) "ni nipiskan 3. -e8, *je suis jongleur, je pense;*" "ni nipitau, *je le pense en jongleur*" | ABEN nebizon, *medicine* (Day, 1995); ANISH Cuoq (1886) "Nipiki, *pratiquer la jonglerie médicinale;*" MIAMI nepil-, *to doctor sb* (ILDA, 2017); nepihkii-, *to doctor* (ILDA, 2017) limited to | *t³ see | *kē² compare | *ato² discussion | Note that the extended form ***nipiskē** is an antipassive formed from the VTA stem ***nipit** + ***kē**.

*nipākwē

INITIAL (VERB, ANIMATE, INTRANSITIVE)

— thirst

evidence | PC nipākwēsimow, *to dance in a sundance;* WI (Pessamit) nipakueshkaku [nəpākwēʃkāku], *to be thirsty because of sth;* Laure (ca. 1726) "ni nipag8an, *j'ai soif*" see | *āpākwē

*nipē

INITIAL (VERB, ANIMATE, INTRANSITIVE)

— sleep

evidence | PC nipēwin, *bed;* MC nipehew, *to put sb to sleep;* AT nipāw, *to sleep;* SEC nipewikamikʷ, *bedroom;* WI nipakan [nəpākən], *bedspread;* Watkins (1865) "Nipākasoo, *v.i.4. He pretends to be asleep*" | ANISH nibekaazo, *to pretend to sleep* (Livesay & Nichols, 2021) compare | *nip¹

*nipiy

INITIAL (NOUN, INANIMATE)

— **1** water

— **2** body of water

evidence | PC nipiy, *water;* MC nipiy, *water;* SEC nipīwan, *to be wet;* NEC nipī, *water;* WI (Uashat) nipi [nəppī], *water; a lake;* EI (Sheshatshiu) nipi [nəppī], *water; a lake;* Laure (ca. 1726) "ni-nipiuihau, *je lui jette de l'eau;*" Silvy (ca. 1680) "nipi, *boisson*" origin | PA ***nepyi** (Hewson, 1993) see | *ɪp, *ɪpiy

*nisāw

INITIAL

— prepare for a journey

evidence | MC nisāwīw, *to gather up one's things in preparation for a trip;* AT (Wemotaci, Jeannette Coocoo) nisawihew [nizāwīhēw], *to prepare sb;* SEC nisāwīw, *to get one's things ready for a trip* limited to | *ī¹

*nisk¹

INITIAL (NOUN, ANIMATE)

— Canada goose (Branta canadensis)

evidence | PC niska, *a Canada goose;* WC niskihkānihkīw, *to make a goose decoy;* MC niskiskāw, *to be many geese;* SEC nisk, *a Canada goose;* oniscimiw, *to have goose;* Silvy (ca. 1680) "niska, *outarde;*" "nistchich, *petite outarde*" | ANISH nika, *a Canada goose* (Livesay & Nichols, 2021); MESK anehka, *a Canada goose* see | *ɪsk¹

*nisk²

INITIAL (NOUN, DEPENDENT INANIMATE)

— forearm (including the hand)

evidence | Mackenzie (1801) "o nisk, *arms*" | ANISH onik, *one's arm* (Livesay & Nichols, 2021); MENO nenɛ·h(kan), *my hand, my arm*

*nisk³

MEDIAL (NOUN INCORPORATION)

— forearm (including the hand)

evidence | PC sakiniskēnitowak, *to hold hands;* MC kakweciniskenew, *to arm-wrestle sb;* SEC sōhciniscew, *to have strong hands;* WI (Pessamit) napatenisseu [nəpətēnəssēw], *to use only one hand* | ANISH izhinike, *to have such an arm or such arms* (Livesay & Nichols, 2021)

*ništ¹

INITIAL

— three

evidence | PC nistinwa, *to be three;* WC nisto, *three;* MC ništiwak, *to be three;* SEC ništwāw, *three times;* Laure (ca. 1726) "nichturiniu, *trente;*" Silvy (ca. 1680) "nichtin8ai, *3 choses*" | ANISH nising, *three times* (Livesay & Nichols, 2021) origin | PA ***neʔθ** (Hewson, 1993) discussion | Derivations beyond the basic VAI and VII forms are built on the numeral stem ***ništw**.

*ništ[2] (~ *nihš)

INITIAL

— overpower

evidence | PC nistāpāwēw, *to drown;* ESC (Severn) nishimew, *to embarrass or offend sb;* MC ništāhpiw, *to laugh hysterically;* nišikanew, *to feel weak to the bones;* SEC ništāpāwew, *to drown;* ništēyihtam, *to be overpowered by an emotion;* NEC nishipāu, *to pass out from drinking;* NSK nistaapaauyaau, *to drown sb* | ANISH nisaabaawe, *to get wet; to drown* (Livesay & Nichols, 2021) origin | PA ***neʔθ** (Hewson, 1993) see | *nihšiwanāt

*ništ[3]

INITIAL

— travel upriver against current

evidence | AT nictaham [ništaham], *to travel upriver by canoe;* NEC nishtiham, *to paddle upriver through a strong current or rapids;* Laure (ca. 1726) "ni-nichtahen, *je monte une rivière*" | ANISH nita'am, *to go upriver against the current* (Livesay & Nichols, 2021)

*ništam

INITIAL

— first

evidence | PC nistamohtēw, *to walk first;* WC nistamōsān, *firstborn;* MC nīštamahtāw, *to prioritize sth, to prefer sth;* AT nictam [nīštam], *first;* SEC nīštam, *first;* WI (Pessamit) nishtamushan [līstəmūʃān], *eldest child of a family;* Watkins (1865) "Nistumoosan, *n.an. The first-born;*" Silvy (ca. 1680) "nichtam, *le 1er*" | ANISH nitamige, *to live in the first house;* MENO nɛ·qtam, *first in time, earliest, at first, before* compare | *nīštām

*ništaw

INITIAL

— together

evidence | PC Lacombe (1874) "nistāwittin, wa, (a.in.) *confluent de deux rivières;*" SEC ništawaham, *to gather things using sth;* NEC nishtiwaau, *to be a convergence of streams;* WI (Pessamit) nishtuaukuat [nəstwāwkūt], *to be piled up by the waves;* Watkins (1865) "Nistowisāwukinum, *v.t.in.6. He scrapes the embers together;*" Laure (ca. 1726) "ni-nichtaukuaten, *je couds de vieux lambeaux ensemble*"

*nīcān

INITIAL (NOUN, ANIMATE)

— child

evidence | PC onīcāniw, *a female quadruped not currently with a calf;* AT (Opitciwan, Patrick Awashish) onitcaniw [onīcāniw], *a female moose;* (Opitciwan, Joey Awashish) nitcanicak [nīcāniššak], *children;* Silvy (ca. 1680) "nichanich, *enfant*" | ANISH oniijaaniw, *a doe;* giniijaanis, *your child* (Livesay & Nichols, 2021); MENO ni·cianok, *children;* neni·cianɛhsak, *my children* compare | *awāhs

*nīht (~ *nīhš)

INITIAL

— down

evidence | PC nīhtāstan, *to be blown down;* MC nīhtinam, *to lower sth;* AT (Opitciwan, Nadia Awashish) niciporo [nīššiporow], *to travel down the rapids;* SEC nīšāhtawīw, *to climb down;* Laure (ca. 1726) "ni-nichikuaskutin, *je mets pieds à terre, je descends de cheval;*" Silvy (ca. 1680) "ni nitinen, *j'abaisse, je descends qqch*" | MESK nīsīwa, *descend* origin | PA ***nīhθ** (Hewson, 1993)

*nīk

INITIAL

— slack

evidence | MC nīkipaliw, *to slacken;* NEC nīkāpihkātim, *to ease the ties on sth;* Laure (ca. 1726) "ni-nikabiterin, *je desserre les dents*"

*nīkān

INITIAL

— at the fore, ahead

evidence | PC nīkānapiw, *to sit at the head;* MC nīkānīw, *to lead;* SEC nīkānohtew, *to walk ahead;* Fabvre (ca. 1690) "Niganameg8an, *p(ar)tie de poiss(on) entre La teste et La queue*" | ANISH niigaanabi, *to sit in the front* (Livesay & Nichols, 2021)

*nīkihikw (~ *nīkihiko)

INITIAL (NOUN, DEPENDENT ANIMATE)

— parent

evidence | PC onīkihikomāw, *a parent;* SEC ni nīcihikw, *my parent;* NSK uniichihiikwa, *one's parent(s)* | ANISH oniigi'igoon, *one's parent(s)* (Livesay & Nichols, 2021); MENO nene·kehekok, *my parents*

*nīm

INITIAL

— **1** aloft

— **2** dance

— **3** take along

evidence | [1]PC nīminēw, *to hold sb aloft;* SEC nīminam, *to hold sth up;* Watkins (1865) "Nemaskoohum, *He lifts it or holds it out, with a pole, &c.*" [2]MC nīmihew, *to make sb dance;* NEC nīmiu, *to dance* [3]MC nīmaskihkwew, *to take a pot along;* PC Lacombe (1874) "Nimikkumānew, *il a un couteau avec lui*" see | *nīmā

*nīmā

INITIAL (VERB, ANIMATE, INTRANSITIVE)

— bring provisions along

evidence | PC nīmāhēw, *to give sb provisions for a journey, to make a lunch for sb to take along;* MC nīmāwinihkew, *to prepare provisions to take along, to make a lunch;* SEC nīmāwin, *food taken along, a lunch;* EI (Sheshatshiu) nimau [nīmāw], *to bring a snack or supply of food for a trip* compare | *nīm

*nīp

INITIAL

— leaf, leafy plant

evidence | PC nīpimināna, *highbush cranberries;* MC nīpimin, *an unidentified type of red berry;* SEC nīpiskāu, *to be many willows* (CSB, 2018); WI (Pessamit) nipiminan [nīpmənān], *berry of a type of plant, possibly the mountain holly;* Watkins (1865) "Nepiminana, *n.in.pl. A species of red berries*" see | *nīpiy compare | *nīpin, *nīpisiy

*nīpaskō

INITIAL (VERB, ANIMATE, INTRANSITIVE)

— kneel upright

evidence | WC nīpaskōw, *to kneel upright;* nīpaskōpiw, *to sit in a kneeling posture;* MC nīpaskōw, *to kneel upright; to stand one one's toes; to stand on one's hind legs, speaking of an animal;* NEC nīpiskū, *to kneel;* WI (Pessamit) nipashkutsheshtapu [nīpəʃkūtʃēstəpu], *to sit on one's heels;* EI (Sheshatshiu) nipashkupu [nīpəʃkūpu], *to kneel;* Watkins (1865) "Nepuskoo, *v.i.4. He kneels upright;*" Laure (ca. 1726) "ni-nipaskun, *je me mets à genoux*" | ANISH Cuoq (1886) "Nipakwi, *Être debout sur les genoux, Être à genoux*" compare | *nīpawi

*nīpawi

INITIAL (VERB, ANIMATE, INTRANSITIVE)

— stand

evidence | PC nīpawiw, *to stand;* MC nīpawihkwāmiw, *to sleep in a standing position, as a horse;* SEC nīpawištawew, *to stand by sb;* nānīpawiw, *to stand around;* Silvy (ca. 1680) "ni nipa8in, *je suis debout*" compare | *nīpaskō

*nīpē

INITIAL

— at night

evidence | MC nīpecimew, *to paddle at night;* SEC nīpehkwew, *to eat supper;* WI (Pessamit) nipepishtueu [nīpēpīstwēw], *to sit by sb at night;* Silvy (ca. 1680) "niperăbatau, *je l'ai pris la nuit au rets*"

*nīpin

INITIAL (VERB, INANIMATE, INTRANSITIVE)

— summer

evidence | WC nīpinisiw, *to summer;* ESC nīpin, *to be summer;* MC nīpinākohtew, *to be bare ground as the snow melts;* SEC nīpinihow, *to be dressed for summer* see | *nīp, *ın

*nīpisiy

INITIAL (NOUN, INANIMATE)

— willow

evidence | PC nīpisiy, *a willow bush or branch;* ESC nīpisiy, *a willow;* MC nīpisiyāhtik^{w}, *a willow bush or branch;* SEC nīpisiy, *a willow bush;* NEC nīpisīhtik^{w}, *a dry willow stick;* Watkins (1865) "Nepiseskow, *v.imp. Willows abound*" see | *nīp compare | *alısisiy discussion | The absence of a preaspiration on the sibilant cannot be confirmed due to the lack of an Atikamekw cognate.

*nīpitē

INITIAL

— in a row

evidence | PC nīpitēkotāw, *to hang things up in a row;* MC nīpitekāpawiwak, *to stand in line;* SEC nīpiteštāw, *to place things in a row* | ANISH niibidebiwag, *to sit in a row* (Livesay & Nichols, 2021)

*nīpiy

INITIAL (NOUN, INANIMATE)

— leaf

evidence | PC nīpiya, *leaves;* MC nīpīšak, *leaves;* SEC nīpīšac, *leaves;* NEC nīpīū, *to have leaves or flowers;* Silvy (ca. 1680) "nipi, nipia, *feuilles, choix*" see | *nīp compare | *nīpin, *nīpisiy

*nīram

INITIAL

— weak

evidence | PC niyamāw, *to be frail;* MC līlamisīw, *to be weak;* AT niramisiw, *to be slow;* SEC nīyaminākwan, *to appear weak;* Silvy (ca. 1680) "ni niramȣtan 3. -teȣ, *je vais doucement, je ne puis marcher*" | ANISH niinamitaagwad, *to sound weak* (Livesay & Nichols, 2021)

*nīš

INITIAL

— two

evidence | PC nīsinwa, *to be two;* WC nīso, *two;* MC nīšiwak, *to be two;* AT (Wemotaci, Jeannette Coocoo) nico [nīʒo], *two;* SEC nīšwāw, *two times;* Laure (ca. 1726) "nichuriniu, *vingt;*" Silvy (ca. 1680) "ni nichinan, *nous sommes deux*" | ANISH niizhing, *twice* (Livesay & Nichols, 2021) discussion | Derivations beyond the basic VAI and VII forms are built on the numeral stem ***nīšw**.

*nīšk[1]

INITIAL

— moist, humid

evidence | PC nīskāw, *to be damp;* WC nīskāw, *to be damp;* MC nīškicāpiw, *to tear up;* Silvy (ca. 1680) "nichkabiskau, *cela est humide, de re solida*"

*nīšk[2]

INITIAL (NOUN, DEPENDENT ANIMATE)

— gland, such as the thyroid, thymus, or salivary glands

evidence | PC Lacombe (1874) "nisk, wok, *(n.r.) partie de viande sous l'oreille, v.g. ni nisk, ki nisk, oniskwa;*" SEC onīšk, *glandular flesh from the upper chest of a beaver;* NEC unīshk, *meat from the upper chest of a beaver;*

EI (Unaman-shipit) unishka [unīhka], *one's salivary gland(s)* | ANISH oniishkwan, *one's gland* (Livesay & Nichols, 2021); Cuoq (1886) "O nickwan, *sa glande*" compare | *rihkw

*nīštām

INITIAL

— at the fore

evidence | WC nīstāmohkīw, *to be at the bow;* MC nīštāmohkew, *to be at the bow;* WI (Pessamit) nishtamitak[u] [nīstāmətuk[w]], *front of the canoe;* Laure (ca. 1726) "ni-nichtamapin, *je tiens le premier rang*" compare | *ništam

*nō

INITIAL

— be perceptible

evidence | PC nōkosiw, *to be visible;* Lacombe (1874) "Nokuttowew, *il lui fait voir;*" MC nōkwan, *to be visible;* SEC nōhtākwan, *to be audible* | ANISH noondam, *to hear* (Livesay & Nichols, 2021)

*nōhr

INITIAL (VERB, TRANSITIVE, ANIMATE)

— breastfeed, suckle

evidence | PC nōhēw, *to breastfeed sb;* WC nōhðīw, *to breastfeed sb;* Watkins (1865) "Nòonāo, *v.t.an. She suckles him, she nurses him;*" "Nòohāo, *v.t.an. She suckles him;*" "Nòonoo, *v.i.4. He sucks (as an infant), he draws the breast;*" Laure (ca. 1726) "ni-puninurau, *sevrer, je le sèvre, ne lui donne plus [le sein];*" La Brosse (1766) "Nurrhau, *n. Lacto, mammam do.;*" Fabvre (ca. 1690) "n8ha8as8n 8, *donner à teter à un enfant;*" Silvy (ca. 1680) "ni n8hau, *je l'allaite*" | ANISH noonaawaso, *to nurse a baby* (Livesay & Nichols, 2021); MIAMI noon-, *to breastfeed (of a baby)* (ILDA, 2017); cf. ABEN noni, *to suckle* (Day, 1994); MESK nōnwa, *to suck at the breast* origin | PA ***nōnr** (***no:nl**, Hewson, 1993) compare | *nōhšē, *nōhto, *nōnē

*nōhso (~ *nōhsaw, *nōhsō)

INITIAL

— follow

evidence | PC nōsawi, *following;* ESC nōsoneham, *to follow sth;* MC nōsonehwew, *to follow sb;* AT (Opitciwan, Nadia Awashish) nosowictew [nōssowištēw], *to be easy to follow, speaking of a story;* nosswa:pam-, *to follow him with one's eyes* (Béland, 1978); SEC nōsowāpamew, *to follow sb with one's eyes;* NEC nūshūshkim, *to follow sth;* Laure (ca. 1726) "ni-nuchaui-tepuatau, *je le rappelle sortant de chez-moi*" | ANISH noosom, *to call, yell after sb* (Livesay & Nichols, 2021)

*nōhšē

INITIAL (VERB, ANIMATE, INTRANSITIVE)

— have a breastfeeding baby

evidence | PC nōsēstim, *a female dog or horse;* WC nōsīmisk, *female beaver;* ESC nōšēšip, *a female duck;* MC nōšāniw, *to suckle;* nōšānihew, *to breastfeed sb;* AT no:šša:nih-, *to feed (child) at the breast;* no:ššeskw, *female bear* (Béland, 1978); SEC nōšāniw, *to suckle;* nōšesk[w], *a female bear;* WI (Pessamit) nusheu [nūʃēw], *to have a nursing child;* nushanu [nūʃānu], *to breastfeed, speaking of the infant;* nusheiapush [nūʃējāpuʃ], *a female hare of reproductive age;* EI (Unaman-shipit) nusheu [nūhēw], *to be pregnant;* Watkins (1865) "Noosanehāo, *v.t.an. She nurses him, she suckles him;*" "Noosāmāk, *n.an. A spawner;*" Laure (ca. 1726) "ni-nuchan 3. -eu, *je lui donne à téter;*" "ni-nuchanin 3. nuchaniu, *je tète;*" Fabvre (ca. 1690) "N8chesk8e8, *femelle qui allaite;*" Silvy (ca. 1680) "n8chestim8, *chienne ayant des petits*" see | *ōšē compare | *nōhto, *nōhr, *nōnē discussion | In most contemporary dialects the sense of this root has become generalized to "female" when referring to fauna, even replacing ***ıskwē** for this purpose in some regions.

***nōhtaw**

INITIAL

— before the expected time, prematurely

evidence | PC nōhtaw, *short of, prematurely;* MC nōhtaw, *short of;* SEC nōhtāš, *short of;* NEC nūhtāshīsh, *short of, before;* EI (Sheshatshiu) nutashkueu [nūtāʃkwēw], *to turn back before reaching sb*

***nōhtē**

INITIAL

— insufficient

evidence | PC nōhtēham, *to shoot short of the a target;* MC nōhtetāmow, *to be short of breath;* SEC nōhtesiw, *to be wanting;* WI (Pessamit) nutekushu [nūtēkuʃu], *to fall asleep before the end;* Laure (ca. 1726) "nutebariu mitchim chachai, *les vivres sont consumées, il n'y en a plus;*" Silvy (ca. 1680) "ni n8techinin, *je n'ai pas assex de place pour m'étendre*" | ANISH noondese, *to run short* (Livesay & Nichols, 2021)

***nōhto**

INITIAL (VERB, ANIMATE, INTRANSITIVE)

— breastfeed, suckle

evidence | WC nōhtow, *to suck on a breast or bottle;* WSC nōhtow, *to breastfeed;* Watkins (1865) "Nòotoo, *v.i.4. He sucks (i.e. he draws the breast)*" | cf. MESK nōtāwasowa, *to nurse a baby;* nōtēwa, *to breastfeed sb;* MIAMI nōnt-, *to breastfeed sb;* noonšici, *she breastfeeds me* compare | *nōhr, *nōhšē, *nōnē

***nōm**

INITIAL

— partially

evidence | PC Lacombe (1874) "Nomihew, *il n'en fait qu'une partie;*" MC nōmake, *a short while;* NEC nūmikāpū, *to stop walking before reaching one's destination;* WI (Pessamit) numishkam[u] [nūməʃkəm], *to cover part of the distance on foot* | MESK nōmatamwa, *to eat part of sth*

***nōnē**

INITIAL

— suck

evidence | PC nōnātam, *to suck sth;* SEC nōnācicew, *to suckle;* WI (Pessamit) nunamew [nūnāmēw], *to suckle from her;* Fabvre (ca. 1690) "ni N8nāten 3 tam8, *Sucer La moile d'un os v.g.*" compare | *nōhšē, *nōhto, *nōhr

***nōrkwē**

INITIAL

— lick

evidence | PC nōhkwācikēw, *to lick;* WC nōskwācikew, *to lick;* MC nōhkwātaham, *to lick sth;* SEC nōhkwātaham, *to lick sth;* WI (Pessamit) nukuateu [nūkwātēw], *to lick sb;* Laure (ca. 1726) "ni-nukuatchiraganan, *je lèche un plat*" | ANISH nooskwaanzo, *to lick sap* (Livesay & Nichols, 2021) limited to | *t³, *t⁴

***nōt¹ (~ *nōc, *nōs)**

INITIAL

— work on, busy oneself on

evidence | PC nōtamēsēw, *to fish;* WC nōtihkomīw, *to check for lice;* ESC nōtinikew, *to fight;* MC nōtaštimwew, *to be busy taking care of dogs;* AT no:sipe-, *to play in the water* (Béland, 1978); SEC (Waswanipi) nōcimīkisew, *to do beadwork;* WI (Pessamit) nutshishatshimeueu [nūtʃʃətʃəmēwēw], *to go about killing mosquitoes;* Watkins (1865) "Noochetow, *v.t.in.2. He works at it, he works with it;*" Fabvre (ca. 1690) "N8tattik8an e8, *à la chasse des cer(f)s, carib8s*" origin | PA ***nōt** (Hewson, 1993)

***nōt² (~ *nōš)**

INITIAL

— to have no room, to not fit

evidence | MC nōtapiw, *to have no room to sit;* PC nōtiskam, *to wear an article of clothing that is too small;* WI (Pessamit) nutishkueu [nūtəʃkwēw], *to wears an article of clothing that is too small;* Laure (ca. 1726) "nutastinahutan, nutastinahurhau, *je ne puis l'embarquer;*" Fabvre (ca. 1690) "N8tinen n. nau, *ne p8uoir embrasser qlq che v.g. che trop grosse, v.g. toy, moy*" | ANISH noonabi, *to have no room to sit* (Livesay & Nichols, 2021) origin | PA ***nōθ*** discussion | The expected allomorph ***nōš*** has yet to be corroborated by written sources. Lacombe (1874) lists a possible candidate, "Nosatchikew, ok, *(v.n.) il ne peut tout manger.*" Although probably a match, the allomorph is unexpected given the phonological environment. On the other hand, in MC the allomorph ***nōc*** replaces the expected form, as in **nōcišin**, *to have no room to lie down.*

*nōtim

INITIAL

— spherical, cylindrical

evidence | PC nōtimisiw, *to be round;* MC nōtimatinam, *shape soft substance into a ball;* SEC nōtimāw, *to be round;* Watkins (1865) "Nootimikwuk, *n.in. A round-pointed needle*"

*nōtimē

INITIAL (VERB, ANIMATE, INTRANSITIVE)

— walk without snowshoes

evidence | PC nōtimēw, *to walk without snowshoes;* MC nōtimēw, *to walk without snowshoes;* SEC nōtimēw, *to walk without snowshoes;* WI (Pessamit) nutimeu [nūtəmēw], *to walk without snowshoes* see | *nōt², *ım²

O

*o

FINAL (VERB, ANIMATE, INTRANSITIVE, ABSTRACT)

— **1** forms reflexive verb stems when suffixed to transitive animate verb stems

— **2** forms the antipassive when suffixed to transitive animate verb stems

— **3** forms functional verb stems when suffixed to certain initials and medials

evidence | [1]PC pimācihow, *to make a living for oneself;* kawisimow, *to lie down for bed;* MC āhcihow, *to change clothes;* tepiškolow, *to eat enough, to satiate onself;* WI (Pessamit) apatelimu [āpətēləmu], *to think oneself important* [2]MC tipācimow, *to tell a story;* SEC ošimow, *to flee;* WI (Pessamit) puamu [pwāmu], *to dream* [3]PC kanawēyimāwasow, *to babysit;* SEC pwecitow, *to fart;* Silvy (ca. 1680) "ni ta8ak8at8n, *j'ai perdu une dent*"

*ohtah (~ *htah)

FINAL (VERB, TRANSITIVE, ANIMATE)

— walk sb

evidence | PC kīwēhtahēw, *to take sb home;* MC pimohtahew, *to walk sb; to carry sb along on foot;* Laure (ca. 1726) "ni-pimuttahau, *j'aide à marcher*" see | *ohtē, *ıh

*ohtatā (~ *htatā)

FINAL (VERB, ANIMATE, INTRANSITIVE)

— walk sth

evidence | PC kīwēhtatāw, *to take sth home;* MC pimohtatāw, *to carry sth along on foot;* Laure (ca. 1726) "ni-urauitatan, *j'emporte quelque chose dehors*" see | *ohtē, *tā

*ohtē (~ *htē)

FINAL (VERB, ANIMATE, INTRANSITIVE, CONCRETE)

— walk

evidence | PC pimohtēw, *to walk along;* MC kikasāmohtew, *walk with snowshoes;* SEC nīkānohtew, *to walk ahead;* Fabvre (ca. 1690) "Naska8etahau, *pr(en)dre qlqn. en chemin par terre;*" Silvy (ca. 1680) "ni petisk8tan 3. -e8, *je viens en deçà sur la glace*" | ANISH ondose, *to walk from* (Livesay & Nichols, 2021) origin | PA ***ohθē*** (Aubin, 1975; Hewson, 1993)

*ok

MEDIAL

— dwelling

evidence | PC kīsokēw, *to finish erecting a dwelling;* WC wītokīmīw, *to live with sb;* MC pīhtokew (archaic), *to enter a dwelling;* MC matokahp, *a deserted camp;* kīšakwew, *to finish erecting a dwelling;* SEC āhtocew, *to move;* Silvy (ca. 1680) "ni pitȣkahau, *je le porte dedans;*" "ni mamenȣganan, *nous demeurons çà et là*" | ANISH agwanoge, *to cover a lodge* (Livesay & Nichols, 2021) compare | *īk

*or

MEDIAL

— canoe

evidence | PC Lacombe (1874) "astoyuw, ok, *(v.n.) il fait un canot;*" "astoyawew, *(v.a.) il lui fait un canot;*" WC astoðiw, *to make a canoe;* EI (Mamit) ashtunu [ahtunu], *to build a canoe;* Laure (ca. 1726) "nit-asturin 3. -iu, *je fais un canot;*" Fabvre (ca. 1690) "Natȣrȣn ȣ, *aller querir, chercher canot;*" Silvy (ca. 1680) "nit'achtȣraȣau, *nob. je lui fais un canot*" compare | *ot

*osw (~ *oso)

MEDIAL, FINAL (NOUN INCORPORATION)

— moose

evidence | PC nōsēs, *mother moose with offspring;* AT (Opitciwan, Joey Awashish) kitohoswew [kitohozwēw], *to call moose;* SEC mištos^{w}, *cow;* Fabvre (ca. 1690) "Achtȣsȣan eȣ, *cacher en neige l'orig(na)l;*" Silvy (ca. 1680) "kichesȣ, *gros orignal*" origin | Likely PA ***osw**. see | *mōsw

*ot (~ *oš, *otak)

MEDIAL, FINAL (NOUN INCORPORATION)

— canoe

evidence | WC māhkotīw, *to have a big canoe or boat;* MC kinotakāw, *be a long canoe;* mihtot, *a raft;* SEC nātotāw, *to fetch a canoe;* āmoteŝhin, *to fall out of a canoe;* peyakotac, *one canoe;* NEC āmutāpiyiu, *to fall out of a canoe;* WI (Pessamit) mitush [mətəʃ], *a raft;* EI (Sheshatshiu) peikutat [pējkutət], *one canoe;* Laure (ca. 1726) "uanaskutagu, *proue, le devant du navire;*" Silvy (ca. 1680) "ni pȣchkȣtechinin, *je romps mon canot en heurtant;*" "nit'amȣtenau, *je le jette par-dessus bord, à l'eau;*" "ni natȣtaȣau, *je vais quérir son canot*" | ABEN oskidolagwa, *deck of a ship* (Day, 1994); ANISH anaamoonag, *under the boat* (Livesay & Nichols, 2021); MENO ana·monak, *under the canoe* origin | PA ***oθ**. see | *ōt compare | *or

*otam

FINAL (VERB, TRANSITIVE, ANIMATE)

— travel a long distance on foot to reach sb, journey to sb

evidence | SEC cīwotamew, *to visit sb;* Silvy (ca. 1680) "ni kihȣtamau, *je m'en vais le voir*" see | *otē

*otē

FINAL (VERB, ANIMATE, INTRANSITIVE, CONCRETE)

— travel a long distance on foot, journey

evidence | PC Lacombe (1874) "kiyutew, *visiter à une distance;*" WC mānotīw, *a stranger;* MC mānteW, *a stanger;* SEC cīwotew, *to visit;* Laure (ca. 1726) "ni-tchiutan, *je voyage;*" Fabvre (ca. 1690) "manȣtan eȣ, *arriuer d'un autre pays, en apporter nȣuelles;*" Silvy (ca. 1680) "ni manȣtekaȣau, *j'arrive en son quartier*" | ANISH biiwide, *a visitor, a stranger* (Livesay & Nichols, 2021) see | *otam

*ōhkom (~ *ōhko)

INITIAL (NOUN, DEPENDENT ANIMATE)

— grandmother

evidence | PC ohkomiw, *to have a grandmother(s);* MC ohkomimāw, *a grandmother;* AT (Wemotaci, Nicole Petiquay) noko [nōhko], *grandmother!;* SEC nōhkom, *a grandmother;* NEC nūhkū, *grandmother!;*

EI (Sheshatshiu) ukumipana [ūkumpəna], *one's late grandmother(s);* Laure (ca. 1726) "nu-ukumimau 3. -mimeu, *je l'ai pour grand-mère;*" Silvy (ca. 1680) "n8k8m, *ma grand-mère*" discussion | The allomorph listed above is preserved only in the vocative.

*ōhkomihs

INITIAL (NOUN, DEPENDENT ANIMATE)

— **1** paternal uncle

— **2** stepfather

evidence | PC ohkomisimāw, *a paternal uncle; a stepfather;* MC nōhkomis, *my paternal uncle, or uncle married to a maternal aunt, or stepfather;* NEC uhkumisimāu, *a paternal uncle; a stepfather;* WI (Uashat) ukumishu [ukuməʃu], *to have an uncle(s);* Silvy (ca. 1680) "n8k8mis, *mon oncle paternel*" compare | *šihs

*ōhow

INITIAL (NOUN, ANIMATE)

— owl

evidence | PC ōhow, *an owl;* NSK uuhuw, *an owl;* EI (Mamit) uhu [ūhu], *an owl*

*ōhšim (~ *ōhš)

INITIAL (NOUN, DEPENDENT ANIMATE)

— grandchild

evidence | WSC (Misipawistik, Ellen Cook) nōsim, *grandchild!;* AT (Opitciwan, Joey Awashish) nosim [nōssim], *my grandchild;* Laure (ca. 1726) "achtam nuché, *viens, mon petit-fils, petite-fille;*" "nuchiminanets, *nos descendants;*" Fabvre (ca. 1690) "n 8chimak, *mes descend(an)ts, petits fils*" | MENO nohseh, *grandchild!;* MIAMI noohsema, *my grandchild; noohse, my grandchild!* compare | *ōšihsim discussion | The allomorph listed above, likely representative of an older form lacking the possessive ***ɩm**, is preserved only in the vocative, hence its assignment to the allomorph category rather than the primary form.

*ōhtāwiy (~ *ōhtāwī)

INITIAL (NOUN, DEPENDENT ANIMATE)

— father

evidence | PC Lacombe (1874) "eoko awāh weyottāwiyān, *c'est mon père;*" WC kōhtāwiy, *your father;* MC wewohtāwīmāwit, *He who is the father;* SEC nōhtāwiy, *my father;* EI utauia [utāwja], *one's father;* Laure (ca. 1726) "nuttaui-ban, *feu mon père;*" Silvy (ca. 1680) "n8ta8i *voc.* n8ta, *mon père*"

*ōmo

FINAL (VERB, ANIMATE, INTRANSITIVE, CONCRETE)

— tuck

evidence | WSC (Ida Bear) pīhtōmow, *to tuck sth under one's garment;* MC pīlōmow, *to tuck sth under one's garment;* AT (Opitciwan, Joey Awashish) piromow [pīrōmō], *to secretly tuck sth under one's coat;*" Watkins (1865) "Peyoomoo, *v.i.4. He puts (it) into his bosom;* Peyoomoohāo, *v.t.an. He puts it into his bosom (i.e. into another person's);*" Laure (ca. 1726) "ni-birumututauau, *je mets, v.g. l'enfant (dans mon sein);*" Silvy (ca. 1680) "pir8mon, *je mets dans mon sein*" | ANISH Cuoq (1886) "Pindom, o, *mettre dans son sein;*" Baraga (1878) "Pinomon, (nin). *I put it in my bosom;* p. panomod," but also "Pindomowin. *Bosom*" limited to | *pīhr, *pīht[1]

*ōro

INITIAL (VERB, ANIMATE, INTRANSITIVE)

— howl

evidence | PC oyōyow, *to howl;* WC oðow, *to howl;* MC ōlow, *to howl;* AT oro [ōrō], *to howl;* NEC wiyū, *to howl;* WI (Pessamit) ulu [ūlu], *to howl;* Laure (ca. 1726) "uru, *rugir, la bête rugit, crie*" | ANISH waawoono, *to howl* (Livesay & Nichols, 2021) origin | Likely onomatopoeic.

*ōšihsim (~ *ōšihs)

INITIAL (NOUN, DEPENDENT ANIMATE)

— grandchild

evidence | WC kōsisim, *your grandchild;* WSC (Misipawistik, Ellen Cook) nōsisim, *my grandchild;* MC nōsisim, *my grandchild;* NEC nūsisā, *grandchild!;* nūsisim, *my grandchild;* WI (Pessamit) ussimu [ussəmu], *to have a grandchild;* Laure (ca.1726) "nuchichimets, *(mes) descendants;*" Silvy (ca. 1680) "n8chisai, *mon petit fils ou fille*" | ABEN -oses, *grandchild or descendant* (Day, 1995); ANISH noozis & noozhis, *my grandchild* (Livesay & Nichols, 2021); MESK nōshisema, *my grandchild* compare | *ōhšim discussion | degree of uncertainty remains regarding the quality of the sibilants in the above root and the presence of any pre-aspirates, the latter of which is based by analogy on Atikamekw kinship terms that feature a variation between ***hs** and ***sihs**. The allomorph listed above, likely representative of an older form lacking the possessive ***ɪm**, is preserved only in the vocative, hence its assignment to the allomorph category rather than the primary form. The comparative evidence is insufficient to reconstruct a semantic distinction, if any, between ***ōhšim** and ***ōšihsim**.

*ōšē

FINAL (VERB, ANIMATE, INTRANSITIVE, CONCRETE)

— give birth to, bear child

evidence | PC pakwatōsān, *an illegitimate child;* MC sakōšew, *to birth children at short intervals;* AT (Wemotaci, Nicole Petiquay) pikotocan [pikotōʒān], *an illegitimate child;* (Opitciwan, Joey Awashish) peikocew [pēyakōʒēw], *to birth only one child or offspring;* SEC nihtāwōšew, *to be able to bear children;* Laure (ca. 1726) "pikuatuchan, *fils illégitime*" compare | *ɪšē

*ōt (~ *ōš)

INITIAL (NOUN, INANIMATE)

— canoe

evidence | PC ōsi, *a canoe, a boat;* SEC ōt, *a canoe;* WI (Pessamit) ush [ūʃ], *a canoe, a boat;* EI (Mushuau) ut [ūt], *a canoe, a boat;* EI (Mamit) ush [ūh], *a canoe, a boat;* Silvy (ca. 1680) "8ch *pl.* 8tai, *canot, berceau;*" "n'8t8chin, *j'ai un canot*" origin | PA ***ōθ** (Hewson, 1993) see | *ot discussion | Compare the Old Cree singular ***ōši** with its plural, ***ōtahi**.

*ōtēnaw

INITIAL (NOUN, INANIMATE)

— settlement

evidence | PC ōtēnāwiwin, *township;* MC otenaw, *a long-term encampment, a settlement;* SEC otenaw, *town;* EI (Sheshatshiu) utenass [utēnāss], *a village;* Silvy (ca. 1680) "8tenau, *village*" | ABEN odana, *town, village, settlement* (Day, 1995); ANISH oodena, *town* (Livesay & Nichols, 2021)

P

*pah[1]

INITIAL

— singe

evidence | WC pāhtīw, *to singe sb;* ESC pasow, *to be singed;* MC pasam, *to singe sth;* SEC pahtam, *to singe sth;* NEC pihtākwāu, *to singe porcupine;* EI (Unaman-shipit) patam[u] [pātam], *to singe sth;* Watkins (1865) "Pùtāo, *v.t.an. He singes him;*" Laure (ca. 1726) "ni-patau, *je fais griller un cochon;*" Fabvre (ca. 1690) "ni Patau 3 pate8, *bruler duuet, La petite plume doy(seau) Le flambant;*" Silvy (ca. 1680) "ni patag8an 3, -e8, *je brûle un porc-épic*" | ANISH banzo, bande, *to be singed* (Livesay & Nichols, 2021); MENO pahsi·w TA, pahsam TI, *to singe sb or sth* origin | PA ***pan** limited to | *s, *sw, *so[2], *tē[4], *t[5], *t[6]

*pah² (~ *paš)

INITIAL

— emit or detect an odor

evidence | PC pasow, *to catch a scent of sth, to smell sth;* Lacombe (1874) "Paswew, *il le fait sentir;*" MC paštew, *smoke;* NEC pisū, *to catch a scent of sth; to catch a scent of smoke;* piswāu, to alert an animal by one's scent; pishtāu, *smoke from a fire made by a person;* Laure (ca. 1726) "pasteu, *fumée, boucane;*" "akubasteu, akubasu, *tabac fort, piquant*" origin | PA ***paʔ** limited to | *s, *so², *sw, *tē⁴

*pah³

FINAL (VERB, TRANSITIVE, ANIMATE, CONCRETE)

— run with

evidence | PC nakacipahēw, *to leave sb behind as one runs away;* MC pimipahew, *to run along with sb;* SEC cihcipahew, *to run off with sb*

*pahk

INITIAL

— fall

evidence | PC pahkisimēw, *to let sb fall;* WC pāhkisam, *to blast sth;* MC pahkišimon, *sunset;* pahkitew, *to explode;* SEC pahcihtin, *to fall;* NEC pihkihan, *to pulsate or throb;* WI (Pessamit) papatshikun [pāpətʃəkūn], *to drip;* Silvy (ca. 1680) "papakibestan, *il pleut un peu d'une nuée grosse*" | ANISH bangishin, *to fall* (Livesay & Nichols, 2021); MESK pakishinwa, *to land* origin | PA ***pank** (Hewson, 1993)

*pahkān

INITIAL

— separate

evidence | PC Lacombe (1874) "Pakkāneyimew, *il le trouve différent;*" WC pāhkān, *separate;* MC pahkānihew, *to separate sb;* SEC pahkānapiw, *to sit separately* compare | *tipān

*pahko (~ *pahkw)

INITIAL

— **1** remove external layer or skin

— **2** break through the surface of (water)

evidence | [1]WC pāhkonīw, *to skin sb;* MC pahkonamiskwew, *skin beaver;* pahkohaskew, *to remove a piece of moss using a tool;* SEC pahkonew, *to skin sb;* NEC pihkunīu, *to have a blister or for a tree's bark to come off easily;* Watkins (1865) "Pukwatipapitâo, *v.t.an. He scalps him;*" Laure (ca. 1726) "ni-pakuanastchikuan, *j'écorche du loup-marin*" [2]PC pahkopēwaskisin, *rubber boots;* MC pahkopew, *to step in or go in the water;* EI (Sheshatshiu) pakupepatau [pākupēpātāw], *to run into the water;* Silvy (ca. 1680) "ni pakȣban 3. -eȣ, *je me mouille en marchant*" | [1]ANISH bakonamikwe, *to skin a beaver* (Livesay & Nichols, 2021); Baraga (1878) "Bakwabidebina, (nin). *I pull him a tooth out; p. bek...nad*" [2]ANISH bakobii, *to go into the water* compare | *pahkwat, *pahkwē

*pahkwat (~ *pahkwac)

INITIAL

— dislodge

evidence | PC pahkwacipitam, *to loosen and pull sth off;* WC pāhkwacipaðiw, *to become unstuck;* MC pahkwatahaskew, *to remove a piece of moss using a tool;* SEC pahkwatāhkatotew, *to become dislodged from drying;* WI (Pessamit) pakutshitin [pukutʃətn], *to be detached or unstuck;* Silvy (ca. 1680) "papakȣatchitin, *la pièce est ôtée, v.g. l'emplâtre*" see | *pahko, *at² compare | *wīhkwat

*pahkwē

INITIAL

— break piece off

evidence | PC pahkwēsam, *to cut a piece from sth;* MC pahkwenam, *to break off a piece of sth manually;* SEC (Waswanipi) pahkwepayin, *a piece breaks off;* Silvy (ca. 1680) "ni pakȣechamaȣau, *je coupe pour lui;*" "ni pak8achama8au, *je coupe pour lui donner*" compare | *pahko, *pahkwat

*pahrakosiw

INITIAL (NOUN, ANIMATE)

— pancreas

evidence | Lacombe (1874) "opeyakusiw, ok, *rate;*" "o'pehiyakusiw, a, *sa tripe, et, la rate;*" "ni pehiyakusiw, *ma tripe;*" AT (Wemotaci, Nicole Petiquay) opaparakisiwan [opahparakiziwan], *one's pancreas;* NEC uhpaapihiikusiu, *one's pancreas, a sponge-like organ near the stomach;* cf. EI (Unamanshipit) upeminikushu [upēminukuhu], *a spleen*

*pahs[1]

INITIAL

— **1** groove, furrow, fissure

— **2** hew wood

— **3** wear a band or other thin strip of material

evidence | [1]WC pasāw, *to be grooved;* MC pasahcāw, *be a ditch, trench, or furrow in the ground;* pasakihtin, *to sustain a thin fracture on impact;* AT (Wemotaci, Nicole Petiquay) pasatawakaw [passatāwahkāw], *to be a ditch or trench in the sand;* SEC pasākonakāw, *be a furrow or trench in the snow;* Lacombe (1874) "Pasaw, a, (a.in.), *il est creux, concave, cannelé, silloné;*" "Pasikaw, a, (a.in.), *idem;*" "pasakipayiw, ok, a, (a.a. et in.), *il a une fissure, une fente;*" Watkins (1865) "Pusukipuyew, *v.imp. It splinters*" [2]PC pasaham, *to hew and square sth;* WC pasahikīw, *to hew logs;* MC pasahapoyew, *to cut wood for a paddle;* SEC pasahasāmew, *to go and cut wood for snowshoes;* Watkins (1865) "Pusuhum, *v.t.in.6. He square it;*" Fabvre (ca. 1690) "Passahigan 3 ke8, *aller c8per chercher bois à menuyser v.g. pr faire raqttes*" [3]PC Lacombe (1874) "Pasikkwepitew, *(v.a.) il lui bande les yeux, le visage;*" "Pasistikwānepitew, *(v.a.) il lui bande la tête, il lui met une couronne;*" "Pasiskwepisuw, ok, *(a.a.) il a la tête bandée, couronnée;*" WSC (Misipawistik, Ellen Cook) pasiskwēhpison, *a headband;* SEC paskwehpison, *a headband;* NSK piskwaapisuw, *to wear a headband;* EI (Sheshatshiu) pashkuepishun [pəʃkwēpəʃun], *a headband* | [1]ANISH basadinaa, *to be a valley* (Livesay & Nichols, 2021) [2]MENO paqsaham, *to split sth by tool;* paqsekaham, *to split sth with an axe;* MIAMI pahsahaakani, *wedge* (ILDA, 2017) [3]ANISH basikwebizo, *to wear a headband* (Livesay & Nichols, 2021) origin | PA ***paʔs*** discussion | Western dialects display **pasak** as a variant, which likely represents the addition of the post-initial **ak**. Lacombe (1874) also lists the variant **pasik**, analogous to the **kīnik** variant of ***kīn.**

*pahs[2]

INITIAL

— come briefly or lightly into contact; graze, skim, slap, whip

evidence | PC pasastēham, *to whip sth;* MC pasāhkotiyehwew, *to slap sb's bum;* pasipaliw, *to skim the surface of;* AT (Wemotaci, Nicole Petiquay) pasikwehwew [passihkwēhwēw], *to slap sb in the face;* SEC pasitihcehwew, *to slap sb's hand;* Watkins (1865) "Pussipasin, *v.i.7. He skims along the surface of the water (e.g. a goose falling after being shot while flying)*" | ANISH basidiye', *to slap sb on the rear* (Livesay & Nichols, 2021); MESK papasanasitēpahowa, *to run with one's feet barely touching the ground;* pasetonēhwēwa, *to slap sb on the mouth*

*pahs[3]

INITIAL

— be on fire

evidence | PC pasitēw, *to be on fire; to be a wildfire;* MC pasisow, *to be on fire;* AT (Wemotaci, Nicole Petiquay) pasitew [passitēw], *to be on fire;* SEC pasitew, *to be on fire;* Laure (ca. 1726) "pasiteu, *enflammé, pris en feu;*" Silvy (ca. 1680) "ni pachisen, *j'allume, j'enflamme;*" "ni passiss8n, *je me brûle*" limited to | *s, *tē[4]

*pahs[4]

MEDIAL (NOUN INCORPORATION)

— breast of a bird

evidence | WSC (Misipawistik, Ellen Cook) mahkipasēw, *to have a large breast;* AT (Opitciwan, Joey Awashish) tawipasehwew [tāwipassēhwēw], *to shoot a bird right in its breast;* WI (Pessamit) taushpasheueu [tāwʃpəʃēwēw], *to hit a bird right in the chest with a projectile;* Watkins (1865) "Mìkoopusāo, *v.i.3. He has a red breast;*" "wapiskepusāo, *to have a white breast;*" "towipussāwāo, *He hits it (e.g. a bird) on the breast*" see | *spahsēw

*pahsahk

INITIAL

— blink, twinkle

evidence | PC pasahkāpiw, *to blink one's eye(s);* MC papasahkāštawew, *to twinkle;* AT (Wemotaci, Nicole Petiquay) pasakapiw [passahkāpiw], *to blink;* Watkins (1865) "Pusùkapew, *v.i.1. He twinkles (with the eyes)*" | ANISH basangaabi, *to blink or wink* (Livesay & Nichols, 2021)

*pahsēkān

INITIAL (NOUN, ANIMATE)

— head of a cattail (Typha spp.)

evidence | MC pasekān, *head of a cattail;* pasekānaškʷ, *a cattail;* AT pissekan, *NI cat's tail, bulrush* (Béland, 1978); (Opitciwan, Joey Awashish) pisekan [pissēkan], *a cattail;* Faries & Mackay (1938) "Pusāka'n, *n.an. The head of the bulrush;*" Watkins (1865) "Pusākan, *n.an. The head of the bulrush;*" Laure (ca. 1726) "passeganiskau, *plein de roseaux;*" "passegan *pl.* -ets, *roseau;*" Silvy (ca. 1680) "passegan, *roseau;*" cf. PC pasān, *NA cattail* | ANISH Cuoq (1886) "Apakweiack, *herbe à couverture, quenouille. C'est ce qu'en botanique, on appelle typha latifolia, massette à larges feuilles. Le duvet qui entoure les fruits de cette plante, est nommée par les Algonquins pasekanak, ils s'en servent quelquefois pour garnir des coussins.*"

*pahswē

INITIAL

— fatty (food)

evidence | PC paswēyāw, *to be excessively fatty;* MC paswemāštew, *to smell fatty when cooking;* AT (Opitciwan, Joey Awashish) paswespokosiw [passwēspokoziw], *to taste unpleasantly strong;* SEC paswemahcihow, *to feel sick from eating fatty food*

*pahswēwē

INITIAL (VERB, INTRANSITIVE)

— echo

evidence | WC paswīwihtin, *to make an echo;* MC paswewew, *to create an echo with one's voice;* AT pissweššin, *to resound, re-echo (Béland, 1978);* WI (Pessamit) pashueueteu [pəʃēwētēw], *to echo, speaking of a gunshot or explosion;* Silvy (ca. 1680) "pass8e8echinani8i8, *on entend l'écho*" | ANISH baswewe, *to echo or resound* (Livesay & Nichols, 2021) see | *pahs², *wēwē

*pahtā

FINAL (VERB, ANIMATE, INTRANSITIVE, CONCRETE)

— run

evidence | MC pimipahtāw, *to run along;* SEC yāyipahtāw, *to run along the edge;* EI (Sheshatshiu) ueshamipatau [wēʃāmpātāw], *aller trop loin en courant ou en véhicule à roues* | ANISH apiichibatoo, *to run at a certain speed* (Livesay & Nichols, 2021)
origin | PA ***pahtā** (Aubin, 1975)

*pahtwā

FINAL (VERB, ANIMATE, INTRANSITIVE, CONCRETE)

— run with

evidence | PC nakacipahtwāw, *to leave sth behind as one runs away;* MC pimipahtwāw, *to run along with sth;* SEC ispahtwāw, *to run thither with sth*

*pak

MEDIAL (NOUN INCORPORATION)

— leaf

evidence | PC kākikēpakwa, *Labrador tea;* MC apišipakāw, *to have small leaves;* NEC sāchipichīu, *to be budding season;* Fabvre (ca. 1690) "Aga8achtepăgau, *bel ombre d'arbre feuilles etc*" | ABEN mkwibaga, *to be red leaves* (Day, 1994) see | *nīpiy, *ak[2] compare | *pēmak

*pakam

INITIAL

— strike

evidence | PC pakamaham, *to strike sth;* MC pakamākan, *a club;* Watkins (1865) "pukumétin, *v.imp. it falls with force against something;*" Laure (ca. 1726) "pakamichanasku, *coin, massue de bois;*" Fabvre (ca. 1690) "Pakamăgan *pl.* găna, *massüe, casse teste*" origin | PA ***pakam-**, *to strike sb* (Hewson, 1993), from ***pak** + ***am** see | *am[1] compare | *pakaso discussion | This root is derived from a functional VTA in PA but was reanalyzed as a productive initial requiring a final in Old Cree. This root has been replaced in most dialects by ***witām**.

*pakask

INITIAL

— clear

evidence | PC pakaskinam, *to see sth clearly;* WC pakaskinākwan, *to be clearly visible;* WI (Pessamit) pakashkatishiu [pəkəʃkāttʃīw], *to be intelligent;* Laure (ca. 1726) "nema ni-pakassinen, distinguer, *je ne distingue pas bien de loin (à la vue)*" | ANISH bagakaabi, *to see clearly* (Livesay & Nichols, 2021)

*pakaso

INITIAL (VERB, ANIMATE, INTRANSITIVE)

— extract marrow

evidence | MC pakasowin, *marrow;* AT (Opitciwan, Joey Awashish) pakaso [pakazo], *to break a bone to extract the marrow; to eat marrow;* SEC pakasow, *to break a bone to extract the marrow;* Laure (ca. 1726) "ni-pakasun, *je casse un os pour avoir la moelle*" compare | *pakam

*pakān[1]

INITIAL (NOUN, ANIMATE)

— nut

evidence | PC pakānāhtik, *nut tree;* WC pakān, *NA a nut;* AT pakan [pakān], NA *a nut;* SEC pakān, *NA a nut;* WI (Pessamit) pakanakashi, *a beaked hazel tree;* EI (Sheshatshiu) pakan [pəkān], *NA a nut;* Laure (ca. 1726) "pakan *pl.* -ets, *noix;*" "pakanaskuch -a, *noisettier;*" Fabvre (ca. 1690) "pakanask8 *pl.* *8ek, noyers, arbres*" | ANISH bagaaniminzh, *a hazelnut bush;* MENO paka·nawi·hsyak, *butternut trees*

*pakān[2]

MEDIAL (NOUN INCORPORATION)

— nut

evidence | Laure (ca. 1726) "ni-pinahepakanan, *j'abats des noix;*" "ni-chinipakanachauan, *je fais de l'huile de noix*"

*pakēhsē

INITIAL (VERB, ANIMATE, INTRANSITIVE)

— play a dice-like game of chance

evidence | PC Lacombe (1874) "pakessew, ok, *(v.n.) il joue au jeu de hazard (le jeu de main);*" MC pakesānimin, *a fig (biblical translation);* Watkins (1865) "Pukāsāwuk, *v.i.3. pl. They gamble with dice;*" Isham (1743) "perca sa ne ma nuck, *a prunn;*" Laure (ca. 1726) "patchechanets, *dé à jouer à la manière des sauvagesses;*" Silvy (ca. 1680) "patchesaniminets, *prunes*" | ANISH bagese, *to play the dish game;* bagesaan, *a plum* (Livesay & Nichols, 2021) origin | Query noun incorporation of ***ēhsa**. discussion | In the absence of an Atikamekw cognate the preaspirate in this reconstruction is indirectly supported by Anishinabe.

*pakit (~ *pakic)

INITIAL

— release, set down

evidence | PC pakitahwāw, *to set a fishing net;* MC pakitinam, *to set sth down;* pakicīw, *to descend;* EI (Sheshatshiu) patshitinam^u [pətʃitnəm], *to let sth fall from one's hand;* Laure (ca. 1726) "ni-patchitinan 3. -nau, *je le sème*" | MENO pake·tenam, *to set sth down; to give permission regarding sth*

*pako[1] (~ *pakw)

INITIAL

— make hole

evidence | PC pakocepayiw, *to have a rupture;* MC pakoceśwew, *to cut open sb's abdomen to remove the guts;* SEC pakocenew, *to gut sb;* NEC pikuham, *to cut a hole in the ice to set a net or nightline;* Laure (ca. 1726) "pakutche-namesai, *ébreuils de poisson;*" Silvy (ca. 1680) "ni pak8pitau, *je troue, v.g. le rets*" | ANISH bagozhan, *to cut a hole in sth* (Livesay & Nichols, 2021) compare | *pakonē

*pako[2]

FINAL (VERB, ANIMATE, INTRANSITIVE, CONCRETE)

— under one's garment

evidence | MC mōskipakow, *to pull sth out from under one's garment;* Laure (ca. 1726) "ni-mutchibagun, *je tire de mon sein;*" Fabvre (ca. 1690) "nit Achebăk8n 8, *retirer de son sein;*" Silvy (ca. 1680) "nit'ataubak8n, *je retire de mon sein;*" "ni m8stibag8n, *je tire de mon sein;*" "ni pitchipak8s8n, *le feu vole dans mon sein*" | ANISH Cuoq (1886) "mockinebakwi, en avoir tout plein sous ses habits"

*pakohs

INITIAL

— wish or hope for

evidence | PC pakoseyimow, *to wish, to hope;* MC pakoselihtam, *to hope for sth;* AT (Wemotaci, Jeannette Coocoo) pakoserimowin [pakossērimowin], *prayer;* SEC pakoseyimākan, *one from whom people hope they will receive, used as epithet for God* | ANISH bagosendam, *to wish or hope* (Livesay & Nichols, 2021); MENO paki·hseneme·w, *to place hope in sb* origin | PA ***pakwihs** compare | *pakohš

*pakohš

INITIAL

— expect to be fed

evidence | PC pakosīhtāw, *to beg for sth;* MC pakošihew, *to expect food from sb;* AT (Opitciwan, Joey Awashish) pakocihew [pakoššihēw], *to expect food from sb;* WI (Pessamit) pakushitaupu [pukustāwpu], *to sit around hoping for something to eat or drink* | ANISH bagoshi'iwe, *to expect to be fed* (Livesay & Nichols, 2021) compare | *pakohs

*pakonē

INITIAL

— hole

evidence | PC pakonēskam, *to wear a hole into sth;* MC pakoneham, *to make a hole in sth using a tool;* WI (Pessamit) pakunemeu [pukunēmēw], *to make a hole in sth using one's teeth;* Silvy (ca. 1680) "pag8neïau, *cela est troué, v.g. cabane*" | ANISH bagoneyaa, *to have a hole* (Livesay & Nichols, 2021) origin | Query obscure noun incorporation. see | *pako[1]

*pakwahtē

INITIAL

— gird

evidence | PC pakwahtēhow, *to have a belt on;* MC pakwahtehon, *a belt;* WI (Pessamit) pakuateun [pukutēwn], *a belt;* EI (Sheshatshiu) pakuateu [pukwātēu], *to wear a belt;* Watkins (1865) "Pukwùtāhāo, *v.t.an. He girds him;*" Silvy (ca. 1680) "pak8atehau, *je le ceins*" | MENO pakuahtɛh (-onak, -onan)

AN and inan, *belt;* MIAMI pakwanteehwi-, *to put on a belt, to cinch one's clothing* (ILDA, 2017)

*pakwano (~ *pakwanaw)

INITIAL

— without relying on observing a given thing or person

evidence | PC pakwanaw, *instinctively; by chance, at random;* MC pakwanawāspinatew, *to curse sb with illness behind their back;* NEC pikuniwiham, *to sing w/o looking at the lyrics;* Watkins (1865) "pukwunoomāo, *He speaks about him behind his back;*" Laure (ca. 1726) "ni-pagunumuan, *je suis médisant*" | MENO pakuanawe·htaw, *to be off alone by oneself*

*pakwē

INITIAL

— impatient

evidence | PC pakwātēw, *to hate sb;* MC pakwātam, *to feel bad, to be sad;* SEC pakweyeyihtam, *to be anxious about sth;* NEC pikwāhāu, *to keep sb anxiously waiting;* WI (Pessamit) pakueieu [pukwējēw], *to cause sb to be impatient;* Watkins (1865) "Pukwatikwan, *v.imp. It is hateful, it is abominable;*" Laure (ca. 1726) "ni-pakuatau, *je lui souhaite la mort;*" Silvy (ca. 1680) "ni pak8atau, *je l'attends*"

*pam

INITIAL

— tend to, care for

evidence | PC pamihēw, *to take care of sb;* WC pamihākan, *a welfare recipient;* MC pimelimew, *to concern oneself with sb;* AT (Opitciwan, Joey Awashish) mihew [mihew], *take care of sb;* SEC papāmeyihtam, *to concern oneself with sth;* NEC pimīhkim, *to work on sth;* Watkins (1865) "pumestakāo, *He serves;*" Laure (ca. 1726) "ni-pamikauau, *je lui fais l'amour;*" Silvy (ca. 1680) "ni pamita8au, *je lui obéis*"

*panahko (~ *panahkw)

INITIAL

— saggy, loose

evidence | MC panahkošakew, *to have saggy skin;* SEC panahkoškam, *to wear an article of clothing loosely;* Laure (ca. 1726) "panakuabegamu, *lâche, qui n'est pas bien tendu;*" Fabvre (ca. 1690) "papanak8chka8ak, *elles sont desbarrées, raqttes*"

*papak

INITIAL

— thin

evidence | PC papakisam, *to slice sth thinly;* MC papakatin, *to be frozen thin;* SEC papakāw, *to be thin;* Silvy (ca. 1680) "papatchitak, *planche*"

*papakwat (~ *papakwac, *papakwas)

INITIAL

— distract from boredom or tediousness

evidence | PC papakwatēyihtākwan, *to be amusing;* Lacombe (1874) "papakwatch pittwaw, *il fume pour se distraire;*" NEC pipikusihtākusiu, *to sound entertaining;* ESC (Attawapiskat, Angela Sheesheesh) pahpakwac, *as a distraction;* MC pahpakwatelihtam, *to distract oneself with sth;* WI (Pessamit) papakutshikam[u] [pəpukutʃīkəm], *to amuse oneself by doing sth;* Watkins (1865) "Pupukwachehāo, *v.t.an. He amuses him;*" Silvy (ca. 1680) "ni papag8as8mau, *je lui raconte qqch. faite;*" Fabvre (ca. 1690) "Papak8atchir8n 8, *s(')amuser à qlq che pr passer tems*"

discussion | The presence of the preaspirate in ESC and MC suggests ***pahpakwat** may be a reasonable alternative reconstruction.

*papikw (~ *papiko)

INITIAL (NOUN, ANIMATE)

— **1** a large ectoparasite such as a flea or bedbug

— **2** bumpy, lumpy, rough

evidence | [1]WC pipikos, *a flea;* WI (Pessamit) papikᵘ [pəpukʷ], *a bedbug;* EI (Mamit) papikᵘ [papukʷ], *a bedbug;* Watkins (1865) "Pipik, *n.an. A flea;*" Silvy (ca. 1680) "papik8, *puce*" [2]PC pipikwatēhtēw, *toad;* WC pipikosiw, *to be lumpy;* MC pipikonikwan, *to feel lumpy to the touch;* AT pipikorikic [pipikorīkiš], *a toad;* SEC pipikwāw, *to be lumpy;* Watkins (1865) "Pupikoosew, Pipikoosew, *v.i.1. He is rough;*" Laure (ca. 1726) "papikuarikets, *grenouilles*" | [1]ABEN babigwak, *fleas* (Day, 1995); ANISH obabigomi, *to have flea* (Livesay & Nichols, 2021); MENO pape·k(ok), flea(s); nepa·pekom, *my flea* [2]ANISH babigozigwaa, *bumpy ice* (Livesay & Nichols, 2021) origin | PA ***papikwa*** (cf. ***pepikwa**, Aubin, 1975)

*par

PREFINAL

— **1** change automatically or spontaneously (from one state to another)

— **2** move automatically or spontaneously (from one place to another)

see | *pari, *parin

*paracān

INITIAL (NOUN, ANIMATE)

— baby bird

evidence | PC panicāyis, *a baby bird;* SEC payacāniš, *a baby bird* | ANISH banajaanh, *a baby bird* (Livesay & Nichols, 2021); cf. MESK panashāha, *a young animal or bird*

*parasko (~ *paraskw)

INITIAL

— break through or into, breach

evidence | MC palaskoham, *break through or into;* AT (Opitciwan, Joey Awashish) paraskockowew [paraskoškawēw], *to break through sth using one's foot or body;* SEC payaskomew, *to suckle a breast until there is a letdown;* WI (Pessamit) pilishkunamᵘ [pələʃkunəm], *défoncer avec les mains*

*pari

FINAL (VERB, INTRANSITIVE, CONCRETE)

— **1** change automatically or spontaneously (from one state to another)

— **2** move automatically, spontaneously, or smoothly

evidence | [1]WC ðikwākonīpaðiw, *to get covered in snow from a fall;* SEC pācihkwanepayiw, *one's ankle(s) swells;* yōtinipayiw, *wind starts blowing;* EI (Sheshatshiu) pakapanu [pākāpənu], *to burst* [2]MC išpipaliw, *it ascends;* kawipaliw, *to fall over;* SEC pimipayiw, *to move along spontaneously or automatically;* Laure (ca. 1726) "ni-tchikaskamitchiparin, *je rampe comme un serpent;*" Silvy (ca. 1680) "ni nanaman8ebarin, *la joue me frémit*" see | *par, *i²

*parin

FINAL (VERB, INANIMATE, INTRANSITIVE, CONCRETE)

— **1** change automatically or spontaneously (from one state to another)

— **2** move automatically or spontaneously (from one place to another)

evidence | AT isparin, *to happen thus;* PC pimipayin, *to run along;* SEC (Waswanipi) cīwepayin, *to return spontaneously* see | *par, *in²

*parip

INITIAL

— pierce

evidence | PC payipaham, *to bore a hole into sth;* MC palipāw, *have a hole;* Laure (ca. 1726) "paripasteu, *un petit rayon de lumière qui entre dans un lieu obscur;*" Silvy (ca. 1680) "paripau, paripiskau, *cela est troué, percé*"

*pas

INITIAL

— slow

evidence | SEC pasohtew, *to walk slowly;* NEC pisīu, *to be slow;* Watkins (1865) "Pusipuyew, *v.imp. It moves slowly;*" Laure (ca. 1726) "ni-pasutan, *je marche lentement;*" Fabvre (ca. 1690) "Passin ne passiȣin nȣ, *trauailler Lentemt;*" Silvy (ca. 1680) "ni passȣtan, *je vais bellement, je m'amuse*" discussion | The absence of a preaspiration on the sibilant cannot be confirmed due to the lack of an Atikamekw cognate.

*pasako (~ *pasakw)

INITIAL

— sticky

evidence | PC pasakwahikēw, *to paste or glue;* MC pasakwāw, *to be sticky;* AT (Wemotaci, Nicole Petiquay) pasakwaw [pazakwāw], *to be sticky;* SEC pasakosiw, *to be sticky;* Laure (ca. 1726) "ni-passakutchiuatchititchan, *j'ai les mains pâteuses;*" Silvy (ca. 1680) "ni passagȣabin, ni passakȣabin, *j'ai les yeux fermés, je ferme les yeux*" | ANISH bazagwaa, *to be sticky* (Livesay & Nichols, 2021)

*pasikō

INITIAL (VERB, ANIMATE, INTRANSITIVE)

— rise from seated position

evidence | PC pasikōpahtāw, *to gets up in a hurry;* MC pasikōhew, *to make sb stand from a sitting position;* AT (Wemotaci, Nicole Petiquay) pasiko [pazikow], *to stand up from a sitting position;* SEC pasikōw, *to stand from sitting;* Watkins (1865) "Pusikoonāo, *v.t.an. He raises him (properly, form a sitting posture)*" | ANISH bazigonjise, *to stand up suddenly* (Livesay & Nichols, 2021)

*pask[1]

INITIAL

— **1** snap, sever (speaking of string-like objects)

— **2** part (of a whole quantity or number)

— **3** spark

— **4** win

evidence | [1]PC paskinam, *to break sth string-like off;* MC paskewakipaliw, *to tear a muscle;* SEC paskahtam, *to gnaw through sth string-like;* WI (Pessamit) passipiteu [pəssəpətēw], *to break sth string-like by pulling;* Watkins (1865) "Puskipuyew, *v.imp. It snaps (as cotton or twine)*" [2]MC paski, *a portion;* SEC pasc, *some, a few;* EI (Sheshatshiu) passe [pəssē], *some;* Silvy (ca. 1680) "pasti, *partie*" [3]PC paskitēw, *to spark;* WC paskisow, *to have sparks land on oneself;* MC papaskiletew, *to spark repeatedly;* Laure (ca. 1726) "paspassiteu, *étincelle, bluette (elle vole);*" Silvy (ca. 1680) "ni pastisȣn, *le feu est sur moi*" [4]PC paskiyākēw, *to win;* MC paskilawew, *to win against sb;* Laure (ca. 1726) "ni-passiragauin, *la chance tourne, je perds*" | [1]ANISH baka'an, *to break or part sth string-like using sth* [4]ANISH bakinaw, *to win over sb* (Livesay & Nichols, 2021)

*pask[2]

INITIAL

— hunger

evidence | MC paskewew, *to be skinny;* SEC pascewew, *to be skinny;* Isham (1743) "pe skop pa quan, *starvd;*" Laure (ca. 1726) "suka-a tchi-paskabaguan?, *as-tu grande faim?;*" Silvy (ca. 1680) "ni paskabagȣan, *j'ai faim*" | ANISH bakade, *to be hungry* (Livesay & Nichols, 2021)

*paskē

INITIAL (VERB, ANIMATE, INTRANSITIVE)

— moving away from the main course

evidence | PC paskēw, *to go off to the side, to branch off;* WC paskīskanawīw, *one's tracks leave the main path;* MC paskeštikweyāw, *river branches off;* SEC pascehtew, *to walk off the main path;* Fabvre (ca. 1690) "Pasteïau, *embȣchure, degorgemt d'une Riuiere, fleuue*"

*paskihtē

INITIAL

— strike

evidence | Laure (ca. 1726) "ni-paschiteuau 3. -ueu, *je le bats;*" Fabvre (ca. 1690) "Pastitechinin, *se ietter bas, y tber se hurtant à qlq che;*" Silvy (ca. 1680) "ni pastitehȣau, *je le bats;*" "ni pastitechimau, *je le jette bas*" | ANISH obakite'waan, *to hit sb* (Livesay & Nichols, 2021)

*paskit (~ *paskic)

INITIAL

— extending over

evidence | WC paskitāmaciwīw, *to go over a hill;* MC paskiciciwan, *a stream runs over;* SEC pescitaskāw, *to be an overlying expanse of land, name of a portage between Mistissini and Lac Saint-Jean;* Silvy (ca. 1680) "ni pachtitahen, *je saute par-dessus*" | ANISH bakidagoode, *to hang across the top of sth* (Livesay & Nichols, 2021); MESK pashkichipahowa, *to run over the top*

*paskwahciw[1]

INITIAL (NOUN, INANIMATE)

— tree stump

evidence | MC paskwahciy, *a tree stump; a gunstock;* paskwahcīskaw, *to be many tree stumps;* WI (Pessamit) pashkutshu [pəʃkutʃu], *stump of a green tree; gunstock;* Silvy (ca. 1680) "pask8atchi8, *souche de bois*" | ANISH bakwanj, *a stump with exposed roots* (Livesay & Nichols, 2021)

*paskwahciw[2]

MEDIAL (NOUN INCORPORATION)

— tree stump

evidence | Laure (ca. 1726) "ni-tchetchikupaskuatchiuepiten, *je deracine un arbre*"

*pasp

INITIAL

— **1** through hole

— **2** narrowly escape

evidence | PC paspīw, *to narrowly escape;* MC paspinew, *to have a close call;* paspāšikawin, *to leak through a opening;* SEC paspāpiw, *to look through an opening or window;* WI (Uashat) pashpapuakan [pəʃpāpwān], *window or pane of glass;* Watkins (1865) "Puspinusoo, *v.i.4. He has a narrow escape of his life;*" Silvy (ca. 1680) "ni paspibatan 3. -tau, *je sors fort vite non par la porte*"

*paspaškiw

INITIAL (NOUN, ANIMATE)

— ruffed grouse (Bonasa umbellus)

evidence | PC paspaskiw, *a ruffed grouse;* WC paspaskiw, *ruffed grouse;* ESC (Severn) pahpaškiw, *a ruffed grouse;* MC papaškiw, *a ruffed grouse;* AT (Wemotaci, Jeannette Coocoo) packiw [paškiw], *a ruffed grouse;* SEC (coastal) papašciw, *a ruffed grouse;* (inland) pašpašciw, *a ruffed grouse;* NEC pispischiu, *a ruffed grouse;* WI (Pessamit) pashpassu [pəʃpəssu], *a ruffed grouse;* EI (Sheshatshiu) pashpassu [pəʃpəssu], *a ruffed grouse;* Silvy (ca. 1680) "paspastchi8, *perdrix grise;*" cf. MC & SEC pāškiy, *a ruffed grouse* | ANISH bapashki(wag), *ruffed grouse* (Lippert & Gambill, 2023)

*pašk

INITIAL

— spaced, sparse(ly); (of mesh) large

evidence | MC paškaštāw, *to place things sparsely;* paškalapiy, *a fishing net with large mesh;* NEC pishkihwāu, *to make the mesh large;* Silvy (ca. 1680) "pachkahabi, *rets à grande maille;*" "pachkahigani8i8, *cela est à petites [sic] mailles, v.g. le rets, la raquettes*" | ANISH bashkaabide, *to have gaps between one's teeth;* bashkasab, *net with coarse mesh* (Livesay & Nichols, 2021) compare | *sako

*paško (~ *paškw)

INITIAL

— **1** lose or remove hair, fur, or plumage

— **2** burst blood vessel

evidence | [1]WC paskostikwān, *person with a bald head;* MC paškopitew, *to pluck hair, fur, or feathers from sb;* SEC paškohamawew, *to give sb a haircut*[2]ESC (Severn) paskocehwew, *burst sb open;* MC paškocehtam, *to burst sth with one's teeth;* AT (Wemotaci, Nicole Petiquay) packoctonew [paškoštonēw], *to have a nosebleed;* SEC paškoštonew, *to have a nosebleed;* WI (Pessamit) pashkuaimakanapishkᵘ [pəʃkwīmākənāpəʃkʷ], *blade used for bloodletting;* EI (Sheshatshiu) pashkuaimueu [pəʃkwējmwēw], *to draw blood from sb;* Silvy (ca. 1680) "ni pask8ahiman 3. -mau, *je saigne, je perce la veine;*" "ni pachk8cht8nin, *je saigne du nez*"

*pat[1] (~ *paš)

INITIAL

— miss

evidence | PC patapiw, *to miss one's seat;* MC patahwew, *to fail to hit sb;* SEC patakwew, *for an animal miss a snare;* WI (Pessamit) pashipiteu [pəʃəpətēw], *to miss grabbing sb;* Watkins (1865) "Puchepuyetow, *v.t.in.2. He makes it go wrong, he frustrates it;*" Silvy (ca. 1680) "ni patahen, *je manque à viser*" | ANISH bana', *to miss sb* (Livesay & Nichols, 2021); MIAMI palehtaw-, *to mishear sb* (ILDA, 2017) origin | PA ***paθ** (Hewson, 1993)

*pat[2] (~ *paš)

INITIAL

— **1** sexually mature, speaking of an animal
— **2** old, speaking of a man

evidence | WC patamisk, *a three-year old beaver;* SEC patāwān, *a two-year old bear;* WI (Pessamit) patatshikᵘ [pətātʃukʷ], *a two-year old otter;* Silvy (ca. 1680) "patag8chich, *petit porc-épic;*" "pachirinich, *viellard;*" "ni pachirini8in, *je suis vieux*" | ANISH Nicholas (ca. 1670) "pachirini, *vieux homme*" (Daviault, 1994) origin | PA ***paθ**
discussion | In SEC, WI, and EI this root alternates with reflexes of what would reconstruct as ***pašē**, as in SEC pašetihkʷ, *a caribou aged two years or older.*

*patako

INITIAL

— weigh down

evidence | PC patakwaham, *to hold sth down with sth heavy;* NEC pitikushkim, *to hold sth down with one's weight;* Watkins (1865) "Putukooskowāo, *v.t.an. He falls upon him, he holds him down (as by pressing upon him);*" Laure (ca. 1726) "ni-patakuskauau, *je me couche sur lui [par mégarde];*" Silvy "ni patag8chk8tan 3. -tau, *je mets une chose sur une autre pour la fouler*" | ANISH badagoshkan, *to cover sth with one's body* (Livesay & Nichols, 2021) compare | *māhtako

*patap

INITIAL

— lower towards the ground

evidence | WC patapīw, *to crouch;* MC patapāloweliw, *to lower one's tail;* EI (Sheshatshiu) patapishkuepu [pətəpiʃkwēpu], *to sit with one's head bent forward;* Laure (ca. 1726) "ni-patabichekahen 3. -himu, *je rive le clou*"

*patask

INITIAL

— prick

evidence | MC pataskihtitāw, *to pierce with sth;* AT pataskaham, *to pierce sth;* SEC pataskahikan, *syringe, injection;* Silvy (ca. 1680) "ni patastinau, *je pince, je serre, j'égratigne;*" "ni pataskask8ah8en, *je cloue, je fiche un clou, etc.*" | ANISH badakijin, *to be pricked* (Livesay & Nichols, 2021); MESK patahkahwēwa, *to pierce sb*

*patotē

INITIAL

— off to the side

evidence | PC patotēpitam, *to pull to the side;* MC patotehtew, *to walk off to the side;* WI (Pessamit) patutepu [pətətēpu], *to sit next to where one wanted to sit* compare | *pat[1]

*patw

MEDIAL

— lock of hair

evidence | PC sekipatwān, *braid of hair;* MC sekipatowew, *to braid sb's hair or to cut* *the flesh that hangs from the severed head of a bear into strips;* SEC osecipatwānišīš, *waxwing;* WI (Pessamit) shetshipatuau [ʃētʃəpətwāw], *to wear one's hair in buns over her ears;* Watkins (1865) "Sākeputwān, *n.in. An ornament suspended from the hair (used by the heathen Indians);*" Laure (ca. 1726) "nema nichetchipatuan, *je les porte pendants;*" Silvy (ca. 1680) "ni pitik8pat8an, *j'ai la moustache liée en paquet*" | ANISH Cuoq (1886) "Kawin acaie sekibanwesik Wadjaonak, *les Iroqouises ne portent plus de séguiban;*" zegibanwaanishiinh, *cedar waxwing* (Livesay & Nichols, 2021); MIAMI seekipalwaakani, *hair bow, hair tie* (ILDA, 2017) origin | PA ***paθw**

*paw

INITIAL

— to move, turn over, shake, or brush an object to cause what has accumulated on or in it to fall off or out

evidence | PC pawaham, *to brush sth off, to beat sth;* MC pāhpawipitam, *to shake sth to remove what has gathered on it;* SEC pawākonicipitam, *to shake sth to remove the snow that has accumulated on it;* pawinam, *to pour sth;* WI (Pessamit) paunauakueu [pūnāwkwēw], *to pour sand;* Silvy (ca. 1680) "ni pa8ichimau, *je jette, je verse, v.g. ce qui est dans le calumet*"

*pawē

INITIAL (VERB, ANIMATE, INTRANSITIVE)

— **1** be faintly discernible

— **2** dream

— **3** to augur well or perform ritual to augur well

evidence | PC papēwēhēw, *to make sb lucky;* pawātam, *to dream about sth;* WC papīwīw, *to be lucky in hunting;* ESC pawehtin, *to make a shadow or silhouette behind sth;* pawātew, *to dream of sb;* MC paweyāsikew, *to be barely discernible behind the clouds, speaking of the moon or sun;* pawepahkwešin, *to be faintly discernible through the cover of a dwelling;* pawākan, *a spirit helper;* papewew, *to augure food fortune;* SEC paweyāskohtin, *to be faintly discernible through the trees;* pawāmow, *to dream;* papeweyāpošwew, *to perform a ritual to ensure success snaring hares;* WI (Pessamit) pueiashkushinu [pwējāʃkuʃənu], *to be difficult to make out from afar while moving behind trees;* puamu [pwāmu], *to dream;* papeuemesheu [pəpēwēmēʃēw], *to treat the remains of the fish according to the rules hoping to have luck fishing;* Watkins (1865) "Powatum, *v.t.in.6. He dreams about it;*" "Pupāwāo, *v.i.3. He is fortunate, he is lucky;*" Laure (ca. 1726) "ni-papaueriten, *j'ai pressenti en jonglant;*" "ni-pauatau, *je m'imagine le voir en rêve;*" "ni-papeuaguan, *je chante du porc-épic;*" Fabvre (ca. 1690) "Pape8an, e8, *ch(an)ter pr tr8uer à mger Igles;*" Silvy (ca. 1680) "ni pa8ïask8ahen, *je vais dans les bois;*" "ni pa8e8in, *je suis rêveur;*" "ni pa8aten, *je vois en songe;*" "ni pape8an 3. -e8, *je devine, disant ou faisant qqch. pour trouver à manger*" | ANISH bawaajige, *to have dreams* (Livesay & Nichols, 2021); MENO pawa·nɛ·w, pawa·tam, *to dream of sb, sth*

origin | PA ***pawē** discussion | Evidence for the first sense is supported by multiple contemporary dialects as well as early Jesuit dictionaries. Whether the second sense is derived from the first or vice versa is unclear, but the association between the vague character of dream states and the indistinct appearance of objects obscured by interposed things such as clouds, screens, or trees is quite clear. The cultural association between dreams and fortune explains the third sense, always expressed as a reduplicated form. This reduplication may have originally been triggered by the repetitive nature of song, a ritual practice traditionally carried out prior to harvesting wildlife. Note that the English word "powwow" is derived from an Eastern Algonquian, likely Narragansett, cognate of this root.

*payahtē

INITIAL

— distinct

evidence | ESC payahtenākwan, *to be clearly visible;* MC payahtekāpawiw, *to stand out in the open;* SEC payahtehtākosiw, *to be clearly heard;* WI (Pessamit) paitekapaushu [pīttēkāpūʃu], *to stand alone;* Watkins (1865) "Payùtānakoosew, *v.i.1. He is distinctly visible, he can be seen plainly;*" Fabvre (ca. 1690) "ni piatepinan nanau naȣau, *etre assis séparemt*" | ANISH Nicholas (ca. 1670) "paiaté, *séparément*" (Daviault, 1994)

*pāhkā

INITIAL

— break open

evidence | MC pāhkāhtam, *to break sth open with one's teeth;* AT pakatew [pāhkātew], *to burst from the heat;* SEC pāhkāhikan, *man-made hole in the ice;* NEC pāhkāhtitāw, *to break sth open on impact;* EI (Sheshatshiu) pakapanu [pākāpənu], *to burst*

*pāhko (~ *pāhkw, *pāh, *pāš)

INITIAL

— dry

evidence | PC pāhkwāpiw, *to have dry eyes;* WC pāhkwāhcāw, *to be dry ground;* pāsimināna, *dried berries;* MC pāhkoham, *to dry sth;* pāsam, *to dry sth thoroughly;* AT (Wemotaci, Nicole Petiquay) pakotamo [pākkotāmow], *to be thirsty;* pakosiw [pākkoziw], *to be dry;* (Wemotaci, Nicole Petiquay) pasam [pāssam], *to dry sth;* SEC pāhkopayiw, *to become dry;* pāštew, *to be thoroughly dry;* NEC pāsihkwān, *dried caribou blood;* WI (Pessamit) pakutshu [pākutʃu], *to dry out in the cold;* EI (Sheshatshiu) pakuashu [pākwāʃu], *to dry out in the wind;* Laure (ca. 1726) "pakuaskamisteu, *aridité, sécheresse;*" "ni-passiminan, *je sèche du blé d'inde ou des graines;*" Silvy (ca. 1680) "pakȣau *ign. cela est sec*" | ANISH baaso, *to be dry* (Livesay & Nichols, 2021); MENO pa·qsam, *to dry sth;* MIAMI paankosam-, *to boil down till dry* (ILDA, 2017) origin | PA ***pānkw**. compare | *pāko discussion | The allomorph ***pāh** occurs when followed by heat finals ***s**, ***sw**, and ***so**, while ***pāš** occurs when followed by the heat final ***tē**.

*pāhp

INITIAL

— laugh

evidence | PC pāhpihēw, *to laugh at sb;* MC pāhpiw, *to laugh;* SEC pāhpihkweyiw, *to smile;* Silvy (ca. 1680) "ni papichtin, *je suis rieur, de belle humeur*" see | *āhpi

*pāhpāhtēw

INITIAL (NOUN, ANIMATE)

— flat nevus, beauty mark

evidence | PC Lacombe (1874) "Pāpāttewisiw, ok, *(a.a.) il est tacheté;*" MC pāhpāhtewihkwew, *to have a freckled face;* AT (Opitciwan, Joey Awashish) opapatemiw [opāhpāhtēmiw], *to have beauty marks or freckles;* papatewekisiw [pāhpāhtēwēkisiw], *to be spotted, speaking of sth sheet-like;* SEC pāhpāhtewāw, *to be spotted;* NEC pāhpāhtāushikiyāu, *to have freckled skin* compare | *mīn

*pāhpāštēw

INITIAL (NOUN, ANIMATE)

— woodpecker (other than the northern flicker and pileated woodpecker)

evidence | PC pāhpāstēw, *a big woodpecker;* WC pāspāstīw, *a big woodpecker;* ESC pāhpāštew, *a northern three-toed or black-backed woodpecker;* MC pāhpāstēw, *a woodpecker;* SEC pāhpāstēw & pāšpāstēw, *any number of small woodpeckers excluding the northern flicker and pileated woodpecker;* NEC pāshpāshtāu, *a woodpecker;* Laure (ca. 1726) "papasteu, *pique-bois;*" Silvy (ca. 1680) "papachteu, *pique-bois*" | ANISH baapaase, *a red-headed woodpecker* (Livesay & Nichols, 2021); MENO pa·hpa·qnɛw, *a woodpecker;* MIAMI paapaahsia, *red-headed woodpecker* (ILDA, 2017) origin | PA ***pāhpāʔθēwa** compare | *mēmēw, *wirikwanēw

*pāk[1]

INITIAL

— swell

evidence | PC pākāpiw, *to have swollen eyes;* MC pākipaliw, *to swell;* SEC pācihkwanepayiw, *one's ankle(s) swells;* Silvy (ca. 1680) "ni patchigatan 3. -e8, *j'ai la jambe enflée*" | ANISH baagidenaniwe, *to have a swollen tongue* (Livesay & Nichols, 2021)

*pāk[2]

INITIAL

— knock

evidence | MC pāhpākapihtesiw, *a yellow rail;* Laure (ca. 1726) "ni-papakauau 3. - ueu, *je le bats;*" "ni-pakahaman utitch, *je frappe sur le canot en chantant;*" "ni-pakahiman nititchia, *claquer, je claque des mains;*" "pakahatuetau, *jouons à la crosse;*" Fabvre (ca. 1690) "Pagahat8an, *b8les à I8er;*" Silvy (ca. 1680) "ni pagahigan 3. -e8, ni pagahaman, *je frappe la terre en chantant;*" "pagat8anask8, *crosse*" | ANISH baaga', *to pound or knock on sb;* baaga'adowe, *to play lacrosse* (Livesay & Nichols, 2021); MENO pa·kaham, *to pound sth; to drum on sth with a stick;* MESK pākahamawēwa, *to knock at sth for sb;* pākahatowēwa, *to play lacrosse or baseball;* pākikomēshinwa, *to bump one's nose*

*pākaskōkan

INITIAL (NOUN, ANIMATE)

— emaciated specter that flies with the wind and tickles its captives to death

evidence | MC pākaskōkan, *emaciated specter that tickles its captives to death;* Isham (1743) "Paw kus ko cun nuc, *angels;*" Fabvre (ca. 1690) "Pakask8kan, *especes doyseaux;*" "Pagachk8gan, *pl.* găna, *feux folets*" | ANISH baagak, *ultra-thin bringer of death* (Lippert & Gambill, 2023); Cuoq (1886) "Pakak, *Être fabuleux que l'on entend, dit-on, voler au-dessus des forêts, en poussant des cris sinistres;* Pakakon o ki nondawan ni micomis, awekwenitok pakatewin ka nisigokwen, *mon grand-père a entendu le Pakak, quelqu'un sera mort de faim, qui est-ce?*" origin | Possibly PA ***pākaskwa**. discussion | Despite being a widely held belief, data supporting the above reconstruction is exceedingly sparse. In fact, iterations of the name of this spirit being in Plains Cree, Woods Cree, and Atikamekw—**pāhkahkos**, **pākāhkos**, and **pāhkōkan**, respectively—all reflect influence from neighbouring Anishinabe dialects.

*pāko

INITIAL

— (of a body of water) shallow

evidence | PC pāhkwāw, *to be shallow;* AT (Opitciwan, Joey Awashish) pakwaw [pāhkwāw], *to be shallow water;* SEC & NEC pākwāu, *to be a shallow body of water* (CSB, 2018); Silvy (ca. 1680) "pak8achi8 sipi8, *la rivière est basse*" | ANISH baagwaa, *to be shallow* (Livesay & Nichols, 2021); MENO pa·ki·w, *to be a shallow body of water* compare | *pāhko

*pākomo

INITIAL

— vomit

evidence | PC pwākomohēw, *to make sb vomit;* Lacombe (1874) "pākomow, ok, *(v.n.) il vomit;*" WC pwākomow, *to vomit;* MC pākomohkwew, *to vomit blood;* SEC pākomoškākow, *to vomit from having ingested sth;* WI (Pessamit) puakumu [pwākumū], *to vomit;* EI pakumu [pākumū], *to vomit;* Watkins (1865) "*Vomit, v.i.* Pakoomoo;" Laure (ca. 1726) "ni-pagumupan, *regorger à force de boire;*" Silvy (ca. 1680) "pag8m8in, *vomissement*" see | *m[1], *o compare | *šikakwē

*pān

INITIAL

— open or expose broadly

evidence | PC Lacombe (1874) "Pāninew, *il l'évase;*" WC pānīsiw, *to be broad and shallow;* pānisāwīw, *to cut up meat or fish for drying;* MC pānišam, *to butterfly sth;* NEC pānāyāu, *to be rounded on the bottom;* pānipitāu, *to expand or open sth wide by pulling;* pānihāmisū, *to clear snow to access berries underneath;* SEC pānepitam, *to open sth wide by pulling;* pānipayiw, *to open up and expand;* WI (Pessamit) panetakau [pānētəkāw], *to have a flared shape, speaking of a canoe;* Watkins (1865) "Panepuyew, *v.imp. It expands, it opens out;*" "Panuakoonāo, *v.i.3. He clears away the snow (for making a tent, &c.);*" Silvy (ca. 1680) "paniparĭ8, *cela s'ouvre*" | ANISH baanizhaawe, *to cut meat into strips for preservation, to filet fish* (Livesay & Nichols, 2021)

*pāp (~ *pā)

INITIAL

— arrive

evidence | MC pāpahtāw, *to arrive running;* SEC pāpihyāw, *to arrive flying;* WI (Pessamit) papalu [pāpəlu], *to arrive;* papitshu [pāpətʃu], *to arrive on foot hauling a toboggan*

*pāpako (~ *pāpakw)

INITIAL

— peel

evidence | PC pāpakwatahwēw, *to rub sb raw;* MC pāpakokitikwešin, *to scrape one's knee against a surface causing the skin to peel;* SEC pāpakošam, *to peel sth with a knife;* Fabvre (ca. 1690) "Papag8rakeskahikan e8, *Leuer ecorce du bois de fraine*" | MENO pa·pakonam, *to peel sth by hand, to strip sth away*

*pāsk

INITIAL

— uncover

evidence | PC pāskinam, *to open or uncover sth;* WC pāskākonakīw, *to make fresh tracks in the snow;* MC pāskāštan, *to be uncovered by the wind;* WI (Pessamit) passinamᵘ [pāssnəm], *to uncover sth manually;* Laure (ca. 1726) "ni-paschitenen, *j'ouvre porte, fenêtre*" | ANISH bākinige, *to uncover things* (Livesay & Nichols, 2021)

*pāskat (~ *pāskac)

INITIAL

— moreover

evidence | PC Lacombe (1874) "Pāskatch, *(adv.) jusqu'à, même, v.g. mistahi ni kisimaw, pāskatch e matchi ijit, je l'ai beaucoup fâché, jusqu'au point qu'il m'a insulté, pāskatch nama wi-mitjisuw, il ne veut pas même manger...;*" WSC (Misipawistik, Ellen Cook) pāskac, *actually;* ESC (Severn) pāskac, *regretfully;* MC pāskac, *however;* WI (Pessamit) pashkat [pəʃkət], *what is more, moreover, in addition;* Watkins (1865) "Paskuch, *adv. Affirmatively, strengtheningly;*" Fabvre (ca. 1690) "Paskatch i8a, *cependant, interim*"

*pāš

INITIAL

— hurry

evidence | WSC (Misipawistik, Ellen Cook) papāsīw, *to hurry;* MC papāšīw, *to hurry;* SEC pāhpāšīw, *to hurry;* pāhpāšipow, *to eat in a hurry* discussion | The absence of a preaspiration on the sibilant cannot be confirmed due to the lack of an Atikamekw cognate.

*pāšiko (~ *pāšikw)

INITIAL

— **1** lack visibility, disappear, become imperceptible

— **2** to not perceive, to be inattentive

evidence | PC pāsikwātan, *to be stormy;* MC pāšikwātan, *to be a winter storm;* pāšikonākosiw, *to disappear in the distance;* SEC pāšikweyihtam, *to be excited;* AT (Opitciwan, Joey Awashish) pacikweritam [pāʒikwērihtam], *to lose consciousness;* NEC pāshikunākun, *to disappear from sight;* pāshikwāpihtim, *to lose sight of sth, to see it disappear;* NSK paasikwaayihtaakun, *to be frustrating;* WI (Pessamit) pashikunakuan [pāʃəkunākwən], *to suddenly disappear;* Laure (ca. 1726) "ni-passikunagusin, *je m'envole (disparaissant);*" "ni-passikueriten 3. -tamu, *je ne suis point attentif;*" "ni-pachigutauau 3. -ueu, *je ne suis point attentif à ce qu'il dit;*" Fabvre (ca. 1690) "Pachik8an e8, *se taire, ne faire bruit;*" Silvy (ca. 1680) "ni pachig8eriten, *je suis distrait*"

*pāšit (~ *pāšic)

INITIAL

— pass over

evidence | PC pāsitohtēw, *to walk over sth;* MC pāšitaham, *to pass over sth;* AT pa:šita:sko-, *to go over* (Béland, 1978); SEC pāšicipayiw, *to pass over by vehicle;* Silvy (ca. 1680) "ni pachitahen, *je saute par-dessus*" | ANISH baazhijijiwan, *to overflow* (Livesay & Nichols, 2021)

*pāšk

INITIAL

— burst

evidence | PC pāskāpisin, *to burst one's eyeball on impact;* WC pāskipaðiw, *to burst, such as a balloon;* MC pāškipaliw, *to burst;* SEC pāshkaham, *to burst sth with a tool or strike;* NEC pāshkihtim, *to crack sth open with one's teeth;* WI (Pessamit) pashkaimᵘ [pāʃkājm], *to cut lightly into sth (body part);* Silvy (ca. 1680) "ni pachkamik8an 3. -e8, *je mange un pou entre les dents*" | ANISH baashkide, *to explode or burst from the heat* (Livesay & Nichols, 2021); MESK pāshkyāwi, *to be cracked or burst open*

*pāšt

INITIAL

— crack

evidence | PC pāstinam, *to crack sth manually;* WC pāstipaðiw, *to break, speaking of glass or dry wood;* MC pāšcipaliw, *to crack spontaneously;* SEC pāštāhkatotew, *to crack from dryness;* Laure (ca. 1726) "ni-pachtahen, *je les casse (noisettes)*" | ANISH baasisin, *to crack, shatter on impact* (Livesay & Nichols, 2021) origin | PA ***pāʔθ** discussion | Evidence for the expected Old Cree allomorph ***pāhš** has yet to be located in Cree sources.

*pāštā

INITIAL

— invite misfortune by transgressing

evidence | PC pāstāhēw, *to bring evil to sb;* MC pāštāhowin, *a transgression that invites misfortune;* SEC pāštāhow, *to suffer a misfortune due to having transgressed;* NEC pāshtāmū, *to speak blasphemously;* EI (Sheshatshiu) pashta-tutamᵘ [pāstātūtəm], *to commit a sin or serious offence;* Laure (ca. 1726) "ni-pastauan 3. -ueu, *je pèche en paroles;*" "ni-pastaiteriten, *je pèche de pensées*"

*pātimā

INITIAL

— later, eventually

evidence | PC pātimā, *by and by; later; until;* MC pātimā, *afterwards; not until, only after; unless;* SEC pātimāhikow, *to only be affected by sth later;* NEC pātimāhpinău, *to die later than intended, such as an injured animal* | ANISH baanimaa, *later, after a while, eventually* (Livesay & Nichols, 2021) origin | PA ***pāθemā**

*pāw

INITIAL

— turbulent

evidence | PC pāwistikowan, *to be a series of rapids;* NEC pāushtikui, *a rapids;* EI (Sheshatshiu) paushtikushkau [pāwstukuʃkāw], *to be many rapids;* Laure (ca. 1726) "pauistigu, *saut d'eau, chute;*" Fabvre (ca. 1690) "Pa8ichtik8 *v.* pahaustik, *saltus, sault, chute d'eau, rapide;*" "Pa8ichtik a, *pieux plantés pr arester l'eau"* | ANISH baawitigweyaa, *to be a river with rapids* (Livesay & Nichols, 2021) **limited to** | *štikw

*pāwan

INITIAL

— **1** shrink from loss of moisture, shrivel

— **2** emaciated

evidence | PC pāwanīw, *to be skinny;* WC pāwanīw, *to be skinny;* MC pāwanīw, *to be emaciated from lack of food;* SEC pāwanatin, *to be freeze-dried;* NEC pāunīu, *to faint from hunger* | ANISH baawanajidoon, *to freeze dry sth* (Livesay & Nichols, 2021)

*pē

INITIAL

— wait

evidence | PC pēhtāw, *to wait for sth;* MC pehew, *to wait for sb;* SEC pehow, *to wait;* Silvy (ca. 1680) "ni pehau, *je l'attends"* | ANISH bii'o, *to wait* (Livesay & Nichols, 2021) **origin** | PA ***pyē** (Hewson, 1993)

*pēhk

INITIAL

— clean

evidence | PC Lacombe (1874) "Pekkisiw, *il est pur, net;"* WC pīhkan, *to be clean;* WSC (Misipawistik, Ellen Cook) pēhkisiw, *to be clean;* ESC (Severn) payehkanasitew, *to have clean feet;* MC payehkan & palehkan (Biblical form), *to be clean; to be holy; to be ritually pure;* AT pekinakon [pēhkinākon], *to look clean;* (Wemotaci, Jeannette Coocoo) pekiteritamowin [pēhkiterihtamowin], *serenity;* SEC payehkan, *to be clean;* payehcitehew, *to be pure-hearted;* NEC piyāhchihtāu, *to clean sth* | ANISH bekisagaa, *to be a clean floor* (Lippert & Gambill, 2023); MENO pɛckaqtaw, *to place sth well; to put sth properly in place;* MIAMI peehkisam-, *to cook sth well;* peehkinaakosi, *to be generous, to be kind*

*pēhkāt (~ *pēhkāc)

INITIAL

— gently

evidence | PC Lacombe (1874) "Pekkātch, *(adv.) ou, Pekikātchi, tranquillement, lentement, (ce mot est peu usité);"* ESC (Severn) pehkācīw, *to be slow;* pehkāc, *slowly, gently;* AT (Wemotaci, Jeannette Coocoo) pekatc [pēhkāc], *slowly, gently;* SEC pēhkātowew, *to speak slowly or gently,* NEC pāhkāch, *slowly, gently;* Watkins (1865) "P'ākach, *adv. carefully, gently, softly, slowly"* | ANISH Cuoq (1886) "Pekatowe, *parler doucement, d'un ton modéré;"* "Pekatc, *tranquille, sans bouger, en repos; doucement, sans bruit"*

*pēhpēhkw

INITIAL (NOUN, ANIMATE)

— spleen

evidence | SEC nipehpehkʷ, *my spleen;* WI (Pessamit) upepekᵘ [upēpēkʷ], *a spleen;* EI (Sheshatshiu) upepekᵘ [upēpēkʷ], *a spleen;* Silvy (ca. 1680) "pepekȣ, *la rate"* **compare** | *pīhpišk **discussion** | In the absence of a Woods Cree cognate, the status of the preaspiration cannot be confirmed.

*pēhš

INITIAL

— stripe

evidence | PC Lacombe (1874) "pesakunehwew, *il tire des lignes sur la neige;"* ESC pešāw, *to be striped;* MC pešāwikanew, *to have a striped back;* pešišin, *to suffer a cut upon contact with sth;* AT (Opitciwan, Joey Awashish) pecāw [pēššāw], *to be striped;* SEC pešāw, *to be striped;* NEC pāshāpiskāu, *to have a vein, speaking of a rock;* WI (Pessamit) peshaim [pēʃīm], *to paint sth;* Fabvre (ca. 1690) "Pechahigan 3 keȣ, *rayer peaux passées faire des rayes"* | ANISH beshaa, *to have a line, a stripe* (Livesay & Nichols, 2021)

*pēhšo (~ *pēhšw)

INITIAL

— **1** near

— **2** short, when speaking of periods of time

evidence | [1]WC pīsohtawīw, *to hear sb from close;* ESC pešoc, *close by;* MC pešonākwan, *to be near;* AT peššona:kosi-, *to be close* (Béland, 1978); SEC pešwāpahtam, *to be near sth;* Silvy (ca. 1680) "pech8tchich, *il n'y a pas loin, proche*" [2]MC pešo-kīšikāw, *to be a short day;* NEC pāshupipun, *to be a short winter;* Silvy (ca. 1680) "pech8tibiskachi8, *les nuits sont courtes*" | [1]ANISH beshonaagwad, *to appear to be close* (Livesay & Nichols, 2021) [2]ANISH besho-biboon, *to be a short winter* (Livesay & Nichols, 2021)

*pēht (~ *pēhc)

INITIAL

— hear

evidence | PC pēhtākosiw, *to be heard;* MC pēhtam, *to hear sth;* WI (Pessamit) petueu [pētwēw], *to hear sb* see | *ıht³

*pēk

INITIAL

— burp

evidence | PC pēkatēskiw, *to burp frequently;* MC pekatehāwasow, *to burp a child;* SEC pekatew, *to burp;* Silvy (ca. 1680) "ni pekatan 3. -te8, *je rote*" limited to | *at³

*pēkihkāt (~ *pēkihkāc)

INITIAL

— slow

evidence | WC pēkīhkātisiw, *to be slow;* MC pekihkātahcikew, *to eat slowly;* WI (Pessamit) petshikatshish [pētʃəkātʃīʃ], *very slowly or gently;* Laure (ca. 1726) "tchi-petchikatisin, *tu ne te dépêches pas;*" Silvy (ca. 1680) "ni pepetchikat8an 3.-e8, *je parle lentement*" | ANISH Cuoq (1886) "Papekikatis,i, *être lent*"

*pēko (~ *pēkw)

INITIAL

— **1** come to the surface

— **2** awaken

evidence | [1]PC pēkopēw, *to come to the surface of the water;* MC pekopepalihow, *to surface from the water;* SEC pekwākonacīw, *to come out from under the snow;* Silvy (ca. 1680) "ni peg8ban 3. -e8, *je viens au-dessus de l'eau*" [2]PC pēkopayiw, *to awaken;* MC pekociw, *to be awakened by the cold;* SEC pekomew, *to wake sb up with one's voice;* Silvy (ca. 1680) "ni peg8n, *je m'éveille*"

*pēm

INITIAL

— cross

evidence | ESC pemakāmeciwan, *rivers meet;* MC pemahokātepiw, *to sit with legs crossed;* pemiciwan, *current flows into another current perpendicularly;* NEC pāmishtikwāu, *to cross a river;* EI (Unaman-shipit) pemishtikutaushinu [pēmihtikutāwhɨnu], *to lie with legs crossed;* Laure (ca. 1726) "ni-pemiskaman 3. -meu, *je coupe le chemin (traversant);*" Silvy (ca. 1680) "pemabegam8, *il est de travers, de biais*"

*pēmak (~ *āpēmak)

MEDIAL

— leaf

evidence | PC atihkwāpēmak, *birch willow;* MC mihkopemak^w & mihkwāpemak^w, *red-osier dogwood;* SEC sācipemakan, *to bud;* WI (Pessamit) ishipemakau [īʃəpēməkāw], *to be thus, speaking of leaves;* EI (Ekuanitshit) atikupemak^u [atīkupēmuk^w], *dwark birch;* Laure (ca. 1726) "mikuabemagu-miuech, *panier fait d'osier;*" Silvy (ca. 1680) "chachak8pemak8, *espèce d'arbre*" | ANISH miskwaabiimag(w), *red-osier dogwood* (Livesay & Nichols, 2021) origin | PA *(ā) **pyēmak** (Hewson, 1993) see | *nīpiy, *ēmak compare | *pak

*pēmāw

INITIAL

— **1** crossed

— **2** confuse one for another, mismatch

evidence | MC pemāwasinātew, *to be marked with an X;* pehpemāwaskisinew, *to wear a non-matching pair of shoes;* WI (Pessamit) pepemaushtisheu [pēpēmāwstəʃēw], *to wear mismatched mittens;* EI (Sheshatshiu) pemauneu [pēmāwnēw], *to confuse sth for another when taking it;* Silvy (ca. 1680) "pemau, *par-dessus le compte*" see | *pēm

*pēšiw

INITIAL (VERB, TRANSITIVE, ANIMATE)

— bring

evidence | PC pēsiwēw, *to bring sb;* MC pešiwew, *to bring sb;* Fabvre (ca. 1690) "Pech8au, *n. Amener, aporter par terre, v.g.* ki pech8in v. pechi8in, *tu m amene par terre*" paired with | *pētā compare | *pēt¹

*pēt¹ (~ *pēc)

INITIAL

— hither

evidence | PC pētakocin, *to come through the air;* MC pęciciwan, *the tide flows;* SEC petācimow, *to bring news;* Silvy (ca. 1680) "ni peterimau, *je pense qu'il vient en deçà*" | ANISH biidaaboode, *to drift here on the current* (Livesay & Nichols, 2021) origin | PA ***pyēt** (Hewson, 1993)

*pēt² (~ *pēc, *pēs)

INITIAL

— slowly

evidence | PC pēsiskāw, *to go slowly;* papētan, *to be slow;* WC papicīw, *to be slow;* ESC (Severn) papecipahtāw, *to run slowly;* SEC papēčīw, *to be slow* | ANISH bejigi, *to grow slowly* (Livesay & Nichols, 2021); MENO pɛ·cecemɛ·w, *to paddle or swim slowly;* pɛ·sɛhkaw, *to move or go slowly* origin | PA ***pēt** (Hewson, 1993)

*pētā (~ *pētw)

INITIAL (VERB, ANIMATE, INTRANSITIVE)

— bring

evidence | PC pētāw, *to bring sth;* MC petowew, *to bring sth for sb;* ki petwātin, *I bring sth for you;* SEC pētāw, *to bring sth;* Fabvre (ca. 1690) "ki pet8ă8in, *tu m'aporte qlq che par terre;*" Silvy (ca. 1680) "ni petan 3. -tau, *j'apporte par terre*" paired with | *pēšiw compare | *pēt¹ discussion | The ***pētw** allomorph surfaces only for further derivation when suffixing the benefactive ***aw**. Its origin predates what is otherwise a loss of morphological distinction in Old Cree between Proto-Algonquian transitive inanimate verb class II and animate intransitive verbs ending in ***ā** (cf. Pentland, 1999). Note that contemporary dialects have all contracted ***pētw** + ***aw** to a reflex of ***pētow**, but the underlying form is revealed when vowel-lengthening processes occur, resulting in reflexes of ***pētwā** as expected.

*pēyako (~ *pēyakw)

INITIAL

— one

evidence | PC pēyakwan, *to be one or alone;* WC pīyakosāp, *eleven;* MC peyakow, *to be alone;* peyakwāpek, *one string-like object;* SEC peyakopišiw, *to sit alone;* NEC pāyikunāu, *to hold one;* WI (Pessamit) peikuteshu [pējkutēʃu], *to walk alone;* EI (Sheshatshiu) peikutat [pējkutət], *one canoe;* Laure (ca. 1726) "pepéioku, *l'un après l'autre;*" Silvy (ca. 1680) "peïok8au, *une fois*" compare | *nikoto

*picērak

INITIAL

— just now

evidence | ESC (Severn) picenak, *just then, at that point, as yet only;* MC picelak, *just beginning to;* EI (Mamit) pitshenik [pitʃēnak], *to be just beginning;* Silvy (ca. 1680) "pitcherik, *tout maintenant*" | ANISH bijiinag, *after a while, eventually; just now; recently* (Livesay & Nichols, 2021) limited to | *a

*pici[1]

INITIAL (VERB, ANIMATE, INTRANSITIVE)

— haul camp

evidence | PC piciw, *to move camp; to move one's belongings and family;* NEC pichiu, *to leave for winter camp;* WI (Pessamit) pitshu [pətʃu], *to move camp on foot hauling a toboggan;* Silvy (ca. 1680) "ni pitchin, *je décabane*" see | *pici²

*pici[2]

FINAL (VERB, ANIMATE, INTRANSITIVE, DERIVED)

— haul camp

evidence | PC ispiciw, *to move camp thither;* MC māhipiciw, *to haul camp downstream;* WI (Pessamit) papitshu [pāpətʃu], *to arrive on foot hauling a toboggan* see | *pici¹

*picikīškihšīhš

INITIAL (NOUN, ANIMATE)

— chickadee (Poecile spp.)

evidence | PC picikīskosīs, *a chickadee;* WC (Stanley Mission, Solomon Ratt) picikīskisīs, *a chickadee;* AT (Opitciwan, Patrick Awashish) mitcikickacic [mīcikīškaššiš], *a chickadee;* SEC picikīškašīš, *a chickadee;* (Waswanipi) micikīškašīš, *a chickadee;* WI pitshikaishkashish (Pessamit) [pətʃəkīʃkəʃīʃ] & (Uashat) [pətʃəkējʃkəʃīʃ], *a boreal chickadee;* Laure (ca. 1726) "pichikitchich, *pie*"

*pihcikay

INITIAL (NOUN, DEPENDENT INANIMATE)

— pelvis

evidence | MC opihcikay, *one's pelvis;* NEC upihchikī, *pelvis;* EI (Sheshatshiu) upitshikai [upītʃikēj], *a pelvis*

*pihkah

INITIAL

— scorch, toast

evidence | PC pihkasikan, *a toast;* WC pihkasow, *to be burnt black;* SEC pihkasweu, *to toast sth;* NEC pihkihtāu, *to be scorched;* Laure (ca. 1726) "pikasu, *brûlé, trop rôti*" limited to | *s, *so², *sw, *tē⁴ see | *ɪhkahtē, *ɪhkahs, *ɪhkahso

*pihko[1]

INITIAL

— free, escape

evidence | PC pihkohēw, *to free sb;* SEC pihkohtāw, *to earn sth;* NEC pihkuhū, *to get free or loose;* Watkins (1865) "Pìkootow, *v.t.in.2., He earns it, he gains it;*" Laure (ca. 1726) "ni-pikuhitisun 3. -su, *j'échappe du danger;*" Silvy (ca. 1680) "ni pik8h8n, *je suis hors du danger*"

*pihko[2] (~ *pihkw)

INITIAL (NOUN, INANIMATE)

— dust, powder

evidence | ESC pihko, *gunpowder;* pihkotew, *ash;* MC pihkokamikʷ, *a building used for storing gunpowder;* SEC pihkošīš, *blackfly;* NEC pihkutāu, *ashes, soot; fireplace;* WI (Pessamit) pikᵘ [pukʷ], *gunpowder; baking powder;* Watkins (1865) "Pìkoowut, *n.in. A keg of gunpowder, a gunpowder keg;*" Laure (ca. 1726) "piku, *cendre, poussière*" | ANISH bingwi, *ashes; sand;* obingwa'aan, *to throw sand or ashes at sth* (Livesay & Nichols, 2021)

*pihko[3] (~ *pihkw, *pihkwak)

MEDIAL, FINAL (NOUN INCORPORATION)

— dust, powder

evidence | AT pirepikw [pīrepihkw], *ashes;* MC pīhcipihkwew, *to load a firearm;* SEC cicipihkweyāw, *to be a loaded gun;* Laure (ca. 1726) "miramauipikuagan, *poudre éventée;*" Silvy (ca. 1680) "ni pitchipik8an, *je charge l'arquebuse*"

*pihrak

INITIAL

— peel

evidence | PC poyakinam, *to peel sth by hand;* SEC (Waskaganish) pohīkahtam, *to peel sth by mouth;* SEC (Oujé-Bougoumou) opihyakahtaweyāhtik[w] [uphīkāhtaweyāhtikw], *stick gnawed clean by beaver;* EI pinakaim[u] [pīnakējm], *to peel sth using a tool;* Laure (ca. 1726) "upiragataueu -a, *bois rongé par le castor;*" "ni-piratsiteraniuan, *j'ai la langue écorchée;*" Fabvre (ca. 1690) "Pirakinen n. nau 3 nam8, *enleuer en ecorchant*" | ANISH bishagibijige, *to peel things by hand* (Livesay & Nichols, 2021); MESK panakahamwa, *chop or scrape the bark or rind off of sth;* MIAMI palakin-, *to peel or husk sb* (ILDA, 2017)

*pihrēko (~ *pihrēkw)

INITIAL

— to offer resistance against movement, to cause friction (when speaking of a solid, rough; when speaking of a liquid, thick or viscous; when speaking of a moving object, to move with difficulty due to friction)

evidence | PC pihēkwāw, *to be rough and hard to swallow;* WC piðīkwāw, *to be difficult to pull, to feel heavy to pull;* piðīkwākamiw, *to be a thick liquid;* ESC pinekopaniw, *to slide roughly over a surface;* MC pilekwāciwahtew, *to thicken from boiling;* NEC pihyākuhtāu, *to thicken sth;* SEC pihyekoštew, *to thicken from sitting;* WI (Pessamit) pilekuau [pəlēkwāw], *to be rough or coarse;* pilekupanu [pəlēkupəlu], *to have trouble moving forward;* Silvy (ca. 1680) "pireg8tin, *cela tient fort, ut pictura*"

*pihsamē

INITIAL (VERB, ANIMATE, INTRANSITIVE)

— make smudge fire

evidence | PC tisamān, *a smudge fire;* MC pasamew, *to makes smoke to repel mosquitoes;* AT (Wemotaci, Jeannette Coocoo) pisaman [pissamān], *a smudge fire;* Silvy (ca. 1680) "ni pisaman, *je fume les maringouins*" | cf. MESK peswēwa, *to smoke sb out, such as bees or a bear*

*pihšihšiko (~ *pihšihšikw)

INITIAL

— empty

evidence | MC pišišikoskitew, *to be an empty building;* AT (Wemotaci, Nicole Petiquay) picicikw [piššiššik[w]], *all the time;* SEC pišiškwāw [piššikwāw], *to be empty;* WI (Pessamit) pissikuatam[u] [pəssukutəm], *to eat sth without garnish or condiment;* EI (Mamit) pissik[u] [pissuk[w]], *without anything or anyone else, only, nothing but;* Laure (ca. 1726) "pichichiguau, pichichigu, *vide, vidé, où il n'y a rien*" | ANISH bizhishigozi, *to be empty* (Livesay & Nichols, 2021)

*pihšiko (~ *pihšikw)

INITIAL

— detach, unfasten, come loose

evidence | MC pišikonam, *to lose one's grip on sth;* AT (Wemotaci, Nicole Petiquay) picikoparin [piššikoparin], *to come loose or detach spontaneously;* WC pisikwāhcinam, *to misstep on ground;* SEC pišikoškam, *to knock sth loose with one's foot or body;* NEC pishikupiyiu, *to come loose or detach spontaneously;* WI (Pessamit) pishikumeu [pəʃəkumēw], *to dislocate, disconnect, take sth apart with one's teeth;* Fabvre (ca. 1690) "Pichik8parin i8, *se desunir, desfaire;*" Silvy (ca. 1680) "ni pichig8nen, *je laisse tomber qqch*" | ANISH bishigobide, *to slip off* (Livesay & Nichols, 2021)

*pihšikwāt (~ *pihšikwāc)

INITIAL

— licentious

evidence | PC pisikwātiskwēw, *whore, prostitute;* WC pisikwātis, *adulterer;* MC pišikwātisīw, *to be licentious or adulterous;*

pišikwātelihtam, *to think licentiously, to lust;* SEC pišikwātisīwin, *adultery;* Laure (ca. 1726) "pachikuat-iskueu, *prostituée, abandonnée au crime*" | ANISH bishigwaajimaagozi, *to smell nasty* (Livesay & Nichols, 2021) see | *pihšiko, *āt⁵

*pik

INITIAL

— discharge viscous substance

evidence | WC (Stanley Mission, Solomon Ratt) pikistanīw, *to have a nosebleed;* MC pikisihkowinew, *to drool;* SEC picisihkwew, *to drool;* EI (Sheshatshiu) pitshishikueu [pətʃʃīkwēw], *to drool* see | *pikiw

*pikisk

INITIAL

— haze, fog

evidence | MC pikiskanahan, *to be a blue haze during a heatwave;* NEC pichiskin, *to be a misty blue sky during warm weather;* WI (Pessamit) pitshishkan [pətʃəʃkən], *to be a heat haze on the horizon in clear weather;* Laure (ca. 1726) "pitchiskanu, *brouillard de chaleur;*" Silvy (ca. 1680) "pitchiskan, *il fait brouillard*"

*pikišk

INITIAL

— reduce to pieces

evidence | PC pikiskatin, *to be decayed;* MC pikiškišam, *to cut into pieces;* SEC piciškahtam, *to chew sth into pieces;* Silvy (ca. 1680) "pitchichtichȣau, *je le hache en pièces*"

*pikiw

INITIAL (NOUN, ANIMATE)

— gum

evidence | MC pikīhkew, *to make resin or pitch;* NEC pichīwāskun, *to be gummy, speaking of sth stick-like;* Watkins (1865) "Pikèkatum, *v.t.in.6. He pitches it, he smears it with pitch;*" Silvy (ca. 1680) "pitchiȣ, *brai*" | ABEN bego, *gum, pitch, tar, rubber* (Day, 1995); ANISH bigiike, *to apply pitch, tar, or putty* (Livesay & Nichols, 2021) origin | PA ***pekiw**. see | *pik, *skiw

*piko (~ *pikw)

INITIAL

— only

evidence | PC piko, *only;* Lacombe (1874) "pikonata, *(adv.) sans dessein, sans raison, gratis;*" ESC (Severn) piko *only, just;* MC piko, *only; but; any;* neštapiko, *or;* pakwantaw, *any; wrongly; trivially;* mikocika, *at least;* AT pikotc [pikoc], *only;* SEC mikʷ, *only, just;* natamikʷ, *any;* neštamikʷ, *or;* NEC mikw, *only; or;* mikuchī, *for a short while;* WI & EI mukᵘ [mukʷ], *only, just; but;* EI (Sheshatshiu) natamikᵘ [ntəmukʷ], *any;* Laure (ca. 1726) "egu miku, eogu miku, *seulement;*" Fabvre (ca. 1690) "mikȣtchĭgai, mikȣtchĭga mitchisȣïeigȣa, *encore si uȣs auiez m(an)gé;*" Silvy (ca. 1680) "memikȣ, *longtemps*" | ANISH Nicholas (ca. 1670) "pikoutch, *seulement*" (Daviault, 1994)

*pikwat

INITIAL

— unclaimed, wild, uninhabited, isolated

evidence | PC pakwatōsān & pikwatōsān *an illegitimate child;* MC pakwataskamik, *in the wilderness;* NEC pikutiskwāu, *female deity associated with the hunt who assists hunters;* EI (Mushuau) pikutipi [pukutəpī], *enclosed lake (with no feeder or outlet);* Watkins (1865) "Pikwucheayiseyinew, n.an. *A lonely man, a barbarian. The word would answer for a hermit;*" Laure (ca. 1726) "pikuatchirinichich, *esprit follet;*" Silvy (ca. 1680) "ni pikȣatichan 3. -eu, *j'ai un enfant d'autre que de mon mari*" | MENO pekuac, *prenoun: growing wild*

*pikwā

INITIAL

— make hole, pierce through

evidence | PC pikwāhwēw, *to pierce sb with a tool or projectile;* WC pikwāwanipī, *hole in the ice;* NEC (Wemindji) kā pikwāyāwihkāw, *place name, literally 'the hole in the sand'* (Bishop, 2022); pikwāunipī, *open water on lake, bay, river during winter;* pikwāhīpānān, *winter fish net setting hole;* EI (Sheshatshiu) pikuanipeu [pukwānɨpēw], *to set a net under the ice;* Fabvre (ca. 1690) "Pik8a8anipi, *eau d'un tr8 qui ne gele pas;*" Silvy (ca. 1680) "pik8ahiban, *trou en la glace;*" "pik8atin, *il entre, v.g. un bon couteau;*" "ni pik8anen, *je fourre le doigt, la main dans la chair*" | ANISH Cuoq (1886) "Pikwaige, *percer la glace*"

*pim[1]

INITIAL

— along a length of space or time

evidence | PC pimihtin, *to lie extended;* pimotam, *to shoot sth with an arrow;* papāmohtēw, *to walk about;* ESC pimātisiw, *to live;* MC pimišimew, *to lay sb down;* pimwew, *to shoot sb;* SEC pimipayin, *to move along; to run or function;* pimosinātaham, *to throw a stone at sth;* papāmāšiw, *to sail about;* NEC pimuhtāu, *to walk along;* WI (Pessamit) pimueuiatsheu [pmwēwījātʃēw], *to make a sound from one's wings in passing;* pimutakueu [pmūtəkwēw], *to shoot with a bow;* Laure (ca. 1726) "tchiui-pimun, *tu veux en tirer contre moi;*" Silvy (ca. 1680) "ni pimah8tan 3. -tau, *je porte qqch par eau;*" "ni pim8tak8an 3. -e8, *je tire mon arc*" origin | PA ***pem** (Aubin, 1975; Hewson, 1993) compare | *pimo

*pim[2]

INITIAL

— fat, grease

evidence | WC pimihkān, *pemmican;* SEC pimihkān, *pemmican;* NEC pimisāwān, *grease floating on top of cooking liquid;* WI (Pessamit) pimishu [pməʃu], *to produce grease from cooking;* pimiteu [pmətēw], *to produce grease from cooking;* Laure (ca. 1726) "ka pimitetjs, *bouillon gras, épais;*" Silvy (ca. 1680) "ni pimikan, *je sauce, je trempe dans la sauce;*" "ni pimisa8an, *je tire la graisse des os pilés, bouillis*" | ANISH bimide, *grease, oil, lard* (Livesay & Nichols, 2021) origin | PA ***pemyi** (Hewson, 1993) see | *pimiy, *pim³

*pim[3]

MEDIAL (NOUN INCORPORATION)

— fat, grease

evidence | WC pīhcipimīw, *to put gas in, to gas up;* MC mōpimew, *to eat grease;* SEC manahipimātam, *to skim the grease from sth;* WI (Pessamit) ueńutshipimeu [wēlūtʃəpmēw], *to have plenty of grease;* Silvy (ca. 1680) "ni manahipiman, *j'amasse la graisse*" see | *pimiy, *pim²

*pimisow[1]

INITIAL (NOUN, ANIMATE)

— American eel (Anguilla rostrata)

evidence | WI (Pessamit) upimishui [upəməʃwī], *American eel;* EI (Mamit) upimishui [upmɨhwī], *American eel;* Laure (ca. 1726) "pimissu *pl.* -ets, *anguille;*" Silvy (ca. 1680) "pimis8, *anguille*" | ANISH Cuoq (1886) "Pimisi, *anguille*" see | *pim², *so², *pimisow² discussion | In the absence of an Atikamekw cognate, the lack of a preaspirate is presumed etymologically.

*pimisow[2]

MEDIAL, FINAL (NOUN INCORPORATION)

— American eel (Anguilla rostrata)

evidence | Laure (ca. 1726) "ni-uachuan, ni-nutchipimisuan, *je vais au flambeau pêcher de l'anguille;*" Silvy (ca. 1680) "achichtchipimis8, *anguille fraîche*" see | *pimisow¹

*pimit (~ *pimic)

INITIAL

— crosswise, sideways

evidence | PC pimicikāpawiw, *to stand sideways;* MC pimitāskohtin, *to lie crosswise, speaking of a stick-like object;* SEC pimitāštan, *to be blown sideways by the wind;* Laure (ca. 1726) "ni-pimitchipiten, *je déchire de travers;*" Silvy (ca. 1680) "ni pimitapin, *je suis assis de travers, je suis couché*" | ANISH bimidabi, *to sit sideways* (Livesay & Nichols, 2021)

*pimiy

INITIAL (NOUN, INANIMATE)

— fat, grease

evidence | PC pimīwakan, *to smell greasy or oily;* MC pimiy, *fat, grease, or oil obtained from animals or plants;* SEC pimīwan, *to be greasy;* EI (Sheshatshiu) pimi [pmī], *rendered grease; oil; gasoline;* Silvy (ca. 1680) "pimi, *graisse*" origin | PA ***pemyi*** (Hewson, 1993) see | *pim², *pim³ compare | *šōpiy, *wīkw, *wīrinw, *wīhs²

*pimo (~ *pimw)

INITIAL (VERB, TRANSITIVE, ANIMATE)

— throw or shoot a projectile at sb or sth

evidence | PC pimotam, *to shoot sth with an arrow;* MC pimwew, *to shoot sb;* SEC pimosinātaham, *to throw a stone at sth;* WI (Pessamit) pimutakueu [pmūtəkwēw], *to shoot with a bow;* Laure (ca. 1726) "tchiui-pimun, *tu veux en tirer contre moi;*" Silvy (ca. 1680) "ni pim8tak8an 3. -e8, *je tire mon arc*" see | *pim¹, *w²

*pin

INITIAL

— fall down, fall out

evidence | PC pinipayihow, *to throw oneself down;* MC pinatawepaliw, *fur falls out;* SEC pinipayiw, *to fall off in small fragments;* WI (Pessamit) pinassiu [pənāssīw], *leaves fall from trees;* Laure (ca. 1726) "pinacheu tchinebiku, *muer, le serpent mue (peau)*" compare | *pinē¹

*pinat (~ *pinaš)

FINAL (VERB, TRANSITIVE, ANIMATE, CONCRETE)

— harm or affect negatively

evidence | PC kīspinatēw, *to earn enough to purchase sb;* MC nōspinatew, *to follow sb;* SEC nāspinatew, *to chase sb;* Laure (ca. 1726) "ni-naspinatau, *je le poursuis, cours après lui;*" "uir ka iariui-atchitak uir eogu ka tchispinatat, *le plus offrant et dernier enchérisseur*" see | *pinē², *t⁵ compare | *ahpinat, *nat²

*pinē¹

INITIAL (VERB, ANIMATE, INTRANSITIVE)

— give birth, deliver offspring

evidence | WC pinīyāwīw, *to lay eggs;* SEC pinemiskowiw, *to give birth, speaking of a beaver;* WI (Pessamit) pineiaku [pənējāku], *to give birth, speaking of a porcupine;* EI (Sheshatshiu) pineshku [pine:ʃku], *to give birth, speaking of a bear;* Laure (ca. 1726) "ni-pinetutauau 3. -ueu, *j'accouche de lui;*" "ka pinehitchet, *matrone, qui accouche les femmes;*" Silvy (ca. 1680) "ni pinan 3. -e8, *j'accouche;*" "pinea8eu, *l'oiseau pond*" | MENO peni·w, *to bear young* compare | *pin, *pinē²

*pinē²

FINAL (VERB, ANIMATE, INTRANSITIVE, CONCRETE)

— **1** be ill

— **2** harm or affect negatively, of transitive clauses derived from the above stem

evidence | PC taspinēw, *to be ill for such a time;* kīspinatēw, *to earn enough to purchase sb;* Laure (ca. 1726) "ni-naspinatau, *je le poursuis, cours après lui;*" "uir ka iariui-atchitak uir eogu ka tchispinatat, *le plus offrant et dernier enchérisseur*" compare | *ahpinē, *nē³, *pinē¹ see | *ıspinē, *āspinē

*pipikwē

INITIAL (VERB, ANIMATE, INTRANSITIVE)

— blow whistle or flute

evidence | PC pipikwan, *eagle bone whistle, flute;* MC pipikwew, *to play the flute or pipe;* Watkins (1865) "Pipikwun, *n.in. A flute, a trumpet*" | ANISH bibigwe, *to play the flute;* MENO pepe·kow AI, *to blow a flute;* pepi·kwan, nepɛ·pekwan, *flute, whistle* see | *wē¹

*pipon

INITIAL (VERB, INANIMATE, INTRANSITIVE)

— winter

evidence | PC piponawēw, *to have one's winter pelage;* WC piponaskisin, *winter boot;* ESC pipon, *to be winter;* MC piponišiw, *to winter;* SEC piponasiw, *gyrfalcon;* Silvy (ca. 1680) "ni pip8napin, *j'hiverne*"

*piponw

MEDIAL, FINAL (NOUN INCORPORATION)

— **1** winter

— **2** year

evidence | [1]PC pāscipiponēw, *to survives the winter;* MC nakipiponew, *to be stopped (from migrating) due to the winter weather* [2]WC nīsopiponīw, *to be two years old;* SEC peyako-pipon, *one year;* NEC nīshupipunwāsiu, *to be two years old;* Laure (ca. 1726) "tan etatu pipunueshin? *quel âge as-tu*" see | *pipon, *w[1]

*pir

INITIAL

— scale, remove scales from

evidence | PC piyahwēw, *to scale a fish;* WC piðahwīw, *to scale sb;* WSC (Misipawistik, Ellen Cook) pinawēw, *to scale a fish;* Watkins (1865) "Pinuwāo, *v.t.an. She scales him (i.e., the fish);*" "Pinuumāsāo, *v.i.3. She is scaling fish;*" Laure (ca. 1726) "tchi-pirauaganiu, *écaillé;*" Fabvre (ca. 1690) "Pirahamesan e8, *escailler poisson, en oster escailles*" discussion | Contemporary East Cree dialects make use of the initial ***pīw** rather than the above, likely as a result of hypercorrection, while Innu dialects have replaced the above with reflexes of ***pihrak**.

*pirēhsiw

INITIAL (NOUN, ANIMATE)

— bird of a larger species such as raptors and waterfowl and excluding songbirds and grouse

evidence | PC piyēsiw, *thunder; a thunder-bird;* WC piðīsiw, *thunderbird;* MC pilesīskāw, *to be many large birds;* AT (Wemotaci, Jeannette Coocoo) piresiw [pirēssiw], *large bird or duck;* SEC piyesiw, *any bird of a larger species such as raptors and waterfowl and excluding songbirds and gallinaceous birds;* WI (Pessamit) pileshu [pəlēʃu], *a large bird;* Laure (ca. 1726) "pirechiuets, *gibier, generice, voir canard, les sortes de gibier*" | ANISH binesi, *a bird of a large species; a raptor (a hawk or eagle); a thunderbird* (Livesay & Nichols, 2021)

*pirēhšīhš

INITIAL (NOUN, ANIMATE)

— bird of a smaller species such as songbirds and excluding raptors, waterfowl, and grouse

evidence | PC piyēsīs, *a small bird;* WC piðīsīsikamik, *a bird house;* MC pilešīš, *bird of a smaller species such as songbirds and excluding raptors, waterfowl, and grouse;* AT (Wemotaci, Jeannette Coocoo) pirecicak [pirēššīššak], *birds;* SEC piyešīš, *bird of a smaller species such as songbirds and excluding raptors, waterfowl, and grouse;* EI (Sheshatshiu) pineshish [pɨnēʃīʃ], *bird;* Laure (ca. 1726) "pirechich *pl.* -ets, *oiseau;*" Silvy (ca. 1680) "pirechich, *petit oiseau*" | ANISH bineshiinh, *a bird* (Livesay & Nichols, 2021) see | *pirēhšīhšiw

*pirēhšīhšiw

MEDIAL (NOUN INCORPORATION)

— bird of a smaller species such as songbirds and excluding raptors, waterfowl, and grouse

evidence | MC nōcipilešīšiwew, *to hunt small birds;* SEC nōcipiyešīšiwew, *to harvest small birds;* Laure (ca. 1726) "ni-natauipirechichiuan 3. -eu, *je chasse aux oiseaux*" see | *pirēhšīhš

*pirēw

INITIAL (NOUN, ANIMATE)

— grouse

evidence | WC piðīw, *grouse;* MC pilewimākwan, *to smell like grouse;* AT pirew, *grouse;* SEC piyew, *grouse;* piyewiminān, *a snowberry;* WI (Pessamit) pileukan [pəlēwkən], *a grouse bone;* EI (Sheshatshiu) pineuapui [pɨnēwāpwī], *grouse broth;* Silvy (ca. 1680) "pireȣaȣ, *œuf de perdrix*" origin | PA ***perēwa** (***pele·wa**, Hewson, 1993) see | *hrēw

*pirk

INITIAL

— bend

evidence | WC piðkinam, *to bend sth;* MC pihkipitoneliw, *to bend one's arm;* AT pikinam [pihkinam], *to bend sth manually;* SEC pihcipayiw, *it bends at the joint;* Laure (ca. 1726) "pitchetsistahigan, *pli de robe*" | ANISH opiskinān, *to bend sth over* (Livesay & Nichols, 2021)

*pisin

INITIAL

— have speck in one's eye

evidence | PC pisin, *to get sth in one's eye;* WC pisiniw, *to have sth in one's eye;* MC pisiniw, *to have sth in one's eye;* AT (Wemotaci, Nicole Petiquay) pisiniw [piziniw], *to get sth in one's eye;* WI (Pessamit) pishinieu [pəʃənjēw], *to get sth in sb's eye;* Watkins (1865) "pissinew, *v.i.1. He gets something into his eye;*" "pissinehāo, *v.t.an. He blinds him;*" Laure (ca. 1726) "ni-pisinin, *quelque chose m'est entré dans l'oeil;*" Fabvre (ca. 1690) "pissinin iȣ, *aur ordures en Loueil;*" cf. Laure (ca. 1726) "ni-pichirin, *j'ai une ordure dans les yeux;*" Fabvre (ca. 1690) "pistirin, iȣ, *aur ordures en loueil;*" "pissirau, *n. en ietter à qlqn;*" "ki pissirin, *tu m en iette dans les y(eu)x, ordures;*" Silvy (ca. 1680) "Ni pistirin, *j'ai une ordure dans l'oeil;*" "ni pistirau, *je lui en jette une, etc.*" | ANISH binzini, *to have sth in one's eye* (Livesay & Nichols, 2021); MENO pesɛ·hnɛw, *to get sth in one's eye;* nepɛ·sɛhnɛn, *the thing that got into my eye* discussion | Early Jesuit sources from the Saguenay region provide evidence for the alternative reconstruction ***pisir**, which is unsubstantiated by the contemporary dialect continuum and historical sources from other regions.

*pisisk

INITIAL

— notice, pay attention to

evidence | WC pisiskāpamīw, *to notice sb;* MC pāhpisiskelimew, *to be attentive to sb;* AT (Wemotaci, Jeannette Coocoo) pisiskapatcikewin [piziskāpahcikēwin], *observation;* SEC pisiskātam, *to bother with sth;* Laure (ca. 1726) "eka ka pichiskatisit, *idiot, qui n'en a point d'esprit;*" Fabvre (ca. 1690) "Pisisteriten 3 tamȣ, *se souuenir bien*"

*pisk (~ *āpisk)

MEDIAL (CLASSIFIER)

— of mineral composition

evidence | MC mahkāpiskisiw, *large stone;* SEC šōšawāpiskāw, *to be a smooth object of mineral composition;* NEC ātāpischinam, *to lock sth manually;* Watkins (1865) "Papachepiskow, *v.imp. It is a low smooth rock;*" Silvy (ca. 1680) "papakibichkau, papakibiskau, *fond pierreux, lieu pavé*" | ABEN masipskw, mazipskw, *flint, chert* (Day, 1994); ANISH jiigaabik, *by a rock* (Livesay & Nichols, 2021); MENO kaska·pɛhkaham, *to lock sth by key*

*piskiht (~ *piskihš)

INITIAL

— separate, partition

evidence | PC piskihcāw, *to be partitioned;* Lacombe (1874) "Piskis, *(adv.) différemment, d'une autre manière, autrement;*" WC pāhpiskīhc, *separately;* MC piskihtasinahikan, *a chapter;* SEC piscišāw, *to be a room;* NEC pischihtipishiu, *to hibernate alone for the first time, speaking of a bear;* Watkins (1865) "Piskisow, *v.imp. See* Piskèchow;" "Piskèchāyow, *v.imp. It is distinct, it is separate;*" "Piskis, *adv. Apart, asunder, by itself, separately, in another place*"

*pisko (~ *piskw)

INITIAL

— hump, mound

evidence | PC piskwāw, *to have a lump;* MC papeskohcāw, *to be lumpy ground;* SEC piskwāwikanew, *to be humpbacked* | ANISH bikwadinaa, *to be a knoll or hill;* MENO pɛhkuahkamekat (on), *little mound, as in a marsh* origin | PA ***peskw** (***pexkw**, Aubin, 1975; Hewson, 1993)

*piskwan

MEDIAL, FINAL (NOUN INCORPORATION)

— upper back (thoracic region)

evidence | PC kinopiskwanēw, *to have a long back;* WC māhkipiskwanīw, *to have a big back;* MC wākipiskwanepiw, *to sit with one's upper back curved;* NEC sichipiskunāyāpush, *rabbit snared around the back* | MESK wāwāchipehkwanēkāpāwaki, *to stand back to back* see | *spiskwan

*piso (~ *pisw)

INITIAL

— **1** attach on, hook on

— **2** trip, stumble

evidence | PC pisoskam, *to stumble over sth;* ESC (Severn) pisopicikan, *a wool pompom decorating the frame of a snowshoe;* MC pisositešin, *to stumble over one's foot;* SEC (Waswanipi) pišopicikan, *tuft of wool that adorns the frame of a snowshoe;* NEC piswāpākiham, *to trip over sth string-like;* piswāpihchēhtitāu, *to hook sth string-like on sth;* Fabvre (ca. 1690) "ni piss8piten, *j'entoure de corde, v.g. la suerie;*" Silvy (ca. 1680) "ni pich8achtebarin, *je tombe en trébuchant*" | ANISH bizogeshin, *to stumble* (Livesay & Nichols, 2021); MENO peso·mɛ·w, *to stop sb by speech from doing sth* origin | PA ***piso**

*pišic

INITIAL

— heed, obey

evidence | MC pišicihew, *to heed sb;* NEC pishichihāu, *to listen to sb;* pishichishkam, *to walk following sth, such as a river;* WI (Pessamit) pishitshieu [pəʃətʃjēw], *to obey sb;* Watkins (1865) "Pisichetum, *v.t.in. 6. He listens to it, he obeys it;*" Laure (ca. 1726) "pichitchihituin, pichitcheritamuin, *obéissance, docilité;*" Silvy (ca. 1680) "ni pichitchita8au, *j'écoute ce qu'il dit*" discussion | The absence of a preaspiration on the sibilant cannot be confirmed due to the lack of an Atikamekw cognate.

*pišimē

INITIAL

— lace anchor string around a frame

evidence | WC pisimanīyāpiy, *fine caribou hide lacing for snowshoes;* ESC (Severn) pishimew, *to attach the line along the inside of the end sections of a snowshoe frame;* MC pišimew, *to install the lace around a frame;* AT (Wemotaci, Nicole Petiquay & Opitciwan, Joey Awashish) pišimew [piʒimēw], *to lace the line along the inside of a snowshoe frame from which the netting is weaved;* SEC pišiman, *lace around snowshoe frame from which the netting is weaved;* WI (Pessamit) pishimeu [pəʃəmēw], *to put a line through holes pierced around a frame;* Fabvre (ca. 1690) "Pichiman 3 e8, *percer futs de raqttes maneabi cordes*" see | *ɪm²

*pišiskiw

INITIAL (NOUN, ANIMATE)

— beast, wild animal

evidence | PC pisiskīwiw, *to be an animal;* Lacombe (1874) "*Animal,* pijiskiw, ok;" WC pisiskiw, *an animal;* AT (Wemotaci, Jeannette Coocoo) pisiskiwotcakw [piziskīwahcāhkʷ], *a type of small owl;* SEC pisisciw, *animal; black bear, euphemistic name;* Watkins (1865) "Pisiskew, *n.an. An animal, a beast, a black bear;*" "Pisiskiskow, *v.imp. Animals or beasts are numerous*" | ANISH bizhiki, *a cow; a buffalo* (Livesay & Nichols, 2021); MENO pesɛ·kiw, nepɛ·sɛhkyam, *head of cattle, cow, ox; bison* origin | PA ***pešeskiwa** compare | *awēhsīhs

***pišiw**[1]
INITIAL (NOUN, ANIMATE)
— lynx
evidence | PC pisīsis, *a lynx kit;* MC pišiw, *a lynx;* AT pišiw, lynx (Béland, 1978); EI (Unaman-shipit) pishiushtau [pɨhīwahtāw], *to set a trap for lynx;* Fabvre (ca. 1690) "Pichiȣ *pl.* ȣek, *Lȣps ceruiers*" | ANISH bizhiw, *a lynx* (Livesay & Nichols, 2021); MENO pese·w, *lynx; lion, tiger;* MESK peshiwa, *a lynx* origin | PA ***pešiwa** (Hewson, 1993) see | *pišiw²

***pišiw**[2] **(~ *āpišiw)**
MEDIAL, FINAL (NOUN INCORPORATION)
— lynx
evidence | WC nōcipisiwīw, *to kill many lynx;* MC šīpahāpišiwew, *to stretch a lynx pelt;* SEC mišāpišiw, *a cougar;* WI (Pessamit) uipishiukan [wiːpəʃiːwkən], *to smell like lynx;* EI (Unaman-shipit) ushtikuanapishu [uhtukwānāpɨhu], *a lynx head;* Laure (ca. 1726) "ni-natauipichiuan, *je chasse au loup-cervier*" see | *pišiw¹

***pišt (~ *pihc)**
INITIAL
— accidentally, inadvertently
evidence | PC pistisam, *to cut sth accidentally;* pihcipow, *to be poisoned;* MC pištaham, *to hit sth accidentally;* pihcimow, *to blurt sth out;* SEC pištahwew, *to hit sb accidentally;* Silvy (ca. 1680) "ni pichtabistichinin, *je me heurte à une pierre, etc.;*" "ni pitchichkaȣau, *je marche sur lui*" | MENO pɛqtahosow, *to chop oneself by accident* origin | PA ***peʔt** (Aubin, 1975)

***pit**[1]
INITIAL
— net
evidence | MC pitaham, *to be caught in a net;* SEC pitahoyew, *to catch sb in a net;* Laure (ca. 1726) "ni-pitahurau, *je l'y prends (au rets), fais entrer*" | ANISH bida'anaa, *to catch sth in a net*

***pit**[2]
INITIAL
— for the time being
evidence | PC pita, *first of all; wait;* MC pitamā, *for the time being, first;* SEC pitamā, *for the time being;* ekā pitamā, *wait!;* NEC pit & pitimā, *for the time being, for now;* EI (Mamit) pita [pɨta], *firstly, for now, for the time being* limited to | *a

***pit**[3] **(~ *pic)**
FINAL (VERB, TRANSITIVE, INANIMATE, CONCRETE)
— pull
evidence | WC asīpitam, *to pull sth backwards;* MC ocipitam, *to pull sth;* SEC yāyicipitam, *to rip sth by pulling* | ANISH azhebidoon, *to pull sth back* (Livesay & Nichols, 2021)

***pit**[4] **(~ *piš)**
FINAL (VERB, TRANSITIVE, ANIMATE, CONCRETE)
— pull
evidence | PC iskwāpihkēpitēw, *to pull sb a certain distance using a rope;* WC āhcipis, *move him by pulling (imperative);* MC ocipitew, *to pull sb;* kit ōcipišin, *you pull me;* SEC nīhcipitew, *to pull sb down;* e nīhcipišiyan, *when you pull me down* | ANISH azhebizh, *to pull sb back* (Livesay & Nichols, 2021)

***pitihko (~ *pitihkw)**
INITIAL
— resonant sound, thud
evidence | PC pitihkopahtāw, *run thudding;* ESC pitihkopanihow, *make a roaring noise;* MC pitihkohtin, *thud;* Fabvre (ca. 1690) "Kȣikȣan ka pitikȣat, *tremble terre*" | ANISH bidikowe, *have a deep voice* (Livesay & Nichols, 2021)

***pitiko (~ *pitikw)**
INITIAL
— short and thick

evidence | PC pitikonam, *form into balls or patties;* MC pitikosiw, *be stumpy;* NEC pitikwāu, *be short and thick;* Laure (ca. 1726) "ni-pitikutitcherin 3. -iu, *je ferme la main;*" Fabvre (ca. 1690) "pitig8ak8nakinike8, *faire ploton de neige*"

*piton

MEDIAL, FINAL (NOUN INCORPORATION)

— arm; (of a quadruped) front leg

evidence | WC cimipitonīw, *to have short arms;* MC kakānopitonew, *to have long arms;* SEC napatepitonew, *to only have one arm;* Silvy (ca. 1680) "ni pimipit8nin, *j'ai le bras tordu*" origin | Old Cree ***ospitoni*** see | *spiton

*pīcit (~ *pīcic)

INITIAL

— move in a particular direction

evidence | PC pīcicipitam, *to pull sth forth;* WC pīcitinam, *to move sth slowly, a little bit at a time;* MC pīcitāštan, *to be moved by the wind;* WI (Pessamit) pitshitshipalu [pītʃətʃəpəlu], *to move forward or in one direction;*" Silvy (ca. 1680) "pitichibari8, *cela recule*"

*pīh

INITIAL

— in see | *pīht[1], *pīhr

*pīhcitaw

INITIAL

— (into) the mouth of a river

evidence | MC pīhcitawāštan, *to be blown into the mouth of a river;* SEC pīhcitawaham, *to swim into the mouth of a river;* WI (Pessamit) pishtuapuku [pīstwāpuku], *to enter the mouth of the river with the incoming tide;* Laure (ca. 1726) "pitchitauichegau, *(fleuve) qui coule entre deux chaînes de montagnes;*" Silvy (ca. 1680) "ni pitchita8ahen, *j'entre à la voile dans les terres*" | ANISH biinjidawa'o, *to enter a river or bay from a lake in a boat* (Livesay & Nichols, 2021) see | *pīht[1], *taw

*pīhpīkihšīhš

INITIAL (NOUN, ANIMATE)

— falcon

evidence | PC pīhpīkisīs, *sparrow hawk;* MC pīhpīkišīš, *American kestrel;* EI (Sheshatshiu) pipitshish [pīpītʃīh], *merlin;* Silvy (ca. 1680) "pipitichich, *épervier*"

*pīhpīšk

INITIAL (NOUN, ANIMATE)

— spleen

evidence | MC nipīhpīšk, *my spleen;* NEC upīshpīshkh, *one's spleen* | MESK pīhpīshkīhi, *a lung* compare | *pēhpēhkw discussion | The evidence is sufficient to reconstruct both ***pēhpēhkw*** and ***pīhpīšk*** in Old Cree, though the latter may represent an early borrowing from a neighbouring language.

*pīhr

INITIAL

— put in

evidence | MC pilōmow, *to tuck sth under one's garment;* AT (Opitciwan, Joey Awashish) piromow [pīrōmō], *to secretly tuck sth under one's coat;*" Watkins (1865) "Peyoomoo, *v.i.4. He puts (it) into his bosom;* Peyoomoohāo, *v.t.an. He puts it into his bosom (i.e. into another person's);*" Laure (ca. 1726) "ni-birumututauau, *je mets, v.g. l'enfant (dans mon sein);*" Silvy (ca. 1680) "pir8mon, *je mets dans mon sein*" | ANISH Baraga (1878) "Pinomon, (nin). *I put it in my bosom;* p. panomod," but also "Pindomowin. *Bosom*" origin | PA extended root ***pīnr*** (***pi:nl***, Aubin, 1975) limited to | *ōmo compare | *pīht[1] discussion | This root is reconstructed separately from ***pīht*** as it is nonproductive in Old Cree, forming only the stem ***pīhrōmo-*** and further derivatives. The paucity of cognates from contemporary dialects also precludes the reconstruction of the preaspirate, which must instead be reconstructed by analogy with the roots ***pīht**, ***wīh**, and ***koh**, and is confirmed by Bloomfield's Proto-Algonquian reconstruction cited in Aubin, 1975.

*pīhs

INITIAL

— be or reduce to fine pieces

evidence | PC pīsipakāw, *to have small leaves;* MC pīsāw, *to consist of small pieces;* AT (Wemotaci, Jeannette Coocoo) pisinam [pīssinam], *break sth into small pieces by hand;* SEC pīsinew, *to change sth (money) into change* | WI (Pessamit) pishanauakau [pīʃānāwkāʃu], *to be fine as powder* | MENO pi·qsiw, *to be finely divided* origin | PA ***pīʔs** (Hewson, 1993) compare | *pīkin

*pīhsāko (~ *pīhsākw)

INITIAL

— ample in space, quantity, or durability

evidence | WC pīsākwan, *to be roomy;* MC pīsākohtāw, *to make sth last by dividing it up into an ample number of portions; to make sth ample or capacious;* EI (Sheshatshiu) pishakushkamᵘ [pīʃākuʃkəm], *to make an article of clothing last a long time;* Laure (ca. 1726) "pichakuaganiuets pakuechiganets, *multiplication des pains;*" Silvy (ca. 1680) "pisag8an, *grand, capable*" | ANISH Baraga (1853) "bīssāgwan, *u.v. it is profitable; it holds much (a bag, a vessel;) p. bass...ang*" discussion | In the absence of an Atikamekw cognate, the preaspirate in this reconstruction is indirectly supported by Anishinabe.

*pīhsimw[1] (~ *pīhsimo)

INITIAL (NOUN, ANIMATE)

— **1** sun, moon

— **2** month

evidence | PC pīsim, *sun, moon; month;* pīsimotāhk, *towards the south;* ayīki-pīsim, *April;* MC pīsimʷ, *sun, moon; month;* pīsimosinahikan, *a calendar or almanac;* AT kape-pi:ssimwa, *all month* (Béland, 1978); SEC pīsimohkān, *a timepiece;* pīsimōhtew, *mushroom;* NEC pīsimwāyāpī, *a sunray;* WI (Pessamit) pishimᵘ [pīʃəm], *sun, moon; month;* EI (Mushuau) pishimuss [pīʃumuss], *a mushroom;* Watkins (1865) "Pesim, *n.an. The sun, the moon;*" "Pesimookan, *n.an. A clock, a sun dial, a mushroom;*" La Brosse (1766) "Pihissimu, *sol, lune, mensis;*" Laure (ca. 1726) "satchipatau pihissimu, *le soleil se lève;*" "tchiche-pihissimu, *février;*" Fabvre (ca. 1690) "pihissim8, *soleil;*" Silvy (ca. 1680) "piisim8, *soleil;*" "tibistchipiissim8, *lune*" see | *pīhsimw[2] discussion | Jesuit sources suggest the vowel of the first syllable may have been two vowels separated by either a semivowel or aspirate. However, evidence from contemporary dialects is unsupportive. Alternatively, the Jesuit sources may simply represent an attempt at capturing the preaspirate. Note that this root is unattested in other Algonquian languages and may, as Pentland suggested (Denny, 1991), be an example of an early loanword from a non-Algonquian language.

*pīhsimw[2]

MEDIAL, FINAL (NOUN INCORPORATION)

— to be a certain number of months

evidence | MC mitāhtopīsimwesiw, *to be ten months old;* NEC tipihīpīsimwān, *a calendar;* WI (Pessamit) neupishimueshu [nēwpīʃəmwēʃu], *to be four months old; to be four months pregnant;* EI (Ekuanitshit) peikunnuepishimueshu [pajukunwēpīhumwēhu], *to be ten months old* see | *pīhsimw[1]

*pīhswē

INITIAL

— have air pockets

evidence | PC pīswēhkasow, *to rise, speaking of bread;* WC pīswīyāw, *to be spongy;* MC pīswehcāw, *to be an expanse of spongy ground;* NEC pipīswāpiyiu, *to bubble;* WI (Pessamit) pishueiakuteu [pīʃwējākutēw], *to be full of holes as it melts, speaking of snow* | ANISH biisweyiigin, *flannel;* biiswewigwane, *to have fine fluffy feathers* (Livesay & Nichols, 2021) discussion | In the absence of an Atikamekw cognate, the preaspirate in this reconstruction is indirectly supported by Anishinabe.

*pīhšākan

INITIAL (NOUN, INANIMATE)

— leather

evidence | PC pīsākanāpiy, *a rawhide thong or rope;* MC pīšākan, *leather;* EI (Sheshatshiu) pishakan [pīʃākən], *leather;* Silvy (ca. 1680) "pichaganeabi, *courroie*" | ANISH biishaagan, *curried skin* (Lippert & Gambill, 2023) see | ākan² discussion | In the absence of an Atikamekw cognate, the preaspirate in this reconstruction is indirectly supported by Anishinabe.

*pīht¹ (~ *pīhc)

INITIAL

— in

evidence | WSC (Ida Bear) pīhtōmow, *to tuck sth under one's garment;* PC pīhtokēw, *to enter a dwelling;* MC pīhtaškwātam, *to stuff sth with grass;* SEC pīhtaham, *to put insert sth;* NEC pīhtāsū, *to put things into a container;* Silvy (ca. 1680) "ni pitagȣnan 3. -eȣ, *la neige entre dans mes habits*" | ANISH biinjise, *to fall or fly in* (Livesay & Nichols, 2021); Cuoq (1886) "Pindom, o, *mettre dans son sein*" origin | PA extended root ***pīnt** (Aubin, 1975; Hewson, 1993) compare | *pīhr

*pīht² (~ *pīhc)

INITIAL

— long distance or time

evidence | PC pīhcāw, *to be a long way;* WC pīhtāciwanāw, *to be a long rapids;* MC pīhcāw, *to be a long distance to travel;* pīhci-nīpin, *to be a long summer;* WI (Pessamit) pitassekau [pītəssēkāw], *to be a long muskeg to travel through;* pishitin [pīʃətn], *to be a small river that is long to travel;* Laure (ca. 1726) "ni-pichissen 3. -kamu, *je vais faire un long chemin (voyage);*" Silvy (ca. 1680) "pitchau, *bien loin;*" "pitchitchichigau, *les jours sont grands*" | ANISH biichaa, *to be far away* (Livesay & Nichols, 2021) origin | PA ***pīht**

*pīhto (~ *pīhtaw)

INITIAL

— be layered, add or remove layer

evidence | PC pīhtonam, *to peel sth by hand, to take the covering layer off sth;* MC pīhtawekinam, *to add a sheet-like layer to sth;* SEC pīhtawitisān, *inner lining of a gizzard;* La Brosse (1766) "Pabitauisiu, *Folium libri;*" Fabvre (ca. 1690) "Pitaȣau, *Il e dȣble, dȣblé;*" Silvy (ca. 1680) "ni pitaȣachan, *j'ai la peau enflée;*" "pitȣbakȣateu, *la couverture de la cabane est double*"

*pīhtwā

INITIAL (VERB, ANIMATE, INTRANSITIVE)

— to smoke

evidence | PC pīhtwāhēw, *to give sb a smoke;* WC pīhtwāhīw, *to give sb a smoke;* MC pīhtwākew, *to smoke sth;* SEC pīhtwāw, *to smoke;* Silvy (ca. 1680) "ni pitȣan, *je pétune*" origin | Possibly an antipassive derivative of the PA extended root ***pīnt**.

*pīk

INITIAL

— turbid

evidence | WC pikāw, *to be muddy or impure;* MC pikāškāw, *to be turbid from the waves;* SEC picinam, *to make the water turbid from walking through it;* Fabvre (ca. 1690) "Pigan, *cela e trȣblé, v.g. eau;*" Silvy (ca. 1680) "ni pikahen nipi, *je trouble l'eau*" compare | *pīkišē

*pīkin

INITIAL

— be or reduce to small pieces

evidence | PC pīkināw, *to be powdery;* Lacombe (1874) "Pikinikkattew, *il est réduit* *en cendres;"* MC pīkinaham, *to break sth into small pieces by striking or using a tool;* Laure (ca. 1726) "pitchinipagau uabikun, *fleur flétrie"* compare | *pīhs

*pīkiskāt (~ *pīkiskāc, *pīkiskās)

INITIAL

— lonely, desolate

evidence | PC pīkiskācihēw, *to make sb lonely and sad;* MC pīkiskācihew, *to make sb lonely;* SEC pīciskāsinākwan, *to look deserted;* Laure (ca. 1726) "ni-pitchiskateriten, *je fais la mine, je boude;"* Silvy (ca. 1680) "ni pitiskat8tan 3. -e8, *je suis las de marcher"*

*pīkiskwē

INITIAL

— speak indiscriminately

evidence | PC pīkiskwātēw, *to speak to sb;* MC pīkiskwew, *to be given to idle talk;* EI (Sheshatshiu) pitshishkueu [pīttʃkwēw], *to be talkative;* Laure (ca. 1726) "ni-pitchiskuan, *il parle trop sans égard"* see | *wē[1]

*pīkišē

INITIAL

— mist, vapor

evidence | PC pīkisēnam, *to have blurred vision;* MC pīkišeyāw, *to be misty;* AT (Opitciwan, Joey Awashish) pikiseapatamaw [pīkizēyāpahtamāw], *to have blurry vision;* SEC pīcišetew, *to produce steam or mist from the warmth;* Laure (ca. 1726) "pitchichetagau, *fumeux, qui jette de la fumée (v.g.: du bois humide)"* | MENO pi·kesiya·kamiw, *to be fog on the water* compare | *pīk

*pīko (~ *pīkw)

INITIAL

— **1** damage, break

— **2** (of skin) break out

evidence | PC pīkwahtam, *to break sth with one's mouth;* MC pīkwāšiw, *to be broken by the wind;* pīkopaliw, *to break or for skin to break out;* SEC pīkohtin, *to break upon impact;* Watkins (1865) "Pekoopuyew, *v.imp. It breaks, it breaks out (as a sore or eruption);"* Silvy (ca. 1680) "ni pik8nen, *je romps, je troue"*

*pīm

INITIAL

— twist

evidence | PC pīmastēhikan, *spinning wheel;* MC pīmipaliw, *to twist;* SEC pīmikwenew, *to wring sb's neck;* Silvy (ca. 1680) "ni pimabedinen, *je tors, v.g. une corde, etc."*

*pīmaroy

INITIAL (NOUN, INANIMATE)

— intra-abdominal fat of fowl

evidence | WSC (Misipawistik, Ellen Cook) opīmanow, *NI fat from the inner abdomen of fowl;* MC opīmaloy, *NA fat from the inner abdomen of fowl;* NEC upīmiyuyi, *NI fat from around the bottom of a body cavity;* Watkins (1865) "pāmunooi, *n.in. The inside fat of a fowl;"* Fabvre (ca. 1690) "8pim8ri8, *panne, graisse pectorale daal"*

*pīpo

INITIAL

— emit particulate matter

evidence | MC pīposow, *to emit smoke;* NEC pīputāu, *to give off smoke;* EI (Sheshatshiu) piputeu [pīputēw], *to give off smoke* see | so[2], tē[4] discussion | Further derivatives are based on the inanimate intransitive verb stem ***pīpotē**, as in the following examples: ESC (Severn) pīpotenikew, *to make smoke;* SEC pīpoteyāwahkāštan, *to be blowing sand;* NSK piipuutaastin, *to be a blizzard;* WI (Pessamit) piputepalu [pīputēpəlu], *to give off smoke or dust;* EI (Sheshatshiu) piputeshtin [pīputēstn], *to be flurries, to be blowing snow*

*pīrē

INITIAL

— to unravel or loosen the edges or surface of a fabric or substance

evidence | AT pirepikw [pīrepihkw], *ashes;* (Opitciwan, Joey Awashish) pirehipew [pīrēhipēw], *to be water full of debris from flooding along the bank;* SEC pīyepayiw, *to become fluffy;* pīyepihkʷ, *soot;* pīyešikan, *a duffle sock;* pīyeyāpāwew, *to become fluffy from being wet;* NEC piyāpāu, *water is up to the tree roots;* WI (Pessamit) pileiau [pīlējāw], *to be pilled;* pilepalu [pīlēpəlu], *to fray or pill;* pilepeu [pīlēpēw], *shore is flooded;* Fabvre (ca. 1690) "Pireask8be8, *Leau gr(an)dit retenue par chausée*" discussion | The root comes to refer to flooding of the shore when combined with the medial ***ɩp**, "water," likely in reference to the swelling and loosening of the superficial layers of dirt.

*pīrihs

INITIAL

— flavorless

evidence | MC pīlisāciwahtew, *to produce a bland broth;* AT (Opitciwan, Joey Awashish) pirisaw [pīrissāw], *to be flavorless;* Silvy (ca. 1680) "pirisau, *viande légère*" | ANISH biinisaa, *to be plain, bland, numb, flavorless, without sensation* (Livesay & Nichols, 2021) compare | *arihs

*pīškw (~ *pīško)

INITIAL (NOUN, ANIMATE)

— nighthawk

evidence | PC pīskwa, *nighthawk;* WC pīskwa, *nighthawk;* MC pīškʷ, *a nighthawk;* SEC pīškʷ, *a nighthawk; a woman's genitalia;* EI (Sheshatshiu) pishkᵘ [pīʃkʷ], *a common nighthawk*

*pīštēw¹

INITIAL (NOUN, INANIMATE)

— foam, froth

evidence | PC pīstēwataham, *to beat sth (as an egg with a beater);* MC pīštew, *foam;* pīštewāciwahtew, *to foam while boiling;* SEC pīštewāpow, *beer;* WI (Pessamit) pishteutamu [pīstēwtāmu], *to foam at the mouth;* Laure (ca. 1726) "ni-pichteutunan, *j'écume par la bouche;*" Silvy (ca. 1680) "pichteu, *écume du pot*" | ABEN bita, *froth, foam;* ANISH biite, *foam* (Livesay & Nichols, 2021) origin | PA ***piʔtēwi** (Aubin, 1975) see | *pīštēw²

*pīštēw²

MEDIAL (NOUN INCORPORATION)

— foam, froth

evidence | Laure (ca. 1726) "ni-manahipichteuatau nitastikum, *j'ôte l'ecume du pot;*" Silvy (ca. 1680) "ni manahipichte8an, *je ramasse l'écume*" see | *pīštēw¹

*pītohš

INITIAL

— different

evidence | PC pītosisiw, *to be an outsider;* MC pītošinākwan, *to look different;* AT (Nicole, Petiquay) pitocinakon [pītoššinākwan], *to look different;* SEC pītošeyimew, *to consider sb different;* Laure (ca. 1726) "papituchituau, iriniu ka papituchituat, *inégal, inconstant d'humeur;*" Silvy (ca. 1680) "ni pit8chihau, *je le change en autre chose*"

*pītoy

INITIAL (NOUN, INANIMATE)

— sled bridle

evidence | MC pītow, *sled bridle;* SEC pītow, *sled bridle;* NEC pītui, *pull rope or front loop on a sled or toboggan*

*pīw¹

INITIAL

— **1** scatter in pieces

— **2** scorn, contempt

evidence | ¹PC pīwan, *to be a blizzard;* MC pīwikaham, *to chop sth into pieces;* SEC pīwahwew, *to scale sth (a fish);* WI (Pessamit) piupalu [pīwpəlu], *to be scattered or dispersed;* Silvy (ca. 1680) "pi8ichigan, *retaille d'étoffe, de peau, etc.*" ²WC pīwiðimīw, *to have no respect for sb;* NEC pīwāyimāu, *to mock or disrespect sb;* Laure (ca. 1726) "ni-piueriten 3. -tamu, *j'ai du mépris pour cela*" compare | *pīw², *pīway²

*pīw[2]

MEDIAL (NOUN INCORPORATION)

— hair, fur, plumage

evidence | MC meštanipīwān, *a down feather;* SEC cišepīwān, *a contour feather* origin | Old Cree ***wipīwayi*** see | *pīway[1], *pīway[2] compare | *pīw[1]

*pīway[1]

INITIAL (NOUN, DEPENDENT INANIMATE)

— hair, fur, plumage

evidence | MC opīwaya, *one's hair, fur, or plumage;* EI (Sheshatshiu) upiuai [upīwī], *one's body hair;* Fabvre (ca. 1690) "Mipi8e, *cheueux, poil*" see | *pīw[2], *pīway[2] compare | *pīw[1] discussion | Further derivatives are based on the third-person stem **wipīway-** + **-ɪw-** to form a derived initial ***wipīwāw-**, as in Moose Cree **opīwāwāskikanew**, *to have a hairy chest.*

*pīway[2] (~ *pīwayak)

MEDIAL, FINAL (NOUN INCORPORATION)

— hair, fur, plumage

evidence | PC sōnīyāwipīwayēw, *to have golden feathers;* WC mīstanipīwayān, *a down feather;* MC mihkopīwayew, *to have red plumage;* WI (Pessamit) umishtanipiuai [umīstənəpīwī], *duvet, down hair;* Laure (ca. 1726) "ka tchinupiuiet, *qui a une longue chevelure;*" Fabvre (ca. 1690) "Mik8pi8eïagau, *poil r8ge, r8x;*" Silvy (ca. 1680) "8abask8pi8ai, *poil d'ours blanc;*" "kastite8pi8aïagau, *poil noir*" origin | Old Cree ***wipīwayi***, likely derived from the root ***pīw**[1] see | *pīw[2], *pīway[1] compare | *pīw[1]

*pīwit

INITIAL (VERB, TRANSITIVE, INANIMATE)

— shoot rapids

evidence | WC pīwitam, *to shoot the rapids;* SEC pīwitam, *to shoot the rapids;* EI (Sheshatshiu) piutam[u] [pjūtəm], *to shoot the rapids;* Fabvre (ca. 1690) "Pi8iten 3 tam8, *saulter en canot rapidemt*"

*po[1] (~ *āpo)

PREFINAL

— by action of water current see | *poko, *por[1], *poro, *potā[1], *potē

*po[2]

FINAL (VERB, ANIMATE, INTRANSITIVE, CONCRETE)

— eat

evidence | PC pihcipow, *to be poisoned;* Lacombe (1874) "wikkipuw, ok, *(v.n.) il mange avec appétit, il trouve bon ce qu'il mange;*" MC milopow, *to eat well;* SEC cīšpow, *to have eaten one's fill, to be full;* NEC kāchipū, *to eat food one has hidden;* Laure (ca. 1726) "ni-nitchipun, *dévorer, je dévore, je mange avec avidité;*" Silvy (ca. 1680) "nit'achtib8n, *je mange cru;*" "nit'aïsp8n he isp8t, *je mange de ce qu'il mange*" | ANISH bichibo, *to be poisoned* (Livesay & Nichols, 2021); MENO aske·pow, *to eat raw things* origin | PA ***po** (Aubin, 1975)

*poko (~ *āpoko)

FINAL (VERB, ANIMATE, INTRANSITIVE, CONCRETE)

— by action of water current

evidence | MC itāpokow, *swept thither by the current;* SEC wepāpokow, *to be swept away by the current;* NEC uchipukū, *to be swept away by the current;* Silvy (ca. 1680) "nit'achaïab8g8n, *je recule en canot, par la force de la marée contraire*" see | *ā[1], *po[1]

*por[1] (~ *āpor)

FINAL (VERB, TRANSITIVE, ANIMATE, CONCRETE)

— affect or move by use of water current

evidence | MC liskipolew, *to flood sb;* NEC pimāpuyāu, *to let sth float;* Silvy (ca. 1680) "ni s8tchib8rig8n, *l'eau me gagne, la chaussée étant rompue*" see | *ā[1], *po[1], *r

*por²

FINAL (VERB, TRANSITIVE, ANIMATE, CONCRETE)

— **1** to feed sb

— **2** to saw, file, or grind sth

evidence | [1]WC pihcipoðīw, *to poison sb;* MC aškipolew, *to feed sb raw meat;* SEC ispišipoyew, *to feed sb a certain quantity of food;* Laure (ca. 1726) "ni-tatchipurau, *je grossis à force de bien le nourrir;*" Fabvre (ca. 1690) "ni matchib8rau, *donner à qlqn mauuaise portion*" [2]WC tāskipoðīw, *to split sth with a saw;* MC kīnipolew, *to file or saw into a point;* SEC kawipoyew, *to fell by sawing* | ANISH ojaagiboonaan, *to saw or grind sth all up* (Livesay & Nichols, 2021) see | *po², *r paired with | *potā²

*poro (~ *āporo)

FINAL (VERB, ANIMATE, INTRANSITIVE, CONCRETE)

— move with water current

evidence | PC kīwēyāpōyow, *to go home by vehicle;* ESC māhāponow, *to drift downriver;* MC atimāpolow, *to be carried away by the current;* AT kiciaporo [kiʒīyāporow], *aller vite en glissant;* EI pimapunu [pmāpunu], *to let oneself be carried along by the current* see | *ā¹, *po¹, *ro

*posākan

INITIAL (NOUN, ANIMATE)

— tinder fungus (Fomes fomentarius)

evidence | PC posākanaciy, *place name, Touchwood Hills, literally "tinder fungus hill;"* MC posākan, *tinder fungus;* SEC posākan, *tinder fungus;* Silvy (ca. 1680) "p8sagan, *tondre à faire feu*" | ANISH boozaaganag, *puffball mushrooms* (Lippert & Gambill, 2023)

*pošt (~ *pohc)

INITIAL

— put on garment or item

evidence | PC Lacombe (1874) "Pustayonisew, *il revêt ses habits;*" WC postiskam, *to put sth on;* MC poštaskisinahew, *to put shoes on sb;* pohcinikātaham, *to put sth on one's shoulder;* SEC papwehcīw, *to get dressed;* Silvy (ca. 1680) "ni p8chtasianan, *je prends mon brayet*"

*potā¹ (~ *āpotā)

FINAL (VERB, ANIMATE, INTRANSITIVE, CONCRETE)

— affect or move by use of water current

evidence | PC māhāpotāw, *to drift sth downstream;* MC liskipotāw, *to flood sth;* SEC māhīputāu, *to float sth downriver* (CSB, 2018); WI (Pessamit) pimaputau [pmāputāw], *to let sth float along with the current* see | *ā¹, *po¹, *tā

*potā² (~ *pot, *poc)

FINAL (VERB, ANIMATE, INTRANSITIVE, CONCRETE)

— to saw, file, or grind

evidence | PC aciwipotāw, *to reduce the size of sth by sawing;* WC pinipocikan, *a grinder;* MC kīnipotāw, *to file or saw into a point;* kīškipocikew, *to saw;* SEC kawipotāw, *to fell by sawing;* Laure (ca. 1726) "ni-tchimiputagan, *je scie [de travers]*" | ANISH jaagiboodoon, *to saw or grind sth all up* (Livesay & Nichols, 2021) see | *po², *tā paired with | *por²

*potē (~ *āpotē)

FINAL (VERB, INANIMATE, INTRANSITIVE, CONCRETE)

— by action of water current

evidence | MC itāpotew, *swept thither by the current;* SEC wepāpotew, *to be swept away by the current;* NEC sāsiputāu, *the waves lap onto sth;* Watkins (1865) "Yiskipotāo, *v.imp. It is flooded, it is over-flowed;*" Fabvre (ca. 1690) "Acheab8te8, *reculer, eviter par la marée;*" Silvy (ca. 1680) "s8tchib8teu mitchi8ap, *la marée entre dans la cabane*" see | *ā¹, *po¹, *tē²

*poyawēw

INITIAL (NOUN, ANIMATE)

— beaver yearling

evidence | PC pōyawēsis, *a one-year-old beaver;* MC opoyawēw, *a beaver yearling;* WI (Pessamit) upuaiemu [upwījēmu], *to have a beaver between one and two years with it;* Fabvre (ca. 1690) "p8ïa8e8 *pl.* 8ek, *ieunes castors de 2 ans*" | ANISH Cuoq (1886) "poiawe, *castor qui est dans sa deuxième année*"

*pō[1]

INITIAL

— give up

evidence | PC pōyow, *to give up;* WC pōðow, *to quit;* MC pōlew, *to compel sb to give up;* pōlikow, *to be compelled to give up on account of sth;* Laure (ca. 1726) "ni-purun, *je lâche le pied;*" Fabvre (ca. 1690) "P8r8māgan nat8k8r8n, *La medicine n'opere rien;*" Silvy (ca. 1680) "ni p8r8n, *je perds espérance*" limited to | *r compare | *pō², *pōn¹, *pōmē

*pō[2]

INITIAL

— feed fire

evidence | PC pōnam, *to build or feed a fire;* WC pōnam, *to make or feed a fire;* MC pōnikew, *to feed a fire;* NEC pūnim, *to feed a fire;* SEC pōnam, *to feed a fire* | ANISH boonam, *to lay an egg* (Livesay & Nichols, 2021); MENO po·nɛ·w & po·nam, *to put sb or sth in the pot;* MIAMI poonamaw-, *to give sth up to him, to deliver sth to sb* origin | PA ***pō**, "set down" limited to | *ɪn³ compare | *pō¹ see | *pōn²

*pōhk

INITIAL

— feel depressed from loneliness

evidence | Laure (ca. 1726) "ni-putcherimun, ni-mittatau, *je pleure sa mort, son absence;*" Fabvre (ca. 1690) "ni p8kerim8n 8, *etre triste naturellemt v.g. p(en)ser s8uent à la mort, en parler s8uent;*" Silvy (ca. 1680) "ni p8tcherim8n, *je suis triste naturellement*" | ANISH boongzid, *to be lonely;* boongi-yaad, *to act depressed from loneliness* (Rhodes, 1993) origin | PA ***pōnk**

*pōht (~ *pōhc, *pōhs)

INITIAL

— into a receptacle

evidence | WC pōhciwīpinam, *to throw sth in;* MC pōhcišātew, *to urinate in sth;* AT (Opitciwan, Joey Awashish) posapatam [pōssāpahtam], *to look inside sth; to experience a shamanic voyage;* SEC pōhtapiw, *to sit inside a receptacle such as a pot, box, or tub;* SEC (Waswanipi) pōsāpahtam [pūšāphtam], *to look inside sth;* Silvy (ca. 1680) "ni p8tik8s8n, *le feu vole dans ma manche*"

*pōmē

INITIAL (VERB, ANIMATE, INTRANSITIVE)

— be weary of waiting, give up waiting for

evidence | PC pōmēw, *to be discouraged;* MC pōmehew, *to give up on sb;* SEC pōmehtāw, *to tire of waiting for sth;* WI (Pessamit) pumeu [pūmēw], *to lose hope that sth can finally happen;* Fabvre (ca. 1690) "P8mebarin i8, *quitter entreprise enuyant;*" "P8man e8, *etre Las d'attendre qqn. qui tard trop;*" Silvy (ca. 1680) "ni p8man 3. -e8, *je suis las d'attendre*" compare | *pō¹, *pōn¹

*pōn[1]

INITIAL

— cease, quit

evidence | PC pōni-pimātisiw, *to die;* MC pōnawahtān, *to cease raining;* SEC pōneyihtam, *to give up sth planned;* NEC pūnīu, *to quit;* WI (Pessamit) punipalu [pūnəpəlu], *to stop;* Laure (ca. 1726) "ni-punitchin, *je cesse de croître;*" Fabvre (ca. 1690) "P8nihau n., *cesser de p8rsuiure qlqn. v.g. aal, origl*" | MESK pōnishēwa, *to quit urinating* compare | *pō¹, *pōmē

*pōn[2]

INITIAL

— set down

evidence | WC pōnakoskīw, *to set baited fish hooks;* MC pōnikoskew, *to set a night-line;* AT ponapew [pōnāpēw], *pêcher (avec une ligne dormante);* SEC pōnasināpātam, *to anchor sth;* NEC pūnitin, *for smoke to be blown back down from the smoke hole;* pūnākunāu, *to put snow in the broth to congeal the fat;* EI (Sheshatshiu) punashinapan [pūnʃɨnāpān], *large rock sinker for a fishnet;* Fabvre (ca. 1690) "P8na8k8an, *mettre sablon au foyer;*" Silvy (ca. 1680) "p8nisitass8ineabi, *cable d'ancre;*" "ni p8nabedinen, *je descends par une corde*" | ANISH boonakadoon, *to anchor sth* (Livesay & Nichols, 2021) origin | PA ***pō**, "set down" + ***en**, "by hand" see | *pō, *ɪn[3]

*pōrkwā

INITIAL

— go through soft snow

evidence | AT (Opitciwan, Joey Awashish) pokwapitciw [pōhkwāpiciw], *to haul camp over soft snow;* pokwaham [pōhkwāham], *to walk through soft snow;* SEC pohkwāwīw, *to throw oneself down into the soft snow* | ANISH booskwaagonezhimon, *road goes into the snow* (Lippert & Gambill, 2023) discussion | In the absence of a Woods Cree cognate, the reconstruction of the consonant cluster is indirectly supported by an Anishinabe cognate.

*pōs[1]

INITIAL

— grease

evidence | AT posarikwenew [pōzārihkwēnēw], *to cream or grease sb's hair;* Laure (ca. 1726) "tchi-pusetchitan nitagup, *tu engraisse mon habit;*" Fabvre (ca. 1690) "P8chinen p8sinen 3 nam, *frotter ig. v.g. sa barbe qlq che;*" Silvy (ca. 1680) "ni p8sa8enen, *je salis qqch*" | ANISH boozaa, *to be greasy or oily* (Livesay & Nichols, 2021)

*pōs[2]

INITIAL

— board, embark

evidence | PC pōsiw, *to board;* MC pōsāhokow, *for one's boat to ship water;* AT po:si-, *to go in a vehicle, board* (Béland, 1978); posatowiw [pōzāhtowīw], *to climb aboard;* SEC pōsihtāsow, *to load a boat;* WI (Pessamit) pushieu [pūʃjēw], *to take sb aboard;* Watkins (1865) "Poosahun, *v.imp. It ships water, water blows into it*" | ANISH boozi, *to board* (Livesay & Nichols, 2021); MENO po·sew, *to board or ride in a vessel or vehicle* origin | PA ***pōs** (Aubin, 1975; Hewson, 1993)

*pōsā

INITIAL

— deeply, thoroughly

evidence | PC pōsāhkwāmiw, *to sleep soundly;* MC pōsāhkwāmiw, *to sleep soundly;* SEC pōsāhkwāmiw, *to sleep soundly;* NEC pūsānāshin, *to sleep after eating grease;* Laure (ca. 1726) "pusakuamiuin, *profond sommeil;*" Silvy (ca. 1680) "ni p8sak8amin, *je dors profondément*" | ANISH boozaangwaami, *to be sound asleep* (Livesay & Nichols, 2021); Cuoq (1886) "Posase, *pénétrer, s'imbiber*"

*pōsisk

INITIAL

— concave

evidence | PC posiskahcāw, *long, narrow gulley;* posiskatināw, *to be a steep valley;* Lacombe (1874) "posiskisiw, ok, *(a.a.) il est concave;*" "posiskaw, a, *(a.in), idem;*" SEC pōsciyākan, *a bark dish;* WI (Pessamit) pussilan [pūsslān], *a bark containter* | ANISH boozikinaagan, *a bowl* (Livesay & Nichols, 2021); Cuoq (1886) "Posikis,i, Posika, *Être creux, profond (un vase, un vaisseau quelconque);*" MENO po·sɛhkato·w, *humped turtle* origin | PA ***pōsesk**

*pōsko[1] (~ *pōskw)

INITIAL

— half

evidence | WC pōskotipisk, *late that same night;* SEC pōskohtay, *half a dollar;* WI (Pessamit) pushkushinateu [pūʃkuʃənātēw], *to have a line drawn through sth separating it in two;* EI (Unaman-shipit) pushkutshishikua [pūhkutʃīhukwa], *for half a day;* Laure (ca. 1726) "puskutekuteu, *à demi ouvert;*" Fabvre (ca. 1690) "P8chk8stinebatan 3 tau, *r(em)plir, emplir à demy;*" Silvy (ca. 1680) "ni p8chk8piten, *je déchire par le milieu*" | ANISH bookobidoon, *to break sth in two with one hands* (Livesay & Nichols, 2021); Cuoq (1886) "Pokocka, *Être cassé en deux et sur le travers;*" MENO po·hkoskaw, *to break in two;* MESK pōhkonamwa, *to break sth in two using one's hands* compare | *pōsko[2]

*pōsko[2] (~ *pōskw)

INITIAL

— to break open or perforate

evidence | PC pōskwahtam, *to bite a hole into sth;* Lacombe (1874) "Poskupayiw, *ça fait explosion;*" WC pōskohtin, *to get a hole from a fall;* MC pōskotin, *to burst as its contents freeze;* Watkins (1865) "Pooskwow, *v.imp. It has a hole in it;*" Laure (ca. 1726) "nipuskunen 3. -namu, *crever, je crève quelque chose (pressant);*" Fabvre (ca. 1690) "P8chk8skau, *il e creué, deschiré v.g. habit;*" Silvy (ca. 1680) "ni p8chk8techinin, *je romps mon canot en heurtant;*" "ni p8sk8piten, *je romps en tirant*" | MESK pōhkenamwa, *to make a hole into sth with one's finger or hand* compare | *pōsko[1]

*pōt

INITIAL

— maybe

evidence | PC pōti, *exclamation expressing surprise, precedes demonstrative pronouns;* AT (Wemotaci, Jeannette Coocoo) pot [pot], *possibly, maybe;* SEC kayapā pōt, *maybe;* WI (Pessamit) put [pù:t], *maybe;* Silvy (ca. 1680) "p8ti, *peut-être*" | ANISH Nicholas (ca. 1670) "pouri, *peut-estre; soit (soit toi, soi moi)*" (Daviault, 1994) origin | PA ***pōθ**

*pōtaw

INITIAL

— distend

evidence | WC pōtawāw, *to be bloated or thick all around;* MC pōtawihkwew, *to have a puffy face;* pōtācepaliw, *to become bloated;* SEC (Waswanipi) pōtawipayin, *to bulge or distend;* Silvy (ca. 1680) "p8ta8egachtan, *le vent enfle la voile*"

*pōtē

INITIAL

— blow

evidence | PC pōtātēw, *to blow on sb;* MC pōtātaham, *to inflate sth;* EI (Sheshatshiu) ashtue-putameu [āstwēpūtāmēw], *to blow sb out;* Laure (ca. 1726) "ni-putatchiskutauaten, *souffler avec un soufflet;*" Silvy (ca. 1680) "ni p8tatchigan, *soufflet à allumer feu*"

*pōtōhš

INITIAL (NOUN, ANIMATE)

— tadpole

evidence | AT po:co:šš, *a tadpole* (Béland, 1978); (Opitciwan, Nadia Awashish) potcoc [pōcoš], *a tadpole;* SEC pōcōš, *a tadpole;* (Waswanipi) pōcowīš, *a tadpole;* WI (Pessamit) putush [pūtūʃ], *a tadpole* | ANISH boodoonh, *a tadpole* (Livesay & Nichols, 2021); MENO po·to·ne·hsɛh, *polliwog*

*pw

FINAL (VERB, TRANSITIVE, ANIMATE, CONCRETE)

— eat, taste

evidence | PC Lacombe (1874) "wikkipwew, *(v.a.)* stam, *il en aime le goût, il aime cette nourriture;*" WC wīhkipwīw, *to like the taste of sth;* SEC ispwew, *to find sth tastes thus;* NEC ishkupwāu, *to leave some of sth uneaten;*

WI (Pessamit) kutshipueu [kutʃəpwēw], *to taste sth* paired with | *št³ compare | *spw

***pwām¹**

INITIAL (NOUN, DEPENDENT INANIMATE)

— thigh

evidence | PC mipwāmikan, *a femur;* MC opwāmiw, *to have thighs;* SEC cipwām, *your thigh;* WI (Pessamit) upuameukᵘ [upwāmēwkʷ], *thigh muscle;* Fabvre (ca. 1690) "Mip8am, *cuisse*" see | *pwām²

***pwām²**

MEDIAL, FINAL (NOUN INCORPORATION)

— thigh

evidence | MC pasipwāmehwew, *to slap sb on the thigh;* SEC ayāpišipwāmešiw, *to have small things;* Laure (ca. 1726) "nit-aieskupuaman, *je suis las dans les cuisses*" see | *pwām¹

***pwāštaw**

INITIAL

— late, tardy

evidence | WC pwāstawīw, *to be slow;* MC pwāštawipaliw, *to start late, speaking of an event;* SEC pwāštawīw, *to be late;* NEC pwāshtiu, *too late;* Laure (ca. 1726) "ni-puastauin, *tardif, lent, paresseux*" | ANISH Cuoq (1886) "pwatawi- *être lent, être tardif*" origin | PA ***pwāʔtaw**

***pwāt (~ *pwāš)**

INITIAL (NOUN, ANIMATE)

— enemy

evidence | PC pwāsīmow, *to speak Nakota;* pwātisimow, *to dance a pow-wow dance;* WC pwāta, *a Sioux;* SEC (Waskaganish) pwāt, *word said as an exclamation when capturing an opponent's checker piece;* NEC pwāt, *word used in oral history to refer to enemies* (Masty, 2014); Laure (ca. 1726) "n-upuachin 3. upuachiu, *j'ai la guerre, je fais la guerre;*" Silvy (ca. 1680) "n'8p8achin, *je suis soldat, je suis en guerre;*" "p8at *pl.* p8atak, *guerrier*" | ANISH bwaan, *a Dakota* (Livesay & Nichols, 2021) origin | PA ***pwāθ** (Aubin, 1975) discussion | The possibility that this root refers specifically to Siouan people cannot be excluded.

***pwāw**

INITIAL

— **1** burdened by a heavy load

— **2** pregnant

evidence | PC pwāwīw, *to be pregnant;* MC pwāwitāpew, *to haul a burdensome load;* Laure (ca. 1726) "ni-puauinikaten, *je ne saurais lever le poids;*" Silvy (ca. 1680) "p8a8ichtim8, *chienne pleine*"

***pwēkit (~ *pwēkic)**

INITIAL

— fart

evidence | PC pwēkiciminak, *beans;* MC pwekitihkwāmiw, *to fart in one's sleep;* SEC pwecitow, *to fart;* NEC pwechichīu, *to fart when while moving;* Silvy (ca. 1680) "ni p8etchititau, *je lui pète contre*" | MENO pɛ·ketow, *to break wind*

R

***r (~ *ɩr)**

FINAL (VERB, TRANSITIVE, ANIMATE, ABSTRACT)

sound change | ē → a

— forms causative verbs

evidence | WC cimaðīw, *to erect sth;* MC pōlew, *to compel sb to give up;* kālew, *hide somebody;* AT akorew, *accrocher qlqn;* arew, *placer qlqn;* SEC ahyew, *place sb;* ništāpāwayew, *to drown sb;* Watkins (1865) "Apooyāo, *v.t.an. He sends it to him*" paired with | *tā discussion | The preaspirated cluster ***hr** is the Old Cree reflex of PA ***ʔr**, which itself derives from the suffixation of the above root onto a stop.

***rahk**

INITIAL

— **1** increase

— **2** advance

evidence | [1]PC Lacombe (1874) "Yakkihew, *il l'accroit, il le multiplie;*" WC ðāhkikin, *to grow in size;* MC lahkipaliw, *increase;* SEC yahcihtāw, *to increase sth* [2]WC ðāhkaham, *to push sth with sth;* WSC (Misipawistik, Ellen Cook) nahkinam, *to push sth forward with one's hand;* MC lahkīw, *to press forward;* SEC yahkaham, *to push sth forward (using sth);* Laure (ca. 1726) "ni-ratchissen 3. ratchiskamu, *je pousse*"

*raw[1]

MEDIAL

— **1** body

— **2** anger

evidence | [1]MC pīhcilaw, *inside the body;* SEC cinoyawew, *to have a long torso;* WI (Pessamit) mitshashkulueu [mətʃāʃkulwēw], *to have a large waist;* Laure (ca. 1726) "eskuraueuin, *grandeur, hauteur de corps;*" Fabvre (ca. 1690) "Atamĭrau nihiak, *au dedans de mon corps, de ma chair;*" Silvy (ca. 1680) "ni michira8an 3. -e8, *j'ai le corps gros*" [2]PC osāmiyawēsiw, *to be overly angry;* MC sōhkilawesiw, *to be very angry;* SEC āšteyawesiw, *to have one's anger subside;* NEC shākuyiwāsiu, *to be short-tempered;* Laure (ca. 1726) "tchiskuerauesiu, *emporté de colère*"

*raw[2]

FINAL (VERB, TRANSITIVE, ANIMATE, CONCRETE)

— to play a competitive game with, to compete against sb

evidence | PC paskiyākēw, *to win;* wayēsiyawēw, *to get sb by deceit;* MC paskilawew, *to win against sb;* Laure (ca. 1726) "ni-passiragauin, *la chance tourne, je perds;*" Fabvre (ca. 1690) "chak8tirāgan n ra8hau *gagner au ieu;*" Silvy (ca. 1680) "8eïechira8au, *je le trompe au jeu*" | ANISH gabenaw, *to defeat sb in a game;* bakinaw, *to win over sb in a contest or game* (Livesay & Nichols, 2021)

*rā

INITIAL

— finish or arrive before, anticipate

evidence | PC Lacombe (1874) "Yāhew, *il le surpasse, il finit avant lui;*" AT (Wemotaci, Nicole Petiquay) rahew [rāhēw], *to finish before sb;* NEC yāhāu, *to finish before sb* see | *rāh compare | *kirā

*rāh

FINAL (VERB, TRANSITIVE, ANIMATE, DERIVED)

— finish or arrive before, anticipate

evidence | PC Lacombe (1874) "kakweyāhew, *il se hâte de l'emporter sur lui;*" WI (Pessamit) kuetshinaieu [kwētlājēw], *to hurry to complete a task before sb* see | *rā, *h

*rāhk

INITIAL

— lightweight

evidence | PC yāhkan, *to be lightweight;* WC ðāhkasin, *to be lightweight;* MC lāhkašin, *to be lightweight;* NEC yāhkāpiskāu, *to be a light object of mineral composition;* WI (Pessamit) latshitishu [lāstəʃu], *to be lightweight;* Laure (ca. 1726) "ka ragasitgs, *léger;*" Silvy (ca. 1680) "ni ratchitichihau, *je le rend léger;*" "ratchitichi8ets assamak, *les raquettes sont légères*" | ANISH naangitoon, *to make sth light (in weight)* (Livesay & Nichols, 2021) origin | PA ***rānk** (***la·nk**, Hewson, 1993)

*rāho

FINAL (VERB, ANIMATE, INTRANSITIVE, DERIVED)

— to be faster than, to finish before

evidence | PC kakwēyāhow, *to hurry;* AT (Wemotaci, Jeannette Coocoo) kwetciraho [kwēcirāhow], *to hurry to finish before others*

*rāhrak

INITIAL

— curved or bent backwards

evidence | PC yāhyakikotēw, *to be snub-nosed;* WC ðāhðakāw, *to be bent backwards;* MC lālakacihtin, *bent backwards on impact;*

NEC yāhīkicipiyiu, *to be bent over backwards;* WI (Pessamit) lalatshikuteu [lāltʃəkutēw], *to have an upturned nose*

*rāhrā

INITIAL

— swim

evidence | PC yāhyānamowin, *swimming;* WC ðāhðānam, *to swim;* Fabvre (ca. 1690) "Raranen 3 namȣ, *nager, se baig(na)nt, y faire traiets*" limited to | *ɪn³

*rāk

INITIAL

— subside, die down (speaking of the wind)

evidence | WSC (Misipawistik, Ellen Cook) nānākipaniw, *to become less strong, speaking of the wind;* NEC yāhyāchihtin [*sic*], *the wind starts to die down;* Laure (ca. 1726) "raratchirutinu, *le vent cesse de souffler;*" Fabvre (ca. 1680) "Rakipari rȣtin, *Le uent calmit, cesse*"

*rākan

MEDIAL, FINAL (NOUN INCORPORATION)

— dish

evidence | PC kāsīyākanēw, *to wash the dishes;* MC mīsīwilākan, *a toilet;* SEC cištāpāwaciyākanew, *to wash the dishes;* Laure (ca. 1726) "ni-nukuatchiraganan, *je lèche un plat;*" "uabatunistchiragan, *plat de terre*" see | *wirākan

*rān

INITIAL (NOUN, ANIMATE)

— calf of the leg

evidence | ESC (Severn) minān, *NAD a calf;* MC olān, *NDI one's calf;* AT oran [orān], *NDI one's calf;* SEC niyān, *NAD my calf* | ANISH ginaan, *your calf* (Livesay & Nichols, 2021); MENO nena·n, *the calf of my leg* compare | *asiskitān

*rār

INITIAL

— alongside

evidence | WC ðāðakāmīham, *to paddle along the shore;* MC lālakām, *along the shore;* SEC yāyipahtāw, *to run along the edge*

*rārako

INITIAL

— draw out, pull out

evidence | AT (Opitciwan, Joey Awashish) rarakonam [rārakonam], *to remove sth from its container;* WI (Pessamit) lalikupitam[u] [lālukupətəm], *to pull sth out quickly;* Watkins (1865) "Yayikoochìchāpitāo, *v.t.an. He takes it out of his hand;*" Fabvre (ca. 1690) "Raragȣparin iȣ *se detacher v.g. mȣstaches ig. v.g.*" compare | *rārisk

*rārik

INITIAL

— rip

evidence | PC yāyikāw, *to be torn in shreds;* WC ðāðikipitam, *to tear sth;* MC lālikāštan, *to rip in the wind;* SEC yāyicipitam, *to rip sth by pulling;* WI (Pessamit) lalikapeshueu [lāləkāpēʃwēw], *to cut sth into strips;* Laure (ca. 1726) "rararitchiskau, *haillon, habit déchiré en pièces*"

*rārisk

INITIAL

— draw out, pull out

evidence | MC lāliskipitam, *to draw sth out, to pull sth out of sth else;* AT (Opitciwan, Joey Awashish) rariskipitam [rāriskipitam], *to pull sth out;* NEC yāyischipitim, *to pull sth out of sth else;* WI (Pessamit) lalissipalu [lāləssəpəlu], *to come out spontaneously from where it was inserted;* Laure (ca. 1726) "ni-rariskatauatchipiten, *j'arrache les racines;*" Silvy (ca. 1680) "ni raristinen, *je retire;*" Silvy (ca. 1680) "ni raristipiten, *je retire une chose dessus l'autre*" compare | *rārako

*rāš

INITIAL

— **1** drop, descend

— **2** stroke

evidence | PC yāsipayiw, *descend;* ESC (Severn) nānāshinam, *to stroke sth;* MC lāšāhtawīw, *to climb down;* lālāšihkwenew, *to stroke sb's face;* AT ra:šin-, *to lower sth or sb by hand* (Béland, 1978); SEC yāšīw, *to descend;* Silvy (ca. 1680) "ni rachabak8enen, *je retire, je rabaisse l'écorce*" | ANISH naazhiibizo, *fall, fly, or swoop down* (Livesay & Nichols, 2021); naazhgatgwenaa, *stroke sb's forehead* (O&OE, 2021); MENO na·senam, *to lower sth by hand*

*rāw

INITIAL

— **1** far

— **2** barely, only partly

evidence | [1]WC ðāwinam, *to be unable to reach with one's hand;* MC lāwinākwan, *to be far;* SEC yāwāpamew, *to be far from sb;* Watkins (1865) "Yowinakwun, *v.imp. It is far off;*" Silvy (ca. 1680) "ni ra8eriten, *je ne saurais l'atteindre;*" "ni ra8inen, *je n'attains qu'à demi, je ne saurais l'atteindre*" [2]PC Lacombe (1874) "Yāwipayiw, *il manque, il se trouve sans moyen;*" AT (Wemotaci, Jeannette Coocoo) rawonam [rāwnam], *to have a hard time walking through thick snow;* NEC iyaawin, *to contain only a small or insufficient quantity;* Silvy (ca. 1680) "ra8beu, *il n'y en a guère dans le vase*" | [1]ANISH naawinaagwad, *to be barely visible, to be visible in the distance* (Livesay & Nichols, 2021) [2]ANISH naawashkine, *to be partly full;* naawibii, *to be partly full of liquid;* (Livesay & Nichols, 2021); MENO na·wepiw AI, II *to be part full of liquid*

*rēhrē

INITIAL (VERB, ANIMATE, INTRANSITIVE)

— breathe

evidence | WC ðīhðīw, *to breathe;* MC leletotawew, *to breathe on sb;* SEC yehyewin, *breath;* Laure (ca. 1726) "ni-rerhan 3. rerheu, *je respire;*" Silvy (ca. 1680) "ni rehan 3. -e8, ni nehan, *je respire*" | ANISH Cuoq (1886) "nese, *il respire*" origin | PA ***rēhrē** (***le:hle:**, Aubin, 1975; Hewson, 1993)

*rēkaw

INITIAL (NOUN, INANIMATE)

— sand

evidence | PC yēkaw, *sand;* MC lekāwaskisinew, *to be wearing sandy shoes;* SEC yekāwihtakāw, *to be a sandy floor;* NEC yākiu; *sand;* WI (Pessamit) lekau [lēku], *sand;* lekauapui [lēkāwāpwī], *lye made from wood ash;* Silvy (ca. 1680) "regau, *sable;*" "rega8i8, *sablonneux*"

*rēko (~ *rēkw)

INITIAL

— from the corner of one's eyes, askance

evidence | WSC (Misipawistik, Ellen Cook) nēkwāpiw, *to look from the top or corner of one's eyes in disdain;* ESC nekocāpamew & nekwāpamew, *to look at sb from the top or corner of one's eyes;* MC lekwāpamew, *to look at sb from the top or corner of one's eyes;* lekocāpiw, *to look from the top or corner of one's eyes;* AT rekwapamew [rekwāpamew], *to look askance at sb;* SEC yekwāpamew, *to look askance at sb* | ANISH negwaabam, *to glance sideways at sb or look at sb out of the corner of the eye* (Livesay & Nichols, 2021); MENO nɛ·kuapew AI, *to peep from under sth;* MESK nēkwāpamēwa, *to peer up at sb out of the tops of one's eyes*

*ri

FINAL (VERB, ANIMATE, INTRANSITIVE, CONCRETE)

— move body part

evidence | MC itiskweliw, *to move one's head thus;* SEC kāhkapeyiw, *to spread one's thighs;* Laure (ca. 1726) "ni-pitikutitcherin 3. -iu, *je ferme la main;*" Fabvre (ca. 1690) "n 8pikaterin, i8, *Remuer Le pied en L air*" | ANISH googiikweni, *to put one's head underwater* (Livesay & Nichols, 2021)

*rihkw (~ *rihko)

INITIAL (NOUN, DEPENDENT ANIMATE)

— lymph node

evidence | PC wiyihkosa, *one's gland(s) or tonsil(s);* WC oðīhk, *a gland;* MC olihkwa, *one's tonsil(s);* NEC wiyihkwh, *one's tonsil(s);* EI (Sheshatshiu) unikua [unīkwa], *one's lymph node(s), one's tonsil(s);* Laure (ca. 1726) "uriku *pl.* -ets, *amygdales, glandes du gosier;*" Fabvre (ca. 1690) "8 rik8 *pl* 8ek, *glandes, grumeaux de chaire daal v.g. dans le derr(iere) de la cuisse*" compare | *nīšk²

*rihrip

INITIAL

— diligent

evidence | PC Lacombe (1874) "yiyippiw, ok, *(a.a.) il est agile, actif, diligent;*" SEC īhīpīu, *to be a committed worker* (CSB, 2018); Watkins (1865) "Yeyippewin, *n.in. Activity, diligence, industry;*" Laure (ca. 1726) "riripiuin, *diligence*" | MENO nεqnεpew, *to be industrious*

*rikiko (~ *rikikw)

INITIAL

— frosty

evidence | WC ðiðikwatin, *to be frosty;* MC lilikotin & likikotin, *to be frosty;* AT ririkotin [ririkotin], *être givrer;* SEC yicikopayiw, *to become frosty;* WI (Pessamit) litshikushkamikatin [ltʃukuʃkəməkətn], *hoar frost covering the ground;* EI (Unamanshipit) nitshikutshu [ntʃukwatʃu], *to be covered in frost;* Laure (ca. 1726) "ritchikuabiskau, *terni;*" Silvy (ca. 1680) "nitchik8atin nicht8ïa, *ma barbe est blanche gelée*" | ANISH nigigwashkadin, *to be frosty grass* (McGregor, 2004)

*riko (~ *rikw)

INITIAL

— cover with

evidence | WC ðikwākonīpaðiw, *to get covered in snow from a fall;* MC likohaskān, *grave;* SEC yikoskwan, *cloudy;* Watkins (1865) "Yikwùhum, *v.t.in.6 He covers it with snow, earth, &c.;*" Silvy (ca. 1680) "ni rig8ak8neh8n, *je m'enfois sous la neige*"

*rimiskw

MEDIAL (NOUN INCORPORATION)

— catkin

evidence | Laure (ca. 1726) "ni-manimiriskuanen [*sic*], *j'ébourgeonne, j'arrange les bourgeons*" see | *wirimiskw

*riniw (~ *riniwak)

MEDIAL, FINAL (NOUN INCORPORATION)

— **1** man

— **2** pair

evidence | [1]PC kihciyiniw, *a head man;* MC ayahcililiw, *a foreigner;* WI (Pessamit) matshilnutishu [*sic*] [mətʃəlnüttʃu], *to be a bad person;* EI (Uashat) mashinnu [māʃɨnnu], *person of mixed race who has one First Nations parent;* Laure (ca. 1726) "miatchiriniu, *barbare, étranger;*" "ni-machirinikan, *je suis avare;*" "ka maratchiriniuatchichit, *charnel, voluptueux, sale;*" Fabvre (ca. 1690) "ichirini8atĭsin i8, *etre de telle hum(eu)r;*" Silvy (ca. 1680) "aïatchirini8, *étranger*" [2]MC nīšoliliw, *two pairs;* SEC peyakoyiniw, *one pair;* NEC nishtuiyiu, *three pairs;* EI (Sheshatshiu) nishtunnu [nɨstunnu], *thirty;* Laure (ca. 1726) "nikuturiniu, *dix*"

*ripāt (~ *ripāc, *ripās)

INITIAL

— uncomfortably wet or dirty

evidence | MC lipāsinākosiw, *to looks messy or filthy;* lipāci-kīšikāw, *miserably cold and wet day;* SEC yipāteyimow, *to feel miserable due to cold and wet weather;* WI (Pessamit) lipashinam [ləpāʃənəm], *to find the sight of sth wet, damp, or sticky unpleasant;* Fabvre (ca. 1690) "Ripatisin i8, *aur mauu(ai)s tems, humid(e), pluu(ieu)x, u(en)teux*" | ANISH nibaadizi, *to be a greedy eater* (Livesay & Nichols, 2021)

*ripwāhkā

INITIAL (VERB, ANIMATE, INTRANSITIVE)

— prudent, sensible

evidence | WC ðipwāhkāw, *to speak prudently;* MC lipwāhkāmow, *to speak sensibly or prudently;* SEC yipwāhkāw, *to be prudent, smart* | ANISH Cuoq (1886) "nibwaka, *être sage; avoir de l'esprit; avoir sa connaissance;*" MENO nepuahkaw, *to be wise, learned, clever;* MESK nepwāhkāwa, *to be wise, smart, clever* see | *ā²

*rir

MEDIAL (NOUN INCORPORATION)

— urinary bladder

evidence | ESC kiponineškāw, *to suffer of a bladder obstruction;* MC kipoleškāw, *to suffer of a bladder obstruction;* NEC wīyiyāchisiu, *to smell of urine;* Laure (ca. 1726) "tchibirirésiuin, *rétention (maladie, on ne peut uriner);*" Fabvre (ca. 1690) "8irirēgan, *Cela sent un peu mal*" see | *ririy¹, *ririy²

*ririhko (~ *ririhkw)

INITIAL

— break apart

evidence | MC lalihkonam, *to take sth apart;* lalihkohtin, *to break apart on impact;* SEC iyihkuham [*sic*], *to break sth apart by striking or using a tool* (CSB, 2018); WI (Pessamit) lalikushteu [lələkustēw], *to be a heap of rocks from an old rock slide;* Laure (ca. 1726) "ririkukaneparin, *je me suis fracassé une jambe;*" "ririkuabischipariu assini, *morceau de roche;*" Fabvre (ca. 1690) "ririk8hau, *fendre en 2x*" discussion | In the absence of a Woods Cree cognate, the status of the preaspiration cannot be confirmed.

*ririy¹

INITIAL (NOUN, DEPENDENT INANIMATE)

— urinary bladder

evidence | MC oliliy, *one's bladder;* AT oriri [orirī], *one's bladder;* SEC niyiyiy [niyiyī], *my bladder;* WI (Mashteuiatsh) uliliapi [uləljāpī], *a bladder;* EI (Sheshatshiu) uniapi [unjāpī], *a bladder* see | *rir, *ririy²

*ririy²

FINAL (NOUN INCORPORATION)

— urinary bladder

evidence | Laure (ca. 1726) "attiku-riri, *vessie de caribou*" see | *rir, *ririy¹

*risk

INITIAL

— under and out of sight, not visible, disappear

evidence | WC ðiskipīw, *to be flooded;* MC liskipaliw, *to drop out of sight;* liskākonew, *to be covered with snow;* liskihkwāmiw, *to fall asleep;* AT riskipotew, *to be flooded;* SEC yiscipotāw, *to flood sth;* WI (Pessamit) lissinakuan [ləssənākwən], *to disappear in the distance;* Watkins (1865) "Yiskipāpuyew, *v.imp. The tide rises;*" Silvy (ca. 1680) "ni ristigam8tan 3. -tau, *mon nez ne paraît pas, tant je suis gras*" | ANISH nikibii, *to be flooded* (Livesay & Nichols, 2021)

*rišk (~ *riškā)

INITIAL

— angry, anger

evidence | AT (Opitciwan, Joey Awashish) rickihew [riškihēw], *to anger sb;* SEC iškāhew, *to irritate or annoy sb;* iškāsīw, *to be irritated or annoyed;* WI (Pessamit) lishkatishiu [ləʃkāttʃīw], *to be bad-tempered;* lishkaieu [ləʃkājēw], *to make sb angry, to provoke sb;* Laure (ca. 1726) "ni-riskatisin, *je suis fâché, en colère;*" "ni-riskahau, *émouvoir, exciter à la colère, j'émeus, j'excite;*" Silvy (ca. 1680) "ni richterimau, ni risterimau, *je le crois en colère et fâcheux, je le hais comme mon ennemi;*" "nichkam8 mel. richkam8, *il souffle avec effort, étant en colère, v.g. le chien, l'ours, etc.*" | ANISH nishkibii, *to be angry when drinking* (Livesay & Nichols, 2021); MENO nɛhke·hɛ·w, *to anger sb*

*rīhrīk

INITIAL

— toothed, notched

evidence | WC ðīhðīkicihcān, *finger;* MC līlīkāw, *be toothed or notched;* SEC (Waswanipi) yīhīkitihcān, *finger;* EI ninikau [nīnīkāw] *be toothed or jagged;* Fabvre (ca. 1690) "Riritichen 3 chamȣ, *decȣper en fr(an)ge, Leches mince(s) pr secher*" | ANISH niisiigizidaan, *a toe* (Livesay & Nichols, 2021) origin | Possibly a reduplication of ***rīk**. compare | *rīkihtaw

*rīk (~ *rīh, *rīš)

INITIAL

— lose or cause to lose one's shape, collapse, decompose, erode

evidence | PC yīkinikēw, *to milk a cow;* WC ðīkinam, *to squeeze sth out by hand;* MC līsam, līswew, *to digest sth;* AT (Opitciwan, Joey Awashish) risam [rīssam], *to digest sth;* riso [rīssow], *to digest; to be digested;* rictew [rīštēw], *to be digested;* SEC (Nemaska) kā yīkatāwahkāw, *place name, literally "the eroding sand bank"* (Bishop, 2022); (Mistissini) kā yīkānakāw, *place name, literally "the eroding island"* (Bishop, 2022); NEC (Chisasibi) yākatāwihkaw, *place name, literally "the eroding sand bank"* (Bishop, 2022) WI (Pessamit) litshipiteu [lītʃəpətēw], *cause sth to collapse or come apart by pulling;* EI (Nutashkuanit) likapuleu [līkāpwēwlēw], *to cause sth to become undone or collapse by putting it in water;* EI (Sheshatshiu) nishamᵘ [nīʃəm], *to digest sth;* Fabvre (ca. 1690) "Rigatȣi mitai, *v.g. uieux pȣry bois*" | MENO ne·kanɛt, *to go out of shape with decay* origin | PA ***rīk** (***li· k**, Hewson, 1993)

*rīkihtaw

INITIAL

— forked

evidence | MC līkihtawištikweyāw, *river forks;* SEC yīcihtawāw, *to be forked;* Silvy (ca. 1680) "nitchitaȣabiskau, *fer fourchu, fourche de fer*" compare | *rīhrīk

*rīw

INITIAL

— reduce in size, deflate

evidence | PC iyiwatēw, *to have an empty stomach;* MC līwištin, *swelling subsides;* līwaham, *to reduce sth to a powder;* SEC yīwācenam, *to deflate sth manually;* NEC īwāshiu, *to be shallow water;* WI (Pessamit) liupalu [ljūpəlu], *become less swollen or deflate;* liutew [ljūtēw], *to have an empty stomach;* EI (Sheshatshiu) niuashu [nīwą̄ʃu], *to be shallow water;* Silvy (ca. 1680) "ni riȣatan 3. -teȣ, *j'ai bon appétit*"

*rīwan

INITIAL

— feel fatigue or lethargy

evidence | PC iyiwanisiw, *to be short of supplies;* Lacombe (1874) "Iyewanisiw, ok, *(a.a.) il est dans la disette, il souffre de la famine;*" WI (Pessamit) liunatshu [ljūntʃu], *to be weakened by cold and hunger; to suffer of hypothermia;* EI (Sheshatshiu) niuniu [njūnīw], *to be weakened by hunger;* Laure (ca. 1726) "ni-riuanabauan, *la pluie m'endort;*" Fabvre (ca. 1690) "Riȣanăpin iȣ, *rester, demeurer pr La fain;*" Silvy (ca. 1680) "ni ririȣanisin, *je suis à jeun, j'ai appétit;*" "ni riȣanisk8r8n, *j'ai sommeil ayant mange*"

*rīwē

INITIAL

— fringe

evidence | MC līwešam, *to cut a fringe into sth;* AT (Opitciwan, Joey Awashish) riwe-wockwi [rīwē-waškway], *birch bark that hangs loosely from the tree;* SEC yīwekotew, *to hang as a fringe* | ANISH niisiiwezhigaade, *to be cut into a fringe* (Livesay & Nichols, 2021)

*rkīkw (~ *rkīko)

INITIAL (NOUN, DEPENDENT ANIMATE)

— gill

evidence | PC Lacombe (1874) "Okik, wa, *(n.r.) ouïes des poissons;*" WC oskīkwak, *fish gills;* WSC (Misipawistik, Ellen Cook)

okikwak, *fish gills;* ESC ohkīk, *gill of a fish;* MC ohkīhkow, *to have gills;* AT (Opitciwan, Monique Awashish) wikikok [wīhkīhkok], *fish gills;* SEC ohcīhk^{w}, *fish gill;* NEC wihchiikwh, *one's gills;* EI (Unaman-shipit) utshikumeshat [utʃīkumēhat], *fish gills;* Watkins (1865) "Ookek, *n.an. The gill (of a fish);*" Fabvre (ca. 1690) "8kig8 *pl.* 8ek, *os de balaine uers Le col, c8;*" Silvy (ca. 1680) "8tchig8, *os de la baleine vers le cou*" | MENO ohke·k(on), *one's gill(s), speaking of a fish*
discussion | Contemporary reflexes of this root disagree regarding the preaspirate in the final consonant cluster, with the contiguous Moose Cree, Atikamekw, and Southern East Cree dialects departing from the others. However, geographically distant dialects agree in the absence of the preaspirate, suggesting the central dialects share an innovation.

*rkw (~ *rkwak)

MEDIAL (NOUN INCORPORATION)

— blood

evidence | PC mēscihkwēkawiw, *to bleed out;* MC cākihkweyāšikawiw, *to bleed out;* NEC pāsihkwān, *dried caribou blood;* SEC šāpohkokan, *to have blood soak through;* šīwākamihkwew, *to be diabetic;* mehcihkwepayiw, *to bleed out;* Laure (ca. 1726) "rigukuatchichiu, *ensanglanté, empourpré de sang [il est...];*" Silvy (ca. 1680) "matchik8aste8, *le sang cuit dans la chaudière, est gâté*" | ANISH gibichiskwagizi, *to stop bleeding* (Livesay & Nichols, 2021) see | *mirko, *ak^{2}

*ro

FINAL (VERB, ANIMATE, INTRANSITIVE, ABSTRACT)

— forms dynamic verbs

evidence | WC pōðow, *to quit;* MC tepiškolow, *to eat enough;* AT otamiro-, *to work* (Béland, 1978); SEC nāciyōštawew, *to creep up to sb;* EI (Unaman-shipit) pimapunu [pmāpunu], *to let oneself be carried by the current;* Laure (ca. 1726) "n-utamirun, *mes affaires m'empêchent, je suis affairé;*" "nit-aieskurun, *je suis las;*" Silvy (ca. 1680) "ni tibistir8n, *la nuit me prend, je ne vois goutte*" see | *r, *o

*rō

INITIAL

— be air current

evidence | PC yōtin, *wind blows;* yōwahtam, *to draw at sth with suction;* Lacombe (1874) "Yowew, *(v.im.) il prend vent, il fait de l'air;*" MC lōlōhtam, *to suck on sth;* lōhtepaliw, *the door opens;* lōtin, *wind blows;* SEC yōhtenew, *to open a tent flap;* NEC yuwāu, *air goes out of sth;* yūhyūshkim, *to let the cold in by going in and out;* yūhyūmāu, *to resuscitate sb;* EI (Sheshatshiu) nutenam^{u} [nūtēnəm], *to open a door or window;* Watkins (1865) "Yoowāo, v.imp. *It blows;*" Fabvre (ca. 1690) "R8e8, *Le uent entre dans La cabane,*" "r8aïau, *la neige e(st) molle;*" Silvy (ca. 1680) "r8ask8teu, *le feu vesse*" | ANISH Cuoq (1886) "Nowaia, *la neige est molle; il y a un peu d'air;* Kawin ningotiji ondji nowaiasinon, cecenamok, *il ne vient de l'air d'aucun côté, ouvrez (portes et fenêtres);*" MENO no·wa·nemat II, *there is a wind blowing*

*rōsk

INITIAL

— soft

evidence | WC ðōskāhcāw, *to be soft ground;* MC lōskašakew, *have soft skin;* SEC yōscinam, *to soften by hand;* Watkins (1865) "Yoosketow, *v.t.in.2. He softens it*" | ANISH nookaa, *to be soft or tender* (Livesay & Nichols, 2021); MIAMI noohkanwi, *to be soft* (ILDA, 2017)

*rōsp

INITIAL

— gentle, tame

evidence | PC yōspisīhēw, *to tame sb;* MC lōspātisīw, *to have a gentle character;* NEC yūspisīu, *to be meek;* Watkins (1865) "Yoospisew, *v.i.1., He is tame, he is gentle, he is tender, (in disposition);"* Laure (ca. 1726) "eka ka ruspisien tapue, *tu es rustique, grossier*"

*rōwē

FINAL (VERB, INANIMATE, INTRANSITIVE, DERIVED)

— wind blows

evidence | PC sōhkiyowēw, *strong wind;* WC tahkiðōwīw, *cold wind;* MC sōhkilawew, *strong wind;* SEC ohciyowew, *to blow from;* Watkins (1865) "kipìcheyoowāo, *The wind ceases;"* Laure (ca. 1726) "tatchirueu, *il souffle [le vent est froid]*" see | *rō, *wē[1]

*rpan[1]

INITIAL (NOUN, DEPENDENT INANIMATE)

— lung

evidence | PC nihpan, *my lung;* WC miðpan, *a lung;* MC ohpanāspinew, *to have a lung disease;* SEC ohpan, *one's lung;* NSK wiihpin, *one's lung;* WI (Pessamit) upan [upən], *one's lung;* Isham (1743) "us'spun, *the lights;"* Silvy (ca. 1680) "8pan, poumon;" "nipan, *mon poumon*" | ANISH gipan, *your lung;* MENO nɛhpa·n, *my lung* see | *rpan[2]

*rpan[2]

MEDIAL, FINAL (NOUN INCORPORATION)

— lung

evidence | MC pākihpanepaliw, *to have pneumonia;* manihpaneśwew, *to cut out sb's lungs;* SEC otōcihpanew, *to have a bruised lung;* WI (Pessamit) patshipanepalu [pātʃəpənēpəlu], *to have pneumonia;* EI (Sheshatshiu) patshipanepanu [pātʃɨpənēpənu], *to have pneumonia* see | *rpan[1]

S

*s (~ *ɩs)

FINAL (VERB, TRANSITIVE, INANIMATE, CONCRETE)

sound change | ē → a

— heat

evidence | PC mēstisam, *to burn sth up;* MC kisisam, *heat sth;* kiśikanasam, *to heat a bone or object made of bone;* AT oppisikan, *baking powder* (Béland, 1978); SEC tihcisam, *to melt sth;* Laure (ca. 1726) "ni-tchichueuasen, *je fais réchauffer de la viande*" | ANISH iniz, *heat sb a certain way* (Livesay & Nichols, 2021) origin | PA ***(e)s** (Aubin, 1975) paired with | *sw compare | *āciwahs

*sak

INITIAL

— grasp, snag

evidence | PC sakicin, *to get snagged on sth;* MC sakālihkwenew, *to grab sb by the hair;* SEC sacisitenew, *to grab sb by the foot;* NEC sichikwāpitāu, *to grab sb by the neck;* NEC sichipiskunāyāpush, *rabbit snared around the back* | MESK sakikwēnēwa, *to take or hold sb by the neck*

*sakask

INITIAL

— be or make safe (in an enclosed space)

evidence | MC sakaskihtāw, *to close sth up properly;* sakaskapiw, *to settle down;* SEC sakasceyimow, *to feel comfortable or settled in a dwelling;* sakascinam, *to put sth in a safe place;* WI (Pessamit) shakashkau, *to be waterproof or windproof* | MENO saka·hkapew AI, saka·hkaqtɛw II, *to be put away, to be safe in a proper place, to sit in one's proper place*

*sakimēw

INITIAL (NOUN, ANIMATE)

— mosquito

evidence | PC sakimēwayān, *mosquito netting;* MC sakimeskāw, *to be many mosquitoes;* SEC sacimew, *mosquito;* EI (Sheshatshiu) shatshimeu [ʃətʃɨmēw], *mosquito;* Silvy (ca. 1680) "satchimeu, *maringouin*" | ANISH zagime, *mosquito* (Livesay & Nichols, 2021); MENO sake·mɛ·w, *mosquito* origin | PA ***sakimēwa** compare | *sak

*sakīn

INITIAL (NOUN, DEPENDENT INANIMATE)

— upper part of the arm (of a biped) or front leg (of a quadruped) including its associated girdle

evidence | PC Lacombe (1874) "ni'sakin, a, o'sakin, *l'épaule tout entière avec le bras, ou, la patte;*" SEC misichīn, *a blouse* (CSB, 2018); WI (Pessamit) ushatshinakᵘ [uʃətʃīnākʷ], *upper part of a quarter of a porcupine;* Laure (ca. 1726) "usatchin, *depuis l'épaule jusqu'au coude;*" "nisatchinitch nit-iskupan, *je suis dans l'eau jusqu'aux épaules;*" "pasteu-kukuch-usatchin, *jambon;*" Fabvre (ca. 1690) "8sakin, 8sakini, *epaule, mon epaule;*" Silvy (ca. 1680) "8satchin, *épaule*" | ANISH ozagiin, *animal arm, front quarter* (Livesay & Nichols, 2021)

*sako

INITIAL

— placed closely, densely spaced; (of mesh) small

evidence | MC sakolapiy, *a fishing net with a small mesh;* sakopiwak, *to be placed close together; to sit close to one another;* sakōšew, *to birth children at short intervals such that they are close in age;* NEC sikusiu, *to have a small mesh, speaking of a net;* sikuschiskāu, *to be a dense area of jack pines;* Silvy (ca. 1680) "sak8ahiganí8i8, *il est à petites mailles;*" "sak8aapich, *rets à petites mailles*" | MESK sakwākwasowaki, *to lie packed closely together* compare | *pašk

*saniko

INITIAL (VERB, ANIMATE, INTRANSITIVE)

— blow one's nose

evidence | NEC sinikwāu, *to blow one's nose;* WI (Pessamit) shaniku [ʃənuku], *to blow one's nose;* EI (Mamit) shaniku [hanuku], *to blow one's nose;* EI (Unaman-shipit) shanikuan [hanakwān], *handkerchief, tissue;* EI (Sheshatshiu) shaniku [ʃənuku], *to blow one's nose;* Laure (ca. 1726) "ni-sanigunau, *je mouche l'enfant;*" Silvy (ca. 1680) "ni sanig8an 3. -e8, *je me mouche*" | MENO sane·ko·w, *to blow one's nose* origin | PA ***sanikwiwa** (Hewson, 1993)

*sasāk

INITIAL

— stingy

evidence | PC sasākisīw, *to be selfish or stingy;* MC sasākisīw, *to be stingy;* SEC sāchisīu, *to be stingy* (CSB, 2018); Silvy (ca. 1680) "ni sasadisin, *je suis avare;*" "sasatchisin, *j'aime tout, je suis avare*" | ANISH zazaagizi, *to be stingy* (Livesay & Nichols, 2021) origin | Possibly a reduplication of ***sāk**. compare | *sāk

*sask[1]

INITIAL

— use cane

evidence | MC saskahowākew, *to use sth as a cane;* SEC saskahow, *to use a cane or stick for walking;* Fabvre (ca. 1690) "Saskah8n pl h8na, *baston à s(')ap8yer*" | ANISH zaka'o, *to use a cane* (Livesay & Nichols, 2021) origin | PA ***sask** (***saxk**, Hewson, 1993)

*sask[2]

INITIAL

— ignite

evidence | MC saskaham, *to ignite sth;* SEC saskahwew, *to light sth on fire;* Fabvre (ca. 1690) "Saskahĭgan pl găna, *allumettes pr allumer feu*" | ANISH zakizige, *to light or ignite things* (Livesay & Nichols, 2021); MESK sahkahamwa, *to set fire to sth* origin | PA ***sask** (***saxk**, Hewson, 1993)

*sask[3]

INITIAL

— to be wet and granular (speaking of snow)

evidence | MC saskāštew, *to be wet and granular snow from the heat of the sun;* SEC saskan, *to be wet and granular snow;* Fabvre (ca. 1690) "Saskan, *Il degele, La neige fond;*" "Sastite8 k8n, *elle fond au soleil La neige*" |

ANISH zhakipon, *wet snow falls* (Livesay & Nichols, 2021); MENO sahka·konakat II, *the snow is crusty;* MESK shahkanwi, *to be a thaw* origin | PA ***šask**

*sask[4]

INITIAL

— put morsel in one's mouth

evidence | MC saskamow, *to put a morsel in one's mouth;* SEC saskamotiyew, *to put sth in sb's mouth;* EI (Mamit) shashkatamuneikan [hahkatāmunējkan], *medical thermometer;* Fabvre (ca. 1690) "ni Saskamȣrau n. *apaster qlqn. n., Luy porter à La bȣche*" | ANISH zhakamo, *to put sth in one's own mouth* (Livesay & Nichols, 2021); MESK shahkamowa, *to put a bite of food in one's mouth* origin | PA ***šask**

*sāh (~ *sāš)

INITIAL

— fry

evidence | PC sāsāpiskisikan, *frying pan;* MC sāsamekwew, *fry fish;* AT (Wemotaci, Nicole Petiquay) saso [sāssow], *to be fried;* (Opitciwan, Joey Awashish) sactew [sāštēw], *to be fried;* sasapocwew [sāssāpoʒwēw], *to fry rabbit;* sa:ss-, *to fry sth* (Béland, 1976); SEC sāsescihkwātam, *to fry sth;* shāshteu, fat used for frying (CSB, 2018); Silvy (ca. 1680) "ni sasen, *je fais fondre de la graisse*" | ANISH zaasakokwe, *to fry sth* (Livesay & Nichols, 2021) origin | PA ***sāʔ** limited to | *s, *so[2], *sw, *tē[4] compare | *šāštē

*sāhkwatamw

INITIAL (NOUN, ANIMATE)

— large hawk, buzzard (buteo spp.)

evidence | PC Lacombe (1874) "sākwatamow, ok, *(n.r.) gros épervier, oiseau carnassier;*" WC sāhkwatamow, *a large hawk;* MC sāhkotamow, *a buzzard;* SEC sāhkotam^w & sāhkotamow, *a buzzard, a large hawk;* WI (Pessamit) shakutam^u [ʃākətəmwī], *a type of hawk;* EI (Sheshatshiu) shakutam^u [ʃākutum], *a type of hawk;* Faries & Mackay (1938) "sȧko'tumoo, sȧkwu'tumoo, *n.an. The goshawk*" | ANISH Cuoq (1886) "sakwatamo, *oiseau criard du genre épervier*"

*sāk

INITIAL

— **1** protrude, stick out, come into view from behind something

— **2** love

evidence | [1]MC sākaham, *to swim out of one's tunnel or lodge;* NEC sāchipichīu, *to be budding season;* WI (Pessamit) shakatshueu [ʃākətʃwēw], *to arrive at the summit;* Laure (ca. 1726) "sakatapetichiu *enraciné, qui a des racines*" [2]MC sākihtāw, *to love sth;* SEC sācihew, *to love sb;* Laure (ca. 1726) "naspitch satcherimaganiu, *il est aimé de tout le monde;*" Silvy (ca. 1680) "ni satchitan 3. -tau, *j'aime*" | [1]ANISH zaagaabide, *to teeth* (Livesay & Nichols, 2021); MENO sa·keken, *to grow up through the soil;* MESK sākikomēshkēwa, *to stick one's nose out* [2]ANISH zaagi'idiwin, *mutual love* (Livesay & Nichols, 2021) origin | PA ***sāk** (Aubin, 1975; Hewson, 1993) compare | *sasāk

*sākitaw

INITIAL

— (exiting) the mouth of a river

evidence | WC sākitawāhk, *Île-à-la-Crosse;* MC sākitawāpotew, *to be swept out the mouth of the river by the current;* WI (Pessamit) shatshituau [ʃāstwāw], *to be the mouth of the river* see | *sāk, *taw compare | *sākiw

*sākiw

INITIAL (NOUN, INANIMATE)

— mouth of a river

evidence | PC sākiy, *inlet;* ESC (Severn) sākiy, *the outlet of a lake;* MC sākiy, *the mouth of a river;* AT (Wemotaci, Jeannette Coocoo) saki [sākī], *mouth of a river;* NEC sāchīū, *to be the inlet of a lake;* EI (Mamit) shatshu [hātʃu], *head of a lake;* Laure (ca. 1726) "satchiu, satchiuan, *décharge d'un fleuve au lac;*" "tchiche-chatsiu, *fleuve St-Laurent*" | ANISH zaagiing, *at the inlet* (Livesay & Nichols, 2021); MENO sa·ke·wew, *to empty into a body of water, speaking of a stream* see | *sāk compare | *sākitaw

*sām

INITIAL

— touch

evidence | PC sāminēw, *to touch sb;* MC sāmiškam, *to touch sth with one's foot or body;* SEC sāminam, *to lay one's hand(s) on sth;* Watkins (1865) "Saminum, *v.t.in.6. He touches it, he feels it*" | ANISH zaamisin, *to lie touching* (Livesay & Nichols, 2021)

*sāp

INITIAL

— vigorous, strong

evidence | MC sāpelihtam, *to be keen about sth;* NEC sāpākimiu, *it is strong, speaking of a drink;* Laure (ca. 1726) "ni-sabikanan, *je suis allègre;*" Silvy (ca. 1680) "ni sabisin, *je me porte bien, je suis fort*" origin | PA ***sāp** (Aubin, 1975)

*sāskwē

INITIAL (VERB, ANIMATE, INTRANSITIVE)

— whoop

evidence | PC Lacombe (1874) "sāsāskwew, ok, *(v.n.) Voy sākowew;* cf. sākowew, ok, *(v.n.) il pousse des cris pour s'animer, pour s'encourager, crier vivat, il applaudit, il pousse des cris de joie, ou, sāsāskwew, ok;*" MC sāskwew, *to whoop;* sāsāskwew, *to whoop repeatedly;* NSK saaskwaaw, *to give a war cry; to howl* | ANISH zaakwaazh, *to cheer for sb;* zaasaakwe, *to whoop* (Livesay & Nichols, 2021) origin | Possibly from ***sāsk**, a root for which the insufficient evidence is limited to Watkins (1865) "Saskeyuwāsew, *v.i.1. He rages, he is furious,*" and repeated in Lacombe (1874) see | *wē[1]

*sēhkwē

INITIAL

— flared

evidence | PC sēhkwēpitēw, *to be pulled to expand;* MC sehkweyāw, *to be flared;* SEC sehkwešam, *to cut sth into a flared shape;* Laure (ca. 1726) "ni-chekuetitcherin, *j'écarte les doigts*"

*sēhsēk

INITIAL

— hail

evidence | WC sīsīkan, *to hail;* MC sesekanipaliw, *to start hailing;* AT (Opitciwan, Joey Awashish) sesekan [sēssēkan], *to hail;* SEC sesekāhtik[w], *black spruce;* Fabvre (ca. 1690) "Sesegan pl gana, *gresle grdo;*" Silvy (ca. 1680) "sesegatak8, *espèce d'arbre, pin piquant*" | ANISH Cuoq (1886) "Sesekan, *grésil, petite grêle, pluie fine qui se glace en tombant*"

*sēk[1]

INITIAL

— frighten

evidence | PC sēkihēw, *to frighten sb;* MC sekisiw, *to be frightened;* SEC secimew, *to frighten sb with one's voice;* Watkins (1865) "Sāsākinakoosew, *v.i.1. He is frightful*" | MENO sɛ·kehɛw, *to frighten sb*

*sēk[2]

INITIAL

— fancy, showy

evidence | PC sēkipatwāw, *to wear a braid;* MC sekipatowew, *to braid sb's hair; to cut the flesh that hangs from the severed head of bear into strips;* sesekāwihow, *to be splendidly dressed;* SEC osecipatwānišīš, *a waxwing;* NEC sāchipitwān, *a braid;* WI (Pessamit) shetshipatuan [ʃētʃəpətwān], *a bun or roll of hair worn over each ear;* sheshekau [ʃēʃēkāw], *to elevate oneself in an arrogant way;* sheshekaunakushu [ʃēʃēkāwnākuʃu], *to look pretentious;* Laure (ca. 1726) "tchiui-sasegan, *tu t'enorgueillis;*" "niui-sasegauinakuahau, *je célèbre, je loue en l'habillant;*" Watkins (1865) "Sākeputwān, *n.in. An ornament suspended from the hair (used by the heathen Indians);*" Silvy (ca. 1680) "setchibat8an, *moustache liée;*" "ni sasegam8n, *je parle en orgueilleux*" | ANISH zazegaashkime, *to decorate the snowshoe lacing* (Livesay & Nichols, 2021); Cuoq (1886) "saseka, *être fier, orgueilleux, superbe;*" MENO nesɛ·kepan, *my headgear, my coiffure, my braid;* sa·sɛ·ka·w AI, *to put on fine clothes*

*sēk[3]

INITIAL

— injure joint, sprain

evidence | MC sekipaliw, *to suffer a sprain or dislocation;* sekahkwanešin, *to sprain or dislocate one's ankle* | ANISH zegigwayawese, *to sprain one's neck* (Livesay & Nichols, 2021); MENO sɛ·ka·wekanɛ·hsemɛw, *to injure sb's spine*

*sēsikē

INITIAL

— near

evidence | MC sesikenākwan, *to be near;* NEC sāschānākun, *to appear to come closer;* WI (Pessamit) shesseiapameu [ʃēssējāpmēw], *to approach sb* | ANISH zezig, *close, nearly* (Lippert & Gambill, 2023); Cuoq (1886) "Ka ni sesikehasi, *je n'approche pas de sa capacité, je lui suis de beaucoup inférieur*"

*sihko (~ *sihkw)

INITIAL

— spit

evidence | PC sihkow, *to spit;* WC sīhkowin, *spit, saliva;* MC sihkwātew, *to spit on sb;* SEC sihkow, *to spit;* Silvy (ca. 1680) "sik88in, *crachat, salive*" | MENO sɛhkuanɛw, *to spit on sb* see | *sihkwē

*sihkwē

FINAL (VERB, ANIMATE, INTRANSITIVE, DERIVED)

— spit, slobber

evidence | MC lipācisihkwew, *to slobber or spit in a filthy fashion;* SEC picisihkwew, *to drool;* EI (Sheshatshiu) mautshishikueu [māwtʃīkwēw], *to gather one's saliva;* Watkins (1865) "Mìkoosikwāo, *v.i.3. He spits blood, he has a hemoptysis*" see | *sihko

*sihpo (~ *sihpw)

INITIAL

— close (by having both sides come together)

evidence | WC sīhpopicikan, *zipper;* MC sihpokwātam, *stitch sth up;* WI (Pessamit) shiputepalu [ʃəputēpəlu], *tent flaps closes;* Silvy (ca. 1680) "ni sip8nen, *je ferme, v.g. un livre*"

*sihs

INITIAL

— make smooth by rubbing or scraping

evidence | AT sipotisinan, *a sharpening stone;* NEC sisiputāu, *to sharpen or file sth;* WI (Pessamit) shishiputakan [ʃəʃəputān], *metal file;* Watkins (1865) "Sisipootow, *v.t.in.2. He grinds it, he sharpens it, he whets it;*" Silvy (ca. 1680) "sisib8tagan, *aiguisoir*" | ABEN zipodigan, *a file, a rub-smooth implement* (Day, 1995); ANISH zisiboode, *to be filed, to be ground down* (Livesay & Nichols, 2021) discussion | In the absence of an unambiguous Atikamekw cognate, the preaspirate in this reconstruction is indirectly supported by Anishinabe.

*sihswē

INITIAL

— spread, scatter, gradually reach a larger area

evidence | PC siswēhtin, *to scatter about in pieces;* WC siswīwīpinam, *to disperse sth;* AT (Opitciwan, Joey Awashish) sisweckaw [sisswēškāw], *to spread out on foot, to gradually reach a larger area, as in an animal expanding its territory;* Laure (ca. 1726) "chichuehinu, *jaillir l'eau, la fontaine jaillit;*" Silvy (ca. 1680) "sis8ebari8, *cela s'éparpille, se défile*" | ANISH ziswewebin, *to scatter sth by hand* (Livesay & Nichols,

2021); MESK sesweyāmowaki, *to scatter in flight;* cf. ABEN sisawōzi, *to be scattered;* MENO sɛʔsi·hnen, *to fall scattering*

*sikākwan

INITIAL (NOUN, DEPENDENT INANIMATE)

— **1** back of the knee

— **2** hock

evidence | PC misikwākan, *the back of the knee;* ESC misikākwan, *the back of the knee;* MC osikākwan & osikwākan, *one's knee pit; one's hock, speaking of an animal;* SEC osikākwan, *the back of one's knee;* NEC usikākun, *the back of one's knee;* WI (Pessamit) ushikakun [uʃəkākwən], *the back of one's knee; one's hock;* EI (Sheshatshiu) ushikakun [uʃəkākun], *the back of one's knee; one's hock;* Laure (ca. 1726) "nichigaguan, *le dessous du genoux*"

*sikirē

INITIAL

— be glad

evidence | MC sikilesiw, *to be glad;* SEC siciyehew, *to make sb glad;* Watkins (1865) "Sikeyāsew, *v.i.1. He is glad, he rejoices*"

*sikohs

INITIAL (NOUN, DEPENDENT ANIMATE)

— paternal aunt

evidence | PC osikosimāw, *paternal aunt; wife of a maternal uncle; a mother-in-law;* WC nisikos, *my paternal aunt; my mother-in-law;* MC osikosiw, *to have a paternal aunt, or an aunt married to a maternal uncle, or a mother-in-law,* AT (Opitciwn, Joey Awashish) nisikosa [nizikossa], *my mother-in-law;* WI (Pessamit) ushikusha [uʃəkùʃ], *one's mother-in-law;* Laure (ca. 1726) "nichiguch, *tante, la sœur de mon père;*" Fabvre (ca. 1690) "sig8sai, *tante*" | ABEN -zegwes, *mother-in-law* (Day, 1995); ANISH ozigosan, *one's paternal aunt* (Livesay & Nichols, 2021); MENO nesɛ·kihsak, *my father's sisters; my mother's brothers' wives;* MESK nesekwisa, *my paternal aunt;* MIAMI "niseg8ssa, *ma tante paternelle*" (Largillier - ILDA, 2017) origin | PA ***sekwihs*** compare | *sikosihs, *tōhs, *tōsihs

*sikosihs

INITIAL (NOUN, DEPENDENT ANIMATE)

— paternal aunt

evidence | Fabvre (ca. 1690) "sik8sis, *tante;*" Silvy (ca. 1680) "nichig8sis, *ma tante paternelle;*" "nisig8sis, nisik8sis, *ma tante*" | MIAMI "Niseg8sessa, *mon beau pere ou ma belle mere, dit soit bru, soit gendre*" (Largillier - ILDA, 2017); "niseg8sessa, *ma belle mere dit l'homme*" (Pinet - ILDA, 2017) compare | *sikohs, *tōhs, *tōsihs discussion | The comparative evidence is insufficient to reconstruct a semantic distinction, if any, between ***sikohs** and ***sikosihs**. Though evidence for the latter is limited to sources from the seventeenth century, its existence follows what appears to be an established pattern for kinship term doublets such as ***kohs**/***kosihs** and ***tōhs**/***tōsihs**. Both are therefore reconstructed in Old Cree.

*sipihkw[1]

INITIAL (NOUN, DEPENDENT INANIMATE)

— tear, teardrop

evidence | Laure (ca. 1726) "missipiku *pl.* -a, *larme;*" Silvy (ca. 1680) "missibik8, *larme*" | ANISH Cuoq (1886) "ni sipingon, *mes larmes;*" MENO nesɛ·pɛhkok, *my tears;* MIAMI nisepiinkwa, *my tears* (ILDA, 2017) see | *sipihkw[2]

*sipihkw[2]

MEDIAL, FINAL (NOUN INCORPORATION)

— tear, teardrop

evidence | Laure (ca. 1726) "nisutchichipikuan, *je verse des larmes*" | ANISH Cuoq (1886) "Kasisipingwen, *essuie ses larmes avec ta main;*" "kikisiping, *en larmes, tout en larmes*" see | *sipihkw[1]

*siriko (~ *sirikw)

INITIAL

— rub

evidence | PC sinikohtitāw, *to rub sth against sth;* MC sinikwākonešimew, *to scrub sb against the snow;* AT sirikotakaham [sirikohtakaham], *to scrub sth using a scrubber;* SEC sinikoham, *to rub or scrub sth using sth;* NEC sinikunim, *to rub sth with one's hand;* WI (Pessamit) shishilikutin [ʃəʃələkutn], *to rub against an object or surface;* Laure (ca. 1726) "ni-chirigunau astchiku, *je me frotte à la chaudière crasseuse;*" Silvy (ca. 1680) "ni sis8rig8asg8chim8n 3. -m8, *je me frotte à qqch pour me gratter*" | ANISH Cuoq (1886) "Ni sinikona, *je le frictionne;*" zinigonige, *to rub things with sth* (Livesay & Nichols, 2021)

*sit[1] (~ *sic)

INITIAL (NOUN, DEPENDENT INANIMATE)

— foot

evidence | PC misit, *a foot;* MC ositiw, *to have feet;* AT (Wemotaci, Nicole Petiquay) osita [ozita], *one's feet;* SEC ositāskʷ, *axe;* WI (Pessamit) ushitikan [uʃətəkən], *a foot bone;* Laure (ca. 1726) "nichitch *pl.* nichita, *mon pied;*" Silvy (ca. 1680) "8ssitab8i, *bouillon des os des pieds;*" "nisit, *mon pied*" | ANISH kizid, *your feet* (Livesay & Nichols, 2021) see | *sit[2]

*sit[2] (~ *sic)

MEDIAL, FINAL (NOUN INCORPORATION)

— foot

evidence | MC alakaškisitew, *have broad feet;* AT (Wemotaci, Nicole Petiquay) aieskositew [ayēskozitēw], *to have tired feet;* SEC kakānositew, *to have long feet;* WI (Pessamit) tipishitateu [təpəʃətātēw], *measure sb using one's feet;* Silvy (ca. 1680) "nit'aïapisites8n, *je me chauffe les pieds*" | ANISH biinizide, *to have clean feet* (Livesay & Nichols, 2021); MENO mama·hkesetɛ·w, *to have big feet* origin | PA ***sit** (Aubin, 1975) see | *sit[1]

*sīhk

INITIAL

— experience (cold)

evidence | MC šīhkaciw, *to feel cold;* AT (Opitciwan, Joey Awashish) sikatciw [sīhkaciw], *to feel cold;* (Wemotaci, Nicole Petiquay) sikatciw [sīhkaciw], *to feel cold;* SEC (Waswanipi) šīhkatāpāwew, *to be cold from being wet;* NEC shīhkichiu, *to feel cold;* sīhkitipiu, *to be cold while sitting* (CSB, 2018); WI (Pessamit) shikatashu [ʃīkātāʃu], *to catch a chill from the wind;* Laure (ca. 1726) "ni-chikatchinach 3. chikatchiu, *je tremble de froid;*" "ni-chikatchirhauan, *j'ai froid au corps;*" Silvy (ca. 1680) "ni sikatimau, *je lui fais avoir froid*" | MESK sīkatenwi, *to freeze* origin | PA ***sīnk** (Hewson, 1993) limited to | *at[5]

*sīhs

INITIAL

— make liquid

evidence | AT (Wemotaci, Nicole Petiquay) sīsipāskot [sīssipāskot], *sugar;* SEC sīsipew, *to melt snow to make water;* Fabvre (ca. 1690) "Sisiban - nab8i, *eau de neige*" | ANISH ziinzibaakwad, *sugar, maple sugar* (Livesay & Nichols, 2021); MIAMI siihsipaahkwi, *maple sugar* (ILDA, 2017) origin | PA ***sīns** see | *siskaw

*sīht (~ *sīhc)

INITIAL

— tight

evidence | PC sīhcāw, *it is tight;* MC sīhtahāpew, *to weave tightly;* SEC sīhtahpisow, *to be tied tightly;* Silvy (ca. 1680) "ni sitatchabikan, 3. -e8, *je bande l'arc, j'y mets la corde*" origin | PA ***sīnt** (Aubin, 1975)

*sīhtaw

INITIAL

— wedge, shim

evidence | PC sīhtwamon, *to fit on tight;* MC sīhtawihtin, *to be wedged;* SEC sīhtawaham, *to caulk sth;* EI (Sheshatshiu) shitushinu, *to lie in a cramped position*

*sīk

INITIAL

— pour

evidence | PC sīkahāhtawēw, *to baptise sb;* MC sīkinam, *to pour sth;* AT sikiparin [sīkiparin], *to pour out;* SEC sīcinam, *to pour sth;* Watkins (1865) "Sekewāpinum, *v.t.in.6. He pours it*" | MENO se·kaham, *to pour sth* origin | PA ***sīk** (Hewson, 1993)

*sīkīhp

INITIAL (NOUN, INANIMATE)

— boil, furuncle

evidence | WC sīhkīhp, *a boil;* MC sīkīhp, *a boil;* osīkīhpimiw, *to have a boil;* AT (Opitciwan, Joey Awashish) cikipic [šikipiš], *a grebe; a boil* (Wemotaci, Nicole Petiquay) ocikipicima [ošikipiššima], *one's boil;* NEC uchischiihpimh, *one's boil;* WI (Pessamit) tshitship [tʃītʃīp], *a boil;* utshitshipimapu [utʃītʃīpmāpu], *to have a stye;* Faries & Mackay (1938) "sekèp, sekìp *n.in. a boil;*" Laure (ca. 1726) "chitchip pl. -ets, *clou, furoncle, tumeur, aposthume;*" Silvy (ca. 1680) "chitchipich, *apostume; espèce de plongeur;*" "n8 chitchipimin, *j'ai une apostume*" | ANISH zhiingibis, *a boil* (Lippert & Gambill, 2023); MENO sɛ·kemyah(san), *pimple, boil* discussion | Reflexes of this root undergo considerable variation across dialects, with some sources merging it with their respective reflex of ***šihkip**, "grebe."

*sīkwan

INITIAL (VERB, INANIMATE, INTRANSITIVE)

— spring

evidence | PC sīkwanohk, *last spring;* MC sīkwanišiw, *to spend springtime in a particular place;* SEC sīkwan, *to be spring;* Laure (ca. 1726) "chiguanu, *la fonte des neiges, petit printemps*" | ANISH ziigwan, *to be spring* (Livesay & Nichols, 2021)

*sīn

INITIAL

— express contents

evidence | PC sīnipēkinam, *to wring sth out;* MC sīninam, *to express the contents of sth;* SEC sīnipātinam, *to express liquid out of sth by hand;* Silvy (ca. 1680) "ni sinau arabi, *je tors le rets, le presse*" | MENO se·nenɛw, *to squeeze sb, to milk a cow* origin | PA ***sīn** (Aubin, 1975)

*sīpiw

INITIAL (NOUN, INANIMATE)

— river

evidence | PC sīpīwāpoy, *river water;* MC sīpiy, *river;* SEC sīpīskāw, *to be many rivers;* WI (Pessamit) shipu [ʃīpu], *river;* EI (Sheshatshiu) shipu [ʃīpu], *river;* Laure (ca. 1726) "chipiu *pl.* chipiua, *rivière;*" Silvy (ca. 1680) "sipi8, *rivière*" | ANISH ziibi, *a river* (Livesay & Nichols, 2021)

*sīskaw

INITIAL

— for liquid to run out of or drain from

evidence | MC sīskopātaham, *to drain liquid from sth;* SEC sīskaweyikomew, *to have a runny nose;* Laure (ca. 1726) "ni-siskauerikumeuatsin, *le froid me rend morveux*" | ANISH ziikawaabi, *to tear up* (Livesay & Nichols, 2021) see | *sīhs, *kaw²

*sīto (~ *sītw)

INITIAL

— support, brace

evidence | PC sītwāskwaham, *to support sth using a pole;* MC sītoham, *to support or brace sth with sth;* NEC sītwāpihkātim, *to tie sth to hold it together;* Silvy (ca. 1680) "ni sit8nen, *je soutiens*" | ANISH ziidonan, *to support sth with one's hand* (Livesay & Nichols, 2021)

*sk[1]

PREFINAL

— by use of foot or body see | *sk[2], *skē, *skaw

*sk[2]

FINAL (VERB, TRANSITIVE, INANIMATE, CONCRETE)

— by use of foot or body

evidence | PC kēsiskam, *to come in time for sth;* NEC tākisiskim, *to have one's foot fit all the way into sth;* WI (Pessamit) mueshishkam [mwēʃəʃkəm], *to arrive too late for an event* | ANISH bizokan, *to stumble or trip on sth* (Livesay & Nichols, 2021) see | *sk[1] paired with | *skaw compare | *ɩšk[2]

*skahtikw (~ *skahtiko)

INITIAL (NOUN, DEPENDENT INANIMATE)

— forehead

evidence | PC Lacombe (1874) "Mi'iskattik, wa, *le front;*" MC niskahtikohk, *on my forehead;* SEC oskahtikʷ, *one's forehead;* Silvy (ca. 1680) "miskatig8, *front*" | ANISH nikatig, *my forehead* (Livesay & Nichols, 2021) see | *kahtikw

*skam

MEDIAL

— navigable water

evidence | WC miðoskamin, *to be late spring, the period of the year when the ice clears from the rivers;* MC miloskamin, *to be late spring;* SEC miyoskamiw, *to be that period of the year when the rivers are free of ice and the ground is free of snow;* WI (Pessamit) milushkamu [mələʃkəmu], *to be that period of the year when the leaves start growing;* Fabvre (ca. 1690) "Mir8skamik mits mi8, *Le printems;*" Silvy (ca. 1680) "mir8skamik, *le printemps*" | ANISH Cuoq (1886) "Minokami, *l'eau est bonne, le liquide est bon (pour la navigation), c'est le printemps, le printemps est arrive;*" MIAMI miloohkamiwi, *to be spring* (ILDA, 2017) limited to | *miro

*skan

INITIAL (NOUN, DEPENDENT INANIMATE)

— bone

evidence | PC miskan, *a bone;* MC oskan, *one's bone;* SEC oskaniwan, *to be bony;* Silvy (ca. 1680) "8skanab8i, *bouillon d'os*" see | *kan

*skaskwan

INITIAL (NOUN, DEPENDENT INANIMATE)

— shin

evidence | WSC (Misipawistik, Ellen Cook) miskaskwan, *a shin* | ANISH nikakwan, *my shin* (Livesay & Nichols, 2021); MENO nɛhka·hkwan, *my shin*

*skašiy

INITIAL (NOUN, DEPENDENT ANIMATE)

— nail, claw, or hoof

evidence | PC maskasiy, *NDA a fingernail or claw;* MC oškašiya, *NDA one's nail(s), claw(s), or hoof/hooves;* AT (Wemotaci, Nicole Petiquay) ockaci [oškaʒiy], *a nail, a claw;* (Opitciwan, Joey Awashish) nickaciak [niškaʒiyak], my nails; NEC ushkishīh, *NDA one's nail(s) or claw(s);* EI (Mamit) ushkashia [uhkahja], *NDA one's nail, claw, or hoof;* Laure (ca. 1726) "uskachi -ets, *ongle;*" Fabvre (ca. 1690) "Miskachi *pl* chia, *griffe, ongle d(')a(nim)al, a(nim)aux*" | MIAMI ahkaša, *one's nails* (ILDA, 2017) see | *kaš, *kašiy

*skaw (~ *skā)

FINAL (VERB, TRANSITIVE, ANIMATE, CONCRETE)

— by use of foot or body

evidence | PC kēsiskawēw, *to come in time for sb;* SEC ākoskawew, *to head sb off;* WI (Pessamit) tekashishkueu [tēkəʃəʃkwēw], *to put sth completely on one's foot or body;* Laure (ca. 1726) "ni-uirauitichiskauau, *je le fais sortir en poussant;*" Fabvre (ca. 1690) "M8esiskāgan 3 ke8, *uenir tard, Le dernier;*" Silvy (ca. 1680) "nit'achiska8au, *je le devance à porter nouvelles*" | ANISH agwaanizhikaw, *to chase sb ashore* (Livesay & Nichols, 2021); bizokaw, *stumble on sb* (Livesay & Nichols, 2021) see | *sk[1], *aw[3] paired with | *sk[1] compare | *ɩškaw

*skāskikan

INITIAL (NOUN, DEPENDENT INANIMATE)

— chest

evidence | MC niskāskikan, *my chest;* AT oskaskikan [oskāskikan], *one's chest;* SEC oskāscikan, *one's chest;* WI (Pessamit) ushkassikanashk[u] [uʃkāssəkənəʃk[w]], *the ribcage of a bear;* EI (Sheshatshiu) ushkassikan [uʃkāssəkən], *one's chest* | ANISH nikaakigan, *my chest* (Livesay & Nichols, 2021) see | *āskikan

*skāt (~ *skāc)

INITIAL (NOUN, DEPENDENT INANIMATE)

— leg; (of a quadruped) hind leg

evidence | PC miskāt, *a leg;* MC oskātiw, *to have legs;* oskātihkākew, *to make a leg out of sth;* SEC oskātāsk[w], *a carrot;* Silvy (ca. 1680) "miskach, jambe;" "niskach, *ma jambe*" | ANISH okaad, *one's leg* (Livesay & Nichols, 2021) see | *kāt

*skē

FINAL (VERB, ANIMATE, INTRANSITIVE, CONCRETE)

— by use of foot or body

evidence | PC tahkoskēw, *to take a step;* MC tahkoskātam, *to step on sth;* māhtakoskātam, *to step on sth;* NEC tihkuschāu, *to take a step;* tihkuskātim, *to step on sth;* EI (Sheshatshiu) tatakushkateu [tātākuʃkātēw], *to trample on sth* see | *sk[1], *ē

*skēkom

MEDIAL (NOUN INCORPORATION)

— nostril

evidence | WC sīniskīkomīw, *to blow one's nose;* MC sīniskekomew, *to express the mucus from one's nose, to blow one's nose;* SEC (Waswanipi) sīniscekomenitisow, *to blow one's nose* | ANISH ziiniskiigome, *to blow one's nose* (Livesay & Nichols, 2021); cf. Cuoq (1886) "Niskikong, *dans mon nez, dans mes narines*" compare | *tērikom

*skiw

MEDIAL

— gum

evidence | MC manahiskiwew, *to gather gum;* SEC māmākomisciwew, *to chew gum;* WI (Pessamit) mamakumissueu [mamakuməsswew], *to chew gum;* Laure (ca. 1726) "ni-pitchikamissiuan, *je mâche de la gomme*" | ANISH zhaashaagwamikiwe, *to chew gum* (Livesay & Nichols, 2021) origin | Likely PA ***skiw**, as a contraction of PA ***pekiw** by syncope of the first vowel. see | *pikiw

*skiwan[1]

INITIAL (NOUN, DEPENDENT INANIMATE)

— nose, snout, bill, beak

evidence | PC miskiwanikan, *a nasal bone;* MC oskiwaniw, *to have a beak, bill, or nose;* WI (Pessamit) ussuniship [ussūnəʃəp], *upper half of a waterfowl's beak;* Silvy (ca. 1680) "misti8an, *nez*" see | *skiwan[2]

*skiwan[2]

MEDIAL, FINAL (NOUN INCORPORATION)

— nose, snout, bill, beak

evidence | MC mahkiskiwanew, *to have a big nose or bill;* NEC wīyipischiwināu, *to have a black nose;* Fabvre (ca. 1690) "Kipisti8anehau, *b8cher Le nez à qlqn;*" Silvy (ca. 1680) "pisk8sti8an, *nez aquilin*" see | *skiwan[1]

*skon

INITIAL (NOUN, DEPENDENT INANIMATE)

— liver

evidence | PC miskon, *a liver;* SEC oskon, *one's liver;* Silvy (ca. 1680) "8sk8n, *foie*" | ANISH nikon, *my liver* (Livesay & Nichols, 2021); MENO nɛhko·n, *my liver*

***skot** (~ ***skoš**)

INITIAL (NOUN, DEPENDENT INANIMATE)

— **1** nose

— **2** beak

evidence | SEC niskot, *my nose;* oskot, *one's nose or beak;* NEC uskut, *a nose or beak;* WI (Pessamit) ushkush [uʃkuʃ], *a nose or beak;* EI (Sheshatshiu) ushkush [uʃkuʃ], *a nose or beak;* EI (Mushuau) ushkut [uʃkūt], *a nose or beak;* Laure (ca. 1726) "uskuch, *bec*" | ANISH okoozh, *one's beak* (Livesay & Nichols, 2021) origin | PA ***skoθ** (***mexkoši**, Aubin, 1975) see | *kot² discussion | Western dialects have replaced this root with a reflex of its derived form, ***kot**.

***skotākay**

INITIAL (NOUN, DEPENDENT INANIMATE)

— cloak, robe

evidence | PC oskotākay, *one's coat; one's dress;* WC miskotākay, *coat; dress;* WSC (Severn) miskotākay, *a dress;* Isham (1743) "muska togy, *a tockey;*" cf. MC wāpošehkolay, *a weaved rabbit fur blanket* | cf. ANISH okonaas, *one's blanket* (Livesay & Nichols, 2021)

***so¹**

FINAL (VERB, ANIMATE, INTRANSITIVE, ABSTRACT)

sound change | ē → ā

— conveys the semantic role of patient or theme to a participant

evidence | PC akisow, *to be counted;* MC itāpihkāsow, *to be tied thus;* AT (Opitciwan, Nadia Awashish) kackipaso [kāškipāzow], *to shave;* SEC nakwāsow, *to be snared;* EI (Mamit) shapushashu [hāpuhāhu], *to be soaked with urine* paired with | *tē²

***so²** (~ ***ɩso**)

FINAL (VERB, ANIMATE, INTRANSITIVE, CONCRETE)

sound change | ē → a

— heat

evidence | PC kisisow, *to be hot;* MC tihkisow, *melt;* AT (Wemotaci, Nicole Petiquay) kiciso [kiʒizow], *to be hot;* SEC cišākamisow, *to be a hot liquid;* Laure (ca. 1726) "ni-uisatchikatesun, *je me brûle les jambes;*" Silvy (ca. 1680) "nit'itisȣn, *je suis brûlé;*" Silvy (ca. 1680) "ni raȣaȣasȣn, *je suis loin du feu*" | ANISH jaagizo, *to burn* (Livesay & Nichols, 2021); MENO atɛ·hsow AI, *to be dyed, colored, ripe* origin | PA ***(e)so** see | *s, *o paired with | *tē⁴

***soy**

INITIAL (NOUN, DEPENDENT INANIMATE)

— tail of an animal

evidence | PC misoy, *a tail;* AT oso:w, *tail* (Béland, 1978); (Wemotaci, Nicole Petiquay) oso [ozow], *one's tail;* SEC osow, *a tail;* NEC usui, *one's tail;* Silvy (ca. 1680) "ȣsȣi, *queue;*" "ȣsȣȣaȣietch, *brins de la queue du porc-épic*" | ANISH ozow, *the tail of an animal* (Livesay & Nichols, 2021) compare | *šikwanay

***sō**

MEDIAL

— name

evidence | SEC wīcisōmākan, *a namesake;* wīcisōmākanihew, *to name sb after sb else;* NEC wīchisumāu, *to name sb;* EI (Sheshatshiu) uitshishumeu [wītʃʃūmēw], *to give sb a nickname* | MESK wīchīsōmēwa, *to have sb as a fellow clan-member* limited to | *wīt, *m¹ discussion | This reconstruction suffers from the lack of an Atikamekw cognate to confirm the absence of a preaspirate.

***sōhk**

INITIAL

— solid, strong

evidence | PC sōhkatin, *to be frozen solid;* MC sōhkan, *to be strong;* SEC sōhcimāsow, *to smell strong while burning or cooking* | ANISH zoonginike, *to have a strong arm* (Livesay & Nichols, 2021); MENO so·hken, *to be firm, solid, or strong* origin | PA ***sōnk** (Hewson, 1993)

*sōk

INITIAL

— pour water onto

evidence | MC sōkispon, *to snow;* sōkahāhtam, *to pour water on sth;* AT sōkispon, *to snow;* SEC sōcištitāw, *to pour water on or in sth;* WI (Pessamit) shukain [ʃūkāīn], *for waves to swamp the canoe* origin | PA ***sōk** (Hewson, 1993)

*sōp

INITIAL

— suck

evidence | PC sōpamēw, *to suck on sth;* MC sōsōpahtam, *to suck on sth;* SEC sōpahtam, *to suck on sth* | ANISH zoobandan, *to suck out of sth (Livesay & Nichols, 2021);* MENO so·pahtam, *to take a swallow of sth, to take a draw*

*sōsāsiw

INITIAL (NOUN, ANIMATE)

— Arctic char (Salvelinus alpinus)

evidence | PC sōsāsiw, *salmon;* MC sōsāsiw, *arctic char;* SEC sōsāsiw, *arctic char;* NEC sūsāsiu, *arctic char;* WI (Pessamit) & EI (Sheshatshiu) shushashu [ʃūʃāʃu], *arctic char;* Waktins (1865) "Sosasew, *salmon*" discussion | This reconstruction suffers from the lack of an Atikamekw cognate to confirm the absence of a preaspirate.

*sp[1]

MEDIAL (NOUN INCORPORATION)

— rib

evidence | WI (Pessamit) manishpepitam[u] [mənəʃpēpətəm], *to pull off the ribs in a single slab* see | *spiy compare | *spik

*sp[2]

PREFINAL

— taste see | *spit, *spoko, *spw

*spahsēw

INITIAL (NOUN, DEPENDENT INANIMATE)

— breast of bird

evidence | WSC (Misipawistik, Ellen Cook) ospasēw, *breast of a bird;* MC ohpasew, *breast of a bird;* AT (Wemotaci, Nicole Petiquay) opasew [ohpassēw], *breast of a bird;* SEC ospasewikan, *the breastbone of a bird;* NEC uspisāu, *breast of a bird;* WI (Pessamit) ushpasheu [uʃpəʃēw], *one's breast, speaking of a bird* EI (Sheshatshiu) ushpasheu [uʃpəʃēw], *one's breast, speaking of a bird;* Watkins (1865) "oospusāo, *n.in. The breast-bone of a bird; the flesh of the breast;*" Fabvre (ca. 1690) "8spasai, *brechet, poitrine doyseaux*" | ANISH opase, *breast of a bird of fowl* (McGregor, 2004); MENO nɛhpa·nɛw, *my thorax, my chest;* MIAMI ahpaleewi, *one's chest* (ILDA, 2017) see | *pahs, *ēw

*spayaw

INITIAL (NOUN, DEPENDENT INANIMATE)

— uterus and adnexa

evidence | PC Lacombe (1874) "mispayaw, a, (n.r.) ospayaw, a, *l'enveloppe du petit dans le ventre de sa mère;*" MC ospayaw, *her womb;* EI (Sheshatshiu) ushpaiuat [uʃpīwīt], *ovaries;* Fabvre (ca. 1690) "8spaïau, *matrice de femelle daaux*"

*spik

MEDIAL (NOUN INCORPORATION)

— rib

evidence | MC tewispikew, *to have achy ribs;* AT (Wemotaci, Nicole Petiquay) manispikepitew [manispikēpitēw], *to pull out sb's rib;* SEC nātwāspicešin, *to break one's rib in a collision;* WI (Pessamit) taushpitsheueu [tāwʃpətʃēwēw], *to hit sb right in the ribs with a projectile* | MESK pōhkwihpikēshinwa, *to fall and break one's rib* see | *spikay compare | *sp[1]

*spikay

INITIAL (NOUN, DEPENDENT INANIMATE)

— rib

evidence | PC ospikay, *one's rib;* MC ospikekana, *one's ribbone;* SEC nispikay, *my rib;* EI (Unaman-shipit) ushpikai [uhpakēj], *rib cage of a small animal;* Silvy (ca. 1680) "8spigai, *côté de l'animal*" | ANISH nipigay, *my rib* (Livesay & Nichols, 2021);

MENO nɛhpe·kɛ·kan, *my rib;* MIAMI kihpikayi, *your rib* (ILDA, 2017) see | *spik compare | *spiy

*spiskwan

INITIAL (NOUN, DEPENDENT INANIMATE)

— upper back (thoracic region)

evidence | PC mispiskwan, *a back;* WC kispiskwan, *your back;* SEC ospiskwan, *one's upper back;* WI (Pessamit) ushpishkunishtikuanan [uʃpəʃkunəstəkwānān], *the back of the head;* Silvy (ca. 1680) "mispisk8an, *le dos;*" "mispisk8anitichan, *le dehors de la main*" | ANISH opikwan, *one's back* (Livesay & Nichols, 2021); MENO nɛhpɛ·hkwan, *my back, especially the set of ribs at the back* see | *piskwan

*spit

FINAL (VERB, TRANSITIVE, INANIMATE, CONCRETE)

— taste

evidence | PC kocispitam, *to taste sth;* SEC nisitospitam, *to recognize sth by taste;* Laure (ca. 1726) "nit-atuspiten 3. -tamu, *je ne le trouve pas bon, cela n'est point à mon goût;*" Silvy (ca. 1680) "ni nassitamispiten, *je n'aime point à manger de cela, je l'ai en dégoût*" see | *sp², *t⁶ paired with | *spw compare | *št³

*spiton

INITIAL (NOUN, DEPENDENT INANIMATE)

— arm; (of a quadruped) front leg

evidence | PC mispiton, *an arm;* MC ospitoniw, *to have arms;* SEC ospitonikan, *a radius;* Silvy (ca. 1680) "mispit8n, nispit8n, *mon bras*" see | *piton

*spiy

FINAL (NOUN, INANIMATE)

— rib

evidence | PC mitiskwēspiy, *the bottom rib;* Lacombe (1874) "ot'iskwespiya, *les côtes, les plus basses de l'estomac*" | cf. MENO nɛhpiaheh *loc, at my flank* see | *sp¹ compare | *spikay

*spo (~ *āspo)

FINAL (VERB, ANIMATE, INTRANSITIVE, DERIVED)

— eat in such a way or in such a place

evidence | SEC papāmāspow, *to walk about eating;* WI (Pessamit) petashpu [pētāʃpu], *to approaches bringing sth to eat;* Laure (ca. 1726) "ni-papamaspun, *je mange en marchant;*" Silvy (ca. 1680) "ni 8era8isp8n, *je mange dehors*" see | *ɪt¹, *po² compare | *spw

*spoko (~ *spokw)

PREFINAL

— taste

evidence | WC āhkospakwan, *to have a strong taste;* WI (Pessamit) shiushpakuan [ʃīwʃpukwən], *to taste bitter;* Laure (ca. 1726) "miruspuguanu, *savoureux, cela est savoureux, de bon goût*" | ANISH wiingipogozi, *to be delicious* (Livesay & Nichols, 2021) see | *spw, *ɪko

*spon

FINAL (VERB, INANIMATE, INTRANSITIVE, DERIVED)

— snow

evidence | MC āštespon, *snowing subsides;* EI (Sheshatshiu) mamenishpun [məmēnɨʃpun], *occasional snowfalls;* Watkins (1865) "papetitāspoon, *it snows into the tent;*" Laure (ca. 1726) "aruaspun, *beau temps après la neige;*" Silvy (ca. 1680) "sitisp8n, *il commence à neiger*" | ANISH maajipon, *to start to snow* (Livesay & Nichols, 2021) origin | Old Cree ***misponwi**, from PA ***mesponwi** (***mexponwi**, Aubin, 1975; Hewson, 1993) see | *mispo

*spōhkan

INITIAL (NOUN, DEPENDENT INANIMATE)

— tarsus

evidence | SEC uspūhkan, *lower leg bone of a beaver* (CSB, 2018); NEC uspūhkin, *lower leg bone of seal or beaver;* WI (Pessamit) ushpukanakᵘ [uʃpūkənākʷ], *bone of a porcupine leg;* Fabvre (ca. 1690) "Isp8kan, *os de la cheuille du pied*" | ANISH Cuoq (1886) "O ponganing, *à son tarse*"

*spw

FINAL (VERB, TRANSITIVE, ANIMATE, CONCRETE)

— taste

evidence | MC kocispwew, *to taste sth;* WI (Pessamit) matshishpueu [mətʃəʃpwēw], *to dislike the taste of sth;* Laure (ca. 1726) "nit-atuspuau 3. -bueu, *je ne le trouve pas bon, cela n'est point à mon goût*" see | *sp², *w² paired with | *spit compare | *pw

*spwākan

MEDIAL, FINAL (NOUN INCORPORATION)

— smoking pipe

evidence | PC wākispwākan, *a curved pipe;* saskahispwākanēw, *to light one's pipe;* WC kwaðakospwākanīw, *to empty out one's pipe;* MC nīmispwākanew, *to take a pipe along;* Fabvre (ca. 1690) "8sp8aganesi8 *pl.* 8ek, *1.2.3. petunées;*" Silvy (ca. 1680) "kichtimanisp8agan, *calumet de pierre à aiguiser*" | ANISH zaka'ipwaagane, *to light a pipe* (Livesay & Nichols, 2021) see | *wispwākan discussion | The example drawn from Fabvre (ca. 1690) is a medial use of the above root that is meant to be preceded by numerals.

*sw (~ *ɪsw)

FINAL (VERB, TRANSITIVE, ANIMATE, CONCRETE)

sound change | ē → a

— heat

evidence | PC mēstiswēw, *to burn sb up;* MC kisiswew, *heat sb;* kišikanaswew, *to heat a bone or object made of bone;* AT (Opitciwan, Joey Awashish) kicekiswew [kiʒēkizwēw], *to heat sth sheet-like;* SEC tihciswew, *to melt sth;* Silvy (ca. 1680) "ni tikag8nas8au g8n, *je fais fondre la neige, v.g. dans la Chaudière*" origin | PA ***(e)sw** (Aubin, 1975) paired with | *s

Š

*šahšakiw

INITIAL (NOUN, ANIMATE)

— great blue heron (Ardea herodias)

evidence | AT (Wemotaci, Jeannette Coocoo) cakiw [šakiw], *great blue heron;* SEC (Washaw sibi) šašakiw, *a great blue heron;* WI (Pessamit) shashatshu [ʃəʃətʃu], *great blue heron;* Watkins (1865) "Susukew, *n.an. a pelican; a Pelican Indian;*" Laure (ca. 1726) "chachatchiu, *grue, oiseau*" | ANISH zhashagi, *a blue heron* (Livesay & Nichols, 2021); MENO sa·qsakɛw, *a heron;* MESK sakiwa, *great blue heron* discussion | The preaspirate in this reconstruction is indirectly supported by Anishinabe and Menominee.

*šahto

INITIAL

— straighten out

evidence | NEC shihtunāu, *to straighten sb out by hand;* WI (Pessamit) shatuiu [ʃətwīw], *to straighten oneself out;* Watkins (1865) "Sàtoonum, *v.t.in.6. He straightens it, he unrolls it;*" Laure (ca. 1726) "ni-chatuestsinen, *j'étends, ouvrant, dépliant;*" Fabvre (ca. 1690) "chatutitchērin n8 rit, *ouurir la main*" compare | *tašo discussion | An isogloss exists whereby dialects north of Southern East Cree and east of Atikamekw exhibit ***šahto** rather than ***tašo**. Evidence for this dates back to seventeenth-century Jesuit dictionaries. The origin of this isogloss is unclear, but it may point to an early loan from a neighbouring language or to an early case of metathesis. As such, it is possible that either one of these roots does not date back to Old Cree.

*šanašk

INITIAL

— be flat against, be in juxtaposition to an underlying surface

evidence | PC Lacombe (1874) "Sanaskisiw, ok, *(a.a) il est bien joint, uni ensemble;*"

"Sanaskipitew, *(v.a.)* tam, -siwew, -tchikew, *il l'unit, il l'aplatit, v.g. une traîne qui passe sur le foin, l'unit, l'aplatit;*" "*écureuil volant,* sanaskāttawew, ok;" MC šanaškīw, *to crouch down flat;* šanaškicāšew, *to have a flat nose;* AT (Wemotaci, Jeannette Coocoo) canackatwew [šanaškāhtawew], *a flying squirrel;* SEC šamaskapiw, *to sit low to the ground, to sit on the ground;* WI (Pessamit) shanashkapu [ʃənəʃkəpu], *to sit without moving, to not move from where one is seated;* Laure (ca. 1726) "ni-chanaskamuttan 3. -tau, *je cheville, je lie avec une cheville;*" "chanassitchiuan, *nez court;*" Fabvre (ca. 1690) "chanaskataȣeȣ, *esc(u)reux volant;*" Silvy (ca. 1680) "sanastistchiȣan, *nez camard;*" "chanaskataȣeȣ, *écureuil volant*" | ANISH Cuoq (1886) "Camackap,i, *Être assis à plate terre, (se dit surtout de la grenouille et des autres Batraciens)*"

*šaw

INITIAL

— affect

evidence | MC šawišikākew, *to be able to cut with sth;* AT caweritakosiw [šawērihtākosiw], *to be blessed;* NEC shuwishkim, *to be able to break or move sth with one's foot or body;* SEC šawahokow, *for sth (such as medicine) to have an effect on sb, to affect sb;* WI (Pessamit) sheshaunam[u] [ʃēʃāwnəm], *to stretch a muscle or limb to loosen up the joint;* Laure (ca. 1726) "ni-chauerimau, *je m'attendris envers lui, en le voyant affligé*"

*šay

INITIAL

— **1** already

— **2** now (as opposed to previously)

— **3** in the immediate future, without delay

— **4** used to indicate completion of an event or task

evidence | PC sāsay & āsay, *already; without delay* WC sāsay & āsay, *already;* MC āšay, *already; now; in the immediate future; used to indicate readiness or completion of a task;* AT (Wemotaci, Jeannette Coocoo) aci [āʒī], *already; used to indicate readiness or completion of a task;* SEC (Waswanipi) āš, *already; now; in the immediate future; used to indicate readiness or completion of a task;* NEC shāsh, *already;* EI (Sheshatshiu) shash [ʃāʃ], *already; finally; that's enough;* shashish [ʃāʃīʃ], *a long time ago;* Watkins (1865) "Sasai, *adv. Already;*" "Asai, *adv. Already;*" Laure (ca. 1726) "chai, chachai, *déjà; c'en est fait;*" "chachaies taguchinuban, *il était déjà venu;*" Silvy (ca. 1680) "chache, *c'est fait;*" "cha, pro. chache, *déjà*" | ANISH zhaazhaye, *a while ago, already* (Lippert & Gambill, 2023); aazha, *already; now* (Livesay & Nichols, 2021); Cuoq (1886) "Acaie," "Caie," "Cacaie;" MENO saqyɛh, *now; soon; just then; already;* MESK aye, *earlier, already;* MIAMI šaaye, *already, come to pass, goodbye*

discussion | While contemporary dialects display reflexes of the reduplicated form, ***šāšay**, the earliest sources, as well as cross-linguistic cognates, support the above reconstruction.

*šā

FINAL (VERB, ANIMATE, INTRANSITIVE, CONCRETE)

— urinate

evidence | MC išišāw, *to urinate thus;* AT (Wemotaci, Nicole Petiquay) patotecaw [patotēʒāw], *to urinate beside the target;* SEC wīhkwešāw, *to urinate in one's pants* | ANISH miziwezhaazo, *to urinate all over* (Livesay & Nichols, 2021); MESK pōnishēwa, *to quit urinating* origin | PA ***šē** see | *šāso, *šāt[1], *šāt[2] discussion | While ***šē** is a more likely reconstruction, it is precluded by the sparsity of corroborative data within Cree proper.

*šāhkwē

INITIAL

— scrape hide

evidence | MC šāhkwehikan, *knife with a crescent-shaped blade;* SEC šāhkweham, *to scrape sth using a semicircular blade;* NEC shāhkwāham, *to scrape sth;* WI (Pessamit) shakueikan [ʃākwējkən], *a semicircular metal scraper;* EI (Mamit) shakueikan [hākwējkan], *a semicircular metal scraper;* Watkins (1865) "Sakwāhikun, *n.in. A wooden scraper for preparing skins*"

*šāhšak

INITIAL

— onto or towards one's back side

evidence | WC sāsakitastāw, *to place sth face up;* MC šāšakacipaliw, *fall onto one's back;* AT (Wemotaci, Nicole Petiquay) cacakipariw [šāššakipariw], *to fall backwards;* SEC šāšakacīw, *to lie back;* Laure (ca. 1726) "ni-chachatchisin, *je tombe à la renverse;*" "ni-chachakastenen 3. -namu, *je le bande;*" "napaté ispanau, napaté chachakau, *vase haut d'un bord et bas de l'autre;*" Silvy (ca. 1680) "ni chachatchin, *je suis recourbé, couché, à la renverse;*" "ni chachagatab8g8n, *le courant me fait reculer*" | MENO sa·qsakeki·yawɛ·hsen, *to lie with one's head bent back*

*šāhšākir (~ *šāhšākih)

INITIAL

— (of a body part) bare

evidence | PC sāsākinikātēw, *to be barelegged;* sāsākihtiw, *to have bare feet;* ESC sāsākinikātew, *to have bare legs;* MC sāsākilikātew, *to be barelegged;* AT (Wemotaci, Nicole Petiquay) cacakirikatew [šāššākirikātew], *to have bare legs;* SEC šāšāciništikwānew, *to be bareheaded;* šāšācihtiw, *to have bare feet;* WI (Pessamit) shashatshilikat [ʃāʃātləkāt], *bare-legged;* EI (Sheshatshiu) shashatshinikateu [ʃāʃātnəkātēw], *to be bare-legged;* Laure (ca. 1726) "ni-chachatchitin, *je suis déchaussé;*" "ni-chatchatsirikatan, *j'ai les jambes nues*" | ANISH zhaashaaginizide, *to be barefoot* (Livesay & Nichols, 2021); MENO sa·hsake·hnɛw, *to have bare feet*

compare | *šāk

*šāhšāko (~ *šāhšākw)

INITIAL

— **1** grind, pulverize

— **2** slim, speaking of a body

evidence | [1]PC sāsākwahtam, *to chew sth into small pieces;* MC šāšākohikanew, *to crush bones;* AT (Wemotaci, Jeannette Coocoo) cacakomew [šāššākomew], *to chew sth;* SEC šāšākomin, *bunchberry;* NEC shāshākuham, *to break sth into little pieces;* Laure (ca. 1726) "chachakuahigan, *pilon ou pierre à piler la viande*" [2]PC sāsākwāpēwiw, *to be a slim man;* WC sāsākosiw, *to be slender;* SEC šāšākosīw, *to be slim;* Watkins (1865) "Sasakoosēw, *v.i.5. He is slender;*" Silvy (ca. 1680) "ni chachag8sin, *je suis grêle, menu*" | ANISH ozhaashaagwandaan, *to chew sth* (Livesay & Nichols, 2021); MENO sa·qsakuahtam, *to chew sth* compare | *šākaw, *šiko

discussion | Possibly a reduplicated form of ***šiko** or ***šāko**, the latter of which is scarcely supported, examples of which could represent cases of back-formation as in Watkins (1865) "sakwapākinuwāsew, *v.i.1. He has a slender body.*"

*šāk

INITIAL

— bare, uncovered

evidence | MC šākikamin, *to be open water (on an otherwise frozen body of water);* AT (Opitciwan, Nadia Awashish) cakikamin [šākikamin], *to be open water (on an otherwise frozen body of water);* SEC šāšācitihcew, *to have bare hands;* NEC shāshāchishtikwānāu, *to be bareheaded;* WI (Pessamit) shashatshishtikuaneu [ʃāʃāstəkwānēw], *to be bareheaded;* Silvy (ca. 1680) "ni chachatchipit8nin, *j'ai les bras nus*"

compare | *šāhšākir

*šākaw

INITIAL

— narrow

evidence | MC šākawāw, *to be narrow;* SEC šākawišam, *to cut sth narrow;* WI (Pessamit) shakushtikuashu [ʃākūstukwāʃu], *narrow river;* Laure (ca. 1726) "chagautagau *pl.* -a, *canot étroit*"

*šāko (~ *šākw)

INITIAL

— weak

evidence | MC šākwelimow, *to be diffident;* SEC šākotehew, *to be cowardly;* NEC shākuyiwāsiu, *to be short-tempered;* WI (Pessamit) shakutau [ʃākutāw], *to have the strength to do sth;* Laure (ca. 1726) "chakuteheuin, *honte, timidité*" | ANISH zhaagwaagamin, *to be weak liquid;* MIAMI šaakwaci, *to be cold*

*šākōt (~ *šākōc)

INITIAL

— overcome

evidence | PC sākōcihēw, *to defeat sb;* MC šākōtihkwašiw, *to be overcome by sleepiness;* AT ša:ko:tahw-, *to defeat sb by tool;* ša:kosom-, *to beat, defeat him, by speech (Béland, 1978);* WI (Pessamit) shakutshimeu [ʃākūtʃəmēw], *to convince sb with one's words;* Fabvre (ca. 1690) "chak8tirāgan n ra8hau *gagner au ieu*"

*šākwēhšiw

INITIAL (NOUN, ANIMATE)

— mink (Neogale vison)

evidence | PC sākwēs, *a mink;* ESC (Severn) shākweshiw, *a mink;* MC šākwēšiw, *a mink;* AT (Wemotaci, Jeannette Coocoo) cakweciw [šākwēššiw], *a mink;* SEC (Waswanipi) šākwešiw, *a mink;* Watkins (1865) "Sakwāsew, *n.an. A mink. Pāyuk sakwāsew, a quarter of a skin (in value);*" MacKenzie (1801) "Sa quasue, *Minx;*" Isham (1743) "Shar qua she wuck, *a wejack*" | ANISH zhaangweshi, *a mink* (Livesay & Nichols, 2021) discussion | Dialects spoken to the east have replaced this root with a reflex of ***acakāhš**, a diminutive of ***atakay**.

*šāpo (~ *šāpw)

INITIAL

— through

evidence | PC sāpopēw, *to be drenched;* Lacombe (1874) "Sābonew, *il le passe au travers;*" MC šāpopaliw, *to go through;* SEC šāpwāpamew, *to take a radiograph of sb;* Silvy (ca. 1680) "ni chachab8erimau, *je vois sa pensée, son cœur*" | ANISH zhaabwaakide, *to be burned through* (Livesay & Nichols, 2021); MENO sa·puapa·we·w AI, *to be wet through*

*šāso

FINAL (VERB, ANIMATE, INTRANSITIVE, CONCRETE)

— urinate

evidence | MC išišāsow, *to urinate thus;* AT (Wemotaci, Nicole Petiquay) wisakicaso [wīssakiʒāzow], *to feel a burning sensation when urinating;* EI (Mamit) shapushashu [hāpuhāhu], *to be soaked with urine* | ANISH madwezhaazo, *to be heard urinating* (Livesay & Nichols, 2021) see | *šā, *so[1]

*šāštē

INITIAL

— rancid

evidence | WSC (Misipawistik, Ellen Cook) sāstēsiw, *to be rancid;* MC šāšteyāw, *to be rancid;* AT cacteiau [šāštēyāw], *to be rancid;* SEC šāštemākwan, *to smell rancid;* EI (Sheshatshiu) shashteiau [ʃāstējāw], *to be rancid;* Laure (ca. 1726) "chachtéiau, *rance, qui sent le vieux;*" Silvy (ca. 1680) "chasteagami8, *cela est pourri, gâté, v.g. liqueur*" | ANISH zaatepogwad, *to taste rancid or stale* (Livesay & Nichols, 2021) compare | *šāh

*šāt[1] (~ *šāš)

FINAL (VERB, TRANSITIVE, ANIMATE, CONCRETE)

— to urinate on sb

evidence | MC pōhcišātew, *to urinate in sth;* SEC pōhcišātew, *to urinate in sth* see | *šā, *t[3]

*šāt[2] (~ *šāc)

FINAL (VERB, TRANSITIVE, INANIMATE, CONCRETE)

— to urinate on sth

evidence | MC āštawešātam, *to extinguish sth by urinating;* SEC pōhcišātam, *to urinate in sth* see | *šā, *t[4]

*šāwahto

INITIAL (VERB, ANIMATE, INTRANSITIVE)

— extend one's legs

evidence | PC sāwahtow, *to extend one's legs;* SEC shāuhtūpū, *to sit with legs stretched out* (CSB, 2018); Laure (ca. 1726) "ni-chachauatuchinin, *je me couche les jambes étendues;*" "ni-chauatukuamin, *je m'étends les pieds au feu*"

*šāwan

INITIAL

— south

evidence | PC sāwanohk, *to the south;* MC šāwanisiw, *deity of the south wind;* SEC šāwanahan, *south wind;* Silvy (ca. 1680) "chaȣanaskȣn, *en temps chaud*" | ABEN zowanesen, *a breeze from the south;* (Day, 1994); ANISH zhaawanong, *in or to the south* (Livesay & Nichols, 2021); MENO sa·wanɛ·qnen, *to be a south wind;* MIAMI šaawanwa, *a Shawnee person*

*šē

INITIAL

— open

evidence | PC sēwēw, *to ring;* MC šeham, *to open sth;* SEC šewehtin, *to ring or echo;* NEC shāhtiwāyāu, *for a conical lodge to have an opening at the top because the cover is low;* Laure (ca. 1726) "ni-chehen 3. -hamu, *j'ouvre avec un instrument;*" Silvy (ca. 1680) "ni chenen, *je me fais un passage*" | MENO sɛ·hkamiw, *to be open water, free of ice*

*šēhk

INITIAL

— **1** spontaneously, without cause

— **2** willingly, without compulsion

evidence | WC sīhkīð, *on one's own accord;* ESC (Attawapiskat, Bill Loutit) šehken, *willingly, voluntarily;* MC šehkel, *willingly; automatically;* WI (Pessamit) shetshel [ʃētʃēl], *for no reason, for nothing, for free;* Watkins (1865) "S'ākā, S'ākān, *adv. Freely, willingly of one's own accord, without cause;*" Laure (ca. 1726) "chetcher, nit-akusin, *je suis malade par cas fortuit;*" Silvy (ca. 1680) "chetcher, tchecher, *en vain, pour rien*"
limited to | *ēr[2]

*šēhšēhšiw

INITIAL (NOUN, ANIMATE)

— yellowlegs

evidence | PC Lacombe (1874) "Sesesiw, ok, *(n.r.) becassine, cercelle;*" MC šešešiw, *a yellowlegs;* AT (Wemotaci, Jeannette Coocoo & Opitciwan, Joey Awashish) cecečiw [šēššēššiw], *a yellowlegs;* SEC šešešiw, *a yellowlegs;* EI (Mamit) shesheshu [hēhēhu], *a sandpiper* | ANISH ozhesheshiwag, *bitterns* (Lippert & Gambill, 2023)

*šēko (~ *šēkw)

INITIAL

— into a tight space

evidence | PC Lacombe (1874) "Sekunew, *il l'introduit entre avec la main;*" MC šekokwanīw, *to slide oneself under the covers;* SEC šekoc, *in a tight space;* Laure (ca. 1726) "ni-chekutitchechinin, *j'ai une [écharde] dans le doigt*"

*šēmāk (~ *šēmāš)

INITIAL

— **1** without delay

— **2** towards the front, frontwards, onwards

evidence | [1]PC sēmāk, *immediately, right away;* MC šemāk, *immediately;* NEC shāmāch, *a short while (only used in negatives clauses to mean 'a long while');* WI (Pessamit) shemat [ʃēmāt], *as predicted or planned* [2]PC sēmākohtēw, *to walk past one's destination;* SEC šešemāštapiw, *to sit in a tailor's posture, to sit Indian style;* NEC shāmāshtipiu, *to sit with one's knees up;* Laure (ca. 1726) "chematch ni-pimuttan, *je passe outre;*" "ni-chéchémachtapin, *moi homme, je m'accoude sur mes genoux;*" Silvy (ca. 1680) "ni chechemastapin, *je suis accoudé sur mes genoux*" | [1]ANISH zhemaag, *immediately, right away, very quickly* (Livesay & Nichols, 2021) [2]ANISH zhemaagibizo, *to fail to stop in time* (Lippert & Gambill, 2023)

*šēsk

INITIAL

— cross a natural boundary as one moves away from water (e.g., to come onto the shore or go into the woods)

evidence | MC seskaham, *to paddle ashore;* SEC seskāskohtew, *to walk into the woods;* SEC sheschishin, *to lie with one end on the shore* (CSB, 2018); NEC shāshkishtāu, *to be placed with one end on the shore;* WI (Pessamit) sheshkashkupatau [ʃēʃkāʃkupətāw], *to run into the woods;* Silvy (ca. 1680) "ni sestchiparin, *j'échoue*" | ANISH zhekaakwa'am, *to go to the woods on a trail* (Lippert & Gambill, 2023); Cuoq (1886) "Cekise, *aller frapper contre, échouer*"

*šēšk

INITIAL

— dread

evidence | PC sēsēskinākwan, *to look dreadful or frightful;* MC (šē)šeškelihtam, *to be nervous about sth;* NEC sāschāyihtim, *to shiver at the thought of sth unpleasant;* NSK saaschaayituw, *to shudder* discussion | While the existence of this root is secure in Old Cree, the quality of the sibilants cannot be confirmed based on the dialectal reflexes cited above.

*šēštakw (~ *šēštako)

INITIAL (NOUN, INANIMATE)

— a strand of natural fiber used for making thread or rope

evidence | PC sēstak, *skein;* MC šeštakweyāpiy, *a rope;* AT (Opitciwan, Joey Awashish) cectak^w [šēštak^w], *thread;* cectakwapi [šēštakwāpiy], *rope;* SEC šeštak^w, *a thread;* EI (Sheshatshiu) sheshtakuiapi [ʃēstukwjāpī], *a thread;* Laure (ca. 1726) "chestaku, *filasse, prêt à être filée;*" Silvy (ca. 1680) "chestak8, *mèche;*" "ni chestag8kan, *je fais du fil de nerfs*"

*šēw

INITIAL

— **1** fragile

— **2** sensitive

evidence | AT (Wemotaci, Nicole Petiquay) cewatciw [šēwaciw], *to be sensitive to the cold;* SEC šewan, *to be sensitive;* NEC shāunāu, *to be hurt easily;* NSK saawiihtaaw, *to break or damage sth easily;* WI (Pessamit) sheuneu [ʃēwnēw], *to be sensitive to pain;* EI (Sheshatshiu) sheun [ʃēūn], *to be fragile* compare | *wahkēw

*šihk

INITIAL

— stretch out

evidence | PC sīhkipitākan, *frame for stretching hides;* MC šihkipitew, *to stretch a pelt;* SEC šihceyōw-anikocāš, *flying squirrel;* NEC shihkāpāu, *to dry out a fish net on the bushes;* sichipitihtāu, *to stretch and lace a pelt on a frame;* Fabvre (ca. 1690) "chikaban e8, *estendre rez p(ou)r secher*" | MENO sɛhke·hsen, *to lie spread*

*šihkip

INITIAL (NOUN, ANIMATE)

— grebe

evidence | MC šihkipiš, *a grebe;* AT (Opitciwan, Joey Awashish) cikipic [šikipiš], *a grebe; a boil;* SEC šihcip & cihcip, *a grebe;* (Waswanipi) šihkipiš, *a grebe;* Faries & Mackay (1938) "sèkip, *n.an. A water-hen;*" Silvy (ca. 1680) "chitchipich, *apostume; espèce de plongeur*" | ANISH zhingibis, *a grebe* (Livesay & Nichols, 2021)

*šihkohs

INITIAL (NOUN, ANIMATE)

— weasel

evidence | PC sihkos, *a weasel;* sihkosiw, *a weasel;* MC šihkosiw, *a weasel;* AT (Opitciwan, Joey Awashish) sikosiw [sihkossiw], *a weasel;* (Wemotaci, Jeannette Coocoo) sikosiw [sihkossiw], *a weasel;* SEC šihkošīš, *a weasel;* NEC sihkus, *a weasel;* WI (Pessamit) shikushish [ʃəkuʃīʃ], *a weasel;* EI (Unaman-shipit) shikush [hīkuh], *a weasel;*" MacKenzie (1801) "Sigous, *Ferret;*" Laure (ca. 1726) "chikuchich, *belette, espèce d'hermine;*" Fabvre (ca. 1690) "chik8si8 *pl.* 8ek, sik8si8ek, *hermines, bestes blanches;*" Silvy (ca. 1680) "sik8si8, *hermine*" | ANISH zhingos, *a weasel* (Livesay & Nichols, 2021); MESK shekosa, *a weasel* origin | PA ***šenkwehsa** (Hewson, 1993) see | *šihkohsiw

*šihkohsiw

MEDIAL (NOUN INCORPORATION)

— weasel

evidence | MC pahkonišihkosiwew, *to skin a weasel;* EI (Mamit) shipaishikushueu [hīpējhīkuhwēw], *to pull a weasel pelt on a stretcher* see | *šihkohs

*šihs

INITIAL (NOUN, DEPENDENT ANIMATE)

— maternal uncle

evidence | PC osisiw, *to have a maternal uncle or a father-in-law;* kisis, WC *your mother's brother;* MC osisimāw, *a maternal uncle; an uncle married to a paternal aunt; a father-in-law;* AT (Opitciwan, Joey Awashish), nisisinan [nizissinān], *our father-in-law;* (Wemotaci) nicice [niʒiššē], *my father-in-law;* SEC nisis, *my maternal uncle; my father-in-law;* WI (Pessamit) ushisha [uʃə̀ʃ], *one's father-in-law;* Silvy (ca. 1680) "nichis *voc.* nichissay, *mon oncle maternel*" | ANISH gizhishenh, *your mother's brother* (Livesay & Nichols, 2021); MENO nese·hsak, *my mother's brothers;* MESK neshisēha, *my maternal uncle;* MIAMI kišihsa, *your mother's brother* (ILDA, 2017) origin | PA ***šihs** (***nešihSa**, *my cross-uncle,* Aubin, 1975) compare | *šitihs, *ōhkomihs

*šiht

INITIAL (NOUN, ANIMATE)

— conifer

evidence | PC sihta, *an evergreen; a spruce;* WC sīhta, *an evergreen;* WSC (Misipawistik, Ellen Cook) sihta, *a conifer; a conifer bough;* (Ida Bear) Nāsik sihtak! *Fetch some conifer boughs!;* NEC shihtāhkun, *a conifer bough;* NSK siihtaahkun, *a conifer bough;* Watkins (1865) "Setakwunuk, *n.an.pl. Brush-wood;*" Isham (1743) "Sheth taw po, *spruce beer;*" Silvy (ca. 1680) "sitiskau, *sapinière*" | MENO sɛhta·kuahtek(-ok), *cedar, fir, needle tree* origin | PA ***šenta** (Aubin, 1975) see | *āhtak, *āšiht

*šik

INITIAL

— urinate

evidence | PC sikiw, *to urinate;* MC šikitew, *to urinate on sb;* SEC šiciw, *to urinate;* Silvy (ca. 1680) "ni chitchik8amin, *je pisse au lit en dormant*" | MENO seke·w, *to urinate*

*šikakwē

INITIAL (VERB, ANIMATE, INTRANSITIVE)

— **1** hiccup

— **2** vomit, regurgitate

evidence | PC sikokahtāw, *to have hiccups;* AT (Wemotaci, Jeannette Coocoo) cecikokwew [šēššikokwēw] & cikokwew [šikokwēw], *to vomit;* SEC (Oujé-Bougoumou, Eva Coon) šikakohtāw, *to have hiccups;* NEC sikukuhtāu, *to have hiccups;* WI (Pessamit) shikukatau [ʃəkukutāw], *to have hiccups;* EI (Sheshatshiu) shikukatau [ʃəkātāw], *to have hiccups;* Watkins (1865) "Sikwukùtāo, *v.i.3. He hiccups;*" "Sisikòokutāo, *v.i.3. He hiccups;*" Laure (ca. 1726) "chigakutauin, *hoquet;*" Fabvre (ca. 1690) "Sigak8atan 3 tau, *s8pirer 2 aur le hoquet;*" "chigag8ătan 3 tau, *auoir le hoquet;*" "chichigag8atan, *vomir;*" Silvy (ca. 1680) "ni sigak8tan 3. -tau, *j'ai le hoquet, je soupire*" | Cuoq (1886) "Cicikakowe, *se vider par la bouche; vomir*" see | *wē, *ıhtā² compare | *pākomo, *witwāwē

*šikat (~ *šikac, *šikas)

INITIAL

— bored, weary

evidence | PC sikatēyimēw, *to be bored of sb;* saskatahtam, *to be tired of eating sth;* MC šikatapiw, *to be bored or weary of sitting;* šaškasihtam, *to be weary of hearing sth;* AT (Wemotaci, Nicole Petiquay) cikateritam [šikatērihtam], *to be bored;* cikasinam [šikazinam], *to find sth boring to look at;* NEC shishkichihīkū, *to be bored of sth;* siskitipiu, *to be bored of sitting* | ANISH zhigajii, *to be impatient, to grow tired of sth* (Livesay & Nichols, 2021); MENO seka·tahεw, *to tire sb, to make sb restless*

*šikākw (~ *šikāko)

INITIAL (NOUN, ANIMATE)

— skunk

evidence | PC sikākomākwan, *to smell a skunk;* MC šikākoskāw, *to be many skunks;* SEC šikākwāyow, *a skunk tail;* EI (Sheshatshiu) shikaku [ʃəkākʷ], *a skunk;* Silvy (ca. 1680) "chikak8, *bête puante*" origin | PA ***šekākwa** (Aubin, 1975; Hewson, 1993) see | *šik

*šikāp

MEDIAL (NOUN INCORPORATION)

— brook fed by meltwater or rainwater

evidence | SEC kā yīcihtawišikāpāc, *place name, literally "forking brook;"* (Mistissini) kā minahikušikāpāc, *place name, literally "white spruce brook"* (Bishop, 2022); WI (Pessamit) passeshikapau [pəssēʃəkāpāw], *to branch off, speaking of a run-off stream* see | *šikāpiw

*šikāpišiy

INITIAL (NOUN, INANIMATE)

— brook fed by meltwater or rainwater

evidence | MC šikāpišiy, *a brook fed by meltwater or rainwater;* SEC šikāpišiy, *a brook fed by meltwater or rainwater;* NEC shikāpishīsh, *a very small, bushy creek;* Silvy (ca. 1680) "chigabichich, *détroit de fleuve*" compare | *šikāpiw discussion | The absence of preaspiration on the last sibilant cannot be confirmed due to the lack of an Atikamekw cognate.

*šikāpiw

INITIAL (NOUN, INANIMATE)

— brook fed by meltwater or rainwater

evidence | MC Miši-šikāpiy, *place name, Missicabi River, literally "big brook;"* SEC (Waskaganish) miši-šikāpiy, *place name, literally "big brook"* (Bishop, 2022); WI (Uashat) shikapiun [ʃəkāpjūn], *to be full of underground streams;* EI (Sheshatshiu) shikapu [ʃəkāpu], *a subterranean stream that surfaces here and there;* Laure (ca. 1726) "michichigabiu, *la rivière Batiscan*" see | *šikāp compare | *šikāpišiy

*šiko (~ *šikw)

INITIAL

— be or reduce to pulp, crush

evidence | WC sikonam, *to crush sth by hand;* MC šikonam, *to crush sth manually;* AT (Opitciwan, Joey Awashish) cikwaw [šikwāw], *to be ripe;* WI (Pessamit) shikuaimu [ʃəkwīm], *to crush sth using an object or by pounding it* | ANISH zhishigoshkoode, *to be crushed by weight;* zhishigode, *to be cooked mushy;* MESK shekoshkamwa, *to crush sth under one's weight* origin | PA ***šeko** (Hewson, 1993) compare | *šāhšāko

*šikwan

MEDIAL (NOUN INCORPORATION)

— fish tail, tail fin

evidence | MC sākišikwanew, *to have one's tail fin stick out above the water;* Laure (ca. 1726) "ni-satchichikuanenau, *je le prends par la queue (poisson);*" Fabvre (ca. 1690) "8a8ebichig8anerin i8, *remuer la queue ut pisces*" | ANISH mamaangizhigwane, *to have big tail fins* (Livesay & Nichols, 2021) see | *šikwanay

*šikwanay

INITIAL (NOUN, DEPENDENT INANIMATE)

— fish tail, tail fin

evidence | PC osikwanās, *a small fish-tail;* MC ošikwanay, *a fish's tail;* AT (Opitciwan, Joey Awashish) ka ocikonawit [kā oʒikwanāwit], *a mermaid;* NEC ushikunī, *the tail end of a fish or whale;* Silvy (ca. 1680) "8chig8ănai, *queue de poisson*" see | *šikwan, *ay² compare | *soy

*šimat (~ *šimac)

INITIAL

— vertical

evidence | PC simacīw, *to straighten up;* MC šimatapiw, *to sit up;* NEC shimichishin, *to sit in a reclined position;* WI (Pessamit) shamatuteu [ʃəmətətēw], *to walk on one's hind legs, speaking of an animal;* Fabvre (ca. 1690) "chimatăpin i8, *assis à son aise L(')estre;*" Silvy (ca. 1680) "chimatag8si8, *il monte en volant*"

*šimākan

INITIAL (NOUN, INANIMATE)

— spear

evidence | PA simākanis, *soldier; policeman; jack, in cards;* MC šimākanihkākew, *to make a sword out of sth;* AT cimakan [šimākan], *spear, javelin;* cimakanic [šimākaniš], *soldier; jack, in cards;* SEC šimākan, *a harpoon;* EI (Sheshatshiu) shimakan [ʃimākən], *spear for killing caribou; sword;* Watkins (1865) "Simakun, *n.in. A bayonet, a sword;*" "Simakunikooman, *n.in. A sword;*" "Simakunis, *n.in. [sic] A soldier;*" Laure (ca. 1726) "chimaganich, *soldat;*" Silvy (ca. 1680) "chimagan, *épée;*" "chimaganik8man, *couteau à doler*" | ANISH zhimaaganike, *to make a spear or lance* (Livesay & Nichols, 2021) see | *ākan²

*šināw

MEDIAL (NOUN INCORPORATION)

— castor sac

evidence | NEC pihkunishināwānāu, *to remove sb's castor glands;* EI (Unaman-shipit) patshishinauepanu [pātʃɨhɨnāwēpanu], *to have swollen testicles;* Laure (ca. 1726) "ka manichinaueskat, *eunuque de naissance*" see | *wīšināw

*šinot

INITIAL

— edge (non-productive root found only in the noun *šinotākani, a binding line for fishing nets)

evidence | MC šinotākan, *a binding line for nets;* SEC šinotākan, *a binding line for nets;* NEC shunitākin, *twine for net;* WI (Pessamit) shinutakaniapi [ʃəntānjāpī], *line joining upper and lower parts of fishing net;* EI (Sheshatshiu) shinutakaniapi [ʃuntākənjāpī], *line joining upper and lower parts of fishing net;* Silvy (ca. 1680) "chin8tagan, *maître à rets, corde, etc.*" | ABEN senodosa, *to walk ashore;* senojiwi, *at the shore;* PASS sonuciw, *along or at edge (of water, field, etc.)* see | *ākan²

*šipwē

INITIAL

— **1** start

— **2** depart

evidence | PC sipwēcimēw, *to paddle away;* WC sipwīpahtāw, *to run away;* ESC (Severn) shipwewinew, *to carry sb off;* shipwenāw, *to fly away;* Watkins (1865) "Sipw'āhum, *v.i.6. He begins to sing. As v.t. he begins to sing it, he sets a tune;*" Silvy (ca. 1680) "ni chib8emau, *je le console*"

*šišo (~ *šišw)

INITIAL

— spread pasty substance

evidence | PC sisopēkahikan, *paint;* MC šišoham, *to paint sth;* AT (Wemotaci, Jeannette Coocoo) cicocimoro [šiʒoššimorow], *to rub oneself onto sth pasty;* šišo:n-, *to paint, rub, spread sth by hand* (Béland, 1978); SEC šišonitihpātew, *to rub brains on sth* | ANISH zhizhoo'ige, *to spread things on using sth* (Livesay & Nichols, 2021); MENO sesuaham, *to rub sth with sth, to daub, smear, or anoint sth*

*šišot (~ *šišoc)

INITIAL

— at the shore

evidence | WSC (Misipawistik, Ellen Cook) sisocipēk, *at the shore;* MC šišōc & šišōtew, *at the shore;* NEC shishutipāch, *ashore;* NSK sisutischaach, *on the shore of the muskeg;* Watkins (1865) "sisooch, *adv. Ashore, on the beach, on the coast, along the beach;*" "sisootāo, *n.in. The shore; the edge of a plain*" | ANISH zhizhodew, *along the shore* (Livesay & Nichols, 2021)

*šit

INITIAL (NOUN, DEPENDENT ANIMATE)

— parent-in-law

evidence | Fabvre (ca. 1690) "chit, *beau pere, belle mere;*" Silvy (ca. 1680) "nichit, *mon beau-père, ma belle-mère;*" "n'8chitimau, *je suis marié à sa fille*" compare | *šitihs

*šitihs

INITIAL (NOUN, DEPENDENT ANIMATE)

— parent-in-law

evidence | Fabvre (ca. 1690) "chitis, *beau pere, belle mere;*" Silvy (ca. 1680) "nichitis, *mon beau-père, ma belle-mère*" | ANISH ozinisan, *one's father-in-law* (Livesay & Nichols, 2021); MENO ose·nɛhsan, *one's father-in-law* origin | PA ***šiθehs** (Aubin, 1975) compare | *šit discussion | In the absence of an Atikamekw cognate, the preaspirate in this reconstruction is indirectly supported by Anishinabe and Menominee cognates.

*šī

INITIAL

— dull

evidence | SEC šīhtin, *to be blunted;* NEC shīham, *to blunt a cutting implement;* WI (Pessamit) shititau [ʃīttāw], *to dull or blunt a blade by bringing it into contact with sth* | MENO si·kwan, *to be dull, e.g., a spear, mover, or knife* compare | *ašiw

*šīhk[1]

INITIAL

— urge

evidence | PC sīhkiskawēw, *to incite sb;* MC šīhkimew, *to urge sb;* SEC šīhcimew, *to urge sb;* Watkins (1865) "Sèkimitoowuk, *v.recip.4.pl. They conspire;*" Silvy (ca. 1680) "ni chitchimau, *je l'excite, combattant avec un autre*" origin | PA ***šīhk** (Aubin, 1975)

*šīhk[2]

INITIAL

— hate

evidence | AT (Opitciwan, Joey Awashish) cīkerimew [šīkērimēw], *to hate sb;* SEC šīkācihkweyiw, *to make a disdainful facial expression;* NEC shīkātāyimāu, *to disdain sb;* WI (Pessamit) shikateu [ʃīkātēw], *to hate sb;* Laure (ca. 1726) "ni-chikatitunan 3. -tuets, *entre-haïr, nous nous entre-haïssons;*" Silvy (ca. 1680) "ni chikaten, *je hais*" | ANISH zhiingendaagozi, *to be disliked, disapproved of, hated* (Livesay & Nichols, 2021); MENO se·hkanɛw, *to hate sb;* MIAMI šiinkilaweelintam-, *to hate sth* (ILDA, 2017) origin | PA ***šīnk** discussion | AT and EC forms lack the expected preaspirate, possibly due to influence from the neighbouring Anishinabe dialect, while WI has lost preaspirates generally. Additionally, the orthography used in the historical sources cited above do not furnish evidence of preaspirates. On the other hand, reliable cross-linguistic data concur regarding the presence of a consonant cluster and furnish the information assumed to be missing in the Cree data.

*šīhšīkwē

INITIAL (VERB, ANIMATE, INTRANSITIVE)

— make rattling noise

evidence | PC sīsīkwēsis, *little rattlesnake;* sīsīkwan, *rattle;* AT cicikon [šīššīkon], *rattle;* SEC šīšīkwan, *rattle;* EI (Sheshatshiu) shishikun [ʃɪʃīkun], *baby rattle;* Laure (ca. 1726) "chichigueu, *sifflement de serpent;*" Silvy (ca. 1680) "chichig8e8, *espèce de couleuvre*" | ANISH zhiishiigwe, *a rattlesnake;* zhiishiigwan, *a rattle* (Livesay & Nichols, 2021)

*šīhšīp

INITIAL (NOUN, ANIMATE)

— duck

evidence | PC sīsīpiskāw, *to be many ducks;* MC šīšīpihkān, *a duck decoy;* AT (Wemotaci, Jeannette Coocoo) cicip [šīššip], *a mallard;* ši:šši:p, *a duck* (Béland, 1993); SEC šīšīp, *a duck;* Silvy (ca. 1680) "chichipau, *œuf de canard*" origin | PA ***šīʔšīpa** (Hewson, 1993) see | *hšip

*šīk

INITIAL

— comb

evidence | PC sīkahow, *to comb one's hair;* WC sīkahon, *comb;* MC šīkahwew, *to comb sb's hair;* SEC šīkahon, *comb;* WI (Mashteuiatsh) shikaun [ʃīkəhun], *comb;* EI (Mamit) shikau [hīkāw], *to comb one's hair with a fine-toothed comb;* Laure (ca. 1726) "ni-chikahuau, *je le peigne;*" Silvy (ca. 1680) "ni chigah8tis8n, *je me peigne*" limited to | *ah

*šīkawē

INITIAL

— sift, strain

evidence | MC šīkawepalihcikan, *a sieve; sifted matter;* NEC shīkiwāpiyihāu, *to sift sth;* Watkins (1865) "Sekowāpuyetow, *v.t.in. 2. He sifts it*" compare | *šīko

*šīkāw

INITIAL (NOUN, ANIMATE)

— widow

evidence | PC sīkāwihow, *to be in mourning;* WC sīkāwināpīw, *widower;* AT cikaw [šīkāw], *a widow;* Watkins (1865) "Sekowew, Sekowisew, *v.i.1. She is a widow. The former of these words is the one more commonly in use;*" Laure (ca. 1726) "ka chigauit, *veuf;*" Silvy (ca. 1680) "chigau, *veuve*" | ANISH zhiigaa, *a widow or widower* (Livesay & Nichols, 2021)

*šīko (~ *šīkaw)

INITIAL

— empty, deplete of contents

evidence | PC sīkwāhkatosow, *to be lean from starvation;* MC šīkonam, *to empty sth of its contents by hand;* SEC šīkonam, *to empty sth of its contents by hand;* šīkwāhkahtew, *to be empty after its contents burn up;* WI (Pessamit) shikuau [ʃīkwāw], *to be empty;* EI (Sheshatshiu) shikuashkupanieu [ʃīkwāʃkupənjēw], *to sift or filter sth; to shuffle cards;* Watkins (1865) "Sekoonum, *v.t.in.6. He empties it;*" "Sekoopuyew, *v.imp. It empties;*" "Sekoopākinikun, *n.in. A strainer;*" Laure (ca. 1726) "chikauaskuparitagan, *sas pour passer la farine;*" Silvy (ca. 1680) "ni chig8nen, *je vide un vase plein d'eau;*" "chiga8agat8s8, *il est sec, maigre, défait de maladie;*" "ni chiga8ask8parihau karak8na, *je sépare la galette des crottes de rats*" | MENO se·konam, *to empty sth by pouring;* MESK shīkonamwa, *to empty sth* compare | *šīkawē

*šīnašk

INITIAL

— drench

evidence | MC šīnaškāpāwew, *be drenched;* SEC šīnaškāpāwatāw, *to drench sth*

*šīp

INITIAL

— **1** stretch

— **2** resistant to

evidence | [1]PC sīpēkinam, *to stretch a cloth;* MC šīpīw, *to stretch;* SEC šīpaham, *to stretch sth using a tool* [2]MC šīpinew, *to have a high tolerance to pain;* šīpilawew, *to be even-tempered, slow to anger;* SEC šīpaciw, *to have a high tolerance for cold;* WI (Pessamit) shipakateu [ʃīpəkətēw], *to withstand hunger well;* Laure (ca. 1726) "ni-chibiban -beu, *je porte bien la boisson*" origin | PA ***šīp*** (Aubin, 1975)

*šīpā

INITIAL

— **1** in space under something, below

— **2** be a navigable side channel, in reference to rivers

evidence | [1]PC sīpāpayiw, *to go under;* MC šīpāsīw, *to pass under;* SEC šīpāpiw, *to sit underneath* [2]WSC (Misipawistik, Ellen Cook) sīpānak, *a river branch that contours an island, a side channel;* MC šīpāštikowan, *to be a navigable side channel;* EI (Mamit) shipashtik[u] [hīpāhtuk[w]], *side channel of a river* | [1]MENO se·pa·cewan, *to flow under* [2]ABEN sibategw, *a river channel* (Day, 1994); ANISH zhiibaa-minis, *between two islands* (Livesay & Nichols, 2021); zhiibaatig, *a channel between islands* (Lippert & Gambill, 2023)

*šīpē

INITIAL

— free from undergrowth, clearing

evidence | MC šīpeyāw, *to be a sparsely wooded area with no undergrowth;* SEC šīpenākwan, *to look clear from undergrowth;* EI (Mamit) shipetinau [hīpētnāw], *to be a way through two mountains;* Watkins (1865) "Sepāyaskwun, *v.imp. It is free from underwood, the trees stand apart and not entangled;*" Silvy (ca. 1680) "chibeïau, *éclaircie d'arbres*" | ANISH zhiibeshkodeyaa, *to be open prairie* (Lippert & Gambill, 2023)

*šīw

INITIAL

— **1** sweet, sour, or salty

— **2** feel discomfort

evidence | PC sīwaham, *to sweeten sth;* sīwaskatēw, *to feel one's stomach is empty;* Lacombe (1874) "Siwihew, *il le sale, il le sucre;*" MC šīwihtākan, *salt;* šīwāsow, *to be dazzled by a bright light;* SEC šīwāscikanew, *to have heartburn;* šīwāw, *to be sweet or salty;* Silvy (ca. 1680) "chiȣisiȣ, *il est salé;*" "ni chiȣasȣn, *je suis ébloui*" | MENO se·wahcekɛ·w, *to eat sweet things*

*škihtēkom

INITIAL (DEPENDENT ANIMATE)

— earwax

evidence | PC miskihtēkom, *earwax;* MC oškihtekoma, *one's earwax;* AT oškittekom, *earwax* (Béland, 1978); SEC (Waswanipi, Mary Jane Kitchen) niškihtekom, *my earwax;* WI (Pessamit) utshishtekuma [utʃəstēkùm], *one's earwax*

*škiš

MEDIAL (NOUN INCORPORATION)

— upper lip

evidence | SEC cāhciščišew, *to have an upturned upper lip;* papaciščišew, *to have a thin upper lip;* Laure (ca. 1726) "ni-tchispatchisisan, *j'ai de grandes lèvres saillantes;*" Silvy (ca. 1680) "ni kitchi-bistichan, *la lèvre de dessus me tremble*" see | *škišay

*škišay

INITIAL (NOUN, DEPENDENT INANIMATE)

— upper lip

evidence | PC Lacombe (1874) "ni'skisāy, a, *ma lèvre;*" AT ockacai [oškaʒay], *lip;* SEC oščišay, *upper lip;* Watkins (1865) "Miskisai, *n.in. The lip.* Niskisai, *my lip;*" Laure (ca. 1726) "nistchichai, *lèvre d'en haut, ma lèvre;*" Fabvre (ca. 1690) "Michtichai *v.* nichtichai, *La leure, mes Leures;*" "chtichai, *Leures, Labia*" origin | PA ***škešay*** (Hewson, 1993) see | *škiš compare | *kwāskonēw

*škīšikw[1] (~ *škīšiko)

INITIAL (NOUN, DEPENDENT INANIMATE)

— eye

evidence | PC miskīsik, *an eye;* MC oškīšikomin, *a dwarf raspberry;* AT (Opitciwan, Joey Awashish; Wemotaci,

Nicole Petiquay & Jeannette Coocoo) ockicikw [oškīʒikʷ], *an eye;* SEC oškīšikohkānāpiskow, *to wear eyeglasses;* EI (Unaman-shipit) ussishikumesh [ussīhukwamēh], *a fish eye;* Silvy (ca. 1680) "nichtigig8, *mon oeil*" | ANISH oshkiinzhigokaanan, *eyeglasses* (Livesay & Nichols, 2021); MENO neske·hsekon, *my eyes* origin | PA ***škīnšekw** (Hewson, 1993) see | *škīšikw² discussion | The Atikamekw cognate above, verified by three fluent speakers, does not support the reconstruction of a preaspirated sibilant, contrary to what is expected when comparing the Anishinabe and Menominee cognates. While the Atikamekw glossary in Béland (1978) does list "oški:ššikw," evidence for a preaspirated sibilant, it also lists the contradicting "oškišikopicikan." The above reconstruction must therefore be imposed by virtue of the comparative method.

*škīšikw² (~ *škīšiko)

MEDIAL, FINAL (NOUN INCORPORATION)

— eyes

evidence | PC mahkiskīsik, *a big eye;* MC ayeskwākamiškīšikwew, *for one's eyes to be tired;* Laure (ca. 1726) "ni-kassiteutchigiguan 3. -gueu, *j'ai un oeil noir*" | ANISH mamaangishkiinzhigwe, *to have big eyes* (Livesay & Nichols, 2021) see | *škīšikw¹

*škotaw (~ *škotawak)

MEDIAL (NOUN INCORPORATION)

— fire

evidence | NEC nūchishkutiwāsiu, *fire ranger;* WI (Pessamit) nutshishkutueu [nūtʃəʃkutwēw], *to be a fire warden;* EI (Unaman-shipit) nipeshkutuenitsheu [nīpēhkutawēntʃēw], *to sit up at night to watch the fire;* Faries & Mackay (1938) "Kunoweskoo'tawāo, *v.t.in. He takes charge of (looks after) the fire;*" Laure (ca. 1726) "pimuskutauatsigan, *grenade;*" "chaburaué mikuskutauasuets, *leur corps est rouge de feu;*" Silvy (ca. 1680) "mik8chk8ta8agau, *feu follet, charbon ardent, rouge*" see | *ıškotēw, *ak², *škotēw

*škotēw

FINAL (NOUN INCORPORATION)

— fire

evidence | PC cīkiskotēw, *by the fire;* MC tetāwiškotew, *in or above the middle of the fire;* WI (Pessamit) akamishkuteu [kāməʃkutēt], *on the other side of the fire* origin | Old Cree ***ıškotēwi** see | *ıškotēw, *škotaw compare | *aškotēw

*škwāht

FINAL (NOUN INCORPORATION)

— doorway

evidence | MC ītawiškwāht, *both sides of the doorway;* WI (Pessamit) apamishkuat [āpməʃkwāt], *behind the door* | ANISH jiigishkwaand, *by the door* (Livesay & Nichols, 2021) compare | *škwāhtaw

*škwāhtaw

MEDIAL (NOUN INCORPORATION)

— doorway

evidence | MC kanawiškwāhtawew, *to watch the doorway;* WI (Pessamit) tshipishkuatuepu [tʃəpəʃkwātwēpu], *to be seated in front of the entrance;* Watkins (1865) "kipiskwatowāstow, *He puts it in the doorway*" see | *ıškwāhtēm compare | *škwāht

*šow

INITIAL

— stretch out or straighten a limb

evidence | MC šowikāteštāw, *to stretch out one's legs;* šowiniskeliw, *to stretch out one's arm;* SEC šowāhcew, *to glide gently downwards, speaking of a bird with wings stretched out;* NEC shūwinischāyishtiwāu, *to put one's hand out towards sb* | MESK showishinwa, *to lie sprawled out;* showēkinamwa, *to hold sth spread out, such as a blanket* discussion | There is no evidence to reconstruct the expected allomorph ***šō**. Rather, the above root is irregular in requiring an epenthetic vowel when it is followed by a consonant-initial medial or final. The reduplicated root ***šēšāw**, used in many dialects to refer to limbering up or exercising, semantically suggests it may be derived from above root. However, it has instead been associated in this work with the root ***šaw** as it is phonologically better explained by the latter.

*šowahkwē

INITIAL

— slide down slope

evidence | AT (Wemotaci, Jeannette Coocoo) cocokwew [šōššōhkwēw], *to slide;* SEC šōšōhkwepayihow, *to make oneself slide down;* NEC shūshiwihkwāpiyihū, *to slide down;* WI (Pessamit) shushukueu [ʃūʃūkwēw], *to slide down a slope;* Laure (ca. 1726) "ni-chuuakuan 3. -kueu, *je me fais ramasser, je glisse du haut en bas exprès pour me dépêcher;*" "ni-chuchuhakuan 3. -kueu, *je me laisse glisser;*" Fabvre (ca. 1690) "ch8ch8ak8an 3 k8au e8, *glisser ainsy q(ue) les enfants*" origin | Query obscure noun incorporation. compare | *šow

*šō

INITIAL

— warm up

evidence | MC šōpesam, *to warm up sth liquid;* šōpeštew, *to be warm liquid;* AT (Opitciwan, Nadia Awashish) copesam [šōpēssam], *to warm up a liquid;* Fabvre (ca. 1690) "ch8chen, *chauffer q(ue)lq(ue) ch(os)e*" | MESK shōpyēsikēwa, *to blanche ears of green corn to set the milk* compare | *kīšō

*šōhšōp

INITIAL

— bendable, pliable

evidence | Fabvre (ca. 1690) "ch8ch8pichichi8 nitatchabi a? *Il n'est pas fort le bois de mon arc?;*" Silvy (ca. 1680) "ni ch8ch8binan 3. -nau, *j'attire la corde de l'arc à moi;*" "ch8ch8pichichi8, *il n'est guère fort, v.g. l'arc*" | ANISH zhoobizi, *to be tempted* (Livesay & Nichols, 2021); zhoobibidoon, *to bend sth;* zhooshoobaabiigad, *to be a flexible wire* (Lippert & Gambill, 2023); MIAMI "ch8ch8pacat8i, *le bois plie*" (Largillier - ILDA, 2017) compare | *tōštōp

*šōkan[1]

INITIAL (NOUN, DEPENDENT INANIMATE)

— lower back (of a person), rump (of an animal)

evidence | PC misōkan, *backside of the body;* MC ošōkan, *one's lower back; one's rump;* AT (Wemotaci, Jeannette Coocoo) ocokan [oʒōkan], *one's hip;* SEC ošōkan, *a lower back of a person, a rump of an animal;* WI (Uashat) ushukanakup [uʃūkənəkup], *a skirt or slip;* Laure (ca. 1726) "uchugan, *son croupion*" see | *šōkan[2] compare | *šōpiy

*šōkan[2]

MEDIAL, FINAL (NOUN INCORPORATION)

— lower back (of a person), rump (of an animal)

evidence | PC mahkisōkanew, *to have a large bum;* MC apwešōkanew, *to have a sweaty lower back;* SEC tewišōkanew, *to have a lower back ache;* Silvy (ca. 1680) "michich8gan, *grosse fesse*" see | *šōkan[1]

*šōm

INITIAL

— partially thawed

evidence | SEC shūmāu, *to be partially thawed* (CSB, 2018); NEC shūmipiyiu, *to be little bit thawed out;* shūmāyāu, *to be mild weather causing the snow to melt;* shūmāskitin, *to be a little frozen* | ANISH Cuoq (1886) "Comingwen,i, *s'adoucir le visage, se dérider, prendre un air de gaîté;*" MENO so·mehkow, *to smile*

*šōmin

INITIAL (NOUN, ANIMATE)

— grape

evidence | PC sōminak, *grapes, raisins;* MC šōminišak, *raisins, dried currants;* SEC šōminišac, *raisins;* EI (Sheshatshiu) shumin [ʃūmin], *a grape, a raisin;* Laure (ca. 1726) "chuminabui, *jus de raisin, vin;*" Fabvre (ca. 1690) "ch8minagăchi, *vigne*" | ANISH Cuoq (1886) "Cowimin, *fruit doux, raisin;*" MENO so·men, *grape, raisin* see | *min⁴

*šōpiy

INITIAL (NOUN, DEPENDENT INANIMATE)

— lower back fat, rump fat

evidence | WC osōpiy, *fat from the back of animals;* MC ošōpiy, *fat from the lower back of a quadruped;* AT (Wemotaci, Nicole Petiquay) ocopi [oʒōpiy], *fat from the back of animals;* SEC ošōpiy, *fat from the back of a quadruped* | ANISH Cuoq (1886) "Ojopi monz, *l'orignal a du jop*" compare | *šōkan¹ compare | *pimiy, *wīkw, *wīrinw, *wīhs²

*šōriyāw¹

INITIAL (NOUN, INANIMATE)

— silver

evidence | PC sōniyāw, *money; wages; gold or silver;* WC sōniyāw, *money;* sōniyāwasinhikan, *a cheque;* MC šōliyāwat, *a bag or container for carrying money;* AT coriakew [šōriyāhkēw], *to make money;* SEC šōliyāw, *money; figuratively, a pelt;* WI (Pessamit) shuliau [ʃūljāw], *money; silver;* EI (Unaman-shipit) shuniau [hūnjāu], *to be expensive;* Laure (ca. 1726) "churiau *pl.* -a, *argent, métal;*" "churiauuémikuan, *cuiller d'argent*" | ANISH Cuoq (1886) "conia, *argent;*" "ozaw conia, *or;*" MENO su·niyan, *silver; money; dollar;* MESK shōniyāhi, *silver; money* origin | PA ***šōriyāw** (***šo·liya·w**, Hewson, 1993) see | *šōriyāw²

*šōriyāw²

MEDIAL, FINAL (NOUN INCORPORATION)

— silver

evidence | PC nātisōniyāwēw, *to fetch money;* AT notecoriawew [nōhtēšōriyāwēw], *to run out of money;* SEC nīmišōliyāwew, *to bring some money along;* WI (Uashat) natushuniaueu [ntūʃūnjāwēw], *to ask for money;* Laure (ca. 1726) "ni-mauatchichuriauan, *je quête, mendiant;*" "ni-chichuchuriauahen, *je dore un ouvrage*" see | *šōriyāw¹

*šōš

INITIAL

— be glaze ice

evidence | PC Lacombe (1874) "Sosānaskwaw, *(v.im.) c'est glissant (la glace);*" "sosāskwan, wa, *(a.in.) il est glacé, uni (du bois);*" MC sōsāskohtāw, *to make glaze ice;* AT (Opitciwan, Joey Awashish) cocaskwan [šōʒāskwan], *to be glaze ice;* NEC sūsāskun, *to be slippery ice;* Silvy (ca. 1680) "ch8chask8an, *verglas, glissant;*" cf. NEC shusāchipipiyiu, *water comes onto the ice and freezes* | ANISH zhoozhaakwad, *to be slippery ice or road* (Lippert & Gambill, 2023) compare | *šōšaw

*šōšaw

INITIAL

— smooth

evidence | MC šōšawāw, *to be smooth;* AT (Wemotaci, Nicole Petiquay) cocawaw [šōʒawāw], *to be smooth;* SEC šōšawāpiskāw, *to be a smooth object of mineral composition;* WI (Pessamit) shushuau [ʃūʃwāw], *to be smooth to the touch;* Fabvre (ca. 1690) "ch8cha8abiskau, *fer poly, frot(t)er p(ou)r polir*"

*šōško (~ *šōškw)

INITIAL

— **1** slippery

— **2** slip or slide

evidence | PC sōskwaciwēw, *to slide downhill;* MC šōškwāw, *to be slippery;* šōškociwepalihow, *to make oneself slide down;* NEC shūshkupiyiu, *to slide along;* shūshkwāu, *to be sloped;* WI (Uashat) shushkuateim^{u} [ʃūʃkwātējm], *to skate, to play hockey;* EI (Sheshatshiu) shushkuau [ʃūʃkwāw], *to be a gentle slope;* Laure (ca. 1726) "ni-chuskuatahan, *je vais en patin;*" "ni-chuskussen, *je tombe en glissant*" | ANISH zhooshkobide, *to slip or slide;* MENO so·konam, *to have sth slip from one's hand*

*št[1] (~ *hš)

INITIAL (NOUN, DEPENDENT ANIMATE)

— husband

evidence | Laure (ca. 1726) "uchta, *son mari;*" "nichta, *mon mari;*" "tchegat niui-uchin, *je suis sur le point de prendre un mari;*" Silvy (ca. 1680) "nichta, *mon mari, mon cousin;*" "n'8chin, *je me marie;*" "nichtisti8, *mon mari qui m'a quittée*" | ANISH Cuoq (1886) "On disait autrefois ... wican, *son mari;*" "Oci, *avoir un mari;*" MIAMI "8chi8a, *elle est mariée*" (Pinet - ILDA, 2017) origin | PA ***weʔθari** compare | *īw, *īskw

*št[3]

FINAL (VERB, TRANSITIVE, INANIMATE, CONCRETE)

— eat, taste

evidence | WC wīhkistam, *to like the taste of sth;* MC iškoštam, *to leave part of sth uneaten;* wīhkištam, *to like the taste of sth;* SEC kocištam, *to taste sth;* EI (Sheshatshiu) ishkushtam^{u} [iʃkustəm], *to leave part of sth uneaten;* Laure (ca. 1726) "ni-mirustaman, *savourer, je savoure, je goutte avec plaisir*" origin | PA ***ʔt** (Hewson, 1993), possibly from ***p^{w} + *t** paired with | *pw compare | *spit

*štan[1]

MEDIAL

— nasal cavity

evidence | PC kipistanēw, *to have a nosebleed;* WC (Stanley Mission, Solomon Ratt) pikistanīw, *to have a nosebleed;* WSC (Misipawistik, Ellen Cook) kipistaniw, *to have a nosebleed;* ESC (Severn) kipistonepitisow, *to make one's nose bleed;* AT (Wemotaci, Nicole Petiquay) packoctonew [paškoštonēw], *to have a nosebleed;* SEC paškoštonew, *to have a nosebleed;* NSK piskustinuw, *to have a nosebleed;* Silvy (ca. 1680) "ni pachk8cht8nin, *je saigne du nez*" | ABEN bagitana, *to have a nosebleed* (Day, 1994); ANISH gibitan, *to have a nosebleed;* gibitaneshin, *to fall and get a nosebleed* (Livesay & Nichols, 2021)

*štan[2]

FINAL (VERB, INANIMATE, INTRANSITIVE, CONCRETE)

— flow (speaking of body of water)

evidence | PC mācistan, *to be a thawing river, when the ice starts to move downstream;* MC mācištan, *to be break-up;* NEC māchishtin, *to be break-up* | MENO pe·keqtanoh, *on or at the Missouri River;* MIAMI kihcihtan-, *to be a big current or rapids;* pemihtan, *to flow along* origin | PA ***ʔtan**

*štēhs

INITIAL (NOUN, DEPENDENT ANIMATE)

— elder brother

evidence | WC kistīs, *your older brother;* MC oštēsiw, *to have an elder brother;* AT (Wemotaci, Jeannette Coocoo) octesimaw [oštēssimāw], *elder brother; friar;* NEC nistāsā, *older brother, vocative;* Laure (ca. 1726) "uchtecha, *son frère aîné;*" Silvy (ca. 1680) "nichtais *voc.* nichtaisai, *mon frère ainé*" | MENO nɛqnɛ·hsak, *my older brothers* origin | PA ***ʔθēhs**

*štikw (~ *štiko)

MEDIAL, FINAL (NOUN, INANIMATE)

— river

evidence | WC wākistikwīyāw, *to be a bend in the river;* MC līkihtawištikweyāw, *river forks;* SEC miništik^{w}, *island;* WI (Pessamit) shakushtikuashu [ʃākūstukwāʃu], *narrow* *river* | ABEN gichitegw, *a big river* (Day, 1995); ANISH izhitigweyaa, *river flows to a certain place* (Livesay & Nichols, 2021) origin | PA ***ʔtekw** (Hewson, 1993)

***štikwān**[1]

INITIAL (NOUN, DEPENDENT INANIMATE)

— head

evidence | PC ostikwānāpisk, *a metal helmet;* MC oštikwān, *one's head;* SEC oštikwānikan, *one's skull;* Silvy (ca. 1680) "ȣstigȣanigan, *crâne*" see | *štikwān[2]

***štikwān**[2]

MEDIAL, FINAL (NOUN INCORPORATION)

— head

evidence | PC wāpistikwān, *a person with white hair;* MC tewištikwānew, *have a headache;* SEC mihkoštikwānew, *to have a red head;* Silvy (ca. 1680) "nit'apȣechtigȣanan, *je sue à la tête*" see | *štikwān[1]

***štim**[1]

INITIAL (NOUN, DEPENDENT ANIMATE)

— **1** cross-niece

— **2** daughter-in-law

evidence | PC ostimimāw, *a niece; a daughter-in-law;* Watkins (1865) "Wāstimèk, *n.an. A daughter-in-law;*" Laure (ca. 1726) "nichtim, *nièce de sœur, la fille de ma sœur;*" Silvy (ca. 1680) "nichtim *voc.* nechte, *ma nièce, la femme de mon neveu, ma bru, la femme de mon fils*" | ANISH oshimisan, *one's cross-niece* (Livesay & Nichols, 2021); MENO neqnemɛh(-sak), *my sister's daughter(s)* origin | PA ***ʔθem** (Aubin, 1975) compare | *tihkwatim, *tōšim

***štim**[2]

FINAL (VERB, TRANSITIVE, ANIMATE, CONCRETE)

— leak, drip onto

evidence | MC sōkištimew, *to pour water on sb;* SEC sōcištimew, *to pour water on sb;* Watkins (1865) "Sookistimāo, *v.t.an. He puts water on him, he soaks him;*" Laure (ca. 1726) "nit-aguchtimau, *je le trempe dans l'eau;*" Silvy (ca. 1680) "agȣchtimau, *je lui jette de l'eau, le mouille*" paired with | *štitā

***štin**[1]

FINAL (VERB, INANIMATE, INTRANSITIVE, CONCRETE)

— leak, drip

evidence | PC ohcistin, *to leak, speaking of a boat;* MC ohcištin, *to leak, speaking of a boat;* NEC ahkushtin, *to be leaked on;* Watkins (1865) "oochistin, *v.imp. It leaks (as a canoe, the idea being that of water coming into the vessel rather than running out of it);*" Laure (ca. 1726) "utchistinu uch, *il fait eau par fente;*" Silvy (ca. 1680) "agȣchtinȣ nitagȣp, *ma robe est mouillée*" paired with | *hši[2] compare | *štin[2]

***štin**[2]

FINAL (VERB, INANIMATE, INTRANSITIVE, CONCRETE)

— swell

evidence | MC līwištin, *swelling subsides;* WI (Pessamit) mikushtin [mukustən], *be an inflammation;* Laure (ca. 1726) "tchipustinu nikutagan, *j'ai la gorge enflée, envenimée;*" Fabvre (ca. 1690) "Pakichtin, *il grossit, enfle v.g. L apostume*" compare | *štin[1]

***štin**[3]

FINAL (VERB, INANIMATE, INTRANSITIVE, CONCRETE)

— wind

evidence | MC pimweweštin, *wind heard blowing along;* SEC aywāštin, *calm, windless weather;* NEC chimishtin, *wind dies down;* WI (Pessamit) matueshtin [məttwēstən], *wind makes rustling sound through branches;* EI (Sheshatshiu) piputeshtin [pīputēstn], *to be flurries, to be blowing snow* | ANISH anwaatin, *calm weather* (Livesay & Nichols, 2021) origin | PA ***ʔten** (Hewson, 1993) compare | *tin

*štitā

FINAL (VERB, ANIMATE, INTRANSITIVE, CONCRETE)

— leak, drip onto

evidence | MC sōkištitāw, *to pour water on or in sth;* SEC sōcištitāw, *to pour water on or in sth;* Watkins (1865) "Sookistitow, *v.t.in.2. He adds water (or other liquid) to it, he soaks it;"* Laure (ca. 1726) "ni-sutchistitan 3. -tau, *je remets de l'eau dedans"* paired with | *štim[2]

*štow

MEDIAL (NOUN INCORPORATION)

— facial hair

evidence | PC mīhistowēw, *to have facial hair;* WC kinostowīw, *to have a long beard;* MC mīlištowew, *to have a moustache;* SEC cīniščowe-āpikošīš, *a shrew;* Laure (ca. 1726) "ni-pachkuchtauechuau, *je lui rase le poil (la barbe);"* "paskuchtué-uabegaigan, *savonnette à barbe;"* Silvy (ca. 1680) "ni 8abicht8an, *j'ai la barbe blanche"* see | *īštow

*šwāk (~ *šwāš)

INITIAL

— partially melted snow, slushy snow

evidence | MC šwākan, *to be slushy snow;* šwākaham, *to walk in slushy snow;* AT (Wemotaci, Nicole Petiquay) cwakaham [šwākaham], *to walk in slushy snow;* cwactew [šwāštēw], *to be slushy snow from the heat of the sun;* NEC shwāshtāu, *to be melting snow from the warm sun;* EI (Sheshatshiu) shashuakan [ʃāʃwākən], *the wet snow does not offer a solid bottom;* Watkins (1865) "Swastāo, *v.imp. The snow thaws"* | ANISH Cuoq (1886) "coagan, *neige molle, fondante;"* MENO suakan, *to be wet snow, to be slushy underfoot* origin | PA ***šwāk**

T

*t[1]

MEDIAL

— feet

evidence | PC sāsākihtiw, *to have bare feet;* SEC šāšācihtiw, *to have bare feet;* šešemāštapiw, *to sit in a tailor's posture, to sit Indian style;* NEC shāmāshtipiu, *to sit with one's knees up;* Laure (ca. 1726) "ni-chachatchitin, *je suis déchaussé;"* "ni-chéchémachtapin, *moi homme, je m'accoude sur mes genoux;"* Silvy (ca. 1680) "ni chechemastapin, *je suis accoudé sur mes genoux"* | MENO sa·hsake·hnɛw, *to have bare feet* origin | PA *θ

*t[2] (~ *ot)

FINAL (VERB, TRANSITIVE, INANIMATE, CONCRETE)

— to vocalize about or do to or affect by vocalizing

evidence | PC asotam, *to promise sth;* WC ātotam, *to tell about sth;* MC ālimōtam, *to talk about sth;* ātotam, *to give an account of sth;* Laure (ca. 1726) "ni-pagunuten, *je médis"* paired with | *m[3]

*t[3] (~ *š)

FINAL (VERB, TRANSITIVE, ANIMATE, ABSTRACT)

sound change | ē → ā

— conveys the semantic role of patient to a participant

evidence | WC onikātīw, *to carry sb on one's shoulders;* MC aciwāpihkātew, *to reduce the size of sth by tying;* SEC šišonitihpātew, *to rub brains on sth;* Laure (ca. 1726) "amisku ni-pauatau, *je songe un castor;"* Fabvre (ca. 1690) "akaten 8skana, *piller des os, hacher menu;"* "ki nipichin = nipiskāchin, *tu me pense(s) à l(eu)r mode"* origin | PA *θ (Aubin, 1975; Hewson, 1993) paired with | *t[4]

*t[4] (~ *c)

FINAL (VERB, TRANSITIVE, INANIMATE, ABSTRACT)

sound change | ē → ā

— conveys the semantic role of patient to a participant

evidence | MC aciwāpihkātam, *reduce size by tying;* pīhtaškwātam, *to stuff sth with grass;* SEC otāpātam, *to haul sth using a rope* paired with | *m[2], *t[3]

*t⁵ (~ *ɩt, *š, *ɩš)

FINAL (VERB, TRANSITIVE, ANIMATE, ABSTRACT)

sound change | ē → a

— forms causative verbs

evidence | PC nakas̱iwēw, *to leave people behind;* MC šikiṯew, *to urinate on sb;* pakwanawāspinaṯew, *to curse sb with illness behind their back;* SEC miciṯew, *to bark at sb;* cicī nakaš̱in, *you left me behind* | MESK mīchiṉēwa, *to defecate on sb* origin | PA *θ (Aubin, 1975; Hewson, 1993) paired with | *t⁶

*t⁶ (~ *ɩt, *c, *ɩc)

FINAL (VERB, TRANSITIVE, INANIMATE, ABSTRACT)

sound change | ē → a

— forms causative verbs

evidence | PC nakaṯam, *to leave sth behind;* MC kohṯam, *to swallow sth (speaking of a fish);* šikiṯam, *to urinate on sth;* ašahṯam, *to feed sth;* SEC miciṯam, *to bark at sth* paired with | *t⁵, *r compare | *tā

*tahk¹

INITIAL

— cold

evidence | PC Lacombe (1874) "Takkisiw, *il est froid;*" MC tahkāyāw, *to be cold weather;* SEC tahkāw, *to be cold;* Laure (ca. 1726) "tatchirueu, *il souffle [le vent est froid]*" origin | PA ***tahk** (Aubin, 1975; Hewson, 1993)

*tahk²

INITIAL

— strike with tip of

evidence | PC tahkahcikēw, *to stab;* cahkahwēw, *to poke sb with a stick;* WC tahkiskātam, *to kick sth;* MC tahkahtam, *to stab sth;* SEC cahkataham, *to peck at sth;* WI (Pessamit) takamew [təkəmēw], *to stab sb;* EI (Unaman-shipit) tatshishkam [tātʃihkam], *to kick sth;* Laure (ca. 1726) "ni-tatchiskauau, *je lui donne un coup de pied;*" "chatchakahimu, *becqueter, picotter avec le bec, il becquette;*" Silvy (ca. 1680) "ni tchatchakah8au, *je le picotte*" origin | PA ***tank** (Aubin, 1975) compare | *cahk

*tahk³

INITIAL

— constantly

evidence | PC tahki, *constantly, always;* WC tāhki, *always;* MC tahki, *continually;* Watkins (1865) "Tùke, *adv. Continually, incessantly, constantly, all along, the whole time, always, perpetually; the whole space;*" "Tùkinā, *adv. See Tùke*" limited to | *i³, *nē⁴ discussion | Despite the broad geographic distribution of this root, cognates have not been identified in dialects spoken east of Moose Cree. Its inclusion here is therefore tentative.

*tahkakwan¹

INITIAL (NOUN, DEPENDENT INANIMATE)

— wing

evidence | PC mitahtahkwan, *a wing;* WC otāhtāhkwana, *one's wings;* MC otahkakwaniw, *to have wings;* otahtahkwaniw, *to have wings;* AT otatakon [otahtahkon], *a wing;* NEC utihkikun, *one's wing;* SEC otahkakwan *a wing;* otahtahkwan, *a wing;* EI (Sheshatshiu) utatakun [utātākun], *a wing;* Watkins (1865) "Ootùkukoonew, *v.i.1. He has a wing;*" "Ootùtukwun, *n.in. A wing;*" Isham (1743) "U'ta caw quan, *the pinion or wing of a fowl;*" Laure (ca. 1726) "udakakuan *pl.* -a, *aile;*" Fabvre (ca. 1690) "8takak8an *pl.* 8ăna, *ailes d'oyseaux*" discussion | Reflexes of the variant ***tahtahkwan**, obtained by assimilation of the second syllable by the first, are widespread in contemporary dialects. The above form, however, is the earliest attested form that continues to be widely employed, including in MC, SEC, NEC, as well as in WI as a medial. Both forms are listed in Watkins (1865).

***tahkakwan²**

MEDIAL, FINAL (NOUN INCORPORATION)

— wing

evidence | MC kaskitahkakwanehwew, *to break a bird's wings with a projectile;* NEC minitihkikunāshwāu, *to cuts a bird's wings off;* WI (Pessamit) kashteutatakunu [kəstēwtəkəkənu], *to have black wings;* Laure (ca. 1726) "ni-tchimitakakuanesuau, *je rogne les ailes à l'oiseau*" see | *tahkakwan¹

***tahko¹ (~ *tahkw)**

INITIAL

— short

evidence | PC Lacombe (1874) "Takupitunew, ok, *(a.a.) il a les bras courts;*" ESC cahkopitonew, *to have short arms;* MC tahkokāpawiw, *to be short;* SEC tahkwāw, *to be short;* WI (Pessamit) takuapeu [təkwāpēw], *to have a short hauling line* | MENO tasko·sew, *to be short* origin | PA ***tahko** (Aubin, 1975; Hewson, 1993)

***tahko² (~ *tahkw)**

INITIAL

— **1** hold

— **2** steer

evidence | PC tahkwaham, *to hold sth (using a tool); to steer sth;* MC tahkonam, *to hold sth;* tahkohikan, *a rudder;* SEC tahkotehtam, *to hold sth in one's mouth;* EI (Sheshatshiu) takuaitsheu [tākwējtʃēw], *to steer a canoe; to govern;* Laure (ca. 1726) "takuahigan, *gouvernail de navire;*" Fabvre (ca. 1690) "Tak8atemau piki8, *mascher braye, La tenir en La b8che*" origin | PA ***tahko** (Hewson, 1993)

***tahkoht (~ *tahkohc)**

INITIAL

— on top

evidence | PC tahkohtastāw, *to place sth on top of;* WC tāhkohtāpisk, *on top of rock;* ESC tahkohtāmatin, *on top of a hill;* MC tahkohtāmaciwew, *to climb to the top of a hill;* SEC tahkohtāhtawīw, *to climb on top of;* WI (Pessamit) takutapu [təkutəpu], *to sit on the top of;* Watkins (1865) "tàkootustow, *He puts it on the top;*" Laure (ca. 1726) "takutchitchiuapitch, *au faite de la maison;*" "ni-takutchiparihun 3. takutchipariuu, *je monte à cheval*"

***tahsināhkēw**

INITIAL (NOUN, DEPENDENT INANIMATE)

— sternum

evidence | PC Lacombe (1874) "n'tasinākkew, a, otasinākkew, a, *os principal de l'estomac, le brochet;*" MC otasināhkewa, *one's sternum;* AT (Wemotaci, Nicole Petiquay) otasinakew [otassināhkēw], *thorax;* SEC otasināhcew, *a sternum;* Silvy (ca. 1680) "8tasinatcheu, *le thorax, l'os d'entre les mamelles*" | ANISH Cuoq (1886) "Nind asinakeng nind akos, *j'ai mal au bréchet*"

***tahsō**

INITIAL

— trap under a weight

evidence | PC tasōtēw, *to be caught under a tree;* AT (Wemotaci, Nicole Petiquay) tasoso [tassozow], *to be trapped;* WI (Pessamit) tishutau [ttʃūtāw], *to trap sth;* Silvy (ca. 1680) "tiss8ragan, *attrape*" | ANISH dasoonaagan, *a deadfall trap; a trap* (Livesay & Nichols, 2021); MENO taqnosow, *to be trapped* origin | PA ***taʔθō** (Hewson, 1993)

***tahš**

INITIAL

— continuously, incessantly

evidence | PC tasi, *for such a time, for the duration; while, at the same time;* tasinē, *all the time;* MC tašine, *continuously, incessantly;* AT (Wemotaci, Nicole Petiquay) tacine [taššinē], *continuously, incessantly;* SEC tašine, *continuously;* Watkins (1865) "Tussinā, *adv. See Tŭke, of which it is a variation;*" "Tusse, *adv. See Tŭke*" | ANISH nasine, *many times, often* (Lippert & Gambill, 2023) limited to | *i³, *nē⁴ compare | *taht¹

*taht[1] (~ *tahš)

INITIAL

— disengage

evidence | PC tahcipitam, *to undo sth;* tahtinikan, *a trigger;* WC tasipaðiw, *to become unhooked or untied;* MC tahtinam, *to disengage sth manually;* tahtāpiskipaliw, *to disengage, speaking of a mechanism;* Laure (ca. 1726) "tatabissinigan, *la boîte bombée à ressort;*" Fabvre (ca. 1690) "tatinigan *pl* gana, *declin detente de fuzil*" | ANISH nasaabikinigan, *a trigger;* MESK nasahtēwa, *to release the bow or pull the trigger* origin | PA ***θahθ** compare | *tahš

*taht[2] (~ *tahš)

INITIAL

— a certain number, so many

evidence | MC tašiwak, *be a certain number;* AT (Opitciwan, Joey Awashish) taciwok [taššiwak], *to be a certain number;* SEC tahtopiponesiw, *to be so many years old;* Silvy (ca. 1680) "tatatin8ai? *combien y en a-t-il?*" | ANISH dasinoon, *to be a certain number;* MESK tasenwi, *to be so many* origin | PA ***tahθ** (Hewson, 1993)

*tahtakwākan

INITIAL (NOUN, DEPENDENT INANIMATE)

— spine

evidence | AT (Opitciwan, Joey Awashish) otatakwakan [otahtakwākan], *one's spine;* SEC (Waswanipi) citahtakwākan, *your spine;* WI (Pessamit) utatakuakan [utətəkwān], *one's spine;* EI (Sheshatshiu) utatakuakan [utātəkwākən], *one's spine;* Watkins (1865) "Ootutookwakun, *n.in. The back-bone of an animal. This word is of local usage;*" Laure (ca. 1726) "nitatakuagan, *mon échine;*" Fabvre (ca. 1690) "8tak8āgan *pl* găna, *L(')espine du dos, grde areste de poisson;*" Silvy (ca. 1680) "8tatak8agan, *épine du dos, reste du poil*" compare | *āwikan

*tak

MEDIAL (NOUN INCORPORATION)

— penis

evidence | MC tahkotakew, *to have a short penis* | MENO mahke·nakɛw, *he is big at the genitals* origin | PA ***θak** (Aubin, 1975) see | *takay

*takahk (~ *takah, *takaš)

INITIAL

— good

evidence | PC takahkastim, *a good dog or horse;* takahkimākwan, *to smell good;* WC takāhkīthīhtam, *to be satisfied;* SEC takaštew, *to be cooked;* NEC tikisim, *to cook sth;* NSK tikistaaw, *to be cooked;* Faries & Mackay (1938) "tukùkā'yimoo, *v.i.4. He is satisfied with himself, he thinks highly of himself*" | ANISH dagakinaagwad, *to look good* (Lippert & Gambill, 2023)

*takawāhšihš

INITIAL

— few

evidence | PC cikawāsis, *few;* ESC (Severn) cakawāshishiwak, *to be a few;* MC cakawāšišiwak, *be few;* NEC tikiwaashiwich, *be few;* Fabvre (ca. 1690) "8 tiga8achichi8, *pl 8ek, il y en a peu, cela e rare pres(en)temt;*" Silvy (ca. 1680) "ni taga8achichinan, *nous sommes peu en nombre*" | MESK takāwi, *a little;* MIAMI tikawi, *a little (for activities or qualities)* (ILDA, 2017)

*takiš

MEDIAL (NOUN INCORPORATION)

— intestine

evidence | MC āpocitakišenam, *to turn the bowels inside out;* SEC āhkositacišew, *to have abdominal pain;* EI (Sheshatshiu) manitatshisheneu [məntətʃʃēnēw], *to gut sb* | ANISH bikonagizhii, *to have a potbelly* (Livesay & Nichols, 2021) see | *takišiy

*takišiy

INITIAL (NOUN, DEPENDENT INANIMATE)

— intestine

evidence | PC mitakisiya, *intestines;* MC otakišiyāpiy, *one's intestine; one's umbilical cord; a spring;* AT otakišiy, *intestine* (Béland, 1978); SEC (Waswanipi) "citakišiy, *your large intestine;* WI (Pessamit) utatshishiship [utətʃʃīʃəp], *intestines of a waterfowl;* Silvy (ca. 1680) "8tatichi, *boyaux*" | ANISH onagizh, *one's intestine* (Livesay & Nichols, 2021); MENO ona·kes, *one's entrail* origin | PA ***θakišy*** see | *takiš

*tako[1] (~ *takw)

INITIAL

— **1** pound, flatten

— **2** bring together, add

— **3** arrive

evidence | [1]PC takwahamawēw, *to pound sth for sb;* WC takwaham, *to pound sth;* MC tahtakoskamikāw, *be flat ground;* SEC takoham, *to pound sth;* WI (Pessamit) takushiteshkueu [təkuʃətēʃkwēw], *to step on sb's foot;* Laure (ca. 1726) "takuahigan, *mortier, vase à piler*" [2]PC takonam, *to add sth;* MC takoštewa, *to be placed together;* SEC takohtāw, *to add sth;* Fabvre (ca. 1690) "Tak8am8tan 3 tau, *Ioindre qlq che*" [3]PC takohāw, *to arrive flying;* WC takwācimow, *to arrive with news;* MC takopaliw, *to arrive by vehicle;* SEC takošin, *to arrive on foot* | [1]MESK takwahwēwa, takwahamwa, *to grind sth up, to grind things together* [2]MESK takwapitōwa, *to tie sth together with sth else* origin | PA ***tako*** (Aubin, 1975; Hewson, 1993)

*tako[2] (~ *takw, *ıhtako, *ıhtakw)

INITIAL

— be (in a certain location)

evidence | PC ihtakow, *to exist; to be there;* MC takwan, *to be present; to exist;* EI (Sheshatshiu) takuan [təkwən], *to exist, to be some; to be necessary that;* Silvy (ca. 1680) "tak8n, *il y en a*" | ANISH dagon, *to be in a certain place* (Livesay & Nichols, 2021); MENO takuah, *to exist; there is some of sth;* MESK takowa, takowi, *to exist; to be found in numbers* compare | *tē[1]

*takwāk

INITIAL

— autumn

evidence | PC takwākisip, *a fall duck;* WC takwākohk, *last fall;* MC takwākišiw, *to spend autumn in a particular place;* SEC takwācin, *to be autumn;* Laure (ca. 1726) "taguagatai, *peau de castor d'automne*" | ANISH dagwaagin, *to be autumn* (Livesay & Nichols, 2021); MIAMI takwaakiwi, *to be autumn* (ILDA, 2017) origin | PA ***takwāk*** (Hewson, 1993)

*takwāsk

INITIAL

— have cold extremities

evidence | SEC tatakwāsiciw, *to have cold feet;* NEC titikwāschiu, *to have cold feet;* titikwāschāuchiu, *to have cold hands;* EI (Sheshatshiu) takuassu [təkwāssu], *to have cold feet;* Laure (ca. 1726) "ni-tatakuastchichin, *j'ai froid aux pieds;*" Fabvre (ca. 1690) "tatag8achtitche8akin i8, *aur froid aux doigts mains;*" Silvy (ca. 1680) "ni tatag8asisin, *j'ai froid aux pieds;*" "ni tag8atchisite8ach, *j'ai froid aux pied*" | MIAMI takwaahkatwi, *to be frost;* "nitatac8akinama8atchi, *j'ai froid aux mains*" (LeBoullenger - ILDA, 2017) discussion | The evidence supporting this root is marred by contractions in every contemporary dialect and in most of the historical sources. Further complicating the reconstruction is the lack of cognates in western dialects where the expected consonant cluster would have been clearly retained.

*tamahk

INITIAL

— pack

evidence | ESC tamahkīw, *to pack;* MC tamahkinam, *to pack sth;* SEC tamahcīw, *to pack;* WI (Pessamit) tamatshinashu [təmətnāʃu], *to pack one's belongings;* Silvy (ca. 1680) "ni tamatchinamaȣau, *je fais son paquet*"

*tamak

INITIAL

— swell (speaking of a body of water)

evidence | NEC timikin, *to be rising water;* timikāpuwāyāhan, *to be rising water due to high winds;* NSK timikin, *to be rising water;* WI (Pessamit) timikuapuepalu [təməkwāpūwēpəlu], *to be a sudden rise in the water level;* Laure (ca. 1726) "tamaganu, *la rivière se renfle;*" Silvy (ca. 1680) "tamagan, tamagatan, *il est grossi de la pluie, v.g. le ruisseau*" | ABEN tamagan, *to go out, speaking of the tide*

*tamako (~ *tamakw)

INITIAL

— squeeze out

evidence | MC tamakopitam, *to squeeze out the contents of sth by pulling at it;* tamakocenam, *to squeeze out the contents of sth manually;* Watkins (1865) "tumukoonum, *v.t.in.6. He squeezes it out (e.g. pus from a boil)*" | MENO tama·konam, *to press or squeeze sth; to press sth out of place; to pull sth (such as a trigger)*

*tamasko

INITIAL

— grease hair

evidence | PC Lacombe (1874) "Tamaskunew, *il le graisse, il l'oint;*" WC tamaskowin, *hair tonic;* MC tamaskonew, *to grease sb's hair;* Silvy (ca. 1680) "ni tamaskȣn, *je graisse mes cheveux, je les démèle avec la main*"

*tamisk

MEDIAL (NOUN INCORPORATION)

— subcutaneous tissue

evidence | AT (Opitciwan, Joey Awashish) paskitamiskecawew [paskitamiskēʒāwēw], *to remove the subcutaneous tissue from a hide using a knife;* SEC manitamascehwew, *to flesh a hide* see | *tamiskay

*tamiskay

INITIAL (NOUN, DEPENDENT INANIMATE)

— hypodermis, subcutaneous tissue

evidence | PC otamiskaya, *hide-scrapings;* MC otamaskay, *one's subcutaneous tissue;* AT (Opitciwan, Joey Awashish) otamiskai [otamiskay], *subcutaneous tissue;* NEC utimiskī, *the inner layer of skin of fur-bearing animals;* EI (Sheshatshiu) utamishkai [utəmiʃkēj], *the membrane which sticks to the hide of an animal;* Silvy (ca. 1680) "ȣtamiskai, *peau de uiande, graisse*" see | *tamisk, *ay[2]

*tapaht (~ *tapahš)

INITIAL

— low

evidence | PC tapahtakocin, *to hang or fly low;* MC tapahtaškošiwakāw, *to be short grass;* AT (Wemotaci, Jeannette Coocoo) tapacic [tapaššiš], *below, down low;* SEC tapahteyimow, *to be humble;* WI (Pessamit) tapashish [təpəʃīʃ], *at the bottom;* Laure (ca. 1726) "tapatauanu, *petit nuage sur la rivière;*" Silvy (ca. 1680) "ni tapatȣanach, *je parle bas, je parle un peu;*" "nit'abatapinach, *je suis assis bas*" | ANISH dabasabi, *to sit low* (Livesay & Nichols, 2021); MENO tapa·hnakotɛ·w, *to hang low* origin | PA ***tapahθ** (Hewson, 1993)

*tapas

INITIAL

— dodge

evidence | PC tapasīstam, *to flee from sth;* MC tapasīw, *to duck; to escape;* SEC tapasihew, *to dodge sb;* NEC tipisīu, *to duck* | ANISH dabazi, *to dodges or duck; to move* *aside, to get out of the way* (Livesay & Nichols, 2021); MENO tapa·sow, neta·pasin, *to dodge or duck* origin | PA ***tapas**

*tapiskohkēw

INITIAL (NOUN, DEPENDENT INANIMATE)

— first cervical vertebrae, atlas

evidence | PC mitapiskohkēw, *the back of the skull;* MC otapiskohkew, *one's atlas;* NEC utipiskuhchāu, *one's first vertebra;* Laure (ca. 1726) "utabiskutcheuigan, *l'os du chignon du cou*" | MENO neta·pesko·hkan, *AN my upper vertebra*

*taskam

INITIAL

— go across an open space

evidence | PC taskamihāw, *to fly across;* NEC tiskimiskū, *walk directly across the ice;* WI tashkamatinau [təʃkəmətnāw], *a mountain lies from one end to the other;* Fabvre (ca. 1690) "taskamăhen h8rau, *passer en canot etc.*" | ANISH dakamaakwaa, *trees extending across ahead* (Livesay & Nichols, 2021); MENO "tahkamehsɛ·w, *historical man's name 'Flies Straight Across' (Tecumseh);*" MESK tahkamosēwa, *to walk across an open space* origin | PA ***taskam** (***taxkam**, Hewson, 1993)

*tašip

INITIAL

— through the length of, from one extremity to the other

evidence | NEC tishipishim, *to cut sth off at the joint;* WI (Pessamit) taship [təʃəp], *constantly, continually;* tashipau [təʃəpāw], *to be open from one side to the other;* EI (Sheshatshiu) tashipinamᵘ [təʃipɨnəm], *to open sth from one side to the other; to unbutton sth;* Silvy (ca. 1680) "ni tachipichtahen, *je romps, je fais éclater forçant, je fends, je casse, etc.*" discussion | The absence of a preaspiration on the sibilant cannot be confirmed due to the lack of an Atikamekw cognate.

*tašo

INITIAL

— straighten out

evidence | PC tasopayiw, *to straighten out;* MC tašwekalew, *to spread sth sheet-like out;* AT (Wemotaci, Nicole Petiquay) tacopariw [taʒopariw], *to straighten out;* SEC tašokātepayihow, *to straighten out one's leg(s)* | ANISH dazhweginan, *to spread sth out flat* (Livesay & Nichols, 2021) compare | *šahto discussion | An isogloss exists whereby dialects north of Southern East Cree and east of Atikamekw exhibit ***šahto** rather than ***tašo**. Evidence for this dates back to seventeenth-century Jesuit dictionaries. The origin of this isogloss is unclear, but it may point to an early loan from a neighbouring language or to an early case of metathesis. As such, it is possible that either one of these roots does not date back to Old Cree.

*taštas

INITIAL

— upwards

evidence | PC tastasāpahtam, *to look up at sth;* WC tastasāpiw, *to look up;* MC taštasāpiw, *to look up;* SEC taštasāpamew, *to look up at sb;* NEC tāstisāpihtim, *to look up at sth;* NSK taastisaapimaaw, *to raise one's head to look at sb;* Watkins (1865) "tustusapew, *v.i.1. He lifts up his eyes, he looks up*" | ANISH daataganaabi, *to look up* (Livesay & Nichols, 2021); MENO ta·qtanapew, *to look up* compare | *tēštak discussion | The comparative evidence suggests this root was nonproductive, forming words only with finals relating to sight. We reconstruct it as above given the lack evidence for the expected allomorph ***taštat**. The long-voweled reflexes in NEC and NSK appear to be influenced by ***tēštak**, whose reflexes in these dialects are **tāstik** and **tāstic**. A similarly mixed form appears to be used in Anishinabe, as listed above.

*taštaw

INITIAL

— between

evidence | PC tastawic, *between;* WC tastawahikan, *forked pole used for building a tipi;* MC taštawaham, *to straddle sth;* SEC (Waswanipi) taštawišin [tštawšin], *to lie between;* EI tashtutinau [təstūtnāw], *be space between mountains* | ANISH nasawaya'ii, *in between* (Livesay & Nichols, 2021) origin | PA ***θaʔθaw** discussion | Aubin (1975) postulates PA ***θaʔθa:w**, the long vowel in the second syllable being based on the assumption of a reduplication of PA ***θāw**. However, Cree and Anishinabe forms support a short vowel instead.

*tat[1] (~ *tac)

INITIAL

— excessively tight

evidence | PC Lacombe (1874) "tatchisin, wok, *(a.a.) il est trop gros pour entrer;*" "tatchisimew, *(v.a.) ttitaw, simiwew, tchikew, il ne peut le fait entrer, étant trop gros;*" WC tatākan, *a wedge for splitting logs;* NEC titākin, *a wooden wedge used to tighten blade on axe handle or to split wood;* Watkins (1865) "Tuchikatāo, *v.i.3. He is a cripple;*" Silvy (ca. 1680) "tatagan, tatakan, *coin à fendre du bois;*" "tatchitin, *elle serre, v.g. l'écorce, contre les perches*" | ANISH dajise, *to be late, no not have time* (Livesay & Nichols, 2021) origin | PA ***tat**

*tat[2] (~ *taš)

INITIAL

— in a particular place

evidence | MC tatahwew, *to hit sb in a particular place;* tašikāpawiw, *to stand in a particular place;* AT (Wemotaci, Jeannette Coocoo) tacikewin [taʒīhkēwin], *residence;* SEC tašišin, *to lie in a particular place;* Fabvre (ca. 1690) "tataskan e8, *etre de ce paÿs d(') tel paÿs*" | ANISH dazhigin, *to grow in a certain place;* danakii, *to dwell in a certain place* (Livesay & Nichols, 2021); MENO tana·ti·mow, *to weep there, then, through that time;* MESK tanosēwa, *to walk somewhere* origin | PA ***taθ** (Hewson, 1993)

*taw

INITIAL

— space

evidence | PC tawinikēw, *to make space, to ake room;* ESC tawāpiskāw, *to be an opening in a rocky area;* MC tawāw, *to be space;* SEC tawipayiw, *to have an opening in one's schedule;* Fabvre (ca. 1690) "Ta8ak8at8n 8, *aur perdu dent ou dents*"

*tawēmāw

INITIAL (NOUN, DEPENDENT ANIMATE)

— sibling by adoption or marriage

evidence | PC nitawēmāw, *my sibling or parallel cousin of opposite gender;* WC nitawīmāw, *my parallel cousin of the same gender, speaking of a male;* ESC (Attawapiskat) "Ndawēmau *is also used by both sexes for stepbrother & stepsister, not for true brother or true sister*" (Michelson, 1936:61); Fabvre (ca. 1690) "A8ĕmau, *parent d'ad(o)ption; tichan. P(ro)pre;*" Silvy (ca. 1680) "8ta8emat8in, *parenté*" | ANISH gidawemaa, *your sibling of the opposite sex* (Livesay & Nichols, 2021) see | *wāhko compare | *ītišān discussion | Note how Fabvre (ca. 1690) presents a contrast between this root and ***ītišān**, the root referring to natural siblings. The gendered senses in WC and PC may be a result of Anishinabe influence.

*tayakwat (~ *tayakwac)

INITIAL

— contrary to what is expected

evidence | PC tēyakwac, *instead;* Lacombe (1874) "Tiyakwatch & Tiyakutch, *(adv.) au contraire;*" MC tayakoc, *contrary to what is expected, instead;* SEC tayakoc, *contrary to* *what is expected;* NEC tiyikuch, *rather, instead;* Laure (ca. 1726) "tiaguetch, *au contraire;*" cf. WI (Pessamit) tiekunu [tjēkunu, tjākunu], *on the contrary, instead of* limited to | *i³

*tā (~ *ıtā, *c, *ıc, *tw, *ıtw)

FINAL (VERB, ANIMATE, INTRANSITIVE, ABSTRACT)

sound change | ē → a

— forms causative verbs

evidence | PC kācikew, *to hide things;* MC kīwehotāw, *return sth by canoe;* kātāw, *hide sth;* kātowew, *hide sth from sb;* kicištāpāwatāw, *to wash sth;* AT kātowew, *hide sth from sb;* SEC akotāw, *hang sth;* cištāpāwatāw, *to wash sth;* pīhtokatāw, *to bring sth indoors;* kapatāw, *to portage things;* āpotowew, *to bring token of hunt back to sb;* NEC ashtāu, *to place sth;* WI (Pessamit) ashtuau [stwāw], *to set sth aside for later use* paired with | *r compare | *t⁶ discussion | Old Cree ***štā** is a reflex of PA ***ʔtā**, which itself derives from the suffixation of the above root onto a stop. The ***tw** allomorph surfaces only for further derivation when suffixing either the antipassive ***ā** or the benefactive ***aw**. Its origin predates what is otherwise a loss of morphological distinction in Old Cree between Proto-Algonquian transitive inanimate verb class II and animate intransitive verbs ending in ***ā** (cf. Pentland, 1999). Note that contemporary dialects have all contracted ***tw** + ***aw** to a reflex of ***tow**, but the underlying form is revealed when vowel-lengthening processes occur, resulting in reflexes of ***twā** as expected.

*tācikwē

INITIAL (VERB, ANIMATE, INTRANSITIVE)

— scream, shout, yell

evidence | PC tācikwēwin, *a scream;* MC tācikwehpinew, *to scream from the pain;* SEC tācikwātew, *to scream at sb;* NEC tāchikwāu, *to scream, to yell;* Watkins (1865) "Tachikwāo, *v.i.3. He screams, he shrieks, he cries through fear*" see | *wē¹

*tācimo

FINAL (VERB, ANIMATE, INTRANSITIVE, CONCRETE)

— crawl

evidence | PC pīhtokwētācimow, *to crawl inside;* MC kāhkīwetācimow, *to crawl back and forth;* SEC pimitācimow, *to crawl along;* Laure (ca. 1726) "nit-ichitatchimun, *je vais en me traînant*"

*tāhk

INITIAL

— touch

evidence | PC tāhkinam, *to touch sth with one's hand;* WC tāhkīhtin, *to touch ground, to run aground;* SEC tāhkaham, *to touch sth using a tool;* Silvy (ca. 1680) "takaskamitchitin, *il touche à terre, ce qui pend*" | ANISH daangisin, *to lie touching* (Livesay & Nichols, 2021) origin | PA ***tānk**

*tāhkohs

INITIAL (NOUN, DEPENDENT ANIMATE)

— **1** female cross-cousin of a woman

— **2** sister-in-law of a woman

evidence | PC ocāhkosiw, *to have a female cross-cousin or a sister-in-law;* ESC (Fort Severn) cāhkos, *sister-in-law, woman speaking;* MC otāhkosa, *one's female cross-cousin or sister-in-law, speaking of a woman* | ABEN -adōgwsiz, *female cross-cousin of a woman* (Day, 1995); ANISH gidaangoshenh, *your cross-cousin, speaking to a woman;*" odaangweyan, *her sister-in-law* (Livesay & Nichols, 2021); Cuoq (1886) "Mani ot angwan, *la belle-sœur de Marie;*" MESK otākwani, *her sister-in-law;* MIAMI kicaankwa, *your sister-in-law, speaking to a woman* (ILDA, 2017) compare | *īštāw, *ītimohs

*tāhs

INITIAL (NOUN, DEPENDENT INANIMATE)

— legging

evidence | WC mitās, *pants;* MC otāsiw, *to have leggings; to have socks or stocking;* EI (Sheshatshiu) utashu [utāʃu], *to have socks;* Watkins (1865) "Mitasikakāo, *v.i.3. She makes leggins or trowsers of it;*" Laure (ca. 1726) "mitas *pl.* -sa, *bas, chausses;*" "ni-mitassikan, *j'en fais;*" Fabvre (ca. 1690) "Mitas *pl.* mitatai, *bas de chausses;*" Silvy (ca. 1680) "mitas, *pl.* mitatai, *bas-de-chausses;*" "nitas *pl.* nitasa, *mes bas-de-chausses*" | ABEN medasal, *stockings, socks, leggings* (Day, 1995); ANISH Cuoq (1886) "Mitasan kawin gwetc awiia acaie ot aiosin, *il n'y a plus guère personne qui se serve aujourd'hui de mitasses;*" MIAMI "Nitassa, *mes bas, mitasses*" (Largillier - ILDA, 2017); kitaahsi, *your sock* (ILDA, 2017) see | *ıtāhs discussion | The variant plural form provided by Silvy (ca. 1680) and repeated in Fabvre (ca. 1690) likely represents a transcription error as it is uncorroborated cross-dialectally and cross-linguistically. On the other hand, the number ten in Anishinabe and certain Cree dialects may represent cognacy, but no definite link is suggested given the lack of corroboration.

*tāht (~ *tāhc)

INITIAL

— fatten

evidence | PC tāhcipohew, *to fatten sb;* MC tāhcipohākan, *a fatling;* SEC tāhcipow, *to be fat;* WI (Pessamit) tatshipu [tātʃəpu], *to be fattened up, to be fat from eating* | cf. MENO ta·hceqtaw, *to have leisure, to be free as to time*

*tān[1] (~ *tā)

INITIAL

— forms interrogative words such as what, which, when, where, why, and how

evidence | PC tāniwā, *where is s/he?;* tāyispī, *when;* MC tāni, *how;* tānehki, *why;* SEC tān, *how;* tā-ispiš, *when;* NEC tān, *what, which, how, where;* EI (Mamit) tanan [tānan], *which one;* Laure (ca. 1726) "tane, *comment;*" "ta-ispich, *quand;*" "tatasiuets iriniuets? *combien d'hommes?;*" Fabvre (ca. 1690) "Tane 8a, *pl.* 8eka, *ou e it, ou sont ils?;*" Silvy (ca. 1680) "tane8e, *pourquoi;*" "tanita? *où, ubi?;*" "tatat8, *combien;*" "ta espich? *quand?*" | MENO ta·neq, *how is it?*

*tān[2]

FINAL (VERB, INANIMATE, INTRANSITIVE, CONCRETE)

— precipitate as rain or snow

evidence | SEC maskomīwitān, *to hail;* mamenispotān, *to snow here and there;* NEC cimitān, *to stop raining;* WI (Pessamit) mishkumiutan, *to hail;* Laure (ca. 1726) "niskan-tibiskuetanu, *il a plu toute la nuit;*" Silvy (ca. 1680) "ar8atan, *beau temps après la pluie*" | MIAMI waapanelaanwi, *to rain till dawn* (ILDA, 2017) origin | PA ***θān** see | *awahtān, *pēštān

*tānihs

INITIAL (NOUN, DEPENDENT ANIMATE)

— daughter

evidence | PC otānisimēw, *to have sb as a daughter;* MC nitānis, *my daughter;* AT (Opitciwan, Nadia Awashish) otanisa [otānissa], *one's daughter;* SEC (Waswanipi) otānisa, *one's daughter;* Silvy (ca. 1680) "nitanis; neta *voc. ma fille;*" "n'8tanisin, *j'ai une fille*" | ANISH odaanisan, *one's daughter* (Livesay & Nichols, 2021) origin | PA ***tānehs** (Aubin, 1975)

*tāp

INITIAL

— **1** redo, repeat, reset

— **2** match, copy

evidence | PC tāpasinaham, *to copy sth in writing;* WC tāpīhtitāw, *to fit sth in;* MC tāpahāmew, *to walk in the footsteps of another;* SEC tāpakwew, *to set a snare;* Silvy (ca. 1680) "ni tapitap8an 3. e8, *je pronnce des* *mots"* | ANISH naabibii'ige, *to copy things by writing or drawing* (Livesay & Nichols, 2021); MENO na·pa·hkihnɛn, *to have a handle* origin | PA *θāp (Hewson, 1993)

*tāpiko (~ *tāpikw)

INITIAL

— thread

evidence | WC tāpikoham, *to fit sth;* MC tāpikoham, *to thread sth;* SEC tāpikohwew, *to put a noose on sth;* Watkins (1865) "Tapikoonāo, *v.t.an. He backs him (speaking of a net, i.e. he fastens it to the backing-line);*" Silvy (ca. 1680) "nit'abik8ahimitisan, *j'enfile des porcelaines*" see | *tāp compare | *tāpisiko, *tāpiš

*tāpisiko

INITIAL

— pass a line through a hole, thread

evidence | WC tāpisikonam, *to fit sth all around sth by hand;* MC tāpisikohimīkisew, *to thread beads;* AT (Wemotaci, Nicole Petiquay & Opitciwan, Joey Awashish) tapisikoham [tāpizikoham], *to thread sth;* SEC tāpisikoham, *to thread sth* see | *tāp compare | *tāpiko, *tāpiš

*tāpiš

INITIAL

— thread

evidence | PC tāpisahwēw, *to thread sth;* WC tāpisaham, *to thread sth;* MC tāpišaham, *to thread sth;* AT (Wemotaci, Nicole Petiquay) tapicaham [tāpiʒaham], *to thread sth;* SEC tāpišahwew, *to thread sth* see | *tāp compare | *tāpiko, *tāpisiko

*tāpiškōt (~ *tāpiškōc)

INITIAL

— alike

evidence | PC tāpiskōtastāw, *to duplicate sth;* MC tāpiskōc, *both, equally; alike, similarly;* AT (Wemotaci, Jeannette Coocoo) tapickotc [tāpiškōc], *same, alike; together, collectively;* SEC tāpiškoc, *both, equally; alike, similarly;* NEC tāpishkutāyimāu, *to feel the same about them;* EI (Mamit) tapishkut [tāpɨhkūt], *in the same way, identically;* Watkins (1865) "Tabiskootāyimāo, *v.t.an. He compares him or them, he likens them;*" Silvy (ca. 1680) "tetabisk8ch nip8ets, *ils meurent ensemble, en même temps*" | ANISH daabishkoo, *for example; alike* (Livesay & Nichols, 2021); Cuoq (1886) "Tabickotc = Tabiskotc, *égal, pareil, également, ensemble, l'un comme l'autre*" see | *tāp

*tāpitaw

INITIAL

— evenly, equally

evidence | PC tāpitawāw, *to be even;* MC tāpitawāskweyāw, *to be an expanse of trees of equal height;* SEC tāpitawaskamikāw, *to be level ground;* Watkins (1865) "Tapitowināo, *v.t.an. He equals him;*" Silvy (ca. 1680) "tabitau nip8ets, *ils meurent ensemble, en même temps*" | ANISH daabida, *alike; identical; the same* (Livesay & Nichols, 2021) see | *tāp

*tāpwē

INITIAL (VERB, ANIMATE, INTRANSITIVE)

— tell the truth

evidence | PC tāpwēwakēyimēw, *to believe in sb;* MC tāpwemew, *to tell the truth about sb;* SEC tāpwemakan, *to be true;* EI (Sheshatshiu) tapueu [tāpwēw], *to tell the truth, to be correct;* Watkins (1865) "Tāpw'ātowāo, *v.t.an. He believes him, he consents to him, he yields to him, he obeys him;*" Laure (ca. 1726) "ni-tapueieriten, *je suis persuadé, certain;*" Silvy (ca. 1680) "tap8e, *assurément*" see | *tāp, *wē[1]

*tāš

INITIAL

— whet, sharpen

evidence | PC tāsahikan, *whetstone;* MC tāšipotāw, *to sharpen sth;* SEC tāšaham, *to whet sth* discussion | The absence of a preaspiration on the sibilant cannot be confirmed due to the lack of an Atikamekw cognate.

*tāšk

INITIAL

— split

evidence | PC tāskipayiw, *to split;* MC tāškaham, *to split sth;* SEC tāšcišam, *to split sth with a blade;* Silvy (ca. 1680) "tachkarasitan, *fourchure du pied de l'orignal*"

*tāštak

INITIAL

— unenthused, reluctant, loath

evidence | MC tāštakācīw, *to be loath, reluctant;* tāštakātam, *to be loath or reluctant to do sth;* SEC tāštakāteyihtam, *to be unenthused about sth;* EI (Sheshatshiu) tashtakatamᵘ [tāstəkātəm], *to be reluctant to undertake sth, to have no energy for sth;* Silvy (ca. 1680) "ni tachtagȣtan 3. -eȣ, *je trouve qu'il y a loin, marchent*" | MENO ta·qtakacew, *to be unwilling; to refuse*

*tāto (~ *tātw)

INITIAL

— tear or burst open

evidence | PC tātoskam, *to tear sth with one's foot;* MC tātopitam, *to tear sth;* SEC tātošam, *to cut sth open;* Laure (ca. 1726) "tatupariu (mitchi), *crevé (apostume)*" | ANISH daadode, *to split open from heat* (Livesay & Nichols, 2021); MENO ta·tosam, *to cut sth open;* MESK tātwineshiwēshinwa, *to fall and tear one's testicles* origin | PA ***tāto**

*tāw[1]

INITIAL

— centered on, middle of

evidence | PC tāwaham, *to hit a target;* MC tāwiškam, *to step right on it;* SEC tāwištikwānehwew, *to hit sb right on the head;* WI (Pessamit) tautukaneueu [tāwtəkənēwēw], *to hit sb right on the hip with a projectile or blow* | MENO na·wikamek, *at the center of the lodge* origin | PA ***θāw** (Aubin, 1975; Hewson, 1993)

*tāw[2]

INITIAL

— open

evidence | PC tāwatinēw, *to open sb's mouth by hand;* MC tāwatihkwāmiw, *to sleep with one's mouth open;* WI (Pessamit) tautu [tāwtu], *to open one's mouth;* Laure (ca. 1726) "ni-tauatin 3. -tiu, *j'ai la bouche béante;*" Silvy (ca. 1680) "ni taȣatin, *j'ouvre la bouche*" | ANISH daawani, *to open one's mouth* (Livesay & Nichols, 2021) origin | PA ***tāw** (Hewson, 1993) limited to | *at[4] compare | *taw

*tē[1] (~ *ıhtē)

INITIAL (VERB, ANIMATE, INTRANSITIVE)

— **1** be (in a certain location)

— **2** have

limited to | *r, *t[6] evidence | [1]PC ihtāw, *to be there;* MC tāw, *to be present;* SEC (Eastmain) tew, *to be present;* SEC (Waswanipi) tāw, *to be present;* WI (Pessamit) teu [tēw], *to be present;* EI tāu [tāw], *to be present;* Laure (ca. 1726) "enagam teu, *il est en deçà du fleuve;*" cf. MC matew, *to not be present* [2]AT (Opitciwan, Joey Awashish) tatam [tatam] & tarew [tarēw], *to have sth or sb in one's possession;* NEC ihtitim & ihtiyāu, *to keep sth or sb there, to have sth or sb available;* EI (Sheshatshiu) tatamᵘ [tətəm], taneu [tənēw], *to place or put sth away in a container;* Laure (ca. 1726) "nit-itaten, nit-itatau, *j'ai;*" Silvy (ca. 1680) "ni titaten, 3. -tim, *j'ai qqch;*" "ni titatau, *nob. j'ai qqch.;*" "ni titatȣau, ni titatamaȣau, *j'ai qqch pour lui*" | [1]MENO tɛ·w AI, *to exist, to be on hand, to be one* [2]MENO tana·m, neta·htanan, *TI to have sth, to have sth on hand;* tanɛ·w, ɛ·htanacen *TA to have sb, to have sb on hand; to maintain sb, to keep sb, to own sb* compare | *ayā, *tako[2]

***tē²**

FINAL (VERB, INANIMATE, INTRANSITIVE, ABSTRACT)

sound change | 1. ē → ā 2. m → h

— conveys the semantic role of patient or theme to a participant

evidence | PC akihtēw, *to be counted;* MC itāpihkātew, *be tied thus;* SEC nakwātew, *to be snared* paired with | *so¹

***tē³ (~ *ɩtē)**

FINAL (VERB, INANIMATE, INTRANSITIVE, ABSTRACT)

sound change | ē → a

— forms stative verbs

evidence | PC cimatēw, *to stand upright, to be erected;* WC asiwatīw, *to be in a container;* MC aštew, *sits;* SEC akotew, *hangs* paired with | *ɩso²

***tē⁴ (~ *ɩtē)**

FINAL (VERB, INANIMATE, INTRANSITIVE, CONCRETE)

sound change | ē → a

— heat

evidence | PC mēstitēw, *to have boiled away;* MC kišitew, *be hot;* SEC atihtew, *to be dyed, to be ripe;* Laure (ca. 1726) "tchiueteu, *le fruit fait du bruit, la pomme en cuisant fait du bruit;*" Fabvre (ca. 1690) "M8cha8ask8te8, *ou le feu a brulé Les arbres;*" Silvy (ca. 1680) "aba8ite8, *cela est dégelé*" | ANISH gizhaawangide, *to be hot sand* (Livesay & Nichols, 2021); MENO atɛ·htɛw II, *to be dyed, colored, ripe* origin | PA ***(e)tē** (Aubin, 1975) paired with | *so²

***tēh¹**

INITIAL (NOUN, DEPENDENT INANIMATE)

— heart

evidence | PC mitēha, *hearts;* MC otehāspinew, *to have heart disease;* AT oteha:pow, *soup made with the heart of a moose* (Béland, 1978); SEC otehīmin, *strawberry;* EI (Unaman-shipit) uteiakᵘ [utējākʷ], *a porcupine heart;* Laure (ca. 1726) "nithaih, *mon cœur;*" Silvy (ca. 1680) "8tehibak, *le cœur du pétun;*" "nitehik, *dans mon cœur*" see | *tēh²

***tēh²**

MEDIAL, FINAL (NOUN INCORPORATION)

— **1** heart

— **2** having such a character, -hearted

evidence | PC sōhkitēhēw, *to be brave;* MC wīlilotehew, *to have a fatty heart;* SEC miyotehew, *to be good-hearted;* Laure (ca. 1726) "ni-kuikuikutehan, *le cœur me palpite;*" "miruthaih, *bon cœur*" | ANISH zhaagode'e, *to be cowardly* (Livesay & Nichols, 2021); MESK ahkwitēhēwa, *to have one's thought go so far* see | *tēh¹

***tēht (~ *tēhš)**

INITIAL

— on

evidence | PC tēhcikāpawiw, *to stand on sth;* MC tehtapiw, *sit on;* AT teššipita:kan, *rack for drying meat* (Béland, 1978); SEC tehtāpiskapiw, *to sit on top of rock;* tešipitākan, *a platform used as a cache;* EI (Sheshatshiu) teshipitakan [tēʃɨpɨtākən], *a storage platform* | ANISH desabi, *to sit on a raised surface* (Livesay & Nichols, 2021); MENO tɛ·hna·hkwahekan, *a shelf or set of shelves* origin | PA ***tēhθ**

***tēhtakohsiw**

INITIAL (NOUN, DEPENDENT ANIMATE)

— kidney

evidence | MC otehtakosiwaya, *one's kidney(s);* AT (Wemotaci, Nicole Petiquay) otetakosiw [otēhtakossiw], *a kidney;* SEC otehtakosiw, *a kidney;* WI (Pessamit) utetakushua [utētəkuʃù], *one's kidney(s);* EI (Unaman-shipit) utetakushu [utētakuhu], *a kidney;* EI (Sheshatshiu) utetakushu [utētəkuʃu], *a kidney;* Laure (ca. 1726) "tétiguchiu, *rognon*" | ANISH Cuoq (1886) "Nind itikosing nind akos, *j'ai mal aux reins*"

*tēhtēw

INITIAL (NOUN, ANIMATE)

— frog, excluding toads and chorus frogs

evidence | MC tehtew, *a frog, excluding toads and chorus frogs;* AT tetew [tēhtēw], *a green frog;* SEC tehtew, *a frog, excluding toads and chorus frogs;* EI (Sheshatshiu) teteu [tētēw], *a type of frog;* Silvy (ca. 1680) "tete8, *espèce de grosse grenouille*" | MENO tɛ·htɛw, *bullfrog*

*tēkaht (~ *tēkahš)

INITIAL

— complete(ly)

evidence | AT (Wemotaci, Jeannette Coocoo) tekaci [tēkašši], *completely;* SEC tekaš, *thoroughly;* NEC tākihtiham, *to fit all the way into sth;* WI (Pessamit) tekashieu [tēkəʃjēw], *to kill them all;* EI (Sheshatshiu) tekatipeu [tēkātipēw], *the tide is at its maximum level;* Watkins (1865) "Tākusow, *v.imp. It is complete;*" "Tākutustow, *v.t.in.2. He completes the line (as in writing);*" Silvy (ca. 1680) "tegatibeu, *la mer est pleine;*" "ni tegat8an, *j'ai achevé mon discours*"

*tēko (~ *tēkw)

INITIAL

— choke on

evidence | MC tekotāmew, *to aspirate and choke on sth;* SEC tekosimow, *to choke on a liquid;* NEC tākuhtim, *to choke on sth;* WI (Pessamit) tekushipimeu [tēkuʃəpmēw], *to choke on grease* | MENO nɛ·kwahtam, *to choke in water* origin | PA ***θēk** (Hewson, 1993)

*tēp

INITIAL

— adequate, sufficient

evidence | PC tēpipayiw, *to have enough;* MC tepihkahtew, *to be cooked enough;* SEC tepaceyihtākosiw, *to be consider fit or suitable;* Laure (ca. 1726) "ni-tepamesan, *je suis soûl, las de poisson;*" Fabvre (ca. 1690) "Tepachitan e8, *aur assez de sapin pr La Cabane*" | MENO tɛ·paqtɛw, *to be there in sufficient quantity*

*tēraniy

INITIAL (NOUN, DEPENDENT INANIMATE)

— tongue

evidence | PC mitēyaniyāpiy, *a tongue string;* WC mitīðaniy, *a tongue;* MC otelalīwan, *to have a pan, speaking of a trap;* WI (Pessamit) utenni [utēlnī], *a tongue;* EI (Unaman-shipit) utenniuashkᵘ [utēnīwahkʷ], *a bear tongue;* Fabvre (ca. 1690) "Mittelin v. mittelini, *Langue, Lingua mea*" | ANISH gidenaniw, *your tongue* (Livesay & Nichols, 2021) see | *tēranīw

*tēranīw

MEDIAL (NOUN INCORPORATION)

— tongue

evidence | PC sakamotēyanīwēw, *to mumble;* MC tāškitelalīwew, *to have a forked tongue;* SEC sāciteyanīwew, *to stick one's tongue out;* Laure (ca. 1726) "ni-piratsiteraniuan, *j'ai la langue écorchée;*" Silvy (ca. 1680) "ni tag8terini8an 3. -e8, *je bégaie, j'ai la langue attachée*" | ANISH baagidenaniwe, *to have a swollen tongue* (Livesay & Nichols, 2021) see | *tēraniy[1]

*tērikom

INITIAL (NOUN, DEPENDENT ANIMATE)

— nostril

evidence | PC mitēyikom, *a nostril;* WSC (Misipawistik, Ellen Cook) nitēnikom, *my mucus;* MC otelikoma, *one's nostrils; one's snots;* SEC niteyikomac, *my nostrils;* EI (Sheshatshiu) utenikuma [utēnukuma], *one's nostril(s);* Silvy (ca. 1680) "miterig8, miterig8m, *ma narine*" | ANISH odenigoman, *one's nostril* (Livesay & Nichols, 2021) see | *ērikw[2] compare | *ērikw[1], *skēkom discussion | The form of this root and its associated medials ***ērikom** and ***ērikw** suggest a Pre-Cree form, ***ērikw**. Any association with the homophonous ***ērikw**, perhaps by the comparison of nasal hair to the filamentous appearance of ants, must remain conjecture given the state of the comparative evidence.

*tēštak

INITIAL

— position unevenly (with one end or side higher than the other)

evidence | WC tastakiskwīðiw, *to hold one's head up;* MC teštakakotew, *hang unevenly;* SEC teštacišimew, *to lie sb down with trunk elevated;* NEC tāstichiskwāyiu, *to put one's head back;* WI (Pessamit) teshtatshishinu [tēstətʃʃənu] *to lie with trunk raised;* EI (Sheshatshiu) teshtakakutin [tēstəkukūtn], *front end of canoe is raised* | ANISH tetagā, *sloped* (McGregor, 2004); Cuoq (1886) "tetakicin, *être demi-couché, être presque assis sur son lit*" origin | PA ***tēʔtak** compare | *taštas discussion | The short-voweled reflex used in WC appears to have been influenced by ***taštas**.

*tētip (~ *tētipā)

INITIAL

— around

evidence | PC tētipēwēw, *to go round;* MC tetipāhtew, *to walk around the perimeter;* SEC tetipaham, *to paddle around;* WI (Pessamit) tetipatauat [tētəpətāwt], *around the perimeter of a hill*

*tēw

INITIAL

— ache

evidence | PC tēwipitonēw, *to have aching arms;* WC tīyistikwāniw, *to have a headache;* MC tewištikwānew, *have a headache;* SEC tewitihcew, *to have an ache in one's hands;* WI (Pessamit) teiaueu [tējwēw], *to cause pain by hitting sb with a projectile;* Silvy (ca. 1680) "ni teït8ganin, *je suis éhanché*" | ANISH dewizi, *to ache* (Livesay & Nichols, 2021); MENO tɛ·wɛhkow, *to have a headache*

*tēwē

INITIAL (VERB, ANIMATE, INTRANSITIVE)

— be loud

evidence | WSC (Misipawistik, Ellen Cook) tēwēhikan, *a hand drum;* MC tewehikan, *drum;* AT (Wemotaci, Jeannette Coocoo) tewesekahikan [tēwēssēkahikan], *a bell;* SEC tewehikew, *to play the drum;* Laure (ca. 1726) "ni-teueiabegahigan, *je joue du violon;*" Silvy (ca. 1680) "ni te8an, *j'ai grosse voix*" | ANISH dewe'igan, *a drum* (Livesay & Nichols, 2021); MENO tɛ·wɛ·hekan AN, *drum;* MESK tēwēhikana, *a drum*

*tihc

MEDIAL (NOUN INCORPORATION)

— hand

evidence | PC kinocihcān, *middle finger;* MC apwecihcew, *have sweaty hands;* SEC tewitihcew, *to have an ache in one's hands;* Laure (ca. 1726) "ni-pitikutitcherin 3. -iu, *je ferme la main;*" Silvy (ca. 1680) "ni matchititchan, *j'ai de laides mains*" | ABEN gezilja, *to wash one's hands* (Day, 1994); ANISH wiinininjii, *to have dirty hands* (Livesay & Nichols, 2021); MESK kesīnechēwa, *to wash one's hands* see | *tihciy[1], *tihciy[2]

*tihcikan

INITIAL (NOUN, DEPENDENT INANIMATE)

— pectoral fin

evidence | WSC (Misipawistik, Ellen Cook) ocihcikan, *a fish fin;* SEC otihcikan, *its fin;* EI (Ekuanitshit) utitshikanamesh [utītʃakanamēh], *pectoral fin of a fish;* Laure (ca. 1726) "utitchigan, utitsigan, *aileron de poisson*" | ANISH oninjigan, *its fin, speaking of a fish (especially a pectoral fin); its pincer, speaking of a crayfish* (Livesay & Nichols, 2021); MENO onɛ·hcikan, *its fin, speaking of a fish*

*tihciy[1]

INITIAL (NOUN, DEPENDENT INANIMATE)

— hand

evidence | MC ocihcīw, *to have hands;* SEC otihcīkan, *a hand bone;* WI (Pessamit) utitshiak[u] [utətʃījāk[w]], *front paw of a porcupine;* Silvy (ca. 1680) "mititchi, *main*" origin | PA ***θency** (Aubin, 1975; Hewson, 1993) see | *tihc, *tihciy[2]

*tihciy[2]

FINAL (NOUN INCORPORATION)

— hand

evidence | MC itohikanicihciy, *index finger;* SEC nahīwinitihciy, *right hand;* WI (Pessamit) ukunititshi [ukwəntətʃī], *knitted wristband* see | *tihc, *tihciy[1]

*tihk[1]

INITIAL

— melt

evidence | PC tihkāpiskisam, *to melt a metal;* MC tihkisow, *melt;* SEC tihcisam, *to melt sth;* WI (Pessamit) titshiu [tətʃīw], *snowing wet and sticky snow;* Silvy (ca. 1680) "tititeu, *il fond, v.g. le plomb*" | ANISH ningide, *melt* (Livesay & Nichols, 2021); MESK neketēwi, *to melt* origin | PA ***θenk** (Aubin, 1975)

*tihk[2]

INITIAL

— be on cradleboard

evidence | PC tihkinākan, *cradleboard;* MC tihkinākan, *cradleboard;* AT tikinew [tihkinew], *to put sb on a cradleboard;* SEC tihcinākan, *cradleboard* | ANISH dikinaagan, *a cradle board* (Livesay & Nichols, 2021); MENO tɛhke·w AI, *to be on a cradleboard, speaking of an infant;* MESK tehkinēwa, *to put sb on a cradle-board* origin | PA ***tehk** (Hewson, 1993)

*tihko[1]

INITIAL (NOUN, DEPENDENT INANIMATE)

— armpit

evidence | PC otihkōkan, *one's armpit;* MC otihkōkan, *one's armpit;* NEC utihkui, *one's armpit;* WI (Pessamit) utikuai [utəkwī], *one's armpit;* EI (Unaman-shipit) utik[u] [utīhk[w]], *one's armpit;* EI (Sheshatshiu) utihkuai [utīkwī], *one's armpit;* Laure (ca. 1726) "uitikui, *son aiselle;*" Silvy (ca. 1680) "nitik8i, nitik8khi, *mon aiselle*" | ANISH gining, *your armpit* (Livesay & Nichols, 2021) origin | PA ***θenko** (***meθenkwi**, Aubin, 1975) see | *tihko[2]

*tihko[2] (~ *tihkw)

MEDIAL (NOUN INCORPORATION)

— armpit

evidence | SEC sīhtawitihkwāhtam, *to take sth by one's armpit;* Silvy (ca. 1680) "ni miritik8n, *je suis velu sous les aisselles;*" "ni tak8tik8amau, *je le porte sous l'aisselle*" see | *tihko[1]

*tihkom (~ *ıhkom)

MEDIAL, FINAL (NOUN INCORPORATION)

— lice

evidence | PC atimotihkom, *woodtick;* WC nōtihkomīw, *to check for lice;* MC nōtihkomew, *to pick lice;* SEC mwākotihkom, *water strider;* EI (Unaman-shipit) natutikumateu [natawtīkumātēw], *to check sb for lice;* Laure (ca. 1726) "tchitachutikumachin, *tu me donnes des poux*" origin | Old Cree **otihkomahi** see | *ıhkw[1] compare | *ıhkw[2]

*tihkwatim

INITIAL (NOUN, DEPENDENT ANIMATE)

— **1** cross-nephew

— **2** son-in-law

evidence | PC otihkwatimimāw, *a nephew; a son-in-law;* WC mitīhkwatim, *a nephew, specifically a man's sister's son or a woman's brother's son;* EI (Unaman-shipit) utikutima [utīkwatɨma], *one's son-in-law;* Watkins (1865) "Mitikwutimimow, *n.an. A nephew (i.e., a sister's son), a step-son;*" Silvy (ca. 1680) "nitik8atim, nitik8a *voc., mon neveu*" | ANISH oningwanisan, *one's cross-nephew* (Livesay & Nichols, 2021); MENO nenɛ·hkwanɛh, *my sister's son (man speaking), my brother's son (woman speaking);* MIAMI kilenkwala, *your son-in-law* (ILDA, 2017) origin | PA ***θenkwaθ** (Aubin, 1975) compare | *štim¹, *tōšim

*tihp¹

INITIAL (NOUN, DEPENDENT INANIMATE)

— brain

evidence | ESC (Fort Severn) otihp, *penis;* SEC otihp, *a brain;* WI (Pessamit) utipapui [utəpāpwī], *boiled mixture of caribou brain, water and grease used to tan hides;* EI (Unaman-shipit) utipakᵘ [utīpākʷ], *a porcupine brain;* Watkins (1865) "Ootìp, *n.in. The brain;*" Laure (ca. 1726) "nitip, *mon cerveau;*" Silvy (ca. 1680) "mitip, *cervelle*" origin | PA ***temp** (***wetempi**, Aubin, 1975) see | *tihp² discussion | Reflexes of an alternative form reconstructible as ***īritihp** is used in all dialects south and west of SEC. However, the medial forms in these dialects do not feature the intrusive initial syllable. Instead, they are cognates of the medial forms used in eastern dialects. The alternative form with the intrusive first syllable is therefore likely an early borrowing from neighbouring Anishinabe dialects.

*tihp² (~ *ātihp)

MEDIAL, FINAL (NOUN INCORPORATION)

— **1** brain

— **2** head

evidence | ¹AT notipew [nōtihpēw], *to eat brains;* SEC šišonitihpātew, *to rub brains on sth;* nōtihpew, *to eat brains* ²PC paskwātihpēw, *to be bald;* ESC paškwātihp, *a bald man;* MC pasātihpehwew, *to slap or pat sb on the top of the head;* AT mikwatipew [mihkwātihpēw], *to have red hair;* SEC wāšeyātihpew, *to be bald* see | *tihp¹

*tihs

MEDIAL (NOUN INCORPORATION)

— **1** navel

— **2** gizzard

evidence | MC manitiseświew, *to cut out sb's gizzard;* SEC pīhtawitisān, *inner lining of a gizzard;* WI (Pessamit) miliutisheu [məlīwtəʃēw], *to have an abscess in one's navel;* EI (Sheshatshiu) manitisheshueu [məntəʃēʃwēw], *to cut out sb's gizzard* see | *tihsiy

*tihsiy

INITIAL (NOUN, DEPENDENT INANIMATE)

— **1** navel

— **2** gizzard

evidence | PC mitisiyēyāpiy, *an umbilical cord;* MC otisiy, *one's navel or gizzard;* otisiyāpiy, *an umbilical cord;* otisīhkān, *a turnip;* AT (Opitciwan, Joey Awashish & Wemotaci, Nicole Petiquay) otisi [otissiy], *one's navel; one's gizzard;* otissiy, *umbilical cord* (Béland, 1978); SEC otisiy, *a gizzard; a navel;* EI (Sheshatshiu) utishishk [utəʃīʃk], *a goose gizzard;* Laure (ca. 1726) "nitisi, *mon nombril;*" "utichi, *gesier d'oiseau*" | ANISH odis, *one's navel or umbilical cord* (Livesay & Nichols, 2021); Cuoq (1886) "Pine o tising, *dans le gésier de la perdrix*" see | *tihs

*tihšiw¹

INITIAL (NOUN, DEPENDENT ANIMATE)

— testicle

evidence | PC mitisoway, *testicle, scrotum;* MC otišiweyāpiy, *one's vas deference;* AT ocišśiwiy, *dIN testicles* (Béland, 1978); SEC nitišiwac, *my testicles;* NEC utishiuh, *one's testicles;* Silvy (ca. 1680) "nitichi8, *f. testiculus meus*" | ANISH onishiwan, *one's testicle* (Livesay & Nichols, 2021); MESK oneshiwahi, *his testicles;* MIAMI kilehšia, *your testicle* (ILDA, 2017) origin | PA ***θeʔšiw** (Aubin, 1975) see | *tihšiw²

***tihšiw**[2]

MEDIAL (NOUN INCORPORATION)

— testicles

evidence | AT -cišsiw-, *testicles* (Béland, 1978); SEC tewitišiwew, *to have a testicular ache;* Watkins (1865) "Munitisāswāo, *v.t.an. He castrates him*" | MENO mi·heneqsewɛw, *to have filthy testicles;* MESK tātwineshiwēshinwa, *to fall and tear one's testicles* see | *tihšiw[1]

***tiht**[1] **(~ *tihš)**

FINAL (VERB, TRANSITIVE, ANIMATE, ABSTRACT)

sound change | ē → ā

— adds a benefactive argument when suffixed to animate intransitive verb stems, but can also be suffixed redundantly to transitive animate verb themes consisting of the benefactive final *aw

evidence | PC Lacombe (1874) "atāwātittew, atāwestamāwew, ou, atāwestawew, *il achète pou lui, en sa place, en sa favour;*" Laure (ca. 1726) "nit-atauatitau, *je traite pour lui;*" "ni-tchimuttitamauatitau, *je pille pour lui;*" Silvy (ca. 1680) "n'8tabatitau, *je traîne pour lui;*" "ni t8tama8atitau, *je parle pour lui*" | ANISH Cuoq (1886) "Nind agatawanisak, *j'ai honte pour eux;*" "Kijikamaw = kijikamawanic, *paie pour lui;*" MIAMI "Nimant8acarissa, *je prie pour luy*" (Largillier - ILDA, 2017) origin | PA ***θehθ** paired with | *tiht[2] compare | *ıštaw discussion | This final is either obsolete or nonproductive in contemporary dialects, having been replaced by ***ıštaw**.

***tiht**[2] **(~ *tihc)**

FINAL (VERB, TRANSITIVE, INANIMATE, ABSTRACT)

sound change | ē → ā

— adds a benefactive argument when suffixed to animate intransitive verb stems, but can also be suffixed redundantly to transitive animate verb themes consisting of the benefactive final *aw

evidence | WI (Pessamit) atautitamueu [tāwtətəmwēw], *to make a sale for sb;* cf. PC itwēstamawātam, *to translate sth;* SEC itweštamawātam, *to interpret it, to serve as interpreter for sth;* NEC uhtinimuwaatim, *to provide sth for sth* origin | PA ***θeht** paired with | *tiht[1] compare | *ıšt[3] discussion | This final is either obsolete or nonproductive in contemporary dialects, having been replaced by ***ıšt**. Examples drawn from PC, SEC, and NEC likely contain a contracted form of this root. Regarding the redundancy of applying this final to the benefactive VTA ***aw**, compare MC *itweštam* and SEC *itweštamawātam*, both meaning "to serve as interpreter for sth."

***tihtawāw**

INITIAL (NOUN, DEPENDENT ANIMATE)

— parent of one's son-in-law or daughter-in-law

evidence | PC Lacombe (1874) "N'tittāwa, N'tittāwok, Ot'ittāwa, *disent les hommes et les femmes entr'eux, ou les hommes entr'eux et les femmes entr'elles, quand leurs enfants sont mariés ensemble;*" WC (Stanley Mission, Solomon Ratt) otihtāwāwa, *one's co-parent-in-law;* cf. WSC (Misipawistik, Ellen Cook) ocicāwiya, *the parent-in-law of one's child;* Fabvre (ca. 1690) "Tită8ach, *Peres ou m(eres) des mariés*" | ANISH nindindawaa, *my fellow parent-in-law* (Lippert & Gambill, 2023); Fabvre (ca. 1690) "*Alg.* Tinta8ach, *le p(ere), La m(ere), de mon g(en)dre, de ma bru;*" Cuoq (1886) "Nind indawak, *le père et la mère de mon gendre, de ma bru;*" MENO netɛ·htawa·w, *parent of my son-in-law or daughter-in-law* origin | PA ***tentawāw**

***tihtiman**[1]

INITIAL (NOUN, DEPENDENT INANIMATE)

— shoulder

evidence | PC mitihtiman, *a shoulder;* MC otihtimaniw, *to have shoulders;* SEC nitihtimanikan, *my humerus;* Laure (ca. 1726) "utitiman, *son épaule*" see | *tihtiman[2]

*tihtiman[2]

MEDIAL, FINAL (NOUN INCORPORATION)

— shoulder

evidence | PC kaskitihtimanesin, *to break one's shoulder in a fall;* MC alakaškitihtimanew, *to have broad shoulders;* SEC ohpitihtimaneyiw, *to shrug;* Laure (ca. 1726) "ni-pikutitimanesun, *je me brûle l'épaule*" see | *tihtiman[1]

*tihtip

INITIAL

— roll

evidence | PC tihtipipayihow, *to roll oneself;* MC tīhtipahpitam, *to swathe sth;* SEC tihtipipayiw, *to roll;* WI (Pessamit) titipashu [tətəpāʃu], *to be rolled by the wind;* EI (Ekuanitshit) titipiu [tītɨpīw], *to roll oneself;* Silvy (ca. 1680) "ni titipititan, 3. -tau, *j'en tortille, j'environne, v.g. la toupie*" | ANISH ditibibide, *rolls* (Livesay & Nichols, 2021); MENO tetɛ·qtepaha·n, *barrel*

*tim

INITIAL

— deep water (or other substance)

evidence | PC timīw, *to be deep water;* MC timīw, *to be deep water;* NEC timitin, *to be deep (thick) ice;* WI (Pessamit) timakunakau [təmākunəkāw], *to be deep snow* | ANISH dimibiiyaa, *to be deep slush* (Livesay & Nichols, 2021); MENO temi·w II, *to be deep* origin | PA ***tem** (Hewson, 1993)

*tin

FINAL (VERB, INANIMATE, INTRANSITIVE, CONCRETE)

— wind blows

evidence | WC nahitin, *favorable wind;* MC lōtin, *wind blows;* SEC cīwetin, *north wind;* NEC mushāwātin, *to be an offshore wind;* Watkins (1865) "poonetin, *The wind ceases*" compare | *štin[3]

*tināštan (~ *tināštah)

FINAL (VERB, INANIMATE, INTRANSITIVE, CONCRETE)

— navigable stretch of river

evidence | PC Lacombe (1874) "pitchitināstan, *(v.imp.) longue vue dans une rivière;*" MC kā kinotināštahk, *place name, literally "long stretch of river;"* (Bishop, 2022); SEC kā cinotināštahc, *place name, literally "long stretch of river;"* (Bishop, 2022); WI (Pessamit) pitshitinashtan, *to be a river that is navigable in a straight line for a long distance;* Silvy (ca. 1680) "k8eïask8tinastan, *cela va droit;*" cf. Watkins (1865) "tinastun, *n.in. A traverse, a reach (i.e. the distance between two points in a river;*" "tinastunewun, *v.imp. It is a reach*" see | *štan[2] discussion | The entry cited in Watkins (1865) suggests the above final may have been derived from a verb stem. However, in the absence of any corroborative evidence, it is possible Watkins misinterpreted this verb final as an independent noun.

*tiniy

INITIAL (NOUN, DEPENDENT INANIMATE)

— nipple

evidence | Watkins (1865) "Mittine, *n.an. The female breast;*" Fabvre (ca. 1690) "Mitini *pl* nia, *mamelle, mamilla;*" "8tinia, *b8ton ou mamelle d'home, de masle;*" "Tini *pl* tinia, *mamelle d(')home, son b8ton v.* t8t8s, *mamelle de femme;*" Silvy (ca. 1680) "8tinia, *mamelle ou bouton de l'homme*" discussion | Despite being corroborated by Watkins (1865), this root appears to have become obsolete in all contemporary dialects. Note that Faries and Mackay's work (1938) does not include the word, despite being largely based on Watkins' dictionary.

*tip

INITIAL

— to determine or provide measure or equivalence

evidence | PC tipāpēskōhēw, *to weigh sb;* Lacombe (1874) "Tipahwew, *il le mesure, il le paye tant;*" MC tipācimowin, *story or news;* AT tipahaskew, *survey land;* SEC tipaham, *to pay for sth;* WI tipishitateu [təpəʃətātēw], *measure sb using one's feet*

*tipān

INITIAL

— apart

evidence | PC tipān, *apart;* MC tipānalew, *to place sb separately;* AT tipaniwetakon [tipānwehtākon], *to be a verb conjugated in the independent order;* WI (Pessamit) tipanishiu [təpānəʃīw], *to be distinct, apart;* Laure (ca. 1726) "ni-tetipaninauets, *je les éparpille, je les sépare (eux)*" compare | *pahkān

*tipinaw

INITIAL

— shelter from the wind

evidence | PC tipinawaham, *to shelter sth from the wind;* MC tipinawāw, *to be a place sheltered from the wind;* SEC tipinawišimow, *to take shelter from the wind;* Laure (ca. 1726) "tipinauaünikan, *abri*"

*tipisk

INITIAL

— dark sky, night

evidence | PC tipiskohk, *last night;* MC tipiskāw, *to be night;* SEC tipisci-pīsim[w], *moon;* WI (Pessamit) tipishkau [təpəʃkāw], *to be night;* Laure (ca. 1726) "tibiskabateu uasku, *le ciel est caché par une épaisse fumée;*" Silvy (ca. 1680) "ni tibisk8tan 3. -te8, *je marche la nuit, je couche en chemin*"

*tipiskw

MEDIAL, FINAL

— night

evidence | PC kanawitipiskwēw, *to watch all night;* SEC nīšotipiskwew, *to be gone for two nights;* WI (Pessamit) pakunu-tipishk[u] [pukunūtəpəʃk[w]], *in total darkness;* Laure (ca. 1726) "niskan-tibiskuetanu, *il a plu toute la nuit;*" "ni-niskantibiskue-kuamin 3. -miu, *je dors toute la nuit*" see | *tipisk, *w[1]

*tipiškōt (~ *tipiškōc)

INITIAL

— directly in front or above

evidence | PC (Maskwacīs, Rosie Roan) tipiskōc, *opposite, parallel; directly overhead;* MC tipiškōc, *vis-à-vis, directly in front or above, opposite;* NEC tipishkutishim, *to cut sth directly across at a right angle;* EI (Sheshatshiu) tipishkut [tɨpɨʃkūt], *right in front; right above* | ANISH dibishkoodagaam, *directly across the water* (Livesay & Nichols, 2021)

*tiriy

INITIAL (NOUN, DEPENDENT INANIMATE)

— shoulder blade

evidence | WC mitiðiy, *a shoulder blade;* MC otilīkekan, *one's shoulder blade (the bone only);* EI (Sheshatshiu) utinikan [utnīkən], *a shoulder blade;* Silvy (ca. 1680) "mitiri, *os de l'épaule*"

*tisp

INITIAL

— dissolve or disintegrate in water

evidence | ESC (Severn) tispaham, *to stir sth;* MC tispaham, *to dissolve sth into a liquid;* tispāpāwew, *to dissolve, to leach;* tispipaliw, *to dissolve;* tispakohtitāw, *to soak sth to soften it* | ANISH dipaabaawadoon, *to moisten sth, to get sth wet* (Livesay & Nichols, 2021)

*tišah

FINAL (VERB, TRANSITIVE, INANIMATE, DERIVED)

— send, drive away, chase in a particular direction

evidence | PC sipwētisaham, *to send sth away;* MC išicišaham, *to send sth thither;* SEC cīwetišaham, *to send sth back* see | *ıtiš, *ah paired with | *tišahw

*tišahw

FINAL (VERB, TRANSITIVE, ANIMATE, DERIVED)

— send, drive away, chase in a particular direction

evidence | PC sipwētisahwēw, *to send sb away;* MC išicišahwew, *to send sb thither;*

AT a:ttiketišahw-, *to chase sb out of the house* (Béland, 1978); SEC cīwetišahwew, *to send sb back;* WI (Pessamit) maitishaueu [mājttʃwēw], *to send sb downstream;* Laure (ca. 1726) "ni-urauitichauauets, *je fais sortir de la cabane les chiens;*" "ni-miuitissauauets, *je brouille ensemble les amis*" | ANISH izhinizha', *to send sb thither* (Livesay & Nichols, 2021); MIAMI "Nitaïc8arechihag8a, *il m'a poursuivy jusqu'au bout. Metaph. il m'a fait couper, m'ayant interrogé qu'il a decouvert mon mensonge*" (Largillier - ILDA, 2017) see | *ɪtiš, *ahw paired with | *tišah

*tiši

FINAL (VERB, ANIMATE, INTRANSITIVE, DERIVED)

— flee in a particular direction

evidence | MC pecicišiw, *to flee hither;* Silvy (ca. 1680) "ni ki8etichin, *je recule en combattant, je m'enfuis*" see | *ɪtiš, *i[2] compare | *tišimo

*tišim

FINAL (VERB, TRANSITIVE, ANIMATE, DERIVED)

— flee in a particular direction from sb

evidence | SEC nāsipetišimew, *to flee from sb down towards the water;* WI (Pessamit) pamitishimeu [pāməttʃəmēw], *to always be running from sb;* Silvy (ca. 1680) "ni ki8etichimau, *je m'enfuis de lui*" see | *ɪtiš, *m[1]

*tišimo

FINAL (VERB, ANIMATE, INTRANSITIVE, DERIVED)

— flee in a particular direction

evidence | MC išitišimow, *to flee thither;* AT (Wemotaci, Nicole Petiquay) iciticimo [iʒitiʒimow], *to flee thither;* SEC nāsipetišimow, *to flee down towards the water;* WI (Pessamit) uluitishimu [ūlwītəʃəmu], *to go outside to escape* | ANISH bagaminizhimo, *to arrive in flight* (Livesay & Nichols, 2021); MENO mata·pi·nesemow, *to flee down to the water's edge* origin | From ***ɪtišimo-**, "to flee thither." see | *ɪtiš, *m[1], *o compare | *tiši

*tišin

FINAL (VERB, TRANSITIVE, DERIVED)

— push, pass, or hand in a particular direction

evidence | MC išpicišinam, *to push or hand sth up;* SEC āmitišinew, *to push sb off sth;* Laure (ca. 1726) "ni-kurasitetichinen, *je fais couler, je glisse quelque chose dans un lieu*" see | *ɪtiš, *ɪn[3]

*tišisk

FINAL (VERB, TRANSITIVE, INANIMATE, DERIVED)

— drive or chase in a particular direction

evidence | ANISH maajinizhikan, *to start chasing sth* (Livesay & Nichols, 2021) see | *ɪtiš, *sk[2] paired with | *tišiskaw

*tišiskaw

FINAL (VERB, TRANSITIVE, ANIMATE, DERIVED)

— drive or chase in a particular direction

evidence | Laure (ca. 1726) "ni-uirauitichiskauau, *je le fais sortir en poussant;*" Silvy (ca. 1680) "ni ki8etichiska8au, *je le fais reculer, fuir au combat*" | ANISH agwaanizhikaw, *to chase sb ashore* (Livesay & Nichols, 2021) see | *ɪtiš, *skaw paired with | *tišisk

*tiy[1]

INITIAL (NOUN, DEPENDENT INANIMATE)

— buttocks

evidence | PC mitiy, *a bum;* WSC (Misipawistik, Ellen Cook) mitiy, *a bum;* cf. ESC (Severn) manāsitiy, *a bum;* MC olāsitiy, *one's buttocks;* AT (Opitciwan, Nadia Awashish) otiaw [otiyaw], *one's buttocks;* otianan [otiyānān], *one's buttocks* | ANISH gidiy, *your rump, rear end, butt* (Livesay & Nichols, 2021) cf. MENO netɛ·tih, *my rectum* see | *tiy[2]

***tiy²**

MEDIAL, FINAL (NOUN INCORPORATION)

— buttocks

evidence | PC mahkitiyēw, *to have a big bum;* ESC (Severn) otāmitiyehwew, *to hit sb on the buttocks;* MC āhcitiyeliw, *to lose one's bum;* AT (Opitciwan, Joey Awashish) makakotiew [mahkāhkotiyēw], *to have a big bum;* SEC pasāhkotiyehwew, *to slap sb's bum* | ANISH ginagidiye, *to have an itchy butt* (Lippert & Gambill, 2023) see | *tiy¹

***tīhtīhsiw**

INITIAL (NOUN, ANIMATE)

— blue jay (Cyanocitta cristata)

evidence | Laure (ca. 1726) "titisiu *pl.* -ets, *geai;*" Silvy (ca. 1680) "titisi8, *geai*" | ANISH diindiisi, *a blue jay* (Livesay & Nichols, 2021) discussion | In the absence of an Atikamekw cognate, the preaspirate in this reconstruction is indirectly supported by Anishinabe.

***to**

FINAL (VERB, ANIMATE, INTRANSITIVE, ABSTRACT)

sound change | m + to → hto

— forms the reciprocal from animate transitive verbs

evidence | PC wāpahtowak, *to see one another;* MC maskahtowak, *to rob from one another;* Silvy (ca. 1680) "nit'achat8nan, *nous nous entre-donnons des vivres*" compare | *ito

***tokan¹**

INITIAL (NOUN, DEPENDENT INANIMATE)

— hip joint

evidence | PC mitokanikan, *hip bone;* MC otokan, *a hip joint;* WI (Uashat) utukanikan [utəkanəkan], *one's femur;* Laure (ca. 1726) "nitugan, *bout de la cuisse, ma hanche*" | ANISH onoogan, *one's hip* (Livesay & Nichols, 2021) see | *tokan²

***tokan²**

MEDIAL, FINAL (NOUN INCORPORATION)

— hip joint

evidence | PC kaskitokanēsin, *to have a broken hip from falling;* MC kotikotokanešin, *to dislocate one's hip on impact;* WI (Pessamit) tautukaneueu [tāwtəkənēwēw], *to hit sb right on the hip with a projectile or blow;* Silvy (ca. 1680) "ni teït8ganin, *je suis éhanché*" see | *tokan¹

***ton**

MEDIAL, FINAL (NOUN INCORPORATION)

— mouth

evidence | PC wīnitonēw, *to have a filthy mouth;* MC mahkitonew, *to have a big mouth;* SEC apišitonešiw, *to have a small mouth;* Laure (ca. 1726) "ni-tchichistabauatchitunan, *je me lave la bouche;*" Silvy (ca. 1680) "ni kipit8nenau, *je l'étrangle avec la main*" see | *tōn

***tot (~ *toc)**

FINAL (VERB, TRANSITIVE, INANIMATE, ABSTRACT)

— applicative suffixed to animate intransitive verb stems

evidence | PC twēhototam, *to land on sth;* MC kīwetotam, *to return to sth;* SEC mātototam, *to cry about sth;* Silvy (ca. 1680) "nit'achiterim8t8ten, *je suis fort affectionné à ce que je fais*" | ANISH apenimonodan, *to depend or rely on sth* (Livesay & Nichols, 2021) origin | PA ***θot** (Hewson, 1993) paired with | *totaw compare | *tōt

***totaw (~ *totā)**

FINAL (VERB, TRANSITIVE, ANIMATE, ABSTRACT)

— applicative suffixed to animate intransitive verb stems

evidence | PC twēhotōtawew, *to land on sb;* MC kīwetotawew, *to return to sb;* ililīmototātowak, *to speak to one another in Cree;* SEC mātototawew, *to cry about sb;* Silvy (ca. 1680) "ni pag8m8t8ta8au, *je vomis sur lui*" | ANISH apenimonodaw, *to depend or rely on sb* (Livesay & Nichols, 2021); MIAMI pooniteeheelotaw-, *quit having feelings for sb*

(ILDA, 2017) origin | PA *θot (Hewson, 1993) see | *tot, *aw[3] paired with | *tot compare | *tōtaw

*towē

INITIAL

— spin

evidence | WC cowīpicikanis, *spinning top;* AT towekan [towēkan], *a motor;* SEC (Waswanipi) towekan, *offboard motor;* Watkins (1865) "Towāpichikun, *n.in. A top (i.e., a child's toy);*" Laure (ca. 1726) "tuégan & tuebitchigan, *pirouette;*" "ni-tueganan, *nous jouons à la pirouette;*" Silvy (ca. 1680) "ni t8egan 3. -e8, *je la fais tourner (pirouette)*" | Cuoq (1886) "Toweike, *jouer à la toupie*"

*tōhē

INITIAL (VERB, ANIMATE, INTRANSITIVE)

— play ball

evidence | ESC tōhān, *a ball;* MC tōhāw, *to play ball;* SEC tōhew, *to play ball;* WI (Mashteuiatsh) tuan [tūhān], *ball;* Laure (ca. 1726) "tuetau, *jouons au ballon*"

*tōhk

INITIAL

— open (by having both sides spread apart)

evidence | PC tōhkāpiw, *to open one's eyes;* MC tōhkapepiw, *to sit with one's thighs spread apart;* SEC tōhkāskoham, *to spread sth apart using sth stick-like;* Watkins (1865) "Tòokepuyew, v.imp. *It opens (as a slit);*" Silvy (ca. 1680) "ni t8kabin, *j'ouvre mon oeil avec la main*" | ANISH Cuoq (1886) "Ni tongakwawa, *je l'ouvre, le tiens ouvert au moyen d'un bois;*" MESK tōkapiwa, *to sit with one's legs spread apart* origin | PA ***tōnk**

*tōhs

INITIAL (NOUN, DEPENDENT ANIMATE)

— **1** maternal aunt

— **2** stepmother

evidence | AT (Opitciwan, Joey Awashish) nitosa [nitōssa], *my aunt; my stepmother;* (Wemotaci, Nicole Petiquay) otosa [otōssa], *one's aunt(s); one's stepmother(s)* | ANISH ginoshenh, *your mother's sister; your stepmother;* MENO neni·hsak, *my mother's sisters; my stepmothers* origin | PA ***θwihs** compare | *tōsihs, *sikohs

*tōhtan[1]

INITIAL (NOUN, DEPENDENT INANIMATE)

— heel

evidence | ESC otōhtanikekan, *one's heel bone;* MC otōhtan, *one's heel;* NEC mituhtinihāpān, *snowshoe lacing at the heel;* WI (Pessamit) ututanikaniapi [utūtnəkənjāpī], *one's heel nerve;* Laure (ca. 1726) "nitutan -a, *mon talon;*" Silvy (ca. 1680) "mit8tan, *talon*" see | *tōhtan[2]

*tōhtan[2]

MEDIAL, FINAL (NOUN INCORPORATION)

— heel

evidence | ESC māskitōhtanew, *to have a lame heel;* MC išpitōhtaneyāw, *to be high-heeled;* SEC tewitōhtanew, *to have achy heels;* WI (Pessamit) teitutaneshinu [tējtūtnēʃənu], *to feel pain in the heel on contact with sth* | ANISH badakidoondaneshin, *to step on sth sharp and prick one's heel* see | *tōhtan[1]

*tōkw (~ *tōko)

INITIAL (NOUN, DEPENDENT ANIMATE)

— semen

evidence | SEC otōkamek^w, *milt;* WI (Pessamit) utukamek^u [utūkəmēk^w], *milt;* Laure (ca. 1726) "utukamegau, *poisson laité, hareng;*" Fabvre (ca. 1690) "8t8g8, nit8g8, *seman, spermen*" | ANISH otigwag, *milt* (Lippert & Gambill, 2023)

*tōm

INITIAL

— grease

evidence | PC tōmisiw, *to be greasy;* MC tōmihtāw, *to grease sth;* SEC tōmikahtikwenew, *to anoint sb's forehead;* Silvy (ca. 1680) "t8mau, *cela est gras, sale*" | ANISH noominigaade, *to be greased* (Livesay & Nichols, 2021) origin | PA ***θōm** (Hewson, 1993)

*tōn

INITIAL (NOUN, DEPENDENT INANIMATE)

— mouth

evidence | PC mitōn, *mouth;* MC otōniw, *to have a mouth;* SEC otōn, *one's mouth;* WI (Pessamit) utunikueu [utūnəkwēw], *to spread sb's rumours;* Silvy (ca. 1680) "nit8n, ma bouche" origin | PA ***tōn** (Hewson, 1991) see | *ton

*tōsihs

INITIAL (NOUN, DEPENDENT ANIMATE)

— **1** maternal aunt

— **2** stepmother

evidence | PC nitōsis, *to have a maternal aunt, an aunt married to a paternal uncle;* MC otōsisimew, *to have a maternal aunt, an aunt married to a paternal uncle, or a stepmother;* AT (Wemotaci, Nicole Petiquay) nitosis [nitōzis], *my aunt; my stepmother;* WI (Pessamit) utussa [utūssē], *one's maternal aunt; one's stepmother;* Silvy (ca. 1680) "T8sis uoc (atit) t8sisai, *tante, belle mere*" compare | *tōhs, *sikohs discussion | The comparative evidence is insufficient to reconstruct a semantic distinction, if any, between ***tōhs** and ***tōsihs**. Though both can be reconstructed in Old Cree, the former appears to be the one inherited from Proto-Algonquian.

*tōsk

INITIAL

— nudge

evidence | PC tōskwahwēw, *to nudge sb with a tool;* tōskinēw, *to nudge sb with one's hand or elbow;* MC tōskinew, *to nudge sb using one's hand;* tōskiškawew, *to nudge sb using one's foot or body;* NEC tūskuhwāu, *to nudge sb with a tool;* Silvy (ca. 1680) "ni t8stinau, *je le pousse manu;*" "ni t8chtiskaȣau, *je le pousse du pied*" | ANISH dookishkan, *to poke, nudge, or tap sth with one's foot or body;* MENO to·ckenam, *to nudge or prod sth with one's hand or finger* discussion | Some contemporary dialects feature a reflex of ***tōskw**, a variant derived by analogy with the root ***tōskwan**, "elbow."

*tōskwan[1]

INITIAL (NOUN, DEPENDENT INANIMATE)

— elbow

evidence | PC mitōskwan, *an elbow;* MC otōskwanahwew, *to elbow sb;* SEC nitōskwan, *my elbow;* Silvy (ca. 1680) "nit8sk8an, *mon coude;*" "n'8t8sk8anapin, *je m'accoude*" | ANISH odooskwan, *one's elbow* (Livesay & Nichols, 2021); MENO nɛhtu·hkwan, *my elbow* see | *tōskwan[2]

*tōskwan[2]

MEDIAL (NOUN INCORPORATION)

— elbow

evidence | PC iskotōskwanēw, *for one's elbows to be so long;* MC āspacitōskwanepiw, *to sit while leaning on one's elbow(s);* WI (Pessamit) miliutushkunu [məlīwtūʃkwənu], *to have an abscess at the elbow* see | *tōskwan[1]

*tōšim

INITIAL (NOUN, DEPENDENT ANIMATE)

— parallel nephew

evidence | PC otōsimimāw, *a nephew, specifically a man's brother's son or a woman's sister's son;* WC mitōsim, *a nephew (a man's sister's son or woman's brother's son);"* ESC otōšimiskwema, *one's parallel niece;* WI (Pessamit) utushima [utūʃəm], *one's nephew; one's stepson;* Watkins (1865) "Mitoosimimow, *n.an. A nephew (i.e. a brother's son), a step-son;*" Laure (ca. 1726) "nituchimiskuem, *nièce de frère, la fille de mon frère;*" Silvy (ca. 1680) "nit8chim, *mon neveu*" | ANISH odoozhiman, *one's parallel nephew; one's stepson* (Livesay & Nichols, 2021) origin | PA ***tōšim** (Aubin, 1975) compare | *tihkwatim, *štim[1]

*tōštōk

INITIAL

— be of a soft and springy consistency, spongy

evidence | PC Lacombe (1874) "tostokisiw, ok, *(a.a.) il est élastique, mouvant, tremblant;*" WC tōstōkan, *to be boggy;* MC tōštōkanāw, *to be a quaking bog;* Silvy (ca. 1680) "t8cht8gan88i8 sipi8, *le fleuve est bourbeux*" | ANISH Cuoq (1886) "Totogan, *marécage, ce qu'au Canada on nomme vulgairement pays tremblant*"

*tōštōp

INITIAL

— flexible

evidence | PC Lacombe (1874) "tostopisiw, ok, *(a.a.) il est mou, il est élastique, spongieux;*" MC tōštōpāskwan, *to be a flexible stick-like object;* SEC tōštōpāw, *to be flexible;* Laure (ca. 1726) "tustubau, *canot mou, mal bandé, lâche*" compare | *šōhšōp

*tōt (~ *tōc)

INITIAL (VERB, TRANSITIVE, INANIMATE)

— do

evidence | PC tōtamawew, *to do sth for sb;* MC tōcikātew, *to be done;* SEC tōtam, *to do sth;* Silvy (ca. 1680) "ni t8ten, *je fais*" | MENO to·tam, *to do so to sth* origin | PA ***tōt*** (Aubin, 1975; Hewson, 1993) paired with | *tōtaw compare | *tot

*tōtaw (~ *tōtā)

INITIAL (VERB, TRANSITIVE, ANIMATE)

— do

evidence | PC tōtawew, *to treat sb thus;* MC tōtātowak, *to do to one another;* SEC tōtawew, *to do to sb;* Silvy (ca. 1680) "ni t8ta8au, *je lui fais*" | ANISH doodaadizo, *to do sth to oneself* (Livesay & Nichols, 2021) origin | PA ***tōtaw*** (Aubin, 1975; Hewson, 1993) see | *tōt, *aw³ paired with | *tōt compare | *totaw

*tōtēm

INITIAL (NOUN, DEPENDENT ANIMATE)

— kin

evidence | PC otōtēma, *one's friend(s); one's kin;* MC otōtēma, *one's friend(s);* SEC (inland) nitōtem, *my kin, my relative(s);* NEC ututāmh, *one's friend(s); one's relative(s);* NSK utuutaama, *one's relative(s)* | ANISH odoodeman, *one's clan* (Livesay & Nichols, 2021); MENO neto·tɛ·m, *my totem animal, my totemic ancestor*

*tōtōhš

INITIAL (NOUN, ANIMATE)

— mammary gland, breast

evidence | PC tohtōs, *a breast or teat;* MC cōcōš, *a breast;* AT (Wemotacin, Nicole Petiquay) tcotcocak [cōcōššak], *breasts;* SEC nicōcōšimac, *my breasts;* NEC tūtūshināpui, *milk;* WI (Pessamit) tutush [tutūʃ], *a breast;* Silvy (ca. 1680) "t8t8ch, t8t8s, *mamelle*" | ANISH odoodooshiman, *her breast(s)* (Livesay & Nichols, 2021)

*twayēhk

INITIAL

— immediately

evidence | MC twayehk, *immediately;* NEC tīwāhch, *immediately;* EI (Sheshatshiu) tuiet [tujēt], *immediately;* Watkins (1865) "Tweyach, *adv. Immediately, at once, directly, forthwith*" limited to | *i³

*twā

INITIAL

— break through ice

evidence | PC twākonēsin, to fall through the snow crust; MC twāhikew, *to make a hole through the ice;* SEC twāšin, *to fall through the ice;* WI (Pessamit) tuakuneshinu [twākunēʃənu], *to break through the crust of the snow when walking;* Silvy (ca. 1680) "ni t8anen, ni t8at8anen, *j'enfonce dans la neige*"

*twēho

INITIAL (VERB, ANIMATE, INTRANSITIVE)

— alight

evidence | PC twēhototam, *to land on sth;* SEC twehōmakan, *to land, speaking of an aircraft;* NEC twāhū, *to land;* EI (Sheshatshiu) tueu [twēu], *to land*

W

*w[1] (~ *o)

FINAL (NOUN, ABSTRACT)

— **1** forms nouns

— **2** forms numerals when suffixed to numeral roots

evidence | [1]MC pīwāpisk^{w}, *metal;* SEC ahyapiyāpek^{w}, *netting twine;* WI uatshinakanitak^{u}, *dry tamarack;* Laure (ca. 1726) "uanaskutagu, *proue, le devant du navire;*" Fabvre (ca. 1690) "Kichik8, *L air, Le tems, Le I8r*" [2]PC nisto, *three;* MC tahto, *so many;* SEC nīš^{w}, *two*

*w[2]

FINAL (VERB, TRANSITIVE, ANIMATE, ABSTRACT)

— produces transitive animate verb stems when suffixed to certain initials and certain transitive inanimate finals

evidence | PC otāmahwew, *to strike sb;* WC wīcīwīw, *to go with sb;* MC mišwew, *to hit sb on target;* ayāwew, *to have sb;* SEC mātišwew, *cut sb;* tihciswew, *to melt sth;* NEC pimwāu, *to throw a projectile at sb;* EI (Sheshatshiu) aiaueu [jāwēw], *to buy sth;* Laure (ca. 1726) "ni-tchispeu-uau, *je lui donne trop de pied, trop de liberté;*" Silvy (ca. 1680) "nit'abah8au assam, *j'en défais la tissure*" compare | *aw[3], *ıw[2]

*wacaškw (~ *wacaško)

INITIAL (NOUN, ANIMATE)

— muskrat

evidence | PC wacaskowayān, *a muskrat pelt;* MC wacaškokan, *a muskrat bone;* SEC wacaškwāyow, *muskrat tail;* Laure (ca. 1726) "uatchasku, *rat-musqué*" | ANISH wazhashk, *a muskrat* (Livesay & Nichols, 2021) see | *acaškw

*wacēhp

INITIAL

— agile, brisk

evidence | PC wacēhpīw & ocēhpīw, *to be active, nimble, light-footed;* WSC (Misipawistik, Ellen Cook) wacēhpīw, *to be agile;* EI (Ekuanitshit) utshepiw [watʃēpīw], *to hurry;* Watkins (1865) "Wuch'āpisēw, *v.i.5. He is active, he is brisk, he is diligent;*" Laure (ca. 1726) "ni-uatcheputan, *je me dépêche en marchant*"

*waciw

INITIAL (NOUN, INANIMATE)

— hill, mountain

evidence | PC waciy, *a hill or mountain;* MC waciy, *a hill;* AT (Opitciwan, Joey Awashish) watci [waciy], *hill or mountain;* SEC wacīskāw, *to be hilly;* WI (Pessamit) utshu [ūtʃu], *mountain;* EI (Mamit) utshu [watʃu], *mountain;* EI (Sheshatshiu) utshu [utʃu], *mountain;* Silvy (ca. 1680) "ichpatinau 8atchi8, *haute montagne*" see | *aciw[2]

*wahrah

INITIAL

— burst into flames, catch fire

evidence | WSC (Misipawistik, Ellen Cook) wanahtēw, *to flame up;* MC walahtew, walasow, *to be in flames;* SEC (Waswanipi) wahahtepayin, *to burst into flames;* NEC wiyihtāu, *to catch on fire;* Watkins (1865) "Wuyàtāo, *v.imp. It blazes, it flames*" limited to | *so[2], *tē[4]

*wahkā

INITIAL

— bother, irritate

evidence | PC Lacombe (1874) "Wakkānew, *etc. (v.a.) pour le peu qu'il lui touche, il lui cause de la douleur;*" MC wahkātitowin, *mutual hatred;* NEC uhkāsīu, *to be easily irritated;* WI (Pessamit) uakaieu [ukājēw], *to annoy or irritate sb;* EI (Sheshatshiu) uakateu [wākātēw], *to hate sb;* Laure (ca. 1726) "n-ukatau 3. -teu, *j'aboie contre quelqu'un;*" Silvy (ca. 1680) "ni 8akaska8au, *je le chasse;*" "8akachka8au, *je l'importune, badinant sans le respecter*" discussion | This root has merged into ***awahkē** in contemporary MC and SEC.

*wahkēw

INITIAL

— **1** fragile

— **2** sensitive

evidence | PC wahkēwaciw, *to be sensitive to the cold;* ESC (Severn) wahkewan, *to be weak;* MC wahkewikanakāw, *to be a fragile bone;* wahkewašteyāw, *to be easily stretchable, speaking of a string; to have a hair trigger, speaking of a firearm;* WI (Mashteuiatsh) "n-utshêuatsin, *je suis frileux*" (Cooter, 1975) | ANISH wakewan, *to be fragile or weak* (Livesay & Nichols, 2021) compare | *šēw discussion | Despite the broad geographic distribution of this root, cognates have not been identified in dialects spoken east of Moose Cree. Its inclusion here is therefore tentative.

*wahrakēskw

INITIAL (NOUN, ANIMATE)

— bark

evidence | PC wayakēsk(w), *bark;* MC walakesk^{w}, *outer bark of a tree;* SEC wahyaceskw, *bark,* pronounced [uhīceskw] in Waskaganish and [wahaceškw] in Waswanipi; Laure (ca. 1726) "uratchesku *pl.* -ets, *grosse écorce de cèdre, propre à couvrir;*" Fabvre (ca. 1690) "8rakechk8a, *t8te sorte d ecorce d arbres*" & "8aratchech, *ecorce, pellicule de t8t arbre*" | ANISH wanagek(w), *bark of a tree; a piece of bark* (Livesay & Nichols, 2021); MENO wana·kɛh(kok), *piece(s) of bark;* MIAMI alakiihkwi, *piece of tree bark* (ILDA, 2017) see | *ahrakēsk, *ahrakēskw

*wahrā

INITIAL

— disrupt, disarrange

evidence | PC wiyānam, *to scatter sth around;* MC walāškam, *to disrupt the arrangement of sth with one's feet or body;* NEC wihyāpitim, *to make a mess of sth;* WI (Pessamit) ualapitam^{u} [ulāpətəm], *to mess things up;* EI (Nutashkuanit) uanapitam [wānāpɨtam], *to mess things up;* Fabvre (ca. 1690) "8arapǐten 3 tam, *deranger en tirant auec ch(os)e*"

*wahswē

INITIAL

— spray, splash

evidence | PC Lacombe (1874) "Waswepekahwew, *(v.a.) ham, huwew, hikew, il l'asperge;*" WC waswīpīkahwīw, *to splash sb;* MC waswepekinam, *to sprinkle sth with water;* AT (Wemotaci, Nicole Petiquay) osweparin [osswēparin], *to spray;* oswepekaham [osswēpēkaham], *to spray or splash sb;* oswepekihtin [osswēpēkihtin], *to fall with a splash into the water; to be torrential rain;* SEC oswepayiw, *to spray;* NSK uswaapaachiihtin, *to fall with a splash;* WI (Pessamit) ushuepetshipalu [uʃwēpētʃəpəlu], *to make the water splash while moving;* Watkins (1865) "*Splash, v.i.,* Wuswāpākuhikāo;" Laure (ca. 1726) "ni-uachuebegaiten, *je mouille pour arroser*" | ANISH oswese, *to scatter suddenly* (Lippert & Gambill, 2023)

*wan[1]

INITIAL

— mistakenly, wrongly, mis-

evidence | PC wanihtāw, *to lose sth;* WC wanikiskisiw, *to forget;* MC wanipitam, *to say sth wrongly;* SEC wawāneyihtam, *to be perplexed about sth;* (Waswanipi) wanišino, *to be lost;* NEC winihtim, *to misunderstand* *sth;* WI (Pessamit) unipalu [ūnəpəlu], *se tromper;* EI (Sheshatshiu) unitin [untn], *to be lost or mislaid;* Silvy (ca. 1680) "ni ȣaneriten, *je l'oublie*" | ANISH wanagindaaso, *to miscount or misread* (Livesay & Nichols, 2021); MENO waneˑnam, *to mislay sth* origin | PA ***wan** (Aubin, 1975)

*wan[2]

INITIAL

— rise from reclined position

evidence | MC waniškānew, *raise sb from a reclined position;* SEC waniškāw, *to rise from a reclined position;* WI (Pessamit) uniu [unīw], *se lever;* Laure (ca. 1726) "ni-uaninau, *je lui aide à se lever sur son séant;*" Silvy (ca. 1680) "ni ȣanin, *je m'éveille*" | ANISH onishkaa, *to get up from a prone position)* (Livesay & Nichols, 2021); MENO oneˑw, *to get up from lying*

*wanasko (~ *wanaskw)

INITIAL

— at the extremity, at the tip

evidence | PC wanaskoc, *at the tip;* MC wanaskwāskwan, *to be the tip of sth stick-like;* SEC wanaskwāw, *to be the tip or extremity of sth;* Laure (ca. 1726) "uanaskutagu, *proue, le devant du navire;*" Silvy (ca. 1680) "ȣanaskȣaskȣ, *bout, v.g. du bâton*" | ANISH wanakoninj, *a fingertip* (Livesay & Nichols, 2021); MENO wanaˑkoh, *at the top of a tree or plant* compare | *anask

*wanawihšiw

INITIAL (NOUN, ANIMATE)

— Atlantic cod (Gadus morhua)

evidence | WI (Pessamit) unushu [ūnūʃu], *Atlantic cod;* EI (Unaman-shipit) unushu [wanawhwī], *Atlantic cod;* Laure (ca. 1726) "unauichiu *pl.* -ets, *morue;*" Silvy (ca. 1680) "anaȣichiȣ, *morue*" | ANISH Cuoq (1886) "Onawic, *petite morue, nom vulgaire d'une espèce de loche*" discussion | In the absence of an Atikamekw cognate, the preaspirate in the above form is presumed etymologically.

*wanā

INITIAL

— disrupt, interrupt

evidence | PC wanāhēw, *to distract or disrupt sb;* MC wanāhtāw, *to disrupt sth;* SEC wanāhew, *to disrupt sb*

*wanāt (~ *wanāc, *wanās)

INITIAL

— inappropriate, improper, unsuitable

evidence | PC wanācīw, *to have one's genitals exposed;* MC wanācišin, *to lie with one's pubic region indecently exposed;* AT (Wemotaci, Jeannette Coocoo) onatakamin [onātākamin], *to be turbid or dirty water;* SEC wanātan, *to be ruined or spoiled;* wanātapiw & wāwanātapiw, *to sit with one's pubic region indecently exposed;* NEC wināchihtāu, *to destroy sth; to disturb sth;* wāunātāpihchāpiyiu, *to become tangled, speaking of sth string-like;* EI (Sheshatshiu) unatishiu [unātəʃīw], *to be a joker or tease;* Watkins (1865) "wunatisew, *v.i.1. He is unsteady in conduct, he is inconsistent;*" Silvy (ca. 1680) "ni ȣanatisin, *je suis fou, je le fais*" | ANISH Cuoq (1886) "Ni wanatenima, *je le crois perdu, je le considère comme ruiné*" origin | PA ***wanāt** (Hewson, 1993) see | *wan[1], *āt[5] compare | *nihšiwanāt

*wanāwihs

INITIAL

— barely

evidence | MC anāwiš, *barely;* AT (Wemotaci, Jeannette Coocoo) onawis [onāwis], *almost not;* SEC onāwiš, *barely;* EI (Sheshatshiu) minaush [mɨnāwʃ], *barely;* Laure (ca. 1726) "unauich nit-iriniuin, *j'ai une faible santé;*" Fabvre (ca. 1690) "ȣanaȣis v. ȣannaȣis, *a peine, par force;*" Silvy (ca. 1680) "ȣanaȣis, *à peine*"

*wanimōt (~ wanimōc, wanimōs)

INITIAL

— secret, secretly

evidence | WC wanimōc, *secretly;* SEC wanimūchiteheu, *to have a secret in one's heart* (CSB, 2018); NEC winimūsinākun, *to look wrong, false, to give the wrong impression;* Watkins (1865) "Wunemootisew, *v.i.1. He is secret*" | MESK wanimōchi, *perchance, if it should happen to be that*

*waniraw

INITIAL

— very

evidence | PC waniyaw, *any, somebody, just anyone, anyone at random;* AT (Opitciwan, Joey Awashish) orina (also spelled warina in religious texts) [orina], *so much, too much;* Laure (ca. 1726) "uanirau, *beaucoup, grandement, fort;*" "uanirau seatchihak, *je l'aime beaucoup;*" Fabvre (ca. 1690) "8anĭrau, *multu(s)*" | ANISH Cuoq (1886) "Wanina, *beaucoup, bien, fort, extrêmement;*" "Wanina notin, *il vente beaucoup;*" MESK waninawe, *in all directions, on all sides* discussion | While the shape of this root is secure, its sense in Plains Cree differs from historical sources from the Saguenay region. Given the paucity of contemporary cross-dialectal evidence, the historical evidence is here prioritized.

*wanī

INITIAL

— set trap

evidence | PC owanihikēw, *a trapper;* WC wanīhikīw, *to trap, to set traps;* WSC (Misipawistik, Ellen Cook) wanīhamawēw, *to set a trap for sth;* ESC (Severn) wanihamawew, *to set a trap for sth;* NEC winihamuwāu, *to set a trap for an animal;* EI (Mamit) unaueu [wanāwēw], *to set a trap for sth;* Watkins (1865) "wunehikāo, *v.i.3. He is trapping or trapmaking;*" Isham (1743) "wun a higan, *a trap;*" Laure (ca. 1726) "ni-uanihigan, *je tends un piège*" | ANISH Cuoq (1886) "oniiamaw wabiceciwak, *mets des trappes pour les martres;*" wanii'ige, *to trap* (Livesay & Nichols, 2021) discussion | Most contemporary dialects have either shortened the final vowel or lost it entirely.

*wap

INITIAL

— (of a body of water) narrows

evidence | PC wapāsin, *to be a small narrows;* MC opatāwahkāw, *sandy narrows;* AT opitciwan [opiciwan], *narrows in a river, place name;* SEC opāw, *to be a narrows;* Fabvre (ca. 1690) "8abichtig8eïak, *La ville de Kebek;*" Silvy (ca. 1680) "8apau, *détroit*"

*waratoy

INITIAL (NOUN, ANIMATE)

— bracket fungus

evidence | ESC (Attawapiskat) wanatoy, *a bracket fungus;* (Severn) wanatoy, *a mushroom; an eraser;* MC walatow, *a bracket fungus;* Laure (ca. 1726) "uratuitichiskuteganu, *contre-poison*" | ANISH anadowag & onadowag, *mushrooms* (Lippert & Gambill, 2023)

*waraw

INITIAL

— out

evidence | WC waðawīw, *to go out;* MC walawīw, *to exit;* WI (Mashteuiatsh) "n-utshēuatsin, *je suis frileux*" (Cooter, 1975) NEC wiyiwāu, *it (river) empties out in another body of water;* Watkins (1865) "wuyuwetimìk, *outside;*" Laure (ca. 1726) "ni-urauitichauauets, *je fais sortir de la cabane les chiens;*" "ni-uarauitabatau, *je l'en fais sortir avec un chien;*" "ni-uirauin 3. urauiu, *je sors;*" Silvy (ca. 1680) "ni 8era8in, *je sors*"

*wasahswē

INITIAL

— spread, scatter, gradually reach a larger area

evidence | PC Lacombe (1874) "Wasaswepayihew, *il l'éparpille, il le sème;*" ESC (Severn) wasaswewepinam, *to scatter sth about by hand;* MC wasaswemina, *choke-*

cherries; wasaswecišahwew, *to disperse them, to cause them to scatter;* SEC wasaswewepinam, *to scatter sth by hand* | ANISH zaswebidoon, *to scatter sth by hand* (Livesay & Nichols, 2021) discussion | In the absence of an Atikamekw cognate, the preaspirate in this reconstruction is indirectly supported by Anishinabe.

*waskatamoy

INITIAL (NOUN, ANIMATE)

— water lily rhizome

evidence | PC waskatamow, *root of the water lily;* MC oskatamoy, *water lily rhizome;* SEC oskatamoy, *water lily rhizome;* NEC uskitimui, *water lily root;* WI (Pessamit) ushkatamui [uʃkətəmwī], *water lily root;* EI (Mamit) ushkatamui [uhkatamwī], *water lily root* | ANISH Cuoq (1886) "akandamo, ...k, volet, nenuphar" see | *wiškihtē

*waskit (~ *waskic)

INITIAL

— on the surface

evidence | PC waskitatēwēnam, *to walk on the snow's crust;* WC waskicipaðiw, *to come to the top;* SEC oscitākonepahtāw, *to run on top of the snow;* WI (Pessamit) ussitishik[u] [ūssətəʃəkʷ], *on the surface of the ice;* Silvy (ca. 1680) "8astitch, 8astitchi, *dessus, le dehors de qqch*" | ABEN oskidolagwa, *deck of a ship* (Day, 1994); ANISH ogidadewe, *to goe on top of the snow crust;* MENO wahke·cecewan, *to flow over sth* origin | PA ***waθkit** (Aubin, 1975; Hewson, 1993)

*waskw (~ *wasko)

INITIAL (NOUN, INANIMATE)

— cloud

evidence | PC waskowan, *to be cloudy;* WC wasko, *a cloud;* WSC (Misipawistik, Ellen Cook) waskowa, *clouds*; ESC wasko, *cloud;* MC wasko, *a cloud;* AT (Wemotaci, Jeannette Coocoo) osko [osko], *a cloud;* (Opitciwan, Joey Awashish) osko [osko], *a cloud;* Watkins (1865) "wuskoo, *n.in. A cloud*" | ANISH wahko, *a cloud* (Oji-Cree, 2014) see | *askw[1] compare | *wāskw discussion | Eastern dialects have replaced this root by reflexes of Old Cree ***kaškawanwi**, "thick fog." Despite the loss of ***waskw** in these dialects, its medial form ***askw** has been retained as a productive morpheme.

*waspāwē

INITIAL

— awaken inadvertently

evidence | PC waspāwēmēw, *to keep sb awake by speech;* MC ospāwehew, *to wake sb inadvertently;* SEC wawespāwehew, *to wake sb up by accident* | ANISH Cuoq (1886) "opaweh, wapaweh *empêche-le de dormir*"

*wašaškwētoy

INITIAL (NOUN, ANIMATE)

— **1** mushroom

— **2** conifer cone

evidence | WC wasaskwītoy, *a mushroom; a cone;* MC wašaškwecōš, *a conifer cone;* AT (Wemotaci, Jeannette Coocoo) ocockweto [oʒoškwētow], *a mushroom; a conifer cone;* SEC (inland) waškwetow & waškwecōš, *conifer cone;* SEC (coastal) waškwetoy, *conifer cone;* EI (Sheshatshiu) ushkuetui [uʃkwētwī], *a mushroom; a cone;* Fabvre (ca. 1690) "8achachk8et8, *pom(m)e de pin, excrem(en)t de sapinage;*" "8achachk8et8ek, 8achechk8et8ek, 8achichk8et8ek, *excrem(en)t rond*" | ANISH wazhashkwedow, *fungus; a mushroom; a pine cone* (Livesay & Nichols, 2021)

*wašikway

INITIAL (NOUN, INANIMATE)

— bark for canoe-making

evidence | Laure (ca. 1726) "uchikuai *pl.* uchikuéia, *écorce à canot;*" Silvy (ca. 1680) "8achig8ai, *écorce à faire canot;*" cf. MC cīmānišikway, *canoe bark* | cf. ANISH Cuoq (1886) "Pakwaajikwe, *enlever l'écorce d'un bouleau*" see | *kway compare | *kwam, *waškway discussion | The absence of a preaspiration on the sibilant cannot be confirmed due to the lack of an Atikamekw cognate, but the Anishinabe cognate suggests the above form is correct.

*wašištaw

INITIAL

— **1** awkward, not quite right

— **2** impatient, offended, disappointed

evidence | [1]MC wašištawīw, *to have an awkward time;* NEC wishtiwinaakun, *to not appear right;* WI (Pessamit) ushtupu [ustūpu], *to be sitting uncomfortably* [2]MC wašištawelihtam, *to be disappointed in sth;* Fabvre (ca. 1690) "8achichta8isin i8, *etre impatient, facheux*" compare | *nēhsitām discussion | This reconstruction suffers from the lack of an Atikamekw cognate to confirm the absence of a preaspirate.

*wašk

INITIAL

— to turn

evidence | PC waskīw, *to turn;* WC wāwaskipaðihow, *to move in a zigzag manner;* MC waškiškāw, *to turn off on foot* compare | *waškaw, *waškwē

*waškaw

INITIAL

— move

evidence | PC waskawipayiw, *to move;* WC waskawinam, *to move sth;* WI (Pessamit) ushkuiu [uʃkwīw], *to strain or make a physical effort;* Fabvre (ca. 1690) "8achka8inen 3 nam8 n. nau, *Remuer auec La main;*" Silvy (ca. 1680) "ni 8achka8ichten, *je remue qqch;*" "ni 8aska8ichenen, *je remue le feu*" compare | *wašk, *waškwē

*waškway

INITIAL (NOUN)

— **1** (animate) birch

— **2** (inanimate) birch bark

evidence | PC waskwayāhtik, *a birch tree; birch wood;* MC waškwayiwat, *a birch bark basket;* SEC waškway, *a birch tree; birch bark;* waškwāwan, *to be birchy;* EI (Sheshatshiu) ushkuass [uʃkwāss], *a young birch;* Watkins (1865) "Wuskwi, *n.an. The birch (tree);*" "Wuskwi, *n.ina. Birch-bark;*" Silvy (ca. 1680) "8achk8ai, *pl.* 8achk8eïa, *bouleau, écorce de bouleau*" see | *aškw², *ay², *aškway compare | *wašikway

*waškwē

INITIAL

— deviate, veer

evidence | MC waškwehtin, *to be sent off course upon contact with sth;* SEC oškwepayiw, *to take a wrong turn;* WI (Pessamit) ushkueiashu [uʃkwējāʃu], *to be blown off course* compare | *wašk, *waškaw

*watakam

INITIAL

— lack resistance

evidence | PC watakamisiw, *to be grouchy, to be easily angered;* MC watakamisiw, *short-tempered;* WI (Pessamit) utakamipeu, *il manque de résistance à l'alcool;* Watkins (1865) "Wutukumisew, *He is hasty, he is crabbed, he is ill-tempered;*" Silvy (ca. 1680) "ni 8atagamiten, *je suis souple, traitable, facile à faire, à obéir*"

*watapiy

INITIAL (NOUN, INANIMATE)

— fine root

evidence | PC watapīwat, *a woven basket;* MC watapīskāw, *to be many roots;* SEC watapiy, *a secondary root;* Silvy (ca. 1680) "8atapi, *racines à coudre canot;*" "8atapi8ach, *panier d'osier*" see | *atap

*watē

INITIAL

— snow crust being strong enough to walk on

evidence | MC wateyāw, *snow's crust to be strong enough to walk on;* SEC watenam, *to walk on the snow's frozen surface;* WI

(Pessamit) uteiau [utējāw], *to be the time of the year when the snow is hard enough to walk on without snowshoes;* Laure (ca. 1726) "uateiau, *elle est dure et me porte;*" Silvy (ca. 1680) "8atenig8an, *la neige porte*" see | *atēwē

*watihkwan

INITIAL (NOUN, INANIMATE)

— branch, knot

evidence | PC watihkwaniwiw, *to have a knot(s) or a branch(s);* EI (Mamit) utikun [utīkwan], *branch; knot in wood;* Laure (ca. 1726) "utikuanich -a, *branche menue;*" Silvy (ca. 1680) "8atik8an, *nœud, branche d'arbre*" see | *atihkwan

*watoy

INITIAL (NOUN, ANIMATE)

— **1** blood clot

— **2** hide scraping

evidence | [1]PC watow, *NI a blood clot;* watowan, *to be congealed;* SEC watoy, *NA blood clot;* EI (Unaman-shipit) utui [watwī], *NA blood clot;* Silvy (ca. 1680) "8at8, *sang figé. blanc à viser, but*" [2]PC Lacombe (1874) "watow, ok, *raclure des peaux tannées;*" SEC watoy, *NA piece of subcutaneous tissue scraped from a frozen hide;* Silvy (ca. 1680) "8at8ek, *raclure de peau*" | ANISH wadow, *NA a blood clot* (Livesay & Nichols, 2021)

*watōk

INITIAL

— to have a hematoma

evidence | MC watōkahwew, *to give sb a hematoma from a strike;* SEC otōcihpanew, *to have a bruised lung;* WI & EI utukau [utūkāw], *to have a bruise;* Fabvre (ca. 1690) "n 8t8kĭsin i8, *Liuide de c8ps, uiolet*" origin | Possibly related to Old Cree ***watoy**-, *blood clot.*

*wawiyat (~ *wawiyas)

INITIAL

— funny

evidence | PC wawiyatwēw, *to joke;* MC wiyatwew, *to talk humourously;* SEC wiyateyihtākosiw, *to be funny;* Laure (ca. 1726) "tchi-uauiéterimitin, *je me moque de toi, je ne te crains pas;*" Fabvre (ca. 1690) "8a8iatĭsin i8, *eclater de rire, folastrer;*" "8a8iasinam8an e8, *se rire, se moqr de qlq che*" | ANISH wawiyazhinaagwad, *to look funny* (Livesay & Nichols, 2021)

*wayān[1]

INITIAL (NOUN, ANIMATE)

— hide, pelt

evidence | PC wayān, *a hide, skin, or piece of fur;* ESC (Severn) wayān, *fur, pelt;* MC wayān, *a hide, a pelt;* MacKenzie (1801) "Wian, *Skin;*" Isham (1743) "wi an, *a skin of any sort of hide*" see | *wayān[2]

*wayān[2]

MEDIAL, FINAL (NOUN INCORPORATION)

— hide, pelt

evidence | PC wākāyōsiwayān, *a bear pelt;* SEC mōsowayānescisin, *a moose hide moccasin;* NEC mūsuyān, *a moose hide;* EI (Sheshatshiu) atikuian [ətīkwjān], *caribou skin, hide;* Laure (ca. 1726) "attiku ueian *pl.* -a, *cuir, peau de caribou;*" Silvy (ca. 1680) "achtioïan, *peau d'orignal avec le poil*" | ANISH Cuoq (1886) "Awesinsiwaian, *peau de bête*" see | *wayān[1]

*wayēš

INITIAL

— **1** approximate amount, place, or degree

— **2** to treat maliciously, to deceive

evidence | [1]PC wayēs, *around, about, approximately;* MC mōla wayeš, *nowhere;* mōla wayeš ihkin, *to not matter;* SEC namawīy wiyēš in, *to not matter;* wiyeš mihtāhtwāpisc itacihtākwan, *to cost approximately ten dollars;* Laure (ca. 1726) "nema uiech nit-itutan, *je vais nulle part;*" "he uiech apitua auechichets, *retraite de bêtes sauvages*" [2]PC wayēsihēw, *to deceive sb;*

MC wayešimew, *to deceive sb by speech;* AT (Wemotaci, Nicole Petiquay) wiecimew [wiyēʒimēw], *to deceive sb by speech;* SEC wiyeši-tōtawew, *to treat sb maliciously;* Laure (ca. 1726) "eka ka-uaiechimat uchta, *cette femme en a (de la fidélité) pour son mari;*" Silvy (ca. 1680) "8eïechira8au, *je le trompe au jeu*" | ANISH wayezhim, *to deceive, trick, or cheat sb by speech* (Livesay & Nichols, 2021)

*wāhkēyōhs

INITIAL (NOUN, ANIMATE)

— bufflehead (Bucephala albeola)

evidence | SEC wāhceyōš, *a bufflehead;* NEC (Whapmagoostui, Mary George Masty) wāhceyōš, *name of a man* | ANISH Cuoq (1886) "wakeiawic, *espèce de canard fort petit;*" MENO wa·hkayo·hsak, *a teal, a butterball duck*

*wāhko

INITIAL

— have or adopt as kin

evidence | PC wāhkōmākan, *a relative;* ESC wāhkomākan, *a relative;* MC wāhkohtowin, *kinship;* AT (Opitciwan, Joey Awashish & Wemotaci, Nicole Petiquay) wakomew [wāhkomēw], *to be related to sb;* SEC wāhkomew, *to be related to sb;* NEC wāhkumāu, *to be related to sb;* Laure (ca. 1726) "n-uakumau, *je l'adopte*" | ANISH waangoom, *to adopt sb* (Livesay & Nichols, 2021); Cuoq (1886) "wangawis,i, *être apprivoisé (en parlant d'une bête fauve, d'un oiseau); être accoutumé, s'accoutumer dans une maison étrangère (en parlant des personnes), être adopté, être allié, être uni par alliance*" origin | PA ***wānko** (Hewson, 1993) see | *āhkom, *tawēmāw compare | *cīrawē discussion | An isogloss runs with East Cree dialects grouping with more westerly dialects and Western Innu grouping with more easterly dialects. While the dialects spoken to the west of this line display the above root, those spoken to the east instead use reflexes of the root ***cīrawē**. The Atikamekw dialect has retained both roots as synonyms of one another.

*wāhkon

INITIAL (NOUN, ANIMATE)

— lichen

evidence | ESC (Severn) wāhkoniskitān, *lichen found on rocks;* SEC wāhkonac, *lichen; dandruff; cradle cap scales;* wāhkonāpisk^{w}, *rock tripe;* EI (Mamit) uakunapishkuat [wākwanāpɨhkwat], *rock tripe;* Isham (1743) "wa quo nuck, *maws that grows upon the rocks;*" Laure (ca. 1726) "tchichétchiuétinutch uakunattikua, *la mousse est du côté du nord;*" Fabvre (ca. 1690) "8ak8n pl 8ak8nek, *tripes de roches;*" cf. WC asinīwāhkwanak, *rock tripe* | ANISH Cuoq (1886) "wakonan ot amwan, *il mange de la mousse;*" MENO wa·hkonak, *tree lichen*

*wāhkw (~ *wāhko)

INITIAL (NOUN, ANIMATE)

— spawn, roe

evidence | PC wāhkwa, *a lump of roe;* MC wāhko, *an egg of an amphibian or fish;* AT (Wemotaci, Jeannette Coocoo) wakw [wāhk^{w}], *egg of a fish;* SEC wāhk^{w}, *egg of an amphibian or fish;* NEC wāhkw, *a fish egg;* Laure (ca. 1726) "uakuets, *œufs de poisson;*" Silvy (ca. 1680) "8ak8a pl. 8ak8ak, *œufs de poisson*" | ANISH Cuoq (1886) "wak, *œuf de poisson;*" "wakowi kinonje, pine dac wawi, *le brochet fraie et la perdrix pond;*" MENO wa·hkow, *female sturgeon* see | *āhkw compare | *wāhkwan

*wāhkwan

INITIAL (NOUN, ANIMATE)

— spawn, roe

evidence | PC wāhkwanak, *fish eggs;* WC wāhkwanak, *fish roe;* ESC (Severn) wāhkonak, *fish eggs;* MC wāhkon, *an egg of an amphibian or fish;* WI (Uashat) uakunu [wākunu], *to be full of eggs, speaking of a fish,* *lobster, frog, or toad;* EI (Mamit) uakunat [wākwanat], *an eggs of a fish, lobster, frog, or toad;* MacKenzie (1801) "Waquon, *Spawn*" compare | *wāhkw

*wāhraw

INITIAL

— far

evidence | PC wāhyaw, *far;* MC wālaw, *far;* SEC wāhyaw, *far;* Laure (ca. 1726) "uarau, *loin*"

*wāhs

INITIAL

— shine

evidence | PC wāsipitam, *to shine a light on sth;* MC wāsitew, *to shine;* AT (Wemotaci, Jeannette Coocoo) wasapiskiso [wāssāpiskizow], *to shine, speaking of a stone or sth metallic;* SEC wāsāhan, *breaking waves;* Silvy (ca. 1680) "ni 8achte8, *il flambe, il reluit, v.g. le feu*" | ANISH waasizo, *to shine or reflect light* (Livesay & Nichols, 2021); MENO wa·qsenakwat, *to be daybreak* origin | PA ***wāʔs** (Hewson, 1993)

*wāhsē

INITIAL

— clear atmosphere, good visibility

evidence | PC wāsēnamān, *window;* WC wāsīskwan, *clear sky;* MC wāse-tipiskāw, *clear night;* wāseyāskweyāw, *to be a wooded area that is full of light;* AT waseaw [wāsseyāw], *clarité;* SEC wāsepayiw, *weather clears up;* wāsetahkokan, *starry night;* NEC wāsānihtākin, *window;* Silvy (ca. 1680) "8assetibiskau, *la nuit est claire*" | ANISH waaseyaaban, *to be light at dawn* (Livesay & Nichols, 2021) origin | PA ***wāʔsē** (Hewson, 1993)

*wāhswē

INITIAL (VERB, ANIMATE, INTRANSITIVE)

— fish by torchlight

evidence | PC Lacombe (1874) "wāswew, *etc., (v.a.) il l'éclaire, c'est-à-dire en faisant de la lumière pour pêcher les poissons, avec un dard ou, il pêche le poisson au flambeau;*" WSC (Ida Bear) wāswēw, *to go spear fishing at night;* AT (Opitciwan, Joey Awashish) Waswanipi [wāsswānipiy], *place name, literally "torch fishing lake;"* SEC Wāswānipiy, *place name, literally "torch-fishing lake;"* WI uashuau [wāʃwāw], *fish by torch-light;* Silvy (ca. 1680) "8as8an 3. -e8. *je peche au harpon, j'eclaire avec le flambeau les pecheurs*" | ANISH Cuoq (1886) "Ni wij waswa, *je veux pêcher au flambeau;*" MENO wa·qswakan, *torch for hunting or fishing* origin | PA ***wāʔswē** see | *wāhs

*wāhšē

INITIAL

— **1** clear, transparent

— **2** bright, light-colored

— **3** devoid of its covering (thus revealing a lighter-colored surface)

evidence | WC wāsīkamiw, *to be clear liquid;* MC wāšeyāpiskāw, *to be bright, speaking of an object of mineral composition;* wāšeyāskopitew, *to strip sth clean, speaking of a stick-like object such as a tree;* AT (Opitciwan, Joey Awashish) waceatipew [wāššeyātihpew], *to be bald;* SEC wāšetin, *to be frozen clear;* (Waswanipi) wāšēkamin, *to be clear liquid;* NEC wāshāsikwāu, *to be clear ice;* WI (Pessamit) uashetakau [wāʃētəkāw], *to be bare of bark, speaking of wood;* EI (Sheshatshiu) uashessukau [wāʃēssūkāw], *to be clear, speaking of a viscous substance;* uasheiakunakau [wāʃējākunəkāw], *to shine, speaking of an expanse of snow;* Silvy (ca. 1680) "ni 8acheabin, *j'ai les yeux blancs*" | ANISH waashegamaa, *to be a clear lake* (Lippert & Gambill, 2023)

*wāk

INITIAL

— curve

evidence | PC wāwākikātēw, *to be bow-legged;* WC wākināwak, *canoe ribs;* MC wākāw, *to be curved;* wākinākan, *a tamarack;* SEC wākāskwan, *to be a curved stick;* Laure (ca. 1726) "uauatchitinu, *elle tourne, serpente;*" Silvy (ca. 1680) "ni 8atchisten api8agan, *je fais plier le banc*" | ANISH waagaa, *to be bent* (Livesay & Nichols, 2021) origin | PA ***wāk** (Aubin, 1975)

*wānaskē

INITIAL (VERB, ANIMATE, INTRANSITIVE)

— free from difficulty, at ease

evidence | PC wānaskēw, *to be free from an ill; to live at peace;* WI (Pessamit) uanasseielimeu [wā:ssējēləmēw], *to think that one can prevail over sb easily;* EI (Sheshatshiu) uanasse [wānəssē], *without difficulty, easily, in peace;* Watkins (1865) "Waniskā, *adv. At liberty;*" Silvy (ca. 1680) "ni 8anaskan, -e8, *je vis en sûreté sans faire le guet*" | ANISH Cuoq, (1886) "wanaki, *être en paix, vivre en paix*" origin | Likely PA ***wānaskyē**.

*wāp

INITIAL

— **1** see

— **2** white

evidence | [1]PC wapamew, *to see sb;* WC wāpan, *to be dawn;* MC wāpiw, *to see;* SEC wāpahtam, *to see sth;* Silvy (ca. 1680) "8aban, *il est le point du jour;*" "ni 8abaten, ni 8abatchigan, *je vois*" [2]PC wāpisiw, *to be white;* MC wāpāw, *to be white;* SEC wāpākonakāw, *an expanse of white snow;* Silvy (ca. 1680) "ni 8abicht8an, *j'ai la barbe blanche*" origin | PA ***wāp** (Aubin, 1975) see | *āpi

*wāpatonisk

INITIAL (NOUN, ANIMATE)

— clay

evidence | PC wāpatoniskinēw, *to apply white clay on sb;* MC wāpatoniskiwan, *to be clayey;* WI (Pessamit) uapatunishk [wāpətūnəʃk], *clay;* Laure (ca. 1726) "uabatunisk, *terre grasse, argile;*" "uabatunistchiragan, *plat de terre*" | ANISH (Abitibi dialect) wāpanonihk, *clay; common family name* see | *wāp, *atonisk, *āpatonisk

*wāpištān

INITIAL (NOUN, ANIMATE)

— marten

evidence | PC wāpistān, *a marten;* WC wāpiscāniskāw, *to be many martens;* MC wāpištānikan, *bone of a marten;* SEC wāpištānāskweyāw, *to be a wooded area ideal for a marten habitat;* WI (Pessamit) uapishtaniss [wāpəstānīss], *marten less than one year old;* Silvy (ca. 1680) "8abichtanich, *fouine, martre*" see | *wāp, *ιšt[1], *ē, *n[1] see | *āpištān, *āpištāniw

*wāpošw (~ *wāpošo)

INITIAL (NOUN, ANIMATE)

— hare

evidence | MC wāpošoskāw, *to be many hares;* AT wapocokan [wāpoʒohkān], *faux lapin, lapin en peluche, jouet en forme de lapin;* (Wemotaci, Nicole Petiquay) wapococic [wāpoʒoʒiš], *a baby hare;* NEC wāpushwākun, *freshly-fallen, light snow;* Laure (ca. 1726) "uabuchuchich, *levraut;*" Silvy (ca. 1680) "ni 8ab8ch8in, *je suis lièvre*" see | *āpošw

*wār

INITIAL

— depressed, sunken

evidence | PC wāyahcāw, *to be a depression in the ground;* MC wāliškam, *to create a depression in sth under one's weight;* AT waraw [wārāw], *être incurvé, concave (comme un trou), profond;* SEC wāyipeyāw, *to be a puddle;* WI (Pessamit) kualaukau [kwālāwkāw], *to be a depression in the sand;* EI (Sheshatshiu) kuanau [kwānāw], *to be concave, to have a hollow or depression;* Laure (ca. 1726) "uaraskamigau, *fond, vallée;*" Silvy (ca. 1680) "ni 8araskamitchinen, *je fais la fosse du blé d'inde avec la main*" | ANISH waanakamigaa, *to be a depression or hollow in the ground* (Livesay & Nichols, 2021) compare | *wāt[1] discussion | Contemporary eastern dialects feature a reflex with an intrusive velar stop, cognates of which are also found in Eastern Algonquian languages. The evidence at hand suggests this form represents either an innovation or influence from neighbouring languages. On the other hand, an exhaustive survey of Algonquian languages may ultimately provide supporting evidence for this form, in which case the loss of the initial stop in the above reconstruction would represent an early innovation shared by the neighbouring Anishinabe dialects, perhaps by analogy with the root ***wāt**.

*wāron

INITIAL

— curve

evidence | PC Lacombe (1874) "wāyinwew, wāyinopattaw, wāyiniw, wāyinuttew, *il se détourne du chemin;*" SEC (inland) wāyinopayiw, *to take a U-turn;* NEC wāyiyumū, *to be a winding trail, path, or road;* wāyiyuhtāu, *to make a turn while walking;* wāyiyushtikwāu, *to be a bend in the river;* Watkins (1865) "Wanunukamāhum, *v.t.in.6. He coasts it, he goes round the lake, &c.;*" Laure (ca. 1726) "uarunahiganiu, *détroit, passage étroit, bras de rivière;*" "uarunamu, "détroit, passage étroit" | ANISH Cuoq (1886) "wanonicka, *allonger son chemin, faire un circuit*" discussion | Contemporary dialects display reflexes of ***wārino**, a form obtained by metathesis.

*wāskam

INITIAL

— clear, lucid

evidence | WC wāskamātisiw, *to be sensible;* MC wāskamisīw, *to be lucid;* SEC wāskameyihtam, *to think lucidly;* NEC wāskimāu, *to be a clear day;* EI (Sheshatshiu) uashkamakunakau [wāʃkəmākunəkāw], *to be clean snow* | ANISH waakaminaagwad, *to look clear* (Livesay & Nichols, 2021) origin | PA ***wāskam** (***wa:xkam**, Aubin, 1975)

*wāskā

INITIAL

— around

evidence | PC wāskāskam, *to walk around sth;* MC wāskāšam, *to cut around sth;* SEC wāskāštāw, *to place things around;* Laure (ca. 1726) "ni-uaskakuaten 3. -tamu, *je borde une robe*"

*wāskw (~ *wāsko)

INITIAL (NOUN, INANIMATE)

— sky

evidence | AT (Opitciwan, Joey Awashish) wasko [wāsko], *the sky;* WI (Pessamit) uashku [wāʃku], *sky, heaven;* EI (Sheshatshiu) uashku [wāʃku], *sky, heaven;* Laure (ca. 1726) "uasku *pl.* uaskua, *ciel;*" Silvy (ca. 1680) "8ask8k, *le ciel, le temps*" | ANISH waakwiing, *in heaven, Ot.* (Rhodes, 1993); Cuoq (1886) "wakwi, *ciel, voûte du ciel, paradis;*" MESK wahkwi, *sky (song word)* see | *āwaskw, *askw[1] compare | *kīšik, *waskw discussion | Dialects spoken to the north of Atikamekw and Innu dialects, as well as those spoken to the west, use a reflex of Old Cree ***kīšikwi** rather than the above root. This isogloss separates Anishinabe dialects between east and west in a similar manner.

*wāsp

INITIAL

— lace up, wrap up

evidence | PC wāspisow, *to be laced in a moss bag;* MC wāspitaham, *to lace sth up;* SEC wāspitāwasow, *to dress a child;* NEC wāspitim, *to lace sth up;* Laure (ca. 1726) "uaspitiganiu *pl.* -ets, *enseveli, enveloppé d'un suaire;*" Fabvre (ca. 1690) "8aspis8n 8, *se ranger, acomoder ses hardes, paq(ue)ts, besoignes*" | ANISH waapijiibizo, *to be laced up in the cradleboard bag* (Livesay & Nichols, 2021)

*wāš

INITIAL

— bay

evidence | PC wāsāw, *to be a bay;* MC wāšāw, *to be a bay;* AT (Wemotaci, Jeannette Coocoo) wacaw [wāʒāw], *to be a bay;* SEC wāšāw, *to be a bay;* NEC wāshāu, *to be a bay;* EI (Sheshatshiu) uashau [wāʃāw], *to be a bay;* Laure (ca. 1726) "uachau *pl.* -a, *baie;*" "uachau, uachikamau, *bras de mer;*" Silvy (ca. 1680) "8achau, *baie*" | ANISH Cuoq (1886) "Waja, *petite baie*" compare | *wāšah

*wāšah

INITIAL

— bay-shaped, horseshoe-shaped

evidence | PC wāsahāw *to be a bay;* MC wāšahāw, *to be a bay;* wāšahāwahkāw, *to be a sandy bay;* SEC wāšahāw, *to be a bay;* wāšahekan, *to be curved at one end, speaking of sth sheet-like;* NEC wāshihāu, *to be a bay;* wāshihākunikāu, *to be a horseshoe-shaped bank of snow;* WI (Pessamit) uashaiau [wāʃījāw], *to have a u-shaped indentation;* Watkins (1865) "Wasahikumow, *v.imp. It is a bay*" | ANISH Waazha'aamikaag, *Wahjamega, Michigan* (Lippert & Gambill, 2023) see | *wāš, *ah

*wāt[1] (~ *wāš)

INITIAL (NOUN, INANIMATE)

— burrow, tunnel

evidence | PC wācis, *a small burrow;* MC wātiskāw, *to be many animal dens, burrows, or tunnels;* NEC wāt, *a beaver or muskrat tunnel;* Watkins (1865) "Wate, *n.in. A natural cave, a den, a lair;*" Silvy (ca. 1680) "8achi, *trou de cabane à castor;*" "8atikan, *fosse, cave*" | ANISH waazh, *a den, a lair, a cave, a burrow;* waanike, *to dig a hole or trench* (Livesay & Nichols, 2021) origin | PA ***wāθ-** (Hewson, 1993). see | *āt[3], *āt[4] compare | *wār

*wāt[2] (~ *wāc)

INITIAL

— even

evidence | PC wāwāc, *even, even now, even more;* mwāc, *no, no way;* MC wāwāc & wāc, *even;* SEC nama wāc, *not even;* NEC wāwāch, *even;* EI mauat [māwāt], *no, not;* Laure (ca. 1726) "nema uatch, *point du tout*" limited to | *i[3]

*wāw[1]

INITIAL (NOUN, INANIMATE)

— egg of a bird

evidence | PC wāwi, *an egg;* MC wāwi, *a bird egg;* SEC wāw, *a bird egg;* Laure (ca. 1726) "uaui *pl.* uaua, *œuf*" origin | PA ***wāwi** (Aubin, 1975; Hewson, 1993) see | *āw[2]

*wāw[2]

INITIAL

— make strips from a hide, make babiche

evidence | MC wāšwew, *to cut sth into strands;* AT (Wemotaci, Jeannette Coocoo) wacapan [wāʒāpān], *babiche;* SEC wāšam, *to cut babiche (from around the edge of a hide);* Laure (ca. 1726) "ni-uachaban, *je coupe, fais de la babiche pour les raquettes*" | ANISH owaazhwaan, *to cut sth into strips, to filet sth* (Livesay & Nichols, 2021) limited to | *ɪš, *ɪšw compare | *wāwiy discussion | The above root is likely a variant of ***wāwiy**, "circular," aptly used to describe the practice of making babiche by cutting a continuous strip from around the edge of a rawhide until the entire piece of hide has been used up.

*wāwāht (~ *wāwāhc)

INITIAL

— placed opposite one another, vis-à-vis

evidence | ESC wāwāhcihtin, *river runs on each side of an island;* MC wāwāhtapīštātowak, *to sit facing one another;* wāwāhcikāpawiwak, *to stand face to face;* Laure (ca. 1726) "ueuatchitchipahigan tchistukan, *porte à deux battants;*" Silvy (ca. 1680) "ni 8a8atabista8au, ni 8e8atabista8au, *je suis assis vis-à-vis de lui*" | MESK wāwātāsamapiwaki, *to sit facing one another;* wāwāchipehkwanēkāpāwaki, *to stand back to back* discussion | Evidence for this root is limited to reduplicated forms. While the Meskwaki form supports the above reconstruction, Silvy (ca. 1680) and Laure (ca. 1726) support a variant for which vowel lengths cannot be ascertained.

*wāwiy

INITIAL

— circular, round

evidence | PC wāwiyakihkotam, *to whittle sth round;* WC wāwīyāsiw, *to be round, as in a full moon;* MC wāwiyāw, *to be circular;* wāwiyātakan, *to be a round burrow or tunnel; to have a round bore;* WI (Pessamit) uauiapu [wāwījāpu], *to have round eyes;* EI (Sheshatshiu) uauiapekan [wāwjāpēkən], *to be in a circular shape, speaking of sth string-like;* Watkins (1865) "Wowetow, *v.t.in.2. He makes it round (i.e. globular);*" "Woweaskwun, *v.imp. It is round (speaking of wood);*" Silvy (ca. 1680) "ni 8a8iāb8g8n, *la marée me fait tourner çà et là*" | MIAMI waawiyaawi, *to be round* (ILDA, 2017) compare | *wāw, *wāwiyē

*wāwiyē

INITIAL

— circular, round

evidence | PC wāwiyēsin, *to lie in a circle;* MC wāwiyeyāw, *to be circular;* SEC wāwiyekamāw, *round lake;* WI (Pessamit) uauieiau [wāwījējāw], *to be round;* Watkins (1865) "Woweyāhāo, *v.t.an. He maks him round;*" Silvy (ca. 1680) "8a8iesi8 piissim8, *la lune est pleine*" | ANISH waawiyezi, *to be round* (Livesay & Nichols, 2021) compare | *wāwiy

*wē[1]

FINAL (VERB, INTRANSITIVE, CONCRETE)

— make a sound or vocalize

evidence | PC kitowēhkwāmiw, *to snore;* sēwēw, *to ring;* MC itwew, *to say sth to sb;* wiyatwew, *to talk humourously;* SEC cipihtowew, *to hush;* SEC šewehtin, *to ring or echo;* Watkins (1865) "Yoowāo, *v.imp. It blows;*" Laure (ca. 1726) "ni-tchiripuan, *je parle vite;*" Fabvre (ca. 1690) "Achik8an e8, *chanter, parler haut;*" Silvy (ca. 1680) "ni tapat8anach, *je parle bas, je parle un peu;*" "ni tegat8an, *j'ai achevé mon discours*" compare | *wēwē

*wē[2]

FINAL (VERB, ABSTRACT, INTRANSITIVE)

— forms the antipassive when suffixed to transitive animate verb stems

evidence | PC kāsiwēw, *to hide people;* kīhkāyāsowēw, *to shine brightly;* MC sākihiwew, *to love;* SEC mākoniwesiw, *police officer;* Laure (ca. 1726) "ni-pagunumuan, *je suis médisant*" compare | *ā[2], *ıkē, *kē[2], *kēmo

*wē[3]

FINAL (ABSTRACT)

— forms particles when suffixed to certain initials

evidence | MC kihciwē, *earnestly;* SEC misiwe, *all;* WI (Pessamit) tshitshue [tʃətʃwē], *really, truly;* Laure (ca. 1726) "missiué, *partout*" see | *kišt, *mis

*wēhsā

INITIAL

— too much

evidence | PC wēsā, *too much;* AT (Wemotaci, Jeannette Coocoo) wesa [wēssā], *too much;* SEC wesā, *too much;* NEC wāsā, *oh no!* | ANISH gaawesaa, *impossible!, no way!, can't be done!* (Livesay & Nichols, 2021) compare | *wisām

*wēht (~ *wēhc)

INITIAL

— easy

evidence | PC Lacombe (1874) "Wetchihew, *il en vient à bout aisément;*" WC wīhtakīhtam, *to sell sth cheap;* MC wehtan, *to be easy;* wehcihew, *to give sb an easy time;* SEC wehtacihtākwan, *to be inexpensive;* Silvy (ca. 1680) "8etachi8, *aisé, facile, de instrumentibus*"

*wēhwēw

INITIAL (NOUN, ANIMATE)

— snow goose (Anser caerulescens)

evidence | PC wēhwēw, *a snow goose;* MC wehwew, *a snow goose;* SEC wehwew, *a snow goose;* NEC wāhwāu, *a snow goose;* MacKenzie (1801) "Wey Wois, *White Goose*" | ANISH we'we, *a snow goose* (Livesay & Nichols, 2021)

*wēm

INITIAL

— a clear view into the distance

evidence | AT (Opitciwan, Joey Awashish) wemapiw [wēmāpiw], *to look from a lookout;* NEC wāminākun, *to be possible to see a long distance away;* SEC wemāpahtam, *to see sth from a lookout;* Watkins (1865) "Wāminākwun, *v.imp. There is a prospect or view*" | ABEN wami, *enough;* wamipi, *to eat enough, to have enough to eat* (Day, 1995)
compare | *wēmoht

*wēmoht (~ *wēmohc)

INITIAL

— a clear view into the distance

evidence | AT (Wemotaci, Nicole Petiquay) Wemotaci [wēmohtāšši], *place name, Wemotaci, literally "place where one can see into the distance, a lookout;"* NEC wāmuhch, *in clear view;* EI (Sheshatshiu) uemut [wēmut], *absolutely; most certainly*
compare | *wēm discussion | Variant spellings used historically for the community of Wemotaci suggest an Anishinabe cognate of the form *wēmont.* These variants include Weymontachie, the official designation from 1986 to 1997, Weymontachingue, the previous designation from 1932 to 1986, and Weymontachinque in 1829 (Commission de toponymie, 2023). Unfortunately, Anishinabe cognates were not identified in the sources available during this investigation.

*wēp

INITIAL

— propel in a sweeping motion

evidence | PC wēpaham, *to sweep sth away;* WC wīpinitowin, *divorce;* MC wewepāloweštāw, *to wag one's tail;* SEC wepāhokow, *to be swept away by the current;* NEC wāpinim, *to throw sth away;* Silvy (ca. 1680) "8e8epachtan, *le vent pousse, ouvre la porte*" | ANISH webaasin, *to be blown away by the wind* (Livesay & Nichols, 2021)

*wērapisk

INITIAL

— a little while

evidence | MC welipisk, *a little while* SEC weyipiščīš, *a little while;* NEC wāyipisch, *a little while;* WI (Pessamit) uelapissish [wēləpəssīʃ], *a little while;* EI (Sheshatshiu) uenapissish [wēnəpɨssīʃ], *a little while;* Laure (ca. 1726) "uerapischich nit-apinach, *je demeure quelques jours;*" Silvy (ca. 1680) "8erabichi8ets, *ils se sont dépêchés, fait à la légère*" | ANISH Cuoq (1886) "Wenibik, *pour peu de temps*"

*wērōt (~ *wērōc)

INITIAL

— plenty

evidence | WC wīðōtan, *to be plentiful;* WSC (Misipawistik, Ellen Cook) wēnōtisiw, *to be rich;* MC welōcihtāw, *to have plenty of sth;* WI (Pessamit) uelutshipimeu [wēlūtʃəpmēw], *to have plenty of grease;* Silvy (ca. 1680) "ni 8er8tisin, *je suis riche*"

*wēskwā

INITIAL

— at the end, to the end

evidence | Laure (ca. 1726) "ni-ueskuaskanauan 3. –ueu, *me voilà au bout du chemin;*" Silvy (ca. 1680) "8esk8anagau, *le bout d'une île"* | ANISH wekwaabatoo, *to run to the end* (Livesay & Nichols, 2021)

*wēskwāhtēm

INITIAL (NOUN, INANIMATE)

— back end of the interior of a dwelling, area opposite a doorway

evidence | PC wēskwāhtēmihk, *opposite the door of the lodge;* MC wēskwāhtēm, *the area opposite a doorway in a dwelling;* SEC (Waswanipi, Mary Jane Kitchen) weškwāhtem, *the area opposite a doorway in a dwelling;* NEC wāskwāhtāmishtuwikuhch, *the back of the beaver lodge opposite to the door side* see | wēskwā, ht¹, compare | ɩškwāhtēm

*wēškat (~ *wēškac)

INITIAL

— long ago

evidence | PC Lacombe (1874) "Weskatisiw, ok, *(a.a.) il est ancien;*" MC weškacihtin, *to be an old track;* AT (Wemotaci, Jeannette Coocoo) weckatc [wēškac], *long ago;* NEC wāshkichinākun, *to look old;* EI (Sheshatshiu) ueshkat [wēʃkət], *formerly, in the past*

*wētāt (~ *wētāc)

INITIAL

— gradually, more and more

evidence | SEC wetāc, *gradually more, increasingly;* Laure (ca. 1726) "uetatch ni-punitan, *peu à peu je me désaccoutume;*" "ni-uetatchinesin, *je suis tout langoureux*" | MENO we·ta·c, *gradually;* cf. MESK wēta, *alas!*

*wēw

INITIAL

— enfold, wrap

evidence | PC wēwēkīw, *to wrap oneself in a blanket;* MC wewakinew, *to hug sb;* wewekinam, *to wrap sth using sth sheet-like;* AT wewakinew, *to hug sb;* SEC wewacikwenew, *to hug sb;* EI (Mamit) ueutshineu [wēwatnēw], *to hug sb* | ANISH owiiweginaan, *to wrap sb* (Livesay & Nichols, 2021); MENO wi·wetɛ·hpɛ·hpeswan, *veil;* wi·wi·kenɛw, *to wrap or cover sb;* MESK wiiwiikihšim-, *to wrap sb up;* wiiwahosi-, *be wrapped, bandaged, swaddled* (ILDA, 2017)

*wēwē

FINAL (VERB, INTRANSITIVE, CONCRETE)

— make a sound or vocalize

evidence | PC pimwēwēstin, *howling wind;* WC matwīwīstin, *howling wind;* MC kišwewew, *to speak loudly;* SEC itweweham, *to make a certain sound from using a tool on sth or striking sth;* WI (Pessamit) pimueuiatsheu [pmwēwījātʃēw], *to make a sound from one's wings in passing;* Silvy (ca. 1680) "pass8e8echinani8i8, *on entend l'écho"* | ANISH wiimbwewe, *to give a hollow sound* (Livesay & Nichols, 2021); MESK anemwēwēpahowa, *to run off with noise* compare | *wē¹

*wēwēp

INITIAL

— hurry

evidence | AT wewepimew [wēwēpimēw], *to tell sb to hurry;* Laure (ca. 1726) "ni-ueueberiten, *je suis pressé, me dépêche*" | ANISH wewiibishkaa, *to hurry* (Livesay & Nichols, 2021); MENO wɛ·we·pahcekɛ·w, *to eat hurriedly;* MESK wēpisēwa, *to start to fly;* MIAMI waawiipisi-, *to be in a hurry* (ILDA, 2017)

*wēwēriht

INITIAL

— properly, carefully

evidence | MC wewelit & wewelat, *meticulously, carefully; gently;* AT (Wemotaci, Nicole Petiquay) wewerita [wēwērihta], *properly;* (Opitciwan, Joey Awashish) wewerita & werita [(wē)wērihta], *properly;* SEC (Waswanipi) weweyit, *properly; gently* | ANISH wewenind, *carefully;* (Lippert & Gambill, 2023); weweni, *properly, correctly,* *carefully* (Livesay & Nichols, 2021); MENO wɛ·wɛ·nen, *in the proper way; thank you* origin | PA ***wēwērint**

*wicē

INITIAL

— kiss

evidence | PC ocēhtowak, *to kiss one another;* MC ocehtam, *to kiss sth;* SEC ocemew, *to kiss sb;* Silvy (ca. 1680) "n'8tchemau, *je le ou la baise*" | ANISH ojiim, *kiss sb* (Livesay & Nichols, 2021); MENO oci·htam, *to kiss sth* limited to | *am², *aht³

*wicēk

INITIAL (NOUN, ANIMATE)

— fisher

evidence | WC ocīk, *a fisher;* SEC ocek, *a fisher;* WI (Pessamit) utshekashtau [utʃēkəstāw], *to set a trap for fishers;* Laure (ca. 1726) "utchekataku, *chien, constellation;*" Silvy (ca. 1680) "8tchek8, *enfant du diable*" | ANISH ojiigag, *fishers* (Livesay & Nichols, 2021) origin | PA ***wecyēka**

*wicēpihk

INITIAL (NOUN, INANIMATE)

— primary root

evidence | PC ocēpihk, *a root;* SEC ocepihc, *a primary root;* WI (Pessamit) utshepitshitakᵘ [utʃēpətʃətukʷ], *large end of a felled tree;* Laure (ca. 1726) "utchebik, *racine d'arbre;*" "utchebikatinau, *le pied d'une montagne*" | ANISH ojiibikan, *roots* (Livesay & Nichols, 2021); MESK ochēpihki, *root;* MIAMI aciiphka, *root* (ILDA, 2017) see | *cēpihk

*wicēšt

INITIAL (VERB, ANIMATE, INTRANSITIVE)

— draw one's foot towards oneself

evidence | WC ocīstiw, *to pull one's foot towards oneself;* Watkins (1865) "Oochāstew, *v.i.1., He puts his leg forward (as in walking, &c.);*" Silvy (ca. 1680) "n'8tchechtin, *je retire les jambes*" origin | Query obscure noun incorporation. see | *wit¹, *t¹

*wicēw

INITIAL (NOUN, ANIMATE)

— housefly

evidence | PC ōcēw, *housefly; maggot;* MC ocewātam, *to lay one's eggs on sth, speaking for a housefly;* NEC uchāu, *a housefly;* Silvy (ca. 1680) "8tche8, *grosse mouche noire*" | ANISH oojii, *a fly* (Livesay & Nichols, 2021); MENO oci·w, *fly;* MESK ōchēwa, *a fly;* MIAMI oocia, *Musca domestica* origin | PA ***wecyēwa** (Aubin, 1975; Hewson, 2023)

*wicicāhkw (~ *wicicāhko)

INITIAL (NOUN, ANIMATE)

— sandhill crane (Antigone canadensis)

evidence | PC ocicāhk, *a crane;* WC ocicāhk, *a crane; a sharp-pointed hoe;* MC ocicāhkoskāw, *to be many sandhill cranes;* SEC ocicāhkʷ, *a sandhill crane;* Silvy (ca. 1680) "8tchistchak, *grue*" | ANISH ojijaak, *a sandhill crane* (Livesay & Nichols, 2021)

*wicihkē

INITIAL (VERB, ANIMATE, INTRANSITIVE)

— to make provisions, speaking of a beaver

evidence | WC ocīhkana, *a beaver's store of food;* MC ocihkew, *to make one's provisions, speaking of a beaver;* NEC wichihkinh, *a beaver's food store;* WI (Pessamit) utshikanashkᵘ [utʃəkənāʃkʷ], *a piece of wood from the beaver's store of provisions;* Laure (ca. 1726) "utchikanitcheu, *le castor fait sa provision*"

*wicihkwan

INITIAL

— kneel

evidence | PC ocihkwanapiw, *to kneel;* ocihcihkwanipayihow, *to genuflect;* WC ocīhcīhkwanapiw, *to kneel;* MC ocīhcīhkwanapiw, *to kneel;* SEC ocihcīhkwanīw, *to kneel;* Laure (ca. 1726) "n-utchikuanapin, *je m'agenouille sur mes talons;*" "n-utchikunapin 3. -piu, *je m'agenouille, m'accroupissant;*" Silvy (ca. 1680) "n'88tchig8napin, *je suis à genoux*" | ANISH ojijiingwanabi, *to kneels* (Livesay & Nichols, 2021); MENO oci·hcekwaneqtaw, *to kneel down*

*wicīhs

INITIAL

— scar

evidence | PC ocīsisiw, *to be scarred by a burn;* ESC (Severn) ocīsisiw, *to have a scar;* ESC (Attawapiskat, Bill Louttit) ocīsāw, *to be scarred;* MC ocīsicihcew, *to have a scar on the hand;* ocīsāhkasow, *to be scarred by the fire;* SEC uchīsisū, *to have wrinkles* (CSB, 2018); NSK uchiisaapuw, *to have wrinkles or scars around one's eyes;* Laure (ca. 1726) "utchichisiuin *pl.* -a, *cicatrice, marque d'une plaie;*" Silvy (ca. 1680) "8itchichisi8in, *cicatrice*" | ANISH ojiishinike, *to have a scar on the arm* (Livesay & Nichols, 2021); Cuoq (1886) "odjicingwe, *avoir une balafre au visage;*" MENO oce·qsam, *to scorch sth* discussion | In the absence of an Atikamekw cognate, the preaspirate in this reconstruction is indirectly supported by Anishinabe and Menominee.

*wih

INITIAL

— boil

evidence | PC osow, *to boil;* MC osam, *to boil sth;* AT (Opitciwan, Joey Awashish) osam [ossam], *to boil sth;* osso-, *to boil* (Béland, 1978); SEC ohtew, *to boil;* Silvy (ca. 1680) "n'8sen 3. -e8, *je fais bouillir*" | MIAMI wensam-, *boil sth* (ILDA, 2017) origin | PA ***wen** (Aubin, 1975; Hewson, 1993), via debuccalization of the final PA ***n** when followed by consonant-initial verb finals, satisfying the morphophonological constraint on preconsonantal nasals. limited to | *tē⁴, *s, *so², *sw

*wihcitaw

INITIAL

— on purpose, for a reason

evidence | PC ohcitaw, *on purpose;* MC ohcitaw, *on purpose, intentionally; necessarily; pretending, not seriously;* without cause; SEC ohcit, *for a reason, on purpose; jokingly;* NEC wisht, *just for fun, teasingly;* EI (Sheshatshiu) usht [ūst], *above all; for no reason; purposely;* Laure (ca. 1726) "utchita kata irinisiu, *il faut qu'il soit sage (malgré lui n'importe);*" Silvy (ca. 1680) "8tchitau, *tout exprès, à dessein*"

*wihkē

INITIAL (VERB, ANIMATE, INTRANSITIVE)

— bark

evidence | PC ohkohkēw, *to bark;* Lacombe (1874) "Okokkew, ok, *(v.n.) il aboie;*" "Okokkātew, *etc., (v.a.) il aboie après lui;*" Laure (ca. 1726) "ni-ukaukan 3. -tchéu, *j'aboie;*" Silvy (ca. 1680) "n'8ka8katau, *je lui aboie;*" "8ka8ka8katcheu, *in reduplicatio, il aboie*" compare | *mik discussion | The extant cognates display reduplicated elements that do not match, hence the nonreduplicated reconstruction above. Furthermore, in the absence of a Woods Cree cognate the status of the preaspiration cannot be confirmed.

*wihp

INITIAL

— up

evidence | PC ohpikiw, *to grow up;* MC ohpipaliw, *to go up;* SEC ohpinam, *to lift sth by hand;* WI (Pessamit) upatinau [upətnāw], *to be a mountainous rise;* Fabvre (ca. 1690) "n 8pikaterin, i8, *Remuer Le pied en L air*" | ANISH ombagoode, *to hang up in the air* (Livesay & Nichols, 2021) origin | PA ***wemp** (Aubin, 1975)

*wihpimē

INITIAL

— on or to one side

evidence | WC ohpimīhwīw, *to miss sb to the side;* MC ohpimepaliw, *to fall onto one's side;* WI (Pessamit) upimeiapiss [upmējāpəss], *beside a rock;* Laure (ca. 1726) "n-upimechinin 3. -chinu, *je couche sur le côté;*" Fabvre (ca. 1690) "n ȣpimechtan tau, *mettre sur son coste canot*"

*wihsikw (~ *wihsiko)

INITIAL (NOUN, ANIMATE)

— merganser (Mergus spp.)

evidence | WC osik, *a merganser;* MC asikʷ, *a merganser;* AT (Opitciwan, Monique Awashish) asikw [assikʷ], *merganser;* mistassikw, *American merganser* (Béland, 1978); SEC asikʷ & osikʷ, *a merganser;* osikoskāw, *to be many mergansers;* WI (Pessamit) ushikᵘ [uʃəkʷ], *a merganser;* EI (Mamit) ushikᵘ [uhukʷ], *a merganser;* Laure (ca. 1726) "uchiku *pl.* -ets, *bec-de-scie;*" Fabvre (ca. 1690) "ȣsigȣ ȣek, *becscie, plongeon à bec comme des dents;*" Silvy (ca. 1680) "ȣsigȣ, *plongeon à long bec armé de dents*" | ANISH anzig, *a merganser* (Livesay & Nichols, 2021); MENO ose·hkok, *sawbill ducks*

*wihšē

INITIAL

— ridge, crest

evidence | PC osētināw, *to be a ridge;* MC ošetāwahkāw, *sandy ridge;* SEC ošeyaw, *to be a ridge;* EI (Sheshatshiu) ushekatan [uhēkātən], *edge of the tibia* | ANISH oshedinaa, *to be a ridge* (Livesay & Nichols, 2021); oshedaawangaa, *to be a sand ridge* (Lippert & Gambill, 2023) discussion | In the absence of an Atikamekw cognate, the preaspirate in this reconstruction is indirectly supported by Anishinabe.

*wiht (~ *wihc, *wihs)

INITIAL

— from

evidence | PC ohcipahtāw, *to run from;* MC ohtohtew, *to come walking from;* osihtew, *to hear;* AT (Wemotaci, Nicole Petiquay) osapatam [ossāpahtam], *to manage to see sth from a distance; to live long enough to see sth;* SEC ohtāšiw, *to be blown from or come sailing from;* NEC wihchichiwin, *to flow from, speaking of a current;* Silvy (ca. 1680) "n'ȣtaten, *j'attire avec la bouche*" | ANISH ondose, *to walk from* (Livesay & Nichols, 2021) origin | PA ***went** (Aubin, 1975; Hewson, 1993)

*wihtiškaw

INITIAL

— facing

evidence | PC ohtiskawisin, *to lie facing;* MC ohtiškawikāpawīštawew, *stand facing sb;* SEC ohtiškawapiw, *to sit facing;* NEC witiskiwipiu, *to sit facing* | ANISH onjishkawabi, *to sit facing the wind* (Livesay & Nichols, 2021)

*wikāskatātāhkw (~ *wikāskatātāhko)

INITIAL (NOUN, ANIMATE)

— salamander

evidence | SEC kāskatātākʷ & okāskatātākʷ, *a salamander;* SEC mishikāskatātāhkw, *a crocodile or alligator* (CSB, 2018); NEC kāškitātākw, *a crocodile or alligator* | ABEN kakadolōkw, *an alligator or crocodile;* kakadolōkwsizak, *a small land lizard, a salamander* cf. MESK kahkāhkachīha, *a salamander* origin | PA ***wekāskatāθānkwa** compare | *wikīskatātāhkw discussion | Loanwords from an old Anishinabe dialect that corroborate the Proto-Algonquian reconstruction and, indirectly, the Old Cree reconstruction above are preserved in the SEC dialect spoken at Waswanipi and in Atikamekw. The Waswanipi forms include *kāhkatālākʷ*, *okāhkatālākʷ*, and the mixed form *okāskatālākʷ*. These, along with the Atikamekw *kāhkatārākʷ*, display an /l/ or /r/ for what is properly /t/ in Cree, pointing to the Proto-Algonquian /θ/ as its origin. Note that many elderly, monolingual speakers of East Cree prefer diminutive forms of this word, curiously associating the nondiminutive forms with large lizards such as crocodiles and alligators.

*wikāw

INITIAL (NOUN, ANIMATE)

— pikeperch, walleye, sauger

evidence | PC okāw, *a pickerel;* MC okāw, *a walleye or sauger;* okāšiš, *a small walleye or sauger;* WI (Pessamit) ukau [ūkāw], *a walleye* | ANISH ogaa, *a walleye* (Livesay & Nichols, 2021) origin | PA ***wekāwa** (Hewson, 1993)

*wikimāw

INITIAL (NOUN, ANIMATE)

— person in a position of authority, boss, chief

evidence | PC okimāwapiw, *to sit in a seat of authority;* MC okimāw, *a person in a position of authority;* SEC ocimāhkān, *a person elected to a position of authority;* EI (Sheshatshiu) utshimaukupu [utʃɨmāwkūpu], *to wear a suit;* Silvy (ca. 1680) "8tchimau, *capitaine*" origin | PA ***wekimāwa** (Aubin, 1975)

*wikīskatātāhkw (~ *wikīskatātāhko)

INITIAL (NOUN, ANIMATE)

— salamander

evidence | WI (Pessamit) utshishkatataku [utʃīʃkətātākw], *a type of salamander;* EI (Mamit) utshishkatataku [utʃīhkatātāhkw], *a type of salamander;* EI (Sheshatshiu) utshishkatataku [utʃīʃkətātākw], *a type of salamander;* Laure (ca. 1726) "utchiskataku *pl.* -ets, *lézard qui va à l'eau;*" Fabvre (ca. 1690) "8kiskatak, *Lezard a(nim)al tem(éraire);*" Silvy (ca. 1680) "8tchichkatatau [*sic*], *lézard;*" "kiskatatak8, *grand lézard écaillé*" | ANISH Cuoq (1886) "Kikatanang, *lézard;*" ogiikadaanaangw(ag), *lizard(s)* (Lippert & Gambill, 2023); (Abitibi dialect) kīhkitānāk(w), *a salamander* origin | PA ***wekīskatāθānkwa** compare | *wikāskatātāhkw, *wisīkirāwīš discussion | Loanwords from an old Anishinabe dialect that corroborate the Proto-Algonquian reconstruction and, indirectly, the Old Cree reconstruction above are preserved in the SEC dialect spoken at Waswanipi and in Moose Cree. These forms, *okīkayātākw* and *kīhkatānākošiš* respectively, display a /y/ and /n/ for what is properly /t/ in Cree, pointing to the Proto-Algonquian /θ/ as its origin.

*wikīškimanihsiw

INITIAL (NOUN, ANIMATE)

— kingfisher

evidence | PC okīskimanasiw, *a kingfisher;* MC okīškimanisiw, *a kingfisher;* AT (Wemotaci, Jeannette Coocoo) okickamanisiw [okiškimanissiw], *kingfisher;* SEC ocīšcimanisiw, *a kingfisher;* EI (Sheshatshiu) utshissimanishu [utʃīssɨmənəʃu], *a kingfisher;* Fabvre (ca. 1690) "8 tchikismanisi8 [*sic*] *pl* 8ek, *petits oyseaux hupés;*" Silvy (ca. 1680) "tchistchimanisi8, *espèce d'oiseau*" | ANISH ogiishkimanisii, *a kingfisher* (Livesay & Nichols, 2021)

*wimāciskōk

INITIAL (NOUN, ANIMATE)

— chorus frog

evidence | MC māciškōkiš, *a chorus frog;* SEC māciškōciš, *a chorus frog;* NEC māchishkūchish, *a spring peeper;* WI (Uashat) umatshashkut [umātiʃkut], *frog;* EI (Mamit) umatshashkuku [umwātʃahkūkw], *a frog;* Faries & Mackay (1938) "Machi'skokis, *S.C., n.an. A small species of frog;*" Watkins (1865) "Makiskoochis, *n.an. A small species of frog;*" Laure (ca. 1726) "tchituets umatchiskughets, *coassement de grenouilles;*" "umatchaskukats, *les grenouilles*" | ANISH (Abitibi dialect) omācihkokihsi, *a chorus frog*

*wimik

INITIAL

— scabby

evidence | PC omikicihcēw, *to have scabs or sores on one's hands;* MC omikitonew, *to have a scabby mouth;* WI (Pessamit) umitshikueu [umətʃəkwēw], *to have a scratched face;* Laure (ca. 1726) "n-umitchistiguanin, *je suis teigneux, galleux;*" Silvy (ca. 1680) "n'8mitchihau, *je lui fais une gale, une plaie*" | ANISH omiginike, *to have sores or scabs on one's arm* (Livesay & Nichols, 2021) origin | PA ***wemek** (Hewson, 1993), derived from the third-person possessive form of ***mekyi**, *scab* see | *mikiy

*wimīmīw

INITIAL (NOUN, ANIMATE)

— dove, pigeon

evidence | PC omīmīw, *a pigeon or dove;* MC omīmīw, *a dove;* EI (Sheshatshiu) umimiu [umīmīw], *a pigeon or turtle dove;* Fabvre (ca. 1690) "mimi8 *pl.* 8ek v. 8mimi8, *T8rtes, t8rterelles*" | ANISH omiimii, *a pigeon, a dove* (Livesay & Nichols, 2021) origin | PA ***wemīmīwa** (Hewson, 1993)

*win

FINAL (NOUN, INANIMATE, ABSTRACT)

— forms nouns from animate intransitive and transitive inanimate verb stems

evidence | WC maskawisīwin, *strength;* PC nipēwin, *bed;* MC tipācimowin, *story or news;* SEC apiwin, *a seat;* miyweyihtamowin, *happiness;* WI (Pessamit) nikamun [nəkəmūn], *song;* Silvy (ca. 1680) "acht8atche8in, *partie au jeu*" | ANISH awazowin, *a heater* (Livesay & Nichols, 2021); MESK mīchiweni, *food* origin | PA ***wen** (Aubin, 1975) compare | *ıhp, *ın², *n¹

*winikē

INITIAL (VERB, ANIMATE, INTRANSITIVE)

— carry on one's shoulder(s)

evidence | WC onikātīw, *to carry sb on one's shoulders;* MC onikēw, *to carry on one's shoulders;* SEC onikahp, *portage;* NEC winichāu, *to carry a canoe on one's shoulders;* Laure (ca. 1726) "n-unikan 3. -tseu, *je porte sur mes épaules;*" Fabvre (ca. 1690) "n 8nigan kan ke8, *porter canot aux portage*" | ANISH onigam, *a portage* (Livesay & Nichols, 2021) origin | PA ***wenikē** (***wenike:wa**, Aubin, 1975) see | *nikē

*winisk

INITIAL

— be fat

evidence | AT (Wemotaci, Nicole Petiquay) oniskamiskw [oniskamiskw], *a fat beaver;* Laure (ca. 1726) "unichkachtimu, *chien gras;*" Silvy (ca. 1680) "8niskachtim, *chien gras;*" "n'8nistihau, *je l'engraisse;*" "n'8nistihin, *je suis gras*" | ANISH Cuoq (1886) "Minawih,o, *se refaire, reprendre de l'embonpoint* Voy. Onikis,i." discussion | The entry in Cuoq (1886) refers the reader to a headword that must have inadvertently been omitted from the dictionary, but is nonetheless a cognate of the above root.

*wir¹

INITIAL

— **1** make ready, set

— **2** good, nice

evidence | PC oyastāw, *to set sth in place;* WC oðapiw, *to take one's seat;* ESC wanāpamew, *to choose sb;* MC wawelīw, *to prepare;* walaštāw, olaštāw, *to set sth ready for use;* AT oreritam [orērihtam], *to decide on sth;* SEC (Waswanipi) wayišam [wayšam], *to cut sth as a pattern;* wayaštāw [way(a)štāw], *to set sth ready for use;* waweyāwahkaham, *to prepare the sandy ground using sth;* NEC wiyishim, *to cut sth out;* WI (Pessamit) ulapu [ūləpu], to be seated ready to begin; Watkins (1865) "Wuyesum, *v.t.in.6. He cuts it out (as a garment);*" "Oonustow, *v.t.in.2. He puts it in order;*" Laure (ca. 1726) "ni-uarachtan, *j'étale, j'expose en vente;*" "n-urikauau, *je taille un arbre fruitier;*" Fabvre (ca. 1690) "n'ȣrichen, 3 chamȣ, *cȣper, tailler en r(on)d ig. v.g. habit;*" Silvy (ca. 1680) "n'ȣrichamȣau, *je coupe, je taille en rond, v.g un habit pour lui;*" [2]MC olihkopāw, *to be an good area covered in thickets;* AT (Wemotaci, Nicole Petiquay) oramekw [oramēkw], *fatty fish;* SEC (Waskaganish) wayimiskʷ, *place name, literally 'good lake bed'* (Bishop, 2022); Silvy (ca. 1680) "ȣraskȣteïau, *belle terre sans broussaille*"; Fabvre (ca. 1690) "ȣratchikȣ, *gros Loup marin;*" "ȣramēgau gȣchkau, *poisson gras;*" Silvy (ca. 1680) "ni ȣirabin, *j'ai bonne vu;*" "ȣraskȣteïau, *belle terre sans broussaille*" | [1]ANISH onagindaaso, *to set a price* (Livesay & Nichols, 2021); MENO ona·pew, *to sit down* [2]ABEN olapiska, *to be a nice rock;* olakwika, *to be a good forest* (Day, 1994) discussion | The alternative reconstruction ***war**, while well supported, appears to be an innovation of certain dialects rather than an archaic feature. Indeed, even Moose Cree literary sources from the late 1800s favor a reflex of ***or** over ***war**, as do sources from sister languages such as Anishinabe and Menominee.

*wir[2]

FINAL (VERB, TRANSITIVE, ANIMATE)

— convey

evidence | ESC shipwewinew, *to carry sb off;* MC āhciwilew, *to take sb elsewhere;* SEC išiwiyew, *to take sb thither;* NEC chihchiwiyāu, *to take sb along as one sets forth* paired with | *witā

*wiraman

INITIAL (NOUN, ANIMATE)

— ochre

evidence | PC oyaman, *colored paint, vermillion;* oyamanask, *love medicine;* NEC wiyiminichī, *Paint Hills, place name;* WI (Pessamit) ulaman [uləmən], *na red-colored canoe resin;* EI (Sheshatshiu) unaman [unəmən], *na ochre;* Fabvre (ca. 1690) "ȣramanǐhau, *n. peinturer che n.;*" Silvy (ca. 1680) "ȣraman, *peinture*" | ANISH Cuoq (1886) "onaman, *fard, vermillon;*" "onamanines,i, *avoir une érysipèle;*" MENO ona·mon, *vermilion;* MIAMI alamoni, *red ocher, paint, vermillion* (ILDA, 2017) origin | PA ***weraman** (***welaman**, Hewson, 1993) see | *ıraman discussion | This root is inherited directly from Proto-Algonquian as a noun stem. However, the PA form may have ultimately been derived from a verb built on the root ***weram**. Consider the Naskapi word *wiimin*, "ochre," in comparison to *wiimisiiu*, "to be fat," built on an otherwise uncorroborated root that may point to PA ***weram**.

*wirākan

INITIAL (NOUN, INANIMATE)

— dish

evidence | PC wiyākan, *a dish;* MC olākan, *a dish;* Silvy (ca. 1680) "ȣragan *pl.* -gana, *plat, écuelle;*" Le Jeune (1634) "ouragan, *dish*" see | *wir[1], *ākan[2], *rākan

*wirēw

INITIAL

— menstruate, menstrual

evidence | AT Cooper (1945) "oleolagan, *dish used in first menses observance;*" Laure (ca. 1726) "ureuasiku, *pin blanc;*" Silvy (ca. 1680) "ȣreȣastikȣ, *chaudière, ouragan des femmes pendant leur mois*" | ANISH Cuoq (1886) "Onewis,i, *avoir ses menstrues;*" "Onewakik, *chaudière de femme en menstrues*" discussion | The name provided for the white pine by Laure (ca. 1726) reconstructs as ***wirēwāšihkwa**, literally "menstrual pine." This may reflect its traditional use as an analgesic and possibly an antispasmodic. Laure himself describes the medicinal application of the inner bark for burns. However, a comparative review of traditional medicine is presently beyond the scope of this dictionary. Note that, while the above root appears to have been lost in all contemporary dialects, cognates of the name recorded by Laure are preserved in SEC and WI, albeit in a modified form.

*wirikwanēw

INITIAL (NOUN, ANIMATE)

— northern flicker (Colaptes auratus)

evidence | PC wiyikwanēw, *a northern flicker;* MC wīlikwanew, *a northern flicker;* AT wirikonew [wirikonew], *a type of woodpecker;* SEC wiyikwanew & koyikwanew, *a northern flicker;* WI (Pessamit) kunikuneu [kuləkunēw], *a type of woodpecker;* Watkins (1865) "*Woodcock, n.* Weyikoonāo;" Laure (ca. 1726) "uriguaneu, *chat-oiseau*" | ABEN gwelegwena, *a flicker;* MIAMI wiinikolia, *a northern flicker* (ILDA, 2017) cf. ANISH mooningwane, *a northern flicker* (Livesay & Nichols, 2021) see | *wir[1], *kwan compare | *mēmēw, *pāhpāštēw discussion | Literally "nicely-plumed," contemporary reflexes of the name of this bird vary on account of the obsoleteness of the secondary sense of the root ***wir**, leading to hypercorrected forms

*wirimāw

INITIAL (NOUN, INANIMATE)

— bedding of an animal's den

evidence | AT (Opitciwan, Joey Awashish) wirimaskew [wirimāskēw], *to prepare the bedding in one's den, speaking of an animal;* WI (Pessamit) ulimaushkua [ūləmāwʃkwē], *flooring of twigs in bear den;* ulimaumishkua [ūləmāwməʃkwē], *flooring of wood chips in beaver lodge;* Faries & Mackay (1938) "Oni'mowu, *n.in. The fine grass which forms the beaver's bed. S.C.;*" "Oyi'mowu, *P.C., n.in. The beaver's bed*"

*wirimiskw

INITIAL (NOUN, INANIMATE)

— catkin

evidence | MC olimiskwa, *catkins;* AT (Opitciwan, Joey Awashish) oromosk [oromosk], *bud, catkin, pollen;* WI (Pessamit) ulimishk[u] [uləmə̀ʃk[w]], *catkin on pussy willow;* Silvy (ca. 1680) "8remisk8, *bourgeon;*" cf. Watkins (1865) "Oosimisk, *n.in. A lead-bud, a bud*" | ANISH Cuoq (1886) "onimik, ...on, *bourgeon, bouton, jet*" see | *rimiskw

*wirkawēw

INITIAL (NOUN, ANIMATE)

— fish flesh

evidence | NEC uhkiwāu, *fish flesh;* uhkiwāwāpui, fish soup see | *ɪrkaw, *ēw[1]

*wirwā

INITIAL

— divine by use of shivers or twitches

evidence | Lacombe (1874) "oywātchikewin, a, *(n.f.) prédiction de l'avenir d'après certaines sensations du corps;*" "oywāstawew, etc., *(v.a.) il fait des prédictions sur lui. N.B. Ce mot et le suivant s'entendent, quand quelqu'un éprouvant certaines sensations dans son corps, croit de là connaître l'avenir;*" Watkins (1865) "ooywachikāo, *He prophesies;*" Laure (ca. 1726) "n-uruatsikan, *je devine par le frémissement de la mamelle;*" Fabvre (ca. 1690) "n 8r8atchigan 3 ke8, *aur tels pressentim(en)ts en fremiss(an)t;*" "n 8r8atam8n 8 8ek, *les deuiner par la narine, par fretillemt de narines, nez;*" Silvy (ca. 1680) "n'8r8atchigan 3. -e8, *je devine par le frémissement;*" "n'8r8at8m8, n'8r8atam8n, *je devine*" | ANISH onwaataw, *to have a foreboding feeling about sb* (Lippert & Gambill, 2023); Cuoq (1886) "onwadjike, *augurer, deviner par le frémissement;*" MENO onuaqtam, *to have a premonition about sth* discussion | Laure (ca. 1726: 295) describes the use of this type of divination to predict the success of a hunt, specifically describing a ritual to induce the quivering of one's breast. Cuoq (1886: 305) describes this type of divination among the Anishinabe as forgotten by all but a few elderly people, and offers the interpretation of various twitches.

For example, the twitching of the lower lip would predict an upcoming feast; that of the eyelids, that one will soon shed tears; that of the ears, that it will snow; among others. While the ritualistic use of this type of divination may be largely obsolete, people in various regions continue to interpret twitches as premonitions. In Moose Factory, for instance, people speak of the twitching of eyelids as predicting that one will cry, and the twitching of lips as meaning that one will soon receive a kiss.

*wisām

INITIAL

— too

evidence | PC osāmihtāw, *to overdo or overwork sth;* MC osāmaškinew, *to be overfilled;* AT (Wemotaci, Jeannette Coocoo) osam [ozām], *too much; because;* SEC osāmihew, *to do too much to sb;* EI (Sheshatshiu) ueshamipatau [wēʃāmpātāw], *aller trop loin en courant ou en véhicule à roues;* Fabvre (ca. 1690) "ȣesamipiten, v. ȣsamipiten 3 tamȣ, *Tirer trop à soy*" | ANISH onzaamaabaawe, *to be too wet* (Livesay & Nichols, 2021); Nicholas (ca. 1670) "ousam, *beaucoup, trop*" (Daviault, 1994) origin | PA ***wesām** (Aubin, 1975; Hewson, 1993) compare | *wēhsā

*wisāw

INITIAL

— hue ranging from brown to yellow

evidence | PC osāwihtâw, *to make sth yellow;* MC osāwālihkwew, *to have blond or brown hair;* AT osāwāpiskāw [ozāwāpiskāw], *to be brown metal or rock;* SEC osāwāw, *to be a hue ranging from brown and yellow;* NEC usāukimiu, *to be a yellow or brown liquid* | ANISH ozaawaabate, *yellow or brown smoke* (Livesay & Nichols, 2021); MENO osa·waqnεm(-ok), *a yellow or brown dog;* MESK asāwesiwa, *to be yellow* origin | PA ***wesāw** (Aubin, 1975) compare | *wīh[2]

*wisip

INITIAL

— cause water to ripple by one's presence underwater

evidence | AT (Opitciwan, Joey Awashish) wisipiw [wizipiw], *to make the water ripple from one's presence underwater;* NEC usipihtāu, *to observe the water for ripples caused by the presence of an animal underwater;* WI (Pessamit) ushipu [uʃəpu], *to make the surface of the water tremble by one's presence underwater, speaking of a beaver;* Laure (ca. 1726) "n-uchipitan 3. -tau, *je sonde pour trouver son trou*"

*wisīk

INITIAL

— wrinkle

evidence | PC Lacombe (1874) "Osikākatosuw, *il se rétrécit en séchant;*" MC osīkāpāwew, *to be wrinkled from wetness;* AT (Wemotaci, Nicole Petiquay) osikikwew [ozīkihkwēw], *to have facial wrinkles;* WI (Pessamit) ushitshikueu [uʃītʃəkwēw], *to have a wrinkled face;* Laure (ca. 1726) "n-uchitchikuan, *j'ai des rides;*" Silvy (ca. 1680) "n'ȣsitchititchan 3. eȣ, *j'ai les mains ridées*" | ANISH oziiganowe, *to have wrinkled cheeks* (Livesay & Nichols, 2021)

*wisīkirāwīhš

INITIAL (NOUN, ANIMATE)

— salamander

evidence | PC osikiyās & osikiyāwīs, *a lizard, a waterdog;* Lacombe (1874) "Osikiyās, ak, *(n.r.), lézard;*" WC osikiðās, *a lizard;* WI (Pessamit) ushitshinauish [uʃītʃəlāwēʃ], *a type of salamander;* WI (Uashat) ushitshinauish [uʃītʃɨnāwīʃ], *a type of salamander;* EI (Ekuanitshit) ushitshinauish [uhītnāwīh], *a type of salamander;* Watkins (1865) "*Lizard, n.* Oosikeyas;" Laure (ca. 1726) "usitchirauich, *lézard, petit serpent*" | ANISH ozhiginaawishag, *lizards* (Lippert & Gambill, 2023) see | *wisīk compare | *wikīskatātāhkw

*wiskahtāmin

INITIAL (NOUN, INANIMATE)

— seed, pit

evidence | PC oskahtāmin, *a young kernal of corn; a stone of a fruit;* MC oskahtāmin, *a seed, a pit;* NEC uskihtāmin, *a seed, a stone, a pit* | ANISH okandaamin, *pit of a fruit* (Lippert & Gambill, 2023) see | *min[4]

*wiskiciy

INITIAL (NOUN, INANIMATE)

— pipestem

evidence | PC oskicīhkān, *stovepipe;* WC oskiciy, *pipestem;* MC oskiciy, *pipestem;* NEC wishchī, *pipe stem;* Watkins (1865) "Ooskiche, *n.in. A pipe-stem;*" Laure (ca. 1726) "ustitchi *pl.* -a, *bâton de calumet;*" Silvy (ca. 1680) "8stitchi, *bâton de calumet*" | ANISH okij, *a pipe stem;* okijaabik, *a stovepipe; a tailpipe* (Livesay & Nichols, 2021) discussion | This root is the source of the family names Weistche, Weistchee, and Wiscutie.

*wiskisk

INITIAL (NOUN, ANIMATE)

— jack pine (Pinus banksiana)

evidence | PC oskāhtak, *jack pine;* MC oskisk, *a jack pine;* oskiskāmatināw, *to be a bank, hill, or mountain covered in pines;* EI (Sheshatshiu) ussishk [ussiʃk], *a jack pine;* Fabvre (ca. 1690) "8stisk, 8stisk8ai [*sic*], *pins rouges, arbres*" | ANISH okikaandag, *a jack pine* (Livesay & Nichols, 2021)

*wisko (~ *wiskw)

INITIAL

— pile, heap

evidence | ESC oskohtin, *to be piled up;* SEC oskotim, *beaver dam;* WI (Pessamit) ushkushteu [uʃkustēw], *to be gathered in a pile* | ANISH okosijigan, *a haystack* (Livesay & Nichols, 2021)

*wiskwēw

INITIAL (NOUN, ANIMATE)

— maggot

evidence | WSC (Ida Bear) oskwēwak, *maggots;* SEC oskwew, *a maggot;* EI (Sheshatshiu) ushkueu [uʃkwēw], *a fly larva, a maggot;* Fabvre (ca. 1690) "8sk8e8 *pl.* 8ek, *vers eng(en)dréz par Les grosses m8ches in carne*" | ANISH Cuoq (1886) "Okwe, *ver qui provient de l'œuf que la mouche dépose sur la viande, ver qui dévore les morts*"

*wisp

INITIAL

— aspirate

evidence | WSC (Misipawistik, Ellen Cook) ospatāmonēw, *to make sb inhale sth;* MC ospatāmēw, *to aspirate sth;* Fabvre (ca. 1690) "n 8spatam8an he reirek, *pr(en)dre ta fumée, aualer ce q(ue) tu respire, humer ton halaine*" compare | *wispwākan

*wispwākan

INITIAL (NOUN, ANIMATE)

— smoking pipe

evidence | PC ospwākanāpisk, *black pipestone;* MC ospwākanihkew, *to make a smoking pipe;* SEC ospwākan, *smoking pipe;* Laure (ca. 1726) "uspuagan -ets, *calumet, pipe;*" Silvy (ca. 1680) "8sp8agan, *calumet*" | ANISH opwaagan, *a pipe* (Livesay & Nichols, 2021); MESK ahpwākana, *a tobacco pipe* origin | PA ***wespwākana** (***wexpwa·kana**, Hewson, 1993) see | *spwākan compare | *wisp

*wiš

INITIAL

— flee

evidence | PC osahwēw, *to make sb flee;* MC ošimow, *to flee;* AT (Wemotaci, Jeannette Coocoo) ocimew [oʒimēw], *to flee from sb;* SEC ošimew, *to flee from sb;* Laure (ca. 1726) "n-uchiskauau, *je fais fuir la bête;*" Fabvre (ca. 1690) "8chah8au, *faire enfuir, enuoler oyseau v.g.*" | ANISH ozhimo, *to flee* (Livesay & Nichols, 2021)

*wišāhš

INITIAL

— slip, slippery

evidence | WC osāsisin, *to slip;* MC ošāšišin, *to slip;* AT oša:šša:w, *to be slippery* (Béland, 1978); SEC ošāšākonacišin, *to slip on snow;* Laure (ca. 1726) "n-uchachichinin, *je glisse par surprise;*" Silvy (ca. 1680) "n8 chachabistichenin, *je tombe en glissant sur les roches*" | ANISH ozhaashaabikaa, *to be slippery rock* (Livesay & Nichols, 2021)

*wišāšoy

INITIAL (NOUN, ANIMATE)

— fresh snow

evidence | PC Lacombe (1874) "Osāsuw, ok, *(n.r.) neige nouvelle;*" SEC ushāshui, *fresh snow* (CSB, 2018); NEC ushāshui, *fresh powdery snow on surface;* WI (Pessamit) ushashunam [uʃāʃūnəm], *to leave tracks in fresh snow;* EI (Sheshatshiu) ushashui [uʃāʃwī], *swirling snow, powder snow* discussion | This reconstruction suffers from the lack of an Atikamekw cognate to confirm the absence of a preaspirate.

*wišētoy

INITIAL (NOUN, INANIMATE)

— tail end of a snowshoe

evidence | PC Lacombe (1874) "osettuy, a, *(n.r.) la queue de la raquette;*" WC osītow, *the heel of a snowshoe;* WSC (Misipawistik, Ellen Cook) osētoy, *tail end of a snowshoe;* AT (Wemotaci, Jeannette Coocoo) oceto [oʒētow], *tail of a snowshoe;* SEC ošētow, *tail of a snowshoe;* NEC ushātui, *tail of a snowshoe;* Silvy (ca. 1680) "8chet8assam, *raquette à queue*" | ANISH ozhedoowaatig, *snowshoe's tail-section wood* (Lippert & Gambill, 2023)

*wišiko (~ *wišikw)

INITIAL (VERB, ANIMATE, INTRANSITIVE)

— **1** injure

— **2** miscarry

evidence | PC osikohēw, *to cause to miscarry;* MC ošikohitisow, *to have a miscarriage;* AT (Wemotaci, Nicole Petiquay) ocikwatisiw [oʒikwātiziw], *to have a miscarriage;* SEC ošikokātešin, *to injure one's leg(s) in a collision;* NEC wishikushimāu, *to injure sb by dropping;* Fabvre (ca. 1690) "n 8chig8chin, n8, *se blesser t(om)band sur un bois;*" Silvy (ca. 1680) "n'8chig8hau, *je l'ai perdu par malheur, v.g. le calumet; je l'ai blessé, perdu, v.g. l'oiseau*"

*wišk

INITIAL

— new

evidence | PC oskāpēw, *a young man;* MC oškakohpew, *wear new dress;* SEC oškāw, *to be new* | ANISH oshki'o, *to wear new clothes* (Livesay & Nichols, 2021) origin | PA ***wešk** (Aubin, 1975; Hewson, 1993)

*wiškat (~ *wiškac)

INITIAL

— at first

evidence | PC oskac, *at first;* MC oškac, *at first;* SEC oškac, *at first;* Laure (ca. 1726) "uichkatch, *au commencement*" limited to | *i³

*wiškācihkw (~ *wiškācihko)

INITIAL (NOUN, INANIMATE)

— awl

evidence | PC oskācik, *an awl;* WC oskācīhk, *an awl;* MC oškācihkʷ, *an awl;* SEC oškācihkʷ, *an awl;* NEC ushkāchihkw, *an awl;* WI (Pessamit) ushkatshikᵘ [uʃkātʃukʷ], *an awl;* EI (Sheshatshiu) ushkatshikᵘ [uʃkātʃīkʷ], *an awl;* Faries & Mackay (1938) "Oska'chik, *n.in. An awl (used in Indian canoe-making);*" Watkins (1865) "Oskachikoo, *v.i.4. He has an awl;*" Laure (ca. 1726) "uskatziku, *alène;*" Silvy (ca. 1680) "8skatik, *alène*"

*wiškihtē

INITIAL

— water lily

evidence | PC oskihtēpak, *lily pad;* WSC (Misipawistik, Ellen Cook) oskihtēpak, *lily;* MC oškihtepakʷ, *lily pad;* AT oškitepakw, *water lily* (Béland, 1978); SEC oščihtepakʷ, *lily pad;* (Waswanipi, Mary Jane Kitchen) oškihtēsiw, *water lily;* NEC uschihtāsiu, *lily;* WI (Pessamit) ussiteshu [ussətēʃu], *lily pad;* EI (Sheshatshiu) utshishteshu [utʃistēʃu], *lily pad* | ANISH (Cuoq, 1886) "wakite, *nénuphar, nymphoea odorata; volet à feuilles orbiculaires, à fleurs odorantes très-grandes*" see | *waskatamoy discussion | The name of the water lily, as well as the names of its edible leaf and rhizome, can be reconstructed in Old Cree, suggesting this plant was of some importance historically.

*wiškinīki

INITIAL (VERB, ANIMATE, INTRANSITIVE)

— be an adolescent boy, a young man

evidence | MC e oškinīkit, *to be a young man;* Silvy (ca. 1680) "n'8chtinitchin 3. -i8, *je suis jeune*" see | *wišk

*wiškinīkiw

INITIAL (NOUN, ANIMATE)

— adolescent boy, young man

evidence | PC oskinīkihkāsow, *to pretend to be a young man;* MC ošinīkiskwew, *an adolescent girl, a young woman;* AT (Wemotaci, Nicole, Petiquay) ockinikiwiw [oškinīkīwiw], *to be an adolescent boy or young man;* SEC oščinīciw, *an adolescent boy;* EI (Sheshatshiu) ussinitshishu [ūssnītʃʃu], *a young man, a bachelor;* Silvy (ca. 1680) "n8chtinitchimats, *nos jeunes*" see | *wiškinīki, *w[1]

*wištošto (~ *wištoštw)

INITIAL

— cough

evidence | PC ostostotamowin, *cough;* NEC ushtutim, *to cough;* Laure (ca. 1726) "n-ustustuten 3. ustustutamu, *je tousse;*" Silvy (ca. 1680) "n'8cht8cht8at8s8au, *je le fais tousser, pétunant près de lui*" | ANISH Cuoq (1886) "ososotam, *tousser*"

*wit[1] (~ *wic)

INITIAL

— draw towards oneself

evidence | PC ocipitam, *to pull sth;* MC otinam, *to take sth;* SEC otāpew, *to haul sth;* wewacikwenitowac, *to hug one another;* NEC witihtim, *to take sth with one's mouth, to suck sth up;* Silvy (ca. 1680) "n'8tichenen, *j'approche, v.g. le feu*" origin | PA ***wet** (Hewson, 1993)

*wit[2] (~ *wiš)

INITIAL

— make or repair

evidence | WC osīhtāw, *to make sth;* MC ošihew, *to make sth;* AT oših-, *to make sb, to arrange or set sb in order* (Béland, 1978); SEC wawetāspitew, *to mend the weaving, netting, or lacing of sth;* wawešihtāw, *to repair* | ANISH ozhitoon, *to make, build, or form sth* (Livesay & Nichols, 2021)

*wit[3]

MEDIAL (NOUN INCORPORATION)

— antlers

evidence | WC māhkiwitīw, *to have big horns;* SEC maniwitew, *to lose one's antlers;* WI (Pessamit) umilutan [umīlūtān], *velvet;* Watkins (1865) "Kichiwitāo, n.an. *A buck deer under three years of age;*" Laure (ca. 1726) "ni-satchiuitan 3. -uiteu, *elles me sortent*" | ANISH mamaangiwine, *to have big antlers* (Livesay & Nichols, 2021); MESK kakānwiwinēwa, *to have long horns* origin | PA ***wiθ** see | *īwit compare | *ēškē

*witam

INITIAL

— hinder

evidence | PC otamihēw, *to hinder sb;* MC otamiškawew, *to hinder sb with one's foot or body;* SEC otamīw, *to be busy;* Silvy (ca. 1680) "n'8tamimau, *je lui nuis en parlant*" origin | PA ***wetam** (Hewson, 1993)

*witatāsakoy

INITIAL (NOUN, INANIMATE)

— sunscald wood

evidence | MC otatāsakiy, *NI sun scald wood, surface wood from the southwest facing side of a tree that has been hardened by repeatedly being damaged by excessive sunlight, traditionally favored for making bows;* SEC utatāsikw, *NA outside bark of a tree only on one side that is hard-to-carve* (CSB, 2018); NEC witităsikw, *NI tree that has properties that are not good for making implements because it is too hard to carve;* WI (Pessamit) utatashikᵘ [utətāʃəkʷ], *very hard yellow layer of wood on the surface of certain conifer tree, especially on the sunny side;* cf. AT (Opitciwan, Joey Awashish) otaraski [otarāskiy], *layer of wood under the bark that is good making a bow when reddish in color*

*witā

FINAL (VERB, ANIMATE, INTRANSITIVE)

— convey

evidence | WC pīciwitāw, *to convey sth here;* MC āhciwitāw, *to take sth elsewhere;* SEC išiwitāw, *to take sth thither;* NEC chihchiwitāu, *to take sth along as one sets forth* paired with | *wir²

*witāhk

INITIAL

— behind

evidence | PC otāhkikāt, *a hind leg;* otāhkisin, *to be running late, to be behind;* MC otāhk, *behind;* otāhkētakʷ, *a stern;* SEC otāhc, *behind; past;* otāhcew, *to be walking behind;* Silvy (ca. 1680) "8tatch, *derrière, après*"

*witāhšo (~ *witāhšw)

INITIAL

— a nonproductive root of uncertain meaning found only in reflexes of *witāhšwamēkwa, "Atlantic salmon"

evidence | AT (Wemotaci, Jeannette Coocoo) ocacamekw [oʒāššamēkw], *salmon;* SEC ocāšomēkw, *Atlantic salmon;* NSK chaasuumaakw, *sea salmon;* WI (Pessamit) & EI (Sheshatshiu) utshashumekᵘ [utʃāʃumēkʷ], *Atlantic salmon;* EI (Unaman-shipit) ushashumekᵘ [uhāhamēkʷ], *Atlantic salmon;* Laure (ca. 1726) "utchachuamegu, *truite saumonée;*" Silvy (ca. 1680) "8chach8ameg8, *truite saumonée;*" "8tach8ameg, *saumon*" | ANISH odaazhawameg, *salmon trout* (Lippert & Gambill, 2023) discussion | The alternative reconstruction, ***wišāhšo**, appears to be limited geographically, making the above reconstruction more likely.

*witāko (~ *witākw)

INITIAL

— evening

evidence | PC otākosinēhkwēw, *to eat supper;* MC otākošin, *to be evening;* SEC otākoham, *to hunt beaver in the evening by boat;* Silvy (ca. 1680) "8tag8chits, *ce soir, sur le soir*" | ABEN wlōgw, olōgw, *evening* (Day, 1994); ANISH onaagoshin, *to be evening* (Livesay & Nichols, 2021) origin | PA ***weθākw** (Aubin, 1975)

*witām

INITIAL

— bang, hit, strike

evidence | PC otāmaham, *to strike sth;* WC otāmahikīw, *to hit with an object or one's hand;* ESC otatāmaham, *to strike sth repeatedly;* MC otāmihtin, *to bang against sth;* AT otamaskoham [otāmāskoham], *to strike sth with a stick;* SEC otāmihtitāw, *to bang sth against sth;* otāmiskwešin, *to bang one's head against sth;* otatāmahicew, *to strike repeatedly;* NEC utāmihtin, *to bang against sth;* WI (Pessamit) utamaikan [uttāmīkən], *a hammer;* EI (Sheshatshiu) utamishtikuaneshinu [utāmɨstukwānēʃinu], *to bump one's head;* Watkins (1865) "Ootamaskikunāwāo, *v.t.an. He hits him on the breast;*" MacKenzie (1801) "Otamaha, *Beat*"

*witih

INITIAL

— reach

evidence | PC otihtaham, *to reach sth;* MC otihtew, *to reach sb (on foot);* SEC otihtinam, *to reach sth by hand;* NEC witihtim, *to reach sth on foot;* WI (Pessamit) utishinakuan [utəʃənākwən], *to be visible from a distance* | ANISH odita'an, *reach sth by water* (Livesay & Nichols, 2021); MESK otehtenamwa, *to obtain sth* origin | PA ***weteh*θ** & ***weteht** (Hewson, 1993) limited to | *t⁵, *t⁶ discussion | Constructions beyond the basic VTA and VTI are based on the VTA stem ***otiht**.

*witiht (~ *witihš)

INITIAL

— face down

evidence | PC "Otisisin, wok, *(a.n.) il est couché la face contre terre;"* MC otihtapiw, *to sit facedown;* AT (Wemotaci, Nicole Petiquay) oticiparihow [otiššiparihow], *to throw oneself to the ground face down;* SEC otihtāmiwanišin, *to lie facedown;* NEC utihtapiu, *to crouch over;* Laure (ca. 1726) "n-utichichinin, *je me couche sur le visage;"* Silvy (ca. 1680) "n'ȣtichichinin, *je suis couché sur le ventre"*

*witōripiy

INITIAL (NOUN, ANIMATE)

— tullibee, cisco

evidence | WSC ocōnipīs, *a cisco;* MC ocōlipiy, *a cisco;* SEC ocōyipīšš, *a cisco;* SEC (Waswanipi) otōlipiy, *a cisco* | ANISH odoonibiins, *a tullibee*

*witwāwē

INITIAL (VERB, ANIMATE, INTRANSITIVE)

— hiccup

evidence | MC otwāwew, *to hiccup;* SEC (Waswanipi) otwāwew, *to hiccup* | ANISH onwaawe, *to have hiccups;* MENO onuawɛ·w, *to hiccough;* cf. ANISH onwaazi, *to be lucky* (Lippert & Gambill, 2023) origin | PA ***weθwāwē** see | *wē¹ compare | *šikakwē discussion | The above root is based on the otherwise unattested initial ***witwāw**, which likely meant "lucky." To this day, Cree-speaking communities around James Bay consider a hiccuping child a sign of good luck, further supporting this analysis. The existence of the synonymous root ***šikakwē** also suggests that ***witwāwē** may have had a more nuanced sense.

*wī (~ *wīt)

INITIAL

— creates a modifier out of a following noun stem or medial

evidence | MC wīšīšīpakisiw, *to smell like duck;* NEC wītimāsichisiu, *to smell like fish;* EI (Sheshatshiu) uitameshakan, *to smell like fish* see | *akan, *akisi, *wīpihko

*wīcēw

INITIAL (VERB, TRANSITIVE, ANIMATE)

— accompany

evidence | PC wīcēwēw, *to accompany sb;* MC wīcewiskwewew, *to accompany a woman;* SEC wīcewākan, *a friend;* EI (Mamit) uitsheuashtimueteu [wītʃēwāhtɪmwētēw], *to walk with a dog;* Silvy (ca. 1680) "ni ȣitcheȣau, *je l'accompagne"* | ANISH wiijiiw, *to accompany sb* (Livesay & Nichols, 2021); MENO wi·ci·wɛ·w, *to accompany sb* origin | PA ***wīcyēw** (Aubin, 1975; Hewson, 1993) see | *wīt, *w²

*wīh¹

INITIAL

— **1** tell

— **2** name

evidence | PC wīhtamawēw, *to tell sb sth;* MC wīlew, *to name sb;* NEC wīhtim, *to tell about sth;* SEC wīhyew, *to name sb;* WI (Pessamit) uauitamᵘ [wāwītəm], *to discuss sth;* Silvy (ca. 1680) "ni ȣiten, *je dis, je déclame;"* "ni ȣihigaȣin, *je suis dit, nuncupor"* | ANISH wiinzh, *to say sb's name or give sb a name* (Livesay & Nichols, 2021) origin | PA

***wīn**, via debuccalization of the final PA ***n** when followed by consonant-initial verb finals, satisfying the morphophonological constraint on preconsonantal nasals. limited to | *r, *t[6] compare | *koh

*wīh[2] (~ *wīš)

INITIAL

— darken with smoke or soot

evidence | PC wīstēpahkway, *a piece of old leather;* Lacombe (1874) "Wistepakkway, a, *(n.f.) vieux morceau de cuir, peau de loge, toute fumée;*" NSK wiiswaaunaakun, *to look yellow;* WI (Pessamit) uishauapu [wīʃāwāpu], *to have yellow eyes;* EI (Sheshatshiu) uishaushiu [wīʃwāwʃīw], *to be yellow;* Watkins (1865) "Westääkin, *n.in. Smoked leather, a leather tenting;*" Laure (ca. 1726) "ni-uichuauisin, *je suis jaune;*" Fabvre (ca. 1690) "8is8a8ipăgau, *feuille, fleur Iaune;*" Silvy (ca. 1680) "8is8a8au, *cela est jaune*" limited to | *s, *so[2], *sw, *tē[4] compare | *wīskwah discussion | While the existence of this root is certain, the cognates do not provide evidence of productivity in contemporary dialects. Evidence is instead limited to initials derived from verb stems that contain heat finals, reflexes of ***wīštē** in western dialects and ***wīhswāw** in eastern dialects, likely derived from a passive form of ***wīhsw**.

*wīhcēk

INITIAL

— reek, stink

evidence | PC wīhcēkisiw, *to stink, to be soiled;* wīhcekaskosiy, *an onion;* MC wīhcekan, *to reek, to be filthy;* wīhcekatāmow, *to have reeking breath;* EI (Sheshatshiu) witshekan [wītʃēkən], *to smell of shit* origin | Query obscure noun incorporation.

*wīhk

INITIAL

— **1** take pleasure in, enjoy

— **2** pleasant (taste or smell)

evidence | PC wīhkistam, *to like the taste of sth;* Lacombe (1874) "Wikkipew, ok, *(v.n.) il aime à boire, il est ivrogne;*" WC wīhkicisiw, *to be tasty;* MC wīhkimākwan, *to smell good;* wīhkelimew, *to take pleasure in sb;* SEC wīhcitiw, *to taste good;* wīhci-cišiwāsiw, *to be easily angered;* Laure (ca. 1726) "uitcheuagau, *cette viande a bon goût;*" Silvy (ca. 1680) "8ikachi8, *cela a bon gout*" | ANISH wiingashk, *sweet grass (Hierochloe odorata)* (Livesay & Nichols, 2021); MIAMI wiinkihtam-, *to like the taste of sth* (ILDA, 2017) origin | PA ***wīnk** (Aubin, 1975)

*wīhko (~ *wīhkw)

INITIAL

— attract, draw

evidence | PC wīhkōw, *to strain oneself;* Lacombe (1874) "wikkomew *(v.a.) il l'invite à manger au festin;*" "wikkwāstimwew, ok, *(v.n.) elle appelle son chien;*" ESC wīhkopitam, *to pull sth;* MC wīhkomew, *to invite sb to a feast;* wīhkohtowin, *a feast;* SEC wīhkohow, *to free oneself;* Laure (ca. 1726) "ni-uikumau 3. -meu, *je crie pour attirer quelque bête;*" Fabvre (ca. 1690) "8ik8mau, *Apeller son chien v.g. allant En la chasse;*" Silvy (ca. 1680) "ni 8ik8mau, *je l'appelle*" | ANISH wiikobidoon, *to pull sth;* wiikom, *to invite sb to a feast* (Livesay & Nichols, 2021); MESK wīhkomēwa, *to invite sb to eat* origin | PA ***wīhko**

*wīhkwat (~ *wīhkwac)

INITIAL

— free from restraint or obstruction, dislodge

evidence | PC wīhkwacīw, *to free oneself;* MC wīhkwacipitam, *to pull sth free;* NEC wīhkutiham, *to free sth from where it is stuck using sth;* WI (Pessamit) uikutaim[u] [wīkutīm], *to free sth from where it is buried, stuck, or caught using an object;* Laure (ca. 1726) "ni-uikuatchihau 3. -heu, *je l'en* *sauve;*" Fabvre (ca. 1690) "8ik8tahigăn *pl.* găna, *Tire b8re de fuzil, vis de fer*" | ANISH wiikwaji'o, *to try to get free; to endeavor* (Livesay & Nichols, 2021) see | *wīhko, *at² compare | *pahkwat

*wīhp

INITIAL

— hollow

evidence | WC wīhpisiw, *to be hollow;* MC wīhpāpiskāw, *to be a hollow rock;* SEC wīhpisekāw, *to be a hollow in a cliff;* Silvy (ca. 1680) "ni 8ipitagahen, *je troue, je creuse*" | ANISH wiimbwewe, *to give a hollow sound* (Livesay & Nichols, 2021) origin | PA ***wīmp** (Aubin, 1975)

*wīhpē

INITIAL (VERB, ANIMATE, INTRANSITIVE)

— sleep with

evidence | PC wīhpēmiskwēwēw, *sleep with a woman;* MC wīhpew, *sleep with a person of the opposite sex;* SEC wīhpemew, *sleep with sb;* Laure (ca. 1726) "uipeu, *nubile, fille en âge de se marier*" | ANISH wiipendiwag, *to sleep with each other* (Livesay & Nichols, 2021); MENO we·hpɛw AI, *to sleep with sb, to sleep double;* MESK wīhpēwa, *to sleep double*

*wīhs¹

INITIAL

— dead tree

evidence | MC wīsāposkitew, *to be a burnt area with dry, standing trees;* wīsāskopewihtakʷ, *a dead tree standing in water;* AT (Wemotaci, Jeannette Coocoo) wisaskopew [wīssāskopēw], *to be dying, said of trees flooded by a beaver pond;* NEC wīsāskupāu, *to be drowned, speaking of a tree;* WI (Pessamit) uishashkupeu [wīʃāʃkupēw], *to be flooded, speaking of a wooded area;* Watkins (1865) "Wesapooskituk, *n.in. A burnt tree, burnt wood*" | ANISH wiisaakode, *to be a half-burnt forest* (Lippert & Gambill, 2023)

*wīhs²

INITIAL (NOUN, INANIMATE)

— caul fat, peritoneum, mesentery

evidence | PC wīsi, *stomach fat;* MC wīsi, *caul fat;* AT (Wemotaci, Nicole Petiquay) ni wisim [ni wīssim], *my caul fat, speaking of when it is obtained from an animal;* EI (Sheshatshiu) uish [wīʃ], *caul fat of a caribou or moose;* Silvy (ca. 1680) "8isi, 8is, *graisse de boyau*" | ANISH Cuoq (1886) "Wis, *crépine, ce que, dans quelques départements, de France, ainsi qu'au Canada, on appelle vulgairement, coife;*" wiis, *tripe* (Livesay & Nichols, 2021) compare | *pimiy, *šōpiy, *wīkw, *wīrinw discussion | This root may alternatively be reconstructed as ***īhs** if considered a dependent noun as supported by data from Western and Eastern Innu.

*wīhsahkēcāhkw

INITIAL (NOUN, ANIMATE)

— trickster in traditional tales who is associated with the great flood and the subsequent recreation of the world

evidence | PC wīsahkēcāhk, *Cree culture hero and the object of many legends and tales;* WC wīsāhkīcāhk, *hero of Cree legends; Santa Clause;* ESC (Peawunuck, George Hunter) wīsakicāhk, *trickster character in traditional tales;* ESC (Fort Albany, Simeon Scott) wīsakēcāhk, *legendary trickster figure* (Ellis, 1995); MC Wīsahkwecāhkʷ, *trickster figure in traditional tales;* AT (Wemotaci, Nicole Petiquay & Opitciwan, Joey Awashish) Wisaketcakw [wīssakēcāhkw], *legendary character;* Isham (1743) "we su ca cha, *God*" | ANISH Cuoq (1886) "Wisakedjak, *c'était le grand Manitou des Algonquins, celui à qui ils attribuaient la formation de la terre. On le nomme aussi Nenabojo;*" MIAMI "Wissakatchákwa" (Gatschet - ILDA, 2017) discussion | This entry is included due to its morphological opacity and widespread distribution. Despite the dialectal variation largely centered around the third syllable, the above form is supported at least partially by all dialectal reflexes. The character is also known by reflexes of Old Cree ***kwīhkwahākēwa** in eastern dialects and as “Māsu” in Northern East Cree, a name mentioned by Jesuit Paul Le Jeune (spelled “Messou”) in his *Jesuit Relations of 1633 and 1634* (Thwaites, 1897).

*wīhsahkwē

INITIAL (VERB, ANIMATE, INTRANSITIVE)

— to have a shrill voice

evidence | MC wīsahkwew, *to have a shrill voice;* wīsahkwehtākosiw, *to sound shrill;* Silvy (ca. 1680) “ni 8isak8an, *j’ai la voix aigre, rauque*” | ANISH wiisakwe, *to have a high, shrill voice* (Livesay & Nichols, 2021) see | *wē[1] compare | *wīhsak discussion | In the absence of an Atikamekw cognate, the preaspirate in this reconstruction is indirectly supported by Anishinabe.

*wīhsak

INITIAL

— **1** bitter

— **2** smarting pain

evidence | [1]PC wīsakipakos, *bitter leaf;* MC wīsakan, *to be bitter;* AT wi:ssakisi-, *to be bitter, sour* (Béland, 1978); WI (Pessamit) uishakakamu [wīʃəkākəmu], *to be bitter liquid* [2]WC wīsakamīw, *to hurt sb by biting;* MC wīsakelihtam, *to be in pain;* SEC wīsakāpiw, *for one’s eyes to smart;* Laure (ca. 1726) “ni-uisatchikatesun, *je me brûle les jambes*” | [1]ANISH wiisagan, *to be bitter* (Livesay & Nichols, 2021); MENO we·qsaken, *to be bitter;* MESK wīsakenwi, *to be bitter;* MIAMI wiihsakaakani, *pepper* (ILDA, 2017) [2]ANISH wiisagaabaso, *one’s eyes hurt from the smoke* (Livesay & Nichols, 2021); MENO we·qsaka·hpenɛw, *to be painfully or seriously ill;* MESK wīsakamatamwa, *to suffer pain* origin | PA ***wīʔsak** (Aubin, 1975)

*wīhšāko

INITIAL (NOUN, ANIMATE)

— male deer in rut

evidence | WC wīsākow, *to smell of rutting; to have body odor;* MC wīšākow, *to rut;* SEC wīšākokan, *to smell like a rutting deer;* NEC wīshākw, *an adult male caribou in rut;* EI (Mamit) uishak^{u} [wīhāk^{w}], *male caribou in rut;* Watkins (1865) “Wesak, *n.an. A buck deer at the time of rutting. The word is sometimes applied to other animals also.*” | ANISH wiishaagomaagozi, *to have body odor* (Livesay & Nichols, 2021) discussion | In the absence of an Atikamekw cognate, the preaspirate in this reconstruction is indirectly supported by Anishinabe.

*wīhtikow

INITIAL (NOUN, ANIMATE)

— man-eating humanoid, cannibal

evidence | WC wīhtikow, *a cannibal; a glutton;* MC wīhtikow, *a cannibal;* SEC (Waswanipi) wīhcikōšš, *a joker, speaking of playing cards;* Faries & Mackay (1938) “Wètiko, *n.an. A cannibal, a devil, a mysterious evil person or spirit who terrorizes the people;*” Isham (1743) “whit te co, *the Devil;*” Fabvre (ca. 1690) “8itik8, 8itig8ets, *l8ps gar8x;*” Silvy (ca. 1680) “8itig8, *loup-garou*” | ANISH wiindigoo, a winter cannibal monster, a windigo (Livesay & Nichols, 2021); MESK wītekōwa, *owl;* MIAMI miintikwa, *a screech owl* (ILDA, 2017) origin | PA ***wīntekōwa** (Hewson, 1993) compare | *acēn discussion | An isogloss runs with Moose Cree and Atikamekw grouping with more westerly dialects, and Northern East Cree and Western Innu grouping with more easterly dialects. While the dialects spoken to the west of this line display the above root, those spoken to the east instead use the root ***acēn**. This lexical feature can be appreciated in the name for the northern shrike *(Lanius borealis)*, appropriately named “wīhtikōwi-wīškacān” in Moose Cree and “atshenishkatshan” in Western Innu, both translating to “cannibal grey jay.” The Southern East Cree dialect has retained both roots, though in lexicalized derivatives only. In this dialect the word "atōš" has come to replace both roots in common speech.

*wīkopiy

INITIAL (NOUN, INANIMATE)

— bark used for making cordage

evidence | PC Lacombe (1874) "wikupiy, a, *(n.r.) écorce de saule, avec laquelle on fait des cordes, des paniers*" "wikupiyāpiy, a, *(n.f.) corde d'écorce de saule;*" MC wīkopiy, *willow bark traditionally stripped to make lines;* NEC wīkupī, *bark of willows used as string;* Laure (ca. 1726) "uikupimichi *pl.* -a, *bâton de bois blanc*" | ANISH wiigob, *inner bark of basswood* (Livesay & Nichols, 2021); MENO we·kope·hkɛw, *to gather basswood bark* origin | PA ***wīkopyi** (Hewson, 1993) see | *kop, *kopiy

*wīkw (~ *wīko)

INITIAL (NOUN, INANIMATE)

— renal fat

evidence | PC wīko, *kidney fat;* MC wīko, *renal fat;* AT (Opitciwan, Joey Awashish) wikw [wīkʷ], *renal fat;* NEC wīkw, *fat around the organs of large game;* EI (Sheshatshiu) uikᵘ [wīkʷ], *an adrenal gland;* Laure (ca. 1726) "uiku, *gras*" compare | *pimiy, *wīrinw, *wīhs², *šōpiy discussion | This root may alternatively be reconstructed as ***īkw** if considered a dependent noun as supported by data from Western and Eastern Innu.

*wīmā

INITIAL

— avoid

evidence | PC wīmāskawēw, *to avoid sb by going in a circuit;* WC wīmāmow, *to be a detour;* MC wīmāšam, *to cut around sth to avoid cutting through it;* AT wimapariw [wīmāpariw], *to drive around, to take a detour;* SEC wīmāšimohtāw, *to make a trail around sth to avoid it;* EI (Sheshatshiu) uemaueu [wēmāwēw], *to pass right by sb by canoe or swimming;* Silvy (ca. 1680) "ni 8imachten, 3. -kam, *j'entre par un autre endroit, je me détourne du chemin embarassé*" | ANISH Wemackaw, *détourne-toi de lui, fais un circuit de peur de l'effrayer* (Livesay & Nichols, 2021)

*wīn

INITIAL (NOUN, INANIMATE)

— **1** marrow

— **2** foul, dirty

evidence | [1]PC wīni, *bone marrow;* MC wīni, *bone marrow;* NEC wīn, *bone marrow;* Silvy (ca. 1680) "8in, *moelle*" [2]PC wīnihtin, *to spoil or rot;* WC wīnisiw, *to be filthy;* MC wīnimākwan, *to stink;* SEC wīnatew, *to bring up a foul smelling burp or vomit;* WI (Pessamit) uinueu [wīnwēw], *to have dirty fur;* Silvy (ca. 1680) "ni 8inisin, *je pue;*" "ni 8inapin, *je suis chassieux, j'ai les yeux puants*" | [1]ABEN win, *bone marrow* (Day, 1994) [2]ANISH wiinad, *to be dirty* (Livesay & Nichols, 2021); MENO we·nesew, *to be dirty;* MESK wīnyāwi, *to be dirty or filthy* origin | PA ***wīn** (Aubin, 1975; Hewson, 1993)

*wīnaškw (~ wīnaško)

INITIAL (NOUN, ANIMATE)

— groundhog

evidence | PC wīnask, *groundhog;* ESC (Severn) wīnask, *groundhog;* MC wīnaškomākwan, *to smell like groundhog;* NEC wīnishkw, *groundhog;* SEC wīniškw, *groundhog;* EI (Mamit) uinashkᵘ [wīnahkʷ], *groundhog;* Laure (ca. 1726) "uinasku-pihissimu, *mars;*" Silvy (ca. 1680) "8inask8, *siffleur*" | ANISH wiinashk, *groundhog* (Oji-Cree, 2014) see | *wīn

*wīnāštakay

INITIAL (NOUN, INANIMATE)

— rumen

evidence | PC wīnāstakay, *a rumen;* NEC wīnāshtikī, *stomach of caribou or moose;* EI (Unaman-shipit) uinashtakai [wīnāhtakēj], *a rumen* | MENO we·na·qnak, *paunch stomach of slaughtered animal*

*wīnihr

INITIAL (NOUN, ANIMATE)

— cherry birch (Betula lenta)

evidence | WI (Pessamit) uiln [wīlən], *NA an unidentified type of birch;* Fabvre (ca. 1690) "8inir, *pl.* 8iniria, *merisier à futz de raq(ue)ttes;*" Silvy (ca. 1680) "8inir8a, *bois à faire raquettes;*" cf. AT (Wemotaci, Jeannette Coocoo) winikis [wīnikis], *NA tree used for making snowshoes, such as the yellow birch or wild cherry tree* | ABEN wins, *yellow birch, sweet birch* (Day, 1995); ANISH wiinisiibag(oon), *wintergreen* (Lippert & Gambill, 2023); Cuoq (1886) "Winisik, ... an, *merisier;*" MENO we·nεqnamenan, *wintergreen berries* discussion | Known colloquially in French as "*merisier rouge*," the cherry birch is sometimes mistaken for a cherry tree due to the appearance of its bark. Its association with wintergreen in more southern languages is due to its production of methyl salicylate, the same chemical that provides wintergreen with its distinctive scent. The southern range of the cherry birch explains the paucity of cognates from dialects spoken further north, but its form is a clear descendant of Proto-Algonquian. Note the metathesis in the WI cognate and in the Anishinabe borrowing in AT.

*wīpat (~ *wīpac)

INITIAL

— **1** soon

— **2** early

evidence | PC wīpac, *soon; early;* MC wīpac, *soon; early;* SEC wīpac, *soon; early;* EI (Sheshatshiu) uipat [wīpət], *soon; early; as soon as;* Silvy (ca. 1680) "8ibatch, *d'abord, incontinent*" | ANISH wiiba, *early; soon* limited to | *i³

*wīpihko (~ *wīpihkw)

INITIAL

— dusty

evidence | WI (Uashat) uipikutin [wīpukutn], *to be moldy;* EI (Sheshatshiu) uipikushinu [wīpīkuʃɨnu], *to be moldy;* Silvy (ca. 1680) "ni 8ipik8sin, *j'ai la tête sèche, non graissée;*" cf. MC šīpihkwāw, *to be dusty* | MESK wīpekwāwi, *to be blue;* MIAMI wiipinkosi-, *to be gray* (ILDA, 2017) see | *pihko², *wī

*wīpo (~ *wīpw)

INITIAL

— narrow

evidence | PC wīpo-, *narrow;* Silvy (ca. 1680) "8ib8t8n, *la tête ou la bouche du calumet;*" "ni 8ib8t8ninach, *je fais la petite bouche pressant les lèvres*" | ANISH wiibwaa, *to become narrow, to constrict* (Livesay & Nichols, 2021); MESK wīponamwa, *to make sth narrow or closer*

*wīposk

INITIAL

— burnt land

evidence | WC wīposkāw, *to be a burnt area;* MC wīposkāw, *to be a burnt area;* WI (Pessamit) uipushkanakau [wīpuʃkānəkāw], *to be a burnt island;* Watkins (1865) "Wepooskituk, *n.in. A burnt tree, burnt wood;*" Laure (ca. 1726) "uipuskau, *lande, pays brûlé et terre desséchée*" see | *āposk

*wīran

INITIAL

— butcher

evidence | SEC (coastal) wīyihew, *to butcher sb;* wīyāpošwew, *to butcher a rabbit;* EI (Sheshatshiu) uinatikueu [wīntīkwēw], *to butcher a caribou;* Silvy (ca. 1680) "ni 8iranihau, *je le démembre v.g. animal*" | ANISH Cuoq (1886) "Ni winaniha monz, *je dépèce un élan*"

*wīrā

INITIAL

— wear article of clothing

evidence | PC wiyāhtam, *to wear sth;* Lacombe (1874) "Wiyāmew, *(v.a.) ... il le porte sur lui, v.g., un habit. On dit aussi: wiyāmew, il l'a pour femme, c'est son avoir;*" WC wīðāhtam, *to have sth on, speaking of clothing;* ESC (Severn) wīnāhcikan, *article of clothing;* MC wīlāmew, wīlāhtam, *to wear* *sth;* SEC wīyāhcikan, *article of clothing;* NEC wiyāmāu, *to wear sth;* Watkins (1865) "Weyàtahāo, *v.t.an. He clothes him, he dresses him*" limited to | *ht⁴, *m¹ discussion | Lacombe (1874) lists a secondary sense, suggesting the root may have originally meant "to own" rather than "to wear." This would mirror how the root ***ayā**, "to have," is used in many dialects, as in the SEC and MC word *ayān,* "article of clothing." However, in the absence of corroborative data from other sources, Lacombe's secondary sense is deemed a local innovation.

*wīric

INITIAL

— dirty

evidence | MC wīlicāpiw, *to have a dirty face;* AT (Opitciwan, Joey Awashish) wiritcipow [wīricāpow], *to have a dirty mouth from eating;* SEC wīyicāpišīš, *Lapland longspur;* NEC wiyichipū, *to have a dirty face after one eats;* EI (Sheshatshiu) uinitshipu [wīntʃipu], *to have a dirty beak or mouth from eating;* Laure (ca. 1726) "ni-uiritchabin 3. -biu, *je me barbouille, je me salis*"

*wīrinw (~ *wīrino)

INITIAL (NOUN, INANIMATE)

— subcutaneous fat

evidence | PC wiyinohēw, *to make sb fat;* WC wīðin, *fat;* wīðinwāpisk, *quartz;* MC wīlilotehew, *to have a fatty heart;* AT wirino [wīrinow], *to be fat;* SEC wīyinʷ, *subcutaneous fat;* wīyinow, *to be fat;* wīyinwāpiskʷ, *a piece of quartz;* Silvy (ca. 1680) "ni ȣirinȣn, *je suis gras*" | ANISH wiinin, *fat* (Livesay & Nichols, 2021) compare | *pimiy, *šōpiy, *wīkw, *wīhs²

*wīrip

INITIAL

— dirty

evidence | WC wīðipinam, *to dirty sth with one's hands;* MC wīlipašakayew, *have dirty skin;* SEC wīyipāw, *be black;* EI (Unamanshipit) uinipapateu [wīnipāpātēw], *to produce black smoke;* Silvy (ca. 1680) "ȣiripau, *cela est sale*"

*wīrkway

INITIAL (NOUN, INANIMATE)

— bladder

evidence | PC wīhkway, *a bladder; a swim bladder; a balloon;* WC wīskway, *a bladder;* MC wīhkway, *a swim bladder; any membranous sac or hollow organ dried and used as a container for liquids;* NEC wīhkui, *animal bladder or bird's esophagus blown up and dried and used as a container for grease;* WI (Pessamit) uikuaimesh [wīkwīmēʃ], *a swim bladder;* Laure (ca. 1726) "uikuai, *vessie;*" Silvy (ca. 1680) "kȣe, kȣai, *vessie*" see | *wīrkwē, *ay²

*wīrkwē

INITIAL

— closed off, dead end

evidence | PA Lacombe (1874) "wikkwepān, ak, *(n.f.) pantalons, culottes;*" WC wīðkwīyāw, *to have no opening, to be a dead end;* MC wīhkwekamāw, *to have a dead end, speaking of a lake;* SEC wīhkwešāw, *to urinate in one's pants* see | *wīrkway

*wīskāt (~ *wīskāc)

INITIAL

— ever

evidence | PC wīskāc, *ever;* MC wīskāt & wīskāc, *ever;* AT (Wemotaci, Jeannette Coocoo) wiskat [wīskāt], *ever;* SEC wīskāt, *ever* | ANISH wiikaa, *late; ever; seldom* (Livesay & Nichols, 2021)

*wīskwah (~ *wīskwaš)

INITIAL

— darken with smoke or soot

evidence | WC wīskwasikīw, *to smoke dye things;* AT (Wemotaci, Nicole Petiquay) wiskosam [wīskossam], *to darken sth with smoke or soot;* wiskoctew [wīskoštēw], *to be darkened from smoke or soot; to be darkened in the corners, speaking of a home;* SEC wīskošteyecisiw, *to be grey, speaking of sth sheet-like;* NEC wīskusim, *to smoke sth;* wīskutāu, *to be grey from smoke;* WI [Pessamit] uishkushu, *to be smoked, speaking of a hide;* EI (Ekuanitshit) uishkushteiau [wīhkwahtjāw], *to be dark grey;* Watkins (1865) "weskoosum, *v.t.in.6. he singes it;*" "weskoostāo, *v.imp. it is brown (with being smoked), it is smoke-dyed; it smells singed;*" Laure (ca. 1726) "ni-uiskuachen, *je brûle ma viande ou graisse;*" Silvy (ca. 1680) "ni 8ichk8ahen, *je brûle, je noircis au feu, v.g. la chaudière;*" "8ichk8asteu, *cela s'est noirci, jauni à la fumée*" | MENO wi·skwaqtɛw, *to be smoked* limited to | *s, *so[2], *sw, *tē[4] compare | *wīh[2] discussion | Northern East Cree cognates appear to be reanalyzed as reflexes of ***wīsko** while the first example cited from Silvy (ca. 1680) is likely a mistranscription of "ni 8ichk8asen."

*wīskwē

INITIAL

— wrap

evidence | PC wīskwēhpitēw, *to bandage sb;* MC wīskweštikwānehpititisow, *to wrap one's head;* SEC wīskwenam, *to wrap sth;* Silvy (ca. 1680) "8isk8epite8, *il est entortillé, enveloppé*"

*wīsop

INITIAL

— color of bile, bilious

evidence | Laure (ca. 1726) "uichupikueu, *elle a la jaunisse;*" Fabvre (ca. 1690) "8is8bau, 8is8pau, *Iaune, c8l(eu)r de fiel d'a(nim)al*" see | *wīsopiy

*wīsopiy

INITIAL (NOUN, INANIMATE)

— gallbladder, bile

evidence | PC wīsopiy, *gallbladder; bile* WC wīsopiy, *gall or bile;* ESC (Fort Severn) wīsopīwitakišiy, *small intestine;* MC wīsopīwāpow, *bile;* AT wi:sopiy, *gallbladder* (Béland, 1978); NEC wīsupī, *gallbladder;* EI (Sheshatshiu) uishupui [wīʃəpwī], *gallbladder;* Watkins (1865) "Wesoope, *gall;*" Laure (ca. 1726) "uichupiuabui, *eau bourbeuse, puante;*" Fabvre (ca. 1690) "8is8pi, 8is8bi, ni 8is8pi, *fiel d'a(nim)al, mon fiel*" | ANISH giinzob, *your gall bladder* (Livesay & Nichols, 2021); Cuoq (1886) "Ni sop, ki sop, wisop, *mon, ton, son fiel;*" "Winzop, *du fiel*" see | *wīsop discussion | While this word is treated as an independent noun in historical sources and most contemporary dialects, some speakers of SEC, WI, and EI treat it as a dependent noun with the initial w representing the third-person possessor as seen in Anishinabe sources.

*wīšā

INITIAL

— invite to join

evidence | PC wīsāmēw, *to invite sb to come along;* Lacombe (1874) "Wisākkawew, *etc., (v.a.) il l'attire à lui, il le charme de manière à se faire suivre par lui;*" MC wīšāmitowak, *to invite one another along;* AT (Wemotaci, Jeannette Coocoo) wicamew [wīʒāmēw], *to invite sb;* SEC wīšāmiwew, *to invite people along;* WI (Pessamit) uishashkuleu [wīʃāʃkulēw], *to attract sb with food;* Silvy (ca. 1680) "ni 8ichamau, *je le retiens, le mène avec moi*" | ANISH wiizhaam, *to invite sb to join* (Livesay & Nichols, 2021) limited to | *m[3]

*wīšāštaw

INITIAL

— narrow pass

evidence | WI (Pessamit) uishashtuau [wīʃāstwāw], *to be a very narrow pass between two hills;* EI (Sheshatshiu) uishashtushekakamau [wīʃāstūʃēkākəmāw], *to be a lake hemmed in by rocky mountains;* Silvy (ca. 1680) "8ichasta8au, *il est étroit, le fleuve, etc.*" | cf. ABEN wizawogama, *to be a strait, to be a narrowing on a lake;* wizawtegok, *at the narrows of a river* (Day, 1994) discussion | The geographic distribution of this root appears restricted to eastern dialects. However, it is supported by a partial Western Abenaki cognate. Its inclusion here is therefore tentative. This reconstruction also suffers from the lack of an Atikamekw cognate to confirm the absence of a preaspirated sibilant.

*wīšināw

INITIAL (NOUN, ANIMATE)

— castor sac

evidence | PC wīsināw, *castor;* MC wīšināw, *a castor sac; castor;* AT (Wemotaci, Nicole Petiquay) wicinaw [wīʒināw], *castor sac;* WI (Pessamit) uishinau [wīʃənāw], *testicle of an animal; castor sac;* EI (Sheshatshiu) uishinauapui [wīʃɨnāwāpwī], *decoction of castor sac;* Watkins (1865) "Wesinow, *n.an. Castor, castoreum;*" Silvy (ca. 1680) "ȣichinau *pl.* -nauak; -nauek; ȣichinaȣa, *rognons de castors*" | ANISH wiinzhinaa, *a castor sac of beaver or muskrat* (Livesay & Nichols, 2021) see | *šināw

*wīškacān

INITIAL (NOUN, ANIMATE)

— grey jay (Perisoreus canadensis)

evidence | PC wīskacān, *a grey jay;* WC wīskacānis, *a grey jay;* MC wīškacān, *a mechanic; a blacksmith; a grey jay;* NEC wīshkichān, *a mechanic;* wīshkichānish, *a grey jay;* SEC wīškacān, *a mechanic; a blacksmith;* wīškacāniš, *a grey jay;* EI (Sheshatshiu) uishkatshan [wīʃkətʃān], *a grey jay;* Fabvre (ca. 1690) "ȣichkatchana, *pie, pica*"

*wīškop

INITIAL

— palatable

evidence | Isham (1743) "wisko pau, *fatt meat;*" Fabvre (ca. 1690) "ȣichkȣpimin *pl.* mĭna, *bled d'inde echauffée puis seché;*" Silvy (ca. 1680) "ȣichkȣpimin pl. -minak, *petit blé, mil*" | ANISH wiishkobizi, *to be sweet* (Livesay & Nichols, 2021)

*wīšt (~ *wīhš)

INITIAL (NOUN, INANIMATE)

— beaver or muskrat lodge

evidence | PC wīšti, *beaver or muskrat lodge;* AT (Wemotaci, Jeannette Coocoo) wic [wīš], *a beaver lodge;* wi:šš, *beaver's den* (Béland, 1978); SEC wīšt, *beaver or muskrat lodge;* NEC uwīshtimihkiwāu, *to give sb the right to harvest a beaver lodge;* EI (Sheshatshiu) uisht [wīst], *a beaver lodge;* Laure (ca. 1726) "uich, *rel.* uichtiriu, *cabane de castor;*" Silvy (ca. 1680) "ȣich, *cabane de castor ou de porc-épic*" origin | PA ***wīʔθ-** (Hewson, 1993) see | *aštaw discussion | Compare the Old Cree singular **wīhši** with its plural, **wīštahi**.

*wīštini

INITIAL (VERB, ANIMATE, INTRANSITIVE)

— eat (speaking of an animal)

evidence | Watkins (1865) "Westinew, *v.i.1. He sits with his fore legs bended under the body;*" Laure (ca. 1726) "uichtiniu, *ravage d'orignal;*" Fabvre (ca. 1690) "ȣichtiniȣa *pl.* ȣai, *Rauages d a(nim)aux, orign(au)x v.g.;*" Silvy (ca. 1680) "ȣichtiniȣ, *il marque le lieu par ses pas;*" "ȣichtimiȣai, ȣichtiniȣai, *lieu marqué de l'orignal, bois rongé, etc.*" | ANISH wiisini, *to eat* (Livesay & Nichols, 2021); MESK wīseniwa, *to eat;* MIAMI wiihsini-, *to eat* (ILDA, 2017) origin | PA ***wīʔθeni** (Hewson, 1993) discussion | The meager evidence for this now obsolete root suggests its use in the historical period had become ambiguous and limited to quadrupeds. While sources from the Saguenay region refer to damage left behind from an animal's feeding and movement, Watkins (1865) provides a gloss referring to the posture used by moose while feeding on low-lying vegetation. Cross-linguistic cognates are used here to support the above gloss.

*wīt (~ *wīc)

INITIAL

— **1** assist, help

— **2** together with, used in the formation of comitative verbs

evidence | [1]PC wīcihēw, *to help sb;* MC wīcihtwāw, *to help with sth;* SEC wīcihitowac, *to help one another* [2]PC wītapimēw, *to sit with sb;* WC wītokīmīw, *to live with sb;* MC wītāskošimew, *to lie with sb;* SEC wīcihyāmew, *to fly with sb;* Silvy (ca. 1680) "ni 8itchinag8simau, *je lui ressemble*" see | *ht[4], *m[1]

*wītē

INITIAL

— dwell with

evidence | Fabvre (ca. 1690) "8itemit8ek, *ils logent t8s ens(em)ble;*" Silvy (ca. 1680) "ni 8itemau, *je demeure chez lui;*" "ni8itemāgan, *mon hôte qui me loge*" | MESK wītēmēwa, wītētamwa, *to accompany sb or sth;* MIAMI wiitee-, *to accompany, to go along* limited to | *ht[4], *m[1]

*wītoy

INITIAL (NOUN, INANIMATE)

— anal gland

evidence | ESC wītoy, *NA oil gland of animals;* MC wītow, *NI an anal gland;* NEC wītui, *NI beaver anus including surrounding fat;* wītuyāskunim, *to put the scent of musk on a pole to attract lynx to a trap;* WI (Pessamit) uituiapishu [wītwījāpəʃu], *NI musk gland of a lynx*

*wīyahkwē

INITIAL (VERB, ANIMATE, INTRANSITIVE)

— swear

evidence | PC wiyahkwēw, *to swear;* WC wiyāhkwīwin, *swearing;* MC wīyahkwātew, *to swear at sb;* SEC wīyahkwew, *to swear;* Watkins (1865) "Weyùkwāo, *v.i.3. He swears (profanely), he uses bad language;*" Fabvre (ca. 1690) "8a8iak8an e8, *begaÿer*" see | *wē[1] compare | *wīyak discussion | Contemporary dialects to the east and south of where East Cree is spoken employ constructions based on Old Cree ***mār** rather than the above form.

*wīyak

INITIAL

— **1** assorted

— **2** spoil, waste

evidence | [1]Fabvre (ca. 1690) "8a8iagab8kan e8, *faire bouillir plus(iers) ch(os)es ens(em)ble;*" Silvy (ca. 1680) "ni 8iagassinahigan, je figure, je peins" [2]PC wiyakisiw, *to be squandered;* WC wiyakan, *it is wasted;* MC wīyakihew, *to waste sb;* NEC wiyichāyihtākun, *to be a waste;* Watkins (1865) "Weyuketow, *v.t.in.2. He destroys it, he spoils it, he wastes it;*" Laure (ca. 1726) "ni-uiatchitan, *je rends mauvais*" | [1]ANISH wiiyag, *assorted, all kind of* (Lippert & Gambill, 2023); MENO we·yakahamasow, *to sing all manner of songs* [2]ANISH waayagi'aad (changed form), *to do sth regrettable to sb, to waste sb* (Livesay & Nichols, 2021)

Y

*yā (~ *ā)

FINAL (VERB, INANIMATE, INTRANSITIVE, ABSTRACT)

sound change | t (PA *t) → c; t (PA *θ) → š

— forms stative verbs

evidence | PC kinokamāw, *long lake*; sīhcāw, *it is tight;* WC misāw, *to be big;* MC mōtāyāw, *to be deep;* wāpāw, *white*; SEC cikāyāw, *to narrow;* osāwāw, *to be a hue ranging from brown and yellow;* NEC apishāshiu, *to be small;* WI (Pessamit) tipishkau [təpəʃkāw], *night;* EI pitshau [pītʃāw], *to be a long way;* Laure (ca. 1726) "tchitcheiau *pl.* -a, *angle d'une maison;*" Silvy (ca. 1680) "michigamau, *grand, large, fleuve, lac, etc.*" | ANISH gaawaa, *to be rough* (Livesay & Nichols, 2021); MESK pāshkyāwi, *to be cracked or burst open* origin | PA ***yā** (Aubin, 1975) compare | *ī[2] discussion | Proto-Algonquian post-consonantal ***y** is dropped in Old Cree, triggering the allomorph ***ā**.

English Index

A

abandon
— *nakē

abate
— *āštē

abdomen
— *aškat, *aškatay, *ıc, *ıciy

able
— *kašk

abreast
— *mātāpo

abrupt narrowing
— *cikā

abrupt rise or fall in terrain
— *kīšk

abundance of
— *ıskā

accidentally
— *pišt

accompany
— *wīcēw

achc
— *tēw

acquire an expected ability
— *nihtāw

across
— *akām

across or along an open expanse of water
— *akām

active
— *ārim

add
— *tako

addition (in addition)
— *ahšit

adequate
— *tēp

adhere
— *ako

adolescent boy
— *wiškinīkiw

adolescent boy (be adolescent boy)
— *wiškinīki

adopt (adopt as kin)
— *āhkom, *wāhko

advance
— *rahk

affect
— *šaw

affect by or be affected by
— *kato

affect by or be affected by drying
— *āhkatos, *āhkatoso, *āhkatosw, *āhkatotē

affect by or be affected by exposure to the wind
— *āhši, *āštan, *āštitā, *ātim

affect by or be affected by light
— *āhs, *āhso, *āhsw, *āštē

affect by or be affected by sleep or sleepiness
— *ıhkwahši, *ıhkwaštim

affect by or be affected by the application of direct heat
— *ıhkahs, *ıhkahso, *ıhkahsw, *ıhkahtē

affect by or be affected by water
— *āpāwar, *āpāwatā, *āpāwē

affect by vocalizing
— *m, *t

affected by action of waves
— *āh, *āhoko, *āhotē

affect by or be affected by weight of a load or by applied pressure of a moving body
— *ıškōr, *ıškōso, ıškōtā, *ıškōtē

affect or be affected by the cold
— *aci, *atihtā, *atim, *atin

against
— *ahšot

against the wind
— *narim

agile
— *katāštap, *wacēhp

ahead
— *nīkān

air current
— *rō

air pockets
— *pīhswē

alder
— *atōsp, *atōspiy

algae
— *aštākipiy

alight
— *twēho

alike
— *nasp, *tāpiškōt

all
— *kaskinaw, *mis, *misihtaw, *misiwē

allow
— *ır

almost
— *kēkāt

aloft
— *nīm

alone
— *nihš, *nihšihkato, *nihšihkēw

along length of space or time
— *pim

along or across an open expanse of water
— *akām

along the way
— *naskawē

along the way (before reaching the destination)
— *nawat

alongside
— *rār

already
— *šay

also
— *ahšit

amaze
— *maskāt

American bittern (Botaurus lentiginosus)
— *mōrkahōhsiw

American crow (Corvus brachyrhynchos)
— *āhāhsiw

American eel (Anguilla rostrata)
— *pimisow

amidst
— *mēkwē

among
— *ınāhki, *mēkwē

ample space, quantity, or durability
— *pīhsāko

anal gland
— *wītoy

anew
— *kīhtwām, *maštaw

anger
— *kišiw, *raw

angled
— *kīhkē

angled edge
— *ıhšawē

angry
— *kišiw, *rišk

animal, person, or thing
— *ay

ankle
— *ahkwan

ant
— *ērikw

anticipate (finish or arrive before)
— *kirā, *rā, *rāh

antiquated
— *nikān

antlers
— *īwit, *wit

anus
— *cišk

any
— *nataw

anyway
— *mihsawāt

apart
— *tipān

appear
— *nāko

appear (make oneself appear thus)
— *ho

appease
— *kākīt

apprehension
— *kospan

approximate
— *wayēš

area opposite a doorway
— *wēskwāhtēm

arctic char (Salvelinus alpinus)
— *sōsāsiw

arm
— *piton, *spiton

arm (upper arm and shoulder girdle)
— *sakīn

armpit
— *tihko

around
— *tētip, *wāskā

arrive
— *pāp, *tako

arrow
— *ato

arrow (blunt)
— *akaskw

arrow (pointed)
— *atohs

ashore (go ashore)
— *šēsk

askance
— *rēko

aspen
— *mītohs

aspirate
— *wisp

assault
— *kwāro

assist
— *wīt

assorted
— *wīyak

at a loss (be at a loss)
— *kwītaw

at ease
— *wānaskē

at some distance (on the ground or in the air)
— *nayēwat

at the base (of an elevation of land)
— *ēn

at the extremity
— *wanasko

at the fore
— *nīkān, *nīštām

at the ready
— *nēhpēm

Atlantic cod (Gadus morhua)
— *wanawihšiw

Atlantic salmon (Salmo salar)
— *witāhšwamēkw

atlas (first cervical vertebrae)
— *tapiskohkēw

attach on
— *piso

attached to
— *amo

attract
— *wīhko

audible
— *matwē

aught
— *nataw

augur well or perform ritual to augur well
— *pawē

aunt (maternal aunt)
— *tōhs, *tōsihs

aunt (paternal aunt)
— *sikohs, *sikosihs

authority (person in a position of authority)
— *wikimāw

autumn
— *takwāk

avoid
— *wīmā

awaken
— *koško, *pēko

awaken (inadvertently)
— *waspāwē

awkward
— *nēhsitām, *wašištaw

awl
— *wiškācihkw

B

babiche (make babiche)
— *wāw

babiche (thin babiche)
— *atipihs

baby bird
— *paracān

back
— *āwikan

back (in return)
— *kāw

back (lower back)
— *šōkan

back (upper back)
— *piskwan, *spiskwan

back end elevated
— *mōhkit

back end of the interior of a dwelling
— *wēskwāhtēm

back side (onto or towards one's back side)
— *šāhšak

backstrap sinew
— *aštihs, *aštihsiy

backwards (move backwards)
— *ašē

bad
— *mac, *mār

bad luck
— *mahrako

bag
— *ıwat, *īwat, *maškimotay

bald eagle (Haliaeetus leucocephalus)
— *mikisiw

band
— *ēyat

bang
— *witām

bare
— *mohšē, *šāk

bare ground as snow melts
— *ırihtē

bare (speaking of a body part)
— *šāhšākir, *šāk

barely
— *ācištaw, *rāw, *wanāwihs

bark (birch bark)
— *aškw, *aškway, *aškwēmak, *waškway

bark (for making canoes)
— *kwam, *wašikway

bark (for making cordage)
— *kop, *kopiy, *wīkopiy

bark (outer covering of a tree)
— *ahrakēmak, *ahrakēsk, *ahrakēskw, *kway, *wahrakēskw

bark (speaking of a dog)
— *mik, *wihkē

bark container (for collecting or storing liquids)
— *mīkwanākway

barren
— *mohšaw

barter
— *atā

bat (flying mammal of the order Chiroptera)
— *apahkwācīhš

bathe
— *kapā

bay
— *wāš

bay-shaped
— *wāšah

be
— *āt

be (a specified thing or person)
— *āw

be aware of
— *kisk

be (in a certain location)
— *tako, *tē

be (in a certain location or condition)
— *ayā

be in the sky
— *ah, *akocin, *akotē

be in water
— *hcin, *ht, *htin

be next
— *askō, *aškoht

be or move round
— *kīnikwān

beak
— *kot, *skiwan, *skot

bear
— *askw, *maskw

bear paw snowshoe
— *mahkwatoy

beast
— *awēhsīhs, *pišiskiw

beautiful
— *katawat

beauty mark
— *mīn, *pāhpāhtēw

beaver
— *amiskw

beaver lodge
— *aštaw, *wīšt

beaver pelt
— *aht, *ahtay

beaver under a year of life
— *awēt

beaver yearling
— *poyawēw

bed (of a body of water)
— *misk

bed stone
— *atān

bedding of an animal's den
— *wirimāw

bee
— *āmow

beforehand
— *kīšāt

before the expected time
— *nōhtaw

behind
— *āpam, *witāhk

belly
— *ɩc, *ɩciy

below
— *šīpā

bend
— *pirk

bend forward
— *nawak

bend over
— *nawē

bendable
— *šōhšōp

berry
— *min, *mīn
berry (unripe)
— *aticiy
best (the best)
— *nawahšō
better
— *mīskaw
between
— *taštaw
beyond
— *awahs, *āhswē
beyond (go beyond)
— *kāhšispo
beyond what is intended
— *mēhtāt
big
— *mišt
bile
— *wīsopiy
bilious
— *wīsop
bill
— *skiwan
birch
— *waškway
birch bark
— *aškway, *waškway
bird (baby bird)
— *paracān
bird (grouse)
— *hrēw, *pirēw
bird (large bird of prey)
— *apiskw
bird (of a larger species)
— *ahsiw, *pirēhsiw
bird (of a smaller species)
— *pirēhšīhš, *pirēhšīhšiw
birth (give birth)
— *ışē, *ōšē, *pinē
bitch
— *kišk
bitter
— *wīhsak
bittern (American bittern)
— *mōrkahōhsiw
black
— *kašk, *kaškitēw
bladder
— *wīrkway
bladder (urinary bladder)
— *rir, *ririy
blink
— *pahsahk
block
— *kipo
blocked
— *āt
blood
— *mirko, *rkw
blood clot
— *watoy
blow
— *pōtē
blow one's nose
— *saniko
blow whistle or flute
— *pipikwē
blue jay (Cyanocitta cristata)
— *tīhtīhsiw
board
— *pōs
bob
— *nām
body
— *īyaw, *raw
body of water
— *āpān, *ıpiy, *kam, *kamiy, *nipiy
boil
— *āciwahs, *āciwahso, *āciwahsw, *āciwahtē, *wih
boil (furuncle)
— *sīkīhp

bone
— *kan, *skan

bone flesher
— *mirkihkwan

bored
— *šikat

boss
— *wikimāw

bother
— *mikoškāt, *wahkā

both sides
— *ītaw

bottom of a body of water
— *āyaw

bounce
— *kwāškwē

bow
— *ahcāp, *ahcāpiy

brace
— *sīto

bracket fungus
— *waratoy

braid
— *apihkē

brain
— *tihp

branch
— *atihkwan, *watihkwan

branch (of a conifer with needles still attached)
— *āhtak, *āšiht

branch (of a pine or pine-like tree with needles still attached)
— *āšihkw

brandish fist
— *nim

breach
— *parasko

bread (unleavened bread)
— *kārahkonāw

breadth
— *atē

break
— *kask, *pīko

break apart
— *ririhko

break in two
— *nātwā

break off
— *kask

break open
— *pāhkā

break open or perforate
— *pōsko

break out (speaking of skin)
— *pīko

break piece off
— *pahkwē

break through ice
— *twā

break through or into
— *parasko

break through the surface of (water)
— *pahko

breast (mammary gland)
— *tōtōhš

breast (of a bird)
— *pahs, *spahsēw

breastfeed
— *nōhr, *nōhto

breastfeed (have breastfeeding baby)
— *nōhšē

breathe
— *atāmo, *rēhrē

breathe on, breath in
— *atāht, *atām

bright
— *wāhšē

bright sky
— *kīšik, *kīšikan

bring
— *pēšiw, *pētā

bring provisions along
— *nīmā

bring together
— *tako

bring token of hunt
— *āpo

brisk
— *wacēhp

brittle
— *kāsp

brook (fed by meltwater or rainwater)
— *šikāp, *šikāpišiy, *šikāpiw

brother (elder)
— *štēhs

brother-in-law (of a man)
— *īštāw

brother (of a man)
— *īhkānihs

brown (hue ranging from brown to yellow)
— *wisāw

brush (brush off)
— *paw

bufflehead (Bucephala albeola)
— *wāhkēyōhs

build fire
— *kotawē

building
— *kamikw

bulky
— *akwēp

bum
— *cišk

bumpy
— *papikw

bunch
— *ahs

burbot
— *miray

burdened by a heavy load
— *pwāw

burn
— *āskis, *āskiso, *āskisw, *āskitē

burn (speaking of a fire)
— *ahkorē

burnt land
— *āposk, *wīposk

burp
— *pēk

burrow
— *āt, *wāt

burst
— *pāšk

burst blood vessel
— *paško

burst into flames
— *wahrah

burst open
— *tāto

bury
— *ar

bush
— *ıhkop

busy oneself on
— *īhk, *nōt

butcher
— *wīran

buttocks
— *tiy

buzzard (buteo spp.)
— *sāhkwatamw

by and by
— *kēk

by use of foot or body
— *ıšk, *ıškaw, *sk, *skaw, *skē

C

cache
— *aštahciko

calf of the leg
— *asiskitān, *rān

call thus
— *ıt

calm water
— *awip

camp
— *kapēhši
Canada goose (Branta canadensis)
— *ɪsk, *nisk
cane (to use cane)
— *sask
cannibal
— *acēn, *wīhtikow
canoe
— *or, *ot, *ōt
canoe bark
— *kwam
cap
— *aštotin
cape (of land)
— *macitēw
care for
— *pam
carefully
— *wēwēriht, *ayākwām
caribou
— *atihkw
carry (on one's back)
— *nay
carry (on one's shoulder)
— *nikē, *winikē
carve
— *ɪhkot, *mōhko
castor sac
— *šināw, *wīšināw
catch
— *kāhcit
catch fire
— *wahrah
catch just in time
— *kēšt
catkin
— *rimiskw, *wirimiskw
cattail (head of a cattail) (Typha spp.)
— *pahsēkān
caul fat
— *wīhs
cause piercing pain
— *cīšt
cause what has accumulated on or in an object to fall off or out
— *paw
cautiously
— *ayākwām
cease
— *pōn
cedar
— *māšikīsk
centered
— *tāw
certain
— *kēštinā
certainly
— *cikēmā
chance (by chance)
— *kwēšwān, *mīskaw
change
— *āht
change automatically or spontaneously (from one state to another)
— *pari, *parin
channel
— *ātim
chapped
— *kīsp
character (have a certain character)
— *āt
charcoal
— *kaškitēw, *maskatēw
chase in a particular direction
— *tišah, *tišahw, *tišisk, *tišiskaw
cheat
— *cīhš
cheek
— *anow, *anoway
cheerful
— *cīhk
cherry birch (Betula lenta)
— *wīnihr

chest
— *āskikan, *skāskikan

chickadee (Poecile spp.)
— *picikīškihšīhš

chief
— *wikimāw

child
— *awāhs, *āwahso, *nīcān

chisel (ice chisel)
— *ašisoy

chisel through ice (to capture beaver)
— *ēškē

choke on
— *tēko

choke on bone
— *ato

choose the best
— *nawahšō

chop
— *cīk, *kah, *kahw

chorus frog
— *wimāciskōk

circular
— *wāwiy, *wāwiyē

circular frame
— *miskwahtoy

cisco
— *witōripiy

claw
— *kaš, *kašiy, *kaškw, *skašiy

clay
— *atonisk, *āpatonisk, *matonisk, *wāpatonisk

clean
— *kicišt, *kisī, *pēhk

clean anus after a bowel movement
— *kimisā

clear
— *pakask, *wāhšē, *wāskam

clear (speaking of the atmosphere)
— *wāhsē

clear view (into the distance)
— *wēm, *wēmoht

clearing
— *šīpē

cliff
— *ıhsēk

cling
— *ako

cloak
— *akohp, *skotākay

close
— *kip

close an open space or gap
— *kašk

close (by having both sides come together)
— *sihpo

closed off
— *wīrkwē

clothes
— *asāk, *asākay

cloud
— *askw, *waskw

cod (Atlantic cod)
— *wanawihšiw

cold
— *tahk

cold extremities (have cold extremities)
— *takwāsk

cold weather
— *kihsin

collapse
— *rīk

color
— *atih

comb
— *šīk

come apart easily
— *kašk

come into view from behind something
— *sāk

come loose
— *pihšiko

come out of water
— *akwā

come out of container or enclosed space
— *kwarako

come to the surface
— *pēko

common
— *ɪrin

compacted
— *ahsan

compel
— *āyihkam

compete
— *raw

complete
— *kīš, *tēkaht

completely
— *tēkaht

compress
— *māko

concave
— *pōsisk

concealed behind
— *ākaw

cone
— *wašaškwētoy

confuse one for another
— *pēmāw

conifer
— *āhtak, *āšiht, *šiht

conifer branch (with needles still attached)
— *āhtak, *āšiht

conifer cone
— *wašaškwētoy

conjuror
— *mitēw

consider
— *āt, *ēriht, *ērim

conspicuous
— *kīhkā

constantly
— *tahk

consume
— *mēšt

consume completely (speaking of food or drink)
— *kitamw, *kitā

consume (food and drink)
— *hkwē

contact (bring into, come into, or be in contact with)
— *hšim, *hšimo, *hšin, *ht, *htin, *htitā

contempt
— *pīw

contents of a digestive tract
— *mēciy

continuously
— *kēyāpit, *tahš

contrary to what is expected
— *tayakwat

convenient
— *nah

convey
— *āwē, *wɪr, *wɪtā

cook
— *ɪhkahs, *ɪhkahso, *ɪhkahsw, *ɪhkahtē

cook (prepare food)
— *ɪnawē

cook in water
— *kapā

copy
— *tāp

corpulent
— *kāmo

correct
— *kwayasko

cough
— *wištošto

country
— *askiy

cousin (cross-cousin of the opposite gender of the subject)
— *ītimohs

cousin (female cross-cousin of a woman)
— *tāhkohs

cousin (male cross-cousin of a man)
— *īštāw

cover
— *akwan, *ar, *riko

cover a dwelling
— *apahkw, *apahkwē

cover of a dwelling
— *apahkway

covered (be covered by)
— *nasko

co-wife
— *īskw

crack
— *pāšt

cradleboard (be on cradleboard)
— *tihk

crawl
— *tācimo

creak
— *kicīšk

creature (a thievish simian-like creature believed to inhabit rocky banks)
— *mēmēkwēhšiw

crest
— *wihšē

crispy
— *kāsk

crop
— *amotay

cross
— *āšitaw, *āšitē, *āšitonē, *āšo, *pēm

crossbar (of a snowshoe)
— *koskosk

cross-cousin (female cross-cousin of a woman)
— *tāhkohs

cross-cousin (of the opposite gender of the subject)
— *ītimohs

cross-nephew
— *tihkwatim

cross-niece
— *štim

crossed
— *pēmāw

crosspiece (thwart)
— *apihkan

crosswise
— *pimit

crotch
— *cicāskay

crow (American crow)
— *āhāhsiw

crown of the head
— *asakātihp

crunchy
— *kāsk

crush
— *šiko

cry
— *atwēmo, *māto, *mō

cry because of
— *mōsko

cumbersome
— *akwēp

cured (superficially cured)
— *kārk

curl
— *niko

curve
— *wāk, *wāron

curved or bent backwards
— *rāhrak

custom (have custom)
— *htwā

cut
— *ıš, *ıšw

cut across
— *kask, *kaskam

cut short
— *cim

cut with one's teeth
— *kaht, *kam

D

damage
— *pīko

damp
— *miramaw

dance
— *hšimo, *nīm

dangerous
— *nanīsān

dark blue
— *apiht

dark sky
— *tipisk

dark-colored
— *kašk

darken with smoke or soot
— *wīh, *wīskwah

darkening
— *kašk

dart
— *īpihs

daughter
— *tānihs

daughter-in-law
— *štim

day
— *kīšik, *kīšikan, *kīšikw

dead end
— *wīrkwē

dead tree
— *wīhs

deal with
— *āyihkam

deceive
— *kakayēr, *wayēš

decompose
— *rīk

decrease
— *aciw

deem
— *āt, *ēriht, *ērim

deep
— *mōtā

deep water (or other substance)
— *tim

deeply
— *pōsā

deer
— *ıro

defecate
— *mīt

defend
— *kispēw

definitively
— *nāspit

deflate
— *rīw

deformed
— *māsk

degraded
— *kōhpāt

densely (densely spaced)
— *sako

dent
— *ēt

depart
— *šipwē

depend on
— *miš

deplete
— *cāk

deplete of contents
— *šīko

depressed (feel depressed)
— *kašk

depressed (feel depressed from loneliness)
— *pōhk

depressed (sunken)
— *wār

descend
— *rāš

desire
— *moštaw, *moštē

desire (the presence, possession, or fulfillment of)
— *nato

desolate
— *pīkiskāt

destroy
— *nihšiwanāt

detach
— *man, *pihšiko

detect an odor
— *pah

deviate
— *waškwē

devoid of one's natural covering
— *cīhcīko

die
— *nāspit, *nip

die down (speaking of the wind)
— *rāk

different
— *ayaht, *pītohš

different size, shape, or place
— *kāhtap

difficult
— *ārim

dig up
— *mōn

digest
— *rīk

diligent
— *rihrip

directly in front or above
— *tipiškōt

dirty
— *wīn, *wīric, *wīrip

dirty with excrement
— *cicē

disagreeable
— *āspon

disappear
— *pāšiko, *risk

disappoint
— *mihsaw, *wašištaw

disapprove
— *ān, *ānwē

disarrange
— *wahrā

disbelieve
— *ānwē

discernible through
— *mako

discharge viscous substance
— *pik

discomfort (feel discomfort)
— *šīw

discrete
— *kihtāw

disembark
— *kapē

disengage
— *taht

dish
— *rākan, *wirākan

disintegrate in water
— *tisp

dislocate
— *kotiko

dislodge
— *pahkwat, *wīhkwat

dispossess
— *masisko

disregard
— *ātaw

disrupt
— *wahrā, *wanā
dissatisfy
— *mihsaw
dissolve in water
— *tisp
distance (off in the distance)
— *mītākwē
distant (progressively become distant)
— *atim
distend
— *pōtaw
distinct
— *payahtē
distract from boredom or tediousness
— *papakwat
divide
— *māt
divine (try to see or know supernaturally)
— *kot
divine (by use of fire)
— *kohsikē
divine (by use of shivers or twitches)
— *wirwā
divinity (type of divinity)
— *manitow
dizzy
— *kīškwē
do
— *tōt, *tōtaw
dodge
— *tapas
dog
— *aštimw, *atimw
dog (female dog)
— *kišk
done
— *šay
door
— *kištohkan
doorway
— *ıškwāhtēm, *ht, *htaw, *škwāht, *škwāhtaw
doorway (area opposite a doorway)
— *wēskwāhtēm
double
— *napo
doubt
— *ānwē
dove
— *wimīmīw
down
— *nīht
downriver
— *mā
downwards
— *acitaw
downwind
— *nāmiwan
drain from (speaking of liquid)
— *sīskaw
draw
— *wīhko
draw one's foot towards oneself
— *wicēšt
draw out
— *rārisk
draw towards oneself
— *wit
dread
— *naniht, *šēšk
dream
— *pawē
drench
— *šīnašk
drink
— *ıp, *min
drip
— *hši, *kawi, *kawin, *štim, *štin, *štitā
drive in
— *kihcit

drive in a particular direction
— *tišisk, *tišiskaw

drive or be driven thither
— *ɩtiš

drop
— *kitišk

drop (to a lower level)
— *rāš

dry
— *pāhko

duck
— *hšip, *šīhšīp

dull
— *ašiw, *šī

during
— *mēkwā

during (the course of the present day)
— *anoht

dusk
— *awik

dust
— *pihko

dusty
— *wīpihko

dwell with
— *wītē

dwelling
— *kamik, *kiwāhp, *ok

dye
— *atih

E

eagle (bald eagle)
— *mikisiw

eagle (golden eagle)
— *kihriw

ear
— *ɩht, *htawak, *htawakay

early
— *wīpat

earth
— *ask, *askiy

earwax
— *škihtēkom

easy
— *wēht

eat
— *ɩškoro, *mīci, *mīcihso, *mō, *po, *pw, *št

eat (speaking of an animal)
— *wīštini

eat thus or there
— *spo

echo
— *pahswēwē

ectoparasite (large such as a flea or bed bug)
— *papikw

eel (American eel)
— *pimisow

egg
— *āw, *wāw

egg (of a fish or amphibian)
— *āhkw, *wāhkw, *wāhkwan

elbow
— *tōskwan

elderly
— *kihkā, *kišē

emaciated
— *pāwan

embark
— *pōs

ember
— *āškēw, *āškišēw, *ɩšēw

emerge from under a surface
— *mōsk

emit an odor
— *pah

emit particulate matter
— *pīpo

empty
— *pihšihšiko

empty of contents
— *šīko

encounter
— *mēkwā

encounter weather
— *hši

end
— *ıškwā, *kišip, *wēskwā

enemy
— *pwāt

enfold
— *wēw

enjoy
— *wīhk, *cīhk

equally
— *tāpitaw

equivalence (determine or provide equivalence)
— *tip

erect
— *ask, *cimē

erode
— *rīk

escape
— *kī, *pasp, *pihko

esteem
— *mahtāko

even
— *wāt

even if, even though
— *mihsawāt

evening
— *witāko

evenly
— *tāpitaw

eventually
— *kēk, *pātimā

ever
— *wīskāt

every
— *kaskinaw

everyday
— *mēšakwam

every (speaking of periods of time)
— *mēšakwam

everywhere
— *misiwē

exceed
— *ariw

exchange (in exchange)
— *mīškot, *mīškotō

excrement
— *mēy

exhaust
— *nēšto

expanse of water (across or along an open expanse of water)
— *akām

expect to be fed
— *pakohš

experience a sensation
— *amahciho, *amahcihtā, *amaht

experience cold
— *sīhk

expose or be exposed to smoke
— *āpahs, *āpahso, *āpahsw, *āpahtē

express contents
— *sīn

extend
— *ānisko

extend one's legs
— *šāwahto

extending over
— *paskit

extinguish
— *āštawē

extraordinary (be extraordinary, possess extraordinary powers)
— *manitow

extremity
— *kišip, *wanasko

eye
— *āpi, *škīšikw

eyebrow
— *māmāw

F

face
— *hkw, *hkway

face down
— *witiht

face up
— *ētacin

facial hair
— *ištow, *štow

facing
— *wihtiškaw

fail
— *ātaw

fail to obtain
— *aškōraw

faintly discernible
— *pawē

fairly
— *nawat

falcon
— *pīhpīkihšīhš

fall (autumn)
— *takwāk

fall (late fall)
— *mikisk

fall (move downwards)
— *pahk

fall down
— *pin

fall off
— *ām

fall out or cause to fall out of a container
— *kwatap

fancy
— *sēk

far
— *rāw, *wāhraw

fare
— *ıht, *in

far side
— *awahs

fart
— *pwēkit

fast
— *kišī

fast (abstain from food and drink)
— *kīhikohšimo

fasten a cloak or robe
— *aniskamē

faster than
— *rāho

fat
— *pim, *pimiy

fat (intra-abdominal fat of fowl)
— *pīmaroy

fat (lower back fat)
— *šōpiy

fat (subcutaneous fat)
— *wīrinw

fat (to be fat)
— *kāmo, *tāht, *winisk

father
— *ōhtāwiy

fatigue
— *nēšto, *rīwan

fatten
— *tāht

fatty (food)
— *pahswē

favorable
— *nah

fear
— *koš

feast
— *makohšē

feather (flight feather)
— *mīkwan, *kwan

feather (tail feather)
— *ataniy

feces
— *mēy

feed
— *ahš, *ıškor, *ıškotā, *por

feed fire
— *pō
feel
— *mōš
feel a certain emotion about
— *āt, *ēriht, *ērim
female
— *ıskwē
female dog
— *kišk
fervently
— *āšihk
fetch
— *nā, *nāt, *niko
few
— *takawāhšihš
few (a few)
— *ātiht
fight
— *māš, *mīkā
file
— *por, *potā
fill with water
— *mōšk
fin (pectoral fin)
— *tıhcıkan
find
— *misk, *miskaw
fine (be or reduce to fine pieces)
— *pīhs
fine root
— *atap, *watapiy
finish
— *kīš
finish before
— *rāho
finish task or journey
— *mān
fire
— *ıškotēw, *škotaw, *škotēw
firebrand
— *āškēw, *āškišēw, *ıšēw
firewood
— *miht
firm
— *kišt
firmly
— *āyit
first
— *ništam
first (at first)
— *wiškat
first cervical vertebrae (atlas)
— *tapiskohkēw
fish
— *amēhs, *amēkw, *namēhs
fish by torchlight
— *wāhswē
fish flesh
— *ırkaw, *wirkawēw
fish tail
— *šikwan, *šikwanay
fish weir (build a fish weir)
— *miciskē
fisher
— *wicēk
fishhook
— *mikirkan
fishing net
— *ahrap, *ahrapiy
fishing spear
— *anihtoy
fissure
— *pahs
fixed to
— *amo
flame
— *kwāhko
flared
— *sēhkwē
flat
— *napak
flat (be flat against)
— *šanašk

flat (speaking of land)
— *ēn

flatten
— *tako

flavorless
— *pīrihs

flea
— *papikw

flee
— *āmo, *wiš

flee (to flee in a particular direction from sb)
— *tišim

flee (to flee in a particular direction)
— *tiši, *tišimo

flesh
— *īyāhs

flesh a hide
— *mirk

flesh (meat)
— *ēw

flesher (made of bone)
— *mirkihkwan

fletch
— *aštawē

flexible
— *tōštōp

flight feather
— *kwan, *mīkwan

flint
— *apiht

flood
— *mōšk

flooring (lay material down as flooring)
— *anāskē

flow (speaking of a body of water)
— *ciwan, *štan

fly
— *hrē

foam
— *pīštēw

fog
— *awan, *pikisk

fold over onto itself
— *āpot

folktale (tell folktale)
— *ātarōhkē

follow
— *nōhso

food
— *mīcim

foot
— *sit, *t

foot (of an ungulate)
— *arahsit

foot or body (by use of foot or body)
— *ıšk, *ıškaw, *skaw, *sk, *skē

for good (definitively)
— *nāspit

for the time being
— *pit

forbid
— *kit

force that permeates living beings and inanimate things
— *ahcāhkw

forearm (including the hand)
— *nisk

fore (at the fore)
— *nīštām

forehead
— *kahtikw, *skahtikw

foreign
— *ayaht, *mayak

forever
— *kākikē

forked
— *rīkihtaw

forlorn, forsaken
— *kīwahš, *kīwāt

fortification
— *mēnisk

fortuitously
— *mīskaw
foul
— *wīn
four
— *nēw
fox
— *ahkēhšiw, *mahkēhšiw
fragile
— *šēw, *wahkēw
free
— *pihko
free from difficulty
— *wānaskē
free from restraint or obstruction
— *wīhkwat
free from undergrowth
— *šīpē
freeze
— *aci, *atihtā, *atim, *atin, *āskaci, *āskatihtā, *āskatim, *āskatin
freezing rain
— *misik
fresh snow
— *wišāšoy
friable
— *kašk
friend (male friend of a man)
— *īhkānihs
frighten
— *sēk
frigid weather
— *kihsin
fringe
— *rīwē
frog (chorus frog)
— *wimāciskōk
frog (excluding toads and chorus frogs)
— *tēhtēw
from
— *wiht
from beginning to end of a period of time
— *ıskan
from one to another
— *āniskē
from the present time into the future
— *kēyāpit
front end elevated
— *cāhk
front side up
— *ētacin
frontwards
— *šēmāk
frosty
— *rikiko
froth
— *pīštēw
fruit
— *min, *mīn
frustrated
— *akāw
fry
— *sāh
full
— *aškinē, *mōškinē
full-grown (speaking of animals or trees)
— *kišē
fun
— *mōcik
fungus (bracket fungus)
— *waratoy
fungus (mushroom)
— *wašaškwētoy
fungus (tinder fungus)
— *posākan
funny
— *wawiyat
fur
— *aw, *pīw, *pīway
furrow
— *pahs

furtively
— *kīm, *kīmōt

furuncle
— *sīkīhp

fuzzy
— *mīhr

G

gallbladder
— *wīsopiy

game (play against)
— *raw

garter
— *cīskē

gather
— *māwahtō, *māwat

gather fruit
— *awihso, *āmiso, *mawihso

gather together
— *māwasako

gather up
— *mōšahk

gaunt
— *ātaw

gentle
— *rōsp

gently
— *mētinaw, *pēhkāt

geometric design
— *masin

get away from (a negative experience)
— *mīw

gill
— *rkīkw

gird
— *pakwahtē

give
— *mēk, *mīr

give an account
— *ācim, *ācimo, *ātot

give up
— *pō

give up waiting for
— *pōmē

gizzard
— *tihs, *tihsiy

glad
— *sikirē

gland (such as a thyroid, thymus, or salivary gland)
— *nīšk

glaze ice (be glaze ice)
— *šōš

go across open space
— *taskam

go across
— *āšo

go from a vertical to a horizontal position
— *kaw

go inland
— *kosp

go into a hollow in the ground
— *kwarasitē

go or move about
— *kīw

go over edge or apex
— *ām

go through soft snow
— *pōrkwā

go to
— *maw, *nā, *nāt

golden eagle (Aquila chrysaetos)
— *kihriw

gone
— *ıtāpit

good
— *miro, *takahk, *wir

goose
— *ısk, *nisk

gradually
— *ēškam, *wētāt

gradually reach a larger area
— *sihswē, *wasahswē

grandchild
— *ōhšim, *ōšihsim
grandfather
— *mohšōm
grandmother
— *ōhkom
granular substance
— *āwahk
grape
— *šōmin
grasp
— *sak
grass
— *ašk, *aškw, *aškohsiw, *maškohsiw
grassy clearing after a fire
— *aškotē, *aškotēw, *maškotē, *maškotēw
grate
— *kicīšk
grave
— *kāmwāt
graze
— *pahs
grease
— *pim, *pimiy, *pōs, *tōm
grease hair
— *tamasko
great
— *kišē, *kišt
great blue heron (Ardea herodias)
— *šahšakiw
great degree
— *nāšit
grebe
— *šihkip
grey jay (Perisoreus canadensis)
— *wīškacān
grief
— *kīšināt
grievous
— *āhko
grind
— *šāhšāko
grind bones
— *ahkē
grind (smooth by grinding)
— *por, *potā
groin
— *cicāskay
groove
— *pahs
ground
— *ahc, *ask, *askamik, *askiy
groundhog
— *wīnaškw
group
— *ēyat
grouse
— *hrēw, *pirēw
grow
— *ki, *kin
grow crops
— *kištikē
growl
— *nē
guilt (to attribute guilt)
— *atām
gull
— *kiyāškw
gum
— *pikiw, *skiw

H

habituated
— *nakarā
hail
— *sēhsēk
hair
— *ıšt, *ēštakay, *pīw, *pīway
hair (facial)
— *īštow, *štow
hair (head)
— *ītišt
hairy
— *mīhr

half
— *āpihtaw, *pōsko

half (one half of an object)
— *īšikan

hand
— *tihc, *tihciy

hand (by use of hand)
— *ın

hand in a particular direction
— *tišin

hang
— *akocin, *akor, *akotā, *akotē, *košāwē

hang flesh on rack to dry, smoke, or roast
— *akwāwē

happen
— *ıht, *in

happy
— *cīhk

hard
— *maškaw

hare
— *āpošw, *wāpošw

harm
— *ahpinat, *nat

harm or affect negatively
— *pinat, *pine

harm or affect negatively thus
— *āspinat, *āspinē, *ıspinē

harpoon
— *mihcikiw

hat
— *aštotin

hate
— *šīhk

haul camp
— *pici

have
— *aw, *ayā, *tē

have insulating material in the moccasins one is wearing
— *ašikē

have on or in one's body
— *ıšk, *ıškaw

hawk
— *kēhkēhkw

hawk (large hawk)
— *sāhkwatamw

haze
— *pikisk

head
— *ıskw, *štikwān, *tihp

head hair
— *ītišt

headgear
— *aštotin

heal (a wound or sore)
— *kīkē

heal supernaturally
— *nip

heap
— *wisko

hear
— *ıht, *ıhtaw, *pēht

heart
— *tēh

hearted
— *tēh

heat
— *s, *so, *sw, *tē

heat (be in heat, speaking of animals)
— *āwimat

heat haze
— *nāhtē

heavy
— *kosiko

heed
— *pišic

heel
— *tōhtan

height (particular length or height)
— *ısko

held back
— *āt

help
— *wīt

hemangioma
— *mīn

hematoma (to have a hematoma)
— *watōk

herald a bad omen
— *āš

herbaceous vegetation
— *ašk, *aškw, *aškohsiw, *maškohsiw

heron (great blue heron)
— *šahšakiw

hew wood
— *pahs

hiccup
— *šikakwē, *witwāwē

hide
— *kā, *kāt

hide (dressed animal skin)
— *wayān

high
— *ıšp

hill
— *atin, *waciw

hinder
— *witam

hip joint
— *tokan

hit
— *witām

hit and wound target
— *mišo

hit target
— *mīsko

hither
— *pēt

hock
— *sikākwan

hold
— *tahko

hole
— *pako, *pakonē

hollow
— *wīhp

home
— *īk

hoof
— *kaš, *kašiy, *skašiy

hook on
— *piso

hope for
— *pakohs

horsefly
— *misisāhkw

horseshoe-shaped
— *wāšah

hot
— *kiš

housefly
— *wicēw

howl
— *ōro

human being
— *ıriniw

humid
— *nīšk

hump (mound)
— *pisko

hunch
— *nawē

hunger
— *arkatē, *pask

hurry
— *nihk, *pāš, *wēwēp

hurt
— *āhko

husband
— *št

hypodermis
— *tamisk, *tamiskay

I

ice
— *ısiko, *ıskwam, *miskwamiy

ice chisel
— *ašisoy

ignite
— *sask

ill (be ill)
— *pinē

ill (be ill thus)
— *ɪspinē

ill-formed
— *māš

illness
— *āspinē

immediately
— *twayēhk

impatient
— *pakwē, *wašištaw

imperfect
— *māš

impoverish
— *kitim

imprint
— *ēt, *masināw

improper
— *wanāt

in
— *pīh, *pīht

in a row
— *nīpitē

in a while
— *nākē

in spite of
— *natamā

in turn
— *āšitē

inadvertently
— *pišt

inappropriate
— *wanāt

inattentive
— *pāšiko

incessantly
— *tahš

increase
— *rahk

inflame
— *ɪrikā

inform against
— *miš

injure
— *wišiko

injure joint
— *sēk

in-law (brother-in-law of a man)
— *īštāw

in-law (daughter-in-law)
— *štim

in-law (parent-in-law)
— *šit, *šitihs

in-law (parent of one's son-in-law or daughter-in-law)
— *tihtawāw

in-law (sibling-in-law of the opposite gender of the subject)
— *ītimw

in-law (sister-in-law of a woman)
— *tāhkohs

in-law (son-in-law)
— *tihkwatim

inner thigh
— *ap, *apay

instance (an instance of)
— *min

insufficient
— *nōhtē

interrogative (root that forms words such as what, which, when, where, why, and how)
— *tān

interrupt
— *wanā

intestine
— *takiš, *takišiy

into a receptacle
— *pōht

into a tight space
— *šēko
into the mouth of a river
— *pīhcitaw
into the woods
— *šēsk
intra-abdominal fat of fowl
— *pīmaroy
intuition
— *mōš
inverted
— *atimā
invite misfortune by transgressing
— *pāštā
invite to join
— *wīšā
Iroquois
— *nātowēw
irritate
— *wahkā
island
— *ın, *ınak, *min
isolated
— *pikwat
itch
— *kirak

J

jackfish
— *kinošēw
jack pine (Pinus banksiana)
— *wiskisk
jaw
— *āhpiskan
jealous
— *kāhkw
jerk
— *kośko
join together as a pair
— *napo
journey
— *otē
journey to sb
— *otam
jump
— *kwām, *kwāškoht
junction (of two paths or rivers)
— *mātāw
just
— *ıtāp
just now
— *picērak

K

keep
— *kano
kerplunk
— *camohk
kidney
— *tēhtakohsiw
kill
— *ahpinat, *nat
kin
— *tōtēm
kin (have as kin)
— *cīrawē
kin (have or adopt as kin)
— *āhkom, *wāhko
kind
— *kišēwāt
kingfisher
— *wikīškimanihsiw
kiss
— *wicē
knee (back of the knee)
— *sikākwan
knee joint
— *hcikwan
kneecap
— *kitikw
kneel
— *wicihkwan
kneel upright
— *nīpaskō

knife
— *hkomān, *hkomē

knock
— *pāk

knot (on a tree)
— *atihkwan, *watihkwan

know
— *kisk

L

lace anchor string around a frame
— *pišimē

lace snowshoe frame
— *aškimē

lace up
— *wāsp

lack resistance
— *watakam

lack visibility
— *pāšiko

lake trout
— *namēkohs

land
— *ask, *askiy

land (in the land of the)
— * ınāhki

landlocked salmon (Salmo salar)
— *awanān

large
— *kišē, *mahk

large (speaking of a mesh)
— *pašk

last
— *ıškwē, *māhcit

late
— *pwāštaw

later
— *nākē, *pātimā

laugh
— *āhpi, *pāhp

layer
— *pīhto

layer (protective layer)
— *asp

lazy
— *kihtim

leaf
— *nīp, *nīpiy, *pak, *pēmak

leafy plant
— *nīp

leak
— *hši, *kawi, *kawin, *štim, *štin, *štitā

lean against
— *āspat

lean against for support
— *āhso

learn
— *kiskino

leather
— *pīhšākan

leave behind
— *nakē

leave traces of one's presence
— *namē

leech
— *akarkway

left
— *namaht

leftover
— *ıško

leg
— *kāt, *skāt

leg (front leg of a quadruped)
— *piton, *spiton

leg (hind leg of a quadruped)
— *kāt, *skāt

legging
— *ıtāhs, *tāhs

leister
— *anihtoy

length (particular length or height)
— *ısko

lethargy
— *rīwan

lice
— *tihkom

licentious
— *pihšikwāt

lichen
— *wāhkon

lick
— *nōrkwē

lid (for container containing liquid)
— *āpo

lie in wait
— *ask

lie (tell an untruth)
— *kiraw

lightweight
— *rāhk

line used for securing legging to belt
— *anot

link
— *ānisko

lip (lower lip to the chin)
— *kwāskonēw

lip (upper lip)
— *škiš, *škišay

liquid
— *āpo, *kam, *kamiy

little (a little quantity)
— *mān

liver
— *skon

loath
— *tāštak

lobster
— *ahšākēw

local people (of or allied to the local people)
— *nēhiraw

lock of hair
— *patw

lodge
— *mīkiwāhp

log
— *miht

loincloth
— *āsiyān

lonely
— *pīkiskāt

long
— *kino

long ago
— *wēškat

long distance or time
— *pīht

long-tailed duck (Clangula hyemalis)
— *āhāwēw

look
— *nāko

loon
— *mwākw

loose
— *panahko

lose
— *an

lose hair, fur, or plumage
— *paško

lose or cause to lose one's shape
— *rīk

loud (be loud)
— *tēwē

louse
— *ιhkw

love
— *sāk

low
— *tapaht

lower towards the ground
— *patap

lucid
— *wāskam

lumpy
— *papikw

lung
— *rpan

lymph node
— *rihkw

lynx
— *pišiw

M

made
— *mat

maggot
— *wiskwēw

make
— *ɩhkē, *mat, *wit

make canoe
— *aštor

make hole
— *pikwā

make liquid
— *sīhs

make ready
— *wir

male
— *āpēw, *nāpē

mammary gland
— *tōtōhš

man
— *ɩriniw, *nāpēw, *riniw

mana
— *ahcāhkw

mannered thus
— *htwā

manually
— *ɩn

many
— *mištē

many (so many)
— *taht

mark
— *ašākw, *matin

mark for identification
— *kiskinawāt

marrow
— *wīn

marrow (extract)
— *pakaso

marten
— *āpištān, *āpištāniw, *wāpištān

marvelous
— *mahtāw

match
— *tāp

maternal aunt
— *tōhs, *tōsihs

maternal uncle
— *šihs

mature
— *kihtāw

maybe
— *māškot, *pōt

measure (determine or provide measure)
— *tip

meat
— *ēw

mediocre
— *napāt

melt
— *tihk

mend
— *mīš

menstrual
— *wirēw

merely
— *mošt, *mōš

merganser (Mergus merganser)
— *wihsikw

merry
— *mōcik

mesentery
— *wīhs

metal
— *hkomān

metal implement
— *hkwakw

metal (useful metal or rock)
— *ɩhs, *ɩhsēk
middle
— *tāw
mild winter weather
— *kīšopwē
mineral
— *pisk
mink (Neogale vison)
— *šākwēhšiw
mis-
— *wan
miscarry
— *wišiko
miserable
— *kotak
mislead
— *cīhš
mismatch
— *pēmāw
miss
— *pat
mist
— *pīkišē
mistakenly
— *wan
mitten
— *aštihs
mix
— *kirikaw
moan
— *mē
moccasin
— *askisin, *maskisin
moccasins (put on one's moccasins)
— *nihkinākō
moist
— *nīšk
mole (skin blemish)
— *mīn
month
— *pīhsimw
moon
— *pīhsimw
moose
— *mōsw, *osw
more
— *ariw
more (a little more than)
— *ētataw
more and more
— *ēškam, *wētāt
more so
— *āht
more than half
— *ākwāt
moreover
— *pāskat
morning
— *kēkišēp
mosquito
— *sakimēw
moss
— *ask, *askamik, *askiy, *aštāskamikw
mother
— *kāwiy
mould
— *akwāko
mountain
— *atin, *waciw
mouse
— *āpikohšīhš
mouth
— *at, *ton, *tōn
mouth (by use of mouth)
— *aht, *am
mouth (of a river)
— *sākiw
move
— *āht, *waškaw
move about
— *kīw

move (along a surface located above ground or floor)
— *āhtawī

move (along or across an open expanse of water)
— *akā

move (automatically, spontaneously, or smoothly)
— *pari, *parin

move (away from the main course)
— *paskē

move back and forth vigorously
— *miko

move body part
— *ri

move (in a particular direction)
— *pīcit

move (into an open space and away from the shore, forest, or wall)
— *nimitāw

move one's wings
— *āhk

move up and down
— *nām

much
— *mištē, *ırēm

mucus (nasal mucus)
— *akikw

mud
— *ašiškiw, *ıškiw

muscle
— *ēw

mushroom
— *wašaškwētoy

muskeg
— *aškēk, *maškēkw

muskrat
— *acaškw, *wacaškw

muskrat lodge
— *aštaw, *wīšt

mussel
— *ēhs

muzzle
— *cāt

N

nail
— *kaš, *kašiy, *kaškw, *skašiy

name
— *nihkāso, *nihkāt, *nihkātē, *nihkē, *sō, *wīh

narrate
— *ācim, *ācimo, *ātot

narrow
— *šākaw, *wīpo

narrow pass
— *wīšāštaw

narrowing (abrupt narrowing)
— *cikā

narrowly escape
— *pasp

narrows (speaking of a body of water)
— *wap

nasal cavity
— *štan

navel
— *tihs, *tihsiy

navigable side channel
— *šīpā

navigable water
— *skam

near
— *cīk, *pēhšo, *sēsikē

near a source of heat
— *awē

near side
— *āštam

necessarily
— *āyit

neck
— *kw, *kwayaw

need (be in need)
— *kwītamā

needle used for lacing or weaving
— *amahkw

nephew (cross-nephew)
— *tihkwatim

nephew (parallel)
— *tōšim

net (catch in a net)
— *pit

nether millstone
— *atān

netlike (have many holes or spaces)
— *ahrap

nettle
— *masān

nevertheless
— *natamā

new
— *wišk

niece (cross-niece)
— *štim

night
— *tipisk, *tipiskw

night (do at night)
— *nīpē

nighthawk
— *pīškw

nipple
— *tiniy

no
— *nam

no room
— *nōt

noise (high-pitched noise)
— *cīwē

northern flicker (Colaptes auratus)
— *wirikwanēw

nose
— *kot, *skiwan, *skot

nostril
— *ērikw, *skēkom, *tērikom

not centered
— *atiht

not fit
— *nōt

notched
— *rīhrīk

nothing but
— *mošt, *mōš

notice
— *pisisk

notwithstanding
— *natamā

now (as opposed to previously)
— *šay

nudge
— *tōsk

numb
— *kīskim

number (a certain number)
— *taht

nut
— *pakān

O

obey
— *pišic

obscuring
— *kašk

observe
— *nākat

occasionally
— *āskaw

ochre
— *ıraman, *wiraman

odor (create or give off odor while burning or cooking)
— *māhs, *māhso, *māhsw, *māštē

of course
— *cikēmā

off to the side
— *patotē

offend
— *wašištaw

offshore
— *mōšāw

often
— *mān

old
— *kēhtē, *kiyāš, *nikān

old (speaking of a man)
— *pat

omasum
— *māw

on
— *atōt, *tēht

on a bare surface
— *mošt

on fire
— *pahs

on guard
— *ahšo

on or to one side
— *wihpimē

on purpose
— *wihcitaw

on this side (of an open space)
— *ēn

on top
— *tahkoht

once
— *āpitin

once again
— *kāw

one
— *nikoto, *pēyako

one after the other
— *akinē

one half of an object
— *īšikan

one only (when speaking of a pair)
— *napatē

oneself (by oneself)
— *nēhiraw

only
— *piko

only one side
— *napatē

onwards
— *šēmāk

open
— *šē

open (by having both sides spread apart)
— *tōhk

open mouth
— *tāwat

open or expose broadly
— *pān

open water (on an otherwise frozen body of water)
— *askawiy

open water (towards open water)
— *mōšāw

oppose
— *ıriwē

opposite one another
— *wāwāht

opposite position
— *atimā

oppress
— *māko

oral cavity
— *konēw

orderly
— *nahāw

ordinary
— *ırin

ornamental band (such as a bangle or ring)
— *ahtan

otter
— *ārkikw, *nikikw

ouananiche (Salmo salar)
— *awanān

out
— *waraw

out of one's wits
— *kīškwē

out of sight
— *ākaw

out of the mouth of a river
— *sākitaw

out of the way
— *īkatē

outlet of a lake
— *kohpit

overcome
— *šākōt

overwhelm
— *māko

overhang
— *akorē

overpower
— *ništ

overtake
— *atim

owl
— *ōhow

own person or animal
— *awahkē

P

pack
— *tamahk

pack (bag)
— *ıwat, *īwat, *maškimotay

pack (group)
— *ēyat

packed down
— *kišt

paddle
— *apoy

pain (feel or be in a particular state due to pain)
— *ahpinē

pain (piercing pain)
— *cīšt

pain (smarting pain)
— *wīhsak

pain (suffer from pain or sickness)
— *nēsi

pain (suffer pain)
— *nē

pair
— *riniw

pair (join together as a pair)
— *napo

palatable
— *wīškop

palate
— *arakaskw

palisade
— *mēnisk

palm (of hand)
— *arakāsk

pancreas
— *pahrakosiw

parent
— *nīkihikw

parent of one's son-in-law or daughter-in-law
— *tihtawāw

parent-in-law
— *šit, *šitihs

partially
— *nōm

partition
— *piskiht

partly
— *rāw

part (of a whole quantity or number)
— *pask

part way
— *nayēwat

pass a line through a hole
— *tāpisiko

pass by
— *miyāw

pass over
— *pāšit

patch
— *mīš

paternal aunt
— *sikohs, *sikosihs

paternal uncle
— *ōhkomihs

path
— *ām, *ɪm, *ɪskanaw, *mēw, *mēskanaw

pay attention
— *pisisk

pectoral fin
— *tihcikan

peel
— *pāpako, *pihrak

pelt
— *wayān

pelt (beaver)
— *aht, *ahtay

pelvis
— *pihcikay

penis
— *atakay, *ītakay, *tak

perceive
— *maht

perceive not
— *pāšiko

perceptible
— *nō

perch (yellow perch)
— *ahsāwēw

perilous
— *nanīsān

peritoneum
— *wīhs

persist
— *kīhk

person, animal, or thing
— *ay

person living among spouse's social group
— *nahāhk, *nahākan

pick berries
— *awihso, *āmiso, *mawihso

pieces (be or reduce to fine pieces)
— *pīhs

pieces (be or reduce to small pieces)
— *pīkin

pierce
— *cīšt, *ɪštah, *ɪštahw, *parip

pierce through
— *pikwā

pigeon
— *wimīmīw

pike
— *kinošēw

pikeperch
— *wikāw

pile
— *wisko

pileated woodpecker (Dryocopus pileatus)
— *mēmēw

pine or pine-like tree
— *āšihkw

pipe (smoking pipe)
— *spwākan, *wispwākan

pipestem
— *wiskiciy

pit (stone of a fruit)
— *wiskahtāmin

pitiable
— *kitim, *kitimāk

place flesh on rack to dry, smoke, or roast
— *akwāwē

place (in a particular place)
— *tat
place upright
— *cīpat, *cīpē
plain
— *arihs
plain view (in plain view)
— *nēhpēm
plait
— *apihkē
play
— *mētawē
play (to play a dice-like game of chance)
— *pakēhsē
play (to play ball)
— *tōhē
pleasant (taste or smell)
— *wīhk
please
— *atam
plentiful
— *mīšak
plenty
— *wērōt
pliable
— *šōhšōp
plug up
— *kipo
plumage
— *pīw, *pīway
point
— *nē
point (of land)
— *macitēw
point (to point at)
— *ato
pointed
— *cīpo
pointed arrow
— *atohs
pole
— *āhtikw, *mištikw
pole (pole for supporting a tipi)
— *apahšoy
poor
— *kitimāk, *manēw
poorly
— *māš
poplar
— *mītohs
porcupine
— *ākw, *kākw
porcupine quill
— *āwiy, *kāwiy
portage a canoe
— *ıhsihtā
position unevenly
— *tēštak
post
— *kištākan
pot
— *askihkw
pot-hook
— *akahciy
pound
— *tako
pour
— *sīk
pour water onto
— *sōk
powder
— *pihko
praise
— *mahtāko
precipice
— *kask
precipitate as rain or snow
— *tān
pregnant
— *pwāw
pregnant (speaking of animals)
— *ahcē
prematurely
— *nōhtaw

premonition
— *mōr

prepare for a journey
— *nisāw

presage
— *āš

presentiment
— *mōr

press
— *māko

pretend
— *āhk

prick
— *patask

prod
— *āk

produce smoke
— *āpahtē

proficient
— *nihtāw

projectile (pointed projectile)
— *ahkw

projectile (pointed stick used as a projectile)
— *īpihs

pronounced
— *kīhkā

propel (in a sweeping motion)
— *wēp

proper
— *nah

proper place or state
— *kanāt

properly
— *wēwēriht

protective layer
— *asp

protrude
— *sāk

provisions (make provisions, speaking of a beaver)
— *wicihkē

provoke
— *ırikā

prudent
— *ripwāhkā

psalterium
— *māw

pubes
— *ahciw

pull
— *pit

pull out
— *rārisk

pulp
— *šiko

pulse
— *ahan

pulverize
— *šāhšāko

purplish hue
— *apiht

pursue
— *naw

pus
— *mirēk, *miriy

push
— *kāht

push forward
— *kwahko

push in a particular direction
— *tišin

put in
— *pīhr

put in a container
— *asiwē

put in fire
— *matoštē

put in water
— *hcim, *htitā, *kapaštawē

put morsel in one's mouth
— *sask

put on garment or item
— *pošt

put on one's moccasins
— *nihkinākō

put right
— *mēyāw

quadruped
— *ɪro

Q

quake
— *kwīhko

quick
— *katāštap

quickly
— *kirip, *kisiskā

quiet and somber
— *koškwāwāt

quit
— *pōn

quite
— *nawat

quiver
— *nam

R

raccoon
— *ēhsipan

rain
— *awahtān, *kimiwan, *ɪpēštān

rancid
— *šāštē

rapids
— *āciwan

rapids (to shoot rapids)
— *pīwit

raspberry
— *arōskan

rather
— *nawat

rattling noise
— *šīhšīkwē

raven
— *kāhkākiw

raw
— *ašišk, *ašk

rawhide
— *ahpin

reach
— *miš, *witih

reach open space coming from the bush or inland
— *matāw

ready
— *ayēskaw, *kwayāt

rebuke
— *ān

reckon
— *ak, *akiht, *akim

recognize
— *nihsito

rectify
— *mīno

rectum
— *akahc, *akahciy

red
— *mirko

redo
— *tāp

reduce
— *aciw

reduce in size
— *rīw

reduce to pieces
— *pikišk

red-throated loon (Gavia stellata)
— *āhši-mwākw

red-winged blackbird (Agelaius phoeniceus)
— *cahcahkarow

reed
— *aštākanaškw

reek
— *wīhcēk

refrain
— *arihsā

refuse to abandon
— *kišā

regret
— *miht

regurgitate
— *šikakwē

reject
— *ātaw

release
— *pakit

reliable
— *kakāraw

reluctant
— *tāštak

rely on
— *miš

remain (after consumption or destruction of the rest)
— *ıško

remove
— *man

remove article of clothing
— *kēšt

remove everything
— *masisko

remove external layer or skin
— *pahko

remove from over the fire
— *akwā

remove hair, fur, or plumage
— *paško

remove liquid
— *ırk

remove meat from bone
— *cīhcīko

remove superficial layer
— *cīhš

renal fat
— *wīkw

repair
— *wit

repeat
— *tāp

repulsive (arouse repulsive feeling)
— *kwātištak

resemble
— *naspit, *naspitaw

reset
— *tāp

resist
— *arihsā, *ıriwē

resistant to
— *šīp

resonant sound
— *pitihko

respond
— *nasko

rest
— *arwē

restrain
— *māhciko, *micim

retreat (to one's den)
— *āhkwap

return
— *kīwē

return (in return)
— *kāw

revive
— *āpis

rib
— *sp, *spik, *spikay, *spiy

rich
— *mīšak

ridge
— *wihšē

rip
— *rārik

ripple (cause water to ripple by one's presence underwater)
— *wisip

rise (from reclined position)
— *wan

rise (from seated position)
— *pasikō

river
— *sīpiw, *štikw

roast
— *apwē

rob
— *mask

robe
— *akohp, *skotākay

rock
— *ahsin, *ahsiniy

rock face
— *ıhsēk

rock (useful metal or rock)
— *ıhs, *ıhsēk

roe
— *āhkw, *wāhkw, *wāhkwan

roll
— *tihtip

room
— *kamikw

root (fine root, secondary root)
— *atap, *watapiy

root (large root, primary root)
— *cēpihk, *wicēpihk

rope
— *apihs

rotten
— *at, *atin, *atit

rough
— *kāw

rough (of a surface offering resistance against movement)
— *pihrēko

round
— *wāwiy, *wāwiyē

row (in a row)
— *nīpitē

rub
— *siriko

rub antlers against trees or brush
— *nimit

ruffed grouse (Bonasa umbellus)
— *paspaškiw

ruin
— *nāraw

rumen
— *wīnāštakay

rump
— *kīnānihš, *šōkan

rump (of a bird)
— *anarkitiy

run
— *pahtā

run out (speaking of liquid)
— *sīskaw

run with
— *pah, *pahtwā

runny nose
— *akikw

rust
— *akwāko

rut (male deer in rut)
— *wīhšāko

S

sad
— *kašk

safe (be or make safe in an enclosed space)
— *sakask

saggy
— *panahko

salamander
— *wikāskatātāhkw, *wikīskatātāhkw, *wisīkirāwīš

salmon (Atlantic salmon)
— *witāhšwamēkw

salmon (landlocked salmon)
— *awanān

salty
— *šīw

salute
— *atam

same day (within the same day)
— *ayawiš

sand
— *āwahk, *rēkaw

sandhill crane (Antigone canadensis)
— *wicicāhkw

sauger
— *wikāw

saw
— *por, *potā

say
— *i

say thus
— *ıt

scab
— *mikiy

scabby
— *wimik

scale
— *ahak, *ahakay, *arahak, *arahakay

scale (to remove scales from)
— *pir

scar
— *wicīhs

scare off
— *amā

scatter
— *sihswē, *wasahswē

scatter in pieces
— *pīw

scoop
— *kwāp

scorch
— *pihkah

scorn
— *pīw

scrape
— *kāšk

scrape hide
— *šāhkwē

scraping (hide scraping)
— *watoy

scratch
— *kāšk

scratch itch
— *cīk

scream
— *tācikwē

seal
— *ārkikw

season (be certain season)
— *āyā

season (spend season in a particular place)
— *hši

secretly
— *kīm, *kīmōt, *wanimōt

securely
— *āyit

see
— *āpaht, *āpam, *āpi, *n, *naw, *wāp

seed
— *wiskahtāmin

seek (the presence, possession, or fulfillment of)
— *nato

seek to avoid
— *mīw

semen
— *tōkw

send, drive away, chase in a particular direction
— *tišah, *tišahw

sensible
— *ripwāhkā

sensitive
— *šēw, *wahkēw

separate
— *pahkān, *piskiht

set
— *ahr, *aštā

set a fishing line
— *koskē

set a trap
— *wanī
set down
— *pakit, *pōn
set fishing net
— *ahrā
set or place in a particular position, sit or come to sit in a particular position
— *aštō
settlement
— *ōtēnaw
sever
— *cim, *kīšk
sever (of string-like objects)
— *pask
severe
— *āhko
sew
— *kwāhso, *kwāt
sewn
— *kwāhso, *kwātē
sex (have sex)
— *mē
sexually mature (speaking of an animal)
— *pat
shake
— *miko
shake (shake off)
— *paw
shallow
— *pāko
shame
— *akat
sharp
— *kāhš
sharp point
— *kīn
sharp-tailed grouse (Tympanuchus phasianellus)
— *ākiskow
sharpen
— *tāš
shave scalp
— *mōhš
shave wood
— *mōhko
shear
— *mōhš
sheet-like
— *ay, *ēk, *ēkinw
shell bead
— *mīkihs
shelter from the wind
— *tipinaw
shim
— *sīhtaw
shin
— *skaskwan
shine
— *wāhs
shine (speaking of a heavenly body)
— *āštawē
shine (speaking of a light)
— *āštē
shoot a projectile
— *pimo
shoot rapids
— *pīwit
shore (at the shore)
— *šišot
shoreline
— *ēw
short
— *tahko
short and thick
— *pitiko
short of
— *manēw
short (speaking of periods of time)
— *pēhšo
shortcut (to take a shortcut)
— *kask, *kaskam

shoulder
— *tihtiman

shoulder blade
— *tiriy

shoulder girdle (upper arm and shoulder girdle)
— *sakīn

shout
— *tācikwē

shovel
— *makār

showy
— *sēk

shrill voice (to have a shrill voice)
— *wīhsahkwē

shrivel
— *pāwan

shrub
— *ımihšiy

shrub (fruit-bearing shrub)
— *akahšiy

sibling
— *ītišān

sibling (by adoption or marriage)
— *tawēmāw

sibling (younger sibling)
— *hšīm

sibling-in-law (of the opposite gender as the speaker)
— *ītimw

sick
— *āhko

sideways
— *pimit

sift
— *šīkawē

silhouette
— *nihcik

silver
— *šōriyāw

similar
— *nasp

simply
— *ıtāp

since
— *aspin

sinew
— *cēšt

sinew (backstrap sinew)
— *aštihs, *aštihsiy

sing
— *ah, *nikamo

singe
— *pah

sink
— *kosā, *kotāw

sip
— *kwāštiko

sister (elder)
— *mihs

sister-in-law (of a woman)
— *tāhkohs

sit
— *ap, *api, *aštē

size (have a certain size)
— *ıkit

skim (come briefly or lightly into contact)
— *pahs

skin
— *aš, *ašak, *ašakay

skunk
— *šikākw

sky
— *askw, *āwaskw, *wāskw

sky (during the day)
— *kīšik, *kīšikan

sky (during the night)
— *tipisk

slack
— *nīk

slant
— *nakē

snow crust strong enough to walk on
— *atēwē, *watē

snow goose (Anser caerulescens)
— *wēhwēw

snowshoe
— *ahsām, *ākim, *ɪm

snowshoe (bear paw snowshoe)
— *mahkwatoy

snowshoe harness
— *atiman

soft
— *marōk, *rōsk

soft and springy
— *tōštōk

soft and hollow substance
— *ɪc, *ɪciy

soft substance
— *at

solemn
— *kāmwāt

sole (of foot)
— *arakāsk

solid
— *sōhk

solid (firm)
— *kišt

solidly in place
— *āyit

somber
— *kāmwāt

some
— *ātiht

something
— *natohko

sometimes
— *āskaw

son
— *kohs, *kosihs

son-in-law
— *tihkwatim

soon
— *wīpat

sorcerer
— *mitēw

sorrow
— *kīšināt

so-so
— *napāt

soul (of a dead person)
— *cīpay

sound (make sound)
— *wē, *wēwē

sound (make sound)
— *matwē

sour
— *šīw

south
— *šāwan

space
— *taw

spare
— *manāt

spark
— *pask

sparsely (sparsely spaced)
— *pašk

spawn (to spawn, speaking of fish)
— *ām

spawn (roe)
— *āhkw, *wāhkw, *wāhkwan

speak
— *ayam, *kīšwē

speak indiscriminately
— *pīkiskwē

spear
— *šimākan

spear (barbed spear)
— *mihcikiw

spear (fishing spear)
— *anihtoy

spear (used as a projectile)
— *īpihs

speck (have speck in one's eye)
— *pisin

specter (emaciated specter that flies with the wind and tickles its captives to death)
— *pākaskōkan

spend night away from home
— *katikwan

spherical
— *nōtim

spider
— *ēhēpikw

spin
— *towē

spine
— *āwikan, *tahtakwākan

spirit
— *ahcāhkw

spit
— *sihko, *sihkwē

splash
— *wahswē

spleen
— *pēhpēhkw, *pīhpīšk

split
— *tāšk

spoil
— *nihšiwanāt, *wīyak

spongy
— *tōštōk

spontaneously
— *šēhk

spook
— *amā

spoon
— *ēmihkwān

spotted
— *kitak

sprain
— *sēk

spray
— *wahswē

spray (speaking of a skunk)
— *mīt

spread
— *sihswē, *wasahswē

spread apart
— *kāhk

spread pasty substance
— *šišo

spring
— *sīkwan

squeak
— *kisīp

squeeze out
— *tamako

squirrel
— *anikwacāhs

stake
— *kištākan

stand
— *kāpawi, *nīpawi

star
— *atahkw

start
— *kiht, *māt

stay behind
— *mitē

steal
— *kimot

steam bath
— *matot

steer
— *tahko

step
— *ām

stepfather
— *ōhkomihs

stepmother
— *tōhs, *tōsihs

sternum
— *tahsināhkēw

stick (thin piece of wood)
— *āhtikw, *mištikw

stick (adhere)
— *ako

stick out
— *sāk

stick-like
— *ato, *āsko

sticky
— *pasako

stiff
— *cītaw

still
— *kiyām

stingy
— *sasāk

stink
— *wīhcēk

stir
— *ıtē

stomach
— *at, *atay

stone on which food is pounded
— *atān

stoop
— *nawē

stop
— *kipiht

stop (prevent from proceeding)
— *nak, *nakā

store for later use
— *aštahciko

story (tell story)
— *ācim, *ācimo, *ātot

stout
— *pitiko

straight
— *kwayasko

straighten limb
— *šow

straighten out
— *šahto, *tašo

strain
— *šīkawē

strand
— *ahkw

strand of natural fiber used for making thread or rope
— *šēštakw

strange
— *mayak

streak
— *ašākw

stretch
— *šīp

stretch out
— *šihk

stretch out limb
— *šow

strike
— *pakam, *paskihtē, *witām

strike (with fist or tool)
— *ah, *ahw

strike with tip of
— *tahk

string
— *apihs

string (by use of string-like object)
— *āp, *āpihkē

string-like
— *ašt, *āpēk, *āpiy

strip
— *masisko

stripe
— *pēhš

stroke
— *rāš

strong
— *maškaw, *sāp, *sōhk

stuck
— *micimo

stuck to
— *amo

stumble
— *piso

stump (of a tree)
— *paskwahciw

stunned
— *kīškwē
sturgeon
— *namēw
subcutaneous fat
— *wīrinw
subcutaneous tissue
— *tamisk, *tamiskay
submerge
— *kihtāw, *kōk
subside
— *āštē
subside (speaking of the wind)
— *rāk
subsided (speaking of weather)
— *arwā
succeeding
— *askō, *aškoht
successful hunt
— *min
successive
— *āniskē
such an amount, size, extent, or degree
— *ırikohko, *ıspiht
suck
— *nōnē, *sōp
sucker
— *namēpir
suckle
— *nōhr, *nōhto
suffer
— *nanēhkāt
suffer (cause something or someone to suffer for one's own dissatisfaction)
— *mahtonē
suffer from
— *cim
suffer from pain or sickness
— *nēsi
suffer pain
— *nē
sufficient
— *tēp
summer
— *nīpin
sun
— *pīhsimw
sunder
— *māt
sunken
— *wār
sunscald wood
— *witatāsakoy
superimpose
— *ākwīhtaw
superlative
— *māwat
support
— *sīto
surface (come to the surface)
— *pēko
surface (on the surface)
— *waskit
suspect
— *atām
suspended
— *cin
swallow
— *koh
swear
— *wīyahkwē
sweat
— *apwē
sweet
— *šīw
swell
— *ahan, *pāk, *štin
swell (speaking of a body of water)
— *tamak
swim
— *ah, *ātakā, *cimē, *rāhrā

T

tadpole
— *pōtōhš

tail
— *āro, *soy

tail end of a snowshoe
— *wišētoy

tail feather
— *ataniy

tail fin
— *šikwan, *šikwanay

take along
— *nīm

take (from one place to another)
— *āwē, *wir, *witā

take pleasure in
— *wīhk

take out of container or enclosed space
— *kwarako

take out of water
— *akwā

take sides
— *kispēw

talk
— *ayam, *kīšwē

talk about
— *ārimō

tame
— *rōsp

tapeworm
— *kāšak

tardy
— *pwāštaw

tarsus
— *spōhkan

taste
— *pw, *sp, *spit, *spoko, *spw, *št

taste like
— *akan, *akisi

tattoo
— *ašākw

teach
— *kiskino

tear (teardrop)
— *sipihkw

tear open
— *tāto

tease
— *natohko

teeth (by use of one's teeth)
— *aht, *am, *kaht, *kam

tell
— *wīh

tell on
— *miš

temper (take one's temper out on something or someone)
— *mahtonē

tend to
— *pam

tender
— *kašk

territory
— *askiy

testicle
— *tihšiw

thank
— *moyaw

thatch
— *apahkw, *apahkway, *apahkwē

thaw
— *āpaw

thawed (partially thawed)
— *šōm

thick
— *kispak

thick (speaking of a liquid)
— *pihrēko

thicket
— *ıhkop

thickness
— *atē

too
— *mēhtāt, *wēhsā, *wisām

too late
— *mwēšt

tool (by use of a tool)
— *ah, *ahw

tooth
— *āpit, *arkwat, *īpit

toothed
— *rīhrīk

top of a tree
— *anask

top (on top)
— *tahkoht

topple
— *kīp, *kīpat

torment
— *nanēhkāt

touch
— *sām, *tāhk

towards a certain side
— *ɪtēhkē

towards the end
— *ākwāt

track
— *mit

tracks
— *ɪskanaw

trade
— *atā

tranquil
— *kiyām

transparent
— *wāhšē

transport by water
— *ahor, *ahotā

trap (set a trap)
— *wanī

trap (under a weight)
— *tahsō

travel by canoe
— *ah, *aho, *cimē, *ɪškā

travel by water
— *ɪškā

travel on foot
— *ah, *ɪn, *ohtē

travel on hill or mountain
— *aciw

travel over ice
— *ɪsko

travel upriver against current
— *ništ

travel with by canoe
— *cīm

treat maliciously
— *wayēš

treat with something medical
— *natohko

tree
— *āhtikw, *mištikw

tree stump
— *paskwahciw

tremble
— *nam

trickster (in traditional tales associated with the great flood and subsequent recreation of the world)
— *wīhsahkēcāhkw

trip
— *piso

trout
— *amēkohs

trout (lake trout)
— *namēkohs

truth (to tell the truth)
— *tāpwē

try
— *kot

tuck
— *ōmo

tullibee
— *witōripiy

tunnel
— *āt, *wāt

turbid
— *pīk

turbulent
— *pāw

turn
— *wašk

turn around
— *kwēsk

turn back
— *āpas

turn inside out
— *āpot

turn (in turn)
— *mīškot

turn over
— *kwēsk, *kwētip

turtle
— *miskināhkw

twinkle
— *pahsahk

twist
— *pīm

twitch
— *cīp

two
— *nīš

U

unable or barely able despite wanting
— *akāw

unclaimed
— *pikwat

uncle (maternal uncle)
— *šihs

uncle (paternal uncle)
— *ōhkomihs

uncomfortably wet or dirty
— *ripāt

uncover
— *pāsk

uncovered
— *šāk

under and out of sight
— *risk

under one's garment
— *pako

understand
— *nihsito

under the surface
— *atām

undo
— *āp

unenthused
— *tāštak

unhabited
— *pikwat

unfasten
— *āpirko, *pihšiko

unleavened bread
— *kārahkonāw

unload
— *kapatē

unpleasant
— *āspon

unravel
— *pīrē

unripc bcrry
— *aticiy

unseasoned
— *arihs

unseen presence (feel uneasy due to some unseen presence)
— *amatihso

unsuitable
— *wanāt

untie
— *āpirko

up
— *ısko, *wihp

upper part of the arm (of a biped) or front leg (of a quadruped) including its associated girdle
— *sakīn

upriver
— *nat

upriver (travel upriver against current)
— *ništ

upside down
— *acit

upwards
— *taštas

upwind
— *narim

urge
— *šīhk

urinary bladder
— *rir, *ririy

urinate
— *šā, *šāso, *šik

urinate on
— *šāt

uropygium
— *anarkitiy

use
— *āpat

use up
— *mēšt

useless(ly)
— *arāwat

usually
— *mān

uterus and adnexa
— *spayaw

V

vagina
— *āhkay

vamp
— *ašēsin

vapor
— *pīkišē

various
— *nanāhkaw, *natohko

various (do various things)
— *natohko

various (in various places or directions)
— *nanāništ

veer
— *waškwē

vertical
— *šimat

very
— *nāšit, *waniraw

vexatious
— *nayēhtāw

vigorous
— *sāp

vis-à-vis
— *wāwāht

vocalize
— *atāmo, *imo, *kito, *wē, *wēwē

vocalize about
— *m, *t

vomit
— *pākomo, *šikakwē

vulva
— *āhkay

W

wait
— *pē

walk
— *ohtē

walk somebody or something
— *ohtah, *ohtatā

walk without snowshoes
— *nōtimē

walleye
— *wikāw

warm
— *kīšō

warm up
— *šō

wart
— *cīhcīkw

waste
— *wīyak

watch
— *nākat

water
— *ɩp, *ɩpiy, *nipiy

water current
— *ciwan, *štan

water current (be affected or affect by use of water current)
— *poko, *por, *poro, *potā, *potē

water lily
— *wiškihtē

water lily rhizome
— *waskatamoy

waterweed
— *ahsisiy

wave
— *ātikw, *kaskanw

waves run
— *āhan, *āškā

weak
— *nīram, *šāko

wear (a band or other thin strip of material)
— *pahs

wear (article of clothing)
— *ɩšk, *ɩškaw, *wīrā

wear (as a cloak)
— *ako

weary
— *mwēštāt, *šikat

weary of waiting
— *pōmē

weasel
— *šihkohs, *šihkohsiw

weather (be certain weather)
— *āyā

wedge
— *sīhtaw

wedge-shaped
— *ɩhšawē

weep
— *mē

weigh down
— *māhtako, *patako

well
— *miro, *takahk

wet and granular (speaking of snow)
— *sask

whet
— *tāš

which
— *kēko

while
— *mēkwā

while (a little while)
— *aciraw, *nakiskaw, *wērapisk

while (in a while)
— *nākē

whip
— *pahs

whistle
— *kwīškohš

white
— *wap

white spruce
— *minahikw

whole
— *mis, *misihtaw, *misiwē

whoop
— *sāskwē

wide
— *arakašk

wide apart
— *arak

widow
— *šīkāw

width
— *atē

wife
— *īw

wild
— *pikwat
wild animal
— *awēhsīhs, *pišiskiw
wild rice (Zizania spp.)
— *arōmin
willingly
— *šēhk
willow
— *nīpisiy
win
— *pask
wind
— *rōwē, *štin, *tin
windstorm
— *kīštin
wing
— *tahkakwan
winter
— *pipon, *piponw
wipe clean
— *kāhsī
wise
— *ırinī, *kihtāw
wish for
— *pakohs
with
— *kik
withdraw
— *atim
without cause
— *šēhk
without delay
— *šay, *šēmāk
without fail
— *āyit
without relying on observing a given thing or person
— *pakwano
with the wind
— *nāmiwan
wolf
— *mahīhkan
wolverine
— *kwīhkwahākēw
woman
— *ıskwēw
wondrous
— *mahtāw
wood
— *ıht
wood grain
— *ırkaw
woodpecker (other than the northern flicker and pileated woodpecker)
— *pāhpāštēw
woods (into the woods)
— *šēsk
work
— *ato
work on
— *īhk, *nōt
wrap
— *wēw, *wīskwē
wrap up
— *wāsp
wrestle
— *māš
wretched
— *kotak, *kōhpāt
wrinkle
— *wisīk
wrong
— *naspāt
wrongly
— *wan

Y

year
— *piponw
yell
— *tācikwē

yellow (hue ranging from brown to yellow)
— *wisāw

yellowlegs
— *šēhšēhšiw

yellow perch (Perca flavescens)
— *ahsāwēw

yet
— *kēyāpit

yielding
— *marōk

younger sibling
— *hšīm

young man
— *wiškinīkiw

young man (be a young man)
— *wiškinīki

MERCURY SERIES / LA COLLECTION MERCURE

The best resource for peer-reviewed research on the history, archaeology, and culture of Canada is proudly published by the Canadian Museum of History and the University of Ottawa Press.

Le Musée canadien de l'histoire et Les Presses de l'Université d'Ottawa publient avec fierté la meilleure ressource en ce qui a trait aux recherches évaluées par les pairs dans les domaines de l'histoire, de l'archéologie et de la culture canadiennes.

Strikingly Canadian and highly specialized, the Mercury Series presents works in the research domain of the Canadian Museum of History and benefits from the publishing expertise of the University of Ottawa Press. Created in 1972, the series is in line with the Canadian Museum of History's strategic directions. The Mercury Series consists of peer-reviewed academic research, and includes numerous landmark contributions in the disciplines of Canadian history, archaeology, and culture. Books in the series are published in at least one of Canada's official languages, and may appear in other languages.

Remarquablement canadienne et hautement spécialisée, la collection Mercure réunit des ouvrages portant sur les domaines de recherches du Musée canadien de l'histoire et s'appuie sur le savoir-faire des Presses de l'Université d'Ottawa. Fondée en 1972, elle répond aux orientations stratégiques du Musée canadien de l'histoire. La collection Mercure propose des recherches scientifiques évaluées par les pairs et regroupe de nombreuses contributions majeures à l'histoire, à l'archéologie et à la culture canadiennes. Les ouvrages sont publiés dans au moins une des langues officielles du Canada, avec possibilité de parution dans d'autres langues.

The Mercury Series/La collection Mercure

Stacey J. Barker, Krista Cooke, and Molly McCullough, *Vestiges de guerre : récits de femmes canadiennes en temps de conflit, 1914-1945*, 2025.

Alan Bowker, *A Church at War: MacKay Presbyterian Church, New Edinburgh, and the First World War*, 2024.

Yves Frenette, Marie-Ève Harton, and Marc St-Hilaire, eds, *Déploiements canadiens-français et métis en Amérique du Nord (18e-20e siècle)*, 2023.

Frances M. Slaney, *Marius Barbeau's Vitalist Ethnology*, 2023.

Robert von Bitter and Ronald F. Williamson, eds, *The History and Archaeology of the Iroquois du Nord*, 2023.

Kenneth R. Holyoke and M. Gabriel Hrynick, *The Far Northeast: 3000 BP to Contact*, 2022.

Stacey J. Barker, Krista Cooke, and Molly McCullough, *Material Traces of War: Stories of Canadian Women and Conflict, 1914–1945*, 2021.

Michael K. Hawes, Andrew C. Holman, and Christopher Kirkey, eds, *1968 in Canada: A Year and Its Legacies*, 2021.

Steven Schwinghamer and Jan Raska, *Pier 21: A History*, 2020.

Steven Schwinghamer and Jan Raska, *Quai 21 : une histoire*, 2020.

Robert Sweeny, ed., *Sharing Spaces: Essays in Honour of Sherry Olson*, 2020.

Matthew Betts, *Place-Making in the Pretty Harbour: The Archaeology of Port Joli, Nova Scotia*, 2019.

Lauriane Bourgeon, *Préhistoire béringienne : étude archéologique des Grottes du Poisson-Bleu (Yukon)*, 2018.

Jenny Ellison and Jennifer Anderson, eds, *Hockey: Challenging Canada's Game – Au-delà du sport national*, 2018.

Myron Momryk, *Mike Starr of Oshawa: A Political Biography*, 2018.

John Willis, ed., *Tu sais, mon vieux Jean-Pierre: Essays on the Archaeology and History of New France and Canadian Culture in Honour of Jean-Pierre Chrestien*, 2017.

Anna Kearney Guigne, *The Forgotten Songs of the Newfoundland Outports: As Taken from Kenneth Peacock's Newfoundland Field Collection, 1951–1961*, 2016.

Ian Dyck, *The Life and Work of W. B. Nickerson (1865–1926): Scientific Archaeology in Central North America*, 2016.

Brad Loewen and Claude Chapdelaine, eds, *Contact in the 16th Century: Networks Among Fishers, Foragers and Farmers*, 2016.

Mauro Peressini, *Choosing Buddhism*, 2016.

Pierre Bibeau, David Denton, and André Burroughs, eds, *Ce que la rivière nous procurait : archéologie et histoire du réservoir de l'Eastmain-1*, 2015.

Charles Garrad, *Petun to Wyandot: The Ontario Petun from the Sixteenth Century*, 2014.

Gabriel M. Yanicki, *Old Man's Playing Ground: Gaming and Trade on the Plains/Plateau Frontier*, 2014.

Jean-François Blanchette, *Du coq à l'âme : l'art populaire au Québec*, 2014.

Terence N. Clark, *Rewriting Marpole: The Path to Cultural Complexity in the Gulf of Georgia*, 2013.

Michel Plourde, *L'exploitation du phoque à l'embouchure du Saguenay par les Iroquoiens de 1000 à 1534*, 2013.

Stuart E. Jenness, *Stefansson, Dr. Anderson and the Canadian Arctic Expedition, 1913–1918: A story of exploration, science and sovereignty*, 2011.

Co-published by the Canadian Museum of History and the University of Ottawa Press.
Publié conjointement par le Musée canadien de l'histoire et Les Presses de l'Université d'Ottawa.
For a complete list of the University of Ottawa Press titles, visit:
Pour une liste complète des titres des Presses de l'Université d'Ottawa, voir :
www.Press.uOttawa.ca

www.ingramcontent.com/pod-product-compliance
Lightning Source LLC
Chambersburg PA
CBHW052009030426
42334CB00029BA/3143

* 9 7 8 0 7 7 6 6 4 5 4 9 0 *